CAREFULLY TO CARRY

CONSOLIDATED EDITION 2023

WITHERBYS

Since 1740

First edition published 2018

Second edition published 2023

Book ISBN: 978-1-914993-12-1
eBook ISBN: 978-1-914993-13-8

British Library Cataloguing in Publication Data
A catalogue record for this book is available from the British Library.

Cover image credit: Aastels/Shutterstock.com

Published by

Witherby Publishing Group Ltd
Navigation House,
3 Almondvale Business Park,
Almondvale Way,
Livingston EH54 6GA,
Scotland, UK

+44 (0)1506 463 227
info@witherbys.com
witherbys.com

Printed and bound by Trade Colour Printing in Cumbria at www.hardbackbooks.co.uk

Foreword

I am very pleased to endorse this excellent and unique publication which strives to improve crew and vessel safety as well as enhancing loss prevention.

The 2023 consolidated edition of the UK P&I Club's *Carefully to Carry* represents over 60 years' worth of experience from several generations of international cargo experts together with claims and loss prevention specialists at one of the world's leading P&I clubs.

It was back in 1961 that the UK P&I Club first set up its pioneering London advisory committee on cargo matters. The aim was to reduce claims through timely advice to the club's members. The so-called *'Carefully to Carry'* committee consulted widely with technical experts and went on to produce many articles on cargoes and the related issues that lead to claims.

The quality of the advice provided soon established *Carefully to Carry* articles as a key source of guidance for all the world's shipowners and ships' officers, whether entered with the UK Club or not. The articles also began to be used in claims negotiations and settlements, as well as being relied upon in court hearings.

In 2002 all the articles were gathered together, updated and made available as one entity by the Club for the first time. It continued to grow over the next 15 years to reach some 600 pages, prompting the Club to hand over the not-inconsiderable task of publication to leading shipping publisher Witherbys.

The first 'consolidated edition' duly appeared in 2018 and this 2023 edition marks the first of what we predict will be a long-running series of periodic updates of this definitive best practice guide on the carriage, loading and stowage of most types of seaborne cargo. Long may it continue.

Dimitris Fafalios
Chairman of INTERCARGO
Chair of the International Chamber of Shipping Bulk Carrier Panel

Contents

Acknowledgements

A.R. Brink & Associates CC

APC

BMT Surveys

Brookes Bell

Burgoynes consulting scientists and engineers

Cambridge Refrigeration Technology

Crawford & Company

CWA International

de Haas | van Oosterhout

DPS

E.L. Johnsons Sales Ltd

EMCS Limited

IMCS bv

Langlois & Co.

MacGregor

Minton Treharne & Davies Group

Mr. Joel Kruehler – Logistics Compliance Manager, Urenco Ltd

Mr. Marc-Andre Charette – Director, Transportation, Security and Regulatory Relations, Cameco Corporation

Mr. Steve Hansen – Chief Compliance Officer, TAM International (US) Inc

Portpictures.nl

TMC Marine

Van Ameyde Marine

Wavespec Ltd

Part 1 –
Grain

Chapter 1 –
Preparation, Survey and Load

Under SOLAS Chapter VI, the term 'grain' covers wheat, maize (corn), oats, rye, barley, rice, pulses, seeds and processed forms thereof, whose behaviour is similar to that of grain in its natural state. For all grain cargoes, the hold must be cleaned properly prior to loading. If cargo holds are not cleaned sufficiently to prevent cargo contamination, the cargo may be damaged and there will be large financial claims. The requirements for and extent of cleaning the holds depends on:

- The previous cargo carried
- the next cargo to be carried
- the charterers' requirements
- the requirements of shippers and/or the requirements of the authorities and receivers at the load port.

Typical hold cleaning will involve sweeping the tank top before washing the hold. Washing may be conducted twice, with the first round using seawater and the second using fresh water. Alternative chemicals may be needed.

1.1 Hold Cleaning

Prior to the commencement of hold cleaning, a toolbox talk should take place, including all the personnel involved. During the talk, the hold cleaning schedule should be discussed. All equipment and chemicals that will be used should be fully explained and the safety data sheets (SDS) understood by all. The SDS should be available for consultation by the cleaning team and also displayed on the ship's notice boards.

Appropriate permits to work (PTWs), including an enclosed space entry permit, should be completed prior to entry. For operations that take several days, permits should be created on a daily basis, as this will help reduce the risk of accidents.

Safety routines should be established and the wearing of suitable personal protective equipment (PPE) throughout the hold cleaning is essential. Mandatory PPE should include oilskins, safety shoes/safety sea boots, eye protection, hand protection and safety helmets complete with a chin strap. High visibility jackets/waistcoats will help ensure the visibility of the cleaning team in the hold.

Prior to high-pressure hold washing, excess cargo residue on the tank top should be removed by hand sweeping and lifted out of the holds using a portable de-mucking winch.

Regardless of the nature of the previous cargo, all holds should then be thoroughly cleaned by sweeping, scraping and high-pressure seawater washing to remove all previous cargo residues and any loose scale or paint. Particular attention should be paid to anything that may be trapped behind beams, ledges, pipe guards or other fittings in the holds. The seawater washing should be carried out using a high-pressure hold cleaning gun, supplemented by the deck air line to provide increased pressure. This is the most commonly used method of hold cleaning and the hold cleaning gun normally requires two seafarers to safely control the increased water pressure.

Figure 1.1: Crew member operating a cleaning gun within a cargo hold.

Figure 1.2: Hold cleaning equipment in the stowed position above the deck. Note the flange on the deck wash line.

Some ships are fitted with fixed hold cleaning equipment, normally fitted under the hatch covers. This method of hold cleaning is less labour intensive. A flexible high-pressure hose is connected between a flange on the hatch cover and the deck high-pressure hold washing line.

Figure 1.3: Fixed hold cleaning gun under hatch covers and fixed hold cleaning connection on deck.

Other ships have permanent high-pressure hold cleaning equipment that can be lowered through a flange on the main deck, turned 90 degrees and bolted to the high-pressure deck wash service line.

All cargo residues washed down must be removed via the hold eductors or de-mucking winch. Special attention should be paid to cargo residues:

- Wedged behind pipe brackets
- around hold ladders, under-deck girders and transversals
- at the ventilators to ensure that remnants have been removed
- in hold bilges and recessed hatboxes.

After cleaning and removal, bilge suctions must be tested both before and after washing and the results entered in the cargo notebook and/or deck logbook.

Chemical wash
One of the most difficult hold cleaning tasks is the preparation of a ship for grain cargo after discharging a dirty or dusty cargo such as coal or iron ore, particularly if it has left 'oily' stains on the paintwork or other deposits stubbornly adhering to the steel surfaces. Greasy deposits that remain on the bulkheads will require a degreasing chemical wash and a fresh water rinse in order to pass a grain inspection. The degreasing chemical should be environmentally acceptable for marine use and safe for application by the crew. If special training or PPE is required, this must be planned for. Product SDS of any cleaning or degreasing chemical used should be read, understood and followed by all persons involved with the cleaning process.

Figure 1.4: Coal residue in cargo holds.

To remove any greasy deposits from the hold steelwork, all holds should be high-pressure chemical washed using the hold cleaning gun and air line booster.

Numerous degreasing chemicals are available and they work quite effectively when directly injected into the fire main via the general service pump strainer cover. Manufacturer's instructions must always be followed, PPE worn and all safety instructions followed.

A typical 100,000 dwt bulker will require around 100 litres per hold, or 25 litres of degreasing chemical on each bulkhead.

To avoid the use of long lengths of hose to deliver chemicals, the chemical station should be situated as close as possible to the injection point of the fire and general service (GS) pump. The easiest way to control the rate of chemical flow is by fitting a temporary small hand-operated valve on top of the strainer cover.

An alternative method is to use an eductor system to pump the chemical directly from the drum into the discharge nozzle. The quantity of chemical introduced is controlled by the operator lifting the nozzle clear of the drum. However, this method of educting the chemical from the drum into the discharge nozzle is time consuming, awkward for the operator and restricts their movement around the hold. In addition, it carries a greater risk of an accident, or spillage of degreasing chemical, because the chemical drums have to be lowered into each hold.

A degreasing chemical injection station may consist of:

- A transparent container of 120-litre capacity, graduated in 10-litre units
- a 5 m length of transparent reinforced hose, one end fitted with a 40 cm long steel uptake branch pipe and the other end open. The branch pipe is inserted into the chemical container and the open end of the transparent reinforced pipe is connected to the hand valve on the pump strainer cover using two pipe clamps. The small hand valve on the strainer cover may be used to control the flow of chemical into the fire pump.

Prior to starting the high-pressure seawater chemical wash, all fire hydrants and anchor wash hydrants on deck should be checked to confirm they are fully closed. The hydrant serving the hold cleaning gun should be opened and the fire and GS pump started.

To avoid unnecessary chemical waste, predetermined times of injecting the chemical into the fire main should be agreed between the hold cleaning party and the person controlling the rate of chemical injection. As an example, on a 100,000 dwt bulker, it takes approximately 20 minutes to complete a chemical wash in each hold, after which the chemical should be washed off using high-pressure salt water.

At the same time as the chemical wash, the hold should be hand scraped with sharp long-handled steel scrapers. All loose scale and flaking paint must be removed.

Fresh water rinse and general hold preparation

The final stage of hold washing is the fresh water rinse. Whenever salt water washing is used to clean hatches, the relevant holds should always be rinsed with fresh water to minimise the effects of corrosion and to prevent salt contamination of future cargoes.

Arrangements should be made, in good time, to ensure sufficient fresh water is available on board. A ship preparing for a grain cargo will usually carry additional fresh water, often in the after-peak tank, which can be pumped into the fire main via a GS pump. As an example, a typical 100,000 dwt bulk carrier will require around 30 T of fresh water per hold.

Before undertaking a fresh water rinse, the supply line (normally the deck fire main or similar) will need to be flushed through to remove all residual salt water. Therefore, fresh water rinsing of the holds is generally left until the end of hold cleaning operations to minimise the amount of fresh water required. If a GS pump is used, the flushing through typically takes a few minutes. Once the fire main is clear of salt, all deck fire hydrants and anchor washers should be inspected and confirmed as closed.

If a GS pump is to be used for the hold rinse, to prevent possible pump damage a return line into the fresh water tank should be set up using a hose connected from the fire main into the after-peak vent.

On completion of the hold fresh water rinse, all hatch entrances, hatch trunkings and ladders should be hand washed and fresh water rinsed using the fresh water high-pressure gun. It is not advisable to rinse and clean the access ladders and hatches before washing the main hold, because splashings from the hold bulkheads will often contaminate the freshly washed ladders. Bulkheads either side of all the ladders should be hand cleaned and jet washed, as far as can be safely reached, using long-handled Turk's head brushes. Note that Turk's head brushes are a type of cleaning brush where the bristles are arranged to prevent the end of the brush from coming into contact with the surface being cleaned.

Safety body harnesses should always be used when working at height in the tank. If required, a bosun's chair or other approved access arrangement should be used when undertaking this task. A risk assessment must be carried out for any working at height activity.

Figure 1.5: Holds drying after washing.

When it is safe to open the hatches, all the hatch coamings should be hand washed using long-handled Turk's head brushes and jet washed with fresh water using a high-pressure fresh water gun. With the hatch covers open, binoculars should be used to inspect the holds for any cargo remains.

To prevent possible condensation in the hold, all recessed hold eductors (if fitted) must be drained of any water residue and be cleaned, dry and odourless. There is usually a small stainless steel drain plug on the underside of the eductor that can be temporarily removed to allow the eductor water to drain into the bilge area. When the eductor is empty, the drain plug must be replaced and secured. The eductor hold plate must be secured with all the securing bolts. Duct tape should be used to cover both the securing bolts and the recessed lid handles.

Hold bilges should be completely dried out, odourless and in a fully operating condition.

The tank top must be completely dry and any indentations on the tank top must be wiped dry. The hold should be made completely odourless by maximising hold ventilation. Two layers of clean hessian cloth should be fitted to the bilge strainer plate to further restrict cargo particles entering the bilge area. Duct tape is used to cover the small gap between the bilge strainer and the tank top. The hold hydrant area, if fitted, should be cleaned and dried out and the steel cover refitted and secured in place with all its bolts/screws.

To avoid taint problems, fresh paint should not be applied within the holds or under the hatch covers at any time during the hold preparation, unless there is sufficient time for the paint to cure and be free of odour as per the manufacturer's instructions. This is because most marine coatings require at least seven days for the paint to be fully cured and odour free. All paint used in the holds or on the underside of the hatch covers should be certified grain compatible and a certificate confirming this should be available on board.

Freshly painted hatches/covers will normally result in instant failure during the grain inspection. The paint must have been given time to cure.

Processed grains, or grain cargoes that are highly susceptible to discolouration and taint, should only be stowed in holds where the paint covering is intact. It is important that there is no bare steel, rust, scale or rust staining in the hold.

To prevent cargo debris from the main deck being walked into the accommodation or brought into freshly washed cargo holds, the main decks and accommodation block should be washed down as soon as possible after clearing the discharge port.

Always be mindful of potential pollution from the cargo remains. As such, all cargo residue and washings must be removed in accordance with applicable regulations.

Figure 1.6: Ship's main deck covered in previous cargo.

1.1.1   Ballast Hold

If the ship has a ballast hold that has been used to transport cargo, this should be discharged as early as possible in the discharge sequence to allow the ship's personnel time to remove all cargo debris and prepare the hold for ballasting.

A good working relationship with the stevedores may allow the removal of cargo remains from the ballast holds by use of the shore crane or other cargo-handling facilities.

The bilges and strums of the ballast hold should be thoroughly cleaned and all traces of previous cargo removed. The bilge suctions should be tested and confirmed as clear prior to any washing out of the cargo holds, and the bilge spaces should be pumped out and secured with the ballast line blanks.

To prevent ballast water ingress into the bilge area, it is essential that the rubber joint/gasket is in good condition and that all the ballast blank securing bolts are fitted tightly.

1.1.2 Hatch Covers

All the hatch trackways should be swept clean and then carefully hosed down. Compressed air guns should be used with caution and suitable PPE should be worn to ensure both face and body protection.

Figure 1.7: Hatch undersides and rubber packing.

All hatch corner drains, including the non-return valves, should be checked and confirmed as clean and clear. The blanking caps on the hatch corner drains, which are used to ensure hold airtightness, should be attached by a chain to the drain. Blanking caps or plugs are provided where drains do not have an approved automatic means of preventing water ingress into the hold.

Figure 1.8: Hatch drain with cap attached by small chain.

All inner hatch coamings should be washed and then rinsed using a fresh water high-pressure gun. If time permits, it is usually more convenient to wash this area in port where it is sheltered, rather than at sea. If it is permitted by the Port Authority, all hatch tops should be dock water washed, ensuring that cargo remains are retained on board and not washed into the dock. The fitting of plugs to all deck scuppers should help prevent any pollution incidents and claims alongside.

Figure 1.9: Scupper plug fitted.

It is essential that hatch top and deck washing is only carried out with Port Authority permission.

Figure 1.10: In ports where helicopters are used for pilot transfer, it is a normal requirement of the port to wash down the helicopter area and at least one hatch length either side of the helicopter area (ensuring that cargo debris is not washed into the dock).

To prevent cargo claims due to water ingress, all hatch seals (both longitudinal and transverse), hold access lids and seals around the hatch sides should be chalk marked and water tested using deck wash hoses. For more detail on these procedures, see Chapter 55.

A more accurate method of testing a hatch for leakage is to use ultrasonic equipment. However, this is usually carried out by shore personnel who are trained in the use of this equipment.

Figure 1.11: Hose testing and a typical hose test.

Figure 1.12: Ultrasonic hatch testing for leaks.

Faulty or suspect sections of hatch rubber should be replaced in their entirety. Localised replacement or 'building up' of hatch rubbers using sealing tape is discouraged.

Figure 1.13: Poor practice: use of hatch tape to build up a cross joint is discouraged.

1.1.3 Grain Cleaning Checklists

'Grain clean' is by far the most common standard of cleanliness used in the transport of bulk and break bulk cargoes. While exact requirements may vary between regions, the US National Cargo Bureau suggests that, for a hold to be certified 'grain clean' and so fit for loading a cargo such as soya beans, it should be free of:

- Stains and residues of the previous cargo
- loose rust scale and paint scale
- any other contaminants
- insect infestation
- odours
- moisture.

Grain cleaning 'operational' checklist
As soon as the ship starts cleaning preparations, the Master should make regular daily reports of hatch cleaning progress to the operator.

Prior to commencing the grain clean, the Master and crew should check and confirm the following:

- If the previous cargo is likely to cause problems during the cleaning voyage, the Master must advise the operator well in advance so that sufficient cleaning time, manpower and materials can be planned. A lack of communication between ship and shore may result in difficulties for the ship and costly off-hire time for the operator
- if the after-peak tank is to be used for the carriage of additional fresh water, ensure that the after-peak tank can be discharged via the deck service line. If the after-peak tank is filled with fresh water, ensure the ship can still maintain the minimum bow height as per classification rules (details are given in the ship stability book)
- the ship has a fully operational de-mucking winch

- all bilge sounding pipes and temperature pipes (if fitted) are clear with no old sounding rods or any obstructions or blockages
- all sounding pipes have a fully operational screw thread and the gasket is in good condition, ie the sounding cap can be screwed down tightly to prevent water ingress
- the ship has no ballast tank leaks
- the ship's ballast pumps, eductor(s) and GS pumps are working correctly. Advise the operator if there are any problems
- where applicable, the ship has a 'grain certified' paint certificate for inside the holds and hatches
- all hatch corner drains and non-return valves are working correctly and are complete
- all hold ladders on forward and aft bulkheads are in good condition to allow safe access for all personnel
- all hold bilge plates have all the securing bolts fitted and the ship's approved ballast holds have the ballast line blanks in place. This is often a spectacle piece that can be rotated on deck
- all ballast line hold cover plates have all bolts fitted and all are in good condition
- all hatch access lids can have a hatch seal or padlock fitted after loading to prevent unauthorised entry into an oxygen-depleted area
- the ship is free of infestation. This includes all the storerooms, which are also liable to be inspected by grain inspectors
- approved grain stability books are on board and the pre-calculated load conditions (using appropriate grain shift moments) have been completed. In some ports, these calculations have to be approved by the local authorities
- a hold cleaning schedule using realistic times has been prepared.

Order of events	Day 1	Day 2	Day 3	Day 4	Day 5	Day 6	Day 7
(In port) Hatch undersides	X	X					
Wash down decks		X					
HP salt water wash holds		X	X				
Chemical wash holds, scrape and SW rinse				X			
FW rinse and hold preparation					X		
Clean hatch cover undersides					X		
Check holds and hatch water-tightness					X	X	

Table 1.1: An example of a simplified schedule. Note that this schedule assumes that the vessel's previous cargo was coal or iron ore. If the vessel's previous cargo was grain, the chemical wash may not be required, but the holds should still be hand scraped to remove any loose scale and paint.

Grain cleaning equipment list

A typical equipment list should include:

- A fully working high-pressure hold cleaning gun, complete with sufficient deck wash down hoses and air lines, all in good condition

> Fire hoses must not be used as wash down hoses as they are part of the ship's safety equipment.

- a fully operational salvage pump and approved spares
- sufficient fresh water to complete a high-pressure fresh water rinse of all the holds

> It will be more cost effective to over-supply fresh water for hold cleaning than for the ship to run out during hold cleaning. (A typical 100,000 dwt bulker requires around 30 T per hold.)

- 1 × portable pressurised fresh water gun, complete with extended handle and 30 m of pressurised hose
- 6 × long-handled steel scrapers, c/w handles
- 3 × lightweight, strong, aluminium extension poles with capability to extend to approximately 5 m
- 6 × long-handled rubber squeegees complete with 1 m rubber blades
- 10 × heavy-duty bass brooms, c/w handles, suitable for hold cleaning
- 6 × corn brooms, c/w with handles
- 6 × heavy-duty mops, c/w handles
- 6 × spare mop heads suitable for above
- 4 × galvanised, roller wringer mop buckets
- 6 × Turk's head brushes, round head 4 inch, c/w handles
- 6 × small 6 inch wide, hand shovels, steel, suitable for digging out hold bilges
- 3 × 25 m length, lint-free soogee cloth, width approx 30 cm
- 1 × 50 m length burlap, 1 m wide
- 10 × rolls of 50 m length, 10 cm wide, grey, industrial-strength duct tape
- 6 × 20 m length, 'yellow' wash down hoses, duraline, 45 mm diameter, c/w couplings suitable for ship's fire main
- 4 × plastic jet nozzles, suitable for use with hoses
- 4 × 50 m lengths, transparent plastic, reinforced garden hose, c/w male and female plastic couplings to join each section
- 2 × universal tap connectors for use with reinforced transparent plastic garden hose
- sufficient hatch sealing tape to comply with operator's instructions
- 4 × 500 watt, portable lightweight halogen lights to illuminate hatches during cleaning, each lamp to be complete with 50 m of cable and a fitted waterproof plug
- 10 × spare halogen bulbs for above

- 2 × 50 m extension cables each c/w 3 waterproof outlet sockets and a waterproof plug
- 5 × 20 litre drums of concentrated cleaning product
- sufficient drums of degreasing chemical wash suitable for use with seawater.

1.2 Surveys and Inspections

Prior to loading grain, ships are usually subject to a survey by an approved independent surveyor. The surveyor will require the vessel's particulars and details of (at least) the last three cargoes carried. They will inspect the holds for cleanliness and infestation, or the presence of any material that could lead to infestation.

 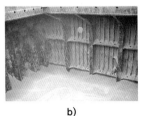 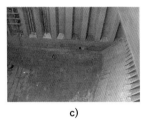

a)   b)   c)

Figure 1.14: a) Discharging soya meal.
b) Tapioca cargo sticking.
c) Cargo hold after discharging minerals.

When the surveyor is satisfied with the condition of the hold, the ship will be issued with a certificate that states which holds are fit to load grain.

1.2.1   Inspection Failures

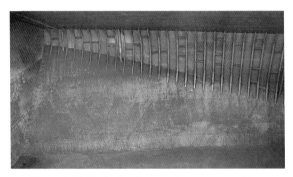

Figure 1.15: Tank showing previous cargo residue.

It is important that the Master and officers are fully aware of the level of cleanliness required for the next cargo to be loaded. A review of Figure 1.15, showing a ship that failed a grain survey, would suggest that:

- The ship's crew completed a very quick salt water wash
- no chemical wash was undertaken
- no hard scraping of the bulkheads was completed
- previous hold cleaning had not been supervised.

Examination of the stiffeners reveals:

- Staining from the previous cargo (coal)
- cargo dust residues
- deposits of previous cargoes in hard to reach places
- flaking paint and scale.

For loss prevention, it is important that:

- Records of cleaning are kept up to date
- photographs are taken as a record of cleaning
- cargo information is recorded and reported accurately
- cargo is observed throughout the loading operation
- cargo is determined as either on or off spec as soon as possible
- any off spec or tainted cargo is segregated
- in the event of contamination, samples and evidence are collected and labelled appropriately.

1.3 Pre-loading

1.3.1 Fumigation

Depending on the quality of the grain to be carried, the charterer may also require the holds to be fumigated. This may be accomplished on passage using fumigant tablets in protective sachets that are introduced into the cargo on completion of loading. It may also be undertaken at the load port (or occasionally at discharge).

The ship will normally be advised of how the fumigation is to be carried out and of any special precautions that will have to be taken. In all cases, the preparations (such as inspecting the holds and hatch covers for gastight integrity) and fumigation must be carried out in accordance with the IMO publication *Recommendations on the Safe Use of Pesticides in Ships* (Reference 1). Most flag and port States also set their own laws and regulations related to fumigation and pesticide use, which must be complied with. Gas detectors and proper PPE must be available and relevant crew should receive appropriate training in their use.

After introduction of the fumigant, an appropriate period should be allowed (normally 12 hours) for the gas to build up sufficient pressure to enable any leaks to be detected. The vessel must not depart from port before this period has expired. For fumigation in port, typically the crew are disembarked until the fumigation is complete.

The entire process should be certified by a qualified fumigator. It is important that the correct dosage of fumigant is used for the cargo/holds. The holds must not be ventilated until the minimum fumigation period has expired and care must be taken to ensure that subsequent ventilation does not endanger any personnel.

1.3.2   Grain Inspection

Prior to the grain inspection, all hatches and access lids must be opened and safely secured with all locking pins/bars. All hatches should be checked for loose scale or flaking paint. There will usually be a little scale on the tank top, which can quickly be removed. If weather conditions permit during the day, the holds should be opened to allow fresh air to assist the hold drying process. Any small pools of water should be mopped dry. All hatch rubbers and centreline seals should be wiped over with a clean dry rag to confirm their cleanliness.

Prior to the inspection, the ship's personnel should lower an aluminium ladder into the first hold, together with a small number of clean brooms, scrapers, a dustpan and brush, a clean bucket and a few clean white rags. If possible, the second hold to be inspected should also be equipped with similar items.

Figure 1.16: Hold ready to load wheat.

The first team to enter the open hold should include the grain inspector and a deck officer.

Grain inspectors should always be escorted by a deck officer when inspecting the hatches.

A second team, consisting of a deck officer and some crew members, should be standing by at the top of the hatch being inspected. The second team should have available additional clean brooms, clean mops, scrapers, buckets, clean heaving lines and clean white rags.

The engineers should be on standby to test the bilges (dry sucking only). Radio contact is essential between all three teams to prevent lengthy delays. Any personnel entering the holds should have clean safety shoes or clean safety sea boots and overshoe covers. It is essential that any debris on the main deck is not walked into the clean holds. If the inspector finds a fault with a hold, it should be identified and recorded and remedial action agreed. If possible, the fault should be rectified immediately and, preferably, before the inspector leaves the ship. If this is not possible, a time should be agreed for re-inspection.

1.4   Loading Grain

The primary sources of reference for the safe loading and carriage of bulk grain cargo are the *International Maritime Solid Bulk Cargoes Code* (IMSBC Code, Reference 17) and the *International Code for the Safe Carriage of Grain in Bulk* (International Grain Code, Reference 3). The International Grain Code sets out specific requirements for the ship to comply with for loading grain. These must be incorporated into the grain loading manual along with a Document of Authorization. The manual contains stability information to allow the Master to safely load grain cargo in accordance with the Code. The ship's loading plan should consider the grain loading stability data for loading, the voyage and discharge. Risk factors that should also be considered include:

- Angles of repose and trimming. All necessary and reasonable trimming should be performed to level all free grain surfaces and to minimise the effect of grain shifting
- stowage factor for particular grains to enable accurate loading
- temperature and moisture. Typically 20°C is considered a favourable temperature for the carriage of grain but the exact requirements will be specified by the charterer
- damage from heat. In some instances, cargo may be damaged by adjacent heated fuel oil tanks
- ventilation/cargo sweat/ship's sweat. Further information on this subject can be found in Chapter 2.

Once loading commences, hatches not in use for loading should be kept closed. All holds, after passing the grain inspection and prior to loading, must be inspected on a daily basis to ensure that they are still completely dry. During loading, it is important to keep the grain cargo dry. If the grain is allowed to become wet, substantial cargo claims may result. Regular visual checks by the ship's personnel throughout the loading should ensure that the grain being loaded is not in a wet condition. These inspections should be recorded in the deck logbook.

During periods of heavy rain precipitation, cargo operations are generally suspended to avoid water damage to cargoes. However, care must be taken by the Master to ensure compliance with charterers' requirements, shipowners' advice and the requirements of the port/terminal. Typically, surveyors attend ships and assist the Master with the loading of grain cargoes during periods of inclement weather. As a general guideline, it is suggested that if grain dust can be seen emanating from the cargo hold during loading in light precipitation, then loading may be continued. As soon as the precipitation is hard enough and sufficient to knock the grain dust down, it is suggested that the Master may want to cease loading as the precipitation is now affecting the cargo. This means that some moisture may be reaching the cargo whilst the hatch covers are closed.

During loading, the inspector should periodically inspect the cargo being loaded and take samples to check for insects, moisture content and odours.

Holds containing grain cargo may be oxygen depleted and, therefore, must not be entered without an appropriate risk assessment, a valid permit to work and adherence to enclosed space entry procedures.

In the event that damaged cargo is discovered, the Master and Members should inform their P&I Club as soon as possible in order to appoint a local surveyor to assess the location, depth and (if possible) extent of the damage. It is often the case that the location of any damage may indicate the cause. Detailed photographs, and even drawings, of the damage location would be useful. In the event that a local surveyor cannot attend immediately, it would assist if the Master/crew photograph and document the damage clearly.

Figure 1.17: Loading grain.

Some importers require grain to be stained with a unique colour if it is being imported for animal consumption. This dyeing process is usually undertaken at the load port and is performed by mixing dyeing agent in water and then spraying the mixture onto the incoming cargo. On completion of loading, the full upper layer of grain is also sprayed with the dyeing agent.

During the loading of grain, dust clouds often develop. These are a health hazard and additional safety precautions, such as the wearing of protective goggles and dust masks, should be observed by all personnel in the vicinity of the dust cloud.

Figure 1.18: Grain dust cloud.   Figure 1.19: Loading barley.

If the Master is in any doubt about the condition of the grain during the load, they must issue a note of protest and seek advice from their operators and/or the applicable P&I Club.

1.4.1   The Separation of Products in the Holds of Bulk Carriers

There is a considerable trade in the bulk carriage of relatively small quantities of cereals, oil seeds and their derivatives, with a number of such similar products shipped simultaneously on board bulk carriers. It is not uncommon for three or more consignments to be stowed in the same hold using separation material to avoid admixtures. However, incidents have arisen where, despite the use of separation cloths, admixtures have occurred and claims have been made by cargo interests.

In addition to separation of different grades, particularly with slack holds (part filled with grain), it is necessary to have the trimmed layer secured to prevent cargo shifting. In such cases, separation principles and/or overstowage with bagged grain are options.

> The steps necessary to avoid any risk of admixture are not complicated, but ships' officers should be aware of them when responsible for the stowage of multiple consignments.

The following measures may be taken:

- Where it is intended to overstow one bulk parcel with another, the lower parcel should be trimmed as flat as possible. If the surface is left uneven, there is a risk that the separation material may be damaged, either as a result of uneven stresses during the sea passage or as a result of contact with the grab or elevator legs and bulldozers. Provided this procedure is followed, a single layer of separation material of good quality is considered adequate. Recommended materials include woven polypropylene, polythene sheets or burlap

- during loading operations, it is essential that the distance between the separation material and either the top of the weather deck hatch coamings or the deckhead of the hold is measured and recorded. This makes it possible to effectively locate the separations between the parcels during discharge and avoid tearing or damaging the separation material

- loading second and third parcels may entail pouring cargo from a considerable height. As a result, the surface of the lower stow inevitably becomes depressed, as shown in Figures 1.20 and 1.21. Because of the need to ensure a relatively even surface between any two parcels, it may be wise to plan the stowage so that commodities with a high angle of repose, such as cereals and oil seed derivatives, are loaded below those with a low angle of repose, such as canary seed or linseed

> Siting the separation material at a level between the slant plating of the upper and lower hopper tanks will eliminate any difficulties caused by cargo settlement.

- ideally, the level of the separation between any two parcels should not be located in the vicinity of the upper ballast tank hoppers. This will ensure that, when the inevitable settling of the cargo occurs during the course of the voyage, the surface area of the separation material will remain adequate and prevent admixture. This problem does not arise in the vicinity of the lower hopper tanks.

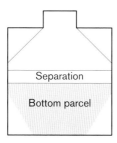

Figure 1.20: Cross-section – situation prior to loading top parcel.

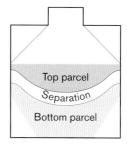

Figure 1.21: Cross-section – situation shortly after commencement of loading top parcel.

1.4.2 Completion of a Hatch

All holds to be loaded must be filled completely. It is essential that the loading spout, or other mechanism, is directed to all corners to avoid any void spaces. The grain should be allowed time to settle and then any spaces (such as hatch corners) refilled.

Figure 1.22: Complete filling of grain cargo.

Figure 1.23: Loading grain to all corners.

When the loading of a hold has been completed, the trackways, hatch drains and channel bars must be swept clean and the hatch closed. Water must not be used to wash down hatch trackways. Dry compressed air used under controlled conditions is very useful for cleaning the hatch area. Ventilators should be tightly secured.

Figure 1.24: Hatch vent to secure.

If the voyage instructions require hatch sealing tape to be used, as an additional precaution to prevent water ingress, then the hatch surfaces must be completely clean before the sealing tape is applied. In cold climates, some brands of tape will adhere better if warmed in the engine room before they are applied. Foam compound should not be used to ensure hatch watertight integrity.

Figure 1.25: Do not use foam to seal hatches.

Figure 1.26: Security seal in place.

To prevent unauthorised access to the grain holds, which may be oxygen deficient or undergoing fumigation, all hold access lids should either be padlocked or have steel security seals fitted.

1.5 Loaded Voyage

Regular checks of all hatch sealing tape (if used) should be completed and any damaged or lifting tape immediately replaced. During the voyage, entry into any cargo space must be strictly prohibited.

Ventilation during the voyage will depend on weather conditions and a comparison between the dew point of the air inside the hold and outside the hold. Under no circumstances should hold ventilation be permitted during adverse weather conditions or before fumigation in transit has been completed.

In good weather, basic cargo ventilation rules should be observed. Generally, the primary purpose of ventilating grain cargoes is to keep moisture to a minimum within the cargo hold by replacing moist air with drier air. Care should be taken to avoid both cargo and ship's sweat during the voyage. Further guidance may be obtained from Chapter 2, as well as from the publication *Bulk Carrier Practice: A Practical Guide* (Reference 2).

It is important that the ship maintains accurate ventilation records throughout the voyage. Details of periods when ventilation was carried out and times when ventilation was not possible should be recorded.

If the ship has any oil tanks adjacent to or under the cargo holds, any steam heating to these tanks should be minimised, but in any case carefully monitored to prevent cargo heating and possible cargo damage. Additionally, some cargoes may have a risk of self-heating so the temperature of the cargo should be monitored regularly. Full records should be maintained.

1.6   Cleaning Alongside After Discharge of Grain

Figure 1.27: Hatch cover underside and clean hatch rubber.

The first consideration before beginning cleaning operations is whether it is safe to enter the space. A test of the atmosphere and a risk assessment should be carried out.

On non-working hatches, remove all cargo remnants, loose scale and flaking paint from the underside of the hatch covers and from all steelwork within the hold. Then commence washing the underside of the hatch covers using a liquid soap, followed by a thorough fresh water rinse with a high-pressure water gun.

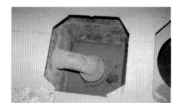 

Figure 1.28: Hold suction arrangement and filter.

The hatch rubber seals should be washed to remove cargo grime, although the water gun should be used with caution to ensure that the hatch rubber seals are not damaged by the high pressure.

After washing, and depending on weather conditions, cargo dust may still lightly contaminate the underside of the hatch covers. However, these dust particles can easily be removed at a later stage using a high-pressure portable fresh water gun.

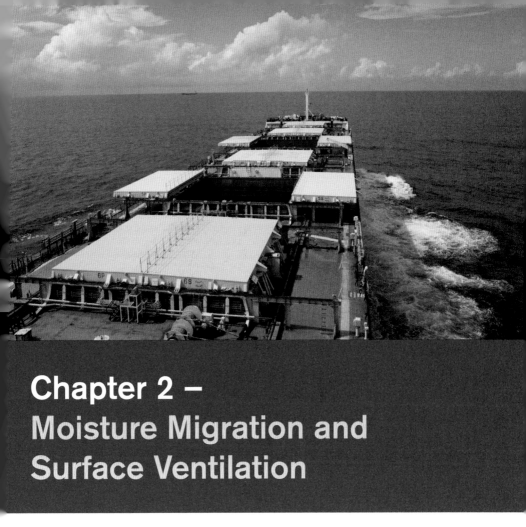

Chapter 2 –
Moisture Migration and
Surface Ventilation

This chapter explains how and why moisture migration takes place and discusses to what extent surface ventilation can reduce or eliminate the damage it can cause to bulk grain cargoes.

2.1 Movement of Moisture

During the voyage it is usual for moisture migration to take place. Part of the moisture migrates to be either lost to the external atmosphere as a result of ventilation, or drained off into the bilges. However, in some cases the total amount of water held in a cargo may be the same at the end of a voyage as it was at the beginning but, as a result of moisture migration, the moisture content of some parts of the cargo may have changed considerably.

In countries such as India and China, grains and other agricultural products might come from a number of locations and so may have different moisture levels. It can be very difficult to obtain a representative sample to determine the correct pre-shipment moisture or to ascertain whether the moisture level is below the threshold that can trigger condensation or 'sweat'.

In addition, grain cargo is often laid into open spaces for drying before it is moved to assembling places, which means that some lots will have higher moisture content than others.

2.2 Physical Considerations

2.2.1 Vapour Pressure (VP) and Relative Humidity (RH)

Vapour pressure (VP)
The earth's atmosphere is a mixture of 78% nitrogen, 20.9% oxygen and approximately 1% of other gases, including water in the form of vapour. Pressure exerted by the atmosphere will partly depend on the pressure exerted by the water in vapour form, and this proportion of the total atmospheric pressure is known as the 'water vapour pressure' of the air at that time.

Saturation vapour pressure (SVP)
As the quantity of water in the atmosphere increases, the VP will increase proportionately. At a given temperature, the air can only hold a specific amount of water vapour and the pressure exerted in the atmosphere when this limiting point is reached is referred to as the 'saturation vapour pressure' (SVP) of the air at that particular temperature.

Super saturation
Any attempt to increase the water vapour in the air once it has reached its SVP will produce 'super saturation', where water is deposited from the air in liquid form, either as droplets to form a fog or cloud or in the form of water drops on suitable surfaces, eg as sweat in a ship's hold.

Relative humidity (RH)
Under most circumstances, the VP of water in the atmosphere is less than the SVP. The percentage value of the actual VP in relation to the SVP is defined as the 'relative humidity' (RH) of the atmosphere. Therefore, if the air only holds half its potential maximum amount of water in the form of vapour, the relative humidity will be 50%. At SVP, the relative humidity will be 100%. Warm air is capable of holding more water vapour than cool air, so the actual weight of water that is required for saturation increases with increasing temperature. Therefore, for a given volume of air containing a constant weight of water vapour, the RH will vary as the SVP changes with the temperature. If the temperature rises, the SVP will increase and the RH will fall.

> If the temperature rises and the water vapour is constant, relative humidity falls.

Relationship at different temperatures
Figure 2.1 shows the relationship between VP and RH at different temperatures, eg 100% relative humidity at 10°C represents a water vapour pressure of 9.2 mm Hg and at 30°C of 32 mm Hg, ie an increase of 20°C has resulted in more than a three-fold increase in the water-holding capacity of the atmosphere.

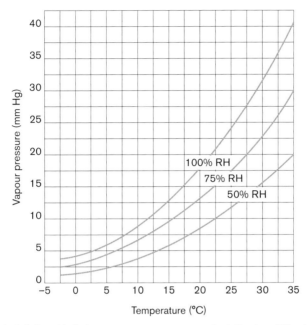

Figure 2.1: Relationship between vapour pressure and relative humidity at different temperatures.

Condensation

If air is cooled to the point where saturation (100% RH) is reached, moisture will begin to be deposited in the form of droplets or mist (ie condensation will occur).

Ship's sweat

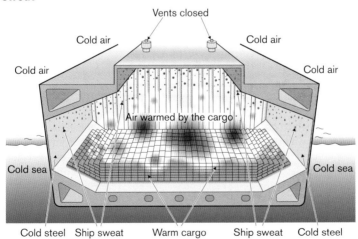

Figure 2.2: Warm cargo in a cold atmosphere resulting in ship's sweat.

If the air in a ship's hold is warm and it comes in contact with the deckhead, which has become cooled by the outside atmosphere, condensation will usually form on the deckhead in the form of sweat.

2.2.2   Equilibrium Relative Humidity (ERH) (Water Activity)

All biological materials normally contain a certain amount of water. The amount of moisture present at any given time is termed the moisture content. If the material comes into contact with dry air, it will tend to lose a small proportion of its water to the air in the form of water vapour. This process will continue until there is an 'equilibrium' of the air in contact with the material of that particular moisture content and at that particular temperature. Equilibrium relative humidity (ERH) is sometimes referred to as 'water activity' and it is measured as a ratio rather than as a percentage, so an equilibrium relative humidity of 50% is equivalent to a water activity of 0.5.

In bulk grain cargoes, where air movement within the bulk is very restricted, the moisture content of the atmosphere within the cargo (which is also termed the 'interstitial' or 'inter-particular' air) is, under normal conditions, completely controlled by the temperature and moisture content of the cargo.

Experimental work with maize has made it possible to construct graphs that equate ERH with moisture content at various temperatures. Such graphs are known as 'desorption isotherms', since all the experiments were constructed so that, to achieve ERH, moisture was given up by the maize to the surrounding air. If the air around the maize is wetter than the ERH, the maize will absorb moisture from the air. Such a process is known as 'adsorption' and a similar series of curves or isotherms may be constructed, called 'adsorption isotherms'. The relationship between adsorption and desorption isotherms is a complex one, but it may be stated that, under conditions of desorption, the ERH at any given moisture content is slightly lower than under conditions of adsorption.

> Normally in the grain trade, from harvesting through to the discharge of cargo, there is a tendency for the grain to lose moisture to the surrounding atmosphere.

2.3   Moisture Migration

Moisture migration can be expressed as follows:

Change of temperature → change of ERH → change of vapour pressure

The mechanism by which moisture migration operates can be illustrated by considering an example cargo of bulk maize, a commodity where migration is generally slow.

The interstitial air, which occupies some 40% of the cargo space in the case of bulk maize, will contain water vapour. The VP in this air will rapidly reach equilibrium with the moisture content of the maize. In maize with a moisture content of 14% and a temperature of 25°C, the RH of the interstitial air will rapidly reach 68% and the water vapour pressure in the air at that time will be 16.3 mm Hg. A change in the temperature of the maize will result in a change of the ERH and in the VP. Table 2.1 shows equilibrium temperatures for maize at 14% moisture content. The temperatures at which SVP occurs (ie 100% relative humidity) are included in the table, and these temperatures are known as the 'dew points'.

Temp (°C)	Equilibrium RH (%)	Vapour pressure (mm Hg)	Dew point (°C)
15	60.0	7.1	7.4
20	64.4	11.2	13.0
25	68.0	16.3	18.7
30	71.5	22.9	24.3
35	75.0	31.5	30.0

Table 2.1: Temp/ERH/VP/DP – Relationship of maize at 14% moisture content.

Table 2.1 shows that air at 25°C and 68% ERH will have a VP of 16.3 mm Hg. If this air is reduced to a temperature of 18.7°C, moisture will be deposited because the SVP will have been reached. If a ship carrying maize of 14% moisture content with a temperature of 25°C passes into a region of colder water, the outside of the cargo will assume the temperature of the cold sides of the vessel. If we assume this to be 15°C, it can be seen that the maize will have an ERH of 60% and a VP of 7.1 mm Hg.

The cooling process of the colder sea will not noticeably affect the maize in the centre of the bulk, since maize is a poor conductor of heat. Therefore, the maize in the centre of the stow will still have a temperature of 25°C and the interstitial air in this region will still have a VP of 16.3 mm Hg.

A VP difference is created between the interstitial air in the maize in the centre and the interstitial air in the maize on the periphery of the stow.

Consequently, there will be a flow of moisture vapour from the high pressure region to the low pressure region in order to equalise the pressure difference, so water will move from the centre towards the periphery.

This movement of water from the inner portion of the cargo will have the immediate effect of causing a reduction in the VP of the air there, but equilibrium conditions will be restored as a result of more water moving from the grain into the interstitial air, so the original VP of 16.3 mm Hg will be maintained. Consequently, there will be a continuous flow of water vapour from the warmer part of the stow to the colder part.

The isotherm graph in Figure 2.3 shows ERH plotted against moisture content.

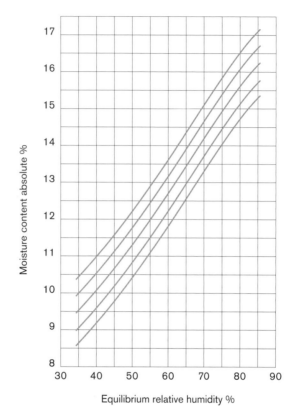

Figure 2.3: ERH plotted against moisture content.

Cargo sweat at periphery

In the example, the overall effect of this transfer of moisture vapour will be to cause deposition of physical water in the periphery of the stow that is in contact with the cold hull. This follows from Table 2.1, which shows that a VP of 16.3 mm Hg at 25°C will have a dew point of 18.7°C. As this dew point is higher than the temperature of the cargo at the periphery, water will be deposited on the cargo and cargo sweat will be produced.

> This example is an oversimplification of what happens in practice, as there is a tendency to set up a temperature gradient in the maize, along the route from the inside of the stow to the outside, and there will be a gradual drop in the temperature of the air that moves and the grain in contact with it. As water vapour will be absorbed en route, lowering the dew point of the air moving towards the periphery of the stow, it is not possible to make an exact prediction of the conditions that are necessary for cargo sweat to occur.

Heating up

If there is a temperature differential between the outside of the stow and the inside, moisture migration will result from the mechanism described. Such moisture migration will also occur when one part of the bulk heats up for any reason, eg insect infestation, microbiological activity or proximity to a hot bulkhead. In all these circumstances, moisture will migrate from the warmer region to colder parts of the stow.

Monitoring the cargo temperature on board, when it is safe to do so, can also provide valuable information regarding whether the cargo is self-heating. With some cargoes, such as soya beans, there will be visible evidence of damage by overheating (as described in Chapter 5).

Warmer to cooler climates

Figure 2.4: Bulk carrier arriving in a colder climate (ice on deck).

The problem of moisture migration is most evident with exports of biological cargo from warmer climates to cooler climates. Moisture migration may occur for many reasons but, irrespective of the cause of the temperature differential, the result will always be (where the moisture content is uniform) a movement of moisture from the warmer to the cooler parts of the cargo.

Moisture migration is observed in cargoes where insect infestation occurs. Here, the respiratory heat from the insects causes centres of heating and moisture migrates from these spots to form a wetter shell in the cooler cargo immediately surrounding the heated zone. As heating becomes progressive, the warmer zone expands and the wetter shell moves outwards.

Another example is where ship's heat causes a localised rise in the temperature of the cargo in contact with the heat source, for example, an uninsulated engine room bulkhead. Here, moisture migrates from the warm cargo and forms a layer of increased moisture content in the cooler cargo adjacent to it.

Unfortunately, the straightforward pattern of moisture movement resulting from a VP differential is not the only phenomenon that results from a temperature differential in a cargo. Where temperature differentials are present, convection currents are set up owing to the fact that warm air is less dense than cold air. Therefore, if heating occurs within a cargo, there will be a tendency for moisture to migrate in all directions from the heating zone. There will also be a tendency for hot air to rise from the heating zone, to be replaced by cooler denser air coming in from the sides and underneath. The warm air will carry more moisture with it, so the pattern of moisture movement will be distorted in a vertical direction.

> Where a hot spot occurs in a cargo, moisture movement is greater in a vertical direction than either laterally or downwards because convection currents reinforce the upward movement of moisture.

Therefore, for grain that is loaded warm and subjected to peripheral cooling, the primary moisture movement will be in a vertical direction, so more water will pass towards the top of the cargo than towards the sides. If it is not possible to remove the water migrating to the top region of the cargo by ventilation, more damage may be anticipated in the top layers than at the sides.

2.3.1 The Rate of Moisture Migration

Difference in vapour pressure (VP)
The rate at which moisture moves from a warm to a cold region depends, to a large extent, on the difference in VP between the warmer and colder parts of the cargo. As shown in Table 2.1, the VP of interstitial air of a cargo of maize at 14% moisture content does not increase directly with temperature. As a consequence, an increase in temperature from 15 to 25°C will give a VP increase of 9.2 mm Hg, while a rise in temperature from 25 to 35°C will give a VP increase of 15.2 mm Hg. It therefore follows that moisture migration will be greater, all other things being equal, when moisture is moving from cargo at 35°C to cargo at 25°C than when moisture is moving from cargo at 25°C to cargo at 15°C, although the temperature difference in both cases is the same.

> When considering the rate of moisture movement within a cargo, the specific temperatures are as important as the relative difference in temperatures.

Another factor is the differential in temperature in relation to distance, as moisture will move more rapidly from cargo at 25°C to cargo at 15°C if the distances are shorter, because the VP gradient is much greater. In this respect, the thermal conductivity of the cargo will be of considerable importance as the lower the conductivity, the slower any heat will move through the cargo.

Initial moisture content
The initial moisture content is also important. If we consider a cargo of maize at 14% moisture content loaded at 35°C, with its periphery cooled down to 25°C, the equilibrium VPs will be 31.5 mm Hg and 16.3 mm Hg respectively, giving a differential of 15.2 mm Hg. Under the same temperature conditions, but with maize at moisture content of 11%, the equilibrium vapour pressures will be 22.4 mm Hg and 11.6 mm Hg, giving a lower differential of 10.8 mm Hg. In addition (and this is of considerable

practical importance), a much greater quantity of water can be absorbed by the cooler grain before the moisture content is raised to a level at which spoilage will commence.

Soya beans are another example where moisture content and temperature are two of the main factors that influence whether the cargo, or part of the cargo, may undergo self-heating (see Chapter 5).

Compactness

Because of the importance of convection currents in moving moisture, the more readily air can move through a cargo, the more rapidly moisture can be carried through.

This means that there will be more rapid moisture movement through a cargo that is less compact (eg pellets) than through a cargo that is powdered, where the movement of air will be very limited.

Relevance to grain

A cargo such as grain, which in this context covers the edible, seed-like fruits of grasses and pulses, has a comparatively low moisture content and the seed itself has a protective outer skin that is relatively impermeable to moisture. Therefore, moisture is released relatively slowly from grain cargoes such as wheat and maize. In addition, whole grain will lose moisture much more slowly than grain that has been milled or pulverised in some way, as the natural protective coating will have been disrupted.

There is little quantitative data for the release of moisture from various products so direct comparisons are difficult. However, in a study of maize, it was found that, in 28 days, a zone of enhanced moisture had moved approximately 1 m in a vertical direction (ie with convection currents reinforcing the moisture movement) from a hot spot. The temperature differential in this experiment was from 40 to 21°C over a distance of approximately 1.25 m. The actual quantities of water involved could not be accurately determined, but there was no doubt that, for many other types of cargo, both the rate of movement and the quantities of water moved would have been many times greater.

When considering the significance of potential moisture migration in a cargo, it is necessary to consider:

- The VP differential in relation to the distance between the hotter and colder zone

- the temperature of the hotter material and the temperature of the colder material to which moisture is migrating

- the initial moisture content

- the nature of the cargo

- the ease with which air may move through it.

Vessels that carry grain in bulk vary in their capability for ventilating the cargo. Considerable quantities of grain are carried in tankers with no ventilation whatsoever. Sometimes grain is carried in vessels fitted with a sophisticated *Cargocaire* system of surface ventilation, which also has facilities for preconditioning the ventilating air. Other vessels have fan-assisted surface ventilation and many others have natural surface ventilation through cowls that is unassisted by any mechanical effort, with the flow of air dependent on the movement of the ship. Some bulk carriers that successfully carry many thousands of tonnes of grain have no means whatsoever of ventilating the surface of the cargo.

However, claimants frequently state that spoilage of grain in transit is a result of unsatisfactory ventilation, or that lack of ventilation has exacerbated damage caused by other factors.

A bulk cargo of grain, if stowed in accordance with the *International Code for the Safe Carriage of Grain in Bulk* (International Grain Code, Reference 3), is not able to be surface ventilated, which suggests that such a cargo is unlikely to be significantly affected by surface ventilation, or from a lack of it. T A Oxley in *The Scientific Principles of Grain Storage* (Reference 4) stated:

"... popular opinion greatly exaggerates the virtues of ventilation ... gaseous diffusion and heat movement in grain are both exceedingly slow and, in the absence of mechanical means to force air through bulks, changes in the atmosphere at the surface have a negligible effect on the intergranular atmosphere and on the water content or temperature of the grain."

Figure 2.5: Loading grain.

To reduce moisture movement and its effects within a grain cargo, it would be necessary to reduce the moisture content throughout the cargo or, alternatively, reduce the temperature differential by cooling the bulk of the grain.

A reduction in moisture content and a reduction in temperature could both be achieved by passing significant quantities of air through the cargo. However, through ventilation, while possible in some silos ashore, is not possible on board ship. In practice, only surface ventilation is available to attempt to control the damaging peripheral effects of moisture migration in bulk grain.

2.4 Cargo Sweat

In the case of tankers, while there is general agreement that little can be done about ship's sweat should it occur, it is suggested that, for vessels fitted with natural or mechanical ventilation, the moist air may be continuously removed from the headspace above the cargo to reduce or eliminate condensation occurring on the deckhead. However, it must be remembered that the air used for ventilation is at the same temperature as, or below, the temperature of the deckhead and hatch covers. If the ventilating air is cool, the immediate effect will be to take up moisture vapour by diffusion from the interstitial air in the surface layers of the cargo, because the vapour pressure of the interstitial air will be higher than the vapour pressure of the ventilating air. At the same time, the surface of the cargo will be cooled, both directly by contact with the cooler ventilating air and as a result of evaporation of moisture. The temperature of the surface layer of the cargo may, therefore, be reduced below the dew point of the warm moist air rising from within the bulk. Water will then condense in the cooler surface layers of the cargo, producing a wet cake just below the surface. Microbiological spoilage will eventually occur in this wet cake. Even if no condensation occurs in the surface layer, the moisture content of these layers may rise as a result of absorption of moisture, to a level where microbiological activity can occur, although this damage does not arise strictly from cargo sweat.

> If the external ambient conditions are such that ship's sweat would occur in the absence of ventilation, cargo sweat will frequently occur just below the surface if ventilation is employed. This means that, under these circumstances, damage will result whether ventilation is used or not.

Surface ventilation is also claimed to be useful in cooling cargo that is heating, minimising the increase in temperature that might cause further deterioration. It is, however, generally agreed that heat transfer through bulk grain is a very slow process. Work carried out using a vertical heat transfer system with a temperature differential of 20°C indicated that about 32 days' continuous heating was required before there was a rise in temperature of 3°C in maize 1 m from the heat source. So, although microbiological spoilage produces serious heating, surface ventilation cannot significantly affect a heating process that is occurring more than about 1 m below the surface.

Figure 2.6: Surface damage to cargo as a result of ship's sweat.

What can occur when the surface of a heating cargo is continuously cooled by ventilation is that the VP differential between the interior of the cargo and the periphery is maintained and, consequently, the phenomenon of moisture migration is encouraged.

2.5 Stowage Regulations

The irrelevance of surface ventilation to the carriage of grain is apparent from the stowage regulations in force in all major grain exporting countries, which insist that the vessel is stowed so that shifting of the cargo is impossible. Under these regulations, a ship's grain carrying compartments are classified as either partly filled or full. Grain in partly filled compartments must be levelled and topped off with bagged grain or other suitable cargo, tightly stowed and extending to a height of 1–2 m above the bulk. The bagged grain or other suitable cargo must itself be supported by a platform made either of close boarded wood or strong separation cloths laid over the whole surface of the bulk cargo.

These regulations also mean that, in compartments totally filled with grain, the grain must be trimmed to fill all the spaces between the beams, in the wings and ends.

Further, to ensure that the compartment is maintained fully filled during the voyage, the compartment must be equipped with a feeder from which grain can flow into the compartment if the cargo settles during the voyage. Alternatively, the grain in the area of the hatch may be trimmed hard up to the deckhead beyond the hatchway to form a saucer. This saucer and the hatchway above are then filled with bagged grain or other suitable cargo extending to a height of at least 2 m in the centre of the saucer. The bagged grain or other suitable cargo must itself be stowed tightly against the deckhead as well as the longitudinal bulkheads, the hatch beams and hatch coamings.

The express purpose of the regulations is to reduce to a minimum, and if possible to eliminate, the headspace between the surface of the cargo and the overlying deck. With cargo stowed correctly in this way, there is no possibility of effective surface ventilation.

2.6 Karnal Bunt

Karnal bunt is a fungal disease that affects certain types of cereal grains such as wheat. The disease develops during the growth phase of the plant and not during post-harvest storage or transportation. However, it can cause potentially serious problems for shipowners and charterers. Many countries prohibit the importation of wheat that is known or, in some instances, is suspected to be affected by Karnal bunt. This can cause lengthy delays to ships while a solution is found for the disposal of the cargo. Definitive identification of the spores of the specific fungus that causes Karnal bunt in a consignment of grain requires specialised and time-consuming test procedures, which can take up to two weeks to complete.

Karnal bunt was first described in Karnal, India in 1931. It has now been identified in all of the major wheat producing regions of India, Pakistan, Iraq and Afghanistan and is also well established in north-western Mexico. More recently, it has also been found in durum wheat from Arizona. Following this discovery, a flurry of surveys and inspections was carried out, resulting in quarantine measures being imposed in the state of Arizona and in counties in New Mexico, Texas and California.

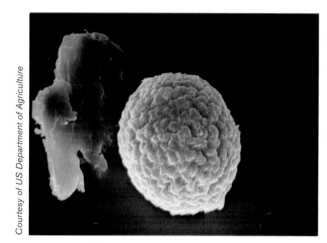

Courtesy of US Department of Agriculture

Figure 2.7: A Karnal bunt spore.

While the disease is not particularly damaging in terms of yield loss, it can cause significant reductions in grain quality. The spores of the infecting fungus are believed to present no health risks to consumers through infected grain or grain products, but wheat containing more than 3% of 'bunted' kernels is commonly considered to be unfit for human consumption. This is because flour produced from wheat containing a significant number of bunted kernels may have a distinctive odour.

Karnal bunt is also known as partial bunt. The fungal organism responsible for the disease is *Tilletia indica*. Spread of the disease occurs by the microscopically small spores of the fungus being distributed by wind and then infecting the host plant during flowering and heading. Symptoms become visible only as the grain matures. Bunted kernels can be very difficult to detect in the field, particularly in cases of mild infection, because normally not all plants in the crop are affected. Bunted kernels, however, each contain millions of spores of the fungus, which means there is potential for further spread.

There are other types of bunt, such as common bunt (sometimes known as 'stinking smut'), which is prevalent in parts of Europe and is caused by a related fungal organism. However, these other types of bunt differ in that infection is spread by spores in the soil, rather than by the wind. This means they can be controlled relatively easily by pre-treatment of the seed with suitable anti-fungal dressings. In EU countries, however, a ban has been imposed in recent years on the application of some effective fungicides previously used to treat seed. This has been held responsible for some resurgence in the incidence of common bunt in certain parts of Europe.

Karnal bunt is much more difficult to control and there is no effective solution as yet.

A number of countries, particularly those in which wheat is a crop of major importance, are extremely concerned by the importation of wheat that is known or suspected to contain kernels affected by Karnal bunt and they regard the disease as a quarantine pest. By early 1997, some 50 countries had adopted phytosanitary measures to prevent the importation of wheat affected by Karnal bunt.

Some countries accept US wheat from quarantined areas if it is certified that the wheat has tested negative for *Tilletia indica* by laboratory analysis on both pre-harvest and pre-shipment samples. Other countries, for example Mexico, require methyl bromide fumigation prior to discharge of the cargo.

It is impossible for ships' representatives to detect, by visual inspection at loading, whether a cereal grain cargo is contaminated with diseased kernels specifically affected by Karnal bunt. However, if during loading of a grain cargo any unusual odour is detected, that may or may not be due to the presence of substantial amounts of grain severely infected with Karnal bunt, the bill of lading should be claused. Other than that, the only realistic course of action open to shipowners wishing to protect their interests as far as possible is to insist on the provision of a certificate, from an authoritative source in the country of exportation, that unequivocally confirms that the cargo is free from Karnal bunt.

It may be advisable for shipowners to avoid carrying cargoes of wheat originating from countries where Karnal bunt is known to be prevalent. This applies particularly to cargoes destined for countries known to adopt a particularly severe approach to the importation of wheat from affected countries.

When a ship has discharged a cargo known to be affected by Karnal bunt, depending on future trading patterns, it may be necessary to carry out sterilisation treatment of the relevant holds to destroy the viability of any residual spores. The following sterilisation treatments are claimed to be effective:

- Wetting all surfaces to the point of run-off with a solution of 1.5% sodium hypochlorite and water and letting stand for 15 minutes. Thereafter, the surfaces should be thoroughly washed down to minimise corrosion
- applying steam to all surfaces until the point of run-off so that a critical temperature of about 80°C is reached at the point of contact
- cleaning with a solution of hot water and detergent under a pressure of at least 2 kg per sq cm (30 pounds per sq inch) at a minimum temperature of 80°C
- fumigating with methyl bromide at a dosage of 240 kg per 1,000 m^3.

Chapter 3 –
Cargo Measurement

During the transportation of bulk cargo, some losses will unavoidably occur. However, when the shortages exceed a percentage regarded as customary in that trade, the carrier is often held responsible. One of the causes of shortage claims is that it is virtually impossible to precisely determine the weight of large quantities of dry bulk cargoes, either afloat or ashore. Chapter 16 describes the measurement of dry bulk cargoes using draught surveys, while this chapter refers to the specifics of bulk grain measurement.

3.1   Determination of Weight Ashore

Various methods are used to determine the weight of a grain cargo when it is still ashore. The common ones are:

- Weighbridges
- mechanical weighing
- fixed and mobile bag weighers
- automatic bulk grain weighers
- automatic load cell gross weighers
- conveyor belt weigh systems.

3.1.1 Weighbridges

These heavy-duty machines for the weighing of empty and fully loaded road vehicles are generally intended to operate in a wide range of temperature conditions, from minus 10°C (−10°C) to +50°C, depending on local regulations. In extreme conditions, where temperatures may be regularly outside these parameters, the manufacturers should be consulted.

Because of the manner in which weighbridge scales are graduated and operated, manufacturers can only guarantee an accuracy of half of one scale division or less.

Therefore, on a 20 T weighbridge, with 10 kg divisions, the error could be ±5 kg (±0.025%). An 80 T weighbridge will have an accuracy of ±10 kg (±0.0125%). Most weighbridge systems can account for any debris, water, ice or snow that may have accumulated between one lorry being weighed and the next.

Figure 3.1: A weighbridge.

3.1.2 Fixed and Mobile Bag Weighers

These include:

- Semi-automatic machines that are suitable for low output, low-cost bagging requirements
- portable automatic bag weighers that can deal with both sacks and bulk
- fully-automatic bag weighers that will record both gross and/or net weights and that are suitable for flow materials such as grain, granular fertiliser, seeds, pulses, pellets, plastic granules, rice, refined sugar and other similar products.

These machines may be accurate to within ±1% for bags weighing between 20 and 50 kg.

When weights increase to 100 and 250 kg, accuracy will improve to between 0.5 and 0.2%.

The degree of accuracy depends on:

- The index allowances set by the operator for the weight of an empty bag
- the degree of care exercised by the operator in maintaining the mechanical system.

3.1.3 Automatic Bulk Grain Weighers

These machines are suitable for weighing grain and free-flowing materials fed from elevators, conveyor belts, storage hoppers or silos. They are produced in various sizes and can record weight cycles from 30 kg up to 5 T. They can deliver at rates of up to 1,000 T/hour. When this machinery is correctly installed and maintained by the manufacturers, and regularly inspected by a reliable local regulatory authority, an accuracy of ±0.1% is likely.

3.1.4 Automatic Load Cell Gross Weighers

These machines are designed to handle grain sizes not greater than 25 mm. They are used in continuous weighing cycles of 10 to 50 kg and their accuracy is better than 0.2% in most cases.

3.1.5 Conveyor Belt Weigh Systems

There are a number of conveyor weigh systems and, at best, their margin of error is likely to be within 0.5% of true weight for capacities of up to 6,000 T/hour, increasing to 1 to 2% of true weight for flow capacities of 2,000 T/hour.

Ivan Kuzukin/Shutterstock.com

Figure 3.2: Conveyor belt system in Canada.

Where an unexplained short-landing occurs at a discharge port, the conveyor belt weigh system may prove to be a worthwhile field of investigation. If the cargo has been loaded and weighed on a conveyor system, both the load port terminal and the discharge port terminal should be asked to produce the manufacturers' full specification and brochures for the equipment utilised. If the guaranteed accuracy is not better than between 1 and 2% of true weight, considerable errors may arise. For a shipment of 100,000 T, for example, an indicated 'loss' of 2,000 T might be possible, where accurate weighing would have probably indicated a discrepancy of no more than 500 T (based on a 'transport' difference of 0.5%).

3.2   Determination of Weight on Board Ship

There are two methods of determining the weight of a dry bulk grain cargo loaded on board a ship:

- On the basis of the free space in a compartment (measurement and stowage factor)
- on the basis of draught surveys (see Chapter 16).

3.2.1   Measurement and Stowage Factor

On completion of loading, the free space in each cargo hold is measured and, from this, the volume occupied by the cargo is calculated. This volume, when divided by an assumed stowage factor, gives the approximate weight of the cargo. This method is no more than an estimation and the exact stowage factor is seldom known, so the assumed figure may be quite inaccurate. The stowage factor can only be ascertained correctly by laboratory analysis of samples from the cargo, which take into account the nature of the cargo, the moisture content, the percentage of foreign matter present and the age of the commodity.

The stowage figure may also vary considerably for other reasons. For example, in grain cargoes, 'spout lines' may develop because grain in a cargo hold tends to separate into heavier and lighter components. In addition, almost all bulk grain cargoes settle during transportation as the kernels and shells collapse. The result of this is an increase in weight per unit volume and a lower stowage factor. In such cases, and if the same assumed stowage factor was used, it would be unsurprising that the weight of cargo calculated on the basis of free space measurement after loading would indicate a greater quantity of cargo than that calculated before discharge.

It is probably reasonable to say that the accuracy of shore weighing of bagged and bulk commodities is unlikely to be better than within 0.2% and, in conveyor belt weigh systems, may be no better than ±2%. There are no technical means by which the exact weight of a dry bulk cargo on a ship may be accurately determined. The weights may be approximately determined by free space measurement or by draught survey, but neither of these methods is sufficiently accurate to verify the weight of a cargo as stated by shippers, nor to determine any loss of cargo in transit.

Chapter 4 –
The Carriage of Genetically Modified (GM) Crops

The term GMO (genetically modified organism) refers to any organism whose genetic makeup has been altered using genetic engineering. In the context of marine cargoes, they are usually seed from GM plant varieties that have characteristics that are different from those of varieties that have been developed through traditional plant breeding techniques. GM crops are not readily detectable by visual inspection.

Figure 4.1: GM cargoes are usually comprised of seed from GM plant varieties.

GM crop varieties have been developed to meet different breeding aims including:

- Herbicide resistance – crops that show minimum damage following herbicide spraying regimes that are designed to eliminate weeds
- disease – crops that are less prone to be damaged by fungal, bacterial or viral diseases
- pest resistance – crops that are less attractive to natural predators such as insects
- stress resistance – crops that are more tolerant to various environmental stresses such as drought, salinity and extreme temperatures
- varieties with altered composition – crops that show improved nutritional values, eg 'golden rice' with an increased level of vitamin A
- use in bioremediation to eliminate pollutants – crops that have the ability to decontaminate land by assimilating hazardous pollutants and toxic compounds. These plants can then be harvested and forwarded for industrial use or incinerated
- pharming (biopharming/molecular farming for the production of pharmaceuticals, enzymes, etc) – crops that produce increased yields of desirable compounds for industrial and pharmaceutical use, eg starch, fuel, antibodies, hormones, etc.

The first GM seeds were planted for commercial use in the USA in 1996. By 2006, the total acreage had increased to 102 million hectares, and today it is estimated that 180 million hectares globally are being cultivated with GM crops (2014 figures). The USA is leading in the cultivation of GM crops with approximately half of the world acreage (73 million hectares in 2014), followed by Argentina, Brazil and Canada. China is rapidly expanding cultivation of GM crops.

Today, a total of 28 countries use genetic engineering commercially. Soya beans, maize, oilseed rape (canola) and cotton account for almost all commercial GM crop production. Other GM crops under cultivation include sugar beet, potatoes, rice and sugar cane. GM ornamental products include roses and carnations.

Figure 4.2: GM crops on board a vessel.

4.1 Conventional Hazards

GM crops present no greater hazard during shipping than that already identified for their conventional counterparts. Similarly, the loading, precautions during carriage, ventilation and discharge operations of GM crops do not differ from those of conventional crops.

Figure 4.3: The loading of GM crops.

4.2 Carriage of GM Crops

When carrying GM crops:

- Cargoes of soya beans, maize, oilseed rape and cotton that are loaded in the USA, Argentina, Paraguay, Uruguay, Brazil or Canada come with an increased likelihood of being genetically modified. It is therefore recommended that these specific cargoes from the above locations are analysed prior to loading. The GM or non-GM nature of the cargo should be certified based on the analysis carried out

- the B/L should clearly state the unique identifier, species and the variety, which, if the cargo is GM, should be on the list of GMOs authorised in the EU (Reference 5)

- it is recommended that any GMO qualitative and quantitative tests carried out at the load port follow the protocols set out by the National Reference Laboratory of the destination country. In this way, the danger of variable results due to laboratory discrepancies is minimised. A list of National Reference laboratories that can carry out analyses of GM material and work under the auspices of the European Central Reference Laboratory (CRL) can be found at https://tinyurl.com/y8w66vpz (Reference 6)

- enquire whether the testing laboratory at the port of origin is accredited to carry out sampling specifically for GM material

- establish whether the import country is a party to the Cartagena Protocol on Biosafety (CBP) through the Biosafety Clearing-House (http://bch.biodiv.org) (Reference 7). The EU is a party

- establish whether the import country has any additional regulations on GM shipments for FFP (food or feed, or for processing), as in the case of the EU Members who accept only previously EU-authorised GM crops

- the International Grade Trade Coalition recommends that the commercial invoice contains the contact information of the last exporter prior to the transboundary movement and the first importer after that movement.

4.3   Carriage of Non-GM Crops with Low Level Presence (LLP) of Adventitious/Chance Contaminants

In conventional cargoes that are found to contain low levels of chance contaminants of GM origin, the fate of the cargo depends on the nature of the GM contaminant and the sampling and testing procedures that are conducted.

4.3.1   Sampling

Correct sampling intensity and good sampling techniques are crucial to minimising the error and inaccurate measurement of LLP involved with sampling. GM contaminations in large shipments are not necessarily random and any sampling methods used should take this into account. Currently, there are two appropriate testing guidelines:

- European recommendation 2004/787/EC. This also specifies the ISO method that should be used for the collection of the material (see Table 4.1) (Reference 8)
- ISO DIS 21568 (Reference 9).

Commodity to be sampled	ISO method to be used
Free-flowing commodities	6644/13690
Oilseeds	542
Pre-packaged food and feed products	2859
Material larger than grains (eg potatoes, fruits, rhizomes)	2859

Table 4.1: ISO methods used for the collection of material for the detection of GMOs.

Material for testing should be collected in intermittent sampling periods, which may be calculated by dividing the estimated total offloading time by the total number of increments. Table 4.2 shows the recommended number of increments, which varies according to the lot size.

Lot size in tonnes	Size of bulk sample in kg	Number of increments
≤50	5	10
100	10	20
250	25	50
≥500	50	100

Table 4.2: Size of bulk samples (kg) and number of increments to be collected for testing for GMOs in cargoes.

4.3.2   Testing

It is recommended that any qualitative and quantitative tests of GM crops that are carried out at the load port follow the protocols set out by the EU or national reference laboratory of the destination European country. In this way, the danger of variable results due to laboratory discrepancies is minimised. A list of national reference laboratories that can carry out analyses of GM material and that work under the auspices of the European Central Reference Laboratory (CRL) can be found at https://tinyurl.com/y8w66vpz (Reference 6).

The analytical steps of cargo testing for the low level presence of GM material are shown in Figure 4.4.

Following a negative result of the screened material, the cargo will be released. However, a positive test to GM material will prompt further investigation for the identification of the exact GMO. If the identified GMO has been authorised to be used as food or feed in the European country of discharge, a quantitative test will be required to determine the level of contamination.

The maximum permitted amount of approved GMO in a non-GM cargo is 0.9%. Above this, the cargo will be labelled as GM cargo. If the GMO has not been previously authorised under EU regulations, the cargo will be deemed illegal and it will be rejected irrespective of the level of contamination (there is a zero threshold for non-approved GMOs in the EU).

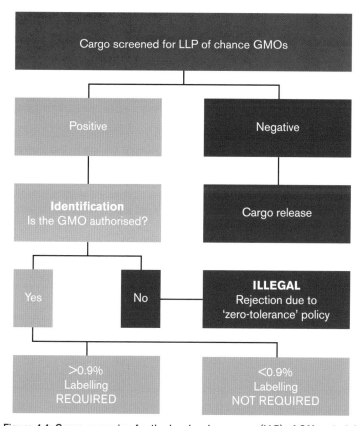

Figure 4.4: Cargo screening for the low level presence (LLP) of GM material.

Products that require labelling
Food that is a genetically modified organism (GMO) or that consists of GMOs (eg canned sweetcorn, approved but not available in the EU).
Food ingredients or additives that are produced from GMOs (eg oil from GM rapeseed or soya beans, starch from GM maize, and sugar from GM sugar beet).
Food ingredients or additives that contain genetically modified organisms (eg beer with GM yeast, blue cheese with GM moulds, yoghurt with GM lactobacilli). NOTE: No GM yeast/bacteria/fungi have been approved for use in food in the EU.

Products that do not require labelling
Food containing GMOs up to a threshold of 0.9%   • The producer/importer of a product needs to supply evidence that the presence of such material is either adventitious or technically unavoidable and that every possible step to minimise the presence of such material has been taken   • the GMO in question has already been classified as safe and has received an EU authorisation.   NOTE: The threshold of unauthorised GMOs is 0% (zero tolerance).
Food that is produced with the aid of genetically modified organisms (eg meat, eggs or dairy products produced from animals fed on GM feed, also additives, flavours and vitamins produced with the help of GM microorganisms such as artificial sweeteners, flavour enhancers and thickening agents)
Substances that are not required to be declared on the list of ingredients   • Enzymes used in food processing (eg chymosin used in cheese production and pectinases used to degrade cell membranes in juice or wine)   • substrates (growth media) for microorganisms (eg baker's yeast cultured on a medium containing GM corn, and vitamin C produced by microorganisms raised using glucose derived from GM corn starch)   • carrier substances; substances used to prolong shelf life, facilitate transportation, etc (eg starch/glucose/dextrin-derived).
Honey containing pollen or nectar from genetically modified plants

Table 4.3: Labelling requirements of GMO-related products.

4.4   The Legal Framework of GMO Importation

4.4.1   The European Regulations

Three laws govern the authorisation and release of genetically modified organisms in the EU:

Regulation 1829/2003 in effect since 19th April 2004 (Reference 10)
(Replaces directive 258/97)

This regulation defines the use of food and feed that has been produced from or contains GM plants. The regulation is set out in 49 Articles which give the detailed requirements for a GMO food or feed that need to be demonstrated in order for authorisation to be granted. It specifies the application for authorisation and the authorisation process, including modifications, revocations, suspensions and renewals of these.

Directive 2001/18/EC in effect since 17th April 2001 (Reference 11)
(Replaces directive 90/220/EC)

This directive contains 38 Articles which define the commercial use of genetically modified plants and their deliberate release into the environment. These have been compiled with the objective of protecting human health and the environment by controlling the risk of the deliberate release of GMOs. It clarifies the obligations, including the notification procedure, consultation with the public, and exchange of information prior to the release, as well as the monitoring and handling of any modifications following the release.

In addition to these two main directives, there is a further regulation concerning the traceability and labelling of GMOs, and a recommendation that encourages the inclusion of GM crops in European farming.

Directive (EU) 2015/412 in effect since 11th March 2015 (Reference 12)
(Amended directive 2001/18/EC)

This directive is an amendment that allows for member States to restrict or prohibit the cultivation of GMOs in their territory or in specific geographical areas.

Regulation 1830/2003 (Reference 13)
This regulation (13 Articles) determines the stages involved in the traceability and labelling of approved GMOs and the traceability of food and feed products produced from these GMOs prior to being placed on the market. It covers the labelling provisions of all GM food or feed that consists of, contains or is produced from GMOs. For any products comprising mixtures of GMOs, a list of the unique identifiers of all GMO components should be made available. Labelling of pre-packaged and non-pre-packaged products consisting of or containing GMOs should include the following statement on the label:

"This product contains genetically modified organisms" or *"This product contains genetically modified [name of organism(s)]."*

Recommendation 2003/556/EC (Reference 14)

This recommendation states that no form of agriculture should be excluded in the EU and includes guidelines to be used by member States for the development of measures for the coexistence of GMO crops and crops developed through conventional breeding. Strategies should be developed on the basis of the best available scientific evidence. The recommendation distinguishes between assessment of the environmental and health aspects, already covered by Directive 2001/18/EC, and the economic aspects still to be assessed. It also emphasises the need for monitoring and evaluation of coexistence and encourages the improvement of the existing segregation measures.

4.4.2 The Cartagena Protocol on Biosafety (CBP) and GMO Trade to the EU

In addition to the EU legal framework, there are regulations that have been agreed in the context of the Cartagena Protocol on Biosafety (CBP, Reference 15), which came into force in 2003. The CBP was designed to promote transparency and control in the international GMO trade, and up to the end of 2021 it had been ratified by 173 countries, excluding the three main GMO producers – USA, Argentina and Canada.

The CBP is an international regulatory framework put in place to reconcile the safety of the biodiversity with the use of products of modern biotechnology. A major component of the CBP was the establishment of the Biosafety Clearing-House (BCH) which was set up to *"facilitate the exchange of information on Living Modified Organisms (LMOs) and assist the Parties to better comply with their obligations under the Protocol".* (Reference 7).

The intentional and unintentional movements of products of modern biotechnology and their handling are described in Articles 6, 11, 17 and 18. It should be noted that the CBP refers to living modified organisms (LMOs). LMOs include genetically modified crops and other GMOs.

Under the protocol, exporters are obliged to provide more information on GM products before the shipment, and it is then up to the receiving country to decide whether or not to accept the shipment or to seek more information. Member States may reject such imports without quantitative justification or scientific evidence but must provide reasons, which may include (for example) potential danger to traditional crops, impacts on local culture or potential impacts on the value of biodiversity.

Figure 4.5: A shipment of GM goods.

CBP – Article 6 – Transit and Contained Use

Article 6 of the CBP exempts material destined for contained use or material in transit from the provisions of the protocol.

CBP – Article 11 – Procedure for Living Modified Organisms Intended for Direct Use as Food or Feed, or for Processing (LMO-FFPs)

Article 11 of the CBP describes the special measures required for LMOs that are intended for direct use as food or feed, or for processing (FFP), including the requirement for accurate information sharing via the BCH.

CBP – Article 17 – Unintentional Transboundary Movements and Emergency Measures

The presence of GM material found in non-GM cargoes is covered in Article 17. According to this Article, the duties of Parties involved in unintentional transboundary movements are:

- To notify affected or potentially affected States, the BCH and, where relevant, international organisations

- to provide the name, identity and details of the characteristics/traits of the LMO

- to provide information on the estimated quantities involved, the date of release, the use of the LMO at origin and any other relevant circumstances

- to inform on the possible adverse effects of the LMO on biodiversity, any risks to human health, and to provide possible risk management measures

- to provide a point of contact for further information and clarifications.

CBP – Article 18 – Handling, Transport, Packaging and Identification

Article 18 describes the requirements for handling, transport, packaging and identification of intentional transboundary movements of LMOs for direct use as FFP (Article 18.2a), for contained use (Article 18.2b) and for intentional introduction into the environment (Article 18.2c).

Central to the requirements of Article 18.2a is that the documentation that accompanies cargoes of LMO-FFPs clearly states that it 'may contain' LMOs. To this effect, the International Grain Trade Coalition (IGTC) recommends that the commercial invoice contains the following or a similar meaning declaration:

"*Cartagena Protocol Provision: This shipment may contain living modified organisms intended for direct use as food or feed, or for processing, that are not intended for intentional introduction into the environment.*"

The European Union goes beyond the Cartagena provisions, with strict rules on the importation of GMOs, based on demanding but clearly set out principles. Following the cessation of the *de facto* moratorium on GMO imports in 2004, Regulation 1829/2003 came into force specifying the labelling provisions for food and feed produced from GMOs (as described under Regulation 1830/2003).

Chapter 5 – Soya Beans

5.1 Hold Preparation

Prior to loading a cargo of soya beans, the ship's holds should be cleaned to 'grain clean' standard (see Section 1.1.3). In some cases, the charterer may provide instructions on cleaning prior to loading. Before loading it would be prudent for the Master to carry out a hose test to make sure that the hatch covers and ventilation windows are weather tight.

5.2 Considerations During the Loading of Soya Beans

Soya bean cargoes can be loaded in a number of ways:

- Directly from barges
- from flat warehouses or silos
- from trucks.

In many cases, the cargo is transferred to the vessel by conveyor belt and loaded by pipe. If loading is conducted from barges, it is worth noting the numbers and/or names of the barges and the holds into which each barge loads. In all circumstances, the sequence of hold loading should be recorded. Clear photographs of how the cargo is delivered to the vessel and how it is loaded will be invaluable in the event of a claim.

While a Master and crew will usually recognise the type of commodity being loaded, they are not cargo specialists and it can be difficult to recognise whether or not soya bean cargoes are loaded *"in apparent good order and condition"*, as described on the B/Ls. This is not helped by the high speed at which the cargo is loaded and the fact that the quality of soya beans can only be accurately assessed by laboratory analysis of representative samples.

Figure 5.1: A ship unloading soya beans.

It is unlikely that the Master will receive either a quality specification for the soya beans to be loaded or a Quality Certificate representing the average quality of the cargo loaded on board. A Quality Certificate is usually issued to the cargo buyer after the vessel has sailed, when the samples obtained by cargo superintendents/sampling attendants throughout loading, on behalf of shippers, have been analysed. While a Quality Certificate can be requested from shippers, the Master may not receive any analytical information regarding the quality of the cargo being loaded and so will have to rely on a visual assessment of condition during loading, which is challenging for non-specialists.

Moisture content and temperature are two of the main factors that influence whether the cargo or part of the cargo of soya beans may undergo self-heating. According to standards issued by the American Society of Agricultural and Biological Engineers (ASABE), it can be inferred that soya beans loaded with a moisture content above 12.4%, at temperatures above 25°C may become unstable during a long voyage. While some commercial contracts allow a soya bean moisture content of up to 14%, this would be too high for the safe carriage of soya beans being shipped over long distances, or on extended voyages. It should be noted that a Quality Certificate generally provides the average moisture content for a bulk cargo of soya beans. Some parcels of beans may therefore be loaded above or below the average moisture content stated on a Quality Certificate.

The Master and crew will have difficulty assessing the moisture content of bulk soya beans being loaded. While hand-held moisture meters are sometimes available, they do not always provide results as accurate as those obtained from analysis undertaken in a laboratory. However, an obvious sign that a consignment, or part of a consignment, has a high moisture content is when the soya beans are visually mouldy. This could indicate that they were not effectively dried after harvest or that they have been subject to poor handling and storage prior to shipment.

Figure 5.2: Sound soya beans.

Figure 5.3: Mouldy soya beans.

If the cargo on board a particular barge or truck is presented for loading with obvious clumps of white or green mouldy soya beans, or the beans are visibly wetted, then the Master should protest and refuse to load this cargo. Mouldy or wetted cargo will further deteriorate during the voyage and, potentially, initiate self-heating within surrounding soya beans.

The crew or cargo superintendent should enter the holds when safe to do so, ie during a loading break, and visually inspect the surface of the cargo for any odours or noticeable moisture, heat or mould in the cargo. Numerous spot samples should be obtained from each hold and labelled clearly. The findings should be noted and photographs obtained.

As with all agricultural cargoes, loading should be discontinued during rain and all holds kept closed until the weather conditions are appropriate. Lack of suitable covering to barges or trucks, especially during poor weather conditions, should be recorded. Any conveyor belts or loading equipment wetted by rain, which is subsequently used for loading, should be photographed and a Protest issued. Any cargo wetted ashore on the conveyor belt, shore equipment or in open barges or trucks, should be rejected from loading.

Monitoring the cargo temperature on board when it is safe to do, can also provide valuable information regarding whether the beans are undergoing self-heating. Soya beans undergo discolouration at high temperatures. The colour of the beans will change from cream to brown as a result of heating over a period of time. At very high temperatures, soya beans appear totally blackened. The Master should refuse to load visually darkened portions of soya beans. Taking temperatures at regular intervals should indicate whether the cargo temperature is stable across the consignment or whether there are hotspots within some cargo parcels, which should not be loaded. It is useful to monitor cargo temperatures at regular intervals during loading. The use of sub-surface calibrated temperature probes will provide more reliable readings than the use of an infrared thermometer.

If mouldy cargo or cargo at a high temperature is loaded on board and later discovered during loading operations, there may be a situation where the cargo needs to be removed from the vessel in order that the Master can sign clean bills of lading. This situation can lead to long negotiations with stevedores and shippers. If the cargo is not successfully removed the Master should issue a Protest and the Member's P&I Club contacted for further advice. Any delays caused by a lack of cargo readiness for loading should be noted. Furthermore, the Master should record any excessive spillage of cargo. Photographs of any significant events regarding the cargo should be obtained.

5.3 Sampling

Members can appoint a cargo superintendent to sample the cargo throughout loading, according to a representative sampling method, in order to obtain representative samples which can be assessed for cargo quality in the event a cargo claim arises. However, this is often a costly exercise. Owners may wish to invite all parties to sample the cargo representatively in order to share costs.

If representative sampling during loading is not feasible, collecting some samples through loading may provide an indication of the cargo condition which was loaded, without being representative. How these samples were collected and from which location needs to be clearly documented.

5.4   Heated Fuel Oil Tanks

Prolonged exposure to high temperatures from heated bunker tanks can also lead to direct heat-related discolouration of soya beans located next to the tank. This will have a direct impact on the oil and protein quality of the beans. The temperature gradient established over time between the tanks and cargo will drive moisture up through the cargo, resulting in further heating of cargo at some distance from the heated tanks.

Ideally, soya beans should not be loaded in holds adjacent to fuel oil tanks which are likely to be heated. Top side wing fuel oil tanks present a lower risk than those located in the double bottom as there is likely to be less cargo in direct contact with the steelwork of a top side wing fuel oil tank. If it is unavoidable that the cargo has to be loaded into holds adjacent to heated fuel oil tanks, the Master should inform the Chief Engineer that a temperature-sensitive cargo is to be loaded to allow for a suitable heating plan to be prepared.

The levels of heat required to facilitate efficient transfer of the fuel oil from the storage tanks to the settling tank will depend on the properties of the fuel oil. As a matter of prudence, it is recommended that the fuel oil be heated to the minimum temperature that will allow for efficient transfer. Heat application to fuel oil tanks that are in direct contact with the cargo should be performed cautiously so that it results in the smallest temperature differential between the cargo and fuel oil tank. The fuel oil temperatures should be recorded in the Engine Room Logbook. Evidence that heating was applied in the most prudent manner will be the best defence against any claims that might arise in this regard.

5.5   Ventilation Throughout the Voyage and During Delays

The cargo should be ventilated in accordance with sound maritime practice and any carriage instructions provided to the vessel. Ventilation should be conducted in accordance with the fumigation instructions where applicable and when the weather/sea conditions permit. It is important to avoid wetting of the cargo. The decision to ventilate should be based on either the Three Degree Rule or Dew Point Rule. During a voyage it is usually only practical to open the ventilation windows for natural surface ventilation, however in some circumstances it may be possible to partially open or crack the cargo hold hatch covers if they are not sealed to allow a more efficient exchange of air. This must only be done under suitable sea and weather conditions. This method is often useful for vessels delayed at anchorage.

The decision to ventilate should be reviewed at least every four to six hours, since frequent changes in weather conditions may affect when ventilation should be undertaken. If possible, ventilation should also be carried out during the night provided the dew point or temperature measurements indicate the conditions are appropriate. During periods of heavy weather or adverse sea conditions, steps should be taken to prevent rain and spray from entering the cargo spaces and may mean that ventilation is stopped until conditions improve. It is important to maintain a Ventilation Log that notes which ventilation rule is being followed as the basis for the decision to ventilate the cargo. The log should record which holds were ventilated and the duration. If the Three Degree Rule is being followed, the average cargo temperature at loading and the ambient dry bulb temperatures need to be recorded. If the Dew Point Rule is being followed, the wet and dry ambient air temperatures and wet and dry hold air temperatures, as well as the dew point temperature calculations, need to be recorded. In addition, any periods when ventilation is stopped or prevented and the reason why (eg during the fumigation exposure period or due to adverse weather) should be noted. If bad weather/shipping seas prevent ventilation, photographs should be taken as evidence and a Sea Protest issued which includes these photographs. These records will provide a valuable defence for owners in evidencing that ventilation was correctly undertaken in the event a claim arises with regards to the care of the cargo.

The Master should ventilate the holds prior to arrival at the discharge port in accordance with any instructions provided by the load port fumigator.

The vessel may be subject to delays at anchorage. Whilst delayed, the crew should continue to ventilate the cargo according to one of the two ventilation rules when conditions deem it necessary and safe. If the vessel is only capable of undertaking natural ventilation, it may be wise, assuming the hatch covers are not sealed, to tent the hatch covers or crack them open when ventilation is appropriate. If suitable, opening the hatches will also provide an opportunity for the crew to inspect the surface of the stow and obtain sub-surface cargo temperatures to determine if there is any evidence of self-heating. Localised hot spots or mouldy cargo should be photographed and recorded. If it is practical, cargo in these hot spots/mouldy areas should be removed from the hold and kept in bags or drums on board the vessel.

5.6   Discharge

The Master should instruct the crew to monitor the discharge operations carefully. This entails noting and photographing how discharge is undertaken. The quantity of spilled cargo should be noted and, if excessive, a Protest issued. Any delays that were not the fault of the vessel should also be recorded. In the event that damaged cargo is discovered, the Master and Members should inform their P&I Club as soon as possible in order to appoint a local surveyor to discern the location, depth and (if possible) extent of the damage. It is often the case that the location of any damage can be used to hypothesise the cause. Detailed photographs and even drawings of the damage location would be useful. In the event that a local surveyor cannot attend immediately, it would assist if the Master/crew photograph and document the damage clearly.

Part 2 –

Ores, Minerals and Fertilisers

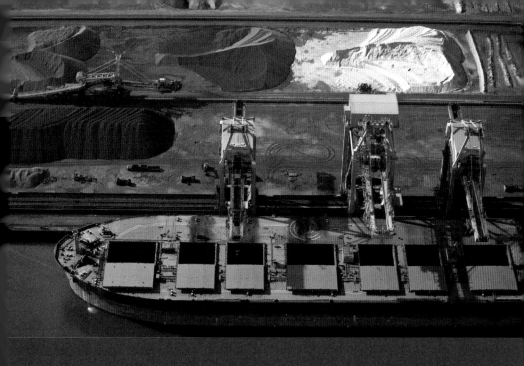

Chapter 6 –
Coal Cargoes

This chapter, and all of the chapters in Part 2, should be read in conjunction with the booklet *Carrying Solid Bulk Cargoes Safely* (Reference 16), published by Lloyd's Register/UK P&I Club/INTERCARGO, which can be found on the UK P&I website.

6.1 Properties and Characteristics

The *International Maritime Solid Bulk Cargoes Code* (IMSBC Code) (Reference 17) categorises coal as Group B (cargoes with a chemical hazard) and Group A (cargoes which may liquefy). The general properties and hazards are as follows:

- Coals may emit methane, a flammable gas. A methane/air mixture containing between 5 and 16% methane constitutes an explosive atmosphere which can be ignited by sparks or naked flame, eg electrical or frictional sparks, a match or lighted cigarette. Methane is lighter than air and so may accumulate in the upper region of the cargo space or other enclosed spaces. If the cargo space boundaries are not tight, methane can seep through into spaces adjacent to the cargo space

- coals may be subject to oxidation, leading to depletion of oxygen and an increase in carbon dioxide or carbon monoxide concentrations in the cargo space. Carbon monoxide is an odourless gas, slightly lighter than air, and has flammable limits in air of 12 to 75% by volume ie, within this range of concentration it may burn.

It is toxic by inhalation with an affinity for blood haemoglobin over 200 times that of oxygen

- some coals may heat spontaneously and this may lead to spontaneous combustion in the cargo space. Flammable and toxic gases, including carbon monoxide, may be produced

- some coals may be liable to react with water and produce acids which may cause corrosion. Flammable and toxic gases, including hydrogen, may be produced. Hydrogen is an odourless gas, much lighter than air, and has flammable limits in air of 4 to 75% by volume

- coal cargoes may liquefy when their moisture content exceeds their transportable moisture limit (TML).

6.2   General Requirement for All Coals

The IMSBC Code states that, prior to loading, the shipper or their appointed agent should provide, in writing to the Master, a cargo declaration containing the characteristics of the cargo and the recommended safe handling procedures. These details should include whether the cargo may be liable to emit methane or self-heat.

> The Master should be satisfied that they have received this information prior to accepting the cargo. This is an essential requirement for safe shipment of the cargo as it determines the method of safe carriage.

- If the shipper has advised that the cargo is liable to self-heat, the Master should seek confirmation that the intended precautions and the intended procedures for monitoring the cargo during the voyage are adequate

- if the cargo is liable to self-heat, or an analysis of the atmosphere in the cargo space indicates an increasing concentration of carbon monoxide, the following additional precautions should be taken:

  - the hatches should be closed immediately after completion of loading in each cargo space. The hatch covers may also be additionally sealed with a suitable sealing tape. Surface ventilation should be limited to the absolute minimum time necessary to remove methane that may have accumulated. Forced ventilation should not be used. On no account should air be directed into the body of the coal as this could promote self-heating

  - personnel should not be allowed to enter the cargo space unless they are wearing self-contained breathing apparatus (SCBA) and access is critical to the safety of the ship or safety of life. The SCBA should be worn only by personnel trained in its use

  - when required by the competent authority (CA), the carbon monoxide concentration in each cargo space should be measured at regular time intervals to detect self-heating

  - if, at the time of loading, when the hatches are open, the temperature of the coal exceeds 55°C, expert advice should be obtained.

If the carbon monoxide level is increasing steadily, self-heating may be developing. The cargo space should be completely closed down and all ventilation ceased. The

Master should seek expert advice immediately. Water should not be used for cooling the material or for fighting coal cargo fires at sea, but may be used for cooling the boundaries of the cargo space.

> Even if the shipper considers that the cargo is not liable to self-heat, the recommendations stated above should be closely followed. Monitoring the atmosphere of the cargo space is essential at least once daily, and twice daily if rapid changes are detected.

During loading, all cargo should be properly trimmed as level as possible to the boundaries of the cargo spaces.

During and after loading, it is important to regularly monitor the temperature of cargo. While measuring temperature by lowering thermometers into sounding pipes may be useful generally, it should not be relied upon to reflect any changes occurring in the bulk of the cargo. This is because temperature monitoring via sounding pipes will only detect heating coal in the immediate vicinity and will not provide information on the bulk of the cargo.

During the voyage, the bilge of the hold should be tested to monitor the pH. If the pH level indicates a corrosion risk, the bilges can be pumped out to avoid the accumulation of acid on the tank tops and throughout the bilge system.

6.3 Gas Monitoring and Ventilation Coal Cargoes

All vessels engaged in the carriage of coal cargoes should have on board an instrument for measuring methane, carbon monoxide and oxygen, as per Section 3.2.5 of the IMSBC Code (Reference 17). SOLAS Chapter VI – Carriage of cargoes and oil fuels (Reference 18) confirms this requirement:

Regulation 3
"Oxygen analysis and gas detection equipment

1. *When transporting a solid bulk cargo which is liable to emit a toxic or flammable gas, or cause oxygen depletion in the cargo space, an appropriate instrument for measuring the concentration of gas or oxygen in the air shall be provided together with detailed instructions for its use. Such an instrument shall be to the satisfaction of the Administration.*

2. *The Administration shall take steps to ensure that crews of ships are trained in the use of such instruments."*

Appendix 1 of the IMSBC Code provides the individual schedules of solid bulk cargoes (Reference 17). This includes the schedule for coal that also contains, as a separate appendix, the procedures for gas monitoring of coal cargoes, the equipment to be used, the design and siting of sample points, and procedures for measurement.

> *"3 The ship shall be suitably fitted and carry on board appropriate instruments for measuring the following without requiring entry in the cargo space:*
>
>   *.1 Concentration of methane in the atmosphere;*
>
>   *.2 Concentration of oxygen in the atmosphere;*

.3 Concentration of carbon monoxide in the atmosphere; and

.4 pH value of cargo space bilge samples."

The appendix goes on to state:

"4 These instruments shall be regularly serviced and calibrated. Ship personnel shall be trained in the use of such instruments. Details of gas measurement procedures are given at the end of this appendix."

The appendix continues:

"8 The atmosphere in the space above the cargo in each space shall be regularly monitored for the concentration of methane, oxygen and carbon monoxide. Details of gas monitoring procedures are given at the end of this appendix. The results of monitoring shall be recorded. The frequency of the monitoring shall be determined based upon the information provided by the shipper and the information obtained through the analysis of the atmosphere in the cargo space.

9 Unless expressly provided otherwise, surface ventilation shall be conducted in all cargo spaces carrying this cargo for the first 24 hours after departure from the loading port. During this period, the atmosphere in the cargo spaces shall be monitored once from one sample point per cargo space and, for the purpose of the gas monitoring, the ventilation shall be stopped for an appropriate period prior to the gas monitoring.

10 When the methane concentrations monitored within 24 hours after departure are at an acceptably low level, the ventilation openings shall be closed and the atmosphere in the cargo spaces shall be monitored. When the methane concentrations monitored within 24 hours after departure are not at an acceptably low level, surface ventilation shall be maintained, except for an appropriate period for gas monitoring, and the atmosphere in the cargo spaces shall be monitored. This procedure shall be followed until the methane concentrations become acceptably low level. In any event, the atmosphere in the cargo spaces shall be monitored on a daily basis."

Other requirements set out in the schedule relate to trimming the cargo, smoking and the use of naked lights etc.

6.4　Special Precautions

Special precautions apply to coals emitting methane and self-heating coals.

Coals emitting methane

Methane is a flammable gas that, within the range of 5 to 16% in air, can form a flammable mixture that can be readily ignited by a spark or naked light. The IMSBC Code, in the Appendix to the schedule relating to coal, requires the following special precautions:

"1. Coals emitting methane

"When the shipper has informed that the cargo is liable to emit methane or analysis of the atmosphere in the cargo space indicates the presence of methane in excess of 20% of the Lower Explosion Limit (LEL), the following additional precautions shall be taken:

.1 *Adequate surface ventilation shall be maintained, except for an appropriate period for the purpose of gas monitoring.*

.2 *Care shall be taken to remove any accumulated gases prior to operation of the hatch covers or other openings for any reason, including discharging. Care shall be taken to operate hatch covers of the cargo spaces and other openings to avoid creating sparks. Smoking and the use of naked flame shall be prohibited.*

.3 *Personnel shall not be permitted to enter the cargo space or enclosed adjacent spaces unless the space has been ventilated and the atmosphere tested and found to be gas-free and to have sufficient oxygen to support life. Notwithstanding these provisions, emergency entry into the cargo space may be permitted without ventilation, testing the atmosphere or both, provided that the entry into the cargo space is undertaken only by trained personnel wearing self-contained breathing apparatus under the supervision of a responsible officer and special precautions are observed to ensure that no source of ignition is carried into the space.*

.4 *The master shall ensure that enclosed working spaces such as storerooms, carpenter's shops, passageways, tunnels, etc., are regularly monitored for the presence of methane. Such spaces shall be adequately ventilated and, in the case of mechanical ventilation, only equipment safe for use in an explosive atmosphere shall be used."* (Reference 17)

Self-heating coals

Low-rank coal types are more prone to oxidation than the high-rank anthracites and are therefore more liable to spontaneous heating. High inherent moisture contents, which can evaporate to create large internal surface areas susceptible to oxidation, will assist this heating process. Frequently, cargoes may consist of coals of different ages and from different mines, which can also lead to spontaneous heating problems.

The Appendix to the coal schedule of the IMSBC Code goes on to state further special precautions as follows:

"2.1 The cargo spaces shall be closed immediately after completion of loading in each cargo space. The hatch covers may also be additionally sealed with a suitable sealing tape. Only natural surface ventilation shall be permitted and ventilation shall be limited to the absolute minimum time necessary to remove methane which may have accumulated.

.2 *Personnel shall not enter the cargo space during the voyage, unless they are wearing self-contained breathing apparatus and access is critical to safety of life and the safety of the ship.*

.3 *Prior to loading, temperature of this cargo shall be monitored. This cargo shall only be accepted for loading when the temperature of the cargo is not higher than 55°C.*

.4 *When the carbon monoxide level is increasing steadily, a potential self-heating may be developing. In such a case, the cargo space shall be completely closed and all ventilation ceased, and the master shall seek expert advice immediately. Water shall not be used for cooling material or fighting coal fires at sea, but may be used for cooling the boundaries of the cargo space.*

.5 *When the carbon monoxide level in any cargo space reaches 50 ppm or exhibits a steady rise over three consecutive days, a self-heating condition may be developing and the master shall inform the shipper and the company of, at least,* the following information if an accurate assessment of the situation is to be achieved:

.1 identity of the cargo spaces involved; monitoring results covering carbon monoxide, methane and oxygen concentrations;

.2 if available, temperature of the cargo, location and method used to obtain results;

.3 time gas sample taken (monitoring routine);

.4 time ventilators opened/closed;

.5 quantity of coal in hold(s) involved;

.6 type of coal as per cargo information, and any special precautions indicated on information;

.7 date loaded, and ETA at intended discharge port (which shall be specified); and

.8 comments or observations from the ship's master."

6.5 Acid Conditions

Many coals contain sulphur and if this is in soluble form it may react with moisture in the coal to form sulphurous and sulphuric acids. These acids will attack steel, corroding bilge systems, tank top areas and, in some cases, bulkheads. For this reason, it is recommended that regular hold bilge testing should be conducted. If acid conditions are indicated, the bilges should be pumped regularly to minimise contact between the acids and the hold structure. This will also prevent the accumulation of water drained from the cargo collecting at lower hold levels and creating problems at discharge.

6.6 Entry to Cargo Spaces

Coal will oxidise, which is a process that removes oxygen from the surrounding atmosphere. The oxygen content of a normal atmosphere should be approximately 20.9% for safe entry. However, tests of the atmosphere in sealed holds carrying coal cargoes have indicated an oxygen content of less than 4%. It is essential that suitable test procedures are followed to confirm sufficient oxygen prior to entry into a cargo space or a neighbouring confined space. Requirements for the safety of personnel are detailed in Section 3 of the IMSBC Code. In addition, Appendix 1 contains the specific risks associated with each cargo type (Reference 17).

The importance of this test procedure cannot be overemphasised. Preventable loss of life continues to occur as a result of entry into cargo spaces and confined spaces without prior testing of the atmosphere. Ships must be equipped with the relevant test apparatus and personnel trained in its use.

6.7 Brown Coal (Lignite) Briquettes

Amendment 03-15 of the IMSBC Code that entered into force on 1st January 2017 and the Supplement (the Code of Practice for the Safe Loading and Unloading of Bulk Carriers (BLU Code)) (Reference 17) include 'brown coal (lignite) briquettes', which are manufactured by pressing dried coal particles into compressed blocks. The briquettes are subject to oxidation, which leads to both oxygen depletion and carbon dioxide increase within the cargo space. They are also liable to self-heating and spontaneous combustion, which in turn may produce flammable and toxic gases.

Boundaries of cargo spaces in which briquettes are stowed should be fire and liquid resistant. The *International Maritime Dangerous Goods Code* (IMDG Code) should be consulted for particular stowage requirements (Reference 19). For full details of pre-loading, loading and post-loading operations and recommendations, the BLU Code (Supplement to the IMSBC Code) (Reference 17) should be consulted.

6.8 The Risk of Liquefaction

Amendment 04-17 of the IMSBC Code that entered into force on 1st January 2019 set out new requirements to manage the risk of liquefaction of coal cargoes. The IMSBC Code (Coal schedule in the Appendix) now classifies all coal cargoes as both Group A (risk of liquefaction) and Group B, unless a test confirms otherwise. The shipper is required to demonstrate that the coal does not belong to Group A, specifically:

"Coal shall be classified as Group A and B unless classified as Group B only by a test determined by the appropriate authority or where it has the following particle size distribution:

.1 not more than 10% by weight of particles less than 1 mm (D10 > 1 mm); and

.2 not more than 50% by weight of particles less than 10 mm (D50 > 10 mm).

Notwithstanding the above, a blend of two or more coals shall be classified as Group A and B unless all original coals in the blend are Group B only."

Figure 6.1: Where coal cargoes are subject to rainfall in the load port, they should be covered where possible but always reinspected and retested to confirm their moisture level.

Before loading, the Master should request evidence of the correct coal classification. Shippers should clearly demonstrate whether the cargo falls under Group A and B or Group B only. If no information is available from the shipper, the Master should assume that the coal is both Group A and B and therefore is at risk of liquefaction. However, as required by the IMSBC Code, the Master should insist that the cargo transportable moisture limit (TML) test documentation and its moisture certificate is presented prior to loading.

Where cargo is ashore for a long period and subject to moisture increase by rain, it is essential that the cargo moisture level is reinspected prior to loading.

For further details of the general risk of cargoes that may liquefy, see Chapter 8.

Chapter 7 –
Bitumen (Natural and Rock) and Petroleum Coke

The terms bitumen and asphalt are interchangeable and both refer to black or dark-coloured solids or very thick liquids that have been distilled from crude oil. The distillation process may occur within a refinery, resulting in processed bitumen/asphalt. It may also happen naturally, either when crude oil is exposed to heating and/or biological activity within the deposit, or when it undergoes weathering at or near the earth's surface. Either way, the distillation process separates the heavy molecular weight hydrocarbons, such as bitumen, from the lighter ones, such as methane and petroleum products.

Bitumen is extensively used in roadway construction as a 'glue' or binder in the production of asphalt concrete. To produce asphalt concrete, the sticky bitumen is heated and mixed with aggregates, such as rock chips, and it is then laid and rolled to form the road surface. Asphalt/bitumen may also be referred to as 'tar' or 'pitch'. These liquid bitumens, or 'natural' bitumens, are carried in tankers.

7.1 Bitumen Rock

As it is necessary to heat bitumen to enable mixing with aggregates during road construction, some companies have decided to exploit alternatives to refined bitumen. One alternative is to use natural asphalt/bitumen deposits where the 'glue' is already mixed into the rocks.

As an example, at Buton Island in South-East Sulawesi, Indonesia, natural bitumen/ asphalt is found at the surface in association with limestone. These deposits are locally referred to as Aspal Buton or asbuton rock asphalt and can be utilised directly (or mixed with traditional road-making materials but with much less processing). This avoids the need for excessive heating of the bitumen to enable it to mix with aggregates during road construction. While the Indonesian deposits have been known since 1920, and it is estimated there are 300 million tonnes available, it is only recently that they have been extensively exploited and offered for shipment.

The asbuton deposits consist of about 20 to 30% bitumen/asphalt integrated into about 70 to 80% limestone and can be divided into several types, based on their physical characteristics. The two main deposits currently being exploited are:

- Kabungka (since 1980) – these are hard deposits (the softening point is about 100°C) with relatively low asphalt content. They break easily when crushed but do not release the asphalt without extensive heating
- Lawele (since 2003) – these are soft deposits (the softening point is about 60°C) with relatively high asphalt content. They require slightly lower temperatures and readily deform during processing, such that the asphalt coats the grains of limestone. This makes the grains better able to stick to other aggregates during the production of asphalt concrete. This variety is the main variety being exported to date.

Figure 7.1: Bitumen rock.

When asbuton rock asphalt is dried and crushed to form a granular material, it is referred to as Buton Rock Asphalt (BRA), and it is this name that may be included on cargo documents when the product is presented for ocean carriage in bulk. Shippers may also refer to the product using the name of the source and then add BRA, for example 'Lawele BRA'. Alternatively, they may simply describe it by the general name 'natural bitumen/asphalt'.

Figure 7.2: Buton Rock Asphalt (BRA) cargo is often loaded from barges.

7.1.1   Application of the IMSBC Code (Reference 17)

Shippers tend to describe their cargo with respect to its intended use, so bitumen rock may be described as 'natural bitumen'. This may cause shipowners, charterers of bulk carriers and P&I Clubs to query the nature of the cargo because natural bitumen is a product carried in a tanker. Even more confusing, it appears that this product is more than 50% 'rock', which means it would be a solid cargo. This is a concern for Masters, owners and P&I Clubs.

Natural bitumen/asphalt or bitumen/asphalt rock is not listed in Appendix 1 (the individual schedules section) of the *International Maritime Solid Bulk Cargoes Code* (IMSBC Code), but the advice is to treat this cargo like any other bulk cargo that is not listed in Appendix 1.

The IMSBC Code makes provision for the carriage of new and unlisted cargoes in Section 1.3. This section describes the processes shippers should undertake to gain certification from the load port competent authority (CA). IMO Circular MSC.1/Circ.1453/Rev.1 sets out guidelines for dealing with cargoes not listed in the Code in a manner that complies with the requirements of the IMSBC Code. This circular may be found in the Supplement to the IMSBC Code (Reference 17).

Section 1.3 of the IMSBC Code states that, for any bulk cargo not listed in Appendix 1, the shipper must provide the IMO CA of the load port with details of the cargo characteristics and properties prior to loading. Based on this information, the CA of the load port will assess the acceptability of the proposed cargo for safe shipment.

- If no specific hazards are identified, the load port CA can authorise shipment, and the competent authorities of the flag State and the port of unloading should be informed of this authorisation
- if hazards have been identified by the load port CA, the flag State CA and the port of unloading CA should confer to agree the appropriate carriage conditions.

In either case, the load port CA should provide the Master with a certificate that states the cargo characteristics and required conditions for carriage and handling. Cargoes that are not listed in the IMSBC Code and non-IMSBC Code cargoes without a CA certificate should not be accepted.

To complete the procedures for dealing with unlisted cargoes, the IMO requires the CA of the load port to submit an application to the Organization, within one year from the issue of the certificate, to incorporate the new solid bulk cargo into Appendix 1 of the IMSBC Code. This mandatory requirement is detailed in Section 1.3.2 of the IMSBC Code, with the format covered in Section 1.3.3.

One of the major problems is that not every state that ships this type of product actually has a CA. Shipowners are advised not to carry insufficiently certified bulk cargoes.

7.2   Petroleum Coke Bulk Cargo: Tank Washing, Cleaning Products and Discharge Implications

Petroleum coke ('petcoke') is a bulk byproduct of oil refining. Most petcoke (approximately 75%) is sold as a fuel for power generation and cement production, with the higher quality petcoke sold for use in the calcining industry. As with most other bulk cargoes, after discharge, the residues that remain in the holds and on deck must be cleaned before new cargoes can be loaded. The cleaning process typically entails dry sweeping, high-pressure water washing, the application of a chemical cleaner and a final high-pressure water wash.

Historically, the dirty wash water was either disposed of at sea or discharged for treatment in land-based reception facilities. However, given increasingly stringent legislative requirements, it is becoming ever more important to ensure that a proper disposal route is followed (see Section 7.2.4). It is also possible for ships carrying petcoke to be involved in an incident that results in loss of the cargo at sea.

Petcoke is not officially classed as harmful to the marine environment and it could, in theory, be discharged while a vessel is en route and at least 12 nautical miles from the nearest land. However, petcoke cargo residue and wash water can contain a number of harmful components such as residual hydrocarbons, heavy metals, cleaning agents or dust suppressants. The presence of such components in sufficient quantity could result in a particular cargo residue being considered harmful to the marine environment by a national authority.

Generally, the impacts of a discharge of petcoke residue and cleaning products within hold wash water will depend on the volume and location of the discharge. However, the most noticeable effect is likely to be an oily sheen that may be visible on the water surface for a short time in the immediate vicinity of the discharge, with a localised and short-term increase in the pH of the seawater. If the discharge is undertaken in sufficient depth of seawater with currents allowing a good water exchange, it is likely that any residues will quickly dissipate and that no environmental effects will be observed.

The legislation regarding the discharge of any hold wash water from ships is complicated, both nationally and internationally. The minimum requirements worldwide tend to be in accordance with the MARPOL recommendations (as outlined in Table 7.2), but may be more stringent in certain locations. As a result, it is prudent for operators to transfer tank wash water to shore side facilities for processing rather than discharge at sea, in order to avoid potential environmental issues and possible litigation or fines. This is also true for petcoke wash water.

7.2.1 Physical Properties

Petcoke, also known as green delayed coke, consists mainly of carbon (84–97%) and is produced during the thermal decomposition of oil in refining. It exists in various forms, including needle coke, sponge coke and shot coke, which have different microstructures and differ in sulphur content and impurity levels. Crude oil quality is key to determining which of these types is produced – cokes produced from feedstocks high in asphaltenes contain higher concentrations of sulphur and metals.

Green petcoke is the product of delayed coking and has significant hydrocarbon content. It has a distinctive hydrocarbon smell and, depending on the heating rate of the refining process, can contain from 4 to 21% of volatile material, which consists mainly of residual hydrocarbons, including polycyclic aromatic hydrocarbons (PAHs).

Property	Fuel-grade coke (green petcoke)	Anode-grade coke (processed calcined petcoke)
Sulphur (wt%)	2.5–6.0	1.7–3.0
Ash (wt%)	0.1–0.3	0.1–0.3
Nickel (ppm)	250–500	165–350
Vanadium (ppm)	1,000–1,500	120–350
Residual hydrocarbon (wt%)	9–21	<0.25
Bulk density (g/cm^3)	Not determined	0.8
Real density (g/cm^3)	Not determined	2.06

Table 7.1: Representative range values for properties of petcoke.

Calcined petroleum coke (which can be further processed to become anode-grade petcoke) is derived from green (or fuel-grade) petcoke by heating to high temperatures (>1,200°C). This process removes virtually all of the hydrocarbon content (ie to <0.1%). It is common to use a fine water spray containing surfactants to suppress dust. The surfactant reduces the surface tension of the water, making it more effective at wetting the cargo and reducing the volume of water necessary for the task. The surfactant is commonly applied in a dilute (between 1:100 and 1:3,000) form and normally classed as non-hazardous.

The exact properties of petcoke depend on the source of the crude oil feedstock and the heating process used. However, major components would be expected to be within the ranges illustrated in Table 7.1. Trace metals such as nickel and vanadium may be present at ppm levels. The specific gravity of petcoke ranges from 0.8–2.1 relative to water. Therefore, the product specification for each cargo must be consulted to determine if it will float or sink. Generally, most petcoke products will sink in seawater. Petcoke is stable and insoluble in water and is therefore likely to form a slurry if discharged at sea.

7.2.2   Environmental Effects of Petroleum Coke

Environmental toxicity studies have shown that, in general, petcoke has a low potential to cause adverse effects on both aquatic and terrestrial endpoints in plants and animals. Consequently, petcoke Material Safety Data Sheets (MSDS), the EU CLP Regulation (on classification, labelling and packaging of substances and mixtures), and the Joint Group of Experts on the Scientific Aspects of Marine Environmental Protection/Evaluation of Harmful Substances (GESAMP/EHS) list of hazard profiles, all indicate that petcoke is not considered a hazard to the marine environment. No updates have been added in relation to petcoke in the latest versions of the IMSBC (2022) and MARPOL Annex V, indicating that the substance is considered non-hazardous. However, recent evidence suggests that petcoke is not as inert as initially thought, with environmentally significant substances (nickel and vanadium) being detected in petcoke water leachates; these might impact the growth of algae when discharged overboard in low-dilution environments.

It is worth noting that, although petcoke is described as non-hazardous, there are potential human health effects relating to the small particulate matter within the powder or granules when inhaled as dust (ie airborne). In order to suppress dust, a small amount of oil may be added to the cargo, which may have implications if there is a spill or discharge at sea that results in surface sheens.

The hydrocarbon content of green or raw coke is likely to form an oily sheen on the water's surface, although in favourable conditions this is likely to be localised and non-persistent. The greatest concern following a bulk release of petcoke (eg, in a ship casualty scenario) is the potential for smothering effects, particularly in low energy or shallow waters where spreading and dilution is reduced. A release near the shoreline may also cause a negative visual effect if significant black solids are washed onto the shore. Any increases in pH or sheen will be short lived, given sufficient water depth and water exchange. As far as the discharge of small quantities of petcoke within otherwise clean wash waters is concerned, it is not expected that there would be harmful effects to the marine environment as long as the hydrocarbon content of the cargo is sufficiently low. However, this comment should be read in the context of governing legislation.

7.2.3   Cleaning Products

The high content of oil in green coke poses difficult cleaning problems during the hold washing process, which typically also involves the use of chemical cleaning agents. A number of specialist cleaning products are available for this purpose. These may be general cleaning agents or marketed specifically for particular cargo residues. Some may contain hydrocarbon solvents, while others cleanse on the basis of their caustic properties. As such, they too must be considered when studying the environmental implications of wash water disposal, particularly at sea.

All cleaning products that are evaluated by the working group on the Evaluation of Safety and Pollution Hazards of chemicals (ESPH) and found by the Marine Environment Protection Committee (MEPC) to meet the requirements for potential discharge, are listed in Annex 10 of MEPC.2/Circ.27. Because of their potential dilution in use and propensity to dissolve in the sea, the key to understanding the potential for environmental impact of any such cleaning agents is the concentration profile over time following a loss or discharge at sea. In other words, the quantity involved, the spill rate and the potential for water exchange.

7.2.4   National and International Guidance and Restrictions on Discharge

It is important to be aware that any hydrocarbon 'sheen' produced by discharged tank wash water would constitute a violation under MARPOL Annex 1 (concerning oil pollution). Discharge from bilge tanks in areas where this is permitted must pass through an oily mixture separator and monitoring system, and the oil content of the discharge must not exceed 15 ppm.

Type of discharge	Ships outside special areas	Ships within special areas
Non recoverable cargo residues contained in wash water	Discharge permitted ≥12 NM from the nearest land and as far as practicable	Discharge only permitted ≥12 NM from the nearest land and as far as practicable if departure and destination are both within the special area and no adequate reception facilities are available at those ports or in an emergency situation
Cleaning agents and additives contained in cargo hold wash water	Discharge permitted	Discharge only permitted ≥12 NM from the nearest land and as far as practicable if departure and destination are both within the special area and no adequate reception facilities are available at those ports or in an emergency situation
Mixed garbage*	When garbage is mixed with or contaminated by other substances prohibited from discharge or having different discharge requirements, the more stringent requirements shall apply	
Oily mixtures from non-tankers >400 GT	Discharge is only permitted if the oil content of any bilge water discharged is below 15 parts per million (ppm); the ship must be >12 NM from nearest land and it must have in operation an approved oil discharge monitoring and control system, oily water separating equipment or oil filtering equipment	Discharge only permitted if the oil content of any bilge water discharged does not exceed 15 parts per million (ppm); the ship must be >12 NM from nearest land; and it must have in operation an approved oil discharge monitoring and control system, oily water separating equipment or oil filtering equipment with an alarm and automatic stopping device

Table 7.2: Summary of MARPOL discharge provisions for petcoke wash water (modified to include oily mixtures).

*Note that cargo residues and cleaning agents from tank washing are defined as 'garbage' under MARPOL.

Legislation in the United States, such as the Clean Water Act (CWA), the Act to Prevent Pollution from Ships (APPS) and several Coast Guard regulations, implement the standards imposed by MARPOL and prohibit discharge of oily residues or MARPOL defined garbage within 12 nautical miles from shore. In its guidance on the at-sea disposal of cargo tank washings and hatch washings in MGN 385, the UK Maritime and Coastguard Agency (MCA) states that:

".... after unloading some bulk cargoes many ships will wash their holds or decks to remove this excess or spilt material as it could contaminate the next cargo. In such cases this material can be disposed of at sea so long as it is inert, has been minimised by removing as much cargo residue as possible and any disposal complies with the 2008 Regulations and any other relevant legislation. If the material is a marine pollutant, a hazardous or noxious material, or a material that could cause secondary pollution on contact with the sea (such as petcoke, which if disposed of at sea, can cause a sheen on the surface, which will put the ship in contravention of Annex 1 of MARPOL 73/78), then any washings should be disposed of on shore through appropriate reception facilities."

Chapter 8 –
Mineral Ore Concentrates and Other Materials that May Liquefy

Section 7 of the *International Maritime Solid Bulk Cargoes Code* (IMSBC Code, Reference 17) contains general procedures for cargo that may liquefy. The recommended procedures for testing materials that may be subject to liquefaction are covered in Appendix 2 and Section 8. Masters should be aware of Amendment 03-15 of the IMSBC Code that entered into force on 1st January 2017. It included an individual and revised schedule for iron ore fines to address the dangers related to liquefaction.

The following points should be borne in mind by shipowners and Masters when contemplating the carriage of concentrates.

Many minerals that are insoluble in water and that contain mainly finely divided material may liquefy on ocean voyages if they contain an excessive amount of water when loaded or if they subsequently become wetted. This applies even though they may appear to be in the form of dry powders or granular materials.

Liquefaction occurs as a result of energy being applied to the cargo in the form of vibration from the ship's engine or due to motion in heavy seas. Liquefaction may become apparent at almost any stage of a voyage. Any cargo of finely divided material that starts to flatten and develop a putty-like surface during a voyage has begun to liquefy.

The presence of water on the surface of the cargo is also indicative of liquefaction. It must be stressed, however, that liquefaction can occur without liquid water being observed on the surface of the cargo. If flattening or a putty-like surface is observed, the ship should take urgent action and should proceed to the nearest port of refuge. It may be prudent to adjust course and speed to reduce the motion of the ship, even if this means having to steam further before reaching a suitable port.

Liquefaction is unlikely to occur if, when loaded, the cargo complies with the IMO requirement that the moisture content is relatively uniform and below the transportable moisture limit (TML) in each hold. There has been no case of liquefaction involving a cargo that in every respect complied with the IMO requirements.

Before loading any cargo with a potential to liquefy, Masters should carefully check all the documentation provided by the shippers or charterers. All cargoes known to liquefy are identified as such under the heading *Hazards* in Appendix 1 of the IMSBC Code, although total reliance on such information alone is not advised.

It is therefore recommended that, where a Master is concerned about possible liquefaction of a cargo of mineral in a finely divided form, they should insist on a written statement from the shippers or charterers confirming that the product will not liquefy if it contains an excess of moisture.

Alternatively, the Master should obtain the required documentation to satisfy their own suspicions. If the Master is not satisfied with the response obtained, it is recommended that they consult the P&I Club, either through the owners or ship managers.

8.1　Documentation

Before loading commences, the Master should receive a letter from the shippers indicating that the Master will be supplied with certificates stating the average moisture content of the cargo loaded into each separate hold. It will be appreciated that sampling before shipment, except in climates where there is no rainfall, is not satisfactory. Many of the larger shippers use an automatic sampling procedure during loading to obtain satisfactory samples for moisture content measurement. Under these circumstances, actual figures for the average moisture content of cargo loaded into each hold can only be given at the end of the loading period.

After completion of loading of materials known to liquefy, and before starting a voyage, the Master should be supplied with a certificate stating the TML for the cargo. It is stipulated by the IMSBC Code that the testing necessary for the provision of such certificates should be carried out not more than six months prior to loading (see Section 4.5 of the Code). Masters should ensure that this certificate is dated within six months of loading and that it is issued by a reliable laboratory. It is reasonable to assume that certificates issued by major shippers of mineral ore concentrates, as listed in the IMSBC Code, are reliable. However, where there are shipments of less common materials, or where shipments are from newly developed sources, the certificates should be issued by a laboratory reliably known to have the necessary equipment and expertise to conduct the test. If there is any doubt about this matter, the Master should notify the shipowners. They should then contact the Association to obtain expert advice on how to check that the laboratory has the necessary equipment and expertise.

Sampling and testing of this cargo for moisture content should be conducted as near as possible to the time of loading.

The IMSBC Code stipulates as follows:

"The shipper shall be responsible for ensuring that a test to determine the TML of a solid bulk cargo is conducted within six months to the date of loading the cargo. Notwithstanding this provision, where the composition or characteristics of the cargo are variable for any reason, the shipper shall be responsible for ensuring that a test to determine the TML is conducted again after it is reasonably assumed that such variation has taken place."

8.2 Careful Examination

Regardless of any evidence provided by the various certificates discussed above, Masters are strongly advised to examine the stockpiles of cargoes before loading. Water draining from stockpiles must be considered to indicate the probability that a part of the material in the stockpile has a moisture content above the TML. A watch should be kept on the condition of the cargo being loaded. Any obviously wet material should be rejected as such cargo might form a shear plane on which a basically sound cargo loaded subsequently might slide.

Masters should be aware of the risk of loading cargo at sub-zero temperatures, when it may contain ice crystals but not appear to be damp. It is recommended that, when cargo is loaded under such conditions, samples are drawn from various levels, including the bottoms of piles, and that these are warmed and then checked by the can test, as described in Section 8.4 of the IMSBC Code.

Under no circumstances should Masters agree to the erection of shifting boards or other temporary arrangements to carry cargoes loaded at moisture contents above the TML. If bulkheads are to be erected to facilitate the carriage of this type of cargo, they must be constructed strictly as required in Section 7.3.2 of the IMSBC Code (Reference 17).

It cannot be too strongly stressed that when carrying cargoes of this nature, failure to ensure that they are accompanied by the correct reliable documentation and to ensure that they are in generally uniform condition at the time of loading can result in the loss of both a ship and its crew.

Figure 8.1: Liquefied ore concentrate in ship's hold.

8.3 Dangerous Reactions

There are two other dangers associated with concentrate cargoes. The first is that some concentrates may heat. Shippers should always be asked specifically about this possibility. Stows of such concentrates should be trimmed roughly flat using a tracked bulldozer or similar machine that also compacts the cargo. It is sometimes helpful to sheet such materials with heavy gauge polythene film, which further restricts the rate of air penetration into the cargo.

The second danger arises from the fact that, even if concentrate cargoes do not heat, they absorb oxygen such that the atmosphere above the cargo, in a hold that is inadequately or not at all ventilated, may become deficient in oxygen and enriched with nitrogen. Air contains roughly 76% nitrogen and 20.8% oxygen and, as the oxygen is absorbed by the cargo, the oxygen content may fall to as low as 4%.

The minimum concentration of oxygen required in the atmosphere to support life is 19.5%. It is vital to gauge the atmosphere before entering the hold. Fatal accidents have occurred where persons have entered fully closed holds loaded with concentrates where the oxygen content was too low.

8.4 Nickel Ore which May Liquefy

Nickel ore cargoes carry a risk of liquefaction during carriage and liquefaction incidents have resulted in several ship losses, such as the *'Emerald Star'* in 2017. In recent years, the majority of liquefaction incidents relate to nickel ore cargoes being exported from Indonesia and the Philippines, although the risk of liquefaction is common to all nickel ore cargoes. The risk is increased at these ports during the rainy season, which is increasingly variable due to changing weather patterns.

Amendment 02-13 of the IMSBC Code, which entered into force on 1st January 2015, includes the addition of nickel ore as a Group A cargo (with a risk of liquefaction). If the moisture content of nickel ore exceeds its transportable moisture limit (TML), it may liquefy. This has the potential to cause instability and capsizing of the ship.

While the can test is a conventional method used by Masters and surveyors for cargo, the actual moisture content (MC) and TML can only be verified during laboratory analysis, as confirmed on the cargo certificates and declaration. The Master should not load the cargo without confirmation of the MC and TML. Additionally, the Master should pay close attention to the weather, particularly rainy weather, and monitor the cargo ashore to ensure it is not loaded wet.

8.5   Carriage of Bauxite which May Liquefy

Following the loss of the Supramax bulk carrier *'Bulk Jupiter'* in January 2015, with the tragic loss of 18 lives, the IMO Sub-Committee on the Carriage of Cargoes and Containers (CCC), at its second session in September 2015, noted that the loss of the ship may have been caused by liquefaction of the cargo. Circular CCC.1/Circ.2 'Carriage of Bauxite which may Liquefy' was issued at that time to raise awareness of the potential risks posed by moisture in the carriage of bauxite. Bauxite was described in the IMSBC Code at that time as a Group C cargo, and the potential for this cargo to liquefy was not specifically addressed. Subsequent work undertaken by the industry Global Bauxite Working Group (GBWG) in conjunction with competent authorities indicated that there was a need to draw a distinction between the types of bauxite cargoes that can liquefy and those that do not. As a result of this work, the IMSBC Code was amended under Amendment 05-19 to include a new Group A cargo BAUXITE FINES and the existing schedule for BAUXITE, classified as Group C, was revised. The two schedules are distinguished primarily on the basis of a particle size distribution (PSD) criterion that, in simple terms, permits BAUXITE FINES to be loaded with a larger percentage of fine particles compared to BAUXITE, although drainage properties also come into consideration. The amended IMSBC Code entered into force on 1st January 2021.

The revised IMSBC Code includes the following amendments:

- A test procedure for determining the transportable moisture limit (TML) for bauxite
- addition of a new schedule for BAUXITE Group A, with the shipping name BAUXITE FINES
- amendments to the schedule for BAUXITE Group C.

Chapter 9 –
Sulphur Cargoes

Sulphur is a relatively cheap commodity that is used in the manufacture of fertiliser. It is both a byproduct of the petrochemical industry and a naturally occurring mineral. After processing, it is often shipped in pelletised/solid form. This type of sulphur is the most common and is classified as IMSBC Code Group C. However, sulphur in crushed, lump and coarse grained form (UN 1350) is classed as IMSBC Code Group B and *International Maritime Dangerous Good Code* (IMDG) Class 4.1, as it carries a risk of fire. The Master should be aware of the form of sulphur being loaded.

Substantial quantities of sulphur are produced in the Alberta province of Canada, most of which is shipped from Vancouver. It is also shipped from ports that include San Francisco, Long Beach, Mariupol, Aqaba, Jubail and Basra. As such, sulphur cargoes are often generally described as 'Canadian bright yellow formed sulphur'. Sulphur suppliers guarantee strict purity specifications to their customers and so are concerned with the risk of contamination. Sulphur cargo should therefore be kept separate from other cargoes that are strong oxidisers (including chlorate, fluorine, etc).

Dry sulphur does not react with bare steel, but wet sulphur (sulphur containing free water) is potentially highly corrosive. Cargoes of sulphur in bulk are normally stored in the open and so are exposed to inclement weather and consequent increased moisture content. Stock will also include a percentage of sulphur dust particles. To prevent contaminated air emissions, it is normal practice, particularly in Canada and the USA, where loading wharves are situated in built-up areas and the dust is considered to be a pollutant, for the environmental authorities to insist upon the use of a water spray during handling to keep down the dust.

This practice, now widely adopted in other countries, may lead to difficulties during and after the period of sea transportation. However, despite the fact that very large quantities of sulphur are carried annually by sea, the vast majority are carried without significant damage to the carrying vessels.

9.1 Corrosion

When sulphur is loaded, any retained free water filters to the bottom of the holds during the voyage. From there, it is pumped out via the bilges. Some water remains on the tank tops and, together with the fines, this produces a sulphurous mud. A great deal of research has been undertaken to understand and mitigate corrosion to vessel structures during the handling and transportation of sulphur.

There are two processes whereby a corrosion reaction can occur: acidic corrosion and electrochemical corrosion.

9.1.1 Acidic Corrosion

This involves a reaction between an acid and elemental iron (steel). The acid involved is sulphuric acid (H_2SO_4). Corrosion does not become significant until the acidity of the solution decreases to pH 2 or below.

9.1.2 Electrochemical Corrosion

This involves a redox (reduction/oxidation) reaction between iron and sulphur. The specific requirements for this reaction to take place are that sulphur and iron must be in direct contact and that the sulphur must be wet.

For further information on the electrochemical process, see Reference 20. Typically, the characteristics of the reaction are as follows:

- The reaction has a maximum rate at around neutral pH (which is 7)
- the reaction displays auto-catalytic behaviour under anaerobic conditions (existing without the presence of oxygen) and the reaction product promotes further reaction to occur
- the reaction proceeds to a greater extent and at a higher rate under anaerobic rather than aerobic conditions
- the initial by-product of the corrosion process is ferrous sulphide (FeS), otherwise known as mackinawite. This is a black/brown substance that is spontaneously combustible when in contact with oxygen (this is a pyrophoric reaction)
- the reaction is temperature dependent as the rate approximately doubles for every 10°C rise in temperature.

Experience has shown that it is electrochemical rather than acidic corrosion that is responsible for the largest proportion of damage to a ship's hold structures on passage.

The *International Maritime Solid Bulk Cargoes Code* (IMSBC Code) (Reference 17) states in Section 9.3.1.10:

"Materials which present corrosive hazards of such intensity as to affect either human tissue or the ship's structure shall only be loaded after adequate precautions and protective measures have been taken."

The following measures should be adopted to minimise the risk of damage as a result of loading sulphur:

- Make good all damage to paint coatings on hopper tank plating, bulkheads, bulkhead stools, internal ship's side plating, frames and internals to the height to which the cargo will be in contact. Loose rust and scale must be removed from the underside of hatch covers. Aluminium or epoxy resin based paints appear to be most effective
- while the current rules of Classification Societies do not require tank top plating to be coated, it is important and accepted that paint coatings provide protection to the plates during the carriage of sulphur, therefore, consider this precaution
- limewash as per the owner's/shipper's/charterer's instructions and to the satisfaction of the pre-load surveyor
- cover the bilge strainer plates with hessian
- during the loaded voyage, maintain bilge levels below tank top level. Keep a careful bilge pumping record, which should also include estimates of the volumes of water ejected from the holds
- remove all residues of sulphur from the holds after completion of discharge and thoroughly wash down the holds with seawater and, finally, fresh water
- if corrosion has occurred, it must be removed by chipping or shot blasting before washing. The bare steel should be touched up with paint coatings.

The presence of chlorides, in the form of salts, such as sodium and potassium chlorides, can hasten the interaction between the moist sulphur and ship's steel. Sodium chloride is a major constituent of both salt cake and dissolved materials found in seawater. Potassium chloride (potash) is regularly shipped from Vancouver. Any trace of these substances will lead to an accelerated corrosion effect, so hold cleanliness prior to loading is of the utmost importance.

To determine whether a vessel is likely to suffer from corrosion damage due to the carriage of wet sulphur, and to what degree, the following factors should be taken into account:

- Cargo-related factors and, in particular, residual cargo acidity
- length and duration of voyage
- temperatures encountered during the voyage
- effectiveness of lime washing and the condition of underlying paint coating
- proper bilge pumping to remove excess water.

9.2   Cleanliness

Prior to loading sulphur, it is recommended that the receiving holds are in a 'grain clean' condition, which requires:

- Removal of all residues of previous cargoes and hard and loose scale from the holds. Air wands should be used to dislodge residues of cargo from otherwise inaccessible areas
- thorough washing out of the holds with seawater
- thorough washing out of the holds with fresh water.

The IMSBC Code (Reference 17) states in Section 9.3.1.12:

"After discharge of cargoes, a close inspection shall be made for any residue, which shall be removed before the ship is presented for other cargoes."

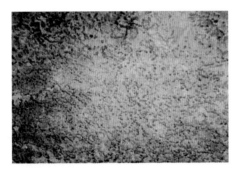

Figure 9.1: Pitting damage caused to tank top after 85 days' sulphur/steel contact.

9.3   Lime Washing

Applying lime wash to cargo hold structures does not totally eliminate corrosive reaction, but only acts to slow or mitigate it. Ideally, the lime wash is, or should be, applied over existing sound paint coatings. The lime wash acts in two respects: as an additional physical barrier and as an alkaline neutralising barrier between the wet sulphur and the bare steel/painted surface. The neutralising action of the lime wash will eventually result in it being 'consumed' by the sulphur. Once this happens, and in the absence of an intact paint coating, the sulphur is once again in direct contact with the ship's structure and the electrochemical corrosion process will resume. Experience with Canadian sulphur has shown that the application of a single layer of lime wash can provide good protection to the steel for about 30 to 40 days, and in some cases even longer.

It is recommended that a mixture of approximately 60 kg of lime to 200 litres of fresh water should be used. The lime wash should also be allowed to dry before loading commences, otherwise the protective 'glaze' may not form properly.

9.4 Gas Emissions

Hydrogen sulphide (H$_2$S)

During the passage and after discharge, bulk sulphur can emit small quantities of H$_2$S gas. As a consequence, all areas where sulphur is stowed or used, or which require the presence of personnel, must be thoroughly ventilated and tested before entry.

Sulphur dioxide (SO$_2$)

SO$_2$ may be generated during repairs involving heating/welding in spaces previously exposed to sulphur. Appropriate safety measures must be taken.

9.5 Flammability

The *International Maritime Dangerous Goods Code* (IMDG Code) (Reference 19) Class 4.1 defines flammable solids as:

"Solids which, under conditions encountered in transport, are readily combustible or may cause or contribute to fire through friction; self-reactive substances (solids and liquids) and polymerizing substances which are liable to undergo a strongly exothermic reaction; solid desensitized explosives which may explode if not diluted sufficiently."

In 1989, following the results of a report from Alberta Sulphur Research, the Canadian Coast Guard declared that:

"Based upon the results of the tests, as submitted, it is agreed that formed sulphur does not meet the criteria for classification in Class 4.1."

Masters should be aware that fire might occur when dry sulphur is being loaded, as a result of static electricity building up on the loading pipes. These fires may be extinguished by dowsing with sulphur or by the use of a fresh water spray. Ferrous sulphide is pyrophoric (ie it may spontaneously combust on contact with air) and can cause fire near the tank top during discharge. Such fires may be controlled with the careful application of a fine jet of fresh water.

However, sulphur that appears in crushed, lump and coarse grained form (UN 1350) carries an ignition risk under Class 4.1 of the IMDG Code. While not combustible, it is readily fusible by heat so should be loaded in a damp or wet condition to reduce the risk of fire/explosion.

Chapter 10 –
Direct Reduced Iron (DRI)

DRI is the raw material for the electric arc process of steel production, which is the primary method of steel production in the world (having superseded the blast furnace process in most countries). DRI is made by passing reducing gases over iron ore, usually in the form of pumps or pellets.

There are three types of DRI:

- Direct Reduced Iron (A) – briquettes, hot-moulded
- Direct Reduced Iron (B) – briquettes, lumps, pellets, cold-moulded
- Direct Reduced Iron (C) – byproduct fines.

Each is covered by a separate schedule in the *International Maritime Solid Bulk Cargoes Code* (IMSBC Code) (Reference 17). DRI is effectively categorised as an IMSBC Code Group B cargo (possesses a chemical hazard which could give rise to a dangerous situation on board ship). The primary hazard in its carriage comes from the risk of reaction with oxygen in the atmosphere. As such, the IMSBC Code requires that DRI B and DRI C cargoes are carried in an inert atmosphere with less than 5% oxygen content. It is important that the Master is aware of what type of DRI is being carried, to comply with the relevant requirements of the IMSBC Code. In some instances, a shipper may seek to obtain an exemption from the Code (under Section 1.5), however in these instances, the Master should seek confirmation from the company and the ship's P&I Club.

Hot-moulded DRI is produced by compressing freshly produced cold-moulded DRI pellets into briquettes at high temperature. The additional processing involved in producing hot-moulded DRI briquettes means this type of DRI is more expensive than cold-moulded DRI, although hot-moulded DRI is a considerably less hazardous product in terms of self-heating. By-product fines are also known to overheat during transit.

10.1   Hot-Moulded DRI

All DRI products are internally porous, but hot-moulded DRI has a considerably lower ratio of surface area to mass than cold-moulded DRI. Consequently, hot-moulded DRI is substantially less reactive with water and so less hazardous than cold-moulded. There have been only isolated serious heating incidents with hot-moulded DRI during transportation.

Therefore, although the product can be hazardous, it is generally acceptable for ocean transportation provided the various requirements set out in Appendix 1 of the IMSBC Code are met. The *Hazard* section in the schedule for Direct Reduced Iron (A) – Briquettes, hot-moulded, states:

"Temporary increase in temperature of about 30°C due to self-heating may be expected after material handling in bulk. The material may slowly evolve hydrogen after contact with water (notably saline water). Hydrogen is a flammable gas that can form an explosive mixture when mixed with air in concentration above 4% by volume. It is liable to cause oxygen depletion in cargo spaces. This cargo is non-combustible or has a low fire-risk."

Figure 10.1: Direct reduction plant which reduces iron ore to produce direct reduced iron.

10.2   Cold-Moulded DRI

Cold-moulded DRI is manufactured in the form of pellets (spheres) about 1 cm in diameter. These are produced from iron ore (principally iron oxide) which is crushed, partially freed from foreign material other than iron oxide and then compressed at normal ambient temperatures into iron oxide pellets. The pellets are passed down through a furnace, in which there is a counter-current flow of 'reducing gas', where they are usually heated to a temperature of between 800 and 1,050°C. This is below the melting point of iron at 1,538°C. The reaction between the iron ore pellets and hot gas removes the chemically-bound oxygen component from the iron oxide ore, leaving metallic iron pellets (cold-moulded DRI) with a sponge-like structure.

Once the pellets, consisting of approximately 90% metallic iron, have been produced and cooled, the product has a tendency to reoxidise (rust) back to iron oxide at normal temperatures if there is sufficient oxygen. This process is, however, extremely slow in dry conditions. The rate of oxidation is substantially increased by the presence of water and, if the water contains dissolved salts such as sodium chloride (as found in seawater), the rate of reaction is further increased very substantially.

The oxidation process is exothermic (heat is generated). All rusting processes are surface reactions and the reason why substantial heating can occur when wet DRI pellets react with atmospheric oxygen is that, because of their sponge-like structure, they have an extremely large surface area. It is important to appreciate that DRI is a poor heat conductor, so heat build-up occurs quite rapidly.

Another property that makes cold-moulded DRI very hazardous is that, although oxidation rates are insignificant in dry air at normal temperatures, the product will react with atmospheric oxygen at a rapid rate if heated to a temperature called the 'autoxidation temperature', which can be as low as 150°C. Therefore, if there is a focus of heating initiated in a cargo due to wetting, and this produces a rise in temperature of the cargo to above the autoxidation temperature, heating can spread to adjacent DRI cargo that would otherwise remain stable.

A final hazard associated with DRI pellets is that, if they become wetted and substantially increase in temperature, water may react with very hot iron to produce hydrogen, which is a potentially explosive gas. To retard or inhibit oxidation, the DRI pellets may receive during manufacture a special treatment called 'passivation'. This is dealt with in both the schedule for cold-moulded DRI in the IMSBC Code (Reference 17) and in a circular to Members on DRI that was issued by the International Group of P&I Clubs (Reference 21). The relevant section in the schedule for Direct Reduced Iron (B) – Lumps, pellets, cold-moulded briquettes, in Appendix 1 of the IMSBC Code reads:

"The ship shall be provided with the means to ensure that the requirement of this Code to maintain the oxygen concentration below 5% can be achieved throughout the voyage. The ship's fixed CO_2 fire-fighting system shall not be used for this purpose. Consideration shall be given to providing the vessel with the means to top up the cargo spaces with additional supplies of inert gas, taking into account the duration of the voyage.

The ship shall be provided with the means for reliably measuring the temperatures at several points within the stow, and determining the concentrations of hydrogen and oxygen in the cargo space atmosphere on voyage whilst minimizing as far as practicable the loss of the inert atmosphere.

The ship shall not sail until the master and a competent person recognized by the competent authority of the port of loading are satisfied:

.1 that all loaded cargo spaces are correctly sealed and inerted;

.2 that the temperature of the cargo has stabilized at all measuring points and that the temperature does not exceed 65°C; and

.3 that, at the end of the inerting process, the concentration of hydrogen in the free space of the holds has stabilized and does not exceed 0.2% by volume." (Reference 17)

With regard to the reference to 'inert atmosphere', it is important to stress that the inerting gas used must be nitrogen. If CO_2 is used, it can be reduced by hot iron to carbon monoxide (CO), which is hazardous in terms of both severe toxicity and flammability.

In the 1980s, there was a lull in transocean shipments of cold-moulded DRI but trade stepped up again in the 1990s. During the 1990s, shipments in bulk carriers were undertaken with no attempts at the outset or during the voyage to maintain the cargoes under an inert gas (nitrogen) atmosphere. Under more recent trading conditions, and with shipments made in ordinary bulk carriers, the practicality and economics on long transocean voyages of shippers or shipowners providing and maintaining such inert conditions must be regarded as questionable. It is understood that shipments of cold-moulded DRI where the cargo was not claimed to be passivated have been carried on relatively short voyages under inert gas with no reports of untoward incidents, and it is presumed that the costs of providing the inert conditions are borne by the shippers.

Some shipments of cold-moulded DRI forwarded for ocean transport in certain regions have undergone a degree of passivation treatment and there are reasonable indications that this treatment does provide satisfactory protection against serious heat-generating oxidative reactions, in circumstances where the product becomes wetted with up to a few percentage units of fresh water.

However, clear evidence has emerged that passivation treatment provides no effective protection against the occurrence of serious heating problems when the product is wetted by seawater. It has been estimated that the containment of a bulk stow of this type of cold-moulded DRI with as little as 60 litres of seawater would be sufficient to initiate very serious heating problems.

10.3 Characteristics of Burning DRI

The characteristics are as follows:

- Hot spots propagate relatively slowly. It may take a day or more for propagation to occur through a stow, which allows the opportunity for action to be taken. Clearing DRI away from bulkheads and making a firebreak between heating DRI and adjacent cargo spaces are two of the few options available

- temperatures can become sufficiently elevated so that, if water is sprayed over DRI, it can evolve hydrogen through catalytic dissociation of the water by the hot metallic surface of the DRI. Sufficient concentration of hydrogen, coupled with a heat source, will result in the hydrogen igniting. A light spray of water, insufficient to quench combustion, can therefore result in burning hydrogen with flames

- neither the fuel, which is iron, nor the combustion products, iron oxides, are gaseous, so no flame appears. Burning DRI is similar in appearance to burning charcoal, glowing red hot but without flame. However, there may be a reaction between very hot DRI and moisture, possibly even atmospheric moisture, which produces hydrogen, as described above, which burns with a blue flame. This flame often appears as a blue haze, best visible in low light conditions

- when fuel oil double-bottom tanks are below a hold containing burning DRI, an added safety measure would be to inert the fuel tanks. Dry ice or CO_2 injected through sounding pipes/breathers is recommended. This does not conflict with earlier advice, as the CO_2 will not be in contact with the burning DRI.

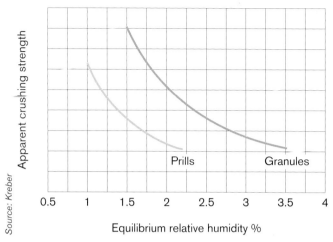

Source: Kreber

Figure 11.2: Granulation properties.

Regardless of whether the fertilisers are prills or granules, the end product should meet these criteria:

- Consistent size
- free from crushed granules and dust
- easily spread
- quickly dissolved
- contaminant free.

11.2   Caking in Fertilisers

Between production and use in soil, fertilisers may need to be stored for long periods, and it is essential that they remain free-flowing during this time. Under certain conditions, lumps or agglomerates (caking) can form in fertilisers, and as fertiliser usage relies on its free-flowing nature, it is important to prevent caking. The contacts formed between fertiliser particles can provide an indication of the cause of caking. Furthermore 'free-flowing' is different for fertilisers than, for example, grain, in that it is inevitable that some fertiliser compaction (adhesion contacts) will occur within the stow. These cliffs are easily collapsed by normal handling during discharge operations of the cargo, for example, using a grab.

The types of contacts that can form between fertiliser particles are detailed as follows. It is noteworthy that adhesion contacts, ie reversible compaction, is distinct from hard caking, the latter being irreversible.

Adhesion contacts, or capillary adhesion, is a relatively weak attraction between the in-contact molecule surfaces. Pressure exerted on the fertiliser particles in bulk can result in adhesion bound particles (ie compaction). Typically, adhesion contacts are easily reverted to a free-flowing state with minimal handling.

Liquid contacts are caused by fertiliser wetting or moisture vapour absorption. The saturated solutions formed between the wetted particles stick them together. As this liquid is mobile, the 'sticking' of the fertiliser particles is relatively easily broken. However, when the wetting is severe, phase contacts will be achieved.

Phase contacts, or salt bridges, are crystal bridges that form between fertiliser particles. These crystal bridges form due to dissolution/recrystallisation and/or thermal effects. The salt bridges are often the most troublesome form of caking, resulting in hard caking that cannot be broken apart easily.

A wide range of factors, both external and inherent to the fertiliser, can affect the propensity for a cargo to cake, as discussed in detail below.

Moisture content at production influences the extent of caking, and fertilisers with higher moisture content, even if they are within contractual specifications, are more prone to caking. The extent of drying required to limit the chances of caking depends on properties such as composition, morphology, size and hardness.

The **uniformity, size and crushing strength** of fertilisers also impacts their likelihood to cake. Fertilisers with a small range in particle size, high crushing strength and larger overall size are less prone to caking due to reduced specific surface area for contact between particles, and decreased likelihood of breaking into smaller particles. Impurities within the fertiliser can also affect caking tendency, for example, iron and aluminium impurities decrease the propensity of caking in diammonium phosphate fertilisers.

Moisture uptake during storage and handling prior to and during loading is another point of consideration. Moisture uptake is a particular risk during loading when all the cargo becomes exposed for at least some time on the conveyor. All fertilisers are hygroscopic, meaning they absorb moisture from the air. This occurs above the critical relative humidity (RH), which differs for individual fertilisers. RH is the amount of moisture in the air relative to the maximum the air can contain at any one temperature. For example, with urea, it is common practice to suspend loading at times of high atmospheric humidity, usually above 75–80% RH. It is also critical that fertilisers are not exposed to moisture during transportation.

Anti-caking agents are often added to fertilisers to minimise caking. These anti-caking agents are usually liquid or powder coatings that act as a barrier to prevent caking and can control the absorption of moisture by creating a hydrophobic barrier. They can also act as a physical barrier between particles or weaken bonds that may have formed between particles. Powder coatings can cause dust issues. Anti-caking agents can also be so-called 'conditioning agents', which improve the crushing strength and decrease dust formation. In the past, there have been issues related to incorrectly or incompletely treated fertilisers.

Inappropriate ventilation can enhance caking, resulting in surface crusting from moisture uptake from humid ventilating air and/or caking in the top layer from excessive cooling. The respective IMSBC Code schedules for all bulk fertilisers specify that they shall not be ventilated during the voyage.

Temperature gradients can enhance caking if there are large temperature differences between the load port and discharge port, resulting in caking along the periphery when cargo cools down. Similarly, if different production batches of fertilisers with different temperatures are loaded, this can also produce temperature gradients within the stow.

11.3   Fertiliser Cargo Issues

The two main issues of fertiliser carriage relate to caking. The first issue arises when the Master observes caking during loading, the second issue being caking from any cause at outturn.

Most often, these issues concern bulk fertilisers rather than bagged, and shippers frequently bring bagged cargo to the vessel and open bags into the holds. If there are any signs of firm caking before loading, caution is advised. For example, fertiliser cargoes have been encountered that were still caked after being loaded from a warehouse onto a truck, followed by a sling and onto a pontoon over the hatch. The caked fertiliser was rendered free-flowing by passing it through a mesh over the hold but re-caked into firm lumps at disport, resulting in a large claim.

Therefore, it is advised that if caked lumps of cargo are observed at any point during the loading process, a protest is made and the Master considers clausing the bills of lading accordingly. Often, lumps or caking seen at outturn are attributed to a condition suspected or observed during loading, and if the Master has not complained or claused documents, then the ship may well be criticised. Therefore, it is recommended that the duty officers take photos of the cargo during normal routine inspection. This can be highly valuable evidence when dealing with such complaints.

Caking might later be blamed on rain during loading, so it is crucial that accurate logs are kept stating whether there were any periods of rain during the loading, and if the hatches were closed in a timely fashion. Ensuring that hatch covers are watertight and that hatch cover surveys are up to date prior to loading can also assist in defending claims.

In the event of wetting during loading, the wetted areas of cargo must be removed as much as possible. However, as the water will be spread quickly and absorbed by the surrounding fertiliser, it will be difficult to remove all of the wetted fertiliser.

11.4   Ammonium Nitrate

Ammonium nitrate is a hazardous compound that has the potential to explode upon contact with ignition sources. The risk of explosion is higher when ammonium nitrate is contaminated by organic material such as fuel oil and/or externally heated, for example by hot work or buried cargo lamps. Some of the most serious cargo-related disasters have been caused by ammonium nitrate, for example in Texas City, Tianjin and Beirut.

There are four entries in the IMSBC Code for ammonium nitrate and ammonium nitrate based fertilisers. There are numerous other entries of ammonium nitrate cargoes within the IMDG Code. The criteria stated in the IMSBC Code for determining which entry a cargo belongs to depends on:

- Percentage of ammonium nitrate
- percentage of total combustible organic material calculated as carbon
- the chemical nature of the components besides the ammonium nitrate
- the outcome of UN standard tests such as the self-sustaining decomposition trough test.

Amendment 05-19 of the IMSBC Code entered into force on 1st January 2021 and reclassified ammonium nitrate based fertiliser as an IMSBC Code Group B cargo (cargoes that possess a chemical hazard which could give rise to a dangerous situation on a ship). This is because the cargo is liable to decomposition leading to flammable and toxic concentrations of ammonia and nitrogen.

Further to this, in May 2021, IMO MSC considered an additional revision of ammonium nitrate cargoes within the IMSBC Code and adopted Amendment 06-21 to the Code. These amendments are due to enter into force on 1st December 2023. The amendments introduced new individual schedules for different ammonium nitrate based cargoes, differentiating these cargoes as follows:

- Ammonium nitrate based fertiliser defined as

"Straight nitrogen fertilisers containing less than 2% chloride, and

.1 not more than 70% ammonium nitrate with other inorganic materials; or

.2 not more than 80% ammonium nitrate mixed with calcium carbonate and/or dolomite and/or mineral calcium sulphate and not more than 0.4% total combustible organic material calculated as carbon; or

.3 mixtures of ammonium nitrate and ammonium sulphate with not more than 45% ammonium nitrate and not more than 0.4% total combustible organic material calculated as carbon.

Compound NPK/NK/NP fertilizers:

.1 mixtures of nitrogen with phosphate and/or potash containing not more than 70% ammonium nitrate and not more than 0.4% total combustible organic material calculated as carbon or not more than 45% ammonium nitrate and unrestricted combustible material; and

.2 either less than 20% of ammonium nitrate content or less than 2% of chloride …"

For these straight cargoes, the IMSBC Code Group is now Group C (neither A nor B).

- Ammonium nitrate based fertiliser MHB defined as

"Ammonium nitrate-based fertilizers transported under conditions mentioned in this schedule are uniform mixtures of nitrogen with or without potash and/or phosphate within the following composition limits:

.1 not more than 70% ammonium nitrate and not more than 0.4% total combustible organic material calculated as carbon or not more than 45% ammonium nitrate and unrestricted combustible material; and

.2 both the ammonium nitrate content is equal to or greater than 20% and the chloride content is equal to or greater than 2% …"

These ammonium nitrate cargoes are still categorised as Group B (possesses a chemical hazard which could give rise to a dangerous situation on a ship). The cargo should be kept as dry as possible and kept away from external sources of heating that may cause its decomposition.

For both cargoes, the shipper should declare the ammonium nitrate content and the chloride content in accordance with Section 4.2 of the Code.

11.4.1 Safety Principles

Before 2021, all ammonium nitrate based fertiliser was categorised as a non-hazardous IMSBC Group C cargo, however the cargo was linked to several serious ship fires, including the *'MV Cheshire'* in 2017. Following this incident, the IMO published a guidance circular on the carriage of ammonium nitrate based fertilisers (CCC.1/Circ.4). Based on guidance from the Fertilizers Europe Organisation, the safety principles for this cargo are as follows:

"• *Avoidance of storage of combustible substances near fertilisers*
• *avoidance of storage of incompatible substances near fertilisers*
• *avoidance of cross contamination with remains of previous cargoes*
• *avoidance of cross contamination of next cargo with fertiliser*
• *avoidance of sources of heat likely to affect the fertiliser*
• *avoidance of application of heat (eg, welding) to any section which may have trapped/confined fertiliser."*

The circular also notes that:

"The best protection for seafarers is awareness of the decomposition process to allow it to be identified at an early stage. Regular monitoring of the cargo throughout the voyage is crucial to detect beginning of decomposition.

When heated strongly, this cargo may decompose and release toxic gases. Timely opening of cargo hatches can prevent the build-up of pressure and help cool the cargo, impeding the development of cargo decomposition.

In case of decomposition or fire involving this cargo:

• *Provide maximum ventilation to remove the gases resulting from decomposition. These gases may include toxic fumes of ammonia and oxides of nitrogen and sulphur*
• *wear, as necessary, protective clothing and self-contained breathing apparatus*
• *application of water is most effective where injection pipes are used to deliver water to hot spots. Water spraying may not be sufficient to control the decomposition*
• *flooding of the cargo space may be considered, giving due consideration to the ship's stability and structural strength*
• *the ship's gas firefighting installation will be ineffective."*

Ammonium nitrate based fertiliser comes in different forms depending on its composition, and the cargo has several UN numbers (UN 1942, 2067, 2071). Ammonium nitrate as a crystal is UN 1438. It is important that the Master is aware of the composition of the cargo being loaded.

Further information on hazards, stowage and segregation is available in the individual schedules of solid bulk cargoes (Appendix 1) of the IMSBC Code (Reference 17).

11.4.2 Self-Sustaining Decomposition (SSD)

The decomposition of ammonium nitrate based fertilisers can be highly exothermic (heat-producing) and violent. Toxic fumes and nitrous oxides (NOx) are produced during this decomposition. The decomposition of ammonium nitrate is referred to as self-sustaining as, whilst a considerable amount of energy is required to initiate the reaction, once the decomposition begins, the energy released (as heat) is enough to support further decomposition, ie the reaction is self-sustaining.

As the decomposition reaction does not involve external reagents, such as oxygen, the decomposition cannot be controlled using inert gases, or by restricting oxygen. Instead, cooling the cargo is necessary to stop further decomposition. SSD can be controlled by quenching the reaction with water, whilst opening the hatch covers prevents over-pressurisation. The IMSBC Code states that in the event of a fire, copious amounts of water should be used and the heat source should be isolated.

Decomposing ammonium nitrate in one hold can act as a heat source for adjacent holds, therefore care needs to be taken to prevent SSD from spreading. The IMSBC Code states that hatch covers of adjacent holds should be opened to allow for maximum ventilation and dividing bulkheads should be cooled.

The decomposition of ammonium nitrate is complex but thought to initially involve an unfavourable, energy absorbing proton (H+) transfer, which is why heat is required to begin the decomposition. Without a sufficient heat source, there would not be enough energy in the system to begin SSD. Temperatures of around 160–170°C are thought to be necessary before decomposition can initiate. Examples of ship-related sources of heat found to have caused SSD in the past include energised lights in the cargo hold and thermal oil heating pipes.

The propensity of ammonium nitrate based fertilisers to undergo SSD can also be influenced by the presence of trace levels of transition metals, chlorides or contamination by chemicals or fuel oil. The IMSBC Code relies on the trough test (UN Manual of Tests Methods Part III, Section 38.2.4) to determine whether nitrates containing fertiliser are capable of undergoing SSD. In this test, the trough (see Figure 11.3) is filled with fertiliser and decomposition is initiated at one end of the trough. Around 20 minutes after the removal of the initial heating source, the propagation of decomposition is measured. If the decomposition has continued after removal of the source, then the fertiliser is considered capable of showing SSD behaviour. One major limitation of this test is that in bulk, fertilisers are excellent insulators. This means that, in case of exposure to external heat sources, such as a light in the hold, the heat is unable to dissipate, causing the temperature of the fertiliser surrounding the heat source to rise. Over an extended period of exposure to the heat source, the temperatures could feasibly reach the point where the fertiliser begins to undergo decomposition.

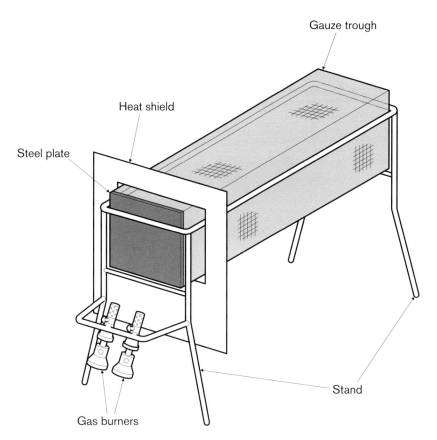

Figure 11.3: Granulation test equipment.

Part 3 –
Steel and Other Metals

Chapter 12 – Steel

This chapter discusses the susceptibility of steel cargoes to damage, particularly pre-shipment. Where damaged cargo is presented for shipment, bills of lading (B/Ls) should be rigorously claused and any damage that is claimed on outturn should be properly surveyed.

In steel trading, profit margins are small and the competition is intense. This trading climate has produced an industry that is highly automated and where plant is expensive and needs to be used to its utmost potential if it is to be worked economically. Anything that leads to delay on the production lines, or that requires extra manual handling, increases the cost of the product.

> Therefore, any steel delivered damaged or blemished will almost certainly be the subject of a claim from the receivers. If the cargo is discharged in anything other than the condition described in the B/Ls, claims against the carrier may be expected.

Steel is often imported by merchants who work to very narrow profit margins and are, accordingly, extremely claims conscious. A merchant may, for example, order coils of say 1,120 mm width, knowing that they have buyers for coils of 510 and 610 mm widths, intending to cut them to the required size. If, however, the coils arrive with their edges crimped or cut, this may not be possible. In the same way, while the bending of the flange at the extreme end of a beam may in itself seem unimportant, this beam may have been ordered in a 20 m length, with the merchant knowing that they have a market for 3 m and 6 m long beams. In both cases, the merchant may find that, after cutting to the width and length needed, they are left with material of a width and length that is not readily marketable. Current business methods do not encourage large stock holding and merchants do not want to keep capital tied up in goods that are deteriorating while they are in their custody.

Finally, the merchant is affected by the steel market where rapid fluctuations in demand mean fluctuations in price, which may leave large quantities of steel for which the merchant cannot get a profitable price. In these circumstances, an aggressive attitude may be expected towards carriers with regard to any damage for which they can possibly be held responsible.

> The import of steel into the USA gives rise to more claims against ocean carriers than in any other part of the world.

This chapter describes the more common types of steel products transported and their susceptibility to damage. It emphasises the importance of accurately clausing the B/Ls and makes some recommendations on stowage and the way in which cargoes found damaged on outturn should be examined.

12.1 Types of Steel Products

Rolled steel.　　　　　　Sheet steel.　　　　　　Steel rods.

Figure 12.1: Steel products.

Courtesy of Danny Cornelissen/portpictures.nl

12.1.1 Sheet Steel

Sheet steel is mainly carried in the form of coils, although smaller quantities are often carried in packs.

Hot rolled coils
Coils are produced by heating and rolling steel ingots through reduction mills. As the thickness of the steel is reduced, its length increases and, for convenience in handling, the long narrow sheet is rolled into a coil. The coil is tightly strapped through the core and around the circumference and made ready for transportation to the load port. The coils are described as hot rolled coils or raw steel and they will require further processing at their country of destination.

Figure 12.2: Coils of hot rolled steel.

The coils are usually between 1.20 and 4.50 m in diameter and weigh between 5 and 15 T each.

Cold rolled coils

Rather than being prepared for shipment as hot rolled coils, the steel may be further processed in the country of manufacture to create cold rolled coils. The steel is passed through baths filled with a weak acid solution to remove rust and scale, a process known as pickling. The sheet is then washed, dried, oiled and re-coiled before being passed on to the cold reduction mill, where it will be cold rolled under tension. The end result is a product of better temper and improved finish.

Figure 12.3: Coils of cold rolled steel.

The higher quality surface finish of cold rolled steel makes it much more susceptible to rust damage, so it is usually packed in bituminous paper and kept away from moisture.

Cold rolled steel may be processed further by dipping the sheet into a bath of zinc to produce coils of galvanised steel sheeting. Alternatively, tin plate may be produced by covering one or both surfaces of the sheet with a thin layer of tin.

Cold rolled steel, galvanised steel sheet and tin plate are much more valuable than hot rolled sheet. They will be strapped in the same way as hot rolled coils but, before leaving the factory for transportation to the load port, will normally be wrapped in bituminous paper and then covered with fine gauge steel sheeting that is itself secured in place with metal strapping.

Packed sheets
Cold rolled sheets, galvanised sheets and tin plate may be carried in packs instead of coils. The bundle of cold rolled sheets that forms a pack is secured with steel strapping. It is then usually completely wrapped in bituminous paper and covered with a metal envelope. The package will be secured, by metal straps, to wooden skids.

12.1.2   Rolled Sections or Construction Steel

Rolled sections or construction steel are generally large sections in the form of 'H', 'I' or 'U' (channel) beams. They are produced by passing the steel ingots through a series of rollers.

12.1.3   Small Section Material, Rods and Wire

Small section material
This may be composed of special steel alloys or of steel that has been given a special finish at the factory. Small section material is usually destined for use in the manufacture of machine tools, for components for electrical machinery or for steel furniture. Other uses include the construction of ladders for fire escapes, racks in factories or warehouses, railings and numerous other appliances or fittings where a quality finish may be required. Small section material is shipped in bundles and may be wrapped.

Reinforcing bars
Reinforcing bars are often referred to as 'rounds', 'concrete iron', 'deformed reinforcing bars' or 're-bars'. The use of the word 'deformed' means that the bars have ridges introduced into their surface during production. The ridges improve the bond of the bar with the concrete and so increase the constructional strength of a finished structure.

Wire rod
Wire rod is mainly produced by drawing larger bars through dies. It is prepared for shipment at the factory by being rolled into coils and, usually, 4 or 5 coils are strapped together to form a unitised coil bundle (see Figure 12.4).

Figure 12.4: Unitised coil – bundles of wire rods.

Bright basic wire

In the country of destination, the wire may be cold drawn through dies so that the gauge is reduced and the wire elongated and polished to form what is called bright basic wire.

Wire rod is used in the manufacture of numerous goods such as nails, wire mesh and galvanised wire. A large quantity of this wire is chromed and used in the manufacture of supermarket shopping baskets and trolleys.

12.2   Susceptibility to Damage

12.2.1   Rust

Figure 12.5: Coils showing external rust.

All steel is susceptible to damage by rusting, which is a continuous and progressive process. The longer it continues, the greater the damage to the product. Rust that appears insignificant at the time the consignment leaves the mill or is loaded on board the ocean-going ship may develop to a serious extent by the time the consignment reaches either the load port or the discharge port, even though there has been no failure on the part of the inland or ocean carrier to care properly for the cargo.

Mill scale

When raw steel leaves the mill, it is covered by a thin layer of hard oxide known as mill scale. This will protect the steel from deterioration by rust as long as it remains an unbroken skin covering all surfaces of the product. Unfortunately, mill scale is very brittle and is easily shattered or splintered off the steel and, when this happens, rusting takes place. Rusting is accelerated in areas where bare steel and mill scale are in close proximity.

> The ordinary shocks to which steel products are subjected in their transport to the carrying ship are sufficient to jar some of the scale off the surface of the steel. The scale will also gradually fall away if the steel is left exposed to the weather for any significant length of time.

Rust damage to coils

The coiling process is itself often sufficient to loosen the scale and expose the steel to rusting. With hot rolled coils, much of the rust will probably be removed in the normal course of further processing in the country of destination. However, if the rust has developed to the extent that the surface of the steel is damaged or pitted, the steel may be unfit for the purpose for which it was originally intended.

Rust damage to construction steel

Construction steel is not usually packed and will almost always be rusted to some extent. It is not unusual for steel producers to fill orders for constructional steel from stock that has been held on their premises for some time. It is usually transported from the factory to the load port by rail, either in open or covered wagons, or in lighters that are usually covered but may not be weathertight, so there is a danger of free water collecting in the bottom. Cargoes are frequently assembled a week or a fortnight before the ship arrives at the loading berth and, as this steel is usually stored unprotected in the open, it will be exposed not only to the weather but also to the atmosphere. Where the atmosphere contains salts and/or is polluted, the steel can be seriously attacked.

Rust damage to small section material

Small section material may be wrapped, but should still be transported and stored under cover, protected from the elements. Unfortunately, this is not always done and frequently piles of small section steel rods are to be seen stored in the open, covered by very patched or old tarpaulins. Claims may be expected if material of this type is received rusty since much of it is used in the production of furniture and fittings, where appearance is very important. This is particularly true of painted material, which is highly susceptible to rusting where the surface has been scratched.

Rust damage to reinforcing bars

Reinforcing bars are normally shipped unprotected in bundles, which can retain a lot of water if they have been exposed in open storage for any length of time. As the wetness on the outside of the bundles dries quickly, the interior of the bundle may be considerably rustier than is apparent from an examination of the outside. Unfortunately, the 'purpose-built' deformations on the bars are susceptible to erosion by rusting.

> If the reinforcing bars are subject to strict specifications (as for example in any US federal project), erosion of the deformation may mean that the goods are off-specification.

Rust damage to wire rod

Wire rod is usually shipped unprotected and, in many cases, the pickling and other processing that the wire rod later undergoes will be sufficient to remove any rust that may have formed. However, if the surface of the wire has been damaged or pitted, it may be necessary to eliminate this by reducing the diameter of the wire, in which case the wire may be off-specification.

Figure 12.6: Typical small section steel.

12.2.2 Physical Damage

The nature of the steel industry is such that any physical damage, such as bending or denting, is likely to give rise to a claim.

Loose and deformed coils

Care should be taken not to displace or break the steel strapping. Where coils are brought forward in railway wagons, it is particularly important that they are well secured so that they do not come adrift with the motion of the train (which may be considerable if the wagons are shunted). If the strapping is displaced or broken, the coil will become loose and possibly deformed. An added danger with loose coils is that abrasive matter may get between the turns of the steel and chafe or scratch the surface. Any deterioration of the surface of either hot or cold rolled steel may be serious since, if pitting, scoring and chafing are not removed, the surface of the finished plate may be marred. Blemishes of this type cannot usually be eradicated without some waste of material.

Telescoping

Coils may also become telescoped, ie some laps may be projecting on one side of the coil. If the telescoping is excessive, it may be difficult to put the coil onto the de-coiling machine at the receiver's premises.

Figure 12.7: Hot rolled coils that have telescoped.

Crimped edges

The edges of coils may be crimped by careless use of lifting equipment. The misuse of handling gear can lead to chafing damage even when the coils are wrapped. The edge of packaged sheets may be crimped, bent or cut if they overhang the wooden bearers.

Distortion

Constructional steel may be damaged if the flanges are bent by the careless use of lifting gear. If the bundle is incorrectly packed, the whole section may be distorted.

Kinked or bent smaller section material

If smaller section material is bent or wire rod is kinked, the value of the material will be reduced. If the rod is kinked or bent, it may damage the dies through which it is drawn and the finished product may have a score mark or nick that can only be removed by reducing the diameter of the wire, which involves the risk of putting it off-specification. Heavily twisted or nicked wire cannot be straightened satisfactorily and, therefore, it may be regarded as scrap.

12.3   Clausing Bills of Lading for Pre-shipment Damage

Before steel cargoes are loaded into the ship, they will have already been subject to considerable risk of damage, both by exposure to the elements and by the number of times they have been handled.

It is extremely important, therefore, that any pre-shipment damage is noted on the B/Ls. The services of a skilled and conscientious surveyor are usually necessary.

For steel shipments, some qualification of pre-existing damage does appear in the mate's receipt or B/L, although this should not necessarily make the B/L a 'foul' B/L. Letters of credit need to be amended or there will be a tendency to issue a clean B/L against a Letter of Indemnity (LoI).

Masters and agents of ships stemmed to load steel cargoes should contact the local UK P&I Club correspondent, who can normally arrange for a surveyor to be instructed to attend the loading of cargo.

12.3.1 Rust Damage

Nowhere is the need to clause B/Ls greater than in the case of rust. Without exception, whenever a consignment is rusty, this should be stated in the B/L. Cargo interests may insist that the rust is normal or customary, or will not affect the value of the cargo, or will be removed in any event by further processing and that the B/L can be issued clean without any danger of prejudicing the interest of the carrier. However, representations of this type are to be ignored. The best way of protecting the carrier's interests is to clause the B/L. If the rust is normal or customary, there should be no difficulty in the B/Ls being negotiated through the banks. Masters should not concern themselves with the marketability of the cargo but should focus on describing the condition of the cargo as seen.

When clausing B/Ls against rust, it is essential not to qualify the word rusty in any way (eg by using words such as 'atmospherically' or 'superficially' or 'slightly'). The reason for this is that rust that may appear, on loading, to be only slight may have worsened progressively during the voyage (without there being any fault on the part of the carrier in the care of the cargo) to such an extent that the cargo is pitted or otherwise seriously affected on discharge. If the damage on outturn is more severe than the damage noted on loading, a court may be tempted to attribute the deterioration in the condition of the cargo to some alleged fault of the carrier in the care of the cargo. This danger is minimised by simply describing the cargo as 'rusty'.

In the 20th century, London based P&I Clubs issued circulars setting out clauses that were suitable for describing pre-shipment rust damage to steel. These included:

- Rusty
- rusty edge
- rusty end
- top sheets rusty
- rust on metal envelopes
- goods in rusty condition
- wet before shipment
- covered with snow.

However, to avoid misunderstanding, it is now recommended simply to describe the cargo as 'rusty'.

12.3.2 Physical Damage

Any physical damage, such as denting or bending, should also be entered on the B/L. Where packaging is damaged, this should be noted as well, together with any obvious damage to the contents.

12.4 Loading and Stowage

Courtesy of Danny Cornelissen/portpictures.nl

Figure 12.8: Steel coils ready for loading.

The most suitable ships to be engaged in steel trade, from the point of view of loading and stowing, are bulk carriers with wide, large hatches and unobstructed holds. Residues of previous cargoes that may have an adverse effect on steel, particularly salt and fertilisers, should be very carefully removed.

Loading and stowage of steel cargoes requires skilled and experienced stevedores. Steel can easily be damaged, or damage the ship, if not handled with care as each separate lift is likely to weigh in the region of 5 to 12 T.

Cranes used for loading and discharging containers are the best equipment for handling steel cargoes. Lifting gear such as wire slings, spring laid rope strops or chains should be adequately protected to avoid damaging the edges of coils. Winch drivers should be instructed to avoid violent acceleration or braking when lifting or lowering coils.

Forklift trucks should have the forks adequately protected with timber unless they are specially designed for use with steel cargoes. Crowbars should only be used when handling material not capable of being damaged by them.

Locking coils
Generally, coils should be given bottom stow. A method of stowing coils that has been used with success is stowing them in athwartships rows with their major axes horizontal and in the fore and aft line. The bottom tier of coils should stand on double lines of good dunnage, placed athwartships, so that any moisture that may collect on the tank top or ceiling of the hold can run to the bilges without damaging the cargo. This dunnage also helps to spread the weight of the coils over the tank top plating. The first coils loaded are placed in the wings against the bulkhead and then the row is extended inwards towards the centreline of the ship. Invariably, a gap will be left on the centreline

and the first coil of the second tier in that row will be placed in that gap. The next coils of the second tier will be placed in the wing above and outboard of the extreme wing coils of the first tier and these three coils, ie the one on the centreline and the one in each wing, will effectively jam and block off the first tier of that row (see Figure 12.9). These three coils are known as the locking coils. The remainder of the second tier in that row will be placed in the cantlines of the coils beneath them. The same procedure is followed for each further tier until the first row has been built up to the required number of tiers.

Coils of up to 10 or 12 T in weight may be stowed in 3 tiers, but over this weight it is better that a new row is started in the same way, ie loading the first 2 coils in the wings, against the first row loaded.

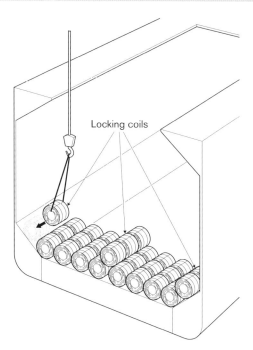

Locking coils

Figure 12.9: Locking coils.

Loading and stowing coils

It may be difficult to manipulate coils into positions out of the reach of the crane or derrick, and attempts to swing the coils into position in the wings or at the fore or aft ends of the hold may cause damage. The use of dedicated trucks and equipment has improved the means by which steel coils may be properly handled.

It is better to stow coils at least 2 tiers high. A single tier of coils nearly always allows movement and, as result, the stow may work loose. If there are insufficient coils to make 2 complete tiers over the whole surface of the hold, the hold should be partially floored out with 2 tiers of coils so that the stow ends in a brow or wall across the hold. The face of the coils should be protected by a strong timber fence when other cargo, such as constructional steel, is stowed adjacent to them.

Each individual coil in the top tier of the stow should be secured by driving wedges between it and its adjacent coils on either side and fore and aft.

12.5 Securing Shipments of Steel Coils by Flexible Metal Bands

Steel coils may be successfully secured by using flexible flat metal banding secured by clips. Securing clips around the bands and tensioning the bands is undertaken using pneumatically-operated tools.

When utilising strapping bands, it is essential that the manufacturer's instructions are strictly observed and that the correct procedures are closely followed at the time of loading. The following points should be carefully borne in mind when using bands:

- The strapping band system uses fewer personnel to secure the cargo as straps are easier to thread through the coils, and rigging/bottle screws and bulldog clips are not required
- the straps can be rendered bar tight at the outset of the voyage (in contrast to wires, which may still not have reached the full limit of their elasticity and may subsequently slacken off during the voyage)
- it is necessary to utilise an air compressor when strapping bands are used

Remember that such pneumatic tools need regular servicing and require trained operators.

- normal lashing wire of 16 mm diameter loses 30% of its strength in the area of the bulldog clips. The actual breaking strain may, therefore, be considered as 5.6 T. Metal strapping bands have, in general, a breaking strain of 4 T
- when a 'key coil' is secured with 16 mm wire lashings through the core and with additional cross lashings over the top, a breaking strain of 44.8 T can be achieved (8 lashings × 5.6 T = 44.8 T). This compares with a breaking strain of 32 T when single strapping bands are used, which would be considered adequate for coils weighing up to 15 T. Where very heavy coils are carried, double strapping bands should be applied.

When properly utilised, the strapping band securing system meets all the necessary requirements, ie it is of adequate strength and is acceptable for securing average steel cargoes.

Owners are advised to appoint a surveyor on their behalf in the load port to ensure that the securing system has been properly applied and that the manufacturer's instructions are carefully followed.

Forward compartments
Particular attention should be paid to cargo in the forward compartment of a ship, where the effects of heavy pitching are more pronounced.

Coils of differing dimensions

When coils of differing dimensions and weights are being stowed, the lighter, smaller coils should be given a top position. Precautions should be taken to ensure that the smaller coils cannot work down too far into the cantlines of the rows of larger coils underneath, as this may cause them to become deformed. There is no objection to overstowing a coil cargo with wire rods, bales or other cargo. Whether a floor of dunnage over the stow of coils is necessary will depend on the nature of the overstowing cargo.

Sheet steel in packs

Sheet steel in packs should also be stowed on double lines of athwartships dunnage. The ordinary principles of cargo stowage may be applied to the stowage of these packs. They are less likely to shift than coils as they stow more compactly.

Dunnage for constructional steel

The recommended method of stowing constructional steel entails the use of considerable quantities of dunnage. Quantities of timber, amounting to between 75 and 100 T per 10,000 T, of cargo are quite common.

Dunnage, which is usually 6 × 1 inches (15 × 3 cm), should be laid in double lines athwartships at intervals along the length of the steel that is stowed fore and aft. The dunnage is inserted to assist in reslinging the steel for discharge and to help bind the steel into a solid block. As the steel is very heavy, it needs to be supported at intervals of about 10 ft (3 m) along its length.

Care should be taken to ensure that each line of athwartships dunnage is vertically over the line immediately beneath it (see Figure 12.10). If this precaution is not taken, the steel may become warped.

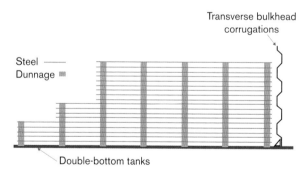

Figure 12.10: Dunnaging constructional steel.

When stowing beams, it is important that the webs are kept vertical and that the flanges overlap in an 'in and out' manner (see Figure 12.11) as the beams can become severely distorted when all flanges are overlapping in the same direction. The stow should be kept level and complete. Efforts should be made to avoid mixing sizes as this may create gaps that can later lead to the whole stow collapsing. Athwartships stowage of steel beams should be avoided if at all possible. In particular, try to avoid the ends of beams stowed at the bottom of the hold in a bulk carrier resting against, or terminating adjacent to, the sides of the hopper tanks in the wings of the compartment. If the dunnage compresses during the voyage, the beams may settle, leaving the ends resting against the hopper tanks and the middle of the beams unsupported. As a result, the beams will probably be permanently bowed (and there is risk of damage to the tanks).

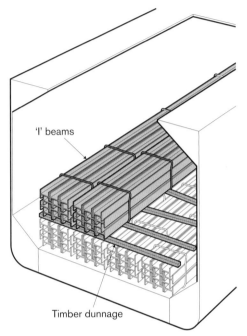

'I' beams

Timber dunnage

Figure 12.11: Constructional steel ('I' beams).
Note that the beams are stacked correctly, with the flanges 'in and out'.

12.6   Stowing and Securing Steel Slabs

The correct and safest method of carrying steel slabs, and heavy steel plates, is to stow with the longitudinal axis athwartships. This entails winging the stow out to the ship's sides and results in overlapping of horizontal layer ends. In the case of slabs, this method of stowage entails handling each slab individually in the hatch, using a forklift truck. Similarly, steel plates, depending on their weight per unit, can only be handled a few at a time.

Figure 12.12 shows a satisfactory method of stowage. An acceptable variation, that is useful when the complete tank top area is not to be utilised, is for Slab 1 to be stowed athwartships and Slabs 2, 3 and 4 stowed longitudinally to prevent movement of the stow.

It is essential that wooden dunnage is placed between plates or slabs, in order to correct any tendency to shift. In some cases, consideration may be given to the lashing of such stows with steel wires, preferably attached to steel eye pads. This applies particularly in the upper decks of tween deck vessels.

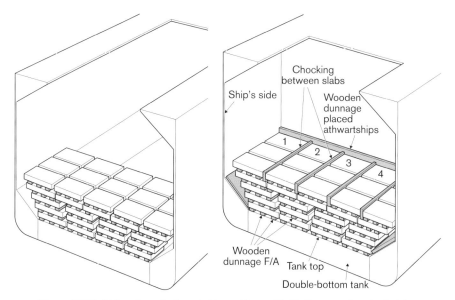

Figure 12.12: Slabs stowed athwartships. Figure 12.13: Dunnage for steel slabs.

Figure 12.14: Correct stowage of plate steel.

In recent years, other methods of stowage have been devised with the aim of speeding up the turnaround of ships and reducing expenses. One such system involves a series of heavy lifts into the ship, with each weighing up to 36 tonnes or more. Each lift is landed in a convenient position and succeeding lifts are landed adjacent to each other, in the square of the hatch, where all the cargo is stowed. No dunnage is used between the individual stacks and there is a gap between the cargo and the ship's side, both to port and starboard. Sometimes timber framings are erected to fill these gaps (see Figure 12.15). Metal strapping bands are sometimes used to secure each stack but, due to the sinkage of whatever wooden dunnage may be placed between slabs, these are often slack before the ship sails.

The use of such strapping bands for steel slabs should not be encouraged as they can be dangerous. The main criticism relates to their use in block stowage of bundles of steel slabs by direct loading into the hatch squares of bulk carriers, leaving the space above the sloping lower wing tanks free of cargo. Whatever lashing or securing is used in these circumstances, there is still the potential for a shift of cargo. It is of paramount importance that the stowage extends out to the ship's sides and that the top of the stowage is level. The only alternative would be to construct, and weld in position, substantial steel framing between the ship's side and the cargo above the sloping lower wing tanks. There is no objection to using block stowage methods in ships with box-shaped holds as long as the stowage extends to the full width of the ship and again the top of the stowage is level.

Figure 12.15: Flimsy timber framing.

Masters should be on guard against situations where steel plates may be presented for shipment that are too large to fit the hatch opening dimensions. Attempts may be made to persuade the Master to carry such plates on hatch covers or weather decks. If steel plate is loaded on deck, care should be taken to ensure that the plates are individually stowed, dunnaged, chocked and lashed. There should be no plate-on-plate interfaces. It is also important, in such circumstances, to clause the mate's receipts appropriately to reflect stowage on deck.

Small section material

Small section material, particularly rods and bars, should, wherever possible, be given a top stowage position and also stowed in a fore and aft direction. The stow should be kept level to ensure that the material is adequately supported at frequent intervals along its length. Rods and bars should only be handled with rope slings, and crowbars should never be used in manipulating the bundles into their stowage positions.

Unitised bundles of wire rods are usually stowed in the ship with their axes in a fore and aft direction and in a manner similar to that described for coils. It is not recommended to stow the bundles of rod more than 6 tiers high as the weight on the lower bundles may be excessive, causing the lower bundles to become deformed and the stow to collapse. As with coils, a two tier stow in part of the hold is preferable to a single tier over the whole floor of the hold. The face or brow of the stow also needs to be fenced or secured in the same way. Loading slings should be made of composition fibre or of wire rope covered with rubber tubing. When forklift trucks are used, the forks should either be covered with timber or fitted with a specially constructed metal tube.

One common fault with bundles of wire rod is that, if the strapping bands break or work round the coil to one particular point on the coil, the unsecured turns open out and become crushed, distorted and twisted in the stow.

Reinforcing bars

Reinforcing bar bundles should be given good, level stow and should be well supported throughout their length to avoid any bending or distortion that may make them unsuitable for the purpose for which they are intended.

Pipes

Figure 12.16: Steel pipes ready for loading.

Pipes are usually shipped in bundles unless the diameter is very large, when they are usually presented for shipment in single pieces. Special stowage is frequently called for, particularly in the case of lighter pipes where top stowage is preferred. Where top stowage is preferred, pipes should be stowed fore and aft in the hold. On occasion, where pipes have been stowed with some fore and aft and some athwartships, one or other tier has become deformed owing to the weight of the overstowed cargo. These goods are most vulnerable at their ends and great care should be taken particularly where the ends are threaded to ensure that the threads are not nicked or otherwise damaged.

12.7   Care on Board

To avoid rust damage, effort should be made to avoid loading (or discharging) during wet weather and all the hatches should be covered during rain showers.

Where the ship's personnel request to stop loading in wet weather, shippers frequently object and attempt to convince the Master and ship to continue loading. However, such pressure should be firmly resisted.

It is not advisable to continue loading in the rain even if the steel already inside the hatch has been covered with tarpaulins or plastic sheeting, since protection of this type has not been found to be of any great assistance in avoiding rust damage claims.

12.8   Fact Finding on Discharge

If damage is suspected on arrival at the discharge port, the Master should contact the P&I Club's local correspondents directly and ask for the appointment of a competent surveyor to examine the hatches and the stowage of the cargo.

> Contacting them direct is usually preferable to contacting the ship's agents at the discharge port as these may be appointed by, and closely identified with, the cargo interests.

Photographs
The receivers of the cargo or the cargo underwriters often appoint surveyors who will want to board the ship and inspect the hatches and other openings into the holds. In the USA, cargo interests can obtain a court order granting them access to the ship for this purpose. When cargo interests' surveyors are on board the ship, they should be accompanied by the shipowner's surveyor wherever they go. Photographs taken by the cargo interests' surveyor should, if possible, be countered with photographs taken by the shipowners' surveyor. This will avoid selected images being used to support a claimant's case by giving the impression that the whole cargo was damaged to the same extent as the cargo actually photographed. High resolution colour photographs are recommended to reveal the extent of damage.

Seawater entry or condensation?
Sometimes, on opening hatches, a pattern of rust extending right down through the stow and coinciding with the hatch coamings or hatch joints, is discovered. While this may indicate that the hatches have leaked during the voyage, it may also be indicative of heavy condensation. In any event, it is imperative that the pattern of damage in each compartment is accurately noted, as only in this way will it be possible to distinguish between pre-shipment damage and damage incurred during the course of the voyage.

A careful examination should be made of any rust that is not pre-shipment in origin to establish whether it is caused by seawater or fresh water. An experienced surveyor should be able to distinguish the cause without resorting to silver nitrate tests, which can be misleading.

Stevedore damage
Any damage caused by the discharging stevedores should be noted so that recovery can be made from them for any claims lodged in relation to the damage.

12.9   Carriage of Steel in Containers

Special containers are available for the carriage of steel, which will reduce the risk of handling and water damage provided the steel is well secured within the container and the containers have been checked for holes prior to acceptance. However, unless precautions are taken and experts are involved in the securing of steel coils inside the container, there is a risk of damaging the coils as well as the container, with a risk of injury if the container breaks loose from the sling.

Chapter 13 –
Scrap Metal

13.1 Borings, Shavings, Cuttings and Turnings

Ferrous materials (those that contain iron), in the form of iron swarf, steel swarf, borings, shavings or cuttings, are classified in the IMO *International Maritime Solid Bulk Cargoes Code* (IMSBC Code) as materials liable to self-heating and spontaneous ignition (Reference 17).

Turnings are produced by the machining, turning, milling, drilling, etc of steel. When produced, the turnings may be long and will form a tangled mass, but they may be passed through a crusher or chip breaker to form shorter lengths. Both forms of turnings are shipped and shipments are frequently a mixture of short and long chips. The density of short chips is approximately 60 pounds per cubic foot, twice the density of longer chips as they tend to compact more readily.

Borings are produced when iron castings are made. Because of the nature of the parent metal, borings break up more readily than turnings, tend to be finer and have a greater bulk density.

Turnings and borings may be contaminated with oils, such as the cutting oils used in the manufacturing processes. Oily rags and other combustible matter may also be found among the loads.

Iron will oxidise (rust), and in a finely divided form will oxidise rapidly. This oxidation is an exothermic reaction, ie it will release heat. In a shallow, level mass of turnings, this heat will be lost to the surrounding atmosphere. However, in large compact quantities, such as would be found in a cargo hold, this heat will be largely retained and, as a result, the temperature of the mass will increase. The oxidation process is accelerated if the material is wetted or damp or contaminated with cutting oils, oily rags or combustible matter.

The turnings may heat to high temperatures but will not necessarily produce flames. In one incident, temperatures in excess of 500°C were observed 6 ft below the surface of the cargo. Temperatures of this order may cause structural damage to the steelwork of the carrying vessel. Flames are frequently seen in cargoes of metal turnings, but they are usually the result of ignition of the cutting oils, rags, timber and other combustible materials that are mixed with the turnings.

Spontaneous heating of metal turnings has caused several major casualties. In one incident, the ship was moved from port to port in attempts to agree discharge. After weeks of delay, all the holds were eventually flooded to reduce the heating for safe discharge of the cargo. Following discharge, the ship loaded a cargo of conventional scrap. During the subsequent voyage, rough weather was encountered and cracks developed in the shell plating. The holds flooded and the ship was lost with 29 lives.

In another incident, heated turnings formed a solid mass in the hold and had to be mechanically broken into pieces before discharge by grab. In a further incident, following a normal passage, it was not possible to discharge the cargo by grabs as the surface of the stow had crusted to a hard mass. Bulldozers were used to loosen the surface of the cargo and, several hours later, fire was observed in all of the holds.

The *International Maritime Solid Bulk Cargoes Code* (IMSBC Code) (Reference 17) has special requirements for the loading of turnings and borings, including:

- Prior to loading, the temperature of the material should not exceed 55°C. Wooden battens, dunnage and debris should be removed from the cargo space before the material is loaded
- the surface temperature of the material should be taken prior to, during and after loading and daily during the voyage. Temperature readings during the voyage should be taken in such a way that entry into the cargo space is not required, or alternatively, if entry is required for this purpose, sufficient breathing apparatus, additional to that required by the safety equipment regulations, should be provided.

  If the surface temperature exceeds 90°C during loading, further loading should cease and should not recommence until the temperature has fallen below 85°C. The ship should not depart unless the temperature is below 65°C and has shown a steady or downward trend in temperature for at least 8 hours. During loading and transport, the bilge of each cargo space in which the material is stowed should be as dry as practicable
- during loading, the material should be compacted in the cargo space as frequently as practicable with a bulldozer or other means. After loading, the material should be trimmed to eliminate peaks and should be compacted.

While at sea, any rise in surface temperature of the material indicates a self-heating reaction problem. If the temperature rises to 80°C, a potential fire is developing and the ship should make for the nearest port.

Early application of an inert gas to a smouldering fire may be effective. If possible, the Master should not use water to fight fire at sea and instead should proceed to a port of refuge. In port, copious quantities of water may be used but due consideration should still be given to stability

- entry into cargo spaces containing this material should be made only with the main hatches open, after adequate ventilation and when using breathing apparatus.

Compacting the cargo by loading with a bulldozer is recommended as this creates a dense mass, pushing the short turnings into the bundles of long turnings and tending to exclude air from the stow. However, some authorities argue that compacting the stow tends to break up the long turnings, creating greater surface area for the oxidation process. Shorter turnings should compact more readily than the longer forms, reducing the area exposed to oxidation.

Trimming level ensures that there is less cargo surface exposed to the air than cargo in a peaked condition. In addition, while air will theoretically pass across the top of a level trim, it can pass through the stow if loaded in a peaked condition, creating a 'chimney' effect that accelerates the heating process.

The requirements for safe entry into cargo spaces must be followed at all times. Many lives have been lost as a result of officers and crew members entering a hold to inspect a heating problem without taking adequate precautions.

13.2   Metal Dross and Residues

Aluminium dross

Aluminium dross is formed during the recovery of aluminium from scrap and in the production of ingots. Dross may constitute about 5% of the metal where clean mill scrap is involved, but will constitute greater quantities where painted or litter scrap is recovered. The main components of dross are aluminium oxide and entrained aluminium. Small amounts of magnesium oxide, aluminium carbide and nitride are also present.

The dross is recovered and re-melted under controlled conditions to provide aluminium metal, which is then treated to remove hydrogen and other impurities, including trace elements. Storage or transport of aluminium dross should be conducted under carefully controlled conditions.

Contact with water may cause heating and the evolution of flammable and toxic gases, such as hydrogen, ammonia and acetylene. Hydrogen and acetylene have wide ranges of flammability and are readily ignited.

Aluminium dross, aluminium salt slags, aluminium skimmings, spent cathodes and spent potliner are included in the IMSBC Code (Reference 17), categorised as aluminium smelting by products.

The Code recommends that hot or wet material should not be loaded and a relevant certificate should be provided by the shipper stating that the material was stored under cover, but exposed to the weather in the particle size in which it is to be shipped, for not less than 3 days prior to shipment. The material should only be loaded under dry conditions and should be kept dry during the voyage. The material should only be stowed in a mechanically ventilated space. The ventilation equipment should be intrinsically safe.

Zinc dross

Zinc dross, zinc skimmings, zinc ash and zinc residues are all materials obtained from the recovery of zinc. They may be recovered from galvanised sheets, batteries, car components, galvanising processes, etc. Zinc ashes are formed on the surface of molten zinc baths and, while primarily zinc oxide, particles of finely divided zinc will also adhere to the oxide. The different types of zinc are processed to produce pure zinc metal.

The ashes, dross, skimmings and residues are all reactive in the presence of moisture, liberating the flammable gas hydrogen and various toxic gases.

The materials are also listed in the IMSBC Code, which states that any shipment of the material requires approval of the competent authorities of the countries of shipment and the flag State of the ship.

The Code recommends that any material that is wet, or is known to have been wetted, should not be accepted for carriage. Furthermore, the materials should only be handled and transported under dry conditions. Ventilation of the holds should be sufficient to prevent build-up of hydrogen in the cargo spaces. All sources of ignition should be eliminated, including naked light work such as cutting and welding, smoking, electrical fittings, etc.

An incident where an explosion occurred in a hold containing zinc ashes was said to have been caused by a lamp used to warm the sealing tape to seal the hatch covers. The flame of the lamp ignited hydrogen gas leaking from the hold. The flame flashed back into the hold, igniting an explosive concentration of hydrogen/air. The explosion lifted the hatch covers and collapsed a deck crane. There was also loss of life. The hydrogen had been generated by reaction of the zinc ashes with water as the zinc ashes had been loaded in a damp condition. They were discharged and later spread on the quayside in a thin layer to dry. Seven days later, hydrogen gas was still being detected.

Part 4 –

Timber and Forestry Products

Chapter 14 – Timber Deck Cargoes

There are several incidences of timber deck cargoes being lost overboard, sometimes with catastrophic results for ship and crew. It is important to ensure that the carriage, stowage and securing of timber deck cargoes does not fall short of any currently accepted codes, rules, regulations or formal recommendations.

14.1 Regulations

The regulations that support the carriage of timber deck cargoes are contained within the following IMO Codes and guidelines:

- *Code of Safe Practice for Cargo Stowage and Securing* (CSS Code) (Reference 22)
- *Code of Safe Practice for Ships Carrying Timber Deck Cargoes* (TDC Code) (Reference 23)
- *Revised Guidelines for the Preparation of the Cargo Securing Manual* (MSC.1/Circ.1353/Rev.2) (Reference 24)
- Regulation 44 of the *International Convention on Load Lines, 1966* (Reference 25).

The provisions in these codes and guidelines are recommended for all vessels of 24 m or more engaged in the carriage of timber deck cargo (ie timber cargo carried on an uncovered part of a free board of superstructure deck). It includes logs and sawn timber, either loose or packaged.

This chapter should be read in conjunction with Chapter 54, Lashing and Securing Deck Cargoes.

14.2 Types of Timber Cargo

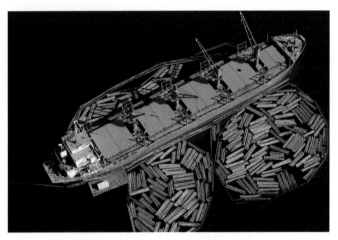

Figure 14.1: Ship preparing to load logs.

Timber (also referred to as 'lumber') cargoes come in many forms and sizes that may consist of logs, cants, ragged end packages, packages that are square (or flush) both ends, etc.

Packaged timber should not be stowed on deck if the bundles are ragged at both ends. Generally, only bundles square at both ends should be used for weather-deck stows, although the Asia trade region usually requires stowage of a proportion of packages that are square at one end and ragged at the other. Wherever possible, care should be taken to ensure that ragged ends are kept to a minimum, are stowed inboard of the perimeter and that broken stowage is avoided.

As far as possible, timber should be stowed fore and aft. On some ships, it may be common practice for the ragged ends to face the aft direction. However, this is not a requirement. As such, all deck officers should consult their ship-specific Cargo Securing Manual and the relevant provisions of the TDC Code when stowing timber cargoes.

The IMO *Code of Safe Practice for Ships Carrying Timber Deck Cargoes* (TDC Code) (Reference 23) does not allow the transverse stowage of packages to the outer sides of the deck and any packages stowed athwartships must be contained within a perimeter of square-ended packages that are stowed fore and aft.

Logs come in a variety of lengths and may be of widely varying diameter. It is essential that uprights are used correctly, supported by transverse hog wires, with wiggle wires, securing wires or chains pitched at the correct distance apart.

Cants are logs that are 'slab cut', ie ripped lengthways so that the resulting thick pieces have two opposing parallel flat sides. In some cases, a third side is sawn flat as well. Cant cargoes require similar arrangements to those for logs.

Some timber cargoes are precut, for example a manufacturer of kitchen cupboards would import precut timber pieces in pallets in order to fix the pieces together to make cupboard carcasses. These pallets should be stowed under deck for protection. Generally, palletised timber cannot be treated as a timber deck cargo, as the pallets are too small to allow securing.

Any deviation from the lashing arrangements recommended in the IMO Code may lead to a loss of cargo and threaten the stability of the ship.

14.3   Loading

Before loading timber cargoes, the holds and hatch covers should be cleaned to a reasonable standard to prevent damage to the timber. This should include the removal of oil, grease, ore remnants and similar residues that may stain the timber. Appropriate dunnage should be used to protect timber and keep it clear of metal structures. Timber should be stored away from, or covered to protect from, rust which may also stain the timber. Where fork lift trucks are used, the underlying timber should be protected by a steel plate.

14.4   Timber Load Lines

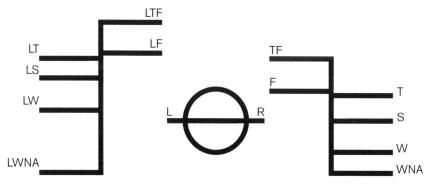

Figure 14.2: Typical timber load lines.

Ships that carry timber cargoes are marked with timber load lines, in addition to the normal load lines, which are calculated on the premise that a full timber deck cargo will be carried. An entirely separate set of cross curves of stability is produced for this full timber deck cargo condition. The timber load lines allow the vessel to load to a deeper draught (and so a larger displacement) than would otherwise be the case because of the overall buoyancy effect from loading timber.

Disputes have arisen between Masters and charterers about the strict application of timber load lines. The following guidelines should be applied:

- When a ship is assigned a timber load line, in order to load to this mark the vessel must be loaded with a timber deck cargo that is correctly stowed in accordance with the deck cargo regulations and the TDC Code

Figure 14.3: Timber logs being loaded in the fore/aft direction.

- the *International Convention on Load Lines, 1966* (Reference 25) requires that the timber is stowed as solidly as possible and to at least the standard height of the superstructure. For example, in ships of 125 m or more in length, this equates to a uniform height of not less than 2.3 m. In ships under 125 m in length, the stow should reach a uniform height of not less than the height of the break of the forecastle head
- if the timber is stowed to a lesser height, or is not correctly stowed in any other way, such as not the full length of the well or not from side to side, then the ship is not permitted to load to the timber line
- when timber is correctly stowed on deck, the ship may load to the timber load line, regardless of the quantity or type of cargo stowed below decks. The reduction in freeboard on a ship that is assigned timber load lines is permitted because of the buoyancy contribution of the timber deck cargo to the ship's stability characteristics
- ships using a timber freeboard assignment should be aware of the load line changes that occur with seasonal zones, as specified in Regulation 6, Annex I of the Load Line Convention. These include Summer Timber Load Line (LS), Winter Timber Load Line (LW), Winter North Atlantic Timber Load Line (LWNA), Tropical Timber Load Line (LT), Fresh Water Timber Load Line (LF) and Tropical Fresh Water Timber Load Line (LTF). For example, it should be noted that the LWNA is the same as the standard Winter North Atlantic Load Line (WNA) for all ships, as this season warrants no additional allowance for timber cargoes.

Figure 14.4: Timber cargo poorly stowed and improperly secured.

When a full timber cargo is carried on deck and the ship is loaded to the timber load line, the static stability curve may be derived from the cross curves of stability, which have been computed taking into account the timber deck cargo. When the timber deck cargo is not correctly stowed, due to deficient height or other reason, the static stability curve must be derived from the cross curves that are computed for the ship without timber deck cargo.

14.5 Strength, Pitch and Tending of Lashings

Once loaded, deck cargoes must be correctly secured. Full details of the exact securing arrangements are provided in the Cargo Securing Manual. Methods include chain lashings, wire lashings and web lashings. However, fabricated web lashings must not be used in conjunction with chains or wires.

It is important to remember that Regulation 44 of the *International Convention on Load Lines, 1966* (Reference 25) still applies to the 2011 IMO *Code of Safe Practice for Ships Carrying Timber Deck Cargoes*, 2011 (TDC Code) (Reference 23), but that the spacing of the transverse lashings within the Code, although still determined by height, does not permit an interpolation between cargo heights of 4 and 6 m. The straightforward interpretation of such spacing applies to a compact stow of square-ended bundles (flush at both ends), or near square-ended bundles, in the following manner:

- Each package (along the sides) shall be secured by at least two transverse lashings spaced 3 m apart for heights not exceeding 4 m above the weather deck at the sides

- for heights above 4 m, the spacing shall be 1.5 m above the weather deck at the sides

- when timber in the outboard stow is in lengths less than 3.6 m, the spacing of the lashings shall be reduced as necessary (to comply with the requirement for each package to be secured by at least two transverse lashings)

- the stowage of timber deck cargo should be tight and compact. Where packages are involved, they should be square-ended (flush) at both ends so far as this is possible. Broken stowage and unused spaces should be avoided. There is no absolute requirement for uprights to be used for packaged timber cargo, although some national administrations may insist on their use when lashing arrangements are not otherwise fully satisfactory. Bundles of regular form when stowed in 'stepped-in' truncated, pyramid fashion will not benefit from uprights, even if they are fitted. The TDC Code (Reference 23) does not allow uprights to be used instead of lashings. Where uprights are used, they are in addition to the full number of lashings, properly pitched and of full strength

- the use of uprights when carrying logs on deck is necessary and it is most important always to rig and attach hog wires between such uprights. The uprights' strength relies upon the weight of logs above the hog wires. This rule applies whenever hog wires are rigged, even with packaged timber. Never use uprights without rigging hog wires

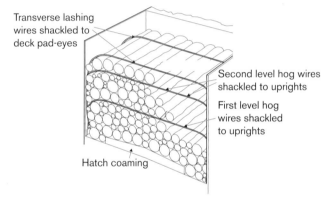

Figure 14.5: Always rig hog wires when using the deck side uprights for logs, packages and loose timber.

Figure 14.6: Rigging hog wires for deck-stowed log cargo, as required by the TDC Code.

Figure 14.7: The correct use of wiggle wires through snatch blocks, which are used to bind and consolidate the log stow and are independent of the number and pitch of cross lashings required. Photo shows chain cross lashings pitched 3 m apart for a stow not exceeding 4 m in height above the weather deck at the ship's side.

- wires or chains used for lashings should have a break load of not less than 13.6 T force (133 kN). With wire and grips, the TDC Code (Reference 23) recommends that four grips per eye are used. If that recommendation is followed, with the eye made up around a thimble, the holding power of the eye will be not less than 90% MBL. Therefore, a 6 × 24 galvanised wire rope of 19 mm diameter will fully comply with the Code's strength requirements (see Section 54.11)

- where thimbles are not used, the slip load of an eye properly made up will be about 70% of the wire's nominal strain. More complex additional securing arrangements are required for cants and reference should be made to the drawings and illustrations given in Annex B of the TDC Code

- at sea, all lashing and securing arrangements should be tended daily, adjusting as necessary to take up any slack that may occur as the cargo settles. Where intermediate ports of discharge are involved, great care must be taken to ensure that the remaining deck cargo is levelled out and resecured in accordance with the Codes.

If necessary, to reach the focsle or to inspect the lashings, it may be possible to rig a walkway over the stow. This should be done carefully, with safety handlines either side in order to prevent injury in case of any cargo movement. Due regard should be made to the relevant chapters of the *Code of Safe Working Practices for Merchant Seafarers* (COSWP).

14.6 Weight and Height of Cargo – Stress and Stability Aspects

14.6.1 Weight

The weight of the deck cargo should not exceed the maximum permissible loading of weather decks and hatch covers. Everyone involved with the loading and safe carriage of timber deck cargoes should be fully conversant with the stability requirements, as set out in the TDC Code (Reference 23), and the ship's 'standard conditions' stability book.

It is important that the correct weight of the cargo is known and allowed for in the stability calculations. Instances have occurred where, because the standard stability booklet has indicated a given height of cargo as representing a given weight, the Master and charterers have assumed that any cargo of the same height will have the same weight. This assumption has proved to be incorrect and can have serious consequences.

An example of the issues with weight can be seen in the losses of packaged timber deck cargoes from Brazil (see UK P&I Club *Packaged timber deck cargo – dangerous densities* (Reference 26)). In this example, investigations revealed that the density of the timber involved was greater than 1,000 kg/m³. In other words, the timber as a whole, and as loaded dry, was heavier than fresh water. Samples cut from the cargo and scientifically analysed confirmed that 78% of the deck cargo, by weight, had specific gravities between 1.0 and 1.4, and that the remaining 22% had an average SG of 0.93. The overall average SG for this deck cargo was 1.080 (compared to SG 1.033 for oceanic salt water).

The average SG of packaged timber deck cargo is generally about 0.6. The data for timber conditions in most standard ship stability books indicates an SG of 0.4 where 'condition volume' is set against 'condition weight'. This underlines the technical philosophy of the TDC Code (Reference 23), which is that a timber deck cargo should float and that if it shifts and causes a severe transverse list, it will provide buoyancy to prevent the ship listing further towards capsize.

It follows, therefore, that lashings approved for cargoes of x metres³ volume and y tonnes weight will be required to hold the same volume when timber of excessive density is involved, but the weight may be as much as 2.7 y tonnes, an increase of 270% in weight. It follows that the cargo itself could not be assumed to provide buoyancy.

The ship's officers should conduct draught surveys at regular intervals to check the weights of cargo coming on board. This is particularly important when all the under-deck cargo has been loaded and before on-deck cargo loading commences. Such draught surveys will, if carefully carried out, provide acceptable information for stability calculations. To enable this, the Master needs to know the correct density (or correct SG) of the timber being loaded. As such, it is a SOLAS requirement for such information to be supplied to the Master by the shipper.

Stability calculations should take into account the changes expected during the duration of the voyage. Annex C of the TDC Code contains instructions on the calculation of the mass change of a timber deck cargo due to water absorption. This is done using a formula involving the planned duration of the voyage in days, and extracting the relevant figure from a table of daily wood mass change (depending on port area and wood type).

GM calculations
The calculation of the metacentric height (GM) of a ship provides some measure of transverse stability, but additional calculations need to be made to produce the curve

of statical stability (the GZ graph). The ship's dynamical stability characteristics can then be established for various angles of heel and can be compared with the minimum characteristics required by the load line rules and the vessel's stability booklet.

There have been examples of written instructions, issued by some charterers or shippers, requiring that 'the metacentric height (GM) should be maintained at 1.5% of the vessel's beam and should never exceed 2 ft (61 cm)'. These instructions could be considered as poorly worded and incomplete, and potentially dangerous for vessels of less than 10 m beam, where 1.5% would produce a GM of less than 0.15 m when 0.15 m is the statutory minimum. Masters should call for expert advice if they face instructions to the contrary, and follow the IMO *International Code on Intact Stability* (IS Code), which says:

"for ships loaded with timber deck cargoes, and provided that the cargo extends longitudinally between superstructures (...) transversely for the whole ship after due allowance for a rounded gunwale not exceeding 4% of the breadth of the ship ..." (Reference 27).

14.6.2 Height

If the timber deck cargo is to be carried through tropical or summer zones only, the following points should be observed:

- The height of the cargo must not restrict or impair visibility from the bridge
- for any given height of cargo, the weight should not exceed the designed maximum permissible loading on weather decks and hatch covers
- any forward facing profile of the timber deck stowage should not present overhanging shoulders to a head sea.

If a timber deck cargo is to be carried through a winter zone, or a seasonal winter zone in winter, the height of the cargo above the weather deck should not exceed one third of the extreme breadth of the ship. For example, if the extreme breadth of the vessel is 15 m, the height of the timber deck cargo should not exceed 5 m. Similarly, a vessel of extreme breadth 21 m could stow cargo to 7 m above the weather deck, providing this does not contravene any of the other requirements of the TDC Code.

It is important to appreciate that the 'weather deck' means the uppermost complete deck exposed to weather and sea. It is not permitted to commence the vertical measurement at hatch cover level.

14.7 Measures to Jettison Cargo

The present regulations for the jettison of cargo involve the use of senhouse slips or equivalent fittings and require personnel to stand on top of the stow to release the individual lashings (see Figures 14.8 and 14.9 for the two systems typically used). This is a dangerous undertaking and serves to emphasise the importance of ensuring, at the outset of the voyage, that the cargo will not shift. If, despite that care, the timber does shift to a dangerous degree, great caution must be exercised in any attempt made to jettison all or part of the cargo.

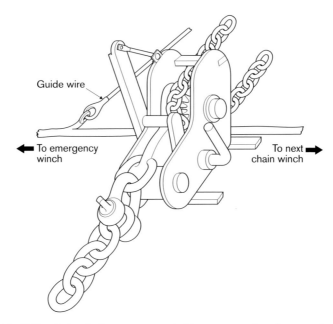

Figure 14.8: All the chain winches are connected by a rope system. In case of emergency, the guide wire has to be pulled by means of a rope winch or warping head. The slip hook will be released and the timber load will be set free at once.

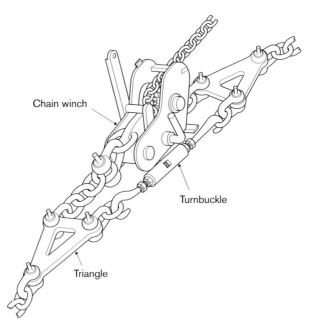

Figure 14.9: A turnbuckle fitting to a triangle plate allows ongoing tightening of lashing. Emergency remote release cannot operate with the turnbuckle fitted as shown.

14.8 Sounding Pipes, Air Pipes and Ventilation

The safe working of a vessel, whether in port or at sea, depends to a large degree upon the ability to obtain quick and safe access to all sounding pipe caps and air pipes. With this in mind, it is imperative that any deck cargo is not stowed over such pipes nor should it interfere with safe access to them.

> Numerous instances have arisen where ships and crew have been placed in danger because it is not possible to walk safely across the cargo to sound tanks or bilges or to effectively close off the upper apertures of air pipes, as is required by the Load Line Rules.

Care must also be taken to ensure that all ventilators, of whatever type, serving the cargo holds are kept clear and free for operation.

14.8.1 Hatchway Coaming Drainage Channels

Hatchways fitted with steel covers are generally provided with drain holes from the coaming channels that, in turn, exit through drainage pipes. The lower open ends of these pipes are sometimes provided with loose canvas socks that close off with the pressure of seas shipped on board, acting as simple (and effective) non-return valves so long as they remain supple and unpainted.

Drainpipes are also frequently fitted with patent non-return valves of one form or another, which are designed to exclude water on deck from working back into the hatchway coaming channels. Before loading timber deck cargoes, Masters should ensure that all such non-return facilities are in efficient working order so that they do not require maintenance or supervision during the course of the voyage.

14.9 Bills of Lading (B/Ls)

The trade in timber from tropical countries has resulted in more and more packages being offered for shipment as 'kiln-dried' and requiring under-deck stowage. Serious claims have arisen against some vessels where kiln-dried timber has been stowed on the weather deck. Masters must ensure that all such timber, even if wrapped, sheeted or otherwise covered, is afforded below-deck stowage.

Where shippers or charterers insist on the vessel carrying such timber on the weather deck, Masters should issue a clear note of protest, ensure that all mate's receipts are claused accordingly, accept no letters of indemnity and instruct the local agents to clause the bills.

A switched B/L may be used when a trader does not want their buyers to know the identity of the actual seller. This means that logs are often loaded in ports of Malaysia with B/Ls showing the Malaysian seller as the 'Shipper or Consignor' and the Trader (say in Singapore) as the 'Consignee'. Later, the B/Ls are 'switched' showing the Trader as the 'Shipper' and the ultimate buyer in various countries as the 'Consignee'. Sometimes, such 'switching' of B/Ls causes disputes over the quantity loaded.

Chapter 15 – Forestry Products

15.1   Softwood and Hardwood Timber, Plywood and Paper Products

It is important to be aware that all forms of forestry products are at risk of causing oxygen depletion in the cargo hold. Safe entry procedures should be followed by all personnel entering the cargo space, including testing of the atmosphere.

Softwood timber

The main areas from which softwood timber is shipped are the Baltic and North America. Very few claims arise from the Baltic or the east coast of North America trades, but large claims have arisen on shipments of timber from the north west coast of North America, mainly due to the wet climate in this area. Softwood timber is commonly shipped in bundles or packages of planks of various lengths and sizes and secured with flat metal strapping bands. The timber is usually unprotected unless it has been kiln-dried, when it is normally protected by a loose plastic wrapper or shroud.

Softwoods, and pinewoods in particular, carry a great deal of sap and are susceptible to fungal growth, known as sap staining, which is relevant only where strength or appearance is of prime importance as clean timber is always a more attractive product. Blue staining occurs mainly in hardwoods and may be prevented by chemical treatment. This must be done within one day of sawing the timber into planks or it may not be effective and may not prevent blue staining. This timber is often stored in the open, exposed to inclement weather, and the water may destroy the effect of the chemicals. Fungal development is associated with the moisture content of the timber and, therefore, kiln-dried timber that has been properly dried is normally not affected by fungal growth.

Due to the extent of rainfall in the British Columbia area of the north west coast of North America, timber is often loaded during pouring rain and may be wet before shipment. The problem is further exacerbated because the rain enters the ship's hatchways and the tank tops can become partially flooded. Apart from the bottom packages of timber becoming thoroughly soaked, the water may stain the timber with rust marks picked up from the ship's structure. It is, therefore, recommended that provision is made to keep the bilges pumped dry at all times when loading during rain. A further problem occurs when the metal strapping bands securing the bundles of timber become rusty and the rust runs into the timber, with resulting stain.

It is important to emphasise that many thousands of tonnes of softwood timber have been shipped over the years in a thoroughly wet condition on long voyages, with no ventilation between the planks or packages in the stow and with the timber remaining saturated for the entire voyage, without developing any defects as a result.

Invariably, B/Ls are signed 'clean', as it is well known that timber shipped from the British Columbia area is likely to be shipped in a wet condition. However, claims may arise as a result of blue staining, rust staining or, in some rare instances, rotting. Claims may also arise after discharge for drying the timber. It is, therefore, recommended that B/Ls are claused with appropriate remarks to reflect the condition of the timber as shipped, such as 'timber rust stained' or 'wet before shipment'.

Hardwood timber
Hardwood and semi-hardwoods are shipped from many tropical and semi-tropical countries. Much of this timber, particularly from West Africa, is shipped as logs. Shipments of logs do not usually generate any cargo claims. However, logs are likely to cause condensation and may also contain insects. It is therefore important to keep logs segregated from cargoes that may be damaged by condensation or insects.

Hardwoods and semi-hardwoods shipped from South East Asia, particularly to Europe, are commonly shipped as boards in bundles or packages secured by metal bands. Most are unprotected. The following types of timber are often shipped from South East Asia:

- Meranti. This is a relatively light semi-hardwood suitable for general construction, interior fittings and furniture. The subgroups include meranti bakau, dark red meranti, light red meranti, white meranti and yellow meranti. This timber is not durable under tropical conditions and is difficult to treat with preservatives. However, it is easy to work and seasons without trouble. It is shipped into Europe in large quantities and used extensively for doors, window frames and other outdoor fittings
- merbau. This is a heavy, relatively strong and durable wood used mainly for heavy construction. It is bronze or red/brown in colour, weathering to dark red brown

- ramin. This is a moderately hard, moderately heavy utility wood, easily treated with preservatives. It seasons quickly but is very liable to blue stain and is usually dipped in anti-stain chemicals after sawing. The timber is white in colour and usually free from quality defects. It is used extensively in the furniture trade and is highly susceptible to claims.

15.2 Loading and Care of Timber Cargo

It is important that cargo holds are thoroughly cleaned before any timber cargo is loaded. Any grease and oil should be removed from the vessel's structure, as contact can stain the timber. All remnants of previous cargoes should be removed from the overhead beams and the underside beams of the hatch panels, as claims have arisen as a result of remnants of previous cargoes contaminating the timber. For example, iron ore dust, when made wet by condensation, can turn into a red liquid that may stain the timber. Ores or sand of an abrasive nature, such as ilmenite ore, can damage sawmill machinery if the timber has been contaminated.

If the steelwork in the hold is rusty, the timber should be protected from rust staining by the use of dunnage. Ship's sweat developing during the voyage and dripping on the timber may also result in rust stains, so correct ventilation and dunnaging is of great importance.

Bad stowage often results in breakage of the bands securing the bundles. This is usually as a result of not keeping the stow level or crossing the bundles in stow, or a combination of the two. It is the practice for stevedores to work forklift trucks on top of the timber, in the square of the hatches in bulk carriers, when the stow has reached about half the height of the hold. The surface of the timber in contact with the trucks usually becomes damaged by scuffing and through oil dripping from the trucks. If this method of loading is to be used, protective steel plates should be carefully laid over the exposed timber.

Care should always be taken to use the correct equipment during loading and discharge. Wire slings tend to score the lower corner planks in the bundles, particularly when the slings are overloaded and so rope or webbing slings are preferable. Forklift truck damage, caused by the forks of the truck being driven into the planks, is common. This results in deep score marks in the timber and, in many instances, splitting of the timber.

Careful supervision by the ship's officers can prevent much of this type of damage.

15.3 Seasoning of Timber

Reduction of the moisture content of timber is achieved by either air or kiln drying. Timber is fully seasoned when the moisture content has been reduced to between 15 and 18%. The moisture content may also be reduced further depending on the purpose of the timber.

Air-dried timber
Air-dried timber is timber that has been allowed to dry naturally, usually by stick piling in covered storage. This involves piling wood in stacks with 'sticks' between them to allow natural air circulation between the planks. The time required for this process will

depend on the type of timber and the climate. Once seasoned, the planks are secured in bundles with a number of flat metal strapping bands and are ready for shipment.

Often, these bundles are stored in the open and exposed to the elements, resulting in moisture infiltrating the individual planks. Although this may result in the planks on the outside of the bundles having a higher moisture level than expected, these planks will quickly dry naturally. The condition of the internal parts of the bundles will depend on how long free moisture has been trapped within the bundles and also the nature of the timber, ie its resilience to the effects of wetness. In the worst situation, the planks will be mouldy, still wet and severely black stained.

In general, high moisture contents for air-dried timber, without staining, do not provoke claims. However, if the moisture content is excessive, it is not unknown for receivers to claim the costs of stick piling to re-dry the timber. If such timber is not dried and remains in store, mould may develop and could lead to staining of the timber.

Air-dried timber is often carried on deck, with shipper's approval, without protection.

Kiln-dried timber
Bundles of kiln-dried timber are generally protected by plastic wrappers and typically have a stencil on the outside of the bundle denoting the fact that the timber is kiln-dried.

Kiln-drying certificates usually specify to what degree the timber has been dried. The usual parameters are 8 to 12%, 14 to 16% or 16 to 18%. Provided the timber has spent sufficient time in the kiln and has been properly treated, the moisture content at the heart of each plank should show the correct degree of drying to within 1 to 2%, even though the surface of the plank may show a higher level of moisture through natural absorption after the kiln-drying process. Sometimes, the moisture content reading from the heart of the plank shows a higher reading than the outside of the plank and much higher than the drying certificate. This is a clear indication that the timber has not been properly dried.

Claims for re-drying of kiln-dried timber represent a large proportion of claims on timber cargoes.

It is often alleged by cargo interests that, to stow kiln-dried timber in the same cargo hold as air-dried timber, is not caring properly for the cargo. However, provided the air-dried timber has not been exposed to rain before shipment and become saturated, allegations of this nature should be rejected. Whether timber is air-dried or kiln-dried, it will eventually adjust to the optimum moisture level compatible with its equilibrium relative humidity, developed in due course, through contact with the ambient air. Therefore, loading of air-dried and kiln-dried timber in the same ambient air will not affect the kiln-dried timber to any noticeable degree during the voyage.

If dry timber is stowed in the same hold as saturated timber, the moisture content of the outer planks of the dry timber will increase through absorption. Experience has proved that, in these circumstances, the inner planks within the bundles are not affected during the course of a normal sea voyage. It is also true that wet timber, or timber with too high a moisture content, will not dry, regardless of how well the bundles are ventilated in the stow. On a normal sea voyage, the timber will not deteriorate. However, if the timber is not dried when discharged, it will eventually decay.

If timber is kiln-dried too quickly or the moisture level reduced too far, this can result in the timber cracking. Usually, any damage of this nature will not be seen at the time of shipment. Claims for this type of damage should be rejected.

15.4   Plywood

Plywood is transported in large quantities throughout the world. It is highly susceptible to damage and often insufficiently packed for shipment.

The manufacture of plywood has been described as *"the unrolling of logs of wood"*. Very long thin sheets are shaved from the log and, after being cut to size, they are glued together to form plywood of various thicknesses. These thicknesses vary from around 4 to 25 mm and the sheets vary in size, the most popular being 96 × 48 inches (244 × 122 cm). Moisture content of this manufactured product has been found to be about 9%.

The method of transporting plywood is to stack the sheets into bundles of about 50 sheets or more, depending on the thickness of the plywood, which are secured together with metal strapping bands across the width of the base of each bundle. It is not unusual for plywood to be transported in a completely unprotected condition. In some trades, the plywood is partly packed and, on rare occasions, it is completely packed and protected.

When packing is used, it is often deficient, failing adequately to protect areas that are vulnerable to handling damage, such as the corners of the bundles. One of the most common forms of packing is an arrangement where the stack of plywood is enfolded in a plastic sheet and placed on a wooden frame. The sides, ends and top are then covered with plywood sheets and strapped up with flat metal strapping bands. If carried out properly and with care, this packing can adequately protect the plywood from normal handling and stowage problems.

Figure 15.1: Plywood bundle showing torn plastic sheeting and loose
and broken strapping bands.

Often, this packing is applied without sufficient care. Any deficiency or tear in the plastic sheeting can allow moisture penetration into the bundle of plywood. The strapping bands are sometimes of inadequate strength and the method of joining them is often unsatisfactory. This results in a lack of rigidity of the bundle, causing the plywood sheets to become misaligned during handling. In the worst cases, the bundle becomes loose, with the potential for considerable damage to the edges of the plywood. If the side, end and top packing is too short, corner damage may occur.

> It is important, therefore, that bundles of plywood are examined by the ship's crew before loading, paying particular attention to the packing of the plywood. Deficiencies in packing should be noted and suitable remarks inserted on the mate's receipts and B/Ls.

Careful attention should be paid to stowage to prevent corner damage, both during the stowage and in securing of the stow. The stow should be properly secured to prevent movement of the bundles.

Plywood can be easily damaged by moisture. Therefore, proper ventilation should be carried out during the voyage to minimise any possible staining from condensation. If possible, stowage should be away from the hatch square to prevent the possibility of moisture dripping down, particularly where the plywood is totally unprotected.

15.5 Paper Pulp (Wood Pulp)

Paper pulp is primarily composed of cellulose fibres that are normally produced from timber, although certain other raw materials that have a high cellulose content, such as sugar cane residues, may be used.

Two basic procedures are used for separating cellulose fibres from timber. The first is a purely mechanical process, where logs are stripped of bark, knotted and ground, using water as a coolant and transport medium for the fibres produced. The slurry of fibres is passed through screens and strainers to remove oversized material, which is returned to the grinders. It then passes over a cylinder board machine to convert it into sheet form. The sheets then pass through hydraulic presses to remove excess water. The sheets of pulp may be baled at this stage but, for overseas trade, are normally further dried to a moisture content of about 10% before baling in hydraulic presses and banding.

Different grades of mechanical wood pulp are used for the manufacture of different types of paper or board.

The second process involves stripping and knotting, after which the timber is cut into wood chips. The wood chips are the raw materials for a chemical treatment process that produces pulp.

Courtesy of Canaveral Port Authority

Figure 15.2: Discharging bales of wood pulp, each weighing two tons.

The pulp may be bleached to varying degrees to produce white pulps for paper or board manufacture. Cargo shipments of paper pulp usually involve the carriage of bleached material in the form of compressed bales.

The bales are banded under compression using special equipment. If the bands are broken, it is not possible to restore the bales. This is of particular significance because modern paper/board-making processes rely on bales being in sound condition up to the time the pulp sheets are fed into a repulping machine.

For this reason, the same paper pulp that forms the sheets within the bales is used to form the protective outer wrapping. Shippers/receivers often claim that the outer protective wrappers form part of the contents.

Figure 15.3: Unitised wood pulp. Note the use of airbags to secure the stow.

Wetting

If bales become seriously wetted, the cellulose will absorb water, like blotting paper, and swell, breaking the bands, with consequent problems. Prolonged wetting, such as would occur if bales were partly immersed in water, can also affect the strength of cellulose fibres. High quality pulps that have been wetted are sometimes considered unsuitable for their original purpose and the pulp is sold for manufacturing a different product at a reduced price. Comparatively minor wetting can result in rusting of certain types of bands. Any resultant rust staining produces localised spots of discolouration on finished white papers, which is unacceptable. This type of wetting may be the result of inappropriate ventilation of cold cargoes. It must be remembered that much of the wood pulp traded around the world is shipped from countries that experience very cold winters, and Masters must, therefore, ventilate cargoes and record their adopted ventilation regime.

In theory, localised wetting of paper pulp can result in mould growth on the surface. However, there is normally sufficient moisture transfer through a bale to prevent this occurring, particularly as cellulose does not provide adequate nutrition for most mould species.

There have been occasions when the swelling of seriously wetted bales has resulted in structural damage to the ship. While this is only a remote possibility, the consequences can be dangerous.

Soiling

Although paper machines are fitted with strainers, magnetic screens and similar devices, soiling of the outside of bales may result in particles of foreign material being incorporated in finished paper or board. Soiled bales, particularly where the soiling consists of particulate material such as grain or plastics granules, may be unacceptable to receivers. They can overcome the problem by tearing off the outer wrappers, but this not only results in loss of material but is also labour intensive. In an industry that is largely mechanised, providing suitable labour may be difficult and is costly.

Regenerated cellulose, which is used to produce viscose rayon textiles and cellophane film, is produced from very high quality bleached cellulose pulp. Because this process involves ejecting a solution of the cellulose through fine dyes, any particulate matter in the solution can completely ruin the product. Pulp sold for this end use must be kept in scrupulously clean condition. It is important that cargo spaces are thoroughly cleaned, particularly following cargo sounds as grain can easily contaminate the wood pulp.

Taint

Cellulose will absorb odour and become tainted, although many taints can be removed in the paper-making operation. Because massive amounts of water are used in paper making, the water is recycled. Paper makers are particularly wary of introducing tainting materials into the water because, in some instances, the taint may be absorbed by the finished product. Such tainting would not be acceptable in products to be used in the food or other sensitive industries.

Fire

Paper pulp will burn. During handling, abrasion between bales can produce significant quantities of cellulose fluff, which is particularly flammable. If a fire in a paper product gains hold, a massive amount of heat is produced, which is sufficient to cause structural damage to a ship. Extinguishing a fire at this stage is a major operation, almost certainly requiring flooding of a hold.

> Masters are advised that it is imperative that no smoking is allowed in or near a cargo of paper pulp and stringent precautions must be taken to avoid sparks from any source entering cargo holds.

Care must be taken to prevent bales of paper becoming contaminated with oil, particularly vegetable oil. Cellulose has a large surface area, so atmospheric oxidation of the contaminating oil can result in self-heating to the point of combustion.

Mechanical damage
Although this is less of a problem with paper pulp than with paper reels, bad handling may result in the breaking of bands or puncturing and contamination.

15.6　Reels of Paper and Board

Figure 15.4: Reels of paper ready for shipment.

Paper and board are manufactured from paper pulp. A large number of different types of paper may be produced by using different types of paper pulp and by various treatments during the paper-making operation, such as sizing, pacifying, treatment to produce wet strength, polishing (calendering), coating, etc. More complex papers are commercially more valuable than less complex papers. Paper products that are unacceptable for the intended purpose must either be sold for scrap or returned for repulping. The pulp produced will inevitably be used for low grade products.

Major uses of paper are for print (newsprint, books, etc) and the manufacture of corrugated fibre board. Newsprint reels are used on high-speed printing presses. Any interruption in the printing process, due to a fault in the paper, results in a substantial financial loss. Users take particular care to ensure that only sound reels, or reels that can easily be handled to make them sound, are accepted.

Although the users of kraft paper are not constrained by time in the same way as newspaper publishers, they also employ high-speed machinery of high capital cost and take the utmost care to prevent any interruption on a production line.

The two main forms of damage that cause problems with reels of paper are mechanical damage and wetting.

Mechanical damage
This may take the form of tears, cuts or snags. Where such damage occurs, the reels have to be unwound until completely sound paper is reached.

Another form of mechanical damage is distortion, which may result from unsatisfactory use of clamp trucks or any form of impact. Where distortion occurs, the paper web is subject to non-uniform tension during unreeling on a press or other machine. Because the web is under considerable tension, any non-uniformity can result in rupture.

Wetting

Newsprint reels are normally overwrapped with a wrapping system incorporating a waterproof barrier. Kraft reels are not so protected. However, significant wetting of newsprint can result in the reels themselves being damaged.

Wetted reels, even after drying, normally present the same problems as distorted reels and again must be stripped down to undamaged paper before they can be used. Due to swelling of the fibres, severely wetted reels are likely to split.

 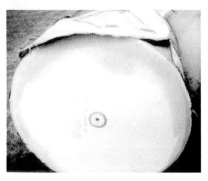

Figure 15.5: Reels of newsprint showing tears and cuts both in the wrappers and paper before shipment.

Figure 15.6: Reel of newsprint that has been standing in water before shipment.

All reels should be examined at the time of loading for evidence of damage. As paper frequently originates from countries that are very cold in winter, they may sometimes be coated in a thin layer of ice, which is not detectable without careful checking. When found during loading, damaged reels should be rejected. If this proves impractical, mate's receipts should be claused giving details of affected reels, including the nature of the damage. B/Ls should be claused in the same terms as the relevant mate's receipts.

Ship's holds should be clean and dry before loading commences and, preferably, the tank tops should be covered with kraft paper or boards.

Great care should be taken to ensure reels, which are always stowed vertically, are not subject to uneven pressure from such fittings as horizontal cargo battens or dunnage. Any objects that can snag reels, such as projecting nails, should be removed. Other projections should be cased in dunnage. Rough sawn dunnage should not be used in contact with reels. The most suitable contact material is plywood sheets. Reels should never be secured in a way that results in direct contact with wires or chains.

Reels of different widths are often loaded in one hold and special care must be taken to ensure a stable stow. Care should also be taken to prevent wetting on board. Hatch covers must be closed when rain is threatened. The ship should be watertight and, if the ventilation system is used, ventilators should be closed whenever bad weather threatens. Paper reels originate from the same areas as wood pulp, ie often from ports where the temperature is very low in winter. Masters should either check the temperature of the reels, which is difficult to do as there may be significant variation through a reel, or assume the reels are at the same temperature as the ambient atmosphere and adopt a ventilation regime accordingly.

Ventilation should not be used after loading in ports where the temperatures are low and when proceeding through/to areas of higher ambient temperatures.

Conversely, there have been claims due to wetting of relatively warm reels by ship's sweat when atmospheric temperatures are falling or when ventilation is interrupted during a period when the outside air temperature is lower than the dew point of the air in the cargo compartment, ie the ambient air surrounding the reels that is influenced to a degree by the peculiarities or characteristics of the actual cargo.

Another problem that may give rise to claims is taint. While this is discussed in relation to paper pulp in Section 15.5, it is not always easy to detect taint to paper reels, particularly when it originates from residual odours from previous chemical cargoes. For example, a case arose where bleached board was used for the manufacture of milk cartons and no taint was detected until complaints were made by consumers. The taint was traced to an earlier cargo of herbicides.

> Masters should check, or arrange for surveyors to check, that holds to be used for paper products are not only scrupulously clean but also odour free. Detection of odour is very difficult when the atmospheric temperature is low and, therefore, when loading takes place under such conditions, it is recommended that known properties of earlier cargoes are reviewed.

Wetting and mechanical damage may occur at the time of discharge. Officers should supervise discharging operations and, where damage is seen to arise as a result of mishandling by stevedores, the occurrence and nature of such damage should be reported in writing to the stevedoring company and recorded in the ship's logbook.

15.7   Carriage of Wood Pellets

Figure 15.7: Wood pellets.

Wood pellets are the most common type of pellet fuel. The manufacture and carriage of wood pellets has increased because of their use as a renewable heating fuel. The main areas of manufacture are North America and Scandinavia.

The pellets are typically produced from sawdust and wood shavings. Pellets can contain additives and/or binders or be additive/binder free. As such, different pellet types are listed separately under the IMSBC Code.

During production, the sawdust and shavings are dried and then milled into particles of up to approximately 2 mm particle size. These are then compressed approximately 3.5 times into pellets that are typically 10 to 20 mm long and 3 to 12 mm in diameter. The compression leads to an increase in temperature. The pellets typically have a moisture content of 4 to 8% and vary in colour from blond to brown, depending on the types of wood used.

Due to transport movements and physical handling, some breakage of the pellets occurs and this means that the material loaded for transport consists of pellets, pieces of broken pellets and wood dust.

The wood pellets are combustible and may be ignited by a range of ignition sources. In addition, the dust associated with the pellets, when dispersed and ignited, may give rise to a dust explosion under certain conditions of containment. Stored bulk piles of wood pellets can self-heat in parts with a high moisture content and it is reported that this process can lead to the spontaneous combustion of the material after a long period of time. This is especially likely when the moisture content is over 15%. High levels of dust concentration from the handling of wood pellets also carries an explosive risk.

In addition to the combustion hazards, wood pellets also undergo oxidation to produce carbon monoxide (CO) and carbon dioxide (CO_2). In a closed space, such as an unventilated ship's hold, this can lead to a dangerous reduction in the oxygen concentration and the development of a dangerous concentration of CO, which is toxic and flammable. Therefore safe entry procedures must be followed at all times by all personnel.

Figure 15.8: The loading of wood pellets.

In one example, a CO concentration of approximately 1% was measured in the sealed cargo hold of a ship containing wood pellets some 18 days after the cargo was loaded. Furthermore, the oxygen concentration at this time was less than 1%. Emission rates for CO from wood pellets of up to 100 to 885 mg/ton/day have been reported.

It is well known that CO is produced when wood products are burned in reduced oxygen environments, but the low temperature emission of the gas from wood products may be unexpected. It has been suggested that the gas is generated by the autoxidation of fats and fatty acids in the wood, but the factors that promote the production have not been fully identified.

The CO hazard associated with wood pellets was referenced in the 2016 and subsequent editions of the IMSBC Code (Reference 17). The hazard associated with oxygen depletion and the generation of CO is now recognised. Safe entry procedures should be followed and all personnel should routinely employ gas detectors in spaces that contain or have contained wood pellets.

Part 5 –

General Guidance

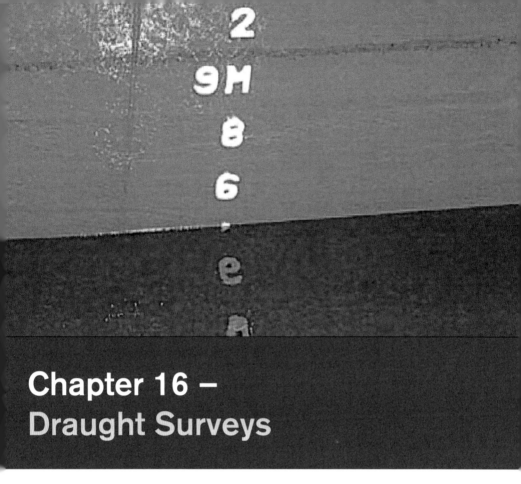

Chapter 16 –
Draught Surveys

If, during loading and discharging, no shifting of weights was to take place, other than the movement of cargo, then calculating the weight of cargo by draught survey could be considered to be reasonably accurate. In practice, this seldom occurs.

The weight of the ship is determined both before and after loading and allowances made for differences in ballast water and other changeable items. The difference between these two weights is the weight of the cargo.

In order to do this, the depth that the ship is floating at is assessed from the draught marks, and the vessel's stability book is consulted to obtain the hydrostatic particulars such as the displacement and other necessary data.

Several corrections are required and the quantities of ballast and other consumable items need to be assessed so as to obtain the net weights as follows.

The weight of an empty ship consists of three elements:

1. Empty ship   Fixed item

2. Stores   Considered fixed

3. Ballast, oil and fresh water   Changeable

Empty net weight = Empty ship + Stores

The weight of a loaded ship consists of four elements:

1. Empty ship   Fixed item

2. Stores   Considered fixed

3. Ballast, oil and fresh water   Changeable

4. Cargo   Fixed item

Loaded net weight = Empty ship + Stores + Cargo

Therefore, the cargo weight is the difference between the net weights.

> Although a draught survey is simple in principle, in practice it is frequently a complicated and time consuming way of attempting to ascertain the weight of cargo loaded on board a ship. Many factors are involved, few of which can be established with a complete degree of accuracy.

A draught survey starts with a reading of the ship's draught, on both sides; forward, amidships and aft. There are a number of limiting factors:

- It is often difficult to accurately read the draught because of prevailing weather conditions and the presence of waves on the water surface. A vessel may have also developed a slight roll, leading to further inaccuracies

- the draught should be read from a position as close to the waterline as possible to avoid parallax, although this may not always be practicable

- a ship moored in a tidal stream or current will be affected by squat, particularly in shallow water, and this will have a further effect

- a draught can be affected when there is a large difference between the temperatures of the air and the water. This will cause a difference in the expansion of the submerged and emerged sections of the ship. There is currently no acceptable method of correcting for this

- when a ship is not on an even keel (as is always the case before loading and after discharge), the draught readings must be corrected for trim. It should be borne in mind that, at such times, the draught marks are not in line with the forward and after perpendiculars

- the draught must be corrected for the density of the water in which the vessel is floating. It is difficult to obtain a reliable average density because this will vary at different levels and locations around the ship

- the draught has to be corrected for hog and sag. This correction is generally calculated on the basis that a ship will bend parabolically, although this is not always the case.

A mean draught figure is obtained (a double mean of means) which, by comparison with the ship's displacement scale, provides the corresponding displacement. The ship's displacement table may not, however, always be completely accurate. This is usually supplied by the shipbuilder and the methods used to make up the tables may not always be totally reliable. Similarly, the trim correction may be derived by the use of various formulae, not all of which are entirely accurate.

16.1   Draught Surveys – Practice

The Master of a vessel should be advised in adequate time that a draught survey will be taking place. If it is an initial light ship survey, they should be requested, subject to the safety of the vessel, to ensure that individual ballast tanks are either fully pressed up or empty and that the vessel is upright with a trim that is within the limits of the tank calibration tables.

When draught surveys are undertaken by independent surveyors, cooperation of the ship's officers is essential. The survey sections should be undertaken with the vessel's chief officer and chief engineer or their appointed deputies.

> Before undertaking the survey, it is recommended that the surveyor makes time to inspect a general arrangement plan to confirm the number and position of the various ballast, fresh water and oil bunker tanks on the vessel.

Equipment used in the survey may include:

- Strong torch
- boat/ladders
- binoculars
- patent draught mark indicator or measuring devices (draught tubes, indicators, etc)
- calibrated inclinometer or manometer
- steel tape measure with plumb bob/stainless steel sounding tape with plumb bob (preferably calibrated)
- seawater sampling bucket or can of sufficient volume
- calibrated patent draught survey hydrometer
- calibrated salinity refractometer
- ballast water sampling device
- computer/calculator.

Reading the draught marks

At the time of reading the draught marks, the vessel should be upright and on an even keel, or with a minimum of trim. The trim at survey should never exceed the maximum trim for which corrections may be included in the vessel's stability book.

To avoid errors when reading the draught marks, the vessel should, ideally, be lying in still, calm water. For example:

- For vessels lying at exposed berths or anchorages, where wave and swell surface disturbance is almost inevitable, even to the extent that the vessel may be rolling and pitching, it is usual to assess the actual mean water level over a number of readings to be at two-thirds of the distance between the lowest and highest levels of water as seen against the draught marks. Some experts advocate that, after studying wave patterns, a mean of the average highest and lowest draught readings should be used

- draught marks on vessels that are lying at a river berth or in tidal conditions when strong currents are running should, ideally, be read over periods of slack water (provided that at a low water slack there is sufficient UKC)
- currents of appreciable strengths are likely to cause the vessel to change trim or pitch slightly and/or sink bodily into the water from her static draught ('squat'). This phenomenon becomes more pronounced in shallow waters (shallow water effect)
- strong currents will result in raised water levels against the leading edge of a stationary vessel lying in flowing water. This is especially true when the flow is in the direction of a vessel's bulbous bow.

Draught marks must be read on both sides of the vessel, ie forward port and starboard, amidships port and starboard, and aft port and starboard. Alternatively, if additional marks are displayed on large vessels, they should be read at all the designated positions.

Should draught marks not be in place amidships, distances from the deck line to the waterline on both sides of the vessel must be measured. The amidships draughts can then be calculated from load line and freeboard data extracted from the vessel's stability booklet.

Draught marks should be read with the observer as close to the waterline as is safe and reasonably possible to reduce parallax error.

Although it is common practice to read the offside draught marks from a rope ladder, a launch or small boat provides a more stable environment and brings the observer to a safer position closer to the waterline.

A vessel's remote draught gauge should never be used for surveys due to lack of the necessary accuracy and the possibility of errors, which may accumulate over the working life of the instrument.

When adverse weather conditions are being experienced, access to the offside draught marks may prove difficult or impossible. At these times, the draughts on the nearside can be read and the offside draughts calculated using a manometer.

This method should never be used when the offside draughts can be safely observed and accurately read. If, as a final resort, this method cannot be undertaken, the use of a fully calibrated inclinometer, graduated to minutes of arc, is strongly recommended. The type of inclinometer fitted to vessels is not usually of sufficient accuracy to be used.

Draught marks
Draught marks (the depth at which the ship is floating) are designed to make reading simple. Metric marks are 10 cm high and are placed 10 cm apart. The steel plate they are made from is 2 cm wide. On the few vessels that still use the imperial system, the numbers are 6 inches high and located 6 inches apart, with the numbers constructed from 1 inch wide steel plate.

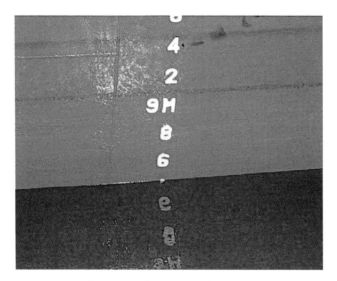

Figure 16.1: Typical draught marks.

Figure 16.1 shows depths from 8.49 to 9.64 m. The water level is at 8.49 m as half the width of the top of the '4' is visible above the water level. Some numbers are easier to assess than others. For example, in Figure 16.2, each pair of lines is 2 cm apart and it can be seen that the assessment of the depth is easy when the water level is across the '8'.

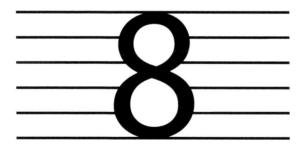

Figure 16.2: Mid number marks.

Some small coasters are only marked at the amidships point with a designated line (again 2 cm wide) called the deck line. The upper edge of this is at a known distance from the keel ('K'), which is the summation of the vessel's official summer freeboard and summer draught. Draughts are then calculated by measuring the actual freeboard (distance of the upper edge of the deck line from the water level) with a measuring tape and deducting it from 'K'.

Density of the water in which the vessel is floating

It is prudent to obtain samples of the water in which the vessel is floating at, or very close to, the time at which the draught marks are read. This is particularly relevant when the vessel is lying at an estuarial or river berth, when the density of the water may be changing due to the ebb or flow of the tide. The density should be checked quickly after obtaining the sample as there may be temperature differences between the actual sampling of the dock water and the time of determination of its density, which may lead to errors in density.

Depending on the length of the vessel under survey, a number of samples, say between one and three, should be taken. To overcome the problem of layering, the samples should be obtained using a closed sampling can at a depth of approximately half the existing draught of the vessel. Alternatively, a slow-filling container may be used to obtain an average sample from keel to waterline.

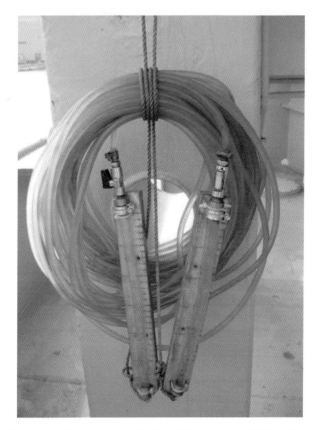

Figure 16.3: Manometer showing plastic tubing (30 to 40 m long), fitted at each end with a valve and scale. The valves are to allow the water in the tube to be retained without any air bubbles when the device is not in use.

Figure 16.4: Manometer, showing scale and water level. When a scale is fitted and used for the reading, care must be taken that the scale is fixed at the same height on each side of the vessel.

When reading the hydrometer floating in the sample of water, the eye of the observer should be as close to the water level as possible to avoid parallax errors and errors due to the meniscus. The hydrometer should also be given a 'twirl' to free it of any air bubbles.

Ballast water tanks

Ballast water tanks, including peaks and those said to be empty, must be carefully sounded or proven to be full by pressing up and overflowing from all air pipes when local regulations permit. If the ballast hold contains ballast water, this compartment must not be fully pressed up but should be sounded and the weight of the water carefully calculated.

Spaces such as the duct keel and voids, particularly those of the lower stools situated at the base of transverse bulkheads, between cargo holds, must be checked when safe to do so and proved in the same condition at initial and final surveys.

These voids often contain the manhole access covers to the adjacent double-bottom tanks. If these covers are not totally watertight, the voids will flood, or partially flood, during ballasting or pressing up of the tanks, potentially resulting in huge errors in the lightship or ballast survey. Surveyors have been known to refuse to conduct draught surveys when it has been established that there is an unknown amount of water in such void spaces.

> The calculation of the weight of ballast water is undoubtedly the main source of error in a draught survey and may result in very large, and unacceptable, inaccuracies in the quantity of cargo calculated.

Density of the ballast water
It should be established where the various ballast tanks were filled. If they were from a single source, a few random samples of the water will confirm the density. If from different sources, samples must be taken from tanks containing water from each of the various sources and relevant densities of the water in individual tanks established.

The ballast tanks may contain significant amounts of muck in the form of sand, silt, shingle, rust scale, etc. The density of these deposits will differ significantly from the ballast water. Also, it may not be possible to determine the amounts of these solids that are in the tanks. The results are usually assumed in the constant, but the value may be significantly inaccurate.

The tanks should not be overflowed substantially to obtain samples unless local regulations permit. Instead, sampling equipment that is suitable for tanks that are only partially filled should be used.

When small samples are obtained, a salinity refractometer should be used to establish density. When larger samples have been obtained, a draught survey hydrometer may be used.

Establishing the correct weight of oils on board
This can be established either by sounding or ullaging of the tanks or, in the case of the engine room daily service and settling tanks, by reading the gauges.

> The volume of oils in each and every tank should be measured and recorded.

The relative densities of the most recently delivered oils on board can be obtained from the bunker delivery certificates. However, bunkers are almost inevitably mixed with oils already on board, the densities of which are likely to differ. The relative density of the contents may be calculated using the following formula:

$$\text{RD of tank contents at survey} = \frac{(\text{Old oil volume} \times \text{Old RD}) + (\text{New bunker volume} \times \text{New RD})}{\text{Total volume of oil in tank}}$$

After completion of the bunker survey, the totals of each oil found must be agreed with the Chief Engineer and the Master.

Water removed from hold bilges

Certain bulk cargoes, such as ores, concentrates and some types of coal, are sprayed with water during loading to keep the dust levels down. In addition, the stockpiles of cargo at the terminal are exposed to rain and other forms of moisture. During the passage, some or all of this water content settles to the bottom of the hold and accumulates in and around the bilges. For safety reasons, this water will be pumped out. A record of bilge pumping would usually be maintained on board, but the volumes pumped out are never known exactly. This volume of water is one of the sources of variation between load port and discharge port figures.

Calculation and corrections of vessel's displacement from draught readings

Before extracting hydrostatic data from the vessel's stability book, care should be taken by surveyors to familiarise themselves with the format and methods used to display the various particulars, especially the means of depicting positions of LCF (longitudinal centre of flotation) etc, relative to amidships or to the after perpendicular.

When using a recommended draught survey computer programme or when calculating directly from data extracted from the hydrostatic particulars contained within the vessel's stability book, it is essential that the data is carefully and properly interpolated or, rarely, extrapolated.

> One of the areas where significant errors often result is from the incorrect application of the sign in respect of the position of the LCF (in the first trim correction).

When undertaking initial and final displacement draught surveys to establish the weight(s) of cargo loaded, or alternatively unloaded, the difference between the net displacement weights provides the total cargo quantity. However, it is recommended for a cross check that, at the light ship/ballast survey, the vessel's light ship weight is deducted from the net displacement found. The resultant then provides the vessel's 'constant' at that time. These unknown weights might also be termed the vessel's 'stores variable'. Although variable, for a number of reasons, it should serve as a guide to the accuracy of the light ship/ballast survey.

Comparison between 'stores variable' quantities, or mean thereof, established at previous surveys should be treated with caution unless the variable is a direct comparison that can be made. For example, all surveys include a check and a record of the engine lubricating oil held in storage tank(s) etc. Occasionally, surveyors report a negative stores variable, which is theoretically impossible unless, in extremely rare instances, the vessel has been subject to modification and large quantities of structural steel removed.

Charterparties often contain reference to an approximate quantity for the vessel's constant, which may well create a discussion between the Master and the surveyor should the constant found by survey be substantially larger than that quoted by the owners. The surveyor, after relevant checks, should remain confident in the figure obtained, but always record on documents issued to the Master and clients any unusual factors or difficulties experienced during the survey. These include any differences between surveyors should owners, charterers or shippers each appoint separate survey companies to act on their behalf.

Documentation

At completion of the survey, a work sheet or computer printout should be placed on board the vessel recording the data and calculations used to obtain the cargo loaded/unloaded quantity. This document is usually produced by individual survey companies, or by shipping companies for use by their officers.

A formal survey report should be submitted to clients at a later date. Specific formal documentation has been drawn up by bodies such as the IMO and the various P&I Clubs.

The formal report document should include details of the survey as well as:

- Dates and times of surveys
- vessel particulars
- vessel location
- weather conditions (and whether these were within acceptable limits)
- sea conditions (and whether these were within acceptable limits)
- tidal/current conditions (and whether these were within acceptable limits)
- a record of any difficulties or defects in a ship's documentation or equipment that might cause the calculated weight by draught displacement survey to be outside acceptable limits of normal draught survey measurement error.

Cumulative errors

Errors can occur when reading and correcting the draughts. The final fully corrected 3/4 mean draught should be within ±10 mm of the true mean draught.

- Errors of calculation. The main error to be avoided in this section is incorrect positioning of the LCF relative to LBP/2, the amidships point
- error of the water density in which the vessel is floating. Always ensure that an average sample, or alternatively the average of a number of water samples, is obtained and that the correct type of certificated hydrometer is used to obtain the density
- sounding of tanks. Leaving aside documented tables which may not be accurate, the way of avoiding the main errors in this section of the survey is by ensuring, as best as possible, that all volumes of liquids on board, particularly ballast water, are both correctly quantified and attributed with correct densities. These factors, particularly when applied to ballast water, undoubtedly contribute to the largest number and degree of errors likely to be encountered in draught surveying.

Bearing these reservations in mind, a well-conducted draught survey under reasonable prevailing conditions is capable of achieving an absolute accuracy of ±0.5%.

Worked example

From the following information, calculate the corrections to perpendiculars and the draughts at the perpendiculars. Also calculate the true trim.

Vessel LBP = 181.8 m
Density at the time of draught reading = 1.0185 T/m³

	port side	stbd side	distance marks from perp
Forward draughts	4.61 m	4.65 m	Fd = 2.94 m aft
Midships draughts	4.93 m	5.10 m	Md = 1.44 m aft
Aft draughts	5.58 m	5.60 m	Ad = 7.30 m forward

Forward mean	= (4.61 + 4.65)/2	**= 4.63 m**

Midships mean = (4.93 + 5.10)/2 **= 5.015 m**

Aft mean = (5.58 + 5.6)/2 **= 5.59 m**

So apparent trim is: 5.59 – 4.63 = 0.96 m

And LBM is: 181.8 – 2.94 – 7.30 = 171.56 m

Forward correction $= \dfrac{\text{Apparent Trim} \times \text{Fd}}{\text{LBM}} = \dfrac{0.96 \times -2.94}{171.56}$ **= –0.0165 m**

Midships correction $= \dfrac{\text{Apparent Trim} \times \text{Md}}{\text{LBM}} = \dfrac{0.96 \times -1.44}{171.56}$ **= –0.0081 m**

Aft correction $= \dfrac{\text{Apparent Trim} \times \text{Ad}}{\text{LBM}} = \dfrac{0.96 \times 7.3}{171.56}$ **= +0.0408 m**

Now:

Forward draught = 4.63 – 0.0165 m = 4.6135 m

Midships draught = 5.015 – 0.0081 m = 5.0069 m

Aft draught = 5.59 + 0.0408 m = 5.6308 m

True trim = 5.6308 – 4.6135 m = 1.0173 m = 101.73 cm

¾ mean draught[1] $= \dfrac{(6 \times 5.0069) + 4.6135 + 5.6308}{8}$ = 5.0357 m

---

[1] This is also known as the true hydrostatic draught, which accounts for hog and sag, and indicates the value for the hydrostatic particulars tables.

From the original surveys, the following data was given in the vessel's hydrostatic particulars:

Scale density of hydrostatic particulars 1.025 T/m³

Draught	Displacement	TPC	LCF		Draught	MCTC	Draught	MCTC
5.00	19,743	42.32	−4.354		**5.50**	445.5	4.50	434.9
5.10	20,167	42.37	−4.289		**5.60**	446.6	4.60	435.9

The stability book stated that a negative (−) sign for LCF indicated forward of midships.

Interpolating the data from the table (it is easier to use centimetres in the interpolation rather than metres), the difference in the tabulated draughts is 10 cm and the draught we are looking for is 3.57 cm more than 5 m.
Therefore:

Displacement for 5.0357 m draught
$$= 19{,}743 + \frac{(20{,}167 - 19{,}743)}{10} \times 3.57 \quad = \textbf{19,894.37}$$

TPC for 5.0357 m draught $= 42.32 + \dfrac{(42.37 - 42.32)}{10} \times 3.57 \quad = \textbf{42.338}$

LCF for 5.0357 m draught $= -4.354 + \dfrac{(4.354 - 4.289)}{10} \times 3.57 \quad = \textbf{−4.331}$
(ford of mid)

MCTC for 5.0357 + 50 cm $= 445.5 + \dfrac{(446.6 - 445.5)}{10} \times 3.57 \quad = \textbf{445.89}$

MCTC for 5.0357 − 50 cm $= 434.9 + \dfrac{(435.9 - 434.9)}{10} \times 3.57 \quad = \textbf{435.26}$

Therefore (dm ~ dz) $= 10.63$

The first trim correction is $= \dfrac{101.73 \times -4.331 \times 42.338}{181.8} \quad = \textbf{−102.61 T}$

Second trim correction $= \dfrac{1.0173^2 \times 50 \times 10.63}{181.8} \quad = \textbf{+3.03 T}$

Then vessel's displacement at a density of 1.025 T/m³ is calculated as follows:

Displacement for 5.0357 m $= 19{,}894.37$ T

First trim correction $= -102.61$ T

Second trim correction $= +3.03$ T

Corrected displacement in salt water $= \textbf{19,794.79 T}$

This is the weight of the ship at the draught if it was in salt water of density 1.025 T/m³, which is the density of the ship's hydrostatic scale.

However, it is floating in water of apparent density 1.0185 T/m³.

So true displacement $= \dfrac{\textbf{19,794.79} \times \textbf{1.0185}}{\textbf{1.025}} = \textbf{19,669.26 T}$

Draught surveying is based on Archimedes' Principle, which states that anything that floats will displace an amount of the liquid it is floating in that is equal to its own weight.

16.2 Equipment

16.2.1 Manometer

In some circumstances, the wave and swell activity can be such that it is too rough to use a boat, or the wave damping tube may be difficult or even impossible to position on the hull. This situation can often be resolved by the use of a manometer to measure the list across the deck at midships, which is then added to, or subtracted from, the inboard draught reading to obtain the outboard draught.

It is not necessary for the manometer to be fitted with a scale at the ends as the height of the water in the tube is measured from the deck on each side using a tape measure. Where the list is large, the end of the manometer on the low side must be positioned higher than the end on the high side to avoid the water in the tube running out. However, when a scale is fitted and used for the reading, care must be taken that the scale is fixed at the same height on each side.

A simple manometer is constructed from a length of plastic tubing about 35 to 40 m long of 10 mm outside diameter, 6 mm inside diameter, filled with water. On each end is a valve connected to a short section of 19 mm tube. The valves allow the water in the tube to be retained without any air bubbles in it when the device is not in use. This is important, as any entrapped air will prevent the manometer working properly. The short sections of 19 mm tube provide a damping action to the movement of water in the system that is caused by ship movement.

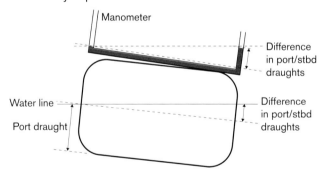

Figure 16.5: Use of a manometer to measure list.

In Figure 16.5, the starboard draught is equal to the port draught plus the difference in port and starboard draughts from the manometer.

If the manometer is not long enough to reach the vessel's sides, the true difference may be calculated from the measured difference by the use of similar triangles. In this case, the manometer is set to obtain readings at a known distance apart across the vessel.

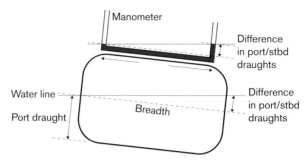

Figure 16.6: Measurement of list using a manometer and similar triangles.

In Figure 16.6:

$$\frac{\text{Difference in port/stbd draughts}}{\text{Breadth}} = \frac{\text{Difference in port/stbd readings}}{d}$$

Therefore:

$$\text{Difference in port/stbd draughts} = \frac{\text{Breadth} \times \text{Difference in readings}}{d}$$

16.2.2   Marine Hydrometers

Two types of hydrometers are commonly used in the maritime industry:

Draught survey hydrometers
These instruments are designed to measure the apparent density of water.

For the purposes of draught surveys:

Apparent density (weight in air per unit volume) (T/m^3) × Volume (m^3) = Weight (T).

Load line hydrometers
These instruments are designed to determine the relative density of water.

For the purposes of load line surveys in determination of a vessel's displacement:

Relative density (specific gravity) × Volume (m^3) = Displacement (m^3).

Marine and draught surveyors should be familiar with the correct usage of both types of instrument so that neither confusion nor errors occur during draught survey or stability calculations.

Draught survey hydrometers
Modern hydrometers of glass manufacture are calibrated at standard temperature, 15°C (60°F), and measure the apparent density of the water sample in kilograms per litre in air. They are usually marked 'for draught (or draft) survey' and 'medium ST' (medium surface tension) and graduated in the range 0.990/1.040 kg/l.

These instruments are used to determine the weight in air (apparent weight) of a vessel, from which the weight of the cargo on board may be calculated.

When manufactured of glass and calibrated at standard temperature, a small error results if the hydrometer is not used at the designed standard temperature.

However, it is accepted that no temperature correction is necessary as it is compensated at survey by the change in volume of the steel vessel itself. The corrections due to the 'coefficients of cubical expansion' of glass and steel are very approximately the same, thus they cancel out.

The older types of hydrometer used for draught surveys and manufactured from brass, or some other metal, are still found on some vessels. These instruments should be accompanied with a table of corrections and the relevant temperature correction should always be applied.

The use of a glass hydrometer is always preferable and it should be kept clean and protected.

Draught survey hydrometers should not be used for load line survey purposes.

Load line hydrometers

Load line hydrometers are used to determine the relative density (specific gravity) of a water sample at a standard temperature (T1) against a sample of distilled water at a standard temperature (T2). The standard temperature used is usually 15°C (60°F). Relative density is a ratio, a number. Load line hydrometers are usually marked 'RD' or 'Sp. Gr.', together with the standard temperatures.

When the temperatures of the water and the distilled water samples have a huge variation, a temperature correction must be applied to allow for the expansion of the hydrometer. These instruments are used to determine the displacement of a vessel at any given waterline in order to comply with the requirements of the *International Convention on Load Lines, 1966* (Reference 25).

Article 12 of the Convention permits a vessel to load to submerge the appropriate load line by an allowance made proportional to the difference between 1.025 and the actual density in which the vessel is floating. This then is relative density, ie the Convention refers to 'density in vacuo', ie mass per unit volume.

16.2.3   Differences Between Hydrometers

The displacement and apparent weight of a vessel have a relationship, as do the relative and apparent densities of the water in which the vessel is floating. The difference between the relative density (specific gravity) as determined by the load line hydrometer and the draught survey hydrometer is known as the 'air buoyancy correction', and can be accepted, at standard temperatures 15°C/15°C or 60°F/60°F, as 0.002 for marine surveys. The density of gases depends on temperature, pressure and moisture content.

The density of dry air at sea level is about $1/800^{th}$ of the density of fresh water, ie 1.25 kg/m^3 when under similar conditions of temperature and pressure. It should also be noted that the actual maximum density of fresh water is 999.972 kg/m^3, which occurs at a temperature of 4.0°C. The density of fresh water at 100.0°C is 958.4 kg/m^3.

A correction should be deducted from the relative density of a load line hydrometer to compare with an actual density of a draught survey hydrometer. For example, for a sample of seawater checked by a load line hydrometer reading relative density 1.025, a draught survey hydrometer would read an actual density of 1.023 kg/l in air.

All hydrometers should be calibrated regularly.

Surveyors should only use a hydrometer manufactured for the relevant type of survey being undertaken.

16.2.4   Salinity Refractometers

Salinity refractometers are used to check the salinity of water samples.

A refractometer uses the fact that light deflects to a varying degree as it passes through different substances. When passing through water, the degree of deflection (refraction) is directly related to the quantity of mineral salts dissolved in the water.

The refractive index of a substance is a measure of how far light is bent by that substance.

For example, at 20°C, the refractive index of distilled water is 1.333 and the refractive index of seawater (relative density 1.025, salinity 35 parts per thousand) at the same temperature is 1.339.

When using a refractometer, a sample is placed on an optical prism in the sample window. As light passes through the sample, the rays are bent according to the salinity of the water, casting a shadow on the scale which is visible through the eyepiece.

A basic hand-held refractometer is used as follows:

- Ensure the refractometer is properly calibrated. If the refractometer scale reads zero, it is properly calibrated. If not, rotate the calibration screw until the shadow boundary lines up with the zero mark
- if necessary, clean the prism using a soft cloth
- rinse the equipment and the prism with part of the sample water to ensure that the sample remains unadulterated
- place several drops of the sample water on the prism, ensuring that the refractometer remains level so that none of the sample runs off the prism
- close the sample cover
- hold the instrument towards a strong light source
- adjust the focus ring until the scale is clearly visible
- read the scale at the shadow boundary
- rinse and clean the instrument before re-use.

Refractometers can be of the analogue or digital type.

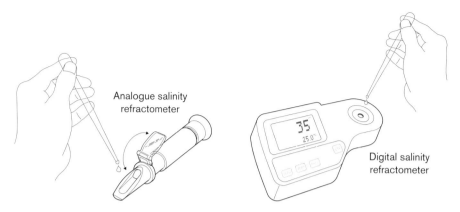

Analogue salinity refractometer

Digital salinity refractometer

Figure 16.7: Typical basic salinity refractometer.

16.3 Draught Survey Documentation Examples

Draught survey certificate

Vessel: _____ B/L (M/T): _____

Port: _____ Date: _____

		Arrival		
	Aft	**Mid**	**Ford**	**L ship**
Port				LBP
Starboard				
Mean				Tpc
Correction to perpendicular				Lcf -(ford)
Draught				Trim
3/4 mean draught				Mct+
Disp @				McT–
Trim correction A				
Trim correction B				Oil
Corrected displacement				Fresh water
Density of dock water				Ballast
Displacement @ density				Other
Variables				Total
Net displacement				

		Departure		
	Aft	Mid	Ford	L ship
Port				LBP
Starboard				
Mean				Tpc
Correction to perpendicular				Lcf -(ford)
Draught				Trim
3/4 mean draught				Mct+
Disp @				McT–
Trim correction A				
Trim correction B				Oil
Corrected displacement				Fresh water
Density of dock water				Ballast
Displacement @ density				Other
Variables				Total
Net displacement				
Cargo				
Surveyor				

Dist of draught marks	Arrival	Departure
From aft perpendicular		
From aft perpendicular		
From aft perpendicular		

Marks forward of perpendicular +ve

Draught survey spreadsheet

File Save Ref			
Date	B/Lading	Tonnes	
Ship Name	Port		
Port of Reg		Draughts	
Flag		Arrival	Departure
Owner	Ford p		
Capt	Ford s		
Cargo Officer	Mid p		
Berth	Mid s		
Agents	Aft p		
Cargo	Aft s		
Arrived	DistFp		
Commenced	DistMidp		
Completed	DistAp		
Year of Build	App Trim	0.0000	0.0000
Gross	True Trim	Calculated	Calculated
Net	3/4 mean	Calculated	Calculated
LOA	Scale density		
LBP	Dock density		
Breadth	Disp @ 3/4 mean	Calculated	Calculated
Depth	Tpc	Calculated	Calculated
Displacement	0.00	Lcf (- if aft)	Calculated	Calculated
Deadweight	Mct+	Calculated	Calculated
Light Ship	Mct–	Calculated	Calculated
Last Port	Total Oil	0.00	0.00
Next Port	Total F.Water	0.00	0.00
Surveyor	Total Ballast	0.00	0.00
	Other		
Weather Conditions and Report	Cargo Wt		Calculated

If the hydrostatics are from the top of the keel, enter keel correction in mm

Hydrostatic Data

Arrival

		Below	Above
Draught			
Displacement			
TPC			
LCF			
MCT+50cm			
MCT-50cm			

Departure

Draught			
Displacement			
TPC			
LCF			
MCT+50cm			
MCT-50cm			
Constant = (Disch)			Calculated
Constant = (Load)			Calculated

Sounding record

Vessel	0				Port	0			Date	0	

Ballast			Trim	Calculated			Trim	Calculated	

			Initial Survey				Final Survey		

Tank	Capacity m³		Sounding	Volume m³	Density	Tonnes	Sounding	Volume m³	Density	Tonnes
Total	0.00		Total	0.00		0.00	Total	0.00		0.00

	Fresh Water						Oil			

Tank	Capacity m³		Initial Survey		Final Survey		Initial Survey		Final Survey	
			Sounding	Tonnes	Sounding	Tonnes		Tonnes		Tonnes
							Heavy		Heavy	
							Diesel		Diesel	
							Lub Oil		Lub Oil	
							Slops		Slops	
							Fecal		Fecal	
Total	0.00		Total	0.00	Total	0.00	Total	0.00	Total	0.00

Draught survey certificate

Vessel:	0			B/L (M/T):		
Port:	0			Date:	0	
			Arrival			
	Aft	**Mid**	**Ford**	L.Ship	0.00	
Port	0.0000	0.0000	0.0000	LBP	0.00	
Starboard	0.0000	0.0000	0.0000			
Mean	0.0000	0.0000	0.0000	TPC	Calculated	
Corr'n to Perpendicular	Calculated	Calculated	Calculated	Lcf (-Ford)	Calculated	
Draught	Calculated	Calculated	Calculated	Trim	Calculated	
3/4 Mean Draught	Calculated			Mct+	Calculated	
Disp @	0.0000	Calculated		Mct–	Calculated	
Trim Correction A	Calculated					
Trim Correction B	Calculated			Oil	0.00	
Corrected Displacement	Calculated			F.Water	0.00	
Density of Dock Water	0.0000			Ballast	0.00	
Displacement @ Density	Calculated			Other	0.00	
Variables	0.00			Total	0.00	
Net Displacement	Calculated					
			Departure			
	Aft	**Mid**	**Ford**			
Port	0.0000	0.0000	0.0000			
Starboard	0.0000	0.0000	0.0000			
Mean	0.0000	0.0000	0.0000	TPC	Calculated	
Corr'n to Perpendicular	Calculated	Calculated	Calculated	Lcf (-Ford)	Calculated	
Draught	Calculated	Calculated	Calculated	Trim	Calculated	
3/4 Mean Draught	Calculated			Mct+	Calculated	
Disp @	0.0000	Calculated		Mct–	Calculated	
Trim Correction A	Calculated					
Trim Correction B	Calculated			Oil	0.00	
Corrected Displacement	Calculated			F. Water	0.00	
Density of Dock Water	0.0000			Ballast	0.00	
Displacement @ Density	Calculated			Other	0.00	
Variables	0.00			Total	0.00	
Net Displacement	Calculated					
Cargo	Calculated					
Surveyor	0					

Dist of Draught Marks	**Arrival**	**Departure**	
From Aft Perpendicular	0.000	0.000	
From Mid Perpendicular	0.000	0.000	Marks forward of perpendicular +ive
From Ford Perpendicular	0.000	0.000	Marks aft of perpendicular -ive

Chapter 17 –
Hold Preparation and Cleaning

This chapter provides an overview of best practice for the carriage of all bulk cargoes. For specific information on hold preparation and cleaning for grain cargoes, see Chapter 1, and for bulk liquids, see Section 18.10.

17.1 Planning

The nature and extent of hold preparation and cleaning will depend on the carriage requirements for the next cargo. Specific guidance should be available from sources such as the ship's SMS and the charterer. It is important that the Master carefully reviews the voyage instructions and charterparty, consulting further if there are any discrepancies in the cleanliness requirements or if further advice is required.

In the event that the ship's holds are in a poor condition, the Master should report this to the owners as additional time and resources may be required to bring the spaces to the require standard of cleanliness.

Figure 17.1: Crew undertaking hold preparation.

The Master should ensure that a hold cleaning schedule is prepared and that the ship has the necessary equipment, materials and chemicals for the task. An example cleaning schedule and equipment list for a 'grain clean' operation is given in Section 1.1.3. The exact cleaning schedule will depend on the cleanliness grade required. Typically, three types of cargo cleanliness category are used in the dry bulk industry. These are:

- 'Hospital clean' is required for certain high standard cargoes. For a 'hospital clean' standard of cleanliness, there should be no rust, no loose rust, no loose paint flakes and no previous cargo residues. Ideally, all steel surfaces and fixtures, including the tank top plating within the compartment, should have good, overall paint coating. This strict cleanliness is usually only achievable by vessels that trade clean cargoes

- 'grain clean' requires the holds to be free from insects, odour, residue of previous cargo, lashing material, loose rust scale and paint flakes, etc. Prior to loading, the holds must be swept, washed down with fresh water, dried and well ventilated. This is the most common requirement. Cargoes such as grains, fertilisers and cement are normally deemed 'moderately clean to moderately dirty cargoes' and typically require the hold to be at a 'grain clean' standard of cleanliness

- dirty cargoes such as bauxite or some types of coal are unlikely to be contaminated by any small amounts of rust or paint from the steel structures within the holds, although it is very important to check the exact cleanliness requirement.

Outside of 'hospital clean' and 'grain clean' standards, additional subcategories may include the following:

- 'Normal clean' requires the holds to be swept to remove all residues of the previous cargo, washed down and dried ready to receive a similar or compatible cargo

- 'shovel clean' does not require washing but only the removal of the previous cargo by rough hand or mechanical sweeping

- 'load on top'. This is only for compatible cargoes where the new cargo can be loaded directly into the hold with existing cargo residues. It usually only occurs on those ships that are routinely trading the same cargo type and grade.

It is important to maintain good records of all hold cleaning and maintenance operations which will assist owners in the event of any cargo claims and show that the ship undertook due diligence. These records should include entries into the log and photographs as appropriate.

Maintenance of the holds should be carried out at appropriate intervals as part of the ship's planned maintenance system and on receipt of any action required following an inspection. Poorly maintained fittings, structures and surfaces within the hold can lead to contamination of the next cargo, so should be repaired. However, if fresh paint is applied it will take time to cure appropriately.

17.2   Hold Cleaning

In general, to avoid contamination, the following areas will need to be prepared and cleaned:

- The bottom, sides and top of the cargo hold or tank, including bulkheads and frames

- the access hatches/lids/covers of the cargo hold or tank

- other fittings such as ladder rails, brackets, pipes and stanchions.

Figure 17.2: The exact type of hold cleaning will be determined by the requirements of the cargo for safe carriage and to prevent taint/spoilage/damage.

The cargo will determine the type of cleaning required but these usually include at one or a combination of:

- Sweeping/brushing/dusting
- saltwater wash
- fresh water wash
- use of chemicals
- use of fumigants.

The use of chemicals and fumigants should be closely controlled and regulations for the use of pesticides must be complied with. Importantly, hazards for crew should be addressed appropriately to prevent health implications.

A permit to work should be carried out for the hold cleaning operation and the team briefed via a toolbox talk. The SDS for cargoes or chemicals should be read and understood. A risk assessment should consider:

- Atmosphere testing within the cargo hold to ensure it is safe to work in
- access arrangements. All ladders and access equipment should be in good condition and properly secured
- PPE. This should be suitable for the job, in good condition and correctly worn
- cleaning equipment, suitable for the task and properly maintained
- proper and effective lighting in the hold/tank
- the number of crew/stevedores required to complete an operation safely
- effective communications between those in the hold and those on deck/on the bridge.

17.3   Hold Inspection

On completion of hold cleaning, time should be given for adequate drying as appropriate. Additionally, any damaged fittings or tank coatings should be repaired and time given for paint curing.

The Master or chief officer should then carry out an inspection of the hold along with the inspector. It is recommended that a small team of crew members also attend the inspection, with equipment, so that any previous cargo residues that have been missed can be cleaned immediately. During an inspection it is important to inspect all tank surfaces, including the tank top, tank top plate, and tank bottom. It is important to look for signs of previous cargo residue but also for rust or paint damage. Additionally, while at the top of the ladder access, the underside of the upper deck and hatch coaming should be inspected. Bright torches and binoculars should be available for those carrying out the inspection. Bilge wells should be dry. For agricultural cargoes, it is also important to look for evidence of insects.

Typically, but not always, the structure, shape and hold members of hold number one on bulk carriers is the more difficult to clean and therefore a close inspection is required to verify cleanliness.

Part 6 –

Bulk Cargoes – Liquid

Chapter 18 –
Bulk Oil Cargoes – Shortage and Contamination Claims

Claims arising from the carriage of oil cargoes are often substantial and may allege either shortage or contamination or both. This chapter provides guidance on how tanker operators can minimise the risk of cargo loss or damage and defend themselves should claims arise.

18.1 Oil Shortages

In general, oil shortage claims are based upon a discrepancy between the quantity of cargo as stated in the B/L and the outturn quantity as calculated in the discharge port. Both these figures are frequently derived from shore tank calibration data. The most common arguments are that:

- The ship is bound by the figure stated in the B/L
- the shore tank calibrations are more accurate than the ship's tank calibrations
- the oil has become contaminated by water after loading
- some oil remains on board the ship.

The carrier's defence is commonly based upon the accuracy of the ship's cargo figures and seeks to demonstrate that they were comparable with the B/L figure, that there was no significant in-transit loss, that any onboard quantity (OBQ) prior to loading has been taken into consideration and that all the cargo has been discharged with none remaining on board (ROB).

The following pages consider each phase of a typical tanker voyage and look at the likely causes of difficulty.

18.1.1 Before Arrival at the Load Port

The cargo officer should prepare a loading plan taking into account stability, trim and stress. Where draught restrictions permit, it may be advisable to plan to leave the load port with a trim that avoids the need for internal transfers of cargo during the loaded passage. The inert gas system, if fitted, should be fully operational in readiness for the forthcoming cargo operation. The oxygen content of the cargo tanks should be as low as possible before arrival and a record of all tank readings should be maintained.

18.1.2 On Arrival at the Berth

Figure 18.1: A berthed ship.

Once the ship is securely moored, it is important to liaise with representatives from the shore loading facility and to ensure continued good communications throughout the loading. All relevant information must be exchanged between ship and shore, including details of the ship's loading plan, maximum loading rates, shutdown procedures, safety regulations and cargo data. The appropriate Ship/Shore Safety Checklists should be completed.

18.1.3 Before Loading

The ship's cargo valves and pipelines should be correctly set for the reception of cargo and the relevant tank valves opened. Before loading, it is customary for a joint inspection of the cargo tanks to be made by the surveyor/shore representatives and ship's officers to confirm that the tanks are properly drained and in a suitable condition to load the designated cargo.

In general, the completion of such an inspection does not relieve the owner of their responsibility to ensure the correct condition of the cargo tanks.

In large tankers and where tanks are inerted to maintain the tank atmosphere, such inspections are difficult and it may be necessary to rely on the ship's gauging equipment rather than any visual inspection. The measurement of any OBQ should be carefully undertaken, preferably jointly with the shore representatives. The depth of any residues should be measured at as many locations as possible, and at least at the forward and after ends of the tanks. A wedge correction should be used, where applicable, to calculate liquid residues. Tank cleaning hatches should be utilised as appropriate.

It is never in the ship's interest for the OBQ to be underestimated. This will result in an overstatement of the ship loaded figure, exposing the ship to an unwarranted short delivery claim.

18.1.4　During Loading

The tank loading sequence should be planned in advance and in accordance with the ship's permissible stability and stress conditions. It is customary to begin loading at a slow rate, with the rate increased to maximum once it is established that cargo is entering the correct tanks and that there are no leaks from hose connections or any other difficulties. It is recommended that, at an early stage, the cargo officer should satisfy themself that the correct grade of cargo is being loaded, either by checking the specific gravity of a sample or, at least, by visual means. The ship's instrumentation may facilitate remote monitoring of temperatures during loading, but in any event it is essential to measure accurately and to record the temperature in each tank during loading. It is not advisable to use an average of the tank temperatures as this leads to inaccurate cargo figures.

The loading rate should be monitored and it is recommended that ullages and corresponding tank volumes, including those in idle tanks, are recorded in the deck log at least at hourly intervals.

The loading rate should be compared hourly with the shore tank discharge rates, where available, to help ensure that the cargo is not being misdirected in the loading terminal. Any changes in the loading rate or any stoppages must also be recorded. During the final stages of loading, the rate should be reduced to a minimum in order to permit measurement of the quantity of cargo so far loaded, to calculate the correct finishing ullage in the last cargo tank and to ensure cargo tanks are topped off safely.

18.1.5　On Completion of Loading

Before the cargo hoses are disconnected, the ship's figures must be calculated to check that the correct quantity of cargo has been loaded. While it is in the ship's interests to measure the cargo on board, it is customary for various witnesses (typically surveyors or loading Masters) to attend this operation and, in some cases, to make independent calculations. These witnesses may include representatives from the loading terminal, the shippers and the charterers. It is of prime importance that the measurements of ullage, temperature and, where appropriate, water dips are agreed by all concerned, although it must be accepted that the methods of calculation employed thereafter may not always be consistent. It is generally accepted that the latest edition of the ASTM-IP-API *Petroleum Measurement Tables* (Reference 28) is more accurate than older tables, but it should be borne in mind that all tables are based on the average characteristics of a range of oils. Where a surveyor is attending on the ship's behalf, they should collaborate with the ship's officers to ensure that no inconsistencies arise in the calculations.

Ship's tanks may be calibrated using imperial or metric units of volume and the quantity of cargo may be expressed in various units including long tons, tonnes or barrels. Whichever units are applied, it is essential to compare like with like. The use of standard volume may be considered preferable as it is less susceptible to misinterpretation by observers or laboratories. The glossary at the end of this chapter lists the common terms and abbreviations used in the measurement of liquid cargoes.

18.1.6 Ullaging

This is the measurement of the distance from the datum point at the top of a tank to the surface of the liquid cargo. Most ships use a combination of fixed and portable gauging equipment to measure the ullage in each tank. It is important to ensure that ullaging equipment has been verified as properly calibrated.

> Ullaging is best carried out when the ship is on an even keel and with no list, otherwise inaccuracies may creep in despite the application of trim corrections.

A ship, whether afloat, alongside a jetty, at anchor or at sea, is a moving platform and even a slight movement will affect the accuracy of measurement. In any single tank, a difference of one inch in the ullage may involve a volume of several hundred barrels. Where a ship is pitching or rolling, it is recommended that five measurements are taken from each tank. The highest and lowest should be ignored and the middle three averaged. Weather and sea conditions at the time of the measurement survey should be logged.

Some factors may affect the calculation of OBQs, particularly residues on tank floors and structures, and these will vary with the age of the vessel and previous cargoes carried. It is not unusual for ullages to be recorded for the purpose of determining ROB and OBQ when the trim of the vessel, at the time of survey, is such that the ullaging tape or sounding rod is not perpendicular to the ship's tank bottom on contact. In such cases, it follows that the depth of ullage obtained must be inaccurate. Clingage is a further consideration because, while crude oil washing (COW) reduces clingage for most crudes, there are a few types where the reverse is true.

18.1.7 Temperature

The temperature of liquid in a ship's tank is obtained by the use of a cup case thermometer or electronic temperature sensing devices. Electronic devices can be fitted in the tank or are part of the portable ullaging system. Cup case thermometers are unreliable and errors of ±2 to 3°C are not unknown. Electronic temperature measurement devices have a greater accuracy, typically ±0.1°C. Great care should be taken when using a manual thermometer to ensure it is not affected by the environmental temperature after it has been removed from the oil.

The vertical positioning of the thermometer in a vessel's tank, particularly at the discharge port, is critical because significant temperature variations can develop within the cargo tanks during the voyage. Cargo temperature may vary at different levels in the tank so, where possible, the temperature should be averaged from at least three readings (upper, middle and lower). Further, as temperatures vary from tank to tank, calculations of quantity must be calculated using individual temperature corrections for each tank.

> The use of an arithmetical average for the whole ship is inaccurate and contributes to 'paper losses'. An error of 1°C in temperature produces an inaccuracy in the volume at standard temperature of approximately 0.1%.

18.1.8   Water Dips

Free water beneath a crude oil cargo is normally measured with a sounding rod. Water finding paste or electronic interface tapes may also be used for the detection of free water. Unfortunately, neither of these methods can be used to distinguish accurately between an emulsion and free water. Each method involves the risk of inaccuracies that can only be determined by proper sampling and analysis techniques.

18.1.9   Sampling

When calculating cargo quantities, the ship has to rely upon certain data supplied from the shore, in particular the density of the cargo that is calculated after the analysis of samples. Shoreline samples may, however, contain inaccuracies and cannot always be accepted as being representative of the cargo loaded. It is recommended that, with crude oils, the standard sampling 'thieves' should not be used. For all oil cargoes, clean sample bottles should be used to acquire individual samples from each level (ie top, middle and bottom of each of the ship's tanks) and from the manifold, as required. Samples should be clearly labelled.

During such an operation, volatile fractions may be lost to the atmosphere with the result that the density established from the final mix does not represent the true density of the cargo in each tank. This, in turn, may later have a significant effect upon the calculation of weight and bottom sediment and water. The importance of sampling as a measure to counter contamination claims is discussed further in Section 18.9.

18.1.10   Density

Despite practical difficulties, it is best practice to ensure that the density of the cargo on board is measured and compared with the figures supplied by the terminal. As an example, an error of 0.01 kg/l can alter the tonnage calculation on a VLCC by 3,000 T.

18.1.11   Measurement Errors

Studies by a major oil company revealed that a measurement error of ±0.21% may occur when calculating the measurement of volumes and an error of ±0.25% when calculating weights. Therefore, measurement errors may easily account for what has previously been termed a 'measurement error loss' or 'measurement tolerance'.

18.2   Completion of Documentation

Once calculation of the ship's figures has been completed, the shore installation will provide a shore figure. It is generally this figure that is used on the B/L. It is most unlikely that the two figures will precisely coincide, although in practice, and in the vast majority of cases, the discrepancy is small and of no great significance. Typically, the Master should have no difficulty in reconciling the figures nor in signing the B/Ls. In each case, the gross figures should be compared and the ship's experience factor should also be taken into consideration.

> If there is an exceptional difference between the B/L figure and the ship's figure, the Master should decline to sign the B/L. They should insist on a thorough check of all measurements and calculations, including those ashore, in order to ascertain the cause of the discrepancy.

When checking the shore figures, difficulties may arise because the measurements taken in the shore tanks before loading cannot be verified once the cargo has been transferred. Checking of the shore figures may, therefore, depend upon the accuracy of the records kept at the shore terminal. In the majority of cases, this investigation is likely to be successful and the figures will be corrected and easily reconciled.

The reasons for gross inaccuracies may include:

- Ullages incorrectly measured
- tanks filled but not taken into account
- the contents of pipelines not allowed for
- incorrect temperatures or densities
- cargo mistakenly loaded on top of ballast
- cargo lost in the shore installation
- incorrect meter proving.

On occasion, despite such exhaustive checks, it may be that the two calculations cannot be reconciled and the Master faces a dilemma. The Hague-Visby Rules provide that:

"No carrier, master or agent of the carrier shall be bound to state or show in the bill of lading any marks, number, quantity, or weight which he has reasonable ground for suspecting not accurately to represent the goods actually received for which he has had no reasonable means of checking." (Reference 29)

However, the Master will be conscious of the commercial pressures, which dictate that the berth must be vacated and that the voyage must not be delayed. There is no one inflexible rule to be followed that will apply in every case.

The Master should make a note of protest, notifying the ship's agents and instructing them to urgently inform the owners of the problem as well as the charterers, the shippers and any consignee or notify party named on the B/L. The Master should give full details of the available figures and ask the parties notified to inform any potential purchaser of the B/L of the discrepancy. It may be difficult for the Master to contact all the parties named, but the owner should do this at the earliest opportunity. Ideally, the Master should be able to clause the B/L, but in practice this creates many difficulties.

The Master should, therefore, decline to sign the B/L, or withhold authority for anyone else to sign, until the dispute has been resolved. In any event, the Master or owner should immediately contact their P&I Club or its correspondents.

18.3   Early Departure Procedures

Figure 18.2: The tanker MT *'Orkim Harmony'*.

In certain busy oil terminals, it is the practice, in the interests of expediting the turnaround of tankers, to offer the Master the opportunity to utilise the early departure procedure. This system was devised in the light of many years' experience of tanker operations and shore figures after loading. On arrival at the loading berth, the Master agrees that, on completion of loading, the loading hoses will be immediately disconnected and the ship will sail. As soon as the B/L figures are prepared, they are cabled to the Master who, if satisfied, authorises the agent to sign the B/L and other related documents on their behalf. On no account should Masters sign the B/L themselves before sailing without the correct figures already being inserted.

18.4   Shipboard Records

It is essential for the defence of possible cargo claims that the tanker maintains certain documentary records of cargo operations. Time charterers, particularly the oil majors, are likely to place their own documentation on board, which they will require to be returned promptly at the end of each voyage. Typical returns would include:

* A voyage abstract (deck and engine)
* notice of readiness (NOR)
* a port log
* pumping/loading records

- stowage plan
- loading and discharge port calculations
- details of any cargo transfers.

They may also include records of all oil transfers, whether loading, discharging or internal, and including bunkering operations. Such records will assist not only with the defence of shortage and contamination claims, but also with the handling of other possible disputes including performance claims and demurrage and dispatch disputes.

> The need to keep full records of bunker quantities and to properly maintain the oil record book cannot be overemphasised.

18.5   During the Voyage

Provided the ship's fittings are properly maintained, the cargo will require little attention during the voyage unless heating is required. In such cases, it is important to follow the charterers' instructions, particularly bearing in mind the specifications of the cargo carried. In some cases, failure to heat the cargo properly may lead to severe difficulties. When crudes that require heating are carried, particularly those with a high wax content, it is important that the charterers provide clear instructions for heating both on the voyage and throughout discharge. Often, heating instructions are not sufficiently precise, with the charterers relying on the experience of the Master. Usually, it is wise to heat early in the voyage to maintain the temperature rather than being obliged to raise the temperature of the cargo more significantly at the end of the voyage. If there is doubt about the heating instructions, the Master should check with the charterers. The tank temperatures should be recorded twice daily.

> Attention should be paid to the condition and operation of the pressure/vacuum (p/v) valves on the tank venting system to ensure that they are functioning correctly. Failure to operate these valves properly may lead to a significant loss of product during the voyage.

Finally, there should be no necessity to transfer cargo between cargo tanks during the voyage, which would create differences between ullages and soundings taken before and after the voyage and invariably lead to disputes when defending shortage claims. Ideally, the two sets of readings should not differ to any degree. Owners should discourage the practice and insist that any transfers that the Master considers urgent and essential be reported and properly recorded in the oil record book. Many charterparties require the Master to notify the charterers of any cargo transfers.

18.6   Arrival

18.6.1   Before Arrival at the Discharge Port

A proper discharging plan should be prepared, taking into account any restrictions or requirements. It must include a careful check of the trim condition during discharge, as well as the stress conditions. Care should be taken to ensure that the parameters laid down by the shipbuilders are adhered to. It is also important to take into account the required discharging temperature and the need to maintain this temperature throughout the discharge. When discharging in ports where low sea temperatures prevail, this may require considerable vigilance. In tankers fitted with inert gas systems, COW or tank washing systems it will be necessary to ensure in advance that the systems are fully operational in readiness for the forthcoming discharge.

18.6.2　On Arrival at the Discharge Port

Figure 18.3: Ship arriving at a discharge port, aided by a tug.

On completion of the arrival formalities, the need to communicate with representatives of the discharging facility is no less important than at the load port. Full liaison should include the exchange of all relevant information about the cargo, including the maximum discharge rates, the discharge plan, safety procedures, shutdown procedures, scheduled shore stops and any local regulations.

If the ship is fitted with COW or tank washing equipment, it must be made clear whether tank washing is to be carried out, particularly bearing in mind any MARPOL requirements (Reference 30).

18.6.3　Before Discharge

As in the load port, the measurement of the cargo is undertaken in the presence of the cargo receivers and possibly other interested parties or their surveyors and including customs authorities. The remarks on cargo measurement in the load port apply equally in this instance. The utmost care should be taken in checking and double-checking the measurements. The measurement of temperature merits particular care, especially where heated cargoes are concerned. Again, it is stressed that apparently small discrepancies in temperature can lead to significant differences in the final calculations, and the temptation to 'round off' temperatures or to use convenient averages should be discouraged. It is essential to note the ship's trim and list at the time of ullaging – the ideal trim is with the ship on an even keel and with no list. When sampling cargo before discharge, and particularly in the case of heated cargoes, samples should be taken from the top, middle and bottom of the cargo tank.

On completion of cargo measurement, a comparison should immediately be made with the loading ullages, tank by tank, to see whether there have been any appreciable changes since leaving the load port. Should any differences be noted, the reasons should be immediately investigated and fully recorded. The ship's responsibility should begin and end at the fixed manifold and the owners have no liability for measurements taken once the cargo has entered the piping that forms the receiving terminal. Claims are frequently presented on the basis of shore figures that are inaccurate and the most effective and economical way of reducing liability may be to recalculate these figures correctly. It would be beneficial for a surveyor representing the shipowner to check the shore reception facility, where it may be possible to witness the taking of shore measurements. They may also be able to check the pipeline system to verify its size and length and the method by which its contents are ascertained before and after discharge, noting whether any valves that lead off the pipelines are in use. Some shore facilities are reluctant to allow ship's representatives to make full checks in their terminals. If an inspection of the terminal or its operations is refused, this should be recorded.

> Where shortage claims arise, they are usually based on the shore figures and the owners must defend themselves not only on the basis of the accuracy of the ship's figures, but also by challenging the accuracy of the shore figures. It will greatly assist if the owners' surveyor has made a thorough inspection of the terminal at the time of the discharge.

18.6.4   During Discharge

Once the necessary preparations have been completed aboard the ship, and the shore installation has confirmed that the discharge can commence, the cargo pumps are started in sequence. Where one or more grades of cargo are carried, it may be possible to discharge each grade simultaneously, subject to stress and trim considerations and any other restricting factors such as the design of the ship's pipeline system. Once it has been established that the cargo is flowing correctly, the discharge rate should be increased to the agreed maximum. The rate may be restricted either by back pressure or by the capacity of the ship's pumps. Ballast operations should then be carried out to ensure that ship stresses are kept within acceptable limits.

The rate of discharge should be carefully monitored throughout and recorded at intervals of no more than one hour. These records should show not only the amount of cargo discharged by volume, but also the shore back pressure, the pressure at the ship's manifold, the speed of the cargo pumps and steam pressure or, in the case of electrical pumps, the amperage. The unloading rate should be compared hourly with the shore tank reception rates, where available, to help ensure that the cargo is not being misdirected in the receiving terminal. If COW is being carried out, this operation must be closely monitored. Careful recording of the discharge in the ship's logs is essential if claims are to be successfully defended.

Effective stripping of the tanks is important since claims will undoubtedly be made against the owner for quantities of cargo remaining on board.

Figure 18.4: Ship discharging its cargo.

Provided the ship has a good stern trim, the tanks were well cleaned and prepared prior to loading, and the ship's pumps and pipelines are in sound condition, it should be possible to ensure that only a negligible quantity of cargo is left on board. Light or clean products should present no problem, although where heavier or heated cargoes are concerned there will inevitably be some clingage and perhaps some sediment remaining. Thorough tank washing will help to reduce these quantities and care should be exercised when stripping heated cargoes to ensure that the tanks are drained quickly as, once the level of the cargo falls below the heating coils, heat will be lost quickly and difficulties may be encountered.

Whatever type of oil is carried, it will be necessary to be able to demonstrate that ship's valves, lines and pumps were in good condition at the time of discharge because this has an impact on the question of 'pumpability'. From the point of view of cargo claims, it must be considered whether the cargo, even if it was liquid, could be pumped by the ship's equipment. It is possible that small quantities of oil, particularly where high gas cargoes are concerned, cannot be picked up by the pumps without the pumps gassing up. It is also possible that due to sediments from the cargo or shore restrictions on trim, the oil is liquid but cannot run to the suction (see Section 18.6.6). If pressure is applied to the ship to sail before the surveyor can attend, the Master should protest to the receivers and to the receivers' surveyor. If the surveyors are not prepared to certify cargo remaining on board as unpumpable, they should be invited to inspect the ship's pumps. The receivers should be informed that, if they consider the cargo to be pumpable, the ship is prepared to continue to attempt to pump it until the Club surveyor arrives. Owners should ensure that the maintenance records for the cargo pumps are carefully preserved and that they are available should such disputes arise. Surveyors who certify cargo as pumpable may be required to prove that they have tested the nature of the cargo and have ascertained that it can and does reach the suction in the cargo tank.

ROB claims may arise in three different ways:

- By loss of heating or inadequate heating on board ships, sometimes coupled with low ambient temperatures at the time of discharge
- as a result of the physical properties of the oil and the ability of the pumps to pump it. The possibility of pumps gassing up and loss of suction must be taken into consideration
- because cargo sediments or trim restrictions prevent the free flow of oil to the tank suction.

In the case of a crude that does not require heating, or that has a high vapour pressure, good COW and a good stern trim will overcome most problems.

Frequently, the charterparty will call for COW 'in accordance with MARPOL' and will allow additional time for discharge when COW is performed. If the receiving installation will not allow satisfactory stern trim, or if they refuse COW either in whole or in part, the Master should protest to the terminal and to the charterers, stating that the vessel cannot be held responsible for any resulting cargo losses.

18.6.5   On Completion of Discharge

When the cargo has been completely discharged, with all tanks and pipelines well drained, the cargo system should be shut down and all tank valves closed. A final tank inspection is then carried out and, inevitably, particular attention will be paid by the shore representatives to any cargo remaining on board. All void spaces, including ballast tanks and cofferdams, should be checked to ensure that no leakage of cargo has occurred.

18.6.6   Dry Tank Certificate

After discharge, a dry tank certificate should be issued, signed by an appropriate shore representative, describing any remaining cargo as 'unpumpable' and carrying an endorsement that the ship's equipment was in good working condition. In many places, shore cargo inspectors are reluctant to describe oil as 'unpumpable' and may prefer to use the terms 'liquid/non-liquid'. This is not satisfactory and should be avoided if at all possible because it leaves cargo owners in a position to claim pumpability and to attempt to activate a charterparty retention clause, albeit unlawfully, if the clause requires the cargo to be pumpable.

> It is strongly recommended that Masters contact their Club representative and the ship's operators for advice if a dry tank certificate showing oil remaining on board as being unpumpable cannot be obtained.

18.7   In-transit Losses and their Potential Causes

The standard defence put forward by a shipowner to a cargo shortage claim used to be that the loss was below or equal to 0.5% of the total cargo. This figure, which originally stemmed from the cargo insurance deductible, was used for many years by shipowners and cargo insurers as an approximate guide for in-transit losses. However, a number of courts, particularly in the United States, have rejected the concept of an automatic 'loss allowance'.

However, there is every indication that the same courts would allow a ±0.5% 'measurement tolerance'. In-transit losses and their causes may be considered under four headings:

- The true in-transit losses during the voyage, where the ship's gross volume at standard temperature on loading is compared with the ship's gross volume at standard temperature prior to discharge
- theoretical in-transit losses, when the comparison of net volume on board at standard temperature on completion of loading is compared with the net volume on board prior to the commencement of discharge
- emptying and filling losses. This is particularly pertinent where a part discharge may take place into a lightering vessel or barge
- additional losses that may occur as a result of COW.

The third and the fourth items become apparent when accounting for volumetric losses on outturn.

The following factors may combine to cause a release of gases and an increase in pressure within the cargo tanks which, combined with the inert gas pressure, may cause venting through the pressure vent valves and consequent loss of product:

- Tanker design
- cargo density
- Reid vapour pressure
- cargo temperature
- ambient temperature and general weather conditions.

18.7.1 Losses During Discharge

The largest volumetric losses are likely to occur when there is transfer from one container to another. Quite large losses can occur when pumping the cargo from the ship to the shore. Where lightering is involved, there will, inevitably, be a greater risk of volumetric losses between the ocean-carrying ship and the shore tanks. Where COW is performed, the potential for volumetric losses is greater since the cargo is being formed into a high-pressure spray and partially atomised.

18.8 The Shore Installation

When assessing a claim for short delivery of an oil cargo, the ship's calculation and figures are scrutinised. It is of equal importance to examine the shore calculations at both the loading and discharge ports. The carrier's liability does not extend beyond the ship's manifold, and claims for apparent oil losses can sometimes be resolved by recalculation of the shore figures. The cargo interests should be asked to provide full details of the shore installation, including a plan showing all the storage tanks and the interconnecting pipelines as well as the position of isolating valves. The shore installation should be able to verify the maintenance of all their equipment and demonstrate that, for instance, all the isolating valves were tight and properly operating at the time of discharge. They should also be asked to demonstrate that the storage tanks were properly calibrated and show that the calibration was accurate. In some oil installations, the accuracy of the tank calibrations may be doubtful, particularly if they are of older construction or built on unstable sites. A small measurement inaccuracy may correspond to a substantial difference in volume. Temperature measurements should also be closely considered as temperature gradients may exist when oil is stored in a large tank. In certain climatic conditions, there may be significant variations in the temperature within the tank. In a cold wind, there may be a horizontal temperature gradient as well as a vertical gradient. In many countries, the measurements taken at the time of custody transfer are witnessed by customs officials and, if appropriate, the official customs documents should be produced.

18.9   Oil Contamination Claims

Many oil shortage claims arise from the presence of excessive quantities of water that have settled out during the voyage and are found in crude oil cargoes at the discharge port. Oil contamination may occur in petroleum products, but a cross contamination between two grades of crude oil would, in most cases, not lead to a cargo claim. Crude oil cargoes are regularly blended before refining and, generally, for a cargo contamination to arise, a large cross contamination would need to take place.

> This is not true of all grades of crude as there are some that have particular properties and must not be contaminated in any way.

Many refineries designed for the reception of cargoes carried by sea have desalination facilities to protect the distillation columns and refinery equipment from excessive corrosion. Such facilities, however, do not always exist. The presence of water in certain crude oil cargoes may also cause emulsions to form with the hydrocarbons. This in turn may cause ROB volumes to be excessive and possible sludging of land tanks if efficient water draining is not carried out.

It is quite possible that any alleged contamination could have taken place ashore before loading. It is recommended that prudent owners protect their interests by ensuring that the ship's personnel take cargo samples from each tank after loading and at the ship's manifold during loading, as a matter of routine, so that hard evidence is at hand to refute claims of this kind. Contamination claims are more likely to occur in the white oil trades, where it is common for a number of grades to be carried simultaneously. As many as eight or ten grades may be carried simultaneously and, on a purpose-built product carrier fitted with deep well pumps and dedicated loading lines, it may be possible to carry a different grade in each tank with complete segregation.

> Aside from leakage, which may occur between cargo pipelines or cargo tanks and may result in contamination, the most likely cause of a product being off-specification is failure to properly prepare the tank or associated pipelines after carrying a previous incompatible grade.

18.9.1   Precautions Before Loading

Every care should be exercised to ensure that proper tank cleaning procedures are rigorously carried out and that tank coatings are in a suitable condition for the intended cargo. Particular care should be taken to ensure that all traces of the previous cargo are removed in the cleaning process.

When carrying multigrade cargoes, effective segregation is of prime importance. A minimum of two-valve segregation between different cargo grades should be considered. When preparing the loading plan, allowances must also be made for trim and draught restrictions. It is common for multigrade cargoes to be loaded in more than one port and for several discharge ports to be involved. In some cases, additional cargo may be loaded during the voyage after the discharge of other products. Careful planning is advisable, taking into consideration the quantity of cargo to be loaded and discharged, draught, trim and stress considerations, as well as the consumption of water and fuel.

Before loading, all concerned should have a clear knowledge of the intended loading plan, and the pipelines and valves must all be carefully set and double-checked. Because product cargoes generally have a low specific gravity, it is likely that the ship may not be loaded down to her marks even with all cargo tanks filled to the maximum permissible. When loading for a voyage that entails passing through areas where higher sea temperatures are expected to be encountered, it is advisable to take into account the expansion of the cargo that will occur as a result of those higher temperatures.

During the loading of sensitive products, it is common for 'foot samples' to be loaded and for samples to be taken and analysed before the rest of the product is taken on board. When carrying multigrades, it is good practice to take as many samples of the cargo as possible at various stages of the loading and discharge, including samples from the shorelines. If claims for contamination arise, the analysis of such samples will often identify the source of the problem and may assist the shipowner in rejecting liability.

If the following points are borne in mind by owners and Masters, there will be a much greater chance of success when defending oil cargo claims:

- Careful attention should be paid to all onboard surveys when loading and discharging with a view to avoiding 'paper losses'

- after discharge, try to ensure that a dry tank certificate is issued showing all cargo remaining on board to be unpumpable and endorsed to confirm that the ship's equipment was working correctly

- employ properly qualified surveyors and protest if it can be demonstrated that a surveyor employed by a cargo interest is not qualified or lacks experience.

18.10 Cargo Tank Preparation

Product and chemical tankers are often required to carry a wide variety of different liquid cargoes. The proper cleaning and preparation of cargo tanks and lines after one cargo and before loading a dissimilar commodity is of utmost importance if successive cargoes are to be carried without cross contamination.

18.10.1 MARPOL Pollution Categories

Tank cleaning and preparation methods are closely tied to the requirements of the MARPOL Convention, intended to prevent marine pollution.

Tanks containing residues of petroleum oil products must be cleaned out in accordance with the requirements of MARPOL Annex I. This Annex focuses on the prevention of discharge of oily residues into the sea by retaining slops on board for later disposal ashore. Annex I only allows the controlled discharge of oily wash water under the conditions set out in Regulation 34. Discharge is only allowed outside special areas under strictly controlled conditions. Full disposal records must be maintained by means of the Oil Record Book.

Tanks containing residues from cargoes of noxious liquid substances (NLS) in bulk must be cleaned in accordance with the requirements of MARPOL Annex II and the *International Bulk Chemical Code* (IBC Code). The IBC Code lists NLS according to their designated pollution category.

The Code requires that tanks containing certain substances must be pre-washed ashore at the receiving terminal before departure. This pre-wash is usually a relatively quick machine flush to remove most of the residues. The residues of cargoes in some pollution categories are permitted to be flushed into the sea under certain conditions, which may be after pre-washing. In all cases, the IBC Code must be consulted for proper compliance with the requirements of MARPOL. Full disposal records of NLS must be maintained by means of the Cargo Record Book.

18.10.2   Tank Cleaning Guides

There are several industry standard guides available to crew to help and inform their decision making regarding suggested tank cleaning methods, depending upon the type of cargo switch that is proposed.

At the simplest end of the scale are the tank cleaning guides produced by the oil majors. These are usually in the form of a matrix listing the typical oil product groups (jet, kerosene, gasoline, diesel fuel oil, etc) and give suggested washing methods from one group to another. The matrix will suggest washing procedures, or indicate when no washing is required at all. Such guides may form an integral part of voyage instructions or charterparty directions when a ship is changing from carrying one listed oil product to another.

On chemical tankers the variety of cargoes likely to be carried is much more extensive and the type of washing required to remove traces of one type of cargo in readiness for the next cargo is more complex. Guides are available in book form which may detail procedures and suggested cleaning steps, including techniques such as: ambient seawater flush, hot chemical recirculation, hot seawater rinsing, fresh water rinsing, ventilation, draining, mopping and drying.

More recently, various online, subscription-based guides have become available (Miracle and Milbro). These are interactive programs that enable the user to choose from a huge range of listed chemicals as last (From) and next (To) cargoes. The search can also be refined as to tank coating type. These online guides can also consider the requirements of the MARPOL regulations pertaining to each commodity and its pollution category.

Some of the major parcel tanker operators have their own interactive computer-based tank cleaning guides to include similar recommendations.

Figure 18.5: Tank cleaning in progress.

18.10.3 Cleaning Chemicals

Numerous off-the-shelf, proprietary tank cleaning chemicals are marketed on a worldwide basis. The chemicals are produced for specific purposes, which may include alkaline degreasers for oils and fats, non-alkaline detergents, acidic based metal brighteners, etc. Each chemical will come with its own MSDS and manufacturer's recommendations. These recommendations will include the optimum dilution dosage, means of application, ideal temperature and whether to use with salt or fresh water. The manufacturer's guidelines should be followed for optimum results.

Those responsible for tank cleaning after any given cargo should ensure that the ship is provided with an adequate stock of the appropriate chemical needed to clean after the cargo being carried, at least before that cargo is discharged. Many chemical tankers will hold a stock of various cleaning chemicals in drums ready for use. They should maintain an inventory of their stocks, noting the litres remaining and including the date of receipt or manufacture. The condition of the containers should also be noted as steel drums can corrode and leak.

Users must be aware of the limitations of certain chemicals in respect of their cargo tank coating types. For example, zinc silicate coatings are liable to be damaged by acidic or alkaline cleaning chemicals, so only those chemicals with an acceptable neutral pH should be considered. The coating manufacturer's recommendations and resistance lists must be consulted regarding the cleaning chemicals, as with the cargo to be loaded.

Degreasing chemicals act as surfactants to help to break down oils and fats in much the same way as washing-up detergent is used to clean greasy crockery. Heat also helps to liquify, break down and remove greasy residues. However, surfactants can cause some fats such as vegetable oils to saponify, causing unsightly white deposits. Acidic metal brighteners can be used to neutralise the deposits in follow-on washing, coatings permitting.

Tanks should be substantially cleaned by hot water washing before cleaning chemicals are employed. Their role is to remove greasiness, not to remove visible residues.

18.10.4 Washing Methods

Physical cleaning of a cargo tank (as opposed to crude oil washing (COW) where the cargo is used as the washing medium) is primarily carried out by water washing. Seawater is usually available in copious quantities and is the principal washing medium employed. There are limitations in its use, as seawater can be damaging to stainless steel and should only be used in accordance with the ship builder's recommendations. If used in a stainless-steel tank, the salt from seawater should be immediately rinsed with fresh water as part of the cleaning plan. Most tank cleaning will include a rinsing stage.

Seawater is usually applied via tank washing machines. These are either fixed (as part of the tank fittings) or portable (where they are introduced on the end of a hose through tank openings). The wash water medium is introduced at pressure either from the ship's washing main or from a cargo pump (when recirculation washing is required). The machines can be programmable, in which their arcs of operation can be limited (ie top, middle or bottom of a tank), or non-programmable where their nozzles describe an overall coverage pattern. Fixed machines should be sited at a sufficient number of locations within a tank and at such positions that shadows (areas not directly impinged by the washing medium) are minimised. Portable machines can be positioned at specific heights and locations to cover shadows, and access openings may be provided in the deck for that purpose. Shadow diagrams should be available to guide mariners as to the best coverage and positions.

In ships with no or few fixed machines, portable machines should be periodically lowered during the wash cycle (drops) to cover all areas of the tanks.

The washing medium can be applied direct (straight from the sea or a freshwater storage tank) or recirculated. Water can be supplied at an ambient temperature or it can be passed through a heat exchanger to raise the temperature, as desired. Any tank coating temperature limits should be observed. Water can be heated up to about 80°C, but above that temperature the water can convert to steam as it leaves the washing machine nozzles and, as a result, the washing effect through mechanical impingement will be lost. During direct washing, chemical cleaners can be injected into the washing medium downstream of the heater by means of a barrel pump. The chemical dose rate can be monitored by adjusting the injection pump rate in relation to the throughput of the washing machines in use. Dosing can be continuous or periodic during the washing cycle depending upon manufacturer's recommendations. After chemical injection has been turned off, the 'clean' washing medium should be continued until all chemicals have been rinsed away.

During washing, the washed tank must be continuously stripped to avoid any build-up of wash water. Any build-up can adversely affect the cleaning efficiency, especially when oils and fats are being cleaned. The spent washing water pumped out will either be stored on board (in the slop tank) or pumped overboard, either directly or after decanting, depending upon the requirements of MARPOL for the previous cargo and the cleaning chemicals used.

The action of stripping out the wash water also ensures that the pump and lines are flushed through and cleaned. This is the main way in which the inside of the cargo lines are cleared of the previous cargo. During washing, all parts of the line system should be flushed, including both sides of manifolds, drop lines, drains and any connecting branches, paying particular attention to ensuring that no dead ends are left unflushed.

Recirculation washing is achieved by formulating a prepared dose of wash medium in a clean cargo tank (the recirculation tank). The wash medium can be heated, either by filling the recirculation tank via the main tank cleaning heat exchanger or by means of the heating coils within the tank. The recirculation wash medium is then pumped out to deck, where hose connection is made to the machines in the tank to be cleaned. The recirculation tank cargo pump is run at sufficient speed and pressure to drive the machines inside the tank being washed. The pump of the washed tank is used to return the medium back to the recirculation tank. The two pump speeds are regulated to ensure that the wash medium is continually stripped out of the washed tank. The volume of the recirculation medium must be sufficient to ensure that the system remains full and effective.

The advantage of direct washing is that the cleaning medium is continuously renewed with clean water. The main disadvantages are that this increases the overall volume of wash water used (which matters if the dirty water must be stored on board) and it is more expensive in terms of heating.

Conversely, the advantages of recirculation are that heat losses are reduced and the volume of wash water is controlled and known. The big disadvantage of recirculation washing is that if the wash medium becomes too dirtied, the washing effect can be minimised, or even reversed if cargo residues are carried back into the tank being washed. In practice, some combination of direct washing and recirculation washing may be employed. This can be advantageous if only a limited cleaning chemical dosage is available, and recirculation is used as the finishing cleaning effort. That is why the cleaning guides will usually specify recirculation washing only as the secondary wash after the tank has been substantially cleaned.

In either case, both methods can be applied to individual cargo tanks or groups of several tanks. Tanks can be washed sequentially in pairs in a rolling programme, so that as soon as one pair has completed a stage, that stage can be rolled forward to the next pair. If recirculation washing is applied to a group of several tanks, there must be sufficient volume and dosage concentration so that the final tank of the batch receives the same cleaning effect as did the first tank of the batch. The recirculation medium must be monitored to ensure that it does not become too contaminated. If necessary, the concentration of the dose can be topped up to maintain its surfactant properties.

Effective tank washing is a balance of wash water pressure, temperature and good stripping. Good pressure and temperature should be maintained by balancing the number of washing machines used at any one time. More machines equal faster water throughflow, resulting in reduced pressure, temperature and cleaning effect. During washing the pressure and temperature of the wash water should be constantly maintained and monitored. It is also important to regularly check that the washing machines are turning correctly. This can be gauged by the sound that impinging water makes on the ship's structure. The water level inside the washed tank should also be constantly checked to ensure that there is no build up.

Figure 18.6: Tank cleaning.

18.10.5   Fresh Water Rinsing

After completion of saltwater washing, and after the cleaning chemical has been rinsed out by clean salt water, all traces of salt should be removed by thorough freshwater rinsing.

After difficult cargoes (such as palm oils) freshwater rinsing can be delayed until a cleanliness evaluation has been made. There is no point in wasting fresh water until the tank is assessed as being sufficiently free from previous cargo to move on to the next cleaning stage.

Hot washing will cause steam in the tanks and condensation on the ship's structure will assist in reducing the salt down to lower levels. However, freshwater rinsing is usually necessary as a final rinsing stage. This is accomplished by running the fresh water through the tank cleaning system. Sometimes, dedicated freshwater washing mains or lines are provided on deck for the purpose.

Some chemical cargoes (such as methanol and MEG) require the tanks to be virtually free from chlorides (a component of salt water) before loading. The chloride levels are assessed by means of wall wash testing. Fresh waters usually contain some trace amounts of salts, which may mean that they are incapable of rinsing to the required very low levels of chlorides. In which case, de-ionised (DI) water, which is chloride free, is used in the final rinsing. DI water can be provided to a ship in drum form. Alternatively, it can be produced on board, by passing the ship's fresh water through special resin filters. The DI water will usually be sprayed on the tank surfaces using a barrel pump and a handheld lance to reach all surfaces from within the tank.

Steaming with live steam (steam under pressure) can also be an effective way of rinsing out salts and odours. The resulting condensation will need to be pumped away. Live steaming should only ever be attempted in gas free tanks, as it can be a source of ignition through static generation.

18.10.6   Inert Gas

Hot water washing after flammable cargoes should always be carried out in accordance with the applicable SOLAS regulations. This will normally be either after the tank has been checked as being gas free or is properly inerted, so that the oxygen content is below 8%. In accordance with SOLAS, in tanks of less than 3,000 m³ capacity in chemical carriers, inert gas may not be required, provided the throughput of the combined washing machines does not exceed 17.5 m³/h and the total combined throughput from the number of machines in use in a cargo tank at any one time does not exceed 110 m³/h (SOLAS Chapter I I-2 B Regulation 4 5.5.2.1).

After cleaning in an inert atmosphere from flammable products, and if it is required to be gas free for the next cargo, the tank should first be purged with inert gas to reduce the hydrocarbon content to 2% or less by volume. This is so that, during the subsequent gas freeing operation, no portion of the tank atmosphere is brought within the flammable range.

18.10.7   Tank Cleaning Plan

Any tank cleaning operation should be well planned and there will usually be a ship-specific tank cleaning form in the safety management system (SMS). If followed correctly, the form can be used as evidence of the nature of washing that was carried out. Those involved can therefore know at any point in the cleaning operation what point has been reached and the likely completion time. Copies of the plan should be circulated amongst all those involved in the operation so that everybody knows the sequence involved.

18.10.8   Drying and Venting

As well as being properly cleaned, cargo tanks will usually need to be presented gas free and dry for the next cargo. Drying will usually require entry into the tank for hand pumping and mopping of any water remaining after stripping, and for final wiping and checking. Tank entry should only be carried out after all the proper procedures for entry into enclosed spaces have been followed.

Figure 18.7: Removing tank cleaning residues.

Venting of tanks by mechanical means will not only remove previous cargo vapours and odours but will also help dry the tank coatings of humidity after washing. The pipes and lines should be opened, thoroughly drained and blown through as part of the tank drying process.

Tank cleaning of any sort may not be permitted alongside some oil terminals in port. Local regulations in that respect should always be followed.

18.11 Glossary of Measurement Terms

API = API gravity
Petroleum industry expression for density of petroleum liquid expressed in API units. API gravity is obtained by means of simultaneous hydrometer/temperature readings, equated to and generally expressed at 15°C (60°F). The relative density to API gravity relation is:

$$\frac{141.5}{-131.5}$$

Relative density 15°C (60°F).

Automatic sampler
A device installed for indicating the level of product from a location remote to the manual gauge site.

Barrel
Petroleum industry measurement unit equal to 42 US gallons.

Clingage
The oil that remains adhered to the inner surface and structure of a tank after it has been emptied.

Crude oil washing (COW)
The technique of washing cargo tanks of oil tankers during the discharge of crude oil cargoes, using the crude oil cargo itself.

Density
The mass per unit volume at a specified temperature used to determine weight for a volume at a standard temperature.

Dip
Depth of liquid. American expression: gauge.

Free water
Water within a container that is not entrained in the cargo.

Gauge reference height
The distance from the tank's strike point to the bench mark or reference point.

Gross observed volume (GOV)
The total volume of all petroleum liquids, including sediment and water (S&W), but excluding free water, at observed temperature and pressure.

Gross standard volume (GSV)
The total volume of all petroleum liquids and S&W, corrected by the appropriate temperature correction factor (Ct1) for the observed temperature and API gravity, relative density or density to a standard temperature such as 60°F or 15°C and also corrected by the applicable pressure correction factor.

Load on top (LOT)
The procedure of allowing hydrocarbon material recovered during tank washing to be commingled with the next cargo.

Net OBQ
Onboard quantity (OBQ) less free water in cargo, slop tanks and lines, and water in suspension in slop tanks.

Net observed volume (NOV)
The total volume of all petroleum liquids, excluding S&W, and free water at observed temperature and pressure.

Onboard quantity (OBQ)
Cargo tank quantities of any material on board a ship after deballasting immediately prior to loading. Can include oil, oil/water emulsions, water, non-liquid hydrocarbons and slops.

Remaining on board (ROB)
Cargo or residues remaining on board the ship after discharge.

Sediment and water (S&W)
Non-hydrocarbon materials that are entrained in oil. Material may include sand, clay, rust, unidentified particulates and immiscible water.

Ship's composite sample
A sample comprised of proportional portions from running samples drawn from each tank on the ship.

Ship figures
Stated volume extracted from ship's calibration tables based on measurements taken from cargo tanks.

Slop tank
A tank into which the tank washings (slops) are collected for the separation of the hydrocarbon material and water, the recovery most often becoming LOT (load on top).

Total calculated volume (TCV)
The total volume of the petroleum liquids and S&W, corrected by the appropriate temperature correction factor (Ct1) for the observed temperature and API gravity, relative density or density to a standard temperature such as 60°F or 15°C and also corrected by the applicable pressure factor and all free water measured at observed temperature and pressure (gross standard volume plus free water).

Total delivered volume (ship)
The total calculated volume less ROB.

Total observed volume (TOV)
The total measured volume of all petroleum liquids, S&W and free water at observed temperature and pressure.

Total received volume (ship)
The total calculated volume less OBQ.

Ullage (outage gauge)
Measurement of the distance from the datum point at the top of a tank to the surface of the liquid cargo.

Volume correction factor (VCF)
The coefficient of expansion for petroleum liquids at a given temperature and density. The product of the petroleum liquid volume and the volume correction factor equals the liquid volume at a standard temperature of either 60°F or 15°C.

Water (dip) gauge
 a) The depth of water found above the strike point, or
 b) To gauge for water.

Water finding paste
A paste applied to a bob or rule to indicate the water/product interface by a change in colour at the cut.

Wedge correction
An adjustment made to the measurement of a wedge-shaped volume of oil, so as to allow for the vessel's trim.

Weight conversion factor (WCF)
A variable factor related to density for use when converting volume at standard temperature to weight.

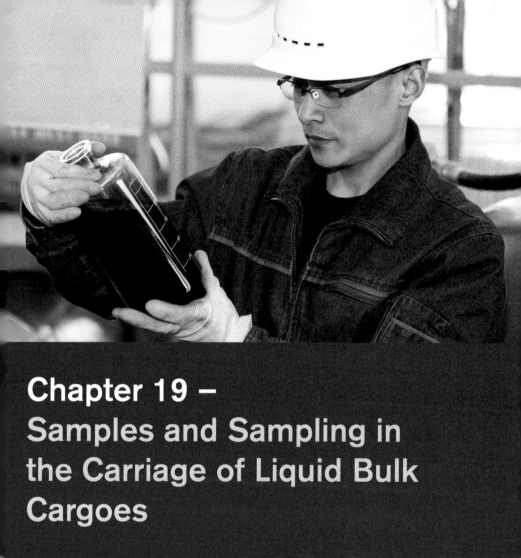

Chapter 19 – Samples and Sampling in the Carriage of Liquid Bulk Cargoes

The period of the carriers' responsibility for liquid bulk cargoes, under the Hague and Hague-Visby Rules, extends from the time when the cargo is loaded until the time it is discharged, including the loading and discharging operations (Reference 29). Under the Hamburg Rules, which came into effect in 1992, the carrier, servants and agents will be responsible from the time the cargo is received by them at the load port until the time it has been delivered at the discharge port (Reference 31).

The carrier, the Master or agent is required to issue to the shipper a B/L showing, among other things, the apparent order and condition of the cargo as received on board. With the exception of cargoes carried in the deep tanks of liner vessels, which may be loaded by the shipper and discharged by the consignee, most loading and discharging operations with bulk liquid cargoes are performed by the actual carrier. There may be different practices in the load and discharge ports and these, together with the nature of the cargo, are important factors. Most B/Ls include the words 'shipped in apparent good order and condition'.

As there is a wide variety of liquid cargoes carried and many different types of ships involved, the subject of sampling is necessarily a very wide one. This chapter deals with the general principles of how to ascertain the apparent order and condition of goods when they are shipped and, just as importantly, how to preserve the evidence.

Many parcel tanker owners have issued instructions to their Masters to sample each type of cargo at the ship's manifold on commencement of loading, after the first test-load (so called 'first run' sample) and from the ship's tank after completion of loading. The samples are numbered and details entered in a sample logbook.

An advantage of this procedure is that the ship's officers who attended the sampling, or who actually drew the samples, are available for questioning at the discharge port. It is sometimes the case that sampling by shippers at the load port is not witnessed by ship's officers and samples allegedly drawn from ship's tanks are handed to the ship's personnel just prior to departure, underlining the need for a joint sampling procedure between shippers and carriers and carriers and consignees.

Owners are strongly recommended to instruct their ship's officers that, whenever they are in doubt as to the apparent good order and condition of a liquid bulk cargo, they should notify both the shipper and the P&I Club's correspondents so that expert advice may be sought and samples analysed at the load port. In case of serious doubt about the condition of the cargo, B/Ls should not be signed until the results of the analysis are available.

It should be emphasised that, as with bulk or general cargo, the description on the B/L relates to the external and apparent condition of the goods. Claims on liquid bulk cargoes often involve the question of quality, which is not usually apparent, and these claims may be based on a detailed analysis that the carrier has no means of checking.

In most instances, the ship's personnel cannot question the condition of a product upon loading, unless they detect the presence of free water, haziness or dull appearance, a strong foreign odour or an obvious deviation in the colour of the product.

It is, therefore, important that samples taken at the time of loading and prior to discharge are truly representative of the condition of the cargo and are available in the event that any dispute arises. Where load port samples have been drawn and retained on board, any uncertainty about the quality of the cargo at the time of loading can be clarified at relatively low expense.

The shipper, however, is in quite a different position because, apart from the sampling and analysis that takes place prior to loading, the shipper may consider it necessary to take first run samples from the ship's tanks at the commencement of loading operations and suspend loading until analysis is available. The ship's personnel may not be involved or even informed about the results of this analysis. Bona fide shippers will usually provide this information, however, and will require the ship to discharge the first run of cargo if this analysis shows it to be off-specification.

When loading operations are resumed, it should not be assumed that the first run of cargo will be in good order and condition as the shipper may have found the product to be only slightly off-specification and decided to blend the cargo during subsequent loading operations. Furthermore, water may be introduced into the product via the installation's pipeline system without the ship's personnel being aware of it.

Carefully cleaned tanks, compatible tank coatings and well maintained pipelines, heating coils, valve systems, hoses and pumps are essential.

When cargo is loaded by shippers and discharged by consignees, it is their responsibility to ensure that the hoses and pumps supplied are suitable for the product concerned. Sampling after the first run of cargo has been loaded, after completion of loading and prior to discharge is important if analysis of whether or not any alleged damage or contamination could have been caused as a result of the use of unsuitable equipment supplied by the shipper or consignee, or by defects in the ship's loading system.

It must also be emphasised that it is the duty of the ship's crew to assist shippers and/or consignees with the proper connection of hoses and to ensure that, in the case of loading over the top, hoses are placed in the proper tanks. The crew should also ensure that, where the ship's integral piping system is involved, the cargo is directed to the correct tank during loading and that the lines used during loading and discharging are properly isolated to avoid contamination with other products on board.

19.1   Sale Contracts

The condition of liquid bulk cargoes when shipped should be in accordance with either the specification in the contract of sale or the usual grade specifications used in the trade. The carrier is not a party to the contract of sale and cannot be expected to have knowledge of a specification that, in most cases, relates only to quality.

Certain limited quality descriptions such as 'clear', 'colourless', etc may be apparent upon visual inspection of samples and the presence of water can usually be detected by an experienced ship's officer. However, the wide variety of products, frequently referred to only by trade names or codes, makes it difficult for ship's officers to detect anything other than the most obvious deviations in the condition of the cargo.

Sale contracts, while regulating the relationship between seller and buyer, also have some bearing on the carrier's position. They usually require certain sampling procedures to be carried out and the appointment of an independent surveyor to certify the fitness and cleanliness of the ship's tank and pipelines. Many standard vegetable oil contracts require discharging samples to be drawn in the presence of both seller's and buyer's representatives and analysed by an independent chemist. Almost all oils and fats are sold subject to such sampling and analysis, but the contracts rarely provide for the carrier to be given such samples.

Evidence of the condition of a liquid bulk cargo on loading is, therefore, extremely important. Claims lodged at the discharge port have frequently been defeated as a result of analysis of loading samples.

Most sale contracts provide for the change of ownership of the cargo to take effect at the time of loading on board ship and for a B/L to be obtained from the carrier. It is, therefore, important for both seller and carrier to have evidence of the condition of the cargo at that time. The carrier's responsibility may, however, commence at an earlier time, depending on the moment of taking charge of the cargo.

The sampling activities of shipper and buyer often lead ship's officers to believe that nothing is required of them as the carrier's position has been sufficiently protected. This, however, is not always the case.

The carrier must take an active part in the sampling procedures, particularly at the load port, and must see that their interests are properly protected.

19.2   Sampling

There are several other important reasons why samples should be taken during loading of bulk liquid cargoes:

- To enable protest to be made to the shipper if the product loaded is not in apparent good order
- to enable the loading operation to be followed in all its stages
- to provide evidence should the ship's tank coatings be found damaged upon discharge
- to enable the carrier to provide evidence should local authorities lodge pollution claims against the ship
- to enable the specific gravity and temperature of the cargo to be established
- to investigate subsequent claims against the carrier for admixture or contamination.

19.2.1   Sampling Prior to Loading

Shippers of liquid bulk cargoes will not, in most cases, allow the carrier to take samples from shore tanks, road tankers, barges or tank wagons, particularly when the shippers are responsible for the loading of the cargo.

It should also be noted that there are many areas of the world where large consignments of vegetable oils are delivered alongside by a wide variety of road tankers, barges or rail tank wagons. With road tankers and rail tank wagons, the product is usually drained into the shore containers before being pumped on board. These tankers are generally used for a variety of commodities, including both vegetable and mineral oils, and their cleanliness should not always be assumed. It is also common practice, in this trade, for shippers to 'borrow' from each other to make up the total quantity loaded into a particular ship, so the cargo may consequently be of variable quality and condition. When loading is from tank barges, sampling takes place prior to loading into the ship. Even if the ship's officers are provided with such samples, they have no control over how they were drawn and there is no certainty about when or from where they were taken.

19.2.2   Sampling During Loading

The first requirement is that, on commencement of loading, samples are taken from the ship's manifold or first run from the ship's tanks, even though the loading operation may have to be suspended while this is done. It is essential that shipper's inspectors take part in this sampling procedure and that the samples are split between the parties. Whenever loading operations are interrupted and hoses, pumps or line systems are changed, sampling of the relevant ship's tanks before and after the changeover will be necessary unless it is certain that the hoses, lines and pumps have been previously used for the same product.

> On completion of loading, a representative sample from each tank should be taken. For a parcel tanker, each consignment should be similarly treated. Shipper's inspectors frequently take first run samples on their own initiative and will usually make up composite samples of all tanks after completion of loading.

19.2.3 Load Port Samples other than those Taken by the Carrier

Samples are sometimes handed to the ship to be delivered to the consignees in accordance with the seller's contractual obligations. In such cases, ship's personnel will be unaware of how or where such samples were obtained and it is rare for the ship to be provided with a duplicate set for its own use. The origin of such samples is uncertain and their labels often bear vague descriptions such as 'average shore tanks', 'average tank trucks', 'average head line', etc. These samples, whether relating to vegetable oils, mineral oils or petrochemicals, may be samples drawn before and/or during and/or after loading, single or duplicate, sealed or unsealed and either against a receipt or not. The carrier has no control over the drawing of such samples and, in many cases, analyses of them will conform to the required specification while the cargo on arrival does not. At the discharge port, such shipper's loading samples are collected by inspectors appointed by the shipper or consignees, who may also measure and sample the ship's tanks. Samples drawn at the load port jointly by ship's officers and shipper's representatives may then serve to prove that the samples handed to the ship's personnel for delivery to consignees do not represent the true condition or quality of the cargo.

19.2.4 Sampling Before Discharge

On arrival at the discharge port, and immediately after tank ullages and temperatures have been carefully checked, samples should be taken of all cargo on board. This sampling is usually carried out by the consignee's surveyor and the procedure should be attended by ship's officers. It is usual to take top, middle, lower and bottom samples, depending on the product. Where a cargo remains homogeneous during the voyage, such samples may be mixed into a composite sample with the largest proportion coming from the middle depth of the tank. It is also desirable to use a water finding instrument to establish whether water is present.

In the case of edible oils and animal oils/fats, bottom samples should always be drawn to check for sediment. These bottom samples must be kept in separate jars, sealed and properly labelled for identification. It must be emphasised that sediments, if any, should always be regarded as belonging to the particular consignment involved.

With many products, it is the practice to defer commencement of discharge until analysis of the samples has been completed. If the receivers indicate that the cargo does not conform to the required specification, the Master should immediately request the P&I Club correspondent to arrange for attendance of an independent surveyor and for analysis of loading samples.

19.3 Sampling Procedures

Cargo sampling is a process that requires careful attention and each sample must be representative of the product concerned. Continuous sampling at the ship's manifold to obtain a so-called 'ship's rail composite' sample, while a time consuming procedure, may be of value in the case of homogeneous cargoes where tank samples taken prior to commencement of discharge have shown the product to be satisfactory at the time the ship arrived. The most important samples are a sample of the first cargo arriving at the ship's manifold, a first run sample from the ship's tank and a sample or set of samples drawn from the tank on completion of loading. In the chemical (parcel) trade, running samples during the first five minutes of loading are sometimes also drawn. The object of all these sampling operations is to obtain a manageable quantity of cargo, the condition and properties of which correspond as closely as possible to the average condition and properties of the parcel being sampled.

The importance of cleanliness cannot be too strongly stressed. All sampling work should be carried out with clean hands and, where protective clothing is necessary, such as in the case of toxic products, clean gloves of a suitable material should be worn. The apparatus used should be of a suitable material that does not react chemically with the cargo being sampled. Various types of sampling bottle can be used, particularly in large tanks, but if glass bottles are employed, care should be taken to avoid breakage.

With edible oils, where smell and flavour is important in quality assessment, scrupulous cleanliness is essential and the sampling devices should be thoroughly washed with hot water and soap and rinsed extensively with hot water before use. All sampling equipment should be protected from the weather, rain, dust, rust, grease, etc, and, before the sample is divided into suitable glass jars, the outside of the sampling apparatus should be wiped clean.

When sampling from the manifold or pipeline, care should be taken to ensure that the sampling cock through which the product is drawn is absolutely clean. This method of sampling is most difficult and must be carefully supervised to ensure that both shipper and carrier obtain a part of the same representative sample. It is important that, when samples are being taken by this method, a constant rate of flow of the product is involved. If there is a variation in the flow rate, the sampling cock must be carefully regulated to ensure that the full sample is taken at a constant rate.

Certain products, such as corrosive liquids, liquefied gases and products that react dangerously with water and/or air cannot be sampled by normal means. It may also be dangerous to keep samples of some products for too long as they become unstable.

19.4 Labelling of Samples

All samples taken jointly should be properly labelled and sealed and identical sets should be kept by all parties. Should shippers refuse to seal the samples jointly, an appropriate entry should be made in the logbook. They should be unilaterally labelled and sealed by a ship's officer and/or the independent surveyor representing the carrier.

The samples themselves must be identical to those taken together with the shippers and the latter must be notified in writing immediately to confirm the joint sampling and record any refusal to seal these identical samples jointly with the carrier.

In some ports, the chief officer may be asked to sign paper labels that state the name of the ship, the shippers, the product, the ship's tank, the date and place of sampling, a seal number (such as the one to appear later on the wax seal) and the signature of shippers' inspectors before the loading operations have been completed or, sometimes, even before they have started. These labels are later attached to the sample containers after they have been filled and closed. This practice should be discouraged as the only way to be certain that the proper label is put on the proper sample container is for ship's personnel to participate in the whole procedure of sampling and sealing and to insist that the sealing and the labelling takes place on board the ship.

All labels should be properly dated and should indicate the local time when they were drawn, the name of the product and its destination, the name of the shippers and whether the sample was drawn jointly with them. The label should also record the quantity, tank number, the tank ullage and temperature, the B/L and voyage number and whether it is a manifold, pipeline, first run or average ship's tank sample after completion of loading. Care must be taken that all these details will remain legible by using permanent washable ink. Having signed the labels, the ship is entitled to retain a set of the samples.

19.5   Storage of Samples

Samples should be stored in a dark, well-ventilated place where daylight cannot enter and away from sources of heat and from living quarters and foodstuff storerooms. Edible oils and chemicals should be stored separately. Samples should be contained in clean, dry and airtight containers, preferably of glass, tinned steel or a plastic material that will not become affected by the contents. They should be closed with corks or suitable plastic stoppers.

A sample logbook should be maintained recording the sample number, the sampling date and place, ship's tank, quantity and kind of product, name of shipper and place of shipment, name of consignee and place of discharge, where stored on board and notes on disposal. Samples should be retained for a period of three months after the ship has discharged.

19.6   Sampling Instruments

Sampling instruments may be made of glass, stainless steel, aluminium, etc, and it is important to use an instrument made of a material that is compatible with the cargo being sampled. It is generally advisable to avoid instruments made of copper or copper-based alloys.

Sampling instruments should be simple, robust and easy to clean. Figures 19.1 to 19.4 illustrate sampling instruments for bulk oil shipments and some other liquid bulk cargoes. The Association is grateful to the British Standards Institution for allowing material from BS EN 627:1996 to be reproduced (Reference 32).

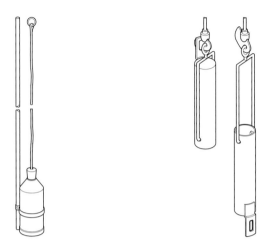

Figure 19.1: Sampling bottle or can.   **Figure 19.2: Sampling tipping dipper.**

The sampling bottle (Figure 19.1) is suitable for sampling large ships and tanks of liquid oil. It consists of a bottle or metal container, which may be weighted, attached to a handle long enough to reach the lowest part to be sampled. It has a removable stopper or top to which is attached a suitable chain, pole or cord. This device is lowered to the desired depth, where the stopper or top is removed and the container allowed to fill.

The tipping dipper (Figure 19.2) consists of a cylinder approximately 6 inches (150 mm) long and 2 inches (50 mm) in diameter, carrying an extension with a hole at its closed end and a stout wire handle at the open end. The handle carries a small metal catch and a rope. The cylinder is inverted in the position shown on the left, and maintained in that position by the insertion of the catch into the hole, and then sunk into the oil in the tank. At the required depth, the rope is twitched to release the catch, whereupon the cylinder rights itself and fills with oil.

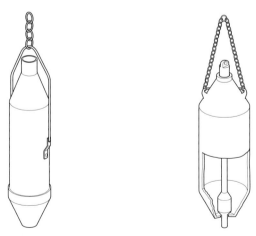

Figure 19.3: 'Go Devil' sampling bottle.   **Figure 19.4: Bottom, or zone, sampler.**

The 'Go Devil' (Figure 19.3) sampling bottle consists of a bottle, heavily weighted at the bottom, with a chain attached. When placed in oil in a tank, it drops so quickly that it does not begin to fill with oil until it reaches a fixed position.

The bottom sampler, or zone sampler, (Figure 19.4) is suitable for withdrawing bottom samples or zone samples at any level from tanks of liquid oil. To withdraw a bottom sample, the apparatus is attached to a cord or chain and lowered empty to the bottom of the tank. On contact with the bottom, the central spindle valve automatically opens and the container fills from the bottom. On withdrawal of the sampler, the valve automatically closes again. To withdraw samples at any level, the apparatus is lowered empty to the required level and then, by means of an additional cord attached to the top of the central valve spindle, the valve may be opened and the container filled. When the sampler has filled, the valve is allowed to close and the container is withdrawn.

Chapter 20 –
Flashpoint Contaminations
of Diesel Oil and Gas Oil

The bulk liquid trade has a history of flashpoint contamination, where high flashpoint cargo (eg diesel oil or gas oil) has been loaded into a tank that previously discharged a low flashpoint cargo, such as naphtha or gasoline. Such contamination can lead to significant delays and subsequent claims for flashpoint contamination of the 'first-foots' of a diesel oil or gas oil cargo.

When first-foots are contaminated, there is an inevitable dispute as to whether the ship can continue loading or whether the contaminated first-foots have to be discharged ashore.

If loading continues, after re-purging with inert gas, it will be hoped that the cargo can be blended back to within specification by dilution with sound cargo. This option is risky as, if the end result does not conform to the calculations undertaken, the ship now has a full flashpoint contaminated cargo on board.

Alternatively, the first-foots may be discharged ashore and the tanks re-purged with inert gas before resumption of loading. This option may lead to significant delays and possibly substantial demurrage disputes between owners and charterers.

20.1 Common Industry Practice

Several options are available to avoid contamination when preparing cargo tanks to load high flashpoint cargo following a discharge of low flashpoint cargo:

1. Cargo tanks are hot water washed (this is not essential but it speeds up the subsequent gas-freeing operation) and gas-freed for entry.

   This option avoids flashpoint contamination of the next cargo loaded and has the advantage of allowing entry for inspection of the cargo tanks.

   This option may not be available because of commercial pressure to load the next cargo as quickly as possible.

2. Cargo tanks are cold water washed, ensuring that all liquid lines are flushed in the process, with recovery of the seawater/oil slops into the vessel's slop tank(s).

   The seawater can then be decanted overboard, from the bottom of the oil/water mixture, before recovering the oil part of the slops into the vessel's oil retention tank, in compliance with Annex I of MARPOL 73/78 (Reference 30). All cargo tanks are then purged with further inert gas until the hydrocarbon content of the vapour phase is less than 2% by volume (ie the industry accepted standard).

3. The most common method is simply to purge each cargo tank with inert gas until the hydrocarbon content of the vapour phase is *'less than 2% by volume'*.

This option is popular because it is quicker and requires fewer personnel than options 1 and 2. However, if it is not carried out properly, it may result in subsequent claims for flashpoint contamination of the next cargo first-foots.

20.2 Hydrocarbon Content of the Vapour Spaces

After discharge of a cargo such as naphtha or gasoline, the cargo tank vapour spaces will contain a mixture of inert gas and predominantly C_{5+} (with some C_3 and C_4 present) hydrocarbon vapours.

Such hydrocarbon vapours are approximately twice as heavy as the inert gas vapours (consisting mostly of nitrogen). Given this disparity in density, it is inevitable that the hydrocarbon vapours will settle towards the bottom of each cargo tank.

The industry accepted standard with regard to flashpoint contamination is to purge cargo tank vapour spaces with inert gas until the hydrocarbon content is less than 2% by volume. This corresponds approximately to 100% of the lower explosive limit (LEL) of the hydrocarbon vapours present, but concerns flashpoint contamination criteria only.

It is often assumed that the dilution method of purging the cargo tanks with inert gas (using inlets at the top of the tank and venting from the top of the tanks) is sufficient to reduce the entire vapour space hydrocarbon content to less than 2% by volume. Unfortunately, this is not always the case and a layer of heavier density hydrocarbon vapour may remain in the bottom of the cargo tank. This layer of hydrocarbon vapour is absorbed into the first-foots of the next cargo loaded, resulting in flashpoint contamination.

If option 3 is the preferred option, the following operational procedures are recommended to ensure that the cargo tank vapour spaces are clear of hydrocarbon vapours (ie lower than 2% by volume) before loading the next high flashpoint cargo:

1. Ensure that all cargo lines and cargo tank sumps are completely clear of the previous low flashpoint cargo.

2. Set the cargo lines so that inert gas is delivered to the top of the tank (as per normal) but the tanks are vented to atmosphere from the bottom of the tanks. This can usually be achieved by opening the liquid lines to the liquid cargo manifolds and, if possible, connecting this outlet to the vent riser(s).

3. Start inerting and venting the bottom of the tanks to atmosphere via the liquid manifolds. This layering method is considered to be more economical than the dilution method and will ensure that all hydrocarbons are removed from the bottom layers of each cargo tank. 1 to 1½ volume changes should be sufficient for each tank.

4. Continue to inert gas purge each pair of wing tanks in turn until the purging operation is complete.

5. Take hydrocarbon readings from the middle and bottom (ie bottom 1 m level) and confirm that hydrocarbon readings are below 2% by volume.

Great care should be taken when using multigas detectors in inert gas atmospheres (usually with oxygen content below 5% by volume). Gas detectors that use *non-dispersive infrared (NDIR) detectors* can be used safely in inert gas atmospheres to give direct gas concentrations in both the *%Volume* and the *%LEL* modes. Some types of gas detector, however, operate using *dual catalytic sensors*. In the *%Volume* mode, with correction factors applied, they will give the correct gas concentrations. In the *%LEL* mode, however, these sensors can only be used in inert gas atmospheres that contain at least 10% by volume oxygen. They cannot be used in normal inert gas atmospheres (ie less than 5% by volume oxygen) and, if used in such circumstances, will give unreliably erratic readings.

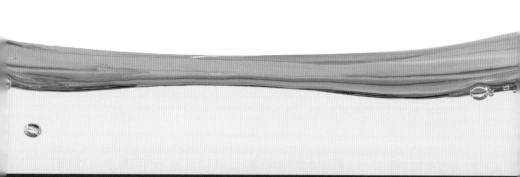

Chapter 21 –
Liquid Natural Oils, Fats and
Fatty Products

This chapter includes crude vegetable, animal and marine oils as well as fats. Some of the oils are edible and others are used in the production of soap, paint, lacquer, cosmetics and medicines. When these products are transported by sea, a variety of difficulties may be encountered, the causes of which generally fall into two categories:

- Handling (usually temperature control)
- contamination.

21.1   Handling

Claims frequently arise that involve allegations of unsatisfactory handling by ships. It is sometimes necessary to apply heat to these cargoes as the temperatures encountered during a sea voyage are likely to be lower than those recommended by the shippers. Many products of this type are adversely affected by heating, so some deterioration is inevitable. The extent of the damage depends on the nature of the product and the length of the voyage.

Unsatisfactory temperature control can cause additional deterioration, usually because the carrying temperature has been too high for all or part of the voyage. It is possible to estimate the level of unavoidable damage, so the extent of further damage caused by poor temperature control can be calculated.

Damage may also result if the carrying temperature is allowed to fall below that recommended by the shippers. The normal procedure for heating this type of product is through the use of heating coils at the tank bottoms and lower sides, with heat being transferred throughout the oil, mainly by convection current. The heat transfer becomes progressively less efficient as viscosity increases. The viscosity of liquid natural fatty products is greatly affected by temperature and a reduction of only a few degrees can have a serious effect. If the heating process is inadequate to maintain sufficient fluidity within the bulk of cargo, the liquid in the vicinity of the heating coils can become overheated.

During the discharge of cargo, if the environmental temperatures are very low, further problems may arise as a result of solidification, which most commonly occurs when a tank is almost empty and the liquid level has fallen below the level of the heating coils. Under such circumstances, the final residues may be removed by sweeping or by steam stripping, provided the receivers are able to accept the fat and water mixture that is produced. Ship's officers responsible for discharging heated products in cold climates should ensure that the maximum pumping rate is maintained and that there are no interruptions during discharge.

21.2   Contamination

The most common contaminant resulting in claims is water, originating from shore or ship tanks, pumps or lines at the time of loading, or introduced by mistake or due to leakage. Some products contain a significant quantity of water when shipped, but the presence of excess water in others may accelerate deterioration.

Traders and governmental authorities also have concerns about the contamination of edible products by traces of chemical substances. Often, but not always, these contaminants have come from residues of previous cargoes.

It is normal practice for samples to be drawn by independent surveyors during loading, or immediately after loading, and at least one set of these samples will be given to the ship. It is important that the ship has a set of loading samples, since most claims are based upon differences in analytical parameters in samples drawn at loading and discharge. If the Master is instructed to deliver a set of samples to the receivers on arrival at the discharge port, it is recommended that the Master requests that the shippers provide a second set of samples for the use of the shipowners. Any such samples handed to the ship should be properly stored during the voyage, preferably in a refrigerated store.

At the time of discharge, samples are always drawn by the receivers or their surveyors. Normal analyses conducted at both load ports and discharge ports are quite straightforward and the typical parameters determined are water, free fatty acid, unsaponifiable matter and odour. If there is evidence or suspicion that, on delivery, the cargo does not conform to either a specification or to the loading samples, more detailed chemical analysis may be performed. Contaminants can be identified and determined at levels as low as 10 parts per billion (ppb); contamination at this level will result from admixture of 10 g of contaminant with 1,000 T of cargo. Most chemical contaminant can be identified and determined at levels of 100 ppb, or 100 g per 1,000 T of cargo.

When cargo is loaded or transshipped, it is essential to consider the nature of previous cargoes. In some cases, it is virtually impossible during tank cleaning to remove all traces of previous cargo to a level that is not detectable by modern laboratory equipment. For this reason, restrictions are laid down in the contracts of sale regarding the immediate previous cargo carried in each of the ship's tanks. Shippers and charterers should be notified in good time of the nature of the three previous cargoes carried in each individual tank. The restrictions are imposed by such bodies as FOSFA (The Federation of Oils, Seeds and Fats Associations) and NIOP (National Institute of Oilseed Products) and their rules should always be checked for periodic updates.

It is important that, before loading, every care and attention is paid to the proper preparation of tanks, pumps and pipelines. It is very important that the tank coating is maintained to a high standard. The coating covering all sections of the tank must be sound because, where any breakdown of the coating takes place, particularly where epoxy and polyurethane coatings are concerned, there is a risk that the remains of previous cargoes may accumulate, creating a potential source of contamination. The breakdown of epoxy coating usually manifests itself in the form of open or closed blisters, forming pockets that cannot be reached by cleaning water. In these areas, there is also a risk that rust may form, which is again likely to trap cargo residues and lead to contamination.

It is not possible to properly clean tanks with damaged coatings. Cases have been recorded where traces of the third previous cargo have been found when samples of damaged coatings were tested.

Another possible source of contamination is the penetration and softening of epoxy and polyurethane coating by a previous cargo, which may later find its way into newly loaded products. Masters should always consult the cargo resistance list provided by the manufacturers of the tank coating, which will list cargoes to which the tank coating is resistant. For cargoes not included in the list, or for cargoes without resistance indicators, or when deviating from the maximum temperatures indicated on the list, the manufacturers should always be consulted.

Tank cleaning

The precise method of cleaning will depend on the previous cargo carried and the state of cleanliness required for the products to be loaded. The relevant tank cleaning guides should always be consulted. Generally, the most important part of the tank cleaning process is 'Butterworthing' with hot or cold seawater at sufficient pressure and at the appropriate tank levels. This should be followed by fresh water washing to remove seawater residues. Tanks that may have contained monomer or drying oils should first be washed with sufficient quantities of cold water to avoid polymerisation of cargo residues. In some cases, it is necessary to employ tank cleaning chemicals, but their use is generally limited as it may be difficult to dispose of slops.

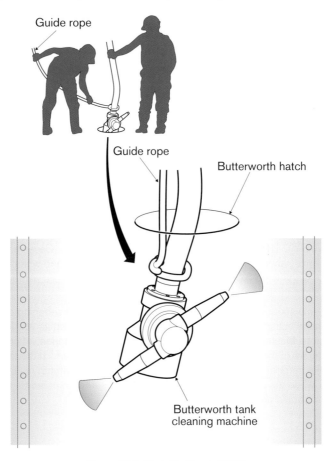

Figure 21.1: Tank 'Butterworthing'.

On completion, the tanks should be clean, dry and free from residual odours. It may also be desirable to take wall-wash samples and have them analysed for traces of previous cargoes, although this requires skilled inspectors. The presence of an odour in a tank that has been cleaned indicates the presence of cargo residues and also indicates the need for further cleaning. When checking for residual odours, it is advisable to do so after the tank has been closed for a period. In any case, checking should be carried out by personnel who have not been working in or near the tanks for at least one hour.

When cargo with a high melting point has been carried, tanks should be washed with hot water. If possible, steam should be used to ensure the residues are effectively melted and cleared. The cleaning process must also include the tank lines, tank lids and vent lines, including pressure vacuum valves and risers. Examples of cargoes with high melting points include phenol and waxes.

Cargo pumps, usually of the hydraulic deep well type, should be dismantled and inspected as recommended by the manufacturer. The pumps should be purged to test the seals that separate the cargo and the hydraulic oil from the void space in the pump. This procedure should always be followed after tank cleaning, before loading and discharging, and after repairs. The results should always be properly recorded in the ship's logbook or other formal records. Where defects to the seals are suspected, cargo should not be handled until corrective measures have been taken. When cleaning pumps, consideration must be paid to the trim of the ship to ensure that any contaminated product is properly drained away. Portable pumps should be tested before being lowered into the cargo tank.

If heating coils are not to be used, before loading commences they should be thoroughly purged and blanked both at the supply and the return ends. Even though coils may have been in use for some time, they should be pressure tested before loading to avoid the possibility of contamination through leaks that might have developed. Pumps not required for cargo handling should always be isolated.

Special attention should be paid to the cleanliness of vent lines, as they may contain residues of previous cargoes, both in a liquid and a solidified state. Vent lines, when not cleaned after discharge, may drain into a newly loaded tank when the vessel changes trim or when encountering heavy weather. Solidified cargo residues in a vent line may melt, due to the heat emitted from a heated cargo, and the melted product may drain back into the tank, causing contamination. The practice of steaming vent lines after the carriage of heated cargoes is recommended as blocked lines may result in overpressuring of cargo tanks.

Drain cocks fitted at the lowest parts of deck and manifold lines, as well as plugs at the bottom of cargo valves, should be opened and rinsed in order to remove any trapped cargo residues. These drain cocks may contain sufficient liquid to result in serious contamination. When clearing deck and drop lines, it is important to ensure that the dead ends of these lines and drop lines are not overlooked. They should be opened and thoroughly cleaned.

Mild steel tanks are sometimes used for the carriage of natural oils and fats but their use is in decline as cargo charterers more frequently stipulate the use of stainless steel or coated tanks. When used, mild steel tanks should be free from rust and scale, since remnants of previous cargoes are likely to be trapped and transferred into subsequently loaded cargoes. Where sensitive cargoes have been carried in mild steel tanks, contamination has been known to occur from the residues of hydrocarbon (petroleum products) cargoes.

The importance of proper tank cleaning procedures and the correct preparation of tanks and all related equipment prior to loading cannot be overemphasised. Masters may wish to consider appointing an independent surveyor to verify the condition of the tank coating, heating coils and hatch openings after the tank preparations have been completed.

On completion of loading, an ullage survey by an independent surveyor may be appropriate, and thereafter valves and hatches should be sealed. This process can be repeated at the discharge port. The practice of taking onboard samples at all stages of the loading and discharging operation is also highly recommended.

Should contamination occur at some stage in the course of transit, it may be possible, by analysis of such samples, to identify the source of contamination. By ensuring that the cargo is carried to the highest standards, the product should be well protected.

Chapter 22 –
Biofuels: Marine Transport, Handling and Storage Issues

The production and use of biofuels as transport fuels has increased significantly in recent years. A number of legislative reforms have mandated the integration of fuels derived from renewable sources into fuel infrastructure. However, the introduction of biofuels has not been without problems and there is considerable research still ongoing into the properties of biofuels and how they behave when blended with conventional fossil fuels.

Generally, the USA and Brazil are the two largest producers of biofuels, mostly ethanol and fatty acid methyl esters (FAME). The EU also has a significant production of hydrotreated vegetable oil (HVO).

22.1 Legislative Targets

Biofuels were originally seen as one answer to the problems of increasing greenhouse gas (GHG) emissions and global warming. Biofuels are produced from renewable sources such as corn, wheat, rapeseed and soya beans, which can be quickly and easily regrown.

Figure 22.1: Potential sources of biofuel.

However, questions were soon raised with regard to the environmental credentials and overall sustainability of commercially available biofuels. Issues included the use of crops that would normally be used for food being put into biofuel production, the questionable CO_2 emissions savings when considering the overall production process, deforestation to make way for biofuel crop plantations and the use of environmentally harmful fertilisers and pesticides employed in growing the crop feedstock.

Amid these growing concerns, as an example of State legislative change, the UK government has amended the targets set out in the *Renewable Transport Fuel Obligation* (RTFO), a directive aimed at reducing GHG emissions from road transport. This legislation has been periodically amended several times since 2007. As of 1st January 2022, it mandates that 13.5% of fuel oil supplied in the UK must be from renewable energy sources (Reference 33). It also aims for this obligation to reach 21% from 2032 onwards.

Annual figures show that the total volume of all UK sourced biofuels used in the UK in 2020 was 293 million litres/kilograms (biogases such as biomethane and biopropane are reported in kg). This was a 5% increase on the 2019 figure. Of this, the volume of UK sourced biodiesel for UK road transport was at 126 million litres and for bioethanol, the figure was 116 million litres.

22.2 Current Types of Biofuel

There are currently two main classes of biofuels in widespread use; biodiesel (or, more correctly, FAME) and bioethanol. The two are very different in their properties and so there are different associated issues to consider if they are to be safely shipped, handled, stored and used.

22.2.1 FAME/Biodiesel

Biodiesel is a fuel derived from vegetable oils or animal fats, and is more correctly called fatty acid methyl esters (FAME). FAME is the product of reacting a vegetable oil or animal fat with an alcohol (methanol, a petrochemical that is generally derived from natural gas or coal) in a process known as transesterification. When compared to conventional diesel derived from crude oil, vegetable oils and animal fats generally have higher viscosities (which means they are more difficult to pump and store without heating) and are more unstable (which means they are more likely to degrade during storage, handling and end use). The transesterification process brings the properties of the raw materials closer to those of a conventional diesel, making the product more suitable for use as a road transport fuel. However, while the FAME produced can be used neat as a fuel, it is more commonly blended with conventional petroleum diesel for use in diesel engines.

ASTM International has described a system of nomenclature for naming FAME/diesel blends (see ASTM D6751) (Reference 34). Pure FAME is denoted B100, representing 100% biodiesel (of which there are four sub-grades). Other common blends include B5 (5% biodiesel and 95% conventional diesel), B7 (the EN 590 European diesel standard allows up to 7% by volume FAME in diesel) and B20 (20% biodiesel and 80% conventional diesel).

Raw materials for FAME production

Various raw materials (feedstocks) may be used for the production of FAME, including palm oil, coconut oil, rapeseed oil, soya bean oil, tallow and used cooking oils. A general FAME cargo might be the product of processing any one of these raw materials or may be a mixture of FAMEs produced from different raw materials. Each raw material would produce FAME of a different chemical composition, with correspondingly different characteristics. For example, a FAME derived from palm oil (PME) is likely to be solidified at normal UK winter temperatures, whereas a FAME derived from rapeseed oil (RME) will be a liquid.

Figure 22.2: Examples of FAME.

One of the most important chemical characteristics of FAME is the structure and composition of the fatty acid methyl ester groups, which will be determined by the fatty acid components of the raw material used in the production process.

FAME types composed of a relatively high proportion of saturated fatty acid methyl esters, such as palm oil derived FAME (denoted PME), will generally be relatively stable to unwanted degradation reactions, but will have poorer cold temperature performance. FAME types composed of a relatively high proportion of unsaturated fatty acid methyl esters, such as soya bean oil derived FAME (denoted SME), will display markedly different behaviour, with better cold temperature properties in comparison to PME, but less stability to degradation reactions.

The presence and composition of other chemical constituents is also important. For example, FAMEs with high levels of vitamin E are thought to be more stable in terms of unwanted oxidative degradation reactions.

22.2.2   FAME Problems

Water contamination

A major problem with regard to the carriage of FAME by sea is the issue of water contamination. FAME is a hygroscopic material, which means that it will absorb water from its surrounding environment, including the atmosphere. This renders FAME very sensitive to water contamination. The current maximum allowable water content in the European EN 14214 and American ASTM D6751 FAME standards is 500 mg/kg, although selling specifications are often lower (300 mg/kg being a typical maximum water content on a sales specification), reflecting the high potential for water pick-up in this material (References 34 and 35).

Figure 22.3: FAME cargoes are extremely sensitive to water contamination, the source of which can be seawater taken in during heavy weather.

Unlike most conventional diesels, in which any undissolved water present will generally settle out over a period of time, FAME can hold water in suspension up to relatively high levels (above 1,000 mg/kg). Apart from the fact this will render the cargo off-specification for water content, the presence of water can promote unwanted hydrolytic reactions, breaking down the FAME to form free fatty acids. These fatty acids not only affect certain specification parameters for the material, but are also corrosive and may attack exposed metal surfaces. Additionally, once a certain threshold level of water content is reached, water can separate out from the FAME, forming a separate (and potentially corrosive) free water phase. The possibility of phase separation occurring is greater for blends of FAME and conventional diesel.

The presence of a FAME/water interface provides ideal conditions for the promotion of unwanted microbiological growth, which may in turn lead to filter blocking and corrosion problems.

Some publications have referenced the greater degree of biodegradability of FAME as a positive factor when dealing with environmental spillages. While this is correct, it also means that FAME is considerably more prone to microbiological attack than a conventional fossil fuel.

Possible sources of water contamination on board a ship range from the obvious, such as seawater ingress or residues of tank washing operations, to the less obvious, for example, moisture in an inert gas blanket produced from a faulty flue gas generating system, or atmospheric humidity in tank ullage spaces that are not under a positive pressure of dry inert gas. Despite having relatively high flashpoints, FAME cargoes are generally carried under a (dry) nitrogen blanket to avoid the potential increase in water due to absorption of moisture from tank ullage spaces.

Stability problems
FAMEs are generally more prone to issues with regard to their stability than conventional petroleum diesel. FAME can degrade under the influence of air, heat, light and water, and this may occur during transport, storage or even during end use. FAME cargoes may display different levels of stability depending on their composition and the feedstock(s) used in their production.

Potential shipping problems include the promotion of degradation reactions by trace metals, as copper heating coils or zinc-containing tank coatings have the potential to cause deterioration in quality. Thermal stability issues may arise if the FAME cargoes are stored next to heated tanks, for example bunker settling tanks. Issues with the promotion of instability by the presence of trace metals are worse for B100 than for lower biodiesel blends such as B5 or B20. Degradation reactions can form insoluble sediments and gums that may increase the viscosity of the FAME, leading to filter blocking, or they may potentially further decompose to other more corrosive species.

Low temperature behaviour
Certain FAMEs form waxy precipitates at low temperatures, which will then not redissolve when the product is reheated, although this appears to be an uncommon problem. However, there is the potential for FAME cargoes shipped from a warm, humid climate to extremely cold conditions, if the correct measures for heating the cargo are not applied, to form unwanted waxy precipitates that may lead to specification failure or pumping problems. It is, therefore, vital that the correct heating instructions are issued and followed. An understanding of the nature of the FAME will inform the necessary heating instructions.

FOSFA (The Federation of Oils, Seeds and Fats Associations Ltd) has now included FAME products in its published heating recommendations (Reference 36):

Oil type	Temperature during voyage		Temperature at discharge	
	Min (°C)	Max (°C)	Min (°C)	Max (°C)
FAME from maize/rapeseed/ soya/sunflower	Ambient		Ambient	
FAME from coconut/palm/palm kernel/tallow	25	30	30	40

Table 22.1: FOSFA heating recommendations for FAME products.

FAME contamination of jet fuel

FAME is a surface active material and can adsorb onto the walls of tanks or pipelines and de-adsorb into subsequently carried products. This may be an issue where multiproduct pipelines or storage tanks are utilised, or where ships carry jet fuel cargoes after carrying FAME/diesel blends.

In May 2008, a number of jet fuel storage tanks at Kingsbury supply terminal and Birmingham Airport were quarantined after it was discovered that samples of the jet fuel in question contained up to 20 ppm of FAME. The cause of the contamination is thought to have been as a result of mixing of jet fuel with B5 diesel in the distillate manifold at Kingsbury terminal. As an indication of the very small quantities needed to cause such contamination, the 5 ppm specification limit would be equivalent to just 1 litre of B5 diesel in 10,000 litres of jet fuel.

When ships may potentially carry jet fuel cargoes following on from FAME or FAME/diesel blends, care must be taken with tank cleaning and flushing and draining of common lines, including sea or jetty loading lines. Switching from a B5 to jet fuel requires at least a hot water tank wash (but preferably also an intermediate FAME-free cargo) to remove FAME residue. Switching from neat FAME to jet fuel requires particular care and some advocate at least three intermediate (FAME free) cargoes plus a hot water wash before loading jet fuel. Jet fuels from a marine terminal storage tank do not require testing for FAME contamination where it can be confirmed that there is no FAME in the marine supply system. Where there is direct knowledge that any diesel on board, or any diesel having any interface with the jet fuel, is B0, and the ship has not carried biodiesel within the last three loads, then the jet fuel may be exempted from testing.

The industry guidelines for the prevention of FAME contamination of aviation jet fuel are as follows[1]:

I. Three intermediate cargoes with a <u>no</u> FAME content between a FAME B100 (100%) cargo or any cargo with a FAME content greater than 15% (above B15) and a subsequent aviation jet fuel cargo.

---

[1] Source: *The Energy Institute Guidelines for the cleaning of tanks and lines for marine tank vessels carrying petroleum and refined products (HM 50) – Section 2.12.7* (Reference 39). While not a legal requirement, these guidelines are based on sensible practice and owners should give serious consideration to adopting such advice.

II. When following cargo with a FAME content of 5% or less (B5 or below), a hot water wash, including flushing of pumps and lines, followed by draining is recommended as a minimum.

III. When following cargo with a FAME content of 15% (B15) or less but above B5, a hot water wash, including flushing of pumps and lines, followed by draining is recommended as a minimum. Tanks must be in good condition and washing needs to be particularly stringent. A single intermediate cargo with no FAME content is suggested as an alternative, followed by a hot water wash, including flushing of pumps and lines, and by draining.

The UK Ministry of Defence Standard 91-91 (Reference 37) states that the maximum permitted level of FAME is 50 mg/kg. It is also suggested that the currently specified method of flushing sample containers three times for jet fuel samples may not be sufficient to remove traces of FAME, which may even be transferred from contaminated gloves. This could potentially lead to false positive detection of FAME in actually on-specification material, resulting in erroneous claims being made. It is therefore recommended that new sample containers and new gloves are used when sampling jet fuel cargoes.

> For product tankers carrying multiple products, the danger of inadvertently contaminating a cargo of jet fuel with traces of FAME is a very real risk, even if it does not initially appear that there is any potential for cross contamination to occur. For example, ultra-low sulphur diesel meeting the EN 590 specification may appear in the shipping documents as ULSD, which would not immediately indicate that the product contained any FAME. However, the EN 590 diesel specification allows up to 7% by volume FAME content (Reference 38). If the ship's tanks and lines are not completely stripped of all the ULSD prior to loading a cargo of jet fuel, the quantity of ULSD containing 7% FAME needed to render the jet fuel cargo off-specification would be very small.

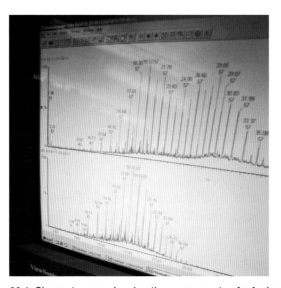

Figure 22.4: Chromatogram showing the components of a fuel cargo.

Solvent behaviour

FAME has the ability to act as a solvent, taking up any organic residue, dirt or scale that may have accumulated on the surfaces of tanks or pipelines. This may have the effect of cleaning out the dirty storage or pumping systems, but it will contaminate the FAME itself and may lead to subsequent fouling of filters or pump blockages.

FAME is known to attack and quicken the ageing process of certain materials, including elastomers (elastic materials that may be used as seals, valves, gaskets, etc). Materials should be checked for compatibility with FAME and FAME/diesel blends by consultation with the equipment manufacturer.

Biodiesel in bunkers

In 2017, the sixth edition of the marine fuels international standard, ISO 8217:2017 (Reference 40), was issued. The third edition of the marine fuels standard, ISO 8217:2005, required under point 5.1 of Section 5 that the fuels to be classified in accordance with the standard should be "*homogeneous blends of hydrocarbons derived from petroleum refining*". This was interpreted as precluding fuel from containing any bio-derived components. During preparation of the fourth edition of the standard, the working group committee considered the topic of biodiesel and the potential for the material to find its way into the marine fuel supply chain. It concluded that it was almost inevitable that, as a result of blending FAME into automotive diesel, some marine distillates and possibly even marine residual fuels would contain a proportion of FAME as a result of cross contamination within the distribution system.

As such, ISO 8217:2012 required, under point 5.4 of Section 5, that "*The fuel shall be free from bio-derived materials other than 'de minimis' levels of FAME (FAME shall be in accordance with the requirements of EN 14214 or ASTM D6751). In the context of this International Standard, 'de minimis' means an amount that does not render the fuel unacceptable for use in marine applications. The blending of FAME shall not be allowed.*"

The current standard, ISO 8217:2017, retains this *de minimis* level requirement but with a wider tolerance to a level of approximately 0.5 volume % FAME and with additional specifications (DF grades) for distillate marine fuels (Reference 40).

Figure 22.5: Bunkering vessel supplying fuel to a cruise ship.

Annex A of the current standard (Reference 40), considers the issue of bio-derived products and FAMEs finding their way into marine fuels in more detail. It states that, notwithstanding the fact that FAME has "*good ignition and lubricity properties together with perceived environmental benefits, there are potentially specific complications with respect to the storage and handling of distillates with a FAME component in a marine environment, such as:*

- *A tendency to oxidation and long-term storage issues*
- *an affinity to water and risk of microbial growth*
- *degraded low-temperature flow properties, and*
- *FAME material deposition on exposed surfaces, including filter elements.*"

It is recognised that there are a number of differently sourced FAME products, each with their own particular characteristics, which may impact upon storage, handling, treatment, engine operations and emissions.

The standard states that in "*... those instances where the use of fuels containing FAME is being contemplated, it should be ensured that the ship's storage, handling, treatment, service and machinery systems, together with any other machinery components (such as oily-water separator systems), are in terms of materials and operational performance* *compatible with such a product. Contact of materials such as bronze, brass, copper, lead, tin and zinc with FAME should be avoided as these may oxidize FAME thereby creating sediments."*

Figure 22.6: Ethanol biorefinery.

22.2.3   Bioethanol

Bioethanol is ethanol produced by the fermentation of renewable sources of sugar or starch crops. Unlike FAME, bioethanol is a single chemical compound, the properties of which are well documented and understood. It is a volatile, colourless liquid that is miscible with water and is hygroscopic. Ethanol is the alcohol found in alcoholic beverages and is also commonly used as a solvent in perfumes, medicines and paints. However, the most common use for ethanol is as a fuel or fuel-additive. Ethanol for use as a fuel is generally dosed with a 'denaturant' to render it unsuitable for human consumption.

There is significant experience worldwide in the use of ethanol as a fuel or fuel-additive. In the USA, there has been over 10 years' successful use of gasoline containing up to 10% ethanol (E10) and in Brazil blends containing up to 85 to 100% ethanol (E85 and E100) are commonly used in flexible-fuel vehicles. The current European gasoline specification, EN 228, allows up to 10% ethanol by volume (E10) (Reference 41). However, in practice, many EU States continue to use up to 5% (E5).

Bioethanol can be produced from a number of raw materials, but they do not impart the same variation in the properties of the end product fuel as is the case with FAME. However, there are still a number of potential hazards for consideration.

22.2.4   Bioethanol Problems

Water contamination
An issue during the carriage of bioethanol and bioethanol-gasoline blends is the potential for water contamination, because ethanol is hygroscopic and highly soluble

in water. Small quantities of water can be dissolved in gasoline/bioethanol blends but, depending on temperature and the gasoline/bioethanol blend ratio, there is a critical threshold level of water that can be dissolved. Once this threshold level has been exceeded, irreversible phase separation will occur where the water causes the ethanol to separate from the gasoline, forming an alcohol rich water/ethanol aqueous phase and an alcohol poor gasoline phase. The alcohol rich aqueous phase will collect at the bottom of the ship's tank or storage tank.

This phase is likely to be highly corrosive and it will not be able to be used as fuel. In addition, if such phase separation does occur, it is possible that the gasoline phase will be classed as *Pollution Category Z*, which means that it is considered to present a *"minor hazard to either marine resources or human health"* if discharged into the sea from tank cleaning or deballasting operations and therefore *"justifies less stringent restrictions on the quality and quantity of the discharge into the marine environment"* (Reference 30). While the regulations do not require ethanol to be carried on a chemical tanker, ethanol is generally shipped on chemical tankers to maintain the integrity of the product.

It should be noted that the terms biodiesel and bioethanol do not appear in the IBC Code (Reference 42). As it is a requirement that the proper shipping name is used to describe any product to be carried that appears in the IBC Code, these terms cannot be used to describe the products being carried.

The situation becomes more confusing when considering how blends of conventional fossil fuels and biofuels are shipped and which Annex of MARPOL they fall under. MARPOL Annex I covers the prevention of pollution by oil and MARPOL Annex II covers the control of pollution by noxious liquid substances carried in bulk (Reference 30). Blends of biofuels and conventional fuels are essentially mixtures of mineral oil based hydrocarbons and noxious liquid substances. The IMO has issued guidelines on biofuels. MSC-MEPC.2/Circ.17 contains *Guidelines for the Carriage of Blends of Biofuels and MARPOL Annex I Cargoes* and was approved in June 2019 (Reference 43). It replaced and revoked an earlier circular (MEPC.1/Circ.761/Rev.1) regarding blends of biofuels and petroleum fuels.

MSC-MEPC.2/Circ.17 contains consequential amendments that reflect the new Annex 12 on energy-rich fuels in the MEPC.2/Circular on Provisional categorization of liquid substances in accordance with MARPOL Annex II and the IBC Code, as well as making reference to SOLAS Regulation VI/5.2. Specifically, the physical blending on board of biofuels and MARPOL Annex I cargoes during a sea voyage to create new products is now prohibited. Circ.17 also defines the following cargo bands:

Band 1: When the biofuel blend contains 75% or more petroleum oil (ie 25% or less biofuel) – the product is carried as a MARPOL Annex I cargo. Oil discharge monitoring equipment (ODME) should be approved/certified for the mixture carried or tank residues and alcohol resistant fire-fighting foams should be used when more than 5% ethyl alcohol blends are used.

Band 2: When the biofuel blends contain more than 1% but less than 75% petroleum oil (ie more than 25% and less than 99% biofuel) – the product is carried as a MARPOL Annex II cargo. A list of existing blends and corresponding IMO IBC carriage requirements is set out in Chapter 17 of the IBC Code. Carriage requirements for new blends of biofuels identified as falling under the scope of MARPOL Annex II will be incorporated into List 1 of the MEPC.2/Circular, as appropriate.

Band 3: Biofuels blended with 1% or less petroleum oil – the products are not considered as blends and are therefore to be shipped in accordance with MARPOL Annex II, under the appropriate product entry in the IBC Code.

22.2.5   Handing and Usage on Board

For use on board as a fuel, separation and purification is still required. The separation temperature will be determined based on the analysis report, which is the same as for Very Low Sulphur Fuel Oil (VLSFO). Difficulty may be experienced in managing the temperature so that it is neither too cold (causing undesirable cold flow properties) nor too warm (causing ageing of the fuel and low viscosity for the engine). This level will be different for every individual fuel, which may increase the level of difficulty for engineers. However, it is also worth noting that VLSFO may still have aluminium/silicon/water present, therefore purification remains essential.

While biofuel is compatible with low sulphur fuel oil, it should never be mixed on board. Instead it must come from a reputable bunker supplier who will supply a stable blend to the ship.

To manage the issue of waxing, it is recommended to keep the temperature in the tank above the waxing point. If this is not possible a purifier can be used to circulate, provided that it has a heater. Again, depending on storage time and temperature, the fuel might age.

Biofuel should always be used as soon as possible. It is also recommended to dewater the bunker tanks, as water contributes to bacterial growth.

Additives
The use of additives is not typically recommended with biofuels since the effect can be unpredictable. Antioxidants and middle distillate flow improvers may be an option, but these should not be blended routinely on board.

Part 7 –

The Carriage of Gas

Chapter 23 –
Liquefied Gases

A liquefied gas is a gaseous substance at ambient temperature and pressure, that is liquefied by pressurisation or refrigeration and sometimes a combination of the two. Virtually all liquefied gases are hydrocarbons and flammable in nature. Liquefaction compresses the gas into volumes suited to international carriage. The principal gas cargoes are liquefied natural gas (LNG) (see Chapter 24), liquefied petroleum gas (LPG), and a variety of petrochemical gases, each associated with specific hazards. By regulation, all liquefied gases when transported in bulk must be carried on a gas carrier, as defined by the IMO. The IMO's Gas Codes (see Section 23.3) provide a list of safety precautions and design features required for each product.

23.1 LPG

LPG covers butane or propane or a mixture of the two. The main use for these products varies from country to country, but sizeable volumes are used as power station or refinery fuels. However, LPG is also sought after as a bottled cooking gas and it can form a feedstock at chemical plants. It is also used as an aerosol propellant and is added to gasoline as a vapour pressure enhancer. LPG may be carried in either a pressurised or refrigerated state. Occasionally, it may be carried in a special type of carrier known as a semi-pressurised ship. When fully refrigerated, butane is carried at minus 5°C (–5°C) and propane at minus 42°C (–42°C). The low carriage temperature required for propane introduces the need for special low temperature (LT) steels.

23.2 Chemical and Other Gases

Ammonia is one of the most common chemical gases and it is carried worldwide in large volumes, mainly for agricultural purposes. It has particularly toxic qualities and requires great care during handling and carriage.

Another important liquefied gas is ethylene. Very sophisticated ships are available for this product as carriage temperatures are minus 104°C (−104°C) and onboard systems require a high degree of expertise. Within this group, a subset of highly specialised ships is able to carry multigrades simultaneously.

The recent exploitation of shale gas has brought an increase in LPG and ethane production, as by-products. Ethane may be used as an alternative to naphtha or LPG as a feedstock for the chemical industry. Liquefied ethane, with a temperature close to minus 89°C (−89°C) at atmospheric pressure, has typically been shipped in small ethylene/ethane carriers. The design characteristics of the cargo containment system for the ships in this trade is in the region of 27,500 to 35,000 m³. The economies of scale needed for a profitable global trade typically require ethane to be shipped in large volumes. The largest VLEC in the world, *'Pacific Ineos Belstaff'*, has a capacity of 99,000 m³ and was built at the end of 2021. It is designed with Type B tanks which can carry LPG, ethylene and ethane.

Significant in the design and operation of all gas carriers is that methane (the main constituent of LNG) vapour is lighter than air, while LPG vapours are heavier than air. For this reason, the current gas carrier regulations allow only methane to be used as a propulsion fuel, with any minor gas seepage in engine spaces being naturally ventilated. With the adoption in January 2017 by the IMO of the *International Code of Safety for Ships Using Gases or Other Low-flashpoint Fuels* (IGF Code) (Reference 44), it has become increasingly likely that LPG will be used as propulsion fuel on future vessels. It is a sulphur-free fuel type, which makes compliance with the latest emission regulations feasible.

The principal hydrocarbon gases such as butane, propane and methane are non-toxic in nature. A comparison of the relative hazards of oils and gases is provided in Table 23.1.

Hazard	Gases		Oils	
	LNG	LPG	Gasoline	Fuel oil
Toxic	No	No	Yes	Yes
Carcinogenic	No	No	Yes	Yes
Asphyxiant	Yes (in confined spaces)	Yes (in confined spaces)	No	No
Others	Low temperature	Moderately low temperature	Eye irritant, narcotic, nausea	Eye irritant, narcotic, nausea
Flammability limits in air (%)	5 to 15	2 to 10	1 to 6	Not applicable
Storage pressure	Atmospheric	Often pressurised	Atmospheric	Atmospheric
Behaviour if spilt	Evaporates forming a visible 'cloud' that disperses readily and is non-explosive, unless contained	Evaporates forming an explosive vapour cloud	Forms a flammable pool which, if ignited, would burn with explosive force; environmental clean-up may be required	Forms a flammable pool; environmental clean-up is required

Table 23.1: Comparative hazards of some liquefied gases and oils.

23.2.1   The Liquefied Gas Fleet

The fleet of liquefied gas carriers of over 1,000 m³ capacity can be divided into the following types:

- Pressurised LPG carriers
- semi-refrigerated LPG carriers (including ethylene)
- fully refrigerated LPG carriers
- LNG carriers
- LNG FSRUs.

Chapter 24 describes the liquefied natural gas (LNG) carrier in more detail.

The sealed nature of liquefied gas cargoes, in tanks completely segregated from oxygen or air, virtually excludes any possibility of a tank explosion. However, the idea of the unsafe ship lingers, and some administrations and Port State Control (PSC) organisations tend to target gas carriers for special inspection whenever they enter harbour.

However, serious accidents related to gas carrier cargoes have been few and the gas carrier's safety record is acknowledged as an industry leader. As an illustration of the robustness of gas carriers, when the *'Gaz Fountain'* was hit by rockets during the Iran/Iraq War in the 1980s, despite penetration of the containment system with huge jet fires, the fires were successfully extinguished and the ship, together with most of the cargo, was salved.

The relative safety of the gas carrier is due to a number of features. One such, almost unique to the class, is that cargo tanks are always kept under positive pressure (sometimes just a small overpressure) and this prevents air entering the cargo system. This means that only liquid cargo or vapour can be present, so a flammable atmosphere cannot exist in the cargo system. In addition, all large gas carriers use a closed loading system with no venting to atmosphere, and a vapour return line (VRL) to the shore is often fitted and used where required.

In 2016, the world's first compressed natural gas (CNG) carrier was launched.

23.3   Regulation of Gas Carrier Design

The regulations for the design and construction of gas carriers stem from practical ship designs codified by the IMO. However, all new ships (from June 1986) are built to the *International Code for the Construction and Equipment of Ships Carrying Liquefied Gases in Bulk* (the IGC Code) (Reference 45). This code also defines cargo properties and documentation provided to the ship (the Certificate of Fitness for the Carriage of Liquefied Gases in Bulk) and shows the cargo grades the ship can carry. In particular, this takes into account temperature limitations imposed by the metallurgical properties of the materials making up the containment and piping systems. It also considers the reactions between various gases and the elements of construction, not only for tanks but also related to pipeline and valve fittings. The IGC Code, adopted by the IMO in 2014, applies to all new ships built (having their keel laid) after 1st July 2016. The latest 2016 edition includes corrections and a supplement added in 2019.

When the IGC Code was produced, an intermediate code was also developed by the IMO – the *Code for the Construction and Equipment of Ships Carrying Liquefied Gases in Bulk* (the GC Code) (Reference 46). This covers ships built between 1977 and 1986.

Gas carriers were in existence before IMO codification and ships built before 1977 are defined as 'existing ships' within the meaning of the rules. To cover these ships, a voluntary code was devised, again by the IMO – the *Code for Existing Ships Carrying Liquefied Gases in Bulk* (the EGC Code) (Reference 47). Despite its voluntary status, virtually all ships remaining in the fleet that are of this age, and because of longevity programmes there are still quite a number, have certification in accordance with the EGC Code.

23.4 Design of Gas Carriers

Cargo carriage in the pressurised fleet comprises double cargo containment. All other gas carriers are built with a double-hull structure and the distance of the inner hull from the outer is defined in the Gas Codes. This spacing introduces a vital safety feature to mitigate the consequences of collision and grounding.

A principal feature of gas carrier design is therefore double containment and an internal hold. The cargo tanks, more generally referred to as the cargo containment system, are installed in the hold, often as a completely separate entity from the ship, ie not part of the ship's structure or its strength members. This is a distinctive difference between gas carriers and oil tankers or chemical carriers.

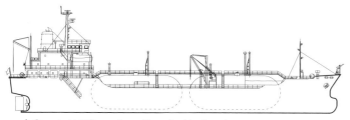

a) Coastal LPG carrier with cylindrical tanks

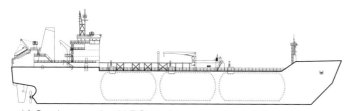

b) Semi-pressurised LPG carrier

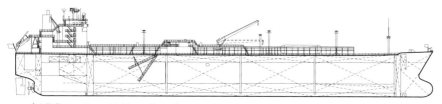

c) LPG carrier with Type A tanks

Figure 23.1: Gas carrier types.

Cargo tanks may be of the independent self-supporting type or of a membrane design. Self-supporting tanks are defined in the IGC Code as being of Type A, Type B or Type C. Type A containment comprises box-shaped or prismatic tanks (ie shaped to fit the hold). Type B comprises tanks where fatigue life and crack propagation analyses have shown improved characteristics. Such tanks are usually spherical but occasionally may be of prismatic types. Type C tanks are pure pressure vessels, often spherical or cylindrical, but sometimes bi-lobe in shape to minimise broken stowage.

The fitting of one system in preference to another tends towards particular trades. For example, Type C tanks are suited to small volume carriage. They are therefore found most often on coastal or regional craft. Large international LPGCs will normally be fitted with Type A tanks.

Type B tanks and tanks following membrane principles are found mainly within the LNG fleet and will be discussed in Chapter 24.

23.4.1 The Pressurised Fleet

Figure 23.1a) shows a small fully pressurised LPGC. Regional and coastal cargoes are often carried in such craft, with the cargo fully pressurised at ambient temperature. The tanks are built as pure pressure vessels without the need for any extra metallurgical consideration appropriate to colder temperatures. Design pressures are usually for propane (about 20 bar) as this form of LPG has the highest vapour pressure at ambient temperature. The ship design comprises the outer hull and an inner hold containing the pressure vessels. These rest in saddles built into the ship's structure. Double bottoms and other spaces act as water ballast tanks and, if problems are to develop with age, the ballast tanks are prime candidates. These ships are the most numerous class, comprising approximately 40% of the fleet. They are relatively simple in design but strong in construction. Cargo operations involve cargo transfer by flexible hose and, in certain areas, ship to ship transfer operations from larger refrigerated ships operating internationally are commonplace.

Figure 23.2: Pressurised LPGC with cylindrical tanks.

23.4.2 The Semi-pressurised Fleet

In these ships, sometimes referred to as semi-refrigerated, the cargo is carried in pressure vessels that are usually bi-lobe in cross-section, designed for operating pressures of up to 7 bar. The tanks are constructed of special grade steel suitable for the cargo carriage temperature and the tanks are insulated to minimise heat input to the cargo. The cargo boils off causing generation of vapour, which is reliquefied by refrigeration and returned to the cargo tanks. The required cargo temperature and pressure are maintained by the reliquefaction plant.

These ships are usually larger than the fully pressurised types and have cargo capacities of up to about 20,000 m³. As with the fully pressurised ship, the cargo tanks are of pressure vessel construction and similarly located well inboard of the ship's side while protected by double-bottom ballast tanks. This arrangement results in a very robust and inherently buoyant ship.

Figure 23.3: Semi-pressurised LPGC.

23.4.3 The Ethylene Fleet

Ethylene is the primary building block of the petrochemicals industry and is used in the production of polyethylene, ethylene dichloride, ethanol, styrene, glycols and many other products. Storage is usually as a fully refrigerated liquid at minus 104°C (–104°C).

Ships designed for ethylene carriage also fall into the semi-pressurised class. They are relatively few in number but are among the most sophisticated ships afloat. In the more advanced designs, they can carry several grades. Typically, this range can extend to ethane, LPG, ammonia, propylene butadiene and vinyl chloride monomer (VCM), all featuring on their certificate of fitness. To aid in this process, several independent cargo systems coexist on board to avoid cross contamination of the cargoes, particularly for the reliquefaction process.

The ships range in size from about 2,000 to 15,000 m³, although several larger ships now trade in ethylene. Ship design usually includes independent cargo tanks (Type C) and these may be cylindrical or bi-lobe in shape, constructed from stainless steel. An inert gas generator is provided to produce dry inert gas or dry air. The generator is used for inerting and for dehydration of the cargo system and the interbarrier spaces during the voyage, when condensation can occur on cold surfaces creating unwanted build-ups of ice. Deck tanks are normally provided for changeover of cargoes.

The hazards associated with the cargoes involved arise from the temperature, toxicity and flammability. The safety of ethane carriers is critical, requiring good management and rigorous personnel training.

Ethane carriers may be seen as a subset of the ethylene fleet and ethane can be carried by ships designed to carry ethylene. The new VLEC class (see Section 23.2) are constructed with a reinforced membrane cargo containment system, similar to that used in LNG carriers.

23.4.4 The Fully Refrigerated Fleet

Figure 23.4: Fully refrigerated LPGC.

These are generally large ships, up to about 85,000 m³ cargo capacity, with those above 70,000 m³ designated as VLGCs. Many in the intermediate range (30,000 to 60,000 m³) are suitable for carrying the full range of hydrocarbon liquid gas, from butane to propylene, and may be equipped to also carry chemical liquid gases such as ammonia. Cargoes are carried at near ambient pressure and at temperatures down to minus 48°C (–48°C). Reliquefaction plants are fitted (to manage boil-off) with a substantial reserve plant capacity provided. The cargo tanks do not have to withstand high pressures and are, therefore, generally of the freestanding prismatic type. The tanks are robustly stiffened internally and constructed of special low temperature resistant steel.

All ships have substantial double-bottom spaces and some have side ballast tanks. In all cases, the cargo tanks are protectively located inboard. The ship's structure surrounding or adjacent to the cargo tanks is also of special grade steel and this forms a secondary barrier to safely contain any cold cargo should it leak from the cargo tanks.

All cargo tanks, whether of the pressure vessel type or rectangular, are provided with safety relief valves amply sized to relieve boil-off in the absence of reliquefaction and even in conditions of surrounding fire.

Figure 23.5: LNG carrier with membrane tanks.

23.5 Crew Training and Numbers

The IMO has laid down a series of training standards for gas carrier crews that are additional to normal certification. These dangerous cargo endorsements are detailed in the STCW Convention (Reference 48). Courses are divided into the basic course for junior officers and the advanced course for senior officers. IMO rules require a certain amount of onboard gas experience, particularly at senior ranks, before taking on a responsible role or before progressing to the next rank.

In addition to the official certification for hazardous cargo endorsements, a number of colleges operate special courses for gas cargo handling. While this provides for a well-trained and highly knowledgeable environment, the continued growth in the fleet currently strains manpower resources and training schedules. To mitigate these pressures, in addition to the STCW requirements, the Society of International Gas Tanker and Terminal Operators (SIGTTO) provides guidance on competency standards and experience levels for officers serving on gas ships. While small gas carriers normally operate at minimum crew levels, on larger carriers it is normal to find increased crewing levels over and above the minimum required by the ship's manning certificate.

23.6 Gas Carriers and Port Operations

Terminals undergo careful risk analysis at the time of construction, helping to ensure that the location and size of maximum credible spill scenarios are identified and that suitable precautions, including appropriate safety distances, are established between operational areas and local populations.

Risk analysis of cargo transfer operations often identifies the cargo manifold as the area most likely to be the source of the maximum credible spill. This is controlled by a number of measures. Primarily, as for all large oil tankers, gas carriers should be held firmly in position while handling cargo, and mooring management should be of a high calibre. Mooring ropes should be well managed throughout loading and discharging.

Safe mooring is often the subject of computerised mooring analysis, particularly for new ships arriving at new ports, helping to ensure a sensible mooring array suited to the harshest conditions. An accident in the UK highlighted the consequences of a lack of such procedures when, in 1993, a 60,000 m³ LPGC broke out from her berth in storm conditions. This was the subject of an official MCA/HSE inquiry, concluding that prior mooring analysis was vital to safe operations. The safe mooring principles attached to gas carriers are similar to those recommended for oil tankers (they are itemised in *Mooring Equipment Guidelines, 4th Edition* (MEG4) (Reference 49).

The need for such ships to be held firmly in position during cargo handling is due in part to the use of marine loading arms (MLAs) (see Figure 23.6) for cargo transfer. Such equipment is of limited reach in comparison to hoses, yet it provides the ultimate in robustness and simplicity in connection at the cargo manifold.

Figure 23.6: MLAs at cargo manifold (on an LNGC).

The use of MLAs for large gas carriers is common and is an industry recommendation. The use of hoses creates concerns over hose care and maintenance, and their proper layout and support during operations to prevent kinking and abrasion. In addition, accident statistics show that hoses have inferior qualities in comparison to MLAs. Perhaps the worst case of hose failure occurred in 1985 when a large LPGC was loading at Pajaritos, Mexico. In this incident, the hose burst and, in a short time, the resulting gas cloud ignited. The consequent fire and explosion impinged directly on three other ships in harbour and resulted in four deaths.

Figure 23.7: MLA quick connect/disconnect coupler (QC/DC).

Figure 23.8: MLA connection to manifold, showing double ball valve safety release.

As ships have grown in size, the installation of VRLs interconnecting ship and shore vapour systems has become more common for LPGCs (and is an integral part of the LNG system – see Chapter 24).

A feature common to both ship and shore is an emergency shutdown system (ESD). It is common to interconnect such systems so that, for example, an emergency on the ship will stop shore-based loading pumps or, conversely, an emergency at an unloading terminal will stop the ship's cargo pumps. It is common for hard arms to be fitted with automatic detection and alarm systems to guard the operating envelope. A further refinement at some larger LPG terminals is to have the loading arms fitted with emergency release devices that allow the hard arms to automatically release with minimal loss of product before they reach the limits of the operating envelope. These devices are commonly referred to as emergency release couplings (ERCs).

23.7 Society of International Gas Tanker and Terminal Operators (SIGTTO)

Valuable assistance in the preparation of these chapters has come from SIGTTO.

SIGTTO is the leading trade body in this field and has 213 members (December 2020), covering nearly 90% of the world's LNG fleet and 50% of the LPG fleet. SIGTTO members also control most of the terminals that handle these products.

SIGTTO's stated aim is to encourage the safe and responsible operation of liquefied gas tankers and marine terminals handling liquefied gas; to develop advice and guidance for best industry practice among its members and to promote criteria for best practice to all who have responsibilities for, or an interest in, the continuing safety of gas tankers and terminals.

Further details on activities and membership are available at www.sigtto.org

Chapter 24 –
Liquefied Natural Gas (LNG)

A liquefied natural gas carrier (LNGC) is a ship with a specialised containment system, designed for carrying LNG in bulk. These ships have heavily insulated, temperature controlled tanks which keep the methane in a liquid state at approximately minus 162°C (−162°C).

LNGCs have been operated since the 1950s. In 1959, the *'Methane Pioneer'* carried the first experimental LNG cargo and, in 1964, British Gas at Canvey Island received the inaugural cargo from Arzew on the *'Methane Princess'*. These two ships formed the core of the Algeria to UK project and the project-based nature of LNG shipping continued until the end of the 1990s. Ships were built specifically for employment within the projects, acting as a floating pipeline between seller and buyer.

Since the year 2000 the demand for LNGCs has grown exponentially. Ship sizes have also drastically increased, with the Q-Max Qatargas ships now topping the scales at 266,000 m³ capacity and 345 m in length.

One unique aspect of an LNGC is that it generally burns the LNG cargo on board as fuel and retains LNG 'heel' on completion of unloading for the ballast passage. This is required not only for propulsion, but also to ensure the vessel arrives cold at the next loading port. A warm LNGC takes approximately 12 hours to 'cool down', which adds considerable time to loading operations, compared to arriving cold.

24.1   LNG Quality

LNG is clear and colourless, comprising mainly methane but with a percentage of constituents such as ethane, butane, propane and nitrogen. It is produced from either gas wells or oil wells and, at the point of production, the gas is processed to remove impurities. The degree to which this is achieved depends on the facilities available, but typically it results in LNG with between 80 and 97% methane content. The resulting LNG can, therefore, vary in quality from loading terminal to loading terminal or from day to day.

Other physical qualities that can change significantly are the specific gravity and the calorific value of the LNG, which depend on the characteristics of the gas field. The specific gravity affects the deadweight of cargo that can be carried in a given volume. LNG is typically bought and sold on the basis of the number of million British thermal units (MMBtu) transferred and, therefore, the calorific value affects both the monetary value of the cargo and the energy obtained from the boil-off gas fuel.

These factors have significance in commercial arrangements and gas quality is checked for each cargo, usually in a shore-based laboratory by means of gas chromatography.

Figure 24.1: LNGC with Type B tanks (Kvaerner Moss system).

Gas quality is also significant from a shipboard perspective. LNGs that have a high nitrogen content naturally allow nitrogen to boil off preferentially, particularly at the beginning of the loaded passage (nitrogen having an atmospheric boiling point of minus 196°C (−196°C)). Methane also boils off preferentially to other heavier components of the LNG such as ethane and propane and this, combined with the boil-off of nitrogen, results in the boil-off gas being used as fuel having a lower calorific value than the bulk LNG cargo from which it originates. This has the reverse effect on the bulk LNG cargo, which increases in calorific value as the lighter components boil off preferentially over the course of laden voyage. Towards the end of a ballast passage, when the remaining heel has all but been consumed, the remaining liquids tend to be high on the heavier components such as the LPGs. This raises the boiling point of the remaining cargo and has a detrimental effect on the cooling capabilities of the LNG heel when used to spray-cool the cargo tanks in readiness for the next cargo.

LNG vapour is flammable in air and, in case of leakage, codes require an exclusion zone to allow natural dispersion and to limit the risk of ignition of a vapour cloud. Fire hazards are further limited by always handling the product within oxygen-free systems. Unlike oil tankers under inert gas, or in some cases air, LNGCs operate with the vapour space at 100% methane. LNG vapour is non-toxic, although in sufficient concentration it can act as an asphyxiant.

The good combustion qualities of LNG make it attractive as a fuel at electric power stations. It is also a 'clean' fuel. It burns producing little or no smoke, and nitrous oxide and sulphur oxide emissions are far better (in terms of environmental damage) than can be achieved when burning normal liquids such as low sulphur fuel oil. Natural gas has become attractive to industry and governments striving to meet environmental targets set under various international protocols such as the Rio Convention and the Kyoto Protocol. The practice of firing marine boilers on LNG provides the further environmental advantage of lesser soot blowing operations and fewer carbon deposits (see Section 24.4).

24.2 The LNG Fleet

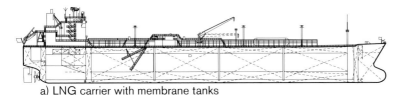

a) LNG carrier with membrane tanks

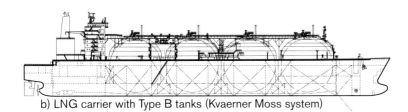

b) LNG carrier with Type B tanks (Kvaerner Moss system)

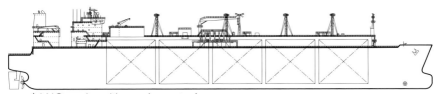

c) LNG carrier with membrane tanks

Figure 24.2: Gas carrier types.

Early LNGCs had carrying capacities of about 25,000 m³. This swiftly rose to about 75,000 m³ for the Brunei LNG project and later ships settled on 125,000 m³. For some years, this remained the norm, giving a loaded draught of about 11.5 m, thus stretching the port facilities of most discharge terminals to their limits. Since then, however, there has been a steady incremental increase in size, usually maintaining the loaded draught (although this has increased marginally to about 12.0 m) but increasing the beam, resulting in a standard ship size of about 175,000 m³. In the main, LNG ports and terminals have adapted accordingly. At the end of 2004, the first orders were placed for LNGCs of more than 200,000 m³ for the Qatar LNG project and currently there are 45 LNGCs trading with a capacity in excess of 200,000 m³, with 14 of these having a capacity of between 260,000 and 266,000 m³ (known as Q-Max). At the other end of the scale is the relatively recent *'Pioneer Knutsen'*, trading at only 1,100 m³ capacity from a facility near Bergen to customers on the Norwegian west coast.

Large modern LNGCs have dimensions approximately as follows:

Capacity (m³)	145,000	215,000	266,000
Length	295 m	315 m	345 m
Beam	48 m	50 m	54 m
Loaded draught	12 m	12 m	12.2 m

Table 24.1: LNGC dimensions.

LNG has a typical density of only 420 kg/m³ which allows ships, even when fully laden, to ride with a high freeboard. They never appear very low in the water as a fully laden oil tanker may do. Ballast draughts are maintained close to laden draughts and, for a ship having a laden draught of 12 m, a ballast draught of 10 m is likely. This means that, for manoeuvring in port in windy conditions, the ships are always susceptible to being blown to the leeward side of the channel, and restrictions on port manoeuvring usually apply with extra tug power commonly specified.

The cargo tanks of LNGCs are thermally insulated and the cargo is carried at or near atmospheric pressure. Cargo tanks may be free standing spherical, or of the membrane type, or prismatic in design. In the case of membrane tanks, the cargo is contained within thin-walled tanks of Invar (a nickel-iron alloy) or stainless steel. The tanks are anchored to the inner hull in appropriate locations and the cargo load is transmitted to the inner hull through the intervening thermal insulation.

All LNGCs have a watertight inner hull and most tank designs are required to have secondary containment capable of safely holding any leakage for a period of 15 days. The simplicity and reliability of stress analysis of the spherical containment designs means that a full secondary barrier is not required, but splash barriers and insulated drip trays protect the inner hull from any leakage that might occur in operation.

No insulation system is 100% efficient and the heat from thermal leakage through the insulation is removed from the cargo by allowing the cargo to evaporate (boil-off). The boil-off gas must be removed from the cargo tanks to ensure that the tanks are maintained at or near atmospheric pressure.

While the majority of LNGCs in operation do not feature a liquefaction plant, an increasing number of new build designs are including these on board. This decreases wastage of cargo boil-off which is beneficial from both a commercial and an operational perspective.

The older propulsion systems for LNGCs were steam turbines supplied by high-pressure boilers. This provided a reliable, low maintenance propulsion system that was capable of burning any combination of gas and conventional fuel in the ship's boilers. The low thermal efficiency of conventional steam turbines has led to the development of a number of alternative propulsion systems that include re-heat steam turbines, which have a higher thermal efficiency than conventional steam turbine systems, and also dual fuel diesel electric (DFDE) systems. LNGCs with DFDE propulsion are equipped with up to four medium-speed diesel generators that provide electrical power to large electric propulsion motors, typically driving a single shaft and propeller through a reduction gearbox. The diesel generators are capable of running on either gas or marine gas oil (and also in some designs, heavy fuel oil) and are therefore able to utilise boil-off gas from the ship's cargo tanks as fuel. The most recent development in propulsion systems for LNGCs is direct drive, gas-injected, slow-speed diesel engines that are more fuel efficient than either steam or DFDE. Two designs are currently available, one working on the Otto process, using low-pressure fuel injection, and the other working on the diesel process using high-pressure fuel injection. The latter requires a gas injection pressure of approximately 300 barg and, where boil-off gas is used as fuel, it is delivered to the engine(s) by a large multistage reciprocating compressor. The compressor also provides the gas pressure required for a partial reliquefaction system in circumstances where not all of the boil-off from the cargo tanks is required as fuel for propulsion.

Figure 24.3: LNGC with Type B tanks (Kvaerner Moss system).

24.3 Cargo Handling

The process of liquefaction is one of refrigeration and, once liquefied, the gas is stored at atmospheric pressure at its boiling point of minus 162°C (−162°C). At loading terminals, any boil-off from shore tanks can be reliquefied and returned to storage. However, on ships this is not usually the case and for the majority of LNGCs not fitted with reliquefaction systems it is the practice to burn boil-off gas in the ship's boilers or engines to provide fuel for propulsion. Depending on the comparative cost of fuel oil, this may be supplemented by either fuel oil or additional natural gas produced by vaporising LNG using a heat exchanger, a process known as 'forcing', to meet the total fuel requirement of the passage.

Cargo volumes at the discharge port will not match those loaded and LNGCs are outfitted with sophisticated means of cargo measurement, referred to as the custody transfer system (CTS) and used in preference to shore tank measurements. These systems normally provide for highly accurate measurement of tank ullages, temperatures and pressures while the tanks themselves are specially calibrated by a Classification Society to a fine degree of accuracy. The system may automatically apply corrections for trim and list using equipment calibrated in dry-dock. The resulting cargo volumes, corrected for the expansion and contraction of the tanks, are normally computed automatically by the system.

Cargo tank design requires carriage at atmospheric pressure and there is little to spare in tank design for over or underpressures. The extent to which pressure build-up can be contained in a ship's tanks is very limited in the case of membrane cargo tanks, although this is normally not a problem as, at sea, the ship is burning boil-off as fuel. In port, the ship has its vapour header connected to the terminal vapour return system. However, there are short periods between these operations when pressure containment is necessary. This is managed by efficient shipboard operations that prevent all possible discharges to atmosphere, apart from minor escapes at pipe flanges, etc. This is part of the design criteria for the class, as it is recognised that methane is not only flammable but is also a greenhouse gas (GHG) that is more than 20 times as damaging to the atmosphere than the equivalent volume of CO_2 over a 100 year period. Over a 20 year period, methane has about 80 times the impact of CO_2.

Boil-off gas (BOG) is limited by tank insulation and newbuilding contracts specify the efficiency required. Usually, this is stated in terms of a volume boil-off per day under set ambient conditions for sea and air temperature. The guaranteed maximum figure for boil-off would normally be about 0.15% of cargo volume per day, although newer ships are capable of achieving closer to 0.10% per day.

While at sea, vapours bound for the boilers or engines must be boosted to the engine room by a low-duty compressor via a vapour heater. The heater raises the temperature of the boil-off to a level suited for combustion and to a point where cryogenic materials are no longer required in construction and where any gas leakage will be lighter than air and so cannot collect in the engine room bilges. LNGCs with high-pressure, gas injected, slow speed diesel engines direct the boil-off gas to the engines via a multistage reciprocating compressor. The boil-off then enters the engine room suitably warmed, but first passes an automatically-controlled master gas valve before reaching an array of control and shutoff valves for direction to each burner or engine. As a safety feature, the gas pipeline through the engine room is of annular construction, with the outer pipe purged and constantly checked for methane ingress. In this area, operational safety is paramount and sensors will trigger shutdown of the master gas valve in alarm conditions. For steam ships, a vital procedure in the case of a boiler flameout is to purge all gas from the boilers before attempting re-ignition. Without such care, boiler explosions are possible and occasional accidents of this type have occurred.

24.4   Cargo Care

The majority of LNG shippers and receivers have a legitimate concern over foreign bodies getting into tanks and pipelines. The main concerns are the risk of valve blockage, eg an old welding rod becomes lodged in a valve seat, damage to the cargo tanks on membrane ships or damage to the cargo pumps' bearings. Such occurrences are not unknown when a ship is discharging first cargoes after newbuilding or recently having come from dry-dock. Accordingly, and despite the economic impact of increased discharge time, it is common practice to fit filters at the ship's liquid manifold connections to prevent any such material from entering the shore system. The ship normally supplies filters fitting neatly into the manifold piping.

Even small particulate matter can cause concerns and the carryover of silica gel dust from inert gas dryers is one example. Another possible cause of contamination is poor combustion in IG plants with ships' tanks becoming coated with soot and carbon deposits during gas-freeing and gassing-up operations. Subsequently, the contaminants may be washed into gas mains. Cargoes can even be rejected on the basis of this. Tank cleanliness is vital and, particularly after dry-dock, tanks must be thoroughly vacuumed and dusted.

An LNG manifold is fitted with a strainer, which prevents any debris from entering the cargo containment system. Debris is particularly common when a loading terminal has been built or has recently undergone maintenance. Cargo equipment can be damaged, and the cargo can even be declared off spec, if debris is found within the cargo/system.

Figure 24.4: Debris recovered from the ship's manifold strainers after loading a commissioning cargo at a new LNG export terminal.

A cargo was once rejected in Japan when, resulting from a misoperation, steam was accidentally applied to the main turbine with the ship secured alongside the berth. The ship broke out from the berth, but fortunately the MLAs had not been connected. This action was sufficient however for cargo receivers to reject the ship, and the cargo could only be delivered after a specialised STS transfer operation had been accomplished. At the time, STS transfer of LNG had only ever been carried out on a few occasions as the operation requires perfect weather, great care and specialist equipment.

Another case of cargo rejection, this time resulting in a distressed sale, involved a shipment to Cove Point in the USA, where the strict requirements that prevail on in-tank pressures on arrival at the berth were not adhered to. The ship had previously been ordered to reduce pressure for arrival.

Pressure reduction is a difficult job to perform satisfactorily and, if it is to be successful, the operation must progress with diligence throughout the loaded voyage by maintaining the cargo tanks at a minimal operational pressure using a compressor to encourage maximum cargo evaporation. This cools the cargo and reduces the saturated vapour pressure (SVP). The process of drawing vapour from the vapour space at the last moment is ineffective because such short-term action will have little effect on reducing the cargo temperature and associated SVP and, once gas burning stops, the vapour space will return to its high equilibrium pressure. The process of reducing the temperature of the cargo and its equivalent SVP on the loaded passage is known as 'cargo conditioning'. In extreme conditions, particularly on short passages, where the amount of boil-off required to condition the cargo is more than that required as fuel, the ship may have to 'dump' excess gas either by steam dumping via the ship's boilers or by use of the gas combustion unit (GCU) on DFDE and diesel-powered LNGCs. Most LNG charterparties require the shipowner to warrant a daily loaded boil-off rate, which may not be achievable where the ship is required to condition the cargo on the loaded passage. In these instances, to avoid a subsequent claim for excess boil-off, the ship's Master should request direct instructions from the charterer with regard to cargo conditioning requirements for the voyage.

Back loading of LNG cargoes from traditional import terminals where the quantity of LNG in storage from long-term supply contracts exceeds the current local pipeline or end user requirements, has become more common in the last decade. This presents the crew of an LNG ship with a number of challenges. The cargo may have come from a number of shore tanks and original sources and the final detailed composition and density of the LNG may not be known until after the cargo has been loaded. The cargo may also be significantly warmer and have a higher saturated vapour pressure than LNG typically loaded at a dedicated LNG export terminal. To ensure that the cargo temperature and associated tank pressures are capable of being maintained within safe limits, particularly during the early part of the loaded passage, it may be necessary to return significant volumes of gas back to the terminal to assist in conditioning the cargo during the loading period. This is typically assisted by the slow loading rate associated with this type of operation, but may be frustrated by the limited capacity of the terminal to receive vapour back from the ship. The key to a successful operation is detailed prior planning between the ship, the charterer, the supplier and the terminal and clear and documented agreement on operational procedures.

LNGCs engaged in a traded LNG market may occasionally be required to carry a number of 'parcels' of LNG loaded at different terminals. In addition to the standard stowage considerations in respect of draught, trim, hull stresses and sloshing limitations on intermediate tank filling levels, the crew of an LNG ship must also consider the risk of rollover where cargoes of different densities and compositions are loaded into the same tank. Shore tanks in LNG receiving terminals are typically provided with top and bottom filling lines and recirculation facilities to promote the mixing of batches of LNG with different compositions and densities loaded into the same tank. This is not the case with LNGCs, which are limited to bottom filling only. Stratification may occur where a heavier LNG, ie an LNG with a higher percentage of ethane and propane, is loaded under a lighter LNG with a higher methane content in the same tank. When stratification occurs, the normal convection currents resulting from heat ingress through the tank insulation are restricted to the individual layers rather than throughout the full depth of the cargo, as is the case where the tank contains a single, homogeneous LNG composition. The top, lighter layer evaporates to the vapour space and, due to the preferential evaporation of methane, becomes progressively denser. The lower, denser layer warms up though heat ingress through the cargo tank insulation, becoming progressively less dense. When the densities of the two layers become similar, the convection currents in the lower layer are able to break through the upper layer to the liquid surface, thus breaking down the stratification, referred to as rollover. The trapped heat in the lower layer may now be released, resulting in a sudden and massive increase in vapour generation and tank pressure causing the tank safety valves to lift and, in extreme cases, overpressure damage to the tank. The risk of rollover can be eradicated by ensuring that each parcel of LNG is loaded into a separate tank.

Where the LNG parcels are loaded into separate tanks but are discharged to a single receiving terminal, the receiver may require the cargo to be received into the terminal with a homogeneous composition. This is to ensure that sampling equipment on the terminal unloading line is able to gather an accurate sample of the average composition of the entire cargo throughout the course of the unloading operation. The composition of the cargo derived from sample analysis determines the price paid for the LNG received. This will require the cargo officer of the LNGC to plan and adjust the unloading rates from individual tanks to achieve a homogeneous blend at the ship's manifolds throughout the unloading.

Rollover may also be a risk where a heavy cargo is loaded under significant quantities of lighter LNG heel. This is not normally an issue with LNGCs on a liner trade and loading at a single export terminal, as the heel will 'weather' on the ballast passage and will always be denser than the cargo to be loaded. It may be an important consideration for LNGCs engaged in an LNG trading market and it is recommended that the *Liquefied Gas Handling Principles on Ships and in Terminals*, published by the Society of International Gas Tanker and Terminal Operators (SIGTTO) (Reference 50) is consulted.

24.5   Ship Care

Most standard materials brought into contact with LNG become highly brittle and fracture. For this reason, pipelines and containment systems are built from the preferred materials of aluminium, Invar (a nickel-iron alloy) and stainless steel. However, these materials do not commonly feature over the ship's weather decks, tank weather covers or hull and so care must be taken to ensure that LNG is not spilt. A spill of LNG will cause significant damage to the decks or hull, normally necessitating emergency dry-docking. Accidents of this nature have resulted in extended periods off-hire, but fortunately there have been no reports of serious injury to personnel.

For cargo operations, a manifold 'water curtain' is established. This usually involves the use of the fire main system to allow a flow of water to cascade down the side of the ship in the vicinity of the manifold. If cargo were to leak or spill from the manifold connections of either the ship or the shore, the water curtain would prevent the cold LNG from coming into contact with the steel of the hull.

Figure 24.5: Brittle fracture of a ship's deck resulting from an LNG spill.

LNGCs are double-hulled ships specially designed and insulated to prevent leakage and rupture in the event of an accident such as grounding or collision. Although sophisticated in control and expensive in materials, they are simple in concept. Mostly, they carry LNG in just four, five or six centreline tanks. Only a few have certification and equipment for cross trading in LPG and/or ethylene. LNG is carried at atmospheric pressure and, although there are four current methods of constructing seaborne LNG tanks, only two are in majority usage. These are the spherical tanks of Moss design and the membrane tanks from Gaztransport or Technigaz (two French companies, now amalgamated as GTT). A number of shipbuilders have their own licensed designs for cargo containment systems based on membrane, spherical or self-supporting prismatic tanks. In each design, the cargo tanks are contained within the double hull with the space between the inner and outer hull being used as ballast water tanks.

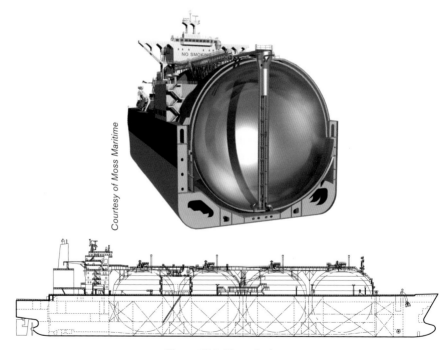

Figure 24.6: Moss design.

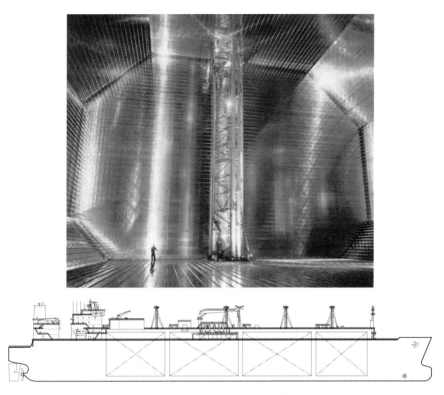

Figure 24.7: Membrane design (GTT).

A small number of spherical tanks are constructed from 9% nickel steel but the majority are constructed from aluminium. A disadvantage of the spherical system is that the tanks do not fit the contours of a ship's hull. LNGCs with spherical containment systems also have a greater lightship displacement than an equivalent membrane ship of the same cargo capacity. In general terms, for two LNGCs of the same carrying capacity, a ship of Moss design will be about 10% longer. It will also have its navigating bridge set at a higher level to comply with SOLAS requirements for visibility from the navigation bridge. However, spherical tanks are robust and relatively simple to install in comparison to the membrane system, with its complication of twin barriers and complex construction requiring in excess of 70 km of precision welding.

The mass of a spherical LNG tank requires a longer cooldown time and a larger amount of LNG to cool down to be ready for loading than an equivalent size membrane tank. Spherical tanks do not, however, have the same restrictions on filling levels that apply to membrane tanks. The large free surface in partially filled membrane tanks may result in damaging overpressures on the membranes and supporting insulation from sloshing motions of the cargo when the LNGC is working in a seaway. The double containment requirements for membrane LNGCs ensure that any damage to the primary membrane will be retained by the secondary membrane and will not prejudice the integrity of the inner hull. Any LNGC suffering damage to the primary membrane will, however, need to be taken out of service for repairs, resulting in lost availability, lost revenue and expensive repair costs. To avoid the risk of sloshing damage, membrane tanks have restrictions imposed by the respective Classification Society on filling levels in the cargo tanks when the LNGC is at sea. The sloshing restrictions typically require the cargo filling level to be either less than 10% of the height of the tank, or greater than 70% of the height of the tank when the LNGC is at sea, with guidance to avoid heavy rolling and pitching, where possible, when tank levels are close to these limits. This may require careful planning on the part of the cargo officer and the Master in circumstances where a long loaded voyage with slack tanks is contemplated, or where a large heel is required for an extended ballast passage.

The demand for LNGCs with spherical containment systems has declined due to the many advantages of membrane based ship types.

Figure 24.8: LNGC with Moss (spherical) tanks.

Figure 24.9: LNGC with membrane tanks.

LNGCs fitted with slow-speed diesel propulsion and burning heavy fuel oil require reliquefaction plants on board to handle boil-off gas (see Section 24.3). All diesel systems require back-up gas disposal facilities – also known as gas combustion units (GCUs) – for occasions when either the reliquefaction plants are not available to process boil-off gas or, in the case of LNGCs with DFDE and gas-injected direct drive diesel propulsion, where the ship's fuel requirement is less than the boil-off generated by the cargo.

LNGCs are expensive to build, but are valuable assets with some hulls and containment systems built with a 40-year fatigue life. Shipowners and ship managers alike recognise this and, assisted by inspection regimes, the overall quality of LNG tonnage is maintained to a high standard.

As some of the older LNGCs reach the end of their lifespan, and where the cost of ongoing maintenance begins to outweigh the cost of running the ship, it has become more common to convert a ship into a floating storage and regasification unit (FSRU).

To ensure that the quality of older LNG tonnage is maintained, many charterers require a Condition Assessment Programme (CAP) rating of the hull and cargo system from a reputable Classification Society for LNGCs older than 15 or 20 years.

24.6   Terminals, FSRU and STS

The cost and the time taken to construct LNG import terminals has led to the development of FSRUs, which are, typically, conventional seagoing LNGCs fitted with onboard regasification systems. An FSRU is designed to regas LNG from its cargo tanks and discharge the resultant high-pressure gas (80 to 100 barg) directly to an end receiver, typically a power plant, or into a gas distribution network. The FSRU enables natural gas to be delivered to a new end user in a shorter time frame and with less capital investment than would be the case with a conventional land-based regas terminal. An FSRU also requires a smaller footprint in a busy port area than a conventional land-based terminal and, when a particular contract has been completed, the FSRU can either be relocated to another project or returned, in the interim, to the LNG trade.

The regas capacity of a modern FSRU is similar to that of a medium size land-based regas terminal with throughput in the region of 3 million tonnes of LNG per annum. The gas is either discharged across a conventional jetty through a high-pressure hard arm or via a submerged turret mooring system into a subsea pipeline. Some FSRUs are converted from existing LNGCs and are de-engined and maintained permanently on station while a significant number are capable of trading as standard LNGCs in between regas contracts. In either case, when an FSRU is on station as a regas facility, it is kept supplied with LNG from standard LNG tankers via a double banked ship to ship transfer (STS) operation, using either flexible hoses or conventional marine loading arms (MLAs). This may be accomplished with the FSRU on station at the jetty or on the turret mooring or at a transshipment location close to the regas station.

The facilities provided for LNG STS transfer are similar in principal to those provided on a conventional LNG jetty. The two ships maintain a common emergency shutdown (ESD) and communications link and the transfer system, whether MLAs or flexible hoses, is fitted with a quick release facility that, in turn, is linked to a position monitoring system. The position monitoring system ensures that the cargo transfer is automatically stopped and the hoses or hard arms disconnected before the relative movement of the two ships exceeds the operating limits of the transfer system.

Courtesy of Excelerate Energy

Figure 24.10: Transshipment of LNG to an FSRU on a regas berth.

24.7 LNG as a Fuel

With the introduction of Environmental Control Areas (ECAs), an advantage of using boil-off gas as fuel is that natural gas provides a clean fuel solution with virtually zero sulphur content. Such is the appeal of natural gas as a clean fuel that LNG is now being increasingly considered as a fuel for ferries and other ships engaged in short sea trades in ECA areas. This concept was recognised in the IMO's Gas Codes from the very earliest days and, with the appropriate safety equipment in place, the regulations allow LNG to be burnt in ships' boilers or engines. This is not the case for LPG, where reliquefaction equipment is a fitment, but specifically because LPGs are heavier than air gases and their use in engine rooms is disallowed. This situation may change with the IGF Code, which may eventually allow for the safe use of low flashpoint fuels other than natural gas.

24.8 Society of International Gas Tanker and Terminal Operators (SIGTTO)

Valuable assistance in the preparation of these chapters has come from SIGTTO.

SIGTTO is the leading trade body in this field and has 213 members (December 2020), covering nearly 90% of the world's LNG fleet and 50% of the LPG fleet. SIGTTO members also control most of the terminals that handle these products.

SIGTTO's stated aim is to encourage the safe and responsible operation of liquefied gas tankers and marine terminals handling liquefied gas; to develop advice and guidance for best industry practice among its members and to promote criteria for best practice to all who have responsibilities for, or an interest in, the continuing safety of gas tankers and terminals.

Further details on activities and membership are available at www.sigtto.org

Part 8 –

Packaged Cargoes, Including Bags, Drums and Flexitanks

Chapter 25 – Sugar

While sugar is found in the tissue of most plants, it is typically produced in commercial quantities from sugarcane and sugar beet. Sugar is used extensively in the production of food, medicine and ethanol. The largest sugarcane producing countries are Brazil, India, China, the United States and Thailand.

Sugar comes in different forms depending on its class, specifically white crystal, raw crystal and liquid. It is then further categorised by type.

25.1 Refined (Crystal) Sugar

Crystal sugar is the most refined type of sugar. Unlike semi-refined or raw sugar, refined sugar is always carried in bags weighing typically 50 kg. In the past, jute outer bags were widely used with a polythene film inner bag, but the outer bags are now typically made from woven polypropylene. The purpose of the plastic inner bag is to keep out moisture but, because the outer and inner bags are often stitched together, the seal is not always effective.

> Substantial claims have arisen on shipments of bagged refined sugar, where the complaint often relates to stickiness or caking of the product, sometimes wrongly attributed to conditions encountered during the voyage.

Refined sugar is normally a dry, free-flowing commodity with very low moisture content.

On delivery, if the sugar is not found to be free flowing, it is important to establish whether this is due to:

- Pressure compaction
- adhesiveness (stickiness)
- caking (agglomeration).

Pressure compaction usually occurs as a result of static pressure exerted by the weight of the sugar itself, particularly when bags are stacked high. This condition can readily be corrected when the bags are handled and transported. However, adhesiveness and caking of refined sugar are both the result of too high a moisture content and possibly, to some extent, the temperature of the cargo at the time of bagging.

Figure 25.1: Raw sugar (left) and refined crystal sugar (right).

Adhesiveness, resulting in poor flow characteristics, occurs as a result of high moisture content, either initially or after packing. Caking may occur when over-moist sugar dries out.

If the product comes into contact with extraneous moisture such as cargo sweat, this may lead to limited, superficial adhesiveness and to subsequent caking of the sugar at the mouth of the bags. This may also occur where bags have been damaged by stevedores' hooks. Extensive adhesiveness and caking may be caused by excessive moisture at the time of packing, particularly if the caking is found at the centre, extending towards the outside of the bag, with the sugar crystals at the edges adhering. This condition may be further affected if, at the time of packing, the temperature of the sugar is high relative to the ambient temperature.

It is of crucial importance that, immediately after production, the amounts of 'free water' and 'bound water' are at satisfactorily low levels. After processing, sugar is normally left in storage for a relatively short period, with appropriate ventilation, to 'condition' or 'mature' the product. The aim of this is to ensure that, when the sugar is bagged, its moisture content is at an acceptably low level. If it is not, comparatively hard caking and possibly some adhesiveness may be expected to occur during subsequent storage and transport. When sugar is bagged with a low moisture content (0.02% or less), there is no risk of adhesiveness or caking being caused by moisture migration.

Some sale contracts stipulate a moisture content of '0.1% maximum', but it should not be assumed that such levels are acceptable if caking is to be avoided. Adhesiveness and caking do not affect the chemical nature of the sugar but may not be acceptable for its intended end use.

25.2 Loading Sugar

Figure 25.2: Raw sugar in Santos, Brazil, being loaded as a bulk cargo directly into the cargo holds.

Figure 25.3: Refined crystal sugar in bags being loaded directly into the cargo holds.

The following general considerations apply:

- The ship's hold, before loading, should be clean, dry and free from any noticeable smell
- for bagged/refined cargoes:
  - bags should be loaded only if outwardly dry and with no apparent lumpiness of the contents
  - bags should not be loaded during any form of heavy precipitation, including rain or snow
  - cargo battens are not essential. Where no battens are fitted, measures should be taken to prevent damage from any protruding cargo batten hooks or fittings. A separation of polyethylene, polypropylene cloth or kraft paper sheeting between the ship's structure and the bags is sufficient
  - tight block stowage is the customary and acceptable method of stowage
  - bags loaded at substantially lower temperatures at the load port should be rapidly discharged to prevent or restrict unwanted condensation on the bags
  - if additional cargo is to be carried in the same hold as refined sugar, it should be a dry cargo
- when loading raw sugar cargoes in bulk quantity:
  - cargo should not be loaded during periods of rainfall and hatches should be closed until the rainfall subsides
  - representative samples should be taken and correctly labelled throughout the loading operation
- the hold should not be ventilated; all ventilators and other openings should be sealed
- on completion of loading, an independent surveyor should carry out a draft or tallying survey, as well as sealing the hatch covers.

The Master should ensure records of the weather conditions are maintained during loading. It is recommended that the deck watch monitors the weather for signs of rainfall throughout the loading operation.

25.3   Stowage and Care of Sugar

Refined sugar is typically carried in containers but can also be loaded as break-bulk depending on the availability of containers in the load port.

Raw sugar is typically carried as a bulk cargo. While sugar is classed as an IMSBC Code Group C cargo (not liable to liquefy), it must be monitored carefully during the voyage because of its high solubility (ability to dissolve) when wet. For bulk raw cargoes, the presence of large volumes of water in the hold could lead to increasing instability of the ship, as well as destruction of the cargo.

In terms of stowage of refined sugar bags, tight block stowage without height limitation is the customary and acceptable method, with the height of the stow limited only by the height of the cargo compartments. Cargo battens are not necessary as it is generally accepted that a separation of paper, cardboard sheets, polyethylene or polypropylene cloth between the ship's structure and the bags is sufficient.

Ventilation of refined sugar is not necessary under any circumstances. The purpose of cargo ventilation is to prevent or restrict the formation of condensation or moisture on the ship's internal structure. However, such condensation originates from within the cargo and will occur only when the cargo itself is moist. Because refined sugar has a low moisture content and is enclosed in plastic film, there is no risk of sweat and so ventilation is not necessary.

Under certain circumstances, ventilation may even be detrimental, such as when holds loaded with cold cargo are ventilated with warm air, which can lead to the formation of sweat.

Sugar has low thermal conductivity, which means that during the voyage it tends to remain at the temperature at which it was loaded, at least in the interior of the stow. If the sugar is loaded cold and later discharged in a relatively hot area, there is a risk of condensation forming, during the discharge, on any bags having a temperature lower than the dew point of outside air. In such cases, rapid discharge is necessary to avoid any adverse consequences.

One of the most common causes of damage to sugar cane is water, particularly rainwater. To prevent this, hatch covers should be in good condition and weathertight, with a particular focus on compression bars and rubber packing around the covers.

As sugar is a seasonal trade, it is possible that smaller or older vessels are used at reduced freight rates. However, hatch covers are more likely to leak on an older vessel, so there is an increased risk of cargo damage.

A careful packing strategy should include control of stacking heights and temperature and moisture control at the producing mills, even before shipping, as this will minimise the chances of caking.

Chapter 26 – Potatoes

Potatoes are grown commercially throughout the world, except in humid tropical lowland areas. They are one of the world's most important food crops and are traded as a commodity. This chapter refers to three basic types of potato, each of which has special considerations for stowage and carriage.

- Early/new or immature
- late/mature
- seed.

Figure 26.1: Three basic types of potato, left to right: early/new; late/mature; seed (notice fragile 'eyes' which produce new growth).

Early new potatoes have thin, relatively loose skins that are easily removed and damaged. Demand for this type of potato is significant and large quantities are shipped from Cyprus, Greece, Israel, Turkey and the Canary Islands during the northern winter and spring seasons.

Late/mature potatoes have firm skins and are, therefore, more resistant to damage and much easier to carry than immature potatoes.

Seed potatoes for shipment are small whole tubers, each with at least one eye to produce the new growth. Seed potatoes are grown under a regulated certification programme to ensure that they are as disease-free as possible.

26.1 Pre-shipment Considerations

Once potatoes have been harvested, they must be stored under optimal conditions until released for shipment.

High temperatures cause the tuber respiration rate to increase, using oxygen and food reserves, potentially resulting in excessive shrinkage. Freezing or chilling temperatures can damage and kill tuber cells. If the air surrounding the tubers has a low humidity, water will move from the tubers to the air, resulting in weight loss. Should the oxygen content of the air fall to a low level, cells within the tubers die and 'blackheart' forms.

Sprouting is a natural function of the tuber, but during shipment it is not desirable as quality and condition will suffer. Sprout suppressant chemicals or other methods may be used prior to shipment to prevent sprouting, but control in stowage can only be maintained by the correct temperature(s).

Potato tuber diseases may be the result of microorganisms, adverse pre-shipment storage conditions, or improper stowage and conditions of carriage. Potatoes are grown under the soil so, when harvested, will always contain spores of invading microorganisms on their surfaces. These will attack the tubers if the natural defence mechanism is ruptured. This can be as a result of mechanical damage, either during harvesting or subsequent handling, or may be the result of other forms of deterioration, such as sunscald. It may also happen if the tuber is subjected to wetting to a point that a film of water is present over its surface.

Figure 26.2: Signs of infestation by the potato tuber moth.

Some of the principal diseases found at the time of harvesting include:

- *Phytophthora infestans* (potato blight)
- a dry mealy rot due to species of *Fusarium* (dry rot)
- a bacterial soft rot principally caused by *Pectobacterium spp.,* formerly known as *Erwinia* (black leg)
- brown rot caused by the bacterium *Ralstonia solanacearum*
- ring rot caused by the bacterium *Clavibacter michiganensis subsp. sepedonicus.*

These are notifiable diseases in many countries.

Post-harvest deterioration, ie storage/stowage deterioration, will normally occur following the development of bacterial soft rot, usually the result of infection by *Pectobacterium (*formerly *Erwinia)* species. This causes collapse of the cells of the infected potatoes, releasing a heavily infected fluid. This gives rise, by contact, to soft rot developing in adjacent tubers. Over a period of time, the contents of whole bags may collapse into an unpleasant smelling slime.

Another cause of deterioration is infestation by insects. The two most serious pests of potato crops are the North American black and yellow striped Colorado beetle (*Leptinotarsa decemlineata*) and the potato tuber moth (*Phthorimaea operculella*).

It is necessary for shippers or charterers to provide phytosanitary certificates, attached to the B/Ls or other trade documents. These certificates are produced by the Authority of the country of origin and indicate that the specified consignment(s) have been inspected or treated according to the importing country's requirements.

While the Master should be able to rely upon a valid phytosanitary certificate, there is a continuing duty in relation to the cargo on board. For example, if infestation is noticed during the voyage, the Master/owners must take reasonable steps to deal with the situation.

Fumigation prior to berthing at an arrived port or, alternatively, rejection of a cargo of potatoes as a result of infestation or infection by serious bacterial diseases may cause massive delays to a ship and considerable problems for the shipowners.

Figure 26.3: Potato tubers infested with Colorado beetle.

Greening may occur in any part of a tuber exposed to light. Exposure to bright light during post-harvest handling, or longer periods (7 to 14 days) of low light, may result in the development of chlorophyll (greening) and bitter, toxic glycoalkaloids, such as solanine.

Experts advise that, while in cultivated varieties green discolouration of the flesh does not cause substantive harm to health, it will, depending upon extent, result in a loss of value of some of the cargo as green flesh tastes bitter and must be cut away before cooking.

When consignments are presented for shipment, the external condition of the packaging should be inspected. Evidence of wet patch staining of the bags, or any associated odours, should alert crew members to likely problems and the ship's P&I Club should be requested to appoint an expert surveyor to investigate and ensure that only healthy and undamaged potatoes are shipped.

Potatoes are often shipped in woven polypropylene bags of varying dark colours making it extremely difficult to recognise wet patches from superficial examination, so close inspection is recommended.

Mechanical damage, which is largely preventable, is one of the most significant factors affecting potato condition. Special care is essential during handling to and from the vessel, particularly when immature/new potatoes are being shipped. Bags of potatoes should not be walked over or handled roughly, with special care taken if palletised units of bags are overstowed by a second tier of pallets.

In light rain, snow or damp weather, cargo must be protected from moisture to preclude the onset of premature spoilage by bacterial soft rot. Potatoes should not be loaded or discharged during heavy rain.

26.2 Packaging and Stowage Considerations

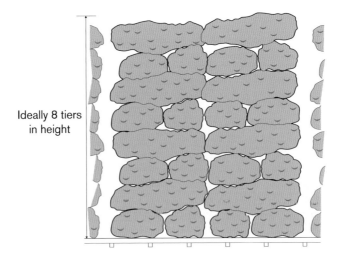

Ideally 8 tiers in height

Figure 26.4: Potatoes packed in mesh bags.

Potatoes may be packed in hessian bags, woven polypropylene bags, sacks lined with an internal perforated polyethylene bag or, sometimes, cartons or crates. Various sizes of bags are utilised and each will usually contain about 25 kg of tubers. They are typically carried on pallets. Alternatively, potatoes may be packed in large open-top lift bags weighing some 2 to 3 T.

Figure 26.5: Potatoes packed in large open-top lift bags.

New potatoes are frequently packed in moist or dry peat moss. The main purpose of the moss is to protect the new tubers and to preclude skin-set to maintain their value. However, excess free water or release of water from the moss during carriage can cause problems that lead to bacterial soft rot of the tubers.

As for any product that may enter the human food chain, preparation of stowages will include ensuring that the cargo spaces are clean and dry. Potatoes are highly sensitive to odours and readily absorb foreign smells from chemicals, mineral oils and some fruits, etc. All compartments destined for stowage of potatoes must be free from odour and volatile substances.

Potato tubers are living organisms that consume oxygen and emit carbon dioxide, water and heat. The principal problem as far as stowage and carriage are concerned is the heat produced and, therefore, good climate control on board is essential to maintain the condition of tubers.

Condensation in the form of ship or cargo sweat should not be allowed to develop during a voyage. Long voyages demand more critical control than short-term voyages.

Table 26.1 sets out the approximate heat that may be produced by cargoes of potatoes. From these figures, it is evident that new/immature potatoes produce considerably more heat per 1,000 kg than late/mature potatoes and so should be considered more difficult to carry.

Type of potatoes	kcal per 1,000 kg per 24 hours				
	At °C	5°	10°	15°	20°
Immature		735	1,070	1,380	1,930
Mature		370	520	550	735

Table 26.1: Approximate heat produced by potato cargoes.

When potatoes are presented for loading in bags, stow heights of up to 8 tiers are preferable. To ensure adequate ventilation of cargo blocks, a maximum stow height of 12 bags should not be exceeded. The stowage must be arranged to ensure a free flow of air throughout the compartments.

Bags shipped on pallets are usually stacked to a height of 8 or 9 bags and are often secured to the pallet baseboards by nylon netting. Care must be taken (particularly when the bags are constructed of woven polyethylene) to ensure that the contents of pallets are fully and properly secured. The frictionless nature of this type of outer bag frequently results in the pallet loads becoming deformed and, in some cases, detached from the baseboards. This slippage may result in additional stevedoring costs for remaking the pallets.

Slippage of woven polyethylene bags from pallets, and also when loose stowed, into ventilation channels will cause restriction of airflow and must be prevented by the use of timber dunnage or dunnage nets.

26.3 Stowage in Refrigerated Cargo Vessels

Written instructions for the carriage temperature regime should always be obtained from the shippers and should be complied with throughout the voyage. Transport temperatures must be such that respiration and weight losses due to evaporation are kept to a minimum.

The approximate lowest safe temperature for the carriage of potatoes is 4°C (39°F) and carriage is usually recommended at 4 to 5°C (39 to 41°F) at a relative humidity of 90 to 95%.

The exact stowage patterns adopted for potatoes will depend on the permanent air circulation systems incorporated in the vessel. Strict supervision of cargo stowage must ensure that airflow will be evenly distributed throughout the compartments for maintenance of optimal temperature control. Detailed records of cargo compartment/flesh temperatures should be maintained throughout the transit period.

When potatoes are discharged from refrigerated stowage, they should, ideally, be landed to stores at a similar temperature to that of carriage. If cold cargoes are discharged into ambient warm humid conditions, there is a risk of condensation forming on the tubers and bacterial soft rot will ensue.

Some shippers/consignees will request the vessel to undertake a dual temperature regime during transit and require the vessel to slowly raise the temperature of the cargo to above the anticipated ambient dew point at the discharge port, commencing some two to three days before discharge is due to begin.

26.4 Stowage in Mechanically Ventilated General Cargo Spaces

The usual system adopted is to use block stowage with air channels around each cargo block. This system relies on convection cooling. The cargo is stowed clear of the deck either by placing it on double dunnage or alternatively on pallet boards.

Cargo blocks should normally not exceed 3 by 3 m square. Smaller blocks may be preferred under certain circumstances, but stability of each block is critical and, when loose stowed, bags must be key-stacked to construct a locking stow precluding slippage or collapse of bags into the air channels, potentially causing a breakdown in the air circulation.

High stows may not only cause compression damage/bruising to the potatoes (particularly new/immature tubers) but may also result in excessive heating due to metabolic processes. Bags should be stowed ideally to 8 tiers in height, but never more than 12 tiers. The width of the air channels around the cargo blocks should be approximately 20 to 30 cm, constructed using dunnage and/or the locking stow noted above.

Cargo should be stowed clear of transverse bulkheads and ship's sides to promote air circulation, with exposed steelwork protected by paper mats or other sheeting to prevent condensation damage.

Potato cargoes should be kept well clear of engine room bulkheads and any other local heat sources situated on the vessel.

The stowage on any vessel should be designed to suit the type of permanent ventilation system fitted. Potato cargoes make heavy demands on ships' ventilation systems and a capacity calculated on the basis of at least 15 air changes per hour in an empty hold is required. At these rates, the ventilation system should be run continuously except when weather and climatic conditions prevent it, eg if there is a risk of shipping water through the weather deck ventilators or condensation forming on the cargo or internal ship's structures.

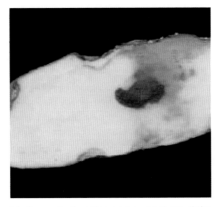

Figure 26.6: Blackheart is formed when the oxygen content of the air falls to a low level.

At higher rates of air changes per hour, consideration should be given, particularly on longer voyages, to either running the fans at lower power (reduction of speed) or for shorter times (ventilate intermittently) to maintain humidity and preclude water loss from the tubers (desiccation).

Details of ambient air wet and dry bulb temperatures, hold air wet and dry bulb temperatures, flesh temperatures, and the ventilation regime undertaken must be recorded in a dedicated ventilation logbook or, alternatively, the deck logbook.

26.5   Stowage in RoRo Vessels

Cargoes of new/immature potatoes are sometimes shipped in the holds of RoRo vessels. Packed in woven polypropylene bags and shipped on pallet boards with bags secured by nylon nets, losses and/or additional costs have been experienced due to the displacement of bags from the pallet boards.

The problem of tuber greening has also been experienced due to the practice of keeping the RoRo deck lights illuminated throughout the voyage. Attempts to prevent this have included covering stowages with polythene sheets, which unfortunately reduces the effectiveness of the hold ventilation system.

Hold lights should never remain continuously illuminated throughout a voyage, even of short duration.

Figure 26.7: Greening occurs when tubers are exposed to bright
light or long periods of low light.

26.6   Transport of Potatoes in ISO Containers

Cargoes of potatoes may be carried in fan-assisted ventilated containers, open-sided
containers, insulated refrigerated containers and 'porthole' insulated containers. For
voyages of short duration, closed cargo containers may be used, but the doors should
remain open whenever possible to promote ventilation. Stowage on deck must include
provisions to protect the cargo from rain, sea spray and sunlight.

Flat racks are also used for below-deck stowage in well-ventilated compartments.
Provisions should be made to afford exposed bags protection against rain and sunlight
prior to loading and subsequent to discharge.

26.7   Seed Potatoes

Seed potatoes are usually shipped in smaller consignments than new or mature
potatoes. The value of seed potatoes is much greater than potatoes destined for
consumption and special care should be taken as any loss in quality or condition will
potentially result in substantial claims. They may be carried in mechanically ventilated
stowage, but for longer voyages involving any prolonged period in warm climatic
conditions (defined as in excess of 20°C), they should be carried under refrigeration at
a temperature of 3 to 4°C. This slightly lower temperature (compared to other potato
carriage) ensures better sprout and weight loss control. Furthermore, seed potatoes
stored at this temperature require less ventilation than potatoes stored at a higher
temperature, as less heat is generated through respiration.

26.8   Safety

Inadequate, or failure of, ventilation in spaces containing cargoes of potatoes can cause life-threatening concentrations of carbon dioxide and oxygen depletion.

Before entry, the compartment(s) must be fully ventilated and a gas measurement conducted to verify the space is safe for entry. As per the *Code of Safe Working Practices* 2015, as amended 2022, the oxygen content must be at least 20% by volume.

Chapter 27 – Cocoa

27.1 Cocoa Beans

Cocoa beans are the dried seeds of the cocoa pod, which is the fruit of the cocoa tree. Cocoa trees are grown in tropical regions of the world. The average number of cocoa beans per pod is 30 to 40.

Following harvesting the cocoa beans are fermented and dried (mainly by the sun).

The cocoa bean is generally of a grey to dark brown appearance (the external grey appearance not necessarily being indicative of inferior quality). The outer shell is brittle and it is the inner 'nib' that is the important part of the cocoa bean. Cocoa beans emit an acidic odour, which varies according to origin. The nib has an odour reminiscent of chocolate.

Cocoa beans are primarily used in the food industry, with alternative uses in cosmetics and, to a limited extent, in pharmaceuticals. The shell is normally discarded, being more or less valueless. The inner nib is used to produce cocoa butter, cocoa liquor, cocoa cake and cocoa powder.

The ideal moisture percentage should be around 7% after drying; the effectiveness of the drying process depends on weather conditions. Cocoa beans are a soft commodity that easily give off moisture during transport from relatively warm countries to relatively colder countries. It is generally accepted that a maximum moisture content of 7.5% is indicative of stable cocoa beans.

Typical problems with cocoa bean cargoes include:

- Damage due to condensation
- damage by seawater
- slack and missing bags
- damage by hydraulic oil
- infestation.

Traditionally, at the country of origin, cocoa beans are packed into jute bags of 60 to 70 kg per bag and are subject to sanitary certification prior to shipment. As cocoa beans and jute (or hessian or sisal, or even polypropylene from Central South American origin) bags are an ideal medium for harbouring infestation, fumigation is frequently carried out prior to shipment.

Figure 27.1: Cocoa beans packed into jute bags.

Ideally, cocoa beans should be shipped in well-ventilated conditions, particularly for transportation from warm tropical producing areas to colder destinations.

When shipped in traditional breakbulk stowage, adequate ventilation should be allowed, with ample dunnage. In particular, bags should not be stowed directly in contact with the ship's side or bare steelwork and they should be given adequate headspace for ventilation. It is imperative that vessels have ventilation capable of a sufficient number of air changes per hour within the cargo holds. The usual recommendation is between 10 to 20 changes per hour. Ventilation of a cocoa cargo requires that a proper regime, based on external air temperatures, cargo temperatures and relative humidities, is drawn up and implemented, with details recorded.

Respiration and post-fermentation factors result in cocoa beans evolving CO_2, so enclosed space entry procedures must be followed before entering cargo spaces.

Figure 27.2: Container lined with kraft paper.

When shipped in containers, it is preferable that fully/super ventilated containers are employed but these types of containers are not usually available.

All containers should be subject to careful inspection to confirm their integrity, cleanliness and freedom from taint. However, while neither shippers nor consignees can dictate to the carriers the stowage location of containers on board, under-deck stowage within cargo holds that are well ventilated is the best that can be offered.

When cocoa beans are shipped in non-ventilated or dry van containers, there is no control over ventilation of the contents. Dry van containers are subject to condensation problems resulting from cargo being loaded in warm climates with temperatures of 25°C upwards and then shipped to colder climates in Northern Europe, USA, etc. The main cocoa shipping season is during the European winter. The mechanics of condensation forming in containers are well understood and various attempts have been made to reduce the effects, but with limited success.

The recommended dressing is for containers to be lined around the side and front walls and over the floor with a single layer of double-wall corrugated board, and then with a double layer of the same over the top of the stow of bags.

Bags of desiccant (known as dri-bags) are then employed (suspended from lashing points at the top of the side walls in the containers) to absorb moisture during the period of transit.

The most effective desiccants are those that contain more than 65% of calcium chloride.

When cocoa beans are shipped with a higher than desirable moisture content, the incidence of condensation with resultant wetting and deterioration (mostly by way of mould to the cocoa beans) increases considerably.

When bags of cocoa beans are offloaded, any bags exhibiting external wet stains and/or external contamination are usually segregated by the receivers. Bags that have become wet damaged may be externally stained and/or mouldy, and cocoa beans within wet bags may show signs of external bloom (white spotting) as well as subsequent mould growth development. In instances of heavy wetting, the beans will become blocked together.

If the bags are found to be contaminated with foreign substances, the contaminant should, wherever possible, be identified and/or analysed as to its likely properties, particularly as cocoa beans are generally destined for use in the human food chain.

Cocoa beans from wet damaged bags may be subjected to a reconditioning operation, but only if this is acceptable to the final receivers. If they are food manufacturers, they may be unwilling and/or unable to accept reconditioned cocoa skimmings, which have a lower value for use in alternative (normally non-food) outlets.

Cocoa beans may also be shipped in open or flat-rack containers, or bolsters, which are essentially containers without sidewalls or roof. The bags are stacked on the base of these containers and secured by lengths of timber, held in place by steel bands around the girth of the stow. Although not common practice, this is an effective method of shipping cocoa beans in bags provided that:

- The bags are well stowed on the flat-rack
- the securing timber is clean and dry
- the securing steel bands do not cut into the bags
- bags do not overhang the base section of the container
- tarpaulin covers are available at both the load port and the discharge port that may be used to cover the laden bolster or flat-rack container when rainfall is experienced.

Shipment of cocoa beans in bags on bolsters allows full all round ventilation and, therefore, allows for the dispersal of moisture from the cocoa.

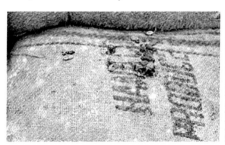 

Figure 27.3: Bags that have become wet damaged may be externally stained and/or mouldy and cocoa beans within wet bags may show signs of white spotting and mould.

Cocoa beans are also shipped in bulk within the cargo holds of ships or in bulk within containers. The reason for shipment in bulk is primarily economic, eg a standard 20 ft container can carry approximately 13 T of cocoa beans in bags but approximately 18 T in bulk.

In some instances, a crust of mouldy cocoa beans forms on parts or all of the surface of bulk cargo, which if possible should be removed and segregated to maintain the good overall quality of the bulk.

Figure 27.4: Bulk shipment of cocoa beans.

A crust may also form when cocoa beans are shipped in bulk containers. These are standard 20 ft, non-ventilated containers that are often plywood lined. However, it is very difficult (more or less impossible) to separate the crust within the container and it may reduce the quality of the bulk overall when discharging.

Care must, therefore, be taken in discussing with consignees/receivers ways of solving the problem effectively. It is possible for some receivers to blend cocoa beans, so an allowance for depreciation can be negotiated in respect of bags that contain a percentage of damaged cocoa beans. If cocoa beans are destined for storage for sampling and sale to the *LIFFE Terminal Market*, reconditioning is not permitted, as reconditioned cocoa beans will not be accepted.

Damaged cocoa beans generally retain a good salvage value.

When loading cocoa beans in bulk, special attention should be paid to the following aspects, in addition to normal bulk carrier practice:

- Fresh air should be ventilated over the top of the cargo. Generally speaking, this means that wooden ducts have to be made between the fixed ducts and the top of the cargo. It must be ensured that wooden ducts cannot collapse during the voyage
- the ballast condition should be such that no alterations have to be made during the voyage. Pumping cold ballast water in ballast tanks around the cargo space will result in damage. Good ballast management is important
- attention should be paid to excessive moisture, lumped cocoa beans and infestation
- sources of ignition, such as cigarette smoke, should be kept away from the cocoa beans as their high fat percentage increases the likelihood of them catching fire.

For bulk cargoes, when sailing from warm to cold regions the cocoa beans will lose considerable quantities of moisture. This warm and humid air has to be ventilated out of the hold, therefore the hold must be ventilated as often and for as long as possible. Ventilation openings on the weather deck can be protected from seawater spray in order to continue ventilation. When a vessel enters the discharge port, the covers have to be opened as soon as possible, all weather permitting.

During the whole voyage records should be made of weather conditions and what ventilation has taken place. Changing the ballast condition should be avoided during the voyage.

27.2   Cocoa Butter

Cocoa butter, in its pure prime pressed form, is produced by pressing the inner nib of the cocoa beans. Cocoa butter is the most valuable product of cocoa beans and usually has a distinctive chocolate-like odour. It is of a cream colour and is customarily packed into blocks of 25 kg and packed within polythene-lined fibreboard cartons. Cocoa butter is normally shipped within containers in such packaging.

Cocoa butter is susceptible to the effects of heating and will become soft and malleable at 30 to 32°C and will melt at 32 to 35°C. Having become warm or molten, it can retain the latent heat and remain in such a condition down to as low as 17°C. Depending on the structure of the constituent fats, the effect of heating cocoa butter is to raise the FFA (free fatty acid) level which, in turn, affects the fat structure and the shelf life of the cocoa butter, and any product that it is used to produce. If severe, it will cause the cocoa butter to become rancid. When heated, the cocoa butter will expand which may, in turn, cause it to burst the polyliner packaging of the cartons and seep out, staining adjacent cartons.

Cocoa butter retains its latent heat for a long period of time, aggravating the extent of any damage or stain.

Bacteria will develop on the fat-stained cartons and may well affect the cocoa butter, rendering it unacceptable to manufacturers of human food chain products. If wet damage is sustained to cartons of cocoa butter and if the water is able to ingress into the blocks of cocoa butter within the inner poly packaging, it will cause the cocoa butter to discolour. Wetting of cocoa butter cartons can also result in microbial contamination, rendering the product unfit for human consumption.

If cartons of cocoa butter are found to be infested, fumigation should not be carried out as the chemical residue will be absorbed by the butter and render it tainted and unfit for use in the human food chain. It is preferable to arrange for a careful stripping, examination and sorting of cartons and their contents according to the degree of infestation.

Other grades of cocoa butter are frequently carried in a molten condition in heated stainless steel tanks at a minimum temperature of 35°C, at which cocoa butter remains liquid, and a maximum temperature of 45°C.

Ships' tanks have to be inspected carefully before shipment to confirm their cleanliness and suitability for carriage of cocoa butter. Details of the ship's previous three cargoes should be established.

Similarly, receiving shore tanks should be inspected.

27.3   Cocoa Liquor/Powder/Butter and Cake

Cocoa liquor is produced from roasted cocoa nibs ground to a paste. The heat of the process causes the cocoa butter in the nibs to melt, forming cocoa liquor. It is similar in all respects to cocoa butter, with the exception that it is a much harder product with a lower fat content than cocoa butter and, therefore, is lower in value. It is otherwise subject to the same difficulties.

Cocoa liquor may be pressed to separate it into cocoa butter and cocoa cake. Cocoa powder is produced from ground cocoa cake. It is customarily packed in multi-ply paper bags, which must be handled carefully to avoid tearing/loss of contents. Cocoa powder is more or less inert, although, if it becomes hot, it may smoulder or burn owing to the residual fat content of the powder.

27.4   Issues with Regard to Shipments of Cocoa Carried in Containers

Cocoa products are prone to mildew damage if wet, so great care is required in handling. It is important to line the inside of ventilated containers to absorb moisture. Moisture, before stuffing or shipment, should be below a certain percentage (typically around 7.5% but advice should be sought from the charterer). During the beginning of the cocoa season, the moisture levels are very high and shipowners often ask for a letter of indemnity from shippers.

Chapter 28 – Coffee

Coffee is processed from coffee beans, the seed of the coffee plant. The beans are processed by either wet or dry processing (typically varying by country of origin). Coffee can be transported as a bulk cargo (break bulk or pre-slung) or in containers.

28.1 Packaging

Traditionally, coffee beans are shipped in woven natural fibre bags, allowing free circulation of air. However, coffee is now most commonly transported by container, particularly from East and West Africa. As the trade has expanded, the methods of shipment have changed from loading coffee bags into containers to loading loose coffee directly into lined containers to save packaging costs and to increase carriage capacity (from 18 to 21 T in a 20 ft container (TEU)).

Figure 28.1: A liner bag fitted in a container for stowage of coffee.

28.2 Stowage and Care of Coffee

Coffee cargoes are highly susceptible to moisture absorption when transported by sea. This is particularly the case for coffee cargoes that are loaded in warm/moist climates and then discharged in the colder climates of Europe/North America. As the low temperature air of the northern hemisphere enters a container loaded in tropical areas, the shipment of coffee suffers more condensation damage than coffee from other sources. The main risk of condensation damage to bagged coffee arises in containers shipped into Northern Europe, particularly if the containers remain on the quayside for long periods after discharge, often exposed to large variations in temperature. Containers on the outside of the stack suffer most damage, with those on the inside being partly protected by the outer containers. Rapid stripping of the containers after discharge, or storage of the containers in a warehouse, are the only solutions to this problem.

For both carriage in bulk and by container, careful ventilation is important to prevent condensation forming on the surfaces of the ship's holds/containers.

Coffee cargoes are sensitive and therefore highly susceptible to taint. Cleanliness of the cargo hold/container is important. Care should be taken not to damage the coffee by fumigation and also to keep the coffee away from exposed internal surfaces with the use of paper.

Figure 28.2: Condensation from the container roof has dripped onto the bags.

Figure 28.3: Sealed ventilation openings.

Another cause of condensation damage is the practice of sealing the container ventilators with tape for fumigation purposes prior to shipment. After fumigation, the tapes are often not removed, preventing airflow and resulting in excessive condensation and mould growth. The volume of the air space at the top of the container should be carefully checked. When containers are loaded with 250 × 70 kg bags, a space of about 50 cm should be left between the top of the stow and the roof of the container.

When loaded with 300 × 60 kg bags, minimal space remains and in this case the cargo is more prone to condensation damage. There is no obvious scientific explanation for this phenomenon but it is well substantiated. Although ships' crew cannot control the stuffing of containers, such damage may well be attributed to the ship, with allegations of incorrect ventilation during the passage.

Figure 28.4: Water has penetrated through all the openings.

It is recommended that containers are lined with heavy duty kraft paper/corrugated paper, which should also cover the floor and the top of the stow of bags, so as to effectively form an 'envelope' around the stow of bags. Bags should be stored in a brickwork fashion in order to minimise the effect of vertical changes between the bags and therefore minimise the rising of moist air towards the roof of the container. The floor of the container will have wooden boarding and this should be treated with wood preservative products. The preservative must be compatible with coffee to avoid contamination and resulting claims.

Shippers are recommended to check the history of containers prior to using them for transportation of coffee.

Chapter 29 – Bagged Rice

Rice is a cereal grain and the staple food for many nations. It can be grown in anything from dry upland soils, to irrigated fields and along flooded river beds. There are over 85,000 varieties of rice in the research stocks of the International Rice Research Institute (IRRI), and over 120,000 cultivars are known to exist. The most common, Asian rice (*Oryza sativa*), is divided into Indica and Japonica varieties. Indica rice is longer and more slender, and generally remains separate when cooked. Japonica rice has shorter, rounder and more translucent grains, which quickly become slightly sticky when cooked.

When harvested, rice typically contains moisture in the range of 15 to 22% (US) or 19 to 25% (Asian) and must be dried to prevent spoilage (generally to between 12 and 14.5%). If well dried and protected, rice can be stored for many years.

After being dried and stored, rice undergoes a milling process to remove the tough outer husk and the inner layers of bran from the edible rice grain. Partial milling removes just the outer husk to produce brown rice. Complete milling also removes the bran layer and cereal germ to produce white rice.

Rice is traded as either paddy or milled rice, but most rice moving in world trade is fully milled and bagged in 20, 25 or 50 kg polypropylene bags. A description of the product is required in cargo documentation, ie paddy/ brown/milled/parboiled, along with the grain type (long or short), origin and the percentage of broken rice (eg Thai white rice, long grain, 5% broken). Standards in most countries define the percentage of 'brokens' and other imperfections permitted in each grade of rice, and the basis on which such percentages are measured, which will have an impact on market value.

Traditionally, rice would have been carried as breakbulk on board general cargo ships designed to accommodate rice, with permanent wooden dunnage and spaces designed for proper ventilation to ensure the cargo arrived in the best condition possible. However, as global demand for staple foods has risen and the shipping industry has faced increasing pressure on freight rates, a large percentage of rice shipments are now transported in bagged form on board traditional bulk carriers, with smaller parcels carried more and more often as containerised cargo.

29.1 Hazards to the Cargo

The primary hazards to bagged rice are water damage, infestation, mishandling of cargo bags during loading, improper stowage in cargo holds and deficiencies in the ship's condition affecting the cargo holds.

Bagged rice needs to be kept dry and well ventilated. Therefore, it is important to inspect the ship's holds, hatch covers and ventilation system for potential defects as these will be critical to the safe carriage of the cargo on even short voyages.

The frequency and cost of claims associated with bagged rice is significant, with wet damage generally accounting for over one third of cargo claims and nearly half of the associated costs. Handling damages generally account for one fifth of the claims. It is also notable that cargo shortage, attributed to short-landings and pilferage, is one of the most costly types of claim.

Seawater ingress	Ingress through cargo hatch covers on passage, bilges, hull damage, pierced ballast tanks or sounding pipes in cargo holds.
Fresh water ingress	Rain ingress during loading or discharging operations, or through leakage on passage. Damaged pipework within cargo hold. Ship/cargo sweat due to variations in climate temperature and humidity.
Condensation	Fresh water condensation on the ship's structure or cargo caused by temperature differences between the air in the hold and the ship's steel structure (or cargo) from poorly managed ventilation.
Contamination	Cargo holds can be contaminated by prior cargoes carried in the hold (residual odours, staining), by general condition (rust, chipped paint) or from fuel leakage.
Infestation	Rice is particularly susceptible to infestation by storage pests if stored for over two months. Cargo can be exposed to granary and rice weevils; flour, drugstore and spider beetles; dried fruit and meal moths; rats and mice.
	The chewing damage caused by cereal pests also brings about increased heat and moisture, which in turn provides favourable conditions for mould and (potentially) bacterial growth.
Heat	As well as the danger of direct heating from halogen lamps that have not been isolated, heat may be generated from spaces adjacent to cargo holds, such as heated bunker tanks, the engine room or adjacent cargo.
Improper stowage	Damage to bagged rice can occur due to improper stowage, causing shifting or collapse of cargo stacks during transit.

Table 29.1: Possible causes of damage to shipments of rice.

Caking, wet rice and mould	Seawater/fresh water ingress or condensation can cause bagged rice to become wet and permanently damaged through 'caking' and can also result in mould development. Affected bags have almost no salvage value.
Odour contamination	Wet rice, particularly rice damaged by seawater, spreads a penetrating odour that is absorbed by the adjacent rice and may spread through the entire hold. Rice is highly odour-sensitive. Brown rice is particularly sensitive to the absorption of foreign odours. Affected cargo has almost no salvage value.
Torn bags	Bags used to carry rice are normally constructed from woven polypropylene, which is a relatively strong material but is still subject to tearing and damage during loading, transit or discharge. Rice from damaged bags can be restowed in spares, but this increases handling costs and can lead to shortage claims.
Stained bags	Bags can be stained due to contact with dirty surfaces, or other factors. If the rice is undamaged, it may be re-bagged, but it will face devaluation and incur additional costs for handling.

Table 29.2: Types of damage associated with shipment of rice.

29.2 Avoidance of Damage: Preparation

29.2.1 Cleaning

A number of factors can affect the condition of the cargo holds, making them unsuitable for carrying bagged rice. Proper precautions should be taken in preparing the cargo hold before loading.

If there is any sign of previous insect or rodent infestation, holds should be sealed and fumigated using an approved method or, if appropriate, sprayed locally with insecticide or rodent repellent.

This operation should only be performed by approved professionals, with due regard to the safety of the crew and contractors.

Rust and scale that might contaminate the cargo should be removed. Paint and lime wash may be applied to avoid contact of the scaled ship side with the bagged rice and also to provide a sound and hygienic space to carry cargo.

Cargo holds should be properly cleaned and prepared. All tank tops/decks and bulkheads (including all difficult to reach areas and areas where dirt and water may become trapped) should be cleaned, swept, washed, rinsed with fresh water, mopped, well ventilated and dried.

All residual odours from cleaning agents should be thoroughly ventilated from the space as they may taint the bagged rice.

The hold bilge wells should be clean and free from any cargo residue, bilge water or moisture. Hold bilge suctions and non-return arrangements should be tested and demonstrated as functional. Double burlap wrapping should be applied on the bilge cover plate and fixed with masking tape.

29.2.2 Hatches and Vents

Bagged rice needs to be kept dry and well ventilated. Therefore, it is important to inspect both the ship's cargo hatch cover systems and ventilators for potential defects as their performance will be critical to the safe carriage of the rice cargo. Attention should be paid to the following areas:

- Hatch cover operation should be reliable, safe and timely, and the hatches should be closed if there is rainfall during loading/discharge in order to protect the cargo. Hydraulics should be free from leaks that may taint cargo

- cargo hatches should be free from piercing damage or deformation, correctly aligned and meet adjoining covers and coamings squarely. To operate correctly, the compression bar, dogs, clamps and cleats must be in line and free from deformation. Dogs should be clear of damage and set for the correct tension when applied

- hatch cover packing should be in good condition (ie not imprinted by more than 25%, hardened, or with any sections missing). Replacement packing should be made in complete lengths only and preshaped corner sections used where necessary. Packing channels should be clear of corrosion and free from damage or deformation

- the full weight of the hatch cover should not be borne by the gaskets alone. Hatch cover landing pads should have minimal wear to avoid overcompression of the packings

- drainage channels should be clear of corrosion and free from damage or deformation and drain non-return valves should be checked and proven to be operational

- ventilator flaps should be inspected to ensure they are in good working condition and seal properly when closed

- the double-bottom ballast tanks and side tanks should be pressed up prior to loading to ensure their watertight integrity

- bilge suctions and tank top openings should be thoroughly examined, tested and proved fully operational and the strainer plate overcovered with burlap (as above). Any openings to the tank top should be examined and proven to be watertight and properly secured

- sounding pipes and other pipework should be examined and cleared of any debris. Any pipes within the holds, including ballast pipes or tank air pipes, should also be closely examined to ensure they are in good working condition. Sounding pipe closures should be checked to ensure they are watertight.

It is the shipowner's responsibility to maintain their cargo hatch covers in good operable condition and establish an adequate inspection/maintenance programme, so that due diligence may be proven in the event of any cargo claim. It is, therefore, also the shipowner's burden to prove that their cargo hatch covers are in good operable condition (see Chapter 55 Steel Hatch Covers).

Hatch covers should be proven to be watertight by hose test or, preferably, ultrasonic testing carried out independently and prior to loading of cargo. Holding valid Class and flag State certificates alone will be no defence against a water ingress claim.

It is important to note that, if charterers ask to use Ram-Nek tape (a brand/type of high adhesive plastic sealing tape) it does not relieve the shipowner from their duty under the charterparty to present their ship in seaworthy and cargoworthy condition.

29.2.3 Dunnage

To prevent damage from condensation, dunnage should be used on steel surfaces. Individual country or Port Authorities may have rules on the use of specific types of dunnage and local agents should be consulted in advance to determine whether there are any local restrictions. Generally, there are two primary types of dunnage used for bagged rice transported on bulk carriers – bamboo or timber – although combinations of Styrofoam, plastic/polythene sheet and kraft paper are also in use.

Bamboo dunnage

Dunnage usually consists of bamboo sticks laid in a crisscross fashion on the steel tank tops and side shells and then overlaid with bamboo mats.

While bamboo is lightweight, re-usable and relatively cheap and easy to access in load ports, it is commonly found that bamboo is not free from moisture and can retain and bleed moisture during passage. Bamboo sticks may appear dry on the outside but may have a moist pulpy interior. Bamboo mats overlaid with kraft paper should never be used as the fragile kraft paper will be destroyed and rendered useless.

When there is condensation or wetness on the tank top, bamboo mats tend to absorb the moisture and pass it on to adjacent bags that rest upon them. The greater the condensation, the more damage is transferred to more adjacent bags, so this method is not recommended.

It is noteworthy that Peru does not allow cargo protected by bamboo mats and sticks to be discharged at their ports. A similar restriction applies in Chile, where disposal of protection materials such as bamboo mats and sticks is not permitted.

Timber dunnage

Timber dunnage (thick planks) should be placed in two layers on the tank top of each hold, with the lowest layer in a fore-aft direction, to provide drain channels, and the second layer at 90°. This will prevent the lower tiers of bags coming into contact with the tank top and avoid wet damage to the cargo. Timber dunnage should be well cured and dried, and the use of fresh sawn timber should be avoided. Kraft/lining paper or corrugated cardboard should be placed on top of the timber dunnage to protect the bags.

In tall or partial loads, timber dunnage should also be used within the stow to avoid stow collapse.

Synthetic materials

For bagged rice, the proper placement and combination of plastic/Styrofoam dunnage materials has proven to be effective in reducing condensation damage caused by direct contact with the ship's steel structure.

In many ports, styrofoam is not easy to obtain and it can be expensive. In addition, plastic and styrofoam dunnage materials may be difficult to dispose of at some ports. Proper care is required to ensure that the stow does not become closed off by polythene sheeting material, reducing the ventilation capacity through the stow or blocking drainage of any condensation.

Caution is important when using Styrofoam near ventilation openings. It should be carefully cut and fitted so that it does not prohibit the flow of air through the ventilation openings.

Location	Plastic sheet	Styrofoam	Kraft paper	Optimal arrangement	Alternative arrangement
Side shell	X	X	X	Plastic and Styrofoam	Plastic and kraft paper
Forward bulkhead, cargo hold no. 1	X	X	X	Plastic and Styrofoam	Plastic and kraft paper
Aft bulkhead adjacent to engine room	X	X		Plastic and Styrofoam	Plastic and kraft paper
All other transverse bulkheads	X	X		Plastic and kraft paper	Kraft paper
Hopper tanks	X	X		Plastic and kraft paper	Plastic or kraft paper
Hatchways	X	X	X	Plastic and Styrofoam	Plastic and kraft paper
Hatch coamings	X	X		Plastic and Styrofoam	Plastic or Styrofoam
Tank tops and tank top sloping plates	X	X		Plastic and kraft paper	Plastic or kraft paper
On top of cargo			X	Kraft paper	

Table 29.3: Placement and combination of dunnage materials.

29.3 Avoidance of Damage: Stowage and Ventilation

Rice should not be stowed near any strong smelling cargo such as bagged cocoa, bulk copra or similar. The impact of any ventilation exhaust should also be considered.

Shipowners, in coordination with the ship's Master and chief officer, should be made aware of the charterer's stowage plan (in writing) in advance of cargo loading operations and all efforts must be made to ensure the cargo is stowed as per the agreed charterer's/shipper's instructions.

Construction of ventilation channels (ie a channel/reasonable gap between groups of bags) should be considered on a case-by-case basis, depending on the volume of cargo, dimensions and configuration of the cargo holds and the ventilation capabilities of the ship to allow the free flow of air. It is common practice that every five tiers of cargo being stowed should interlock and cross bags between adjacent stowage stacks. This practice allows for better stability of the stacks to prevent cargo stack slippage that could potentially block ventilation channels.

29.3.1 When to Ventilate

Bagged rice must be properly ventilated to prevent condensation during the voyage or at any point when the hatch covers are shut. The purpose of this is to remove the warm, moist air surrounding the cargo and replace it with drier air to minimise condensation on the colder steelwork in the hold (ship's sweat). To do this, the ventilation method must be effective and the environmental conditions must be right.

Ship sweat occurs when a ship loads in a warm, moist atmosphere and then sails into cooler climates. As the ship's steelwork cools below the dew point of the surrounding air, moisture will condense onto it.

Ship sweat appears as beads of moisture, typically on the sides of the hold when the sea temperature is low or on upper sides when the air temperature is cold.

If the dew point of the outside air (the air used for ventilation) is lower than that in the hold, it is appropriate to ventilate and, if not, ventilation should be withheld. However, it may be necessary to ventilate for other reasons, such as to comply with fumigators' instructions when the cargo has been fumigated on board. External factors, such as sea spray across the ventilator openings, must also be taken into account to ensure that water does not enter the hold.

While the ship is on passage, the dew point should be regularly monitored to determine whether ventilation of the cargo holds is necessary. Comparison of dew points is usually made by taking readings from wet and dry bulb thermometers on deck and in the hold. Obtaining the ambient readings is generally easy as most ships have a Stevenson screen fitted on each bridge wing. However, obtaining the same readings in a ship's hold can be problematic and during the voyage it may not be safe for crew to enter the hold to obtain temperature readings. If thermometers are simply lowered into the hold from outside, there will be difficulty obtaining sufficient airflow across the wet thermometer.

Where it is possible to safely enter cargo holds to obtain meaningful readings, it may be necessary to stop ventilation to allow the in-hold atmosphere to stabilise. If this is not done, the crew will be measuring the ventilating air rather than the true in-hold atmosphere. If a reading is taken, it should be properly recorded in the cargo ventilation record book.

Where access to the holds is impossible or undesirable, and provided there is no significant airflow, the hold dew point can be determined from traditional wet and dry bulb thermometers placed inside the trunking of an exhaust ventilator or similar pipework leading from the compartment. Again, if this is done, it should be properly noted in the cargo ventilation record book.

Where the cargo has been fumigated, on no account should crew members enter the cargo holds until they have been appropriately ventilated and certified gas-free.

29.3.2 Ventilation Systems

There are three systems of cargo ventilation in general use – mechanical (airflow assisted by fans), natural (without fans) and controlled atmosphere (controlling a space's temperature and carbon dioxide).

Most ships loading full cargoes of rice in the short sea trade in locations such as Thailand generally have only natural ventilation, sometimes assisted by portable fans. For voyages to colder climatic regions, natural ventilation is insufficient and any ships engaged on carriage of bagged rice on longer voyages should be equipped with a proper functioning mechanical ventilation system, with a capacity of 15 to 25 air changes per hour (calculated on the basis of empty hold space). All fans should be checked to ensure they run properly in the correct direction. The carriage of rice in a controlled atmosphere ship does not provide any advantage over a well-ventilated space.

29.4 Fumigation

Most rice cargoes are fumigated after completion of loading, which brings its own set of challenges as substances that kill insects may just as easily kill humans.

Due regard should be paid to the IMO's *Recommendations on the Safe Use of Pesticides in Ships Applicable to the Fumigation of Cargo Holds* (MSC.1/Circ.1264 and Amendments) (Reference 51).

The fumigation process starts with a survey by the fumigator prior to loading. The surveyor will inspect the cargo holds looking for any area that will allow a fumigant to penetrate into spaces that will be inhabited by the ship's crew. This is particularly important at the bulkheads between the accommodation spaces or machinery spaces and cargo holds. If any gaps are known or found, the surveyor will recommend that they are properly and effectively sealed off.

Before the fumigant is applied, the seals on the hatch covers and access trunkways must be marked with warning signs and sealed once completed.

The most common fumigant used is Phostoxin (aluminium phosphide), which creates phosphine gas when it reacts with moisture in the air. For it to activate, there has to be sufficient moisture in the air and the temperature of the cargo must be greater than 7°C.

Phostoxin tablets are often placed in sleeves that are laid across the surface of the cargo. The sleeves keep all of the Phostoxin in a sock-like tube so that the residual ash can easily be removed at the discharge port. If the sleeves are not properly applied, there may be an incomplete reaction, with an insufficient dose applied to the cargo and the danger of production of Phosphine gas when the sleeve is disturbed at the discharge port. A preferred (but more expensive) version is the prepack rope, which spreads the tablets out in a rope-like container across the top of the stow. This ensures greater exposure and thus better reactivity.

The recommended minimum dosage of Phostoxin is 33 g/1,000 ft³ of space. An effective dose is normally 45 g/1,000 ft³. In some instances, owners and/or P&I Clubs hire independent surveyors to witness the fumigation process.

For a charterer, fumigation is usually applied only because it is required in the sales contract and it can, therefore, be a temptation for the shipper to ask a fumigator for a 'full certificate' while only applying a cursory fumigation with less than the required dose for the size of hold. This should be monitored closely and the details of what is actually applied recorded.

29.5   Protection from Claims

Some damages can occur to bagged rice prior to arrival on board ship and it is important to recognise and document any pre-shipment irregularities prior to acceptance.

Cargo can be exposed to damage by wetting during any barge leg of a voyage. Water ingress may occur via the barge hull planking on older wooden barges, or via the deck/hatch cover arrangements on both steel and wooden barges. This is a particular problem during inclement weather and must be watched for. As well as the condition of the cargo, investigation of the condition of any barge should be well documented.

Bagged rice is normally brought on board ship from a barge, or loaded pre-bundled via crane from ashore. Bundles should be examined for any visible damage as much as possible before delivery into the hold and afterwards during stowage.

29.5.1   Cargo Quality and Moisture Content

The ship's Master and chief officer should ensure that the cargo is tested for moisture content as it arrives on board. The maximum moisture content for rice to be shipped is 14.5%. If the cargo moisture is found to be in excess of that amount, there is a significantly higher risk of damage resulting from condensation.

It is important to acquire cargo quality certificates from the shippers. However, this information should not be solely relied upon and the Master should approach the Club correspondent to assist if there are any concerns.

29.5.2   During Loading and Discharge

When the cargo hatch covers are open, the cargo holds are exposed to potential adverse weather conditions. The Master should ensure that during loading and discharge operations, there are crew members on station on the bridge who are constantly monitoring any changes in weather that may require closing of the cargo hatch covers. Monitoring should be informed by visual observation, radar and appropriate weather forecasts. Rain letters must not be accepted.

As well as ensuring hatch covers are in good working order, the crew should know the amount of time it takes to close each hatch cover prior to commencement of cargo operations. Adequately sized, placed and secured tarpaulins should be considered as an additional measure of cargo protection to cover closed or partially closed hatches in the event of adverse weather conditions.

While unlikely, the same applies if cargo hatches are opened during the voyage to ventilate the cargo.

29.5.3   Third Party Surveyors

To protect the ship from false claims, it might sometimes be useful to utilise qualified third party surveyors to properly corroborate and record the condition of the ship, cargo and conduct of the operations. The crew should regularly monitor and ensure that surveyors are performing their assigned survey tasks as required.

An inspection should be made to document the condition of the cargo holds prior to loading to ensure that they are dry and clean, that bilges are in satisfactory condition, ventilation systems are in working order and the hatch covers are in satisfactory weathertight condition. If possible, an ultrasonic hatch test should be witnessed and reported by the attending surveyor.

Where a draught survey is required (and allowed), surveyors representing the shipowner and the shipper's interests should jointly carry this out before and after loading to agree on the quantity of cargo loaded. It should be noted that the weight of cargo may decrease as a result of loss of moisture from the cargo during the voyage and so the moisture content of the rice should also be taken at load and discharge.

A tally surveyor should be positioned at each cargo hold to record the quantity of bags loaded and to liaise with tally clerks, representing the shipper's interests, to agree on the quantity that will ultimately be noted on the mate's receipt.

A cargo surveyor should monitor the cargo being loaded to ensure that it is properly stowed with due consideration to dunnaging and unobstructed ventilation, so that sufficient and proper ventilation channels are allowed for and a stable stow achieved. A cargo surveyor should also monitor the condition of the cargo as it comes on board and during its handling by stevedores, in order to reject on behalf of the shipowner any bags that are caked, mouldy, wet, torn, stained, discoloured or odour contaminated, and reject/remark entire lots that appear to be infested by vermin.

29.5.4 Stevedore Monitoring

During loading and discharge operations, the crew should be aware of the particular cargo damage risks associated with stevedores, which may include:

- Rough handling of cargo bags leading to tearing
- use of steel hooks for cargo handling (which should be strictly prohibited)
- careless loading of heavy slings of bagged rice. Damage may result if cargo is not properly lowered and lifted, and this may go undetected until discharge
- dragging cargo that is wedged in or overstowed by other cargo. This may be avoided by managing the load and discharge sequence
- improper stowage that prevents proper cargo ventilation
- theft/pilferage
- urination and defecation in cargo hold areas due to lack of sufficient sanitary facilities for stevedores while working on board the ship.

If cargo/tally surveyors are not available, as well as manning the gangway (and therefore monitoring any pilferage), the Master should consider stationing crew members above every cargo hold where cargo operations are underway to monitor the activities of all stevedores working in the cargo holds, and in any other locations where cargo is being brought on board or discharged from the ship.

29.5.5 Recording

In the event of damage or incident, the crew should:

- Notify the Master and/or officer on watch of any and all observed activities of concern by third parties on board the ship while loading or discharging cargo
- log the details of the specific incident in the ship's cargo logbook
- collect all possible relevant evidence (video, photographs, statements from witnesses and physical evidence of the incident, if applicable) to be kept as a record of the incident.

The mate's receipt should reflect details of the exact condition of the cargo, any pilferage/theft, receipt of damaged bagged rice upon loading (ie prior to arriving on board ship), improper stowage, etc. Any remarks concerning visual damage should be noted on the mate's receipt, for example 'two torn bags', 'five discoloured bags', 'three mouldy bags', 'evidence of infestation', etc.

29.6 Case Study

A small hold fire occurred on a ship with a cargo of bagged rice. Investigation showed that only empty rice bags had combusted. It was found that, as is customary, a few thousand empty polypropylene bags had been loaded on top of the cargo on completion of loading to allow for rice from split or broken bags to be repackaged during discharge.

From the available evidence, it was deduced that the person doing the fumigation had triggered the solid fumigant capsules and thrown them onto the cargo from the hold access hatch. One or more of the capsules landed on top of the empty bags, which were determined to have been wet, and this additional moisture accelerated the chemical reaction, creating excess heat and causing the fire.

As the hold's fire/smoke detection systems had been isolated as required prior to fumigation, the ship's crew were unaware that there had been a fire in this hold for some days after departure.

To avoid a similar incident, empty bags should always be loaded in a clean and dry condition.

Chapter 30 –
Agricultural Products in
Non-refrigerated Containers

When shipping agricultural products, such as coffee, in ventilated or standard containers, the shipper must ensure that the container, packaging and dunnage are appropriate for both cargo and voyage to ensure cargo arrives in prime condition to the receiver.

A wide variety of agricultural products are carried in non-refrigerated containers, either ventilated or standard dry boxes, including:

- Cocoa
- coffee
- tea
- tobacco
- dried fruit
- rice
- nuts
- oilseeds

- pulses
- spices.

Fresh fruit and vegetables are more commonly carried in refrigerated containers, although produce such as melons, oranges, potatoes, sweet potatoes, yams and onions are sometimes carried in ventilated or open containers.

Two frequent causes of major cargo damage are condensation and taint.

30.1   Condensation (Sweat)

Almost all agricultural products have a considerable intrinsic moisture content. They are hygroscopic cargoes which means they are in equilibrium with the air in the container and can emit as well as absorb moisture. The amount of water available within a container of such cargoes is much larger than for manufactured goods. Translocation of a comparatively small proportion of the total moisture available may cause substantial condensation problems.

> Hygroscopic cargoes change temperature comparatively slowly. Therefore, when a container is shipped across climatic zones, the cargo adjusts to the changing ambient temperatures much more slowly than the container walls and the air. This delay can cause considerable temperature differences within the container and is the driving force for moisture translocation and condensation.

Ventilated containers
Ventilated containers include those with passive ventilation openings, open containers and mechanically ventilated containers. However, these are all comparatively rare and the vast majority of containers have no effective ventilation provision. Although the small air-expansion holes in the walls of standard dry boxes are sometimes called 'ventilation holes', the airflow through them is insufficient to provide significant protection against condensation.

The International Cocoa Organization recommends using ventilated containers for all containerised cocoa shipments. Some coffee and cocoa shippers use such containers, but this is not standard throughout the trade.

> The air inside ventilated containers is largely common with the surrounding air, which may present additional problems, such as more ready transmission of taints. Therefore, the stowage location on board requires careful consideration.

Desiccants
During carriage of hygroscopic cargoes in non-ventilated containers, condensation can be prevented if the relative humidity of the air inside the container is kept sufficiently low that its dew point is always below the ambient temperature. This ideal situation is often unrealistic, but the dew point may be lowered, and the risk of condensation reduced accordingly, by using desiccants.

Desiccants (such as silica gel, Møler clay or certain polymers) are water absorbent and remove moisture from the surrounding air. They may be supplied in bags, specially-lined sheets or as polymer-based paint. Once the maximum absorption capacity of such products is exhausted, they have no further beneficial effect, so their type and amount must be chosen carefully for the type of cargo and the voyage.

Because of their potential for significant moisture exchange with the air inside the container, hygroscopic cargoes place much greater demands on the capacity and sustained absorption rate of desiccants than non-hygroscopic cargoes. Desiccants alone are unlikely to prevent condensation in the event of rapid temperature changes of large magnitude.

Dunnage, sheets and linings

A basic precaution for cargoes sensitive to condensation damage is to apply suitable dunnage to separate the cargo from the container's walls and floors. This cannot prevent the formation of condensation, but can greatly reduce its commercial implications. It is often recommended to use kraft paper or similar material to line the walls and floors of containers or as protective sheets on top of the cargo. Since these quickly become saturated, they cannot afford significant protection against severe sweat, but they can absorb small amounts of condensation and, in some circumstances, prevent or reduce staining and similar damage.

Sheets placed on top of the cargo must be readily permeable to air; plastic is unsuitable for this purpose as condensation could form between sheets and cargo.

30.2   Taint

Many foodstuffs can absorb chemicals and foreign odours from the air. This, typically, affects their taste and severely affects their commercial value, even when there are no significant toxicological implications.

Coffee, tea and cocoa are particularly susceptible to taint. They are traded primarily on the basis of their delicate flavour balance, with sophisticated tastings of every consignment carried out at various stages. A comparatively minor off-flavour or odour causes commercial damage to these high-value cargoes.

Some basic considerations to protect against taint damage include:

- Prior to stuffing, inspect containers for odours, previous cargo residues and staining of floorboards. The container should be kept closed for some time until immediately before inspection

- containers that have recently been used for the carriage of odorous chemicals should not be used for foodstuffs, even if no detectable odour remains. More generally, operators should consider keeping separate pools of containers designated for chemicals and for foodstuffs

- stow containers containing foodstuffs away from strong odours on board. This is particularly relevant when using ventilated containers, where the air exchange rate, and so the potential for transmission of external taints, is much greater than for non-ventilated containers

- floorboards, pallets, crates, etc are often treated with fungicidal wood preservatives containing chlorophenols. These are also contained in mould inhibitors used on jute bags and in the adhesives in some fibreboard cartons. Chlorophenols are themselves a potential source of taint. Although the levels used are usually insufficient to cause commercial problems, they can be converted to chloroanisoles by certain microorganisms, particularly in the presence of excessive moisture such as may result from condensation. Chloroanisoles are an extremely potent source of taint, causing a characteristic musty odour and flavour, even if present only in very minute proportions.

30.3 Production of Gases

Fresh produce continues to go through biological and chemical processes, including respiration, even when in storage. During this process, it will continue to generate heat when it absorbs oxygen (O_2) and releases carbon dioxide (CO_2) and ethylene (C_2H_4). The combination of heat and released gases can have an impact on the 'health' of the products being carried if the respiration process is not controlled.

The quantity of gases and associated heat produced varies between products. For example, pears and apples produce a significantly high quantity of ethylene, which can be controlled in two ways – by lowering the temperature or by increasing the CO_2 concentration combined with reduction of O_2. The latter option, however, is not desirable as it will have a negative impact on the quality of the cargo. The lowering of temperature, therefore, remains the only option to prolong the shelf life and maintain the quality of fresh produce. The atmosphere changed in this way is known as 'Controlled Atmosphere (CA)' or 'Modified Atmosphere (MA)'.

Due to variations in the level of oxygen (O_2) absorption and release of carbon dioxide (CO_2) and ethylene (C_2H_4) even with the same produce, there cannot be any single best method of storage for a particular product. However, shippers may be able to provide some information for the required temperatures and levels of gases required on the basis of their experience. This information must always be complied with and specialist advice sought whenever there is any doubt.

30.4 Containerised Transport of Perishables without Refrigeration

Some perishable commodities are carried without refrigeration, possibly for very short duration journeys, or in ventilated equipment. In these cases, it is wise to consider which of the previous requirements may still apply.

Products with limited temperature sensitivity may be carried under refrigeration for certain journeys only. The following guidelines suggest when this may be appropriate:

- For any goods requiring close temperature control, refrigeration is essential. If temperatures need to be maintained within a band of 2°C or less, refrigeration should be virtually continuous
- at the other extreme, for less sensitive goods with a maximum temperature tolerance of 30°C or above, refrigeration is only necessary for storage on land at high ambient temperatures. For containerised shipments at sea, a protected stow may be requested
- if the maximum permitted temperature is 25°C or lower, refrigeration should be used for any journeys through the tropics and for any journeys anywhere in a summer season

- if cargo requirements are marginal, either in terms of temperature tolerance or in terms of possible delays at high ambient temperatures, the only safe option is to use refrigeration
- frozen foods may sometimes be carried without refrigeration for short journeys as long as the cargo is not subjected to more than the specified maximum temperature. This should only be done with the consent of the owner of the goods.

Chapter 31 – Calcium Hypochlorite

Calcium hypochlorite is a white or yellowish solid, usually found in powder, tablet or granular form. It is soluble in water and has strong decomposing and self-reacting characteristics.

It is mainly used for the disinfection of drinking water and swimming pool water, but can also be used as a bleaching agent for items such as cotton and linen, as well as in household cleaners and weedkillers.

In 2018 'Guidelines for the Carriage of Calcium Hypochlorite in Containers' was jointly published by the Cargo Incident Notification System (CINS) and the International Group of P&I Clubs (IG P&IC). This document (Reference 53) provides additional guidance on cargo hazards and carriage requirements.

Under the *International Maritime Dangerous Goods Code* (IMDG Code, Reference 19), the three most common calcium hypochlorite products are two high strength types: anhydrous (UN1748) and hydrated (UN2880); and a lower strength type, often referred to as bleaching powder (UN2208).

Higher strength calcium hypochlorite substances are less likely to exhibit self-accelerating decomposition, but have more severe consequences in the event of an incident.

Lower strength calcium hypochlorite substances, such as UN numbers 2208, 3486, 1479 and 3077, are more likely to exhibit self-accelerating decomposition, but the consequences are less severe.

31.1   Stowage

Calcium hypochlorite or calcium hypochlorite mixtures should be transported in compliance with the stowage and segregation requirements set out in the IMDG Code.

IMDG Code Special Provision 314, under Part 3, Chapter 3.3, of the Code applies to calcium hypochlorite and states:

314.2 – During the course of transport, these substances shall be shaded from direct sunlight and all sources of heat and be placed in adequately ventilated areas.

In compliance with the IMDG Code (Amendment 41-22) calcium hypochlorite is subject to the provisions of stowage category D and stowage codes SW1 and SW11.

Stowage Category D

- *Cargo ships or passenger ships carrying a number of passengers limited to not more than 25 or to 1 passenger per 3 m of overall length, whichever is the greater number – ON DECK ONLY*
- *other passenger ships in which the limiting number of passengers transported is exceeded – PROHIBITED.*

Stowage Code(s)

SW 1 – Protected from sources of heat.

SW 11 – Cargo transport units shall be shaded from direct sunlight. Packages in cargo transport units shall be stowed so as to allow for adequate air circulation throughout the cargo.

All calcium hypochlorite substances should be stowed out of direct sunlight. If there is a risk that containers could be subjected to long periods of direct sunlight where they are stowed on deck, steps should be taken to restow them. If this is not possible, they should be covered with tarpaulins to provide shade.

Cargoes should ideally be packed in drums, within a container. Packaging this way facilitates airflow through the stow. This is important as airflow will assist in the dissipation of any heat generated. Note that the use of IBCs, bags or sacks for transportation is not permitted. It is also recommended to stow containers of calcium hypochlorite where they are accessible.

According to segregation requirements in the IMDG Code, calcium hypochlorite should be stowed separated from acids, ammonium compounds, cyanides and peroxides. It must not be stored together with combustible material in the same cargo transport unit.

The critical ambient temperature (CAT) for calcium hypochlorite depends on the package shape and size. The CAT is higher for smaller packages because they can dissipate heat in the atmosphere more quickly due to a larger surface area relative to the amount of the contents. The bigger the package, the lower the CAT and, therefore, the higher the risk of exothermic decomposition, ie release of chlorine and oxygen gases if exposed to temperatures of between 30 to 55°C, or above. Exposure to such temperatures can happen if calcium hypochlorite is stowed in direct sunlight or above bunker tanks. When released, oxygen will sustain any fire caused due to the decomposition reaction already taking place. As chlorine is toxic, the IG P&IC recommends that stowage should be clear of living quarters. It also recommends an individual package limit of 45 kg with a maximum of 14 T net weight per container where a CAT of 40°C may be expected.

Dry or reefer containers may be used provided that a proper risk assessment is carried out. The risk assessment should include all aspects of transport including routeing, climatic temperature, duration, etc. The container control temperature should be 10 °C. 20 or 40 ft containers can be used provided that the maximum net weight of calcium hypochlorite does not exceed 14 T. In the event of a mechanical failure or of an interruption of the power supply, the insulation in a reefer container will initially protect the calcium hypochlorite from external heating. However, if there is an extended interruption to cooling, heat produced by calcium hypochlorite decomposition may accumulate faster in a reefer than in a dry container. The longer the interruption, the greater this risk.

Spontaneous decomposition, which may lead to explosion and fire, can occur at temperatures as low as 30°C for freight containers stuffed with large drums (about 200 kg) of UN 2880 (as described in Reference 54). Such temperatures are encountered in the holds of container vessels where there are heated fuel oil tanks. Therefore, the materials should not be stowed where their CAT can be attained.

31.2   Stowage Issues

Calcium hypochlorite has caused numerous fires, explosions and disasters, most of which can be attributed to one or more of the following causes:

- Improper stowage and consequent damage to receptacles in heavy weather
- improper segregation from goods such as combustible solids or liquids, dyes, oils and textiles, non-combustible liquids containing water, ammonium compounds, etc
- contact with rust after spillage of contents
- the decomposing nature of the product itself, the rate of which is heavily dependent on storage temperature and production characteristics.

The stability of calcium hypochlorite has improved in recent years, and now is increasingly replaced by the safer and more stable isocyanurates. In all circumstances, the shipper should deliver a document stating the percentage of free chlorine in the package. For all shipments of calcium hypochlorite containing more than 70% active chlorine, special clearance to carry the substance should be obtained.

The history of ocean transportation of calcium hypochlorite suggests that all forms pose special challenges concerning safe carriage. The safety issues are complex and are aggravated by a high degree of product variability.

31.3 Synonyms for Calcium Hypochlorite

- B-K powder
- bleaching powder
- bleaching powder, containing 39% or less chlorine
- calcium chlorohydrochlorite
- calcium hypochloride
- calcium hypochlorite
- calcium oxychloride
- caporit
- CCH
- chloride of lime (DOT)
- chlorinated lime (DOT)
- HTH
- Hy-Chlor
- hypochlorous acid
- calcium salt
- lime chloride
- lo-Bax
- losantin
- perchloron
- pittchlor
- pittcide
- pittclor
- sentry.

Some calcium hypochlorite shipped out of China is declared as:

- Prechloroisocyanoric acid (UN 2465)
- sodium di-isocyanorate (UN 2466).

31.4 Case Studies

'Eugen Maersk'
In June 2013, the *'Eugen Maersk'* container ship suffered a fire that broke out in one container and spread to several others nearby. The containers had all been declared as containing household goods and none should have held anything hazardous that might have caught fire in such a way. Containers with flammable contents are usually stored on deck to minimise the risks of fire but, if the contents are misdeclared, they may be stored in locations that cause serious hazards to the ship's crew and cargo. No persons were injured by the fire, but a total of 16 containers were damaged or destroyed.

MSC 'Flaminia'
In July 2012, the MSC *'Flaminia'* suffered a severe fire which subsequently led to an explosion on board and the eventual abandoning of the ship by the crew. Three crew

members were killed in the incident. While the exact cause for the initial fire starting was never discovered, it is generally assumed that part of the cargo in the number 4 hold was incorrectly declared, and therefore not stored correctly as per the IMDG Code.

'KMTC Hong Kong'

In May 2019, the South Korean flagged *'KMTC Hong Kong'* suffered a severe explosion and subsequent fire while alongside in Laem Chabang, Thailand. Misdeclared containers of calcium hypochlorite were loaded lower down in the container stacks (contrary to the IMDG Code), and once ablaze, proved difficult to extinguish as the smoke emanating from the fire was highly toxic. 37 people were hospitalised due to the toxic smoke, while 143 people were reportedly affected in some way by chemicals within the smoke.

Chapter 32 –
Thiourea Dioxide

Thiourea dioxide, or formamidine sulfinic acid (UN 3341, Class 4.2), is a white to pale yellow, crystalline powder used as a reductive agent in the paper industry and a bleaching agent in the textile industry. It is produced by oxidation of thiourea with hydrogen peroxide.

During 1996–97, there were several incidents related to the decomposition of thiourea dioxide. In one incident in the Far East, 400 workers were evacuated from a marine terminal and several workers required hospitalisation. At that time, the chemical was not included in the IMDG Code.

32.1 Stowage

The IMDG Code (Reference 19) requires this cargo to be packed in hermetically-sealed drums. Stowage should be in cool dry areas at ambient temperatures. Stowage should be away from heat sources, such as steam pipes, heating coils, heated bunker tanks and main engine bulkheads. Under-deck stowage is not recommended (IMDG Stowage and Segregation, Category D) because ships' holds may reach 65°C in certain tropical zones. However, temperatures in containers carried on deck and exposed to sunlight at the edge of a container stow may also reach 65°C. Containers within the centre of a stow are protected from these high temperatures to some extent.

This cargo must only be transported in hermetically sealed (vapour tight) drums. Any other form of transportation should be rejected by the shipper.

32.2 Decomposition

When exposed to heat above 50°C and/or moisture, thiourea dioxide is likely to decompose visibly and rapidly, a reaction that may be catalysed by metal salts. This decomposition is accompanied by the release of toxic and corrosive gases, including sulphur oxides, ammonia, carbon monoxide, nitrogen oxides, hydrogen sulphide, etc. Sulphur oxides can further react with moisture to form acidic conditions and the acid may then attack neighbouring cargo, leaving solid residue and causing contamination.

Some manufacturers have shipped this cargo under the names 'Thiourea D' or 'Thiourea De', claiming that it is less hazardous than thiourea dioxide, although this is not the case.

Figure 32.1: Decomposition.

Ships' crew should be made fully aware of the hazards concerning the carriage of thiourea dioxide. If there is any doubt as to the safety of its carriage, shipowners should reject the request to carry thiourea dioxide on board.

Chapter 33 –
Expandable Polymeric Beads

Expandable polymeric beads, also known as expandable polystyrene (EPS) (UN 2211 Polymeric Beads, Expandable), are used to produce a moulding material in the form of granules or beads of approximately 3 mm in diameter. The beads or granules may contain 5 to 8% of a volatile hydrocarbon, which is predominantly pentane.

During the moulding process, the beads are heated, causing expansion and fusion, which forms the familiar polymeric packaging material. During storage or transport, the material will release a portion of the pentane. The rate of this release increases with a rise in temperature. Pentane vapours are heavier than air, so higher concentrations can be found closer to the deck level, or at the bottom of cargo holds.

To add more complexity, pentane can ignite at relatively low concentrations, eg 1.3% by volume in the air.

The beads have been found to generate flammable concentrations of gas in enclosed spaces and have been involved in several major explosions, one incident causing severe damage to a container ship.

33.1   Packaging and Storage

Expandable beads are included in the IMDG Code (Reference 19), under Class 9 (miscellaneous dangerous substances and articles). Packaging recommended in the IMDG Code includes outer drums and inner plastic packages. Intermediate bulk containers include composite fireboard or plastic materials.

The IMDG Code (Reference 19) states that storage and segregation is Category A, on deck or under deck, but mechanical ventilation should be provided for under deck stowage to prevent the formation of a flammable atmosphere. The Code advises that, during storage, a small proportion of the pentane may be released to the atmosphere and that this proportion is increased at elevated temperatures. There is also a cautionary note relating to the opening of doors if the material is carried in containers.

The recommended storage is in a well-ventilated space and preferably below 20°C. Warehouse storage below 20°C may be a relatively simple operation. However, stowage in the holds of an ocean vessel may be more difficult and should, at least, be away from heated bunker tanks or engine room bulkheads. Temperatures in ships' holds might be of the order of 65°C in some tropical areas. Adequate hold ventilation with 'suitable equipment' should be stressed because the arcing of an electric fan motor may readily ignite a flammable concentration of pentane in air.

Under deck stowage is permitted, but good ventilation must be ensured so that any ignitable concentrations can be avoided. Use of ventilation containers must be considered with caution as the level of ventilation provided may not necessarily be sufficient to rid any build-up of pentane. When ventilated containers are used, the 'Criteria for the Selection of Ventilated Containers' provided by the Expandable Polystyrene (EPS) Transport Group of Plastics Europe in *Guidelines for Transport and Storage of Expandable Polystyrene Raw Beads* (Reference 55) must be complied with in addition to complying with other requirements of the IMDG Code for labelling, packaging and segregation. This requirement must include additional labelling for closed containers, with markings such as:

- Keep away from sources of ignition
- no smoking or welding
- no fire/flames or naked lights
- no spark producing tools
- distance maintained from hot surfaces or sources of heat.

The Code of Federal Regulations *Title 49: Transportation,* Chapter 1, Part 173 (Reference 56) describes various packaging materials but states that, except for transportation by highway and rail, the packaging must be capable of containing any evolving gases from the contents during normal conditions of transport.

33.2   Shipment

Transportation on ships in closed, non-ventilated containers is permitted, but the consignees must be advised about the risks associated with any accumulated pentane in high concentrations, including additional requirements for making an entry into the container, which should be treated as an enclosed space. This may require use of supplementary labels to warn workers of the hazards.

Deck temperatures in tropical climates can also exceed the recommended limits for safe stowage of the beads. However, if the cargo is containerised, the containers can be placed in a central area of the stow where they will be insulated from the effects of direct sunlight. This arrangement will create extra movement during loading and discharge but can assist toward safe carriage. Pentane released from containers in deck stowage will be dispersed by wind and movement of the vessel and should not create flammable or explosive conditions outside the containers.

33.3   Hazards

Manufacturers are aware of the problems of release of pentane, which is heavier than air, into freight containers. Recommended ventilation periods are suggested prior to entry and unpacking the container. If opened in a container yard, containers should be sited away from drains so that pentane released when the doors are opened does not enter them, creating a potential fire hazard at some nearby location.

Manufacturers are aware of the hazards involved with storage and transportation of the beads and provide detailed lists of precautions to be observed. They also ensure packaging is provided with detailed warning labels, fixed to either the drums or the freight containers, and expressed in several different languages.

Chapter 34 – Flexitanks

A flexitank is a bladder designed to fit inside a 20 ft general freight container, thereby converting the freight container into a non-hazardous bulk liquid transportation unit.
As defined by the IMO/ILO/UNECE *Code of Practice for Packing of Cargo Transport Units* (CTU Code) (Reference 57), a flexitank is a '*bladder used for the transport and/or storage of a non-regulated liquid inside a CTU*'. Flexitanks are not an approved form of packaging for the carriage by sea of dangerous goods classified under the *International Maritime Dangerous Goods Code* (IMDG Code) (Reference 19).

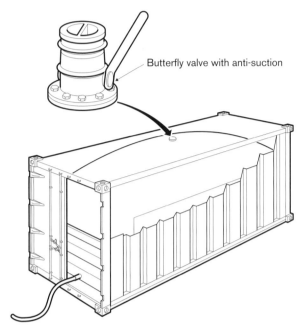

Figure 34.1: Flexitank in a container.

A large number of claims have arisen relating to containers carrying flexitanks, where the pressure placed on the sidewall panels inside the containers has resulted in them bulging beyond accepted ISO external dimensions and tolerances, leading to permanent deformation. The International Organization for Standardization (ISO)/ Institute of International Container Lessors (IICL) deformation limit for sidewall panels is a maximum of 10 mm beyond the plane of the side surfaces of the corner casting fittings. This limit has been exceeded in many incidents, so some operators have imposed limits on the quantity of liquid that may be carried in a flexitank.

Figure 34.2: Bulging flexitanks.

34.1 COA Code of Practice for Flexitanks

In 2011, the Container Owners Association (COA), Flexitank Division, published a Code of Practice to improve the quality and safety of flexitank operations. Compliance with this Code is not mandatory (Reference 58). The current version of the COA *Code of Practice for Flexitanks* was published in 2019 and contains the guidance provided in the IMO/ILO/UNECE *Code of Practice for Packing of Cargo Transport Units* (CTU Code) published on 16th December 2014 (Reference 57).

Under the *Code of Practice*, the COA provides a mechanism for each COA flexitank manufacturer to obtain a COA Compliance Certificate showing their compliance with the Code subsequent to audits for their quality management system, installation and training, material test and rail impact test. The certificate confirms that the manufacturer endorses the COA declaration and has undergone audit in all four areas. The COA also maintains a FQML (Flexitank Quality Management List) on this website to record the manufacturers who have received COA certification.

Alongside the Code of Practice, the British Standards Institution (BSI) has developed specification BSI PAS 1008 *Specification for the performance and testing of a single-use flexitank* (Reference 59). PAS 1008 is sponsored by COA and provides detailed specifications for testing materials, performance and labelling of all components in the flexitank system.

34.2 Perceived Advantages/Disadvantages

In the non-hazardous markets, single-use flexitanks are considered by some to be effective substitutes for ISO tank containers and drums. Some of the reasons for this include:

- Flexitanks are product dedicated and so there is no risk of cross contamination
- relatively low positioning costs (in some areas, 100 empty flexitanks can be positioned for the same cost as one tank container)
- positioning a flexitank with a capacity of up to 24,000 litres inside a 20 ft general freight container enables shippers to dispatch about 40% more cargo per container than a drummed consignment, about 50% more than a bottled consignment and about 15% additional payload when compared to a container filled with intermediate bulk containers (IBCs). No return loads are required
- loading rates are higher compared to drums and IBCs
- flexitank manufacturers obtain approvals from authorities such as the USA's FDA (Food and Drug Administration), the EU-approved Food Safety System Certification (FSSC) 22000 and the UK's HACCP (Hazard Analysis and Critical Control Point) to ensure compliance with food products.

The disadvantages of flexitanks include:

- Products classified as dangerous goods under the IMDG Code (Reference 19) are not permitted to be carried in flexitanks
- pumps are required for unloading older flexitanks, although newer tanks are fitted with loading/unloading valves

- greater preparation is required for flexitanks than for ISO tank containers, although ISO tanks require substantial cleaning, particularly in food applications
- environmental issues arise in connection with the disposal of used single-trip flexitanks
- the risk of leakage of the full contents
- the potential for high costs to clean up spillages
- spillage resulting in the contamination of other cargo, depending upon stowage on board.

Figure 34.3: Flexitanks damage.

34.3   Types of Flexitanks

A range of products are carried in flexitanks, including wine, fruit concentrate, animal fat, fish oil, base oil, detergents, non-hazardous chemicals, drilling mud additives, paint, lubricants, printing ink, latex and potable water. The choice of flexitank is based on the cargo carried and factors such as the duration of the voyage and the temperature difference between load and discharge port.

Flexitanks can be either single layer or multilayer. Single layer flexitanks (SLFs) are generally manufactured from a single thick layer of polyethylene of 40 mm thickness. Multilayer flexitanks (MLFs) can consist of several layers (two, three or more), depending on the type of cargo being carried and the shipper's requirements. Generally, the value of the cargo will determine the protection required in the carriage and, therefore, the number of layers required for the MLF being used. For example, cargoes that require a barrier against taint contamination will use four layers. Each layer of an MLF may be about 125 microns thick. The outer layer of an MLF is normally of a woven type plastic material. A problem with MLFs is that the different layers may, during loading, get caught up and trapped, resulting in a layer tearing.

The first flexitanks were designed on the basis that they would be for multi-trip use, which meant that cleaning and repositioning costs were incurred. However, these costs have been eliminated with the single trip/use flexitank, which is the type now most commonly in use, accounting for more than 95% of the global market.

Flexitanks are required to be marked with the performance test standard, manufacturer's name and logo, unique serial number and capacity at the time of manufacture. These markings must be located on the flexitank in such a way that they are visible when the right-hand door of the container is opened.

34.4 Free Surface Effect

A free surface effect can occur in liquids, or in masses of small solids, if they move about during transport in partly filled tanks, including ballast and fuel tanks. It also occurs in containers that are only partially full and when this happens it can alter the centre of gravity of the ship so that, instead of righting itself as it rolls on passage, the ship leans further over to one side and may capsize.

In October 2002, the container ship 'Westwood Rainier' began to list while in port in Seattle. The upper port ballast tank was seen to be pumping out water immediately prior to the 35 to 40° list developing. While a problem with the ballast water system seems to have been the cause of the list, it may have been exacerbated by a free surface effect in the tanks.

If a flexitank is not filled to near its nominal capacity, a marked free surface effect and hydraulic surging of the liquid may occur, often resulting in damage to the container. A flow meter should be used to ensure that a flexitank has been filled to its correct capacity (±500 litres of its nominal capacity) because a visual inspection alone is unlikely to be sufficient.

A large number of partially filled flexitanks can have a significant adverse impact on ship's stability. Masters must, therefore, be supplied with relevant information so that they can incorporate any loss of stability due to partially filled flexitanks into their stability calculations.

The typical capacity of a flexitank is in the range of 10,000 to 24,000 litres and the weight carried will depend on the density of the commodity. The permitted gross weight of a container should never be exceeded. Current practice is not to load more than 24,000 kg of liquid in a 20 ft freight container, although even this is considered too high by some container operators.

34.5 Flexitank Container Characteristics

The 20 ft containers for carriage of flexitanks should be rated to a minimum 30,480 kg, irrespective of the size of the flexitank. The actual sidewall strength is a function of a container's permitted payload, ie 0.6 × payload (ISO 1496-1 *Series 1 freight containers – specification and testing* (Reference 60)). Therefore, the sidewall panels of a 30 T container will have been tested to a greater load bearing capability than, say, a 24 T container.

The sidewall test requires a general freight container to be subjected to an internal loading uniformly distributed and arranged to allow free deflection of the sidewall and its longitudinal members. This test proves the ability of a container to withstand all forces that can result from the movement of a ship at sea. The ISO Standard requires that, upon completion of the test, the container exhibits neither permanent deformation that will render it unsuitable for use, nor any abnormality that will render it unsuitable for use, and that the dimensional requirements governing handling, securing and interchange are satisfied. Therefore, for a 30 T container, the test load will be of the order of 16.8 T. However, a flexitank does not place a uniform loading over the full area of a sidewall and a gross liquid cargo weight of 24,000 kg is the recommended maximum by some flexitank operators, while some container operators consider that there should be a lower limit. Any general purpose container may be used as currently there is no specific classification of containers for the carriage of flexitanks.

To minimise the stress upon the sidewalls of a freight container, it is recommended that the height of the side of the flexitank in contact with the sidewall panel should be kept to a minimum. An optimum height of 1.3 m has been suggested.

It is also recommended by flexitank operators that the sidewall panels are fully corrugated from end to end and that a container with sidewall decal panels and flat logo panels is not acceptable.

Containers used for flexitanks are required to display a CSC plate and must be part of a valid PES (periodic examination scheme) or ACEP (approved continual examination programme). When used, the containers must be in a good state of repair in compliance with shipping line criteria such as UCIRC (Unified Container Inspection and Repair Criteria).

The container should be fitted with:

- Functioning dual locking bars for each door panel
- left-hand door handles that have a hole to accept a safety bolt seal
- door recesses for bulkhead fixings.

34.6   Inspection of Freight Container Prior to Use

Regardless of whether a single or multi-trip flexitank is being used, a freight container should be inspected to ensure the following:

- The container is structurally undamaged and free from sharp projections on internal side and end wall panels and floor
- the container is in a clean condition and free from the residue of all previous cargoes
- any joints in the welds are smooth, ie no rough edges or cracks in the welding or otherwise in the structure of the container
- there are no floor imperfections:

  - floorboards and their retaining bolts are flush
  - there are no nails in the floor (nails/screws/fastenings should not be hammered into the floor)
  - the underside of the container floor should also be inspected to ensure that no nails are protruding and that all cross members are in place and firmly affixed to the floor and the side rails and do not show signs of excessive deformation and/ or cracking
  - internal weld joints are smooth; rough weld joints can result in a flexitank being abraded (placing tape over the weld joints can provide extra protection)

- cams on both doors are positioned and lock correctly when the doors are closed
- handles are positioned and lock fully in their hatches
- door recesses for bulkhead fixings are in good condition (note: containers are being built without door recess channels which makes them unable to accommodate bulkhead fittings)
- lashing fittings at bottom rails and corner posts should be undamaged to reduce the risk of punctures
- bolts affixing labels etc to the doors are not protruding through to the inside of panels. If they are, they must be covered with foam or cardboard
- any traces of oil found on the container walls or floor must be cleaned. If it cannot be cleaned, such as oil soaked into a timber floor, it must be reported to avoid subsequent claims on an incorrect party.

Some flexitank operators provide a standard practice checklist for container selection. If the container does not meet the criteria laid down, the flexitank operator's technical department should be notified.

To protect the flexitank from abrasion against bare metal, the normal practice is to line the inside of the container. Materials often used include corrugated cardboard, Styrofoam sheets and kraft paper.

Figure 34.4: Use of kraft paper.

To prevent a loaded flexitank bulging outwards when the right-hand door is open, a false bulkhead of plastic panels held in place with horizontal steel bars that fit into the vertical corrugation in the door pillars is placed in the doorway.

To ensure that a flexitank does not bulge through the gaps in a steel framework bulkhead, a sufficiently rigid sheet should be placed on the inside of the bulkhead. This prevents the flexitank chafing against the steelwork. Figure 34.5 shows horizontal steel bars used with cardboard sheeting placed between the flexitank and the steel bars.

Figure 34.5: Use of protective cardboard sheets.

34.7   Stowage of Flexitanks

The stowage of flexitanks on board a vessel needs to be considered in the context of two factors, which may be conflicting, ie the forces acting on the container and the nature of the goods.

To reduce forces acting upon the container and the flexitank, stowage low down in the hold and near to the ship's centreline is preferable. Such forces can be particularly high when the ship is partly loaded and/or has a large metacentric height (GM), resulting in a short rolling period. However, if the nature of the goods is such that they could solidify in the event of a leak (eg latex) and could result in the ship's hold bilge lines becoming blocked, then on-deck stowage is preferable.

Ship operators may also wish to consider whether, due to the nature of the goods, a leak could result in tainting of the hold space and/or other container loads stowed in the same hold.

The information supplied by the shipper should include full details of the nature of the product and whether it could solidify, taint or damage the container in the event of a leak. On balance, the optimum stowage for flexitanks is probably the first tier, on deck.

Even though the cargo carried in flexitanks is considered to be non-dangerous and, therefore, does not necessarily require Safety Data Sheets (SDS), in order for the carrier to be aware of the risks associated with the cargo, the shipper must provide an SDS so that appropriate action can be taken in the event of spillage of cargo on the ship.

34.8   Labelling of Containers

It is normal practice to place a warning label on the left-hand door panel of the freight container to highlight the risk that the container is fitted with a flexitank. The label must be in English and at least one other language of the shipper or the consignee. This label should be printed on a placard of at least A4 size (210 × 297 mm) that is capable of withstanding the harshness of the sea for at least 90 days. It should advise:

- Caution bulk liquid
- flexitank container
- keep left-hand door shut, ie do not open the left-hand door until discharge is complete
- do not loose shunt
- no forklift truck
- emergency contact information.

The *Code of Practice for Flexitanks* recommends only one label, but this presupposes that this single label will be seen by the person handling the container. This may not be the case for the operator of the crane loading or discharging the vessel or the driver of the vehicle moving the container to/from the quayside to its storage location on the terminal (Reference 58). It also presupposes that the label is in a language understood by the person handling the container at any particular time in the transport chain.

Any markings on the container indicating carriage of a flexitank must be removed as soon as the flexitank is discharged.

34.9   Flexitank Safety

For ease of discharge, bottom fittings adjacent to the doorway are generally preferred. However, this can result in a static head of pressure between the flexible body of the tank and the valve construction. Leaks can occur due to the detachment of the double patch around the valve opening of either the top or bottom fittings.

Figure 34.6: Flexitank valve.

A damaged container does not automatically mean that a flexitank will leak. However, if a flexitank does leak and its full load is spilt, then, depending on the commodity being carried, the clean-up costs may be considerable. Additionally, daily demurrage costs on quarantined leaking flexitanks may be charged by shipping lines if the shipper/consignee is unable to provide the emergency assistance required.

A flexitank can sustain severe trauma without leaking. Figure 34.7 shows a flexitank full of synthetic latex stowed at the bottom of a flooded hold. There was no leakage and the product was later sampled, approved and discharged for its intended use.

Figure 34.7: Flood-damaged flexitanks containing undamaged latex.

However, problems do arise, such as with wine which expands excessively if it ferments in a flexitank, see Figure 34.8.

Figure 34.8: Damage caused by fermentation of wine.

In this case, while the sidewall and roof panels of the container were damaged, there was no leakage of the wine. This is one reason why relief valves are not used on some designs. While relief valves are suitable for the rigid design of tanktainers, there are complex problems in designing one suitable for a flexitank. The fitting of relief valves in the early flexitanks led to criticism of the containers, as there was frequently leakage of the contents during shipment.

However, to put the problem into perspective, the number of incidents involving wine, similar to that shown in Figure 34.8, was three or four out of a total of 28,000 carried for one flexitank operator.

As the technology continues to develop, flexitank manufacturers are starting to use 40 ft containers to transport liquid cargoes. It is estimated that these containers will be capable of carrying some 27,000 litres of liquid in one container. These flexitanks will also utilise heating pad systems to heat prior to discharging.

A number of underwriters have refused to insure flexitank shipments due to the risk of leakage, particularly where there is the potential for damage to the environment. It is therefore recommended that the following precautions are taken for all shipments involving flexitanks:

1. The shipper is to provide the carrier with:

   a) details of the product being shipped

   b) details of the manufacturer of the flexitanks to check whether they are on the COA approved list

   c) the serial number of the flexitank, added to the bill of lading (B/L).

2. If the flexitank manufacturer is not on the COA approved list, the carrier may still accept the shipment provided the shipper is able to provide the required information, such as for the criteria specified in the COA *Code of Practice*, and is certified by an independent auditing authority.

3. In all cases, the shipper must provide 24-hour emergency contact details.

4. The personnel operating the flexitank, ie installing it in the container, and loading or unloading cargo, must be trained as required by the COA.

5. Depending on the nature of the cargo being carried, the flexitanks must be filled to their capacity, leaving only 5% space unfilled to allow for expansion. Shippers should establish additional requirements based on the temperature difference between load/discharge ports and transit areas and their impact on cargo expansion etc. If the flexitank is not full to capacity, the Master of the ship must be informed to allow for free surface effect calculations to take place.

6. Carriers must record the condition of the container loaded with a flexitank upon receipt on board, notifying any anomalies to the shipper immediately. The Master must exercise their right to refuse any cargo where a doubt exists as to the integrity of the container or its contents.

34.10　Charterparty Contracts

In charterparty contracts, owners and charterers should identify who will be responsible for costs and damages in the event of leakage from flexitanks while on board. In addition, when B/Ls are issued, they should be claused to identify the party responsible for positioning and loading the flexitank in the container.

Part 9 –

Refrigerated and Controlled Atmosphere Cargoes

Chapter 35 –
Refrigerated Container and Controlled Atmosphere Cargoes

The international transport of temperature controlled raw materials and final products is an essential link between producers and consumers. Most cargoes have properties that will determine their practical storage life (PSL), which is a key factor if they are to be carried by sea.

The container trade has seen changes in recent years, including, for example:

* More countries are exporting by sea, with products including fruit, fish, meat, flowers and other high value items
* some shorter life products spend more than half their PSL in transit
* supermarkets demand all year round supplies, reducing seasonality
* lower stock holding has increased demand for just in time deliveries and inventory control.

35.1 Claims and Incidents

The majority of cargoes are transported without damage as claims represent a fraction of only around 1% of the containers carried. However, for those cargo claims, the following list contains occurrences that are often reported:

- Lack of container preparation for loading, causing issues such as tainting and lack of general cleanliness
- containers off-power and, therefore, off-refrigeration for extended times beyond allowed times for power-off
- wrong settings due to incorrect information supplied or interpreted
- failure to monitor properly leading to failure to correct faults or wrong settings
- poorly pre-cooled or overcooled cargo
- cargoes with insufficient PSL
- badly stowed containers impeding airflow, many with low quality packaging
- use of inappropriate packaging materials
- excess fresh air ventilation for live cargoes causing evaporators to ice up
- physical damage
- broken security seals and issues of potential tampering
- air probe temperature sensor failures
- partial or complete loss of refrigerant and/or generator failure
- incorrect defrost interval where this has to be set manually
- incorrectly booked cargo leading to operational and commercial problems
- Fahrenheit and Celsius temperatures interchanged incorrectly or wrongly converted.

60% of claims can be attributed to human error. For example, mishandling by a gantry crane operator could damage the cooling plant or its controls, leading to incorrect readings on the Partlow charts or Cox recorders.

One of the main causes of damage to cargo carried in containers is poor stowage by the shipper, although as the number of claims is still small, the statistics are difficult to analyse. However, reports indicate a decline in the use of specialised reefer ships and an increase in demand for transport by refrigerated container. As the volume of refrigerated cargo increased, a shift from the use of 20 to 40 ft containers has become evident. Therefore, while the ratio of claims in the trade may not change, the actual number and value of claims is likely to rise.

Most temperature controlled containers contain data loggers that record a variety of information. Some are fitted with data transmission capabilities for remote access for both control and readouts. Increasingly, containers are connected via the SATCOM to allow external monitoring of temperatures and conditions. Independent loggers are also available so that a wide variety of audits and checks can be made. When reviewing a claim/incident, containers equipped with this information download can show:

- Pre-trip inspection records
- set point plus supply and return air temperatures at preset intervals

- defrosts
- times off-power
- basic faults
- relative humidity.

This is a major improvement from just recorder chart details and, when such remotely managed containers are more widely implemented, ships' crews involved in the cool chain should follow cargo care instructions directly from the reefer container operator.

35.2 Future Trends

Future trends are likely to include:

- Integral containers:

  - that are more reliable with improved airflow, calibrated air freshening vents, dehumidifiers and other programmable settings
  - with improved insulation and lower degradation over time
  - with reliable refrigeration machinery, controls and data loggers, with some providing wireless/satellite data transmission and remote access to controls
  - including more use of 40 ft containers making it easy to care, carry and discharge

- increasing uniformity of regulations
- food standards agencies or equivalent developments in some key countries
- majority of container ship operators providing information and guidance through their web-based systems.

35.3 Principles of Controlled Atmosphere (CA) Carriage

CA is a system whereby the gas concentrations to which a cargo is exposed are different from those of normal air.

The atmosphere naturally comprises about 78% nitrogen (N_2), 21% oxygen (O_2) and 0.04% carbon dioxide (CO_2), the remainder consisting of noble gases (eg argon). The aim of CA is to change the ratio of these gases. For example, an atmosphere of 2 to 5% O_2 and 2 to 5% CO_2 can extend the storage life of bananas beyond that which can be achieved by refrigeration alone.

CA is extremely effective on apples and pears but less effective on some other fruit. In general, it can be said that it gives a 50% increase in storage life and, for bananas, their 'green-life' is more than doubled.

Lowering the O_2 concentration results in a reduction of the respiration rate by up to 30%, thereby slowing ageing and also reducing sensitivity to the ripening hormone ethylene. Increasing CO_2 is beneficial in suppressing the growth of moulds. Further, when dissolved in water, it produces carbonic acid which is antibacterial. CO_2 also reduces production of ethylene and lessens its effect on produce.

Chilled produce is still alive and respiring during transport and storage, using O_2 and its own carbohydrate reserves, as shown in Figure 35.1.

Oxygen (O_2)

Ethylene (C_2H_4)

Carbon dioxide + Water $(CO_2 + H_2O)$

Heat

Figure 35.1: Produce respiration.

Regardless of commodity, the strongest influence on the quality of the final cargo outturn is the initial quality of the produce.

As well as prolonging storage life, CA also maintains the firmness, texture, crispness, acidity and appearance of some products. It further opens possibilities for the produce to be harvested in a riper state.

The optimal temperature and gas composition for different perishable cargoes depends on variety, growing area and season. For this reason, the precise values must be defined by the shipper.

CA systems currently in use
The two current CA methods are:

- Nitrogen gas flushing
- fresh air replenishment with CO_2 absorption.

Nitrogen gas flushing employs air and N_2 injection to adjust the balance of O_2 and CO_2 inside a refrigerated hold or refrigerated container. Air separation units are used to obtain N_2 from the outside atmosphere. It is injected to dilute the O_2 in the refrigerated space. If (through respiration of the cargo) the concentration of O_2 becomes too low or that of CO_2 becomes too high, the system automatically adjusts the gas concentrations.

A fresh air exchange system with CO_2 absorption relies on the respiration of the product to vary the gas concentrations. When the CO_2 or O_2 level reaches a preset point, the system activates, drawing in outside air to add O_2 and flush excess CO_2. As respiration consumes O_2 and evolves CO_2, it is not possible for this system simultaneously to achieve low O_2 and low CO_2 levels unless a CO_2 absorption system is used.

Detrimental effects of CA
Generally, CA is beneficial to the long-term storage of produce, but there can be some less desirable consequences.

Inadequate O_2 can result in anaerobic respiration, leading to the production of alcohol and giving the affected produce a characteristic off-taste. Excessive CO_2 can produce tissue damage and 'fizzy' fruit. In apples, the final effect is a condition known as brown heart, where the core tissue turns brown.

Premature ripening of bananas during shipment under air-stored carriage will turn the fruit yellow, easily identified as 'ship-ripes'. Under CA conditions, however, the raised CO_2 concentration prevents de-greening of the peel and the bananas arrive with soft pulp, known as 'green-soft' or 'green-ripes'. If CO_2 levels are excessive, bananas may develop a black blotchy appearance. A combination of elevated temperature and CO_2 levels above 5% can even kill the fruit.

35.4   Safety Issues with CA

Safety is an important consideration for carriers because low oxygen atmospheres are incapable of supporting life. Entering an area during CA operation will have fatal consequences, so all CA areas must be clearly indicated by warning signs. Stevedores, ships' officers and crew should be adequately trained to understand the dangers of CA. Doors should be alarmed and adequate precautions taken against stowaways. Protection for doors may include dedicated safety door locks to prevent easy unauthorised access.

Enclosed space entry procedures must be followed before entering a space that has earlier been subject to CA, or an adjacent space where the O_2 concentration may have been depleted. Anyone entering such a space should carry an O_2 detector with a low-level alarm.

Symptoms of O_2 deficiency are similar to drunkenness and the subject is unaware that they are being affected. Table 35.1 lists the effects at different concentrations.

Oxygen content %	Symptoms
~21	Normal atmospheric concentration
15 to 19	Loss of coordination, impaired work ability
12 to 15	Loss of judgement, confusion and elation
10 to 12	Increased loss of judgement and coordination, general confusion
8 to 10	Mental incapacity, nausea and vomiting
5 to 8	Death in 8 minutes, recovery possible providing exposure less than 5 minutes
<5	Rapid unconsciousness followed by death in under 1 minute

Table 35.1: Symptoms of O_2 deficiency.

Increased CO_2 levels also pose a danger, causing headaches, dizziness, confusion and ultimately loss of consciousness. Long-term exposure limits are 5,000 ppm (8-hour period) and short-term exposure limit 1,500 ppm (15 minutes).

The safety requirements extend to those unloading cargoes. It is essential that workers are adequately trained and that proper fresh air ventilation is applied prior to opening cargo spaces.

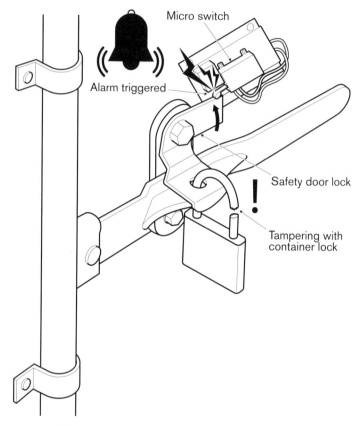

Figure 35.2: Safety door lock in a CA reefer container.

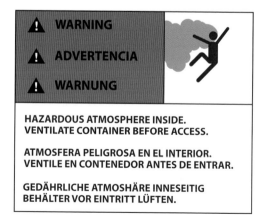

Figure 35.3: Safety decal on a CA reefer container.

35.5 System Failure

Prompt action must be taken in the event of CA system failure. In most cases, the refrigeration system will continue to function and so complete cargo loss is not inevitable. CA failure can be caused by a variety of faults, such as mechanical breakdown, sensor malfunction, unexpected air leakage or even exhaustion of a chemical CO_2 absorbent.

Without intervention, system failure may cause the O_2 to fall too low, causing anaerobic respiration, and/or the CO_2 may increase causing tissue damage.

The crew should be provided with clear guidance to identify those circumstances where it will be necessary to break the CA and introduce fresh air. The procedure should be documented in the CA cargo handling and carriage instructions.

Figure 35.4: Rear door curtain in a CA reefer container.

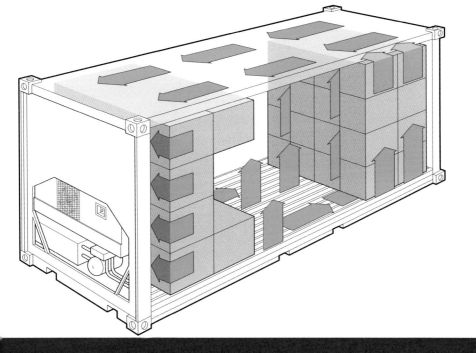

Chapter 36 –
Carriage Instructions for
Refrigerated Cargoes

Refrigerated cargoes are usually perishable and their safe carriage depends on maintaining suitable storage conditions during transportation.

Refrigerated cargoes include frozen products such as meat, fish and seafood, and chilled products such as fresh fruits and vegetables. Chilled products are also known as perishable products. Generally, frozen goods do not suffer if overcooled, but chilled goods can be damaged by temperatures that are too low. Much tropical and sub-tropical produce is liable to chilling injury if subjected to temperatures below those usually experienced in the growing area. Chilled products need to be maintained at temperatures very close to the required set point temperatures. Because they are living and respiring, these products generate heat of respiration, which unless extracted at a sufficient rate will cause an overall increase in temperature and result in damage. This is why the evaporator fans work at high speed for chilled cargoes while for frozen cargoes, since there is no respiration or heat generation, evaporator fans run at slower speed.

Figure 36.1: Transportation of refrigerated cargo.

Successful transportation depends on the carriage instructions, which define the conditions in which the goods are to be carried. If these instructions are incomplete, inadequate, contradictory or wrong, problems can be expected. For the shipper, there is the risk of loss of cargo. For the carrier, there is the risk of a claim even if the goods are undamaged.

Many shippers and carriers seem prepared to accept inadequate instructions, either through ignorance or because of what has been accepted previously by themselves or others. Instructions may be based on goods of different origin, which may have different requirements. For example, there are a few hundred varieties of bananas, each variety requiring its own carriage conditions. It is not acceptable to assume what the carriage requirements are, even if the carrier has carried similar cargo in the past.

36.1   General Requirements

The responsibility for specifying carriage instructions lies with the shipper of the goods and only they know the full nature of the goods, their prior history and their requirements. Frequently, this responsibility is passed to the carrier, but in this case the shipper should agree the acceptability of the specified conditions prior to shipment.

It should be explicitly understood that the responsibility of specifying carriage instructions lies solely with the shipper and not with the carrier.

The exact nature of the cargo needs to be known and, in the case of fruit, for example, carriage requirements may vary depending on type, variety, maturity, origin and growing season conditions. The following general requirements typically apply to refrigerated cargoes:

- If mixed loads of different commodities are to be carried in a single cargo space, it is necessary to consider compatibility of temperature, atmosphere (particularly ethylene levels) and liability to taint. It is possible that gases liberated from one cargo may be detrimental to another. This will usually require specialist cargo care advice

- it may be necessary to ensure that carriage conditions are specified to all carriers in the transport chain, because an international journey may use different carriers at the start and end of the journey

- it is important to pass on the necessary carriage instructions to all carriers in the supply chain, particularly if multimodal transportation is involved

- factors such as relative humidity and maximum time without refrigeration should not be overspecified, but should meet the necessary requirements of the goods

- overspecification of requirements is to be avoided as it tends to lead to more, and sometimes spurious, claims regarding technicalities that have not actually affected cargo quality.

36.2   Requirements for Containerised Cargoes

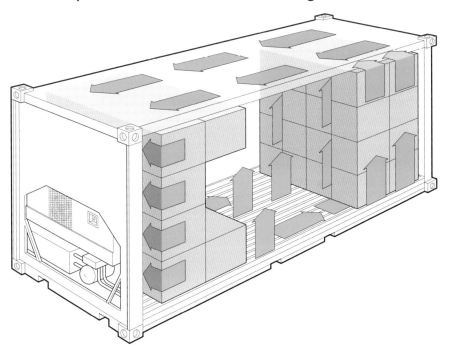

Figure 36.2: Cargo in refrigerated container.

The parameters that may be included in carriage instructions for containerised refrigerated cargo are:

- Pre-trip inspection of containers
Before stuffing the cargo, all refrigerated containers should be subject to pre-trip inspection in which the physical condition of the container is ascertained along with the proper running of the refrigeration equipment.

- pre-stuffing sanitation
Containers to be used for refrigerated goods should be clean and odour free, and any special or particular needs should be identified.

- pre-cooling of containers
  Pre-cooling is only useful when loading from temperature controlled loading bays. In other conditions, it can result in excessive moisture ingress from the atmosphere and is not recommended.

- pre-cooling of the cargo
  Before loading the cargo into the container, the cargo should be pre-cooled to the required carriage temperature. It should be noted that the machinery of a reefer container is not designed to cool the cargo, but only to maintain the cargo temperature. It is not to be used as a cold storage where the temperature of the cargo is brought down rapidly using powerful heavy-duty refrigeration machinery.

- cooling during part-loaded conditions
  Part-loaded containers should be closed and the temperature maintained if there is a delay before complete loading.

- prohibition of loading of hot cargo
  Hot cargo should not be loaded into the container. Many insurance claims have been reported at the consignee's end due to insufficient cooling of the cargo before loading into the container.

- prohibition of stuffing cargo at mixed temperatures
  Properly pre-cooled cargo and substantially warmer cargo should not be mixed.

- stowage requirements
  Any special stowage requirements, such as a protected or under deck stow, should be stated.

- ventilation
  The rate of fresh air ventilation for fresh produce should be specified as an absolute figure in cubic metres per hour. The specification of a percentage rate of ventilation has meaning only if related to a specific container size and a specific model of refrigeration unit.

- carriage temperature
  It is not physically possible to provide refrigeration in the absence of temperature differences, both between the air and the goods, and within the bulk of the goods. The only temperature that can be controlled is the set point, which corresponds to the air delivery temperature for chilled goods and the air return temperature for frozen goods. The term 'carriage temperature' therefore has little meaning, and 'set point temperature' should be specified. If appropriate, this may be augmented by a maximum allowable temperature during periods without refrigeration.

  For the United States Department of Agriculture (USDA) and other cold treatment quarantine requirements, maximum pulp temperature may have to be maintained below a specified temperature throughout a continuous period of days or weeks and only approved equipment may be used.

Although degrees Celsius (°C) are the international standard, degrees Fahrenheit (°F) are still commonly used in the USA. As zero degrees C (0°C) is a common chilled goods temperature and zero degrees F (0°F) is a common frozen goods temperature, great care is needed to avoid possible confusion of units. In case of doubt, clarification should be obtained from the shipper.

- maximum time with refrigeration
  Sometimes, it may be necessary, for statutory or other reasons, to specify a maximum duration of time without refrigeration, either per event or in total for the journey. This should not be necessary if temperature limits are well defined.

- air circulation rate
  Some containers have a high air circulation rate for chilled goods and a lower rate for frozen goods. If a speed change switch is fitted, low-speed operation for chilled goods may be possible, but as this inevitably results in a wider range of cargo temperature, it is not recommended.

- relative humidity
  When equipment with humidity control is used, a range must be specified. It is difficult to measure humidity regularly to better than the nearest 2 to 3%, so an acceptable range of at least ±5% should be specified, albeit with a tighter target. Special equipment is available to maintain either high (90%) or low (50%) humidity. Without such equipment, relative humidity is not controllable and should not be specified.

- defrosting intervals
  The time interval between each consecutive defrost should be specified. Chilled cargoes generally need more frequent defrosting (6 to 8-hour interval) due to respiration and liberation of moisture, and frozen cargoes need less frequent defrosting (24-hour interval). When set as a parameter, the equipment automatically defrosts at the specified intervals.

- measurement and reporting requirements
  It is normal to record air temperature in refrigerated containers and some equipment also records delivery air temperature. Any specific shipper requirement for reporting temperatures should be stated. When the refrigeration unit is not running, the recorded temperatures do not reflect cargo temperatures. Shippers may choose to put their own recording equipment within the cargo, in which case they should inform both carriers and receivers.

- special conditions for cold weather
  Sometimes, special requirements exist for exceptionally cold conditions. However, most transport refrigeration equipment will control temperature, using either cooling or heating as necessary, to maintain specified conditions.

- need to pass instructions to subsequent carrier
  If there is uncertainty at the start of a voyage as to who will be the final carrier, it may be necessary to request the initial carrier to pass on carriage instructions.

- need to notify and whom to notify if limits are exceeded
  Procedures for notification of out of specification conditions should be established prior to acceptance of cargo for shipment. This could apply to warm loading or equipment failures, for example. Standard procedures and safe limits should be available. The party to be contacted if parameters go beyond the set limits should be clearly specified, with contact details provided for second and third back-up options.

36.3 Specific Requirements for Reefer Ships

The parameters for reefer ship carriage instructions may include:

- Pre-loading sanitation
  Compartments to be used for refrigerated goods should be clean and odour free and any special or particular needs should be identified.
- pre-cooling of cargo space
  The pre-cooling of cargo spaces removes heat from steelwork and provides a check on the operation of the refrigeration system. The required pre-cooling temperature may be a few degrees lower than required transport temperature.
- cooling during part-loaded conditions
  Part-loaded spaces should be closed and temperature maintained if there is a delay before completing loading. Care should be taken to ensure that, under these conditions, the temperature is not held at a pre-cooling temperature below the required transport temperature for long enough to damage the cargo.
- prohibition of loading cargo at mixed temperatures
  Properly pre-cooled cargo and substantially warmer cargo should not be mixed at loading.
- stowage requirements
  Any special stowage requirements should be stated.
- ventilation (or lack of) during cooling
  For most refrigerated cargoes, the cargo should be loaded at the required carriage temperature. For some cargoes, notably bananas and the less sensitive citrus varieties, cooling in transit is normal. In these cases, a period of 48 hours should be specified, during which fresh air ventilation is stopped to allow maximum refrigeration.

Reference is sometimes made to the 'reduction period', which is the time from hatch closure to the air return temperature reaching within minus 7°C (–7°C), or 18°F, of the requested air delivery temperature. This is a parameter that may usefully be measured and reported but should not be specified.

After cooling, or throughout in the absence of cooling, the rate of fresh air ventilation for fresh produce should be specified. This may be given as an absolute figure in cubic metres per hour, or as a rate stating the number of air changes per hour of the empty volume of cargo space. Alternatively, it may be linked to measured values of humidity, ethylene or carbon dioxide. Care is necessary to avoid requirements that conflict.

- carriage temperature
  It is not physically possible to provide refrigeration in the absence of temperature differences, both between the air and the goods and within the bulk of the goods. Carriage temperature for chilled goods must therefore be specified as the air delivery temperature. Pulp temperatures may usefully be measured and reported.

It may be necessary to specify a lower temperature for a limited period to ensure rapid cooling of warm cargo, known as 'shock treatment'. Dual-temperature regimes, in which the delivery air temperature is changed after a specified period of days, may also be stipulated.

For frozen cargo, it is usually sufficient to specify a maximum temperature that should not be exceeded. This may be subject to qualification for short periods. For example, the International Council on Clean Transportation (ICCT) note:

"Cargo temperature shall not exceed −18°C, except for short periods during power disconnection or defrosting, when temperatures shall not exceed −15°C. A single specified 'carriage temperature' is a meaningless specification that should never be accepted." (Reference 61)

Although degrees Celsius (°C) are the international standard, degrees Fahrenheit (°F) are still commonly used in the USA. As zero degrees Celsius (0°C) is a common chilled goods temperature and zero degrees F (0°F) is a common frozen goods temperature, great care is needed to avoid possible confusion of units. In case of doubt, clarification should be obtained from the shipper.

For USDA and other cold treatment quarantine requirements, maximum pulp temperature may have to be maintained below a specified temperature throughout a continuous period of days or weeks and only approved equipment may be used.

- air circulation rate
  The rate of circulation of air around and through the cargo controls the range of temperature within the cargo, and also the rate of cargo cooling. Minimum rates may be specified, usually as multiples of the empty volume of the hold per hour. Often, these multiples are misleadingly referred to as 'air changes per hour', or 'ACH', a term best used for ventilation rather than circulation rates.

- relative humidity limits or target
  Relative humidity may not be specifically controllable in shipments. If there are critical requirements, either special equipment or special packaging or both, will be required. A sensible specification is as follows:

"Relative humidity should be maintained at the maximum possible, after the delivery air temperature and fresh air ventilation requirements have been met."

Overspecification of humidity requirements is likely to lead to conflicting instructions. When special equipment with humidity control is used, a range must be specified. It is difficult to measure humidity regularly to better than the nearest 2 to 3%, so an acceptable range of at least ±5% must be specified, albeit with a tighter target.

- carbon dioxide limits or target
  For many fruits, a maximum level of CO_2 may be specified as the overriding parameter for the ventilation rate control. Care is necessary to avoid conflicting ventilation requirements.

- ethylene limits
  The measurement or specification of ethylene levels is rare, as accurate measurement at very low concentrations requires specialised equipment. If limits are to be specified, the measurement and control regime must also be specified.

- measuring and reporting requirements
  It is normal for carriers to measure the temperature of the air in ships' holds. Any specific shipper requirement should be stated, particularly if it involves cargo

rather than air temperature. Shippers frequently choose to put their own recording equipment within the container/cargo, in which case they should inform both carriers and receivers.

- special conditions for cold weather
  Sometimes, special requirements exist for exceptionally cold conditions. However, most transport refrigeration equipment will control temperature, using either cooling or heating as necessary, to maintain specified conditions.

- need to pass instructions to subsequent carrier
  If there is uncertainty at the start of a voyage as to who will be the final carrier, it may be necessary to request the initial carrier to pass on carriage instructions.

- need to notify if limits exceeded
  Procedures for notification of out of specification conditions should be established prior to acceptance of cargo for shipment. For example, this could apply to warm loading or to equipment failures. Standard procedures and safe limits should be made available.

- USDA requirements, if any
  The USDA requires that all refrigerated cargoes entering the US should comply with special requirements of cold treatment and maintenance of cargo temperature during the voyage. This is to prevent entry of insects along with the goods into the US territory. The USDA requires special temperature probes to be inserted into the cargo at various locations within the cargo hold and continuous recording of the temperature. On arrival at US ports, cargo will be allowed to land only if the temperature of the cargo has been maintained continuously within the specified limits.

36.4 Documentation

The importance of documents
Documents are fundamentally important in the investigation of any claim involving damage to cargo. They will be examined by the technical surveyors and may be used as evidence in any subsequent legal proceedings. The following documents are likely to be important in the event of a claim:

- Ship's log
- B/L
- mate's receipts and attached record of the inspection of the cargo prior to and during loading
- stowage plan
- deck log of loading and unloading
- engine room log
- any documentation arising from disputes during unloading and/or receipt of cargo.

In addition, photographs and video recordings can provide important evidence in support of statements in the logs and inspection reports.

Mate's receipts
The mate's receipts should include the record of the pre-shipment inspection. This record should detail all observations on the cargo's condition at the time of receipt,

including results of at least a visual inspection of each part of the consignment. Records should also include temperature measurements, taken at sufficiently frequent intervals to provide a fair indication of the average temperature of the cargo.

Any observations that indicate that the cargo temperature is high or that cargo was delivered in a damaged or deteriorated condition should be supported as far as possible by further evidence. This evidence might include photographs taken during pre-shipment inspection or results of reports by cargo surveyors.

The mate's receipt should include any information on the nature of the consignment supplementary to the B/L as well as details of any labels.

Stowage plan
A stowage plan should be drawn up for all cargoes – an accurate plan is a central piece of evidence in any damage claims arising against the vessel. The stowage plan should indicate the location of each consignment and part of consignment and should include the following information:

- Number of units (pallets, cartons or blocks) in each location
- gross and net weight
- origin of each part
- the corresponding B/L.

Deck log for loading
Loading
Many charterparty agreements specify a minimum rate of transshipment or loading. To demonstrate compliance with this, and to provide evidence in case of claims concerning damage to the cargo during loading, the timing and sequence of events during loading should be noted in the deck log. As a minimum, the log record should include the following:

- Time alongside
- where cargo was loaded from
- times of opening and closing of hatches
- arrival and departure times of stevedores on board
- times when the refrigeration system was turned on and off
- start and finish times of cargo stowage
- any breaks in loading
- weather conditions (sun, wind, rain, ambient temperature)
- any unusual or irregular events that might affect the condition of the cargo during stowage or subsequent carriage.

Deck log for unloading
Unloading
Normally, unloading is the responsibility of the receiver, and the Master of the vessel could consider that their responsibility for the cargo is over. However, the deck log

should continue to record conditions during discharge, logging similar information as listed above for loading.

Engine room log

The engine room log is important since it contributes evidence about the temperature of the ship's cargo during stowage and carriage. The log should document at least the following:

- The locations of temperature sensors in the holds
- temperatures at the sensors in the holds
- times when compressors were turned on and off
- in air-cooled systems, the temperatures in the air streams entering and leaving the holds and compartments
- in pipe-cooled systems, the temperatures of refrigerant to and from the cooling pipes.

36.5 Actions in Case of Dispute

Action by the Master of the ship

The Master must load the cargo in apparent good order and condition and act to maintain it in this state. This section describes actions to be taken when a potential problem is identified.

> In the event of any concern or dispute over the condition of the cargo while loading or unloading, the Master should contact their shipowners or charterers or their P&I correspondent. Best practice would indicate that loading or unloading should cease until instructions have been received, although this may not always be possible.

As soon as any question is raised over the condition of the cargo, the Master should begin to document the events surrounding the discovery of defective material, and the nature and possible extent of the alleged defects.

If possible, loading or unloading of the vessel should be halted and the hatches closed until a cargo surveyor is present. Ideally, cargo should be inspected and sampled while still in the hold, or even during discharge, allowing the surveyor to determine whether the nature and extent of the damage is in any way related to the position in the hold.

Once the cargo has been discharged into store it may be more difficult, or impossible, to relate damage to location in the hold unless the cargo is adequately labelled. Therefore, if loading or unloading must continue, the Master should ensure that each cargo unit is labelled, as it leaves the hold, with the hatch number and deck as well as the location within the hatch and deck. The deck log should also record the destination of the material and the agent responsible for handling it.

Records

The Master should ensure that all records and documents relevant to the dispute are secure and that they are only made available to parties representing the ship's interests.

Services of surveyors

When a problem is identified during loading or unloading, for example if the temperature of the material is too high, loading or unloading should cease until the cargo has been inspected by a specialist surveyor.

If the dispute concerns the quality of the product, it will probably be necessary to call in at least one specialist surveyor to examine the cargo, establish its current quality and determine the nature and cause of any defects.

If it is suspected that defects result from maritime causes, for example physical damage from movement of cargo, or from contamination with seawater, fuel oil or bilge water, an expert in ship operations should be called in. However, if the defects could be attributed to the initial quality of the material when loaded, or to the way the product was stowed and carried on the ship, a specialist surveyor would be more appropriate.

> Many of the surveyors appointed by local shipping agents are general marine surveyors, often with a seagoing background; they are not necessarily skilled in the evaluation of the quality of refrigerated cargoes. Masters and agents are, therefore, advised to check the expertise and qualifications of surveyors carefully to ensure that their technical background and experience are appropriate for the particular job.

As a general rule, a single surveyor should not be commissioned for both a cargo survey and a survey of ship condition. Since the skills required for each type of assessment are very different, it is unlikely that one person would have experience in both areas at the levels of expertise required. For example, a fish cargo surveyor should have a background in food science and the inspection of food products and, ideally, some experience in assessing the quality of frozen fishery products.

Official inspectors and sampling procedures

> Where official inspectors are involved, the Master should document the authority under which the officials visited the ship and the name and status of each official.

The Master is also advised to record the nature and amounts of any samples taken by representatives of the owners or by officials. Such records should include the location of the samples within the hatch or deck, the authority under which the samples were taken and the destination of the samples.

If part of the sample is given to the Master, they should ensure that it is fully labelled and, if possible, that it is sealed in a container and marked as such by the person taking the sample. The Master should store the sample in a secure place, under conditions such that the quality of the sample will not change.

If the cargo is in store, the surveyor should take into account the manner of discharge and delivery to the store, in case these operations could have affected the quality of the product or could in themselves be responsible for any damage.

Chapter 37 –
Fresh Fruit and Vegetables

The transport of fresh fruit and vegetables is complicated because each variety has widely differing requirements for safe preservation. The rate at which living fruits and vegetables age and are attacked by microorganisms depends upon the environment during storage and transit. During these periods, the quality and condition of fruits and vegetables are maintained by retention of their optimum temperatures. For safe carriage, this will usually require the commodities to be pre-cooled and maintained at that temperature prior to being loaded into the transport unit, whether that is a reefer or a refrigerated container.

Reefer containers are not designed to cool the cargo, but only to maintain the cargo temperature. They are not to be used as cold storage, where temperature of the cargo is brought down rapidly using powerful heavy-duty refrigeration machinery.

All fresh fruits and vegetables are living products that respire. Respiration is a complicated sequence of chemical reactions involving conversion of starches to sugars and the oxidation of those sugars to obtain energy. Normal respiration results in the fruit and vegetables consuming oxygen and giving off carbon dioxide, water, ethylene and varying, but significant, amounts of energy in the form of heat.

Figure 37.1: Fruit and vegetable warehouse.

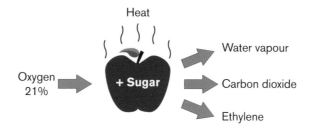

Figure 37.2: Process of respiration in fruits.

The higher the ambient temperature surrounding the commodity, the greater the temperature of the commodity itself and consequently the higher its rate of respiration.

Fruits and vegetables also transpire, which is the loss of water by evaporation that occurs once the fruit or vegetable is removed from the tree or plant that provided water during its growing period. The storage/carriage conditions for fruit and vegetables should be such that excessive water loss does not occur as a result of transpiration.

37.1 Temperature

It is essential to understand that published values of optimum temperatures for storage or transit of fruit and vegetables are not absolute and the accurate optimal requirements are dependent on the variety, climate and other details of the produce. The optimum and required transport temperature should be provided in writing by the shipper who will, or should, have full knowledge of the history of the produce and the temperature that must be maintained by the carrier throughout the period it is under their control.

Optimum temperatures promote low rates of respiration, extend storage life and, in addition, reduce the rate of development of microorganisms. In general, the higher the temperature, the faster the growth of moulds and bacterial infections.

37.2 Freezing Points

The lowest safe limit of temperature for each commodity is its highest freezing point. This temperature is invariably slightly below 0°C, the freezing point of pure water, as natural juices contain dissolved substances in solution that have the effect of lowering the freezing point. Therefore, in general, the sweeter the produce, the lower the freezing point. However, it must be remembered that stalks of fruit contain much less sugar and may freeze at a higher temperature than the fruit itself, resulting in death of the stalk tissue with possible detrimental consequences for other parts of the fruit and a likely loss of market value when the fruit is restored to ambient temperatures.

37.3 Chill Damage

Chilling is another factor that affects the lower safe limit of carriage temperature of some produce. This is a reduction in temperature that does not reach the freezing point of the produce. Numerous commodities, particularly those grown in tropical climates from plants originating from the tropics, are easily affected by low temperatures and are inclined to tissue damage at temperatures well above their freezing point. Typical symptoms include pitting of surface tissues, discolouration of flesh and an increased susceptibility to decay.

37.4 Air and Moisture Considerations

Relative humidity

Relative humidity is the ratio of the water vapour pressure present in air at an existing temperature to the water vapour pressure that would be present if the air were saturated at the same temperature. Relative humidity is usually expressed as a percentage, with saturated air equalling 100% relative humidity.

A difference of vapour pressure may cause water vapour to move from or to the produce within the ambient air. The water retention capacity of air is directly proportional to the temperature of the air, eg a volume of air at 90% relative humidity at 10°C contains a greater mass of water than the same volume of air at 90% relative humidity at a temperature of 0°C.

However, water is lost from produce at about double the rate when carried in a compartment whose air is at 10°C and 90% relative humidity than the same air at 0°C and 90% relative humidity.

The relative humidity of the air within a cargo compartment of a refrigerated vessel or insulated refrigerator container directly determines whether the condition of the products carried can be maintained. Over a period of time, the relative humidity inside a reefer chamber reduces, along with the moisture content in the cargo. The moisture in the air and the moisture released by the cargo due to respiration gets carried over onto the surface of the evaporator coil and settles as condensate. This condensate drips down to the drain pan and is led outside the chamber through a drain pipe. Sometimes, particularly in frozen conditions, when the refrigerant temperature is less than 0°C, the condensate may freeze on the surface of the evaporator tubes in the form of frost, creating a need for periodic defrosting. Frost formed over the evaporator coils has two detrimental effects: a) it blocks the airflow through the evaporator coils, affecting heat transfer and preventing the air from acquiring sufficient coldness from the refrigerant, and b) frost is an insulator and impedes heat transfer across the evaporator coils. Fruits and vegetables, being respiring cargoes, need frequent defrosting (every 4 to 8 hours).

> Relative humidity below the optimum range will result in shrivelling or wilting in most produce. The maintenance of an optimum range of humidity can be difficult to resolve during the carriage of fresh produce.

Relative humidity of air of 85 to 95% is usually recommended for the carriage of most perishable produce in order to preclude/impede wilting or shrivelling caused by moisture loss. Exceptions to this include the carriage of onions, dates, coconuts, ginger rhizomes, yams, dried fruits and some horticultural produce. If the relative humidity increases to 100%, condensation may occur, which would increase the likelihood of mould growth within the compartment and on the produce itself.

Air circulation
The circulation of cooling air within cargo compartments must be kept at an even required temperature throughout. Despite variable heat leakages that may occur in various parts of the system, and the inevitable increase in the circulating air temperature on return compared with delivery, as a result of the removal of respiratory heat from the produce, only a small increase should be acceptable.

> The comparison of delivery air temperatures and return air temperatures is one of the critical monitoring requirements of carriage.

The majority of produce carried, exceptions including cargoes of bananas, should be presented to the ship or container or trailer as pre-cooled with the field heat already removed. The circulating cooling air should, therefore, only be required to remove the respiratory heat of the produce and the heat exchanged via exterior surfaces. A high velocity of circulating air should be unnecessary and is undesirable. Cooling air in refrigerated vessels and containers is usually circulated vertically, from the deck/floor upwards. The system is designed to produce equal air pressures over the full area of the cargo space. However, any elaborate arrangement for air distribution may be rendered useless if incorrect stowage of the produce eliminates or reduces efficient airflow. The difficulties of properly and carefully stowing packages of fresh produce have become more complex with the use of palletised units and pallet boxes/bins.

Air exchange
During the carriage of fresh fruits and vegetables under ordinary conditions of refrigeration, accumulations of gases such as carbon dioxide (CO_2) and ethylene (C_2H_4) will occur. Undesirable odours, or volatiles, may also contribute to off-flavours and hasten deterioration of the produce. These problems can be prevented by repeatedly refreshing the circulating air within the holds by admitting atmospheric air into the system. The introduced air will enter at a point of lowest pressure within the circulation system and the polluted air will exit at the point of highest pressure. Alternatively, an auxiliary air system driven by separate fans may be utilised.

Rates of respiration and heat generation
The rate at which fruits and vegetables produce heat varies: some have high rates of respiration that require more refrigeration to maintain an optimum carriage temperature

than those that respire more slowly. The rates of respiration are determined by temperature and for every 10°C rise in temperature the rates may be doubled or, in some instances, tripled.

The storage life of produce varies inversely with the rate of respiration. This means that produce with short storage expectancy will usually have higher rates of respiration, eg fresh broccoli, lettuce, peas and sweetcorn. Conversely, potatoes, onions and some cultivars of grapes with low respiration rates have longer storage lives. The rate of respiration for any given product will depend on its variety (cultivar), area of growth and the seasonal and climatic conditions experienced during periods of growth.

Some varieties of fruit and vegetables have rates of respiration that do not decline during their ripening period but, instead, their respiration rates increase. This is a critical event or period known as their climacteric. Produce may, therefore, be categorised as climacteric or non-climacteric; the former continues to ripen post-harvest but the latter does not. The ripening processes include development of colour, texture (tissue softening) and flavour.

Many fruits are climacteric, such as peaches, apricots, bananas, mangos, papaya, avocados, plums, tomatoes and guavas, and tend to ripen rapidly during transit and storage. Examples of non-climacteric fruit and vegetables include cucumbers, grapes, lemons, limes, oranges, other citrus fruit (eg satsumas, tangerines, mandarins) and strawberries.

37.5 Weight Loss in Transit

Weight loss from harvested produce can be a major cause of deterioration during transit and storage. Most fruit and vegetables contain between 80 and 95% of water by weight, some of which may be lost by transpiration (water loss from living tissue).

> To minimise loss of saleable produce weight and to preclude wilting and shrivelling, the produce must be maintained at the recommended humidity and temperature. While some weight loss will inevitably occur due to the loss of carbon during respiration, this should only be of relatively minor proportions.

The loss of water will not only result in weight reduction but also in produce of poor quality. Loss of moisture can often be minimised by the use of protective packaging to complement carriage under optimum temperature and humidity.

37.6 Supplements to Refrigeration

Different mechanisms have been tried and tested to slow down ripening after harvest and therefore extend the transit, storage and shelf life of fruit and vegetables, particularly those in the climacteric category. The most successful use:

- Controlled atmosphere (CA) storage and carriage
- modified atmosphere packaging (MAP)
- modified atmosphere (MA) storage and carriage
- edible coatings.

In all cases, the atmosphere created is one of low oxygen (O_2) and high carbon dioxide (CO_2) when compared to atmospheric air. This depresses the production of ethylene (C_2H_4), which accelerates during ripening and in turn expedites the ripening process itself in the form of a chain reaction, particularly in the case of bananas.

> Modified and controlled atmospheres are non-life supporting. Proper ventilation procedures for compartments/containers under CA/MA must be followed prior to entry.

Edible coatings, which will have been tested and tailored for each product, are a simple, safe and relatively inexpensive means of extending the ultimate shelf life of fruit and vegetables provided there are good storage, shipping temperature and humidity controls.

Edible coatings act as a gas barrier, altering the internal atmosphere of the produce and creating an effect similar to that of modified atmosphere packaging (MAP), which can delay ripening of climacteric fruit, delay colour changes in non-climacteric fruit, reduce water loss, reduce decay and maintain quality appearance.

Under ideal conditions of temperature, humidity, atmosphere, packaging and stowing, apples can be preserved for as long as six months or more.

37.7 Carriage of Mixed Produce

Carriers are sometimes required to load and stow different produce in the same vessel, hold or cargo container. Should a mixture be necessary, it is essential that the produce is compatible in respect of:

- Temperature
- relative humidity
- odour production
- ethylene production.

Generally, deciduous fruits with the same temperature requirements can be stowed together.

Cross tainting, where strongly scented fruit and vegetables are stowed together, should be avoided.

Many products produce considerable quantities of ethylene naturally, including apples, avocados, bananas, pears, peaches, plums, melons and pineapples, and should not be stowed with or in adjacent compartments to kiwi fruit, watermelons, lettuce, carrots, etc, all of which can be seriously affected by ethylene.

Two commodities that have produced substantial cargo claims are pears and kiwi fruit.

Pears
Pears are shipped to Europe and North America from South Africa and Chile. They are also shipped in quantity from New Zealand and Australia. Although pears are considered to have a relatively long life, it is essential that they are picked at the right stage of maturity and pre-cooled if optimum life is to be achieved.

Pears are susceptible to various physiological disorders caused by chilling, excess atmospheric CO_2 and skin contact (bruising). They are also subject to microbiological damage resulting from infection by various organisms prior to harvesting. The two most serious types of disease are caused by the fungal species *Monilinia fructigena* and *Botrytis cinerea*. The latter species can grow at temperatures as low as minus 4°C (–4°C) and therefore growth can only be controlled by low temperature storage. The rate of decay increases rapidly as the temperature rises. As invasion usually occurs through damaged tissue, the proper selection of fruit at the packing station is of paramount importance.

The prescribed temperature for the carriage of pears is between 0°C and minus 1.1°C (–1.1°C). Therefore, it is recommended that the carrying temperature should be 0°C, or marginally lower where ships have equipment that can control the delivery air temperature to plus or minus 0.2°C (–0.2°C) or better. The set points for the carriage of pears in containers should be between 0.6 and 1.7°C.

Pears may suffer chilling injury at temperatures below minus 1.5°C (–1.5°C). Certain fruit can tolerate lower temperatures and, even if freezing occurs, very slow thawing at low temperatures can result in the fruit remaining undamaged. Therefore, claims for damage due to the delivery air temperature falling marginally below minus 1.5°C (–1.5°C) for short periods must be viewed with some scepticism.

Because of their comparatively large size and high thermal capacity, cooling of individual fruits through the whole tissue is a relatively slow process. When checking a cargo shipped as pre-cooled, the ship's representative should ensure that spear temperatures are taken at the centre of specimens selected for checking. Other aspects to be checked are the nature of the packaging and the general appearance of the fruit, particularly skin blemishes. Caution is required when attempting to assess the maturity of the fruit and a surveyor should be consulted if in doubt.

Pears are susceptible to damage if the CO_2 concentration in the atmosphere rises much above about 1%, so it is necessary to maintain fresh air ventilation at regular intervals when carrying this cargo.

Where issues occur it is essential that expert advice is obtained as soon as possible.

Kiwi fruit

Kiwi fruit are mainly shipped from New Zealand and California and, increasingly, from Chile. They have a long storage life if picked at the right stage of maturity and stored at temperatures between minus 0.5°C (–0.5°C) and minus 1.0°C (–1.0°C). Storage at a temperature only slightly above this range (+3°C to +4°C) will substantially reduce the storage life.

Kiwi fruit are particularly sensitive to traces of ethylene in the atmosphere, which will prompt rapid ripening. Particular care must, therefore, be taken when kiwi fruit is loaded to ensure that the atmosphere in contact with the fruit cannot be contaminated with the atmosphere from other sources, eg from containers stuffed with cargoes such as apples, which release considerable amounts of ethylene, and even from exhaust fumes from certain types of forklift. As it is necessary for kiwi fruit to be carried using a fresh-air ventilation system, the possibility of cross contamination with the atmospheres from different cargoes must be considered carefully at the time of loading.

Kiwi fruit are also subject to microbiological deterioration, primarily due to invasion by *Botrytis cinerea*.

It is again of paramount importance to obtain expert advice as soon as possible where damage is feared.

Carriage of delicate fruits, exotic fruits and similar products

World trade in delicate products such as strawberries and certain tropical fruits has expanded, although the products concerned frequently have a short shelf life.

It has been known for many years that increasing the CO_2 concentration in a cargo space will depress the metabolic rate of living natural products and this fact has been utilised when carrying apples from Australia to Northern Europe and during storage worldwide. Research has led to the development of more sophisticated gas mixtures, for use in containers or similar carrying units, that not only slow the ripening rate of fruit but also render such products less susceptible to decay and damage caused by microorganisms, insects and physiological disorders.

Controlled or modified atmospheric systems involve initial dosing to produce an atmosphere of the composition required, followed by monitoring. The composition of the atmosphere is automatically maintained using analytical and recycling equipment to remove the excess of some components and increase the concentration of others, as required.

Figure 37.3: Prolonged exposure to high levels of carbon dioxide can cause bananas to become 'green ripe' with soft ripe pulp and green skin.

It has also been established that:

- Ethylene gas, which promotes ripening of fruits, is less effective in atmospheres containing less than 1% carbon dioxide
- if the CO_2 content of the atmosphere is too high, serious physiological damage may result
- at levels of CO_2 in the range of 10 to 15%, *Botrytis* rot of strawberries and some other fruit is substantially inhibited.

Storage in low oxygen levels (2%) can cause problems such as irregular ripening in bananas, pears, etc and the development of black heart in potatoes and brown heart in pears and apples.

Table 37.1 lists some products that benefit from controlled atmosphere storage, showing the optimum conditions for such storage.

Commodity	Temp °C	% O_2	% CO_2
Apples	0.5	2 to 3	1 to 2
Kiwi fruit	0.5	2	5
Pears	0.5	2 to 3	0.1
Strawberries	0.5	10	15 to 20
Nuts/dried fruits	2.25	0.1	0.1
Bananas	12 to 15	2.5	2.5

Table 37.1: Products that benefit from controlled atmosphere storage.

The addition of carbon monoxide at levels of 1 to 5% in atmospheres containing 2 to 5% oxygen has been shown to reduce discolouration of damaged or cut lettuce tissue. At levels of 5 to 10%, it will inhibit the development of certain important plant pathogens. Use of this gas has been the subject of experimentation in some countries.

Table 37.2 lists optimum temperatures, maximum storage, transit and shelf life, etc for a wide range of commodities. This is for guidance only and details of the required temperature and humidity should be provided in writing by the shipper, who has full knowledge of the product's history. The shipper's instructions should be followed at all times.

Commodity	Approx max storage, transit and shelf life	Optimum transit temperature		Container temperature set points		Highest freezing points		Relative humidity
	Days	°C	°F	°C	°F	°C	°F	%
Apples – chilling, sensitive	35 to 45	+1.5 to 4.5	34.7 to 40	+4.4 to +5.6	40 to 42	-1.5	29.3	90 to 95
Apples – non-chilling, sensitive	90 to 240	-1.1 to +1	30 to 33.8	+1.1 to +2.2	34 to 36	-1.5	29.3	90 to 95
Apricots	7 to 14	-0.5 to +1	31 to 33.8	+1.1 to +2.2	34 to 36	-1.1	30	90 to 95
Asparagus	14 to 21	+2.2	36	+2.2	36	-0.6	30.9	90 to 95
Avocados – fuerte and hass	21 to 28	+5 to +8	41 to 46.4	+5 to 12.8	41 to 55	-0.3	31.5	85 to 90
Bananas – green	14 to 21	13 to 14	56 to 58	13 to 14	56 to 58	-0.7	30.6	90 to 95
Blueberries	10 to 18	-0.5	31	1.1 to 2.2	34 to 36	-1.3	29.7	90 to 95
Carrots – topped	30 to 180	0	32	0.6 to 1.7	33 to 35	-1.4	29.5	95
Cherries – sweet	14 to 21	-1.1	30	1.1 to 2.2	34 to 36	-1.8	28.8	90 to 95
Clementines	14 to 28	4.4	40	3.3 to 4.4	38 to 40	-1	30.3	90 to 95
Coconut – flesh	30 to 60	0	32	1.1 to 2.2	34 to 36	-0.9	30.4	80 to 85

Corn – sweet	4 to 6	0	32	0.6 to 1.7	33 to 35	-0.6	30.9	90 to 95
Courgettes	14 to 21	7.2	45	7.2 to 10	45 to 50	-0.5	31.1	90 to 95
Cucumbers	10 to 14	10	50	10 to 11.1	50 to 52	-0.5	31.1	90 to 95
Dasheens	42 to 140	13.3	56	11.1 to 13.3	52 to 56	–	–	85 to 90
Garlic	140 to 210	0	32	0.6 to 1.7	33 to 35	-0.8	30.5	65 to 70
Ginger rhizomes	90 to 180	13.3	56	12.8 to 13.3	55 to 56	–	–	85 to 90
Grapefruit	28 to 42	13.3	56	14.4 to 15.6	58 to 60	-1.1	30	85 to 90
Grapes	56 to 180	-1.1	30	1.1 to 2.2	34 to 36	-2.2	28.1	90 to 95
Guavas	14 to 21	10	50	9 to 10	48 to 50	–	–	85 to 90
Kiwi fruit	28 to 84	0	32	1.1 to 2.2	34 to 36	-0.9	30.4	90 to 95
Kumquats	14 to 28	4.4	40	4.4	40	–	–	90 to 95
Lemons	30 to 180	12.2	54	10 to 12.8	50 to 55	-1.4	29.4	85 to 90
Lettuce – iceberg	10 to 18	0	32	1.1 to 2.2	34 to 36	–	–	90 to 95
Limes	42 to 56	9 to 10	48 to 50	9 to 10	48 to 50	-1.6	29.1	85 to 90
Lychees	21 to 35	1.7	35	1.7 to 2.2	35 to 36	–	–	90 to 95
Mandarins	14 to 28	7.2	45	7.2	45	-1.1	30	90 to 95
Mangoes	14 to 25	13.3	56	12.8	55	-0.9	30.4	85 to 90
Melons – honeydew	21 to 28	10	50	7.8 to 10	46 to 50	-1	30.3	85 to 90
Mineolas	21 to 35	3.3	38	3.9 to 6.7	39 to 44	-1	30.3	90 to 95
Nectarines	14 to 28	-0.5	31	-0.6 to ±1	31 to 32	-1	30.3	90 to 95
Onions – dry	30 to 180	0	32	0.6 to 1.7	33 to 35	-0.8	30.6	65 to 75
Oranges – blood	21 to 56	4.4	40	4.4 to 6.7	40 to 44	–	–	90 to 95
Oranges – California and Arizona	21 to 56	6.7	44	6.7 to 7.8	44 to 45	-0.8	30.6	85 to 95
Oranges – Florida and Texas	56 to 84	1.7	35	1.1 to 2.2	34 to 36	-0.8	30.6	85 to 95
Oranges – Jaffa	56 to 84	7.8	46	7.8 to 10	46 to 50	-0.7	30.6	85 to 90
Oranges – Seville	90	10	50	11	52	–	–	85 to 90
Parsnips	120 to 150	0	32	0.6 to 1.7	33 to 35	-0.9	30.4	95

Peaches	14 to 28	-0.5	31	0.6 to 1.7	33 to 35	-0.9	30.4	90 to 95
Pears – Anjou	120 to 180	-1.1	30	0.6 to 1.7	33 to 35	-1.6	29.2	90 to 94
Pears – Bartlett	70 to 90	-1.1	30	0.6 to 1.7	33 to 35	-1.6	29.2	90 to 94
Peppers – sweet	12 to 18	10	50	10	50	-0.7	30.7	90 to 95
Peppers – hot	14 to 21	10	50	10	50	-0.7	30.7	90 to 95
Pineapples	14 to 36	10	50	10	50	-1.1	30	85 to 90
Plantains	10 to 35	13	57.2	14	57.2	-0.8	30.6	85 to 90
Plums	14 to 28	-0.5	31	1.1 to 2.2	34 to 36	-0.8	30.6	90 to 95
Potatoes – seed	84 to 175	4.4	40	5	41	-0.8	30.5	90 to 95
Potatoes – table	56 to 140	6	42.8	7	44.6	-0.8	30.5	90 to 95
Satsumas	56 to 84	4	39	4	39	–	–	85 to 90
Sweet potatoes	90 to 180	14	57	14	57	-1.3	29.7	85 to 90
Tangerines	14 to 28	7	42.5	7	42.5	-1.1	30.1	85 to 90
Tomatoes – green	21 to 28	13.3	56	13 to 14	56 to 58	-.5	31.1	90 to 95
Tomatoes – turning	10 to 14	9	48.2	10.6	51	-0.5	31.1	90 to 95
Ugli fruit	14 to 21	4.4	40	5	41	-1.1	30.1	90 to 95
Watermelons	14 to 21	10	50	8 to 10	46 to 50	-0.4	30.9	85 to 90
Yams – cured	49 to 112	16	61	16	61	-1.1	30.1	70 to 80

Table 37.2: Guidance for the transportation of fruit and vegetables.

37.8 Table Grapes

Table grapes are a high value commodity that may be carried on pallets either in containers or in breakbulk refrigerated vessels.

As grapes do not continue to ripen once they have been cut from the vine, they must be harvested in fully mature condition. Grapes can easily be physically damaged and poor handling can result in a variety of physiological defects that make them more susceptible to microbiological invasion.

Even comparatively short periods of exposure at normal temperatures, say six hours at 20°C, can result in dehydration and browning of the stems which then often results in bunch 'shattering' during handling. It is, therefore, normal practice to cool grapes as soon as practicable after they have been harvested.

Weather conditions, particularly rain prior to and during the harvest period, can have a significant effect on the storage life of grapes, because wetted grapes are more susceptible to fungal invasion than grapes that have been harvested after a period of dry weather.

Various species of microorganisms will invade grapes and the most common found in transportation is *Botrytis cinerea*, which produces typical grey mould, white mould or some forms of berry rot. This organism can grow at a temperature as low as minus 4°C (−4°C). Fungal infection is more likely to arise if, during the growth period of the fruit, the weather has been wet, but *Botrytis* mould can also develop on grapes that have not been exposed to wet conditions before harvesting. It is impossible to completely control or arrest the spread of infection by this fungal mould, as it will tolerate high levels of sulphur dioxide treatment. Other species of microorganisms that cause deterioration include *Cladosporium herbarum*, *Alternaria* species, *Penicillium* species and *Aspergillus niger*. Identification of the infecting microorganism can only be determined by laboratory examination of specimens of the grapes concerned.

Grapes are stowed in refrigerated containers in pre-cooled conditions. At the normal temperatures for loading, the rate of metabolic heat production is low so there should be no heat load problems. The carrying temperature, ie the air delivery temperature, must be as low as possible and container units are normally set to 0°C. Although grape berries will not freeze at temperatures above approximately minus 2°C (−2°C), the stalks will freeze at minus 1.5°C (−1.5°C) to minus 2°C (−2°C). On thawing, the stalks blacken, shrivel and become brittle, so there can be substantial shatter (ie individual grapes becoming detached from the bunches) with overcooled fruit, even if the berries themselves are unaffected.

The lugs in which the grapes are packed must be carefully stowed and this is normally the responsibility of the shipper. The key responsibility of the ship is to ensure the carrying temperature (0°C) is maintained and that there is a legible record to confirm this.

Grapes infected with *Botrytis cinerea* will continue to deteriorate, even at 0°C, but the rate of deterioration falls as the temperature is lowered, which is why carriers are advised to keep grapes at the lowest practical temperature.

There are many types of physiological disorders that can result in commercial losses of grapes, although some of the causes arise during growing, harvesting and handling rather than during an ocean voyage. If, therefore, damage to grapes is reported, the Master should ensure that a surveyor is called in.

Surveyors should be able to recognise the various conditions of infection or deterioration and take adequate samples to enable specialists to assess the nature of any damage. In cases of fungal infection, it is important that samples are drawn illustrating each particular type of fungal deterioration so that the causative organisms can be identified. This is because the types of infection involved can provide an indication of the underlying cause.

Experience has shown that claims for damage to cargoes of grapes frequently concern shipments made from the same source at about the same time, which could mean there were problems with a particular harvest. It is important for owners to advise their Association as soon as any allegations of damage are received so that the information can be collated and an investigation begun to determine whether any particular pattern is involved.

Chapter 38 –
Frozen Fish

The annual world catch of fish exceeds 100 million tonnes, of which around 25% is processed into frozen fishery products. Each year, a high proportion of these frozen products enters international trade and is carried by sea.

Cargoes of frozen products are sometimes found to be damaged when they are unloaded from ships, leading to rejection and to claims against shipowners and agents alleging that the damage is due to negligence on the part of the Master and crew of the carrying vessel.

A vessel is not liable for damage to cargo that was sustained before loading, or during handling if due to the actions of third parties. However, it is often difficult to establish the precise cause and chain of events leading up to the damage and specialised knowledge is required to sample and inspect fishery products and relate their condition to the events of the voyage. However, vessel operators also need adequate technical knowledge to minimise the risk of problems occurring and to act in the event of a claim.

38.1   Frozen Fishery Products

A variety of frozen fishery products are carried by sea in reefer vessels and reefer containers. The main types, in approximately descending order of frequency, are:

Whole, gutted[1] or dressed[2] fish, individually frozen
Tuna intended for canning is a typical example.

Figure 38.1: Whole fish individually frozen.

Whole, gutted or dressed fish in blocks

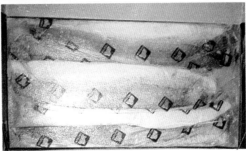

Figure 38.2: Fillets of fish, frozen in a block, wrapped and packed in a carton.

This is a common form of presentation for small and medium-sized fish intended for further processing. Blocks are rarely more than 10 cm thick or more than 50 kg in weight. Common sizes are 25 and 50 kg. Blocks may be unwrapped, or wrapped in plastic film, and are sometimes packed in strapped cartons.

Fillets of fish, frozen in blocks
Fillets of fish are often frozen into geometrically-shaped blocks. Blocks are usually wrapped in plastic film and packed into inner display packs. The display packs are then usually packed in outer cartons.

Fillets of fish, individually frozen
These are fillets frozen as separate pieces and sometimes coated with batter or breadcrumbs.

---

[1] Gutted fish are whole apart from removal of the viscera.
[2] Dressed fish have heads and guts, and perhaps tails and fins, removed.

Fillets are either placed in packages for retail sale or loosely packed in plastic bags. Small display packs are packed in outer cartons while loosely packed fillets may be packed in bags within outer cartons.

Cephalopods, frozen in blocks or as packaged products

Figure 38.3: Cephalopods (squid) frozen in blocks.

Cephalopods include squid, cuttlefish and octopus. Both processed and unprocessed products are, typically, frozen in blocks weighing 10 or 25 kg. Blocks are occasionally individually packaged, but more usually are overwrapped in plastic, with several blocks packed together in a single outer carton.

Crustacean shellfish, frozen in blocks or as packaged products

These include lobster, crayfish, shrimp and crab. Smaller crustaceans and crustacean meats are often frozen in blocks weighing up to 1 kg. Blocks are packed individually in cartons or overwrapped in plastic film and then packed into outer cartons.

Crustacean shellfish, individually frozen

Large crustacea, such as lobsters and crayfish, are individually frozen, whole or as tails and then wrapped and packed in cartons.

38.2 Freezing and Storage of Fishery Products

This subsection provides background to Masters and crew about the technologies involved in freezing and storage of frozen fishery products, and the effects of freezing and storage on product quality.

The Master of a vessel carrying frozen fishery products does not generally need to be concerned with how the products have been frozen and stored before delivery to the vessel. However, the quality of the cargo discharged from the vessel is affected by freezing, storage and distribution practices before transfer to the vessel, as well as by the manner of loading, stowage and carriage on the vessel.

38.2.1 The Freezing Process

When a fish product is cooled in a freezer, its temperature drops rapidly to about minus 1°C (−1°C), when ice begins to form. However, not all the water in the fish turns to ice at this point. As more heat is extracted, more ice forms, but the temperature of the product drops only slowly until about minus 3°C (−3°C). This period, when the product temperature changes very gradually, is known as the thermal arrest period.

The product's temperature then begins to drop rapidly towards the operating temperature of the freezer (see Figure 38.4).

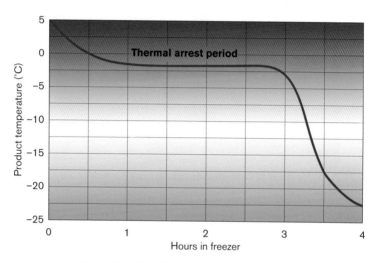

Figure 38.4: Freezing curve of fish initially at 5°C.

To preserve the quality of the product, it is important that the thermal arrest period is as short as possible, preferably less than two hours. This rate of cooling can only be achieved in equipment designed for the purpose; merely placing fish in a cold store will not achieve a sufficiently high freezing rate.

The refrigerated holds of reefer ships are designed as cold stores to maintain the temperature of already frozen products and they do not have the refrigeration capacity to freeze products at the required rate.

When the product is allowed to thaw, the temperature will follow a curve similar to Figure 38.4, but in the reverse direction.

Brine freezing of individual fish

Brine freezing is used for larger, whole fish like salmon and tuna. The technique is used almost exclusively on board fishing vessels, particularly tuna catchers. The fishing vessel is fitted with one or more insulated tanks containing refrigeration coils. Before fishing starts, these tanks are filled with seawater, which is then cooled to around 0°C. As fish are caught, they are dropped into the tanks. When a tank is full, salt is added to lower the freezing point of the brine and the temperature is lowered so that the fish freeze. The optimum temperature to freeze the fish is approximately minus 21°C (−21°C), which is achieved when the brine is saturated. In practice, fishing vessels aim for a solution giving a temperature of around minus 12°C (−12°C). Once the fish are frozen, the brine is drained from the tank and the fish are held in dry condition with the refrigeration system on.

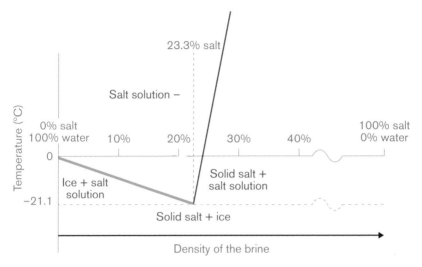

Figure 38.5: Lowering of freezing point of brine.

Freezing of blocks
Small products, including small fish, fish fillets, squid, octopus and shrimps, are often frozen in blocks. The product is laid in trays and frozen, either in a tunnel through which cold air is passed or between pairs of hollow plates through which refrigerant is circulated. The frozen block is knocked out of the tray, protected by some form of overwrapping and usually packed into cartons.

38.2.2   The Quality of Frozen Fishery Products

Complaints about defects in the quality of frozen fishery cargoes usually fall into one or both of two categories:

- Abnormal and offensive odours, flavours or texture, or any other defects that will influence the consumers' perception of quality
- physical damage affecting the processability or merchantability of the product (this can occur during the freezing process, but more usually happens during handling of the frozen product).

Quality defects in both categories can arise during handling, processing and storage of the product before delivery to the vessel, during loading into the holds and while the product is stored on the vessel.

Loss of quality can occur both before and after freezing. However, the nature of the defects differs in the two circumstances and an experienced assessor should be able to distinguish between them.

38.2.3 Loss of Quality Before Freezing

Fish of all kinds are notorious for the speed at which they spoil (even when chilled) and for the unpleasant nature of the spoiled product. Spoilage affects the appearance, odour and flavour of the product. Freezing halts the spoilage process and fixes the quality as it was at the time of freezing. When frozen products are thawed, the quality can be no better than it was at the time of freezing. If defects in the quality of frozen fishery products at the time of delivery are shown to be a consequence of spoilage, no blame can be attached to the carrier of the frozen goods unless the product had thawed out during the voyage.

38.2.4 Loss of Quality During Frozen Storage

Frozen fishery products are not completely stable in the frozen state and will deteriorate over time, resulting in changes in texture, odour and flavour of the product. Changes in texture are similar in character across most fishery products – the product becomes dry, stringy and tough. Changes in odour and flavour depend on the type of fishery product. Lean fish with a low oil content (such as cod) develop the characteristic odours and flavours described as 'musty', 'cardboard' and 'wet dog', while fish with a high oil content (such as tuna, herring and mackerel) develop rancid odours and flavours reminiscent of new leather, linseed oil or old-fashioned oil paints. Changes in odour and flavour in frozen crustacean shellfish and cephalopods are similar to those in lean fish. Oily fish deteriorate faster and produce off-odours more quickly than lean fish during frozen storage.

The main factors influencing the rate at which fishery products deteriorate during frozen storage are temperature of storage and exposure to air. The lower the storage temperature, the slower the product deteriorates. The storage life of fishery products carried at minus 18°C (–18°C) ranges from 3 to 12 months. In general, storage life is halved for each 5°C rise in storage temperature. For example, a product with a storage life of 8 months at minus 18°C (–18°C) will have a storage life of 4 months at minus 13°C (–13°C).

> Since ships' refrigeration systems can maintain products at temperatures below minus 18°C (–18°C), and since voyages are generally less than a month long, there should be no significant loss of quality under the normal conditions of frozen storage during a voyage.

Rate of deterioration is also affected by exposure to air. Block-frozen products are usually protected by close wrapping with plastic film or by coating with a water glaze. To maintain quality, it is important that this cover, film or glaze is not damaged or lost.

Another defect that may arise during frozen storage is excessive loss of moisture from the product, which leads to general or localised dehydration known as a freezer burn. The dehydration is signified by white patches that appear where the glaze is lost or where there are tears or breaks in the protective wrapping. In unprotected material, dehydration occurs first in thin parts of the product, such as the fins of whole fish and the tail-ends of fillets, or at the corners of blocks. These dried areas do not rehydrate when the product is thawed and are indicated by blemishes in the thawed product.

38.2.5   Physical Damage to Frozen Products

Physical damage takes a number of forms, but complaints about the quality of reefer cargoes are usually concerned with distortion or compression of the product. This kind of damage, which affects individually frozen fish or blocks of products, occurs when warm fishery products (ie warm relative to the recommended storage temperature) are subjected to pressure, for example in a stack of fish stored in the ship's hold.

Fish typically contain 70 to 80% water, the exact percentage depending on the species. Water in fish tissues starts to freeze at about minus 1°C (−1°C), but at this point only a proportion of the water is converted to ice. Progressively, more water freezes as the temperature falls. At minus 18°C (−18°C), which is the lowest temperature usually specified for the carriage of frozen fish in reefers, around 90% of the water has turned to ice. It is very difficult to deform frozen fish at this temperature and below, except under extremely high pressure.

If the product warms at all, some of the ice melts. The fish tissue holds an increasing proportion of liquid water and a decreasing proportion of ice as its temperature rises. As the proportion of ice decreases, the fish tissue, though still partly frozen, becomes softer and can be deformed by moderate pressure. At minus 3°C (−3°C), 'frozen' fishery products are soft enough to deform and to sag under their own weight. If the cargo in the hold of a reefer is stacked to a height of 4 or 5 m, as is often the case, there is sufficient pressure to distort fish to some extent at minus 7°C (−7°C), and to distort and compress fish considerably at minus 5°C (−5°C) or higher.

Individually frozen fish can be severely indented where they lie across each other and also tend to take up the shapes of the surfaces they are pressed against, such as ridged floor plates or edges of structures in the hold. In an extreme case, a stack of individual fish can be compressed together into a solid mass with almost no spaces between the fish. Blocks of products can be squeezed, flattened and distorted and will extrude into gaps between cartons and be indented by floor plates or pallet boards.

Figure 38.6: Indentations caused when warmed, soft tuna were pressed onto ridged floor plates by the weight of the stack of fish above them.

Frozen products at low temperatures are often brittle and prone to damage by rough handling. For example, tails are easily broken off whole fish and blocks can be shattered or chipped.

Products can also be damaged by contamination. If oil or chemicals are spilled, they may penetrate the wrappings and affect the contents. When cartons and wrappings are torn, the contents are more vulnerable to both contamination and dehydration.

38.3   Pre-shipment Inspection

The need for inspection

Loss of quality in fishery products can be caused by damage both before and after freezing. Carriage of frozen fish by sea is just one stage in a long sequence of processing, handling, distribution and storage operations, and products can be damaged or decline in quality at any stage. Receivers of damaged cargoes of frozen fishery products might allege that loss of quality occurred solely while the material was in the charge of the shipowner.

Pre-shipment inspection is, therefore, essential to determine as far as possible the condition and quality of the product at the time of loading and to note any circumstances that could lead to an exaggerated loss of quality during carriage in the ship. Such information has an important bearing on any claim that loss of quality or damage occurred during carriage in the ship. The inspection should take into account the nature of the material, its packaging and its presentation.

> Pre-shipment inspection by the ship's officers is generally confined to visual inspection of the cargo and to measurement of physical properties such as temperature. Officers are not expected to carry out detailed evaluations of the quality of the material, which would require examination of material after thawing and perhaps also after cooking.

Nature of the consignment

The deck officer should check that the materials to be loaded are consistent with the B/L. However, information provided on a B/L is usually very brief and a cargo may be described as 'fishery products', which encompasses many different product types. Wherever possible, deck officers should record any additional information, for example, in the case of individually frozen fish, the species or variety, the presentation (whole or dressed) and the name of the fishing vessel.

It is also important to record the details of any labelling on wrapped or cartoned material, particularly production dates or batch codes. The absence of any labelling, particularly of batch or production codes, should also be noted.

Information on the nature of the consignment and all details of labelling should be recorded on the mate's receipt. If labels are detachable, one can be removed and attached to the receipt.

Temperature of the consignment

> It is essential to measure the temperature of frozen fish presented for loading. Since fishery products suffer damage if they are stowed at a high temperature, temperature records provide important evidence of the state of the product at the time of loading.

The terms of carriage normally stipulate the temperature, or at least the maximum temperature, at which the cargo should be carried. Holds of reefer vessels are intended for storage of frozen material loaded at the required temperature of carriage. Refrigeration systems have little spare capacity to lower the temperature of products that are put into the hold at above its operating temperature. Material that is above the operating temperature of the hold will take a long time to cool down and will lose quality as a result.

The terms of contract between the provider of the frozen products and the recipient sometimes specify the maximum temperature at which the products should be stored and delivered to the ship and a temperature no warmer than minus 10°C (–10°C) would be typical for frozen tuna delivered from a tuna fishing vessel. Even if there is no specific requirement for the cargo's temperature on delivery to the ship, the Master may refuse to accept a product if they consider the temperature too high and the product at risk of damage during stowage and carriage.

The deck officer should ensure that sufficient measurements are taken to provide an adequate summary of the temperature of the cargo and that the measurements are accurately recorded.

During loading, supervising officers should note any softening of the flesh of fish during transfer to the vessel; this can be gauged by pressing the surface of the fish with a thumb nail or the point of a temperature probe. Even when the temperature measured at the core of a fish is low, the flesh on the outside can be soft enough to be damaged by the pressure of a stack within the hold.

Condition of the material
It is not easy to assess the intrinsic quality of frozen products by visual examination but, with experience, one can get some indication of pre-freezing quality from the appearance of the eyes and skin in the case of whole fish, from the colour of the shell in the case of shell-on crustacean shellfish, and from the colour of the skin in the case of cephalopods. These indications of quality will not be visible in packaged products unless some of the cartons are opened. Whenever possible, photographs should be taken of any defects.

Visual indication of spoilage in individually frozen fish
The inspecting officer should examine frozen fish individually for signs of spoilage before freezing.

	Good quality fish	Stale fish
Colours	Bright, demarcated	Degraded and dull
Eyes	Clear or slightly cloudy; flat to the head or even projecting slightly	Yellowish or reddish; sunken or missing
Skin	Clean – no discoloured slime or coating	Abraded and covered with yellowish slime or bloodstained brine; head region of tuna takes on a diffuse pinkish hue

	Tuna spoiled prior to freezing – note sunken, discoloured eyes, dull colours, pinkish discolouration of head, loss of skin and dirty, bloodstained slime.

Table 38.1: Signs of spoilage in individually frozen fish.

Nature and integrity of packaging and wrapping

Packaging is intended to protect the product from physical damage. The inspecting officer should record any damage to outer wrappings, particularly if the damage has caused exposure of the contents. Sometimes, the packaging includes strapping, particularly where a carton contains individually wrapped, heavy products such as blocks of fillets. The nature and integrity of any strapping should be noted.

Wrapping, which may or may not be supplemented by further packaging in a carton, is intended to prevent contamination and dehydration. Wrapping is only effective in protecting against dehydration if it is sealed or closely applied to the product. The record should include details of the type and condition of any wrapping.

Figure 38.7: Damage to outer carton, although wrapping and contents appear unharmed.

The officer should note any staining of cartons and outer wrappings, including the character and nature of the stain – lubricating oil, fuel oil, water, fish juices, for example. Oils tend to be dark in colour and leave the wrappings soft, even when frozen. Fish-juice stains are yellowish or reddish. The officer should note whether the staining is extensive, covering all or most of the container or wrappings, or localised. When stains are localised, it should be noted whether they are predominantly on the corners or edges of the packages or on the sides.

Blemishes, stains and contamination of the product

When the surface of the product is visible, it should be inspected for blemishes and contamination. Blemishes include surface damage to whole fish, such as abrasions and tears to the skin or splits in the flesh, and surface damage to blocks, such as patches of freezer burn. An attempt should be made to assess the proportion of the consignment affected.

It is important to record any unusual discolouration or staining and, if possible, the nature of the defect, for example blood or bloody brine (particularly on brine-frozen tuna), oil or chemicals. The product should also be examined for contamination by dust, organic matter such as fish offal or vegetable debris, and any other foreign matter.

In all cases of blemishes or contamination, the inspecting officer should note the extent of the damage and estimate the proportion of the consignment affected.

Signs of thawing or partial thawing
Sometimes, claims are made against shipowners on the basis that a cargo has thawed or partially thawed during the voyage, and has then frozen again to the stipulated carriage temperature. It is, therefore, important to check that a potential cargo does not show signs that it has thawed and refrozen *before* being presented for shipment. Such thawing or near thawing is often indicated by distortion of product shape and release of liquids from the product.

Distortion
Distortion of whole or blocks of fish indicates that the material has thawed or partially thawed since freezing, or was distorted during the freezing process.

Individually frozen whole fish often have slight pressure marks formed during the freezing process. These minor distortions must be allowed for during examination of frozen products. The nature of the marks depends on the freezing process. For example, fish frozen in trays are slightly flattened or have indentations on one side where they have lain on the trays during freezing. Brine-frozen fish tend to float in the brine tanks and are restrained below the level of the brine by a grating. As a result, the fish may have slightly flattened sides where they have been compressed, or shallow cylindrical-shaped depressions where they lay across each other as they froze. Sometimes, the pressure on tuna during brine freezing results in splitting of the skin and flesh, usually on the dorsal surface at the base of the dorsal fin. Any other splitting should be noted by the officer.

Any distortions other than slight flattening or the presence of minor depressions suggest that the product has warmed up, softened and refrozen in the distorted shape. The officer should note the nature and extent of any distortions.

Blocks of fish should reflect the sharp angles and regular, geometrical shape of the tray or former in which they were frozen. Blocks of fish that have thawed while stored on pallets or in stacks will show signs of slumping, bending or compression and material is often squeezed into the spaces between the blocks. Restraints such as strappings and the framing of pallets and shelf-supports cause indentations in blocks of fish. Again, the inspecting officer should note the nature and extent of distortions.

Release of liquid
Fish release liquid as they thaw. The cargo officers should check for pools of liquid collecting within wrappings, and for signs that liquid has been squeezed from the blocks and has refrozen on the sides of the stack or on shelves and pallets. Staining of cartons is sometimes an indication that the contents have thawed and released liquid.

Figure 38.8: Oil-stained cartons.   Figure 38.9: Carton that has been stained by fish juices when the block partially thawed.

38.4   Transfer, Stowage and Carriage

Temperature control during loading

It is very important for maintaining quality that frozen fishery products are held at low temperatures at all times. Although it is inevitable that the product's temperature will rise during loading into the hold, the loading operations must be conducted so as to keep this rise to a minimum. The product's quality suffers not only due to the immediate rise in temperature as material is stowed in the hold, but also because of the time taken to bring the product back down to the required temperature after stowage.

As far as possible, the cargo should be loaded at, or below, the required temperature of carriage, typically around minus 18°C (−18°C). Officers and crew should attempt to minimise warming of the cargo while it is being loaded and stowed in the holds, preferably so that the temperature of the cargo is not above minus 10°C (−10°C) by the time it is stowed. Although the ship's crew may have little control over loading operations, the Master should cooperate with the ship's agent, and particularly with the stevedoring company, to ensure that good practices are adopted during loading and stowing.

Good practices during loading

- Ensure that delivery to the ship's side is matched to loading onto the vessel to reduce the time that products are waiting on the quay
- products should be delivered in insulated containers or lorries, or at least in covered vehicles
- if the material must be unloaded onto the quay or held on the deck of the reefer, it should be placed on pallets or on an insulating base, packed as tightly as possible and covered with a tarpaulin or similar protection against sun and wind
- the cargo should be protected from exposure to wind, rain and sun until it is about to be transferred to the ship
- in tropical climates, avoid loading for two or three hours either side of noon and consider loading the ship at night.

Good practices during stowage

- Ensure that the hold is cooled to below the carriage temperature before loading begins

- during breaks in loading, cover holds or decks with at least the hatch covers, even if the thermal covers are not put in place
- refrigeration to the holds should be turned on during long breaks
- transfer cargo as rapidly as possible from the quay or discharging vessel to the hold
- once loaded, the cargo should be covered with tarpaulins
- where consistent with efficient loading, use only one hatch at a time to avoid through currents of air in the hold.

Maintaining low temperatures during carriage

There is usually an explicit or implicit requirement to hold the cargo below minus 18°C (–18°C) during carriage. The ship's refrigeration system must be capable of delivering air to the holds at a temperature a few degrees below the target temperature to allow for heat leaks through the ship's structures. Cargo spaces in reefers are usually cooled by recirculating air systems, which are only effective if the air can circulate freely through and around the stow.

Most heat leaks into the cargo hold occur through the sides and bulkheads and it is important to ensure that there is free circulation between the cargo and the structures to the hold. Sides and bulkheads should be fitted with vertical dunnage (without horizontal battens which could obstruct airflow) to keep the cargo away from the structures. There should be an even gap of at least 20 cm between the top of the stowed cargo and the lowest part of the deckhead.

Cartons should be stacked with gaps between them, while stows of individually frozen fish will inevitably have spaces unless the fish are deformable and have been compressed.

The ship's engineer should ensure that refrigeration equipment is well maintained and can achieve the design temperatures. Evaporator coils must be defrosted as required to maintain the cooling capacity. Frequent need for defrosting is a sign of high temperatures in the cargo and should be noted in the engine room log. In addition, the engine room log should record temperatures at critical and meaningful positions in the refrigeration system, such as the outlet and return air streams in air-cooling systems and the outlet and return fluid temperatures in pipe-cooled systems.

It is vital to take and record temperature measurements in the hold. How meaningful these measurements are depends on the location of the temperature sensors. Material in the centre of the stow is the slowest to cool because the source of refrigeration is mainly around the sides of the stow. Refrigerated air percolates gaps between fish or between cartons and the cooling effect depends on the existence of uninterrupted spaces. Sensors attached to the sides or bulkheads of the hold are exposed to cold air circulating through the dunnage against the sides or bulkheads and, therefore, tend to indicate temperatures lower than the bulk of the cargo. Sensors should be attached to posts or other structural members running through the hold, where they are more likely to reflect accurately the temperature of the bulk of the cargo.

Protecting the cargo from contamination

Every effort must be made to protect the cargo from contamination. Good shipboard practices will prevent direct contamination by seawater, bilge water, fuel oil and the like, but it is important to be aware that fishery products are rapidly tainted by odours picked up from the ambient air. This is a vital consideration when using air-cooled refrigeration systems – the air must not become polluted by odoriferous materials such as fuel oil, paints or chemicals used on the ship.

A simple guideline is that, if the air circulating through the hold has an odour, then that odour will be picked up by the fish products.

Unloading

When a cargo is unloaded from the ship, similar precautions should be taken to those recommended during loading to minimise warming. Unloading should be completed as quickly as possible and the cargo should be protected from wind, rain and high temperatures.

38.5 Measuring the Temperature of Frozen Fishery Products

Equipment

The most convenient thermometer for measuring the temperature of frozen food products is a water-resistant, K-type thermometer with a digital display reading to 0.1°C. Typically, these thermometers have a measuring range down to minus 50°C (−50°C) and an accuracy of ±0.5°C in the range required when measuring the temperature of chilled or frozen foods. This accuracy is adequate for the purposes described in this chapter.

There are several types of probe available for plugging into the instrument. The best all-round probe for measuring the temperature of fishery products is a 100 mm long, 3 to 4 mm diameter, stainless steel penetration probe on a 1 m lead. There are also stouter, hammer-in probes for forcing into frozen fish (provided the temperature is not too low), but these have long response times. It is usually preferable to drill holes and use a thinner probe.

Measuring the temperature of frozen fish

It is not usually possible to push a probe into frozen products. Normal practice is to drill a hole, with an ordinary engineer's hand or power drill, of such a diameter that the probe fits tightly. The bottom of the hole should be at the thermal centre of the object, ie at the position that will cool down or warm up most slowly. The thermal centre is usually at the backbone in the thickest part of a fish or at the centreline of a block of fillets. The hole should be around 100 mm deep, ie sufficiently long to take the whole length of the probe. This may mean that the hole must be drilled at an angle to the surface of a fish or along the centreline of a block from one of the smaller side faces.

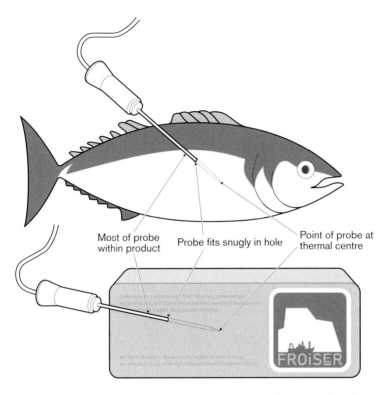

Most of probe within product

Probe fits snugly in hole

Point of probe at thermal centre

Figure 38.10: Inserting temperature probe into frozen fish or block of fish.

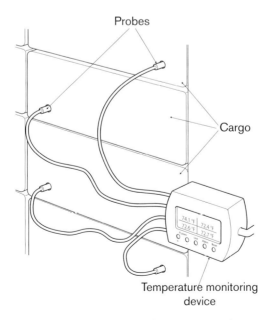

Probes

Cargo

Temperature monitoring device

Figure 38.11: Location of thermometer probes.

Once the probe has been inserted, note the lowest temperature reading given in the next 2 to 4 minutes. While the hole is drilled and the temperature measurement taken, the product warms up, so measurements should be taken as quickly as possible, and preferably while the product is still in the hold.

Measuring the temperature of products in cartons

Products in cartons may be delivered in regular stacks or in random loads. In a regular stack of cartons, for example cartons on pallets, temperatures can be measured by inserting the probe between cartons. The warmest areas are the corners of the stack.

Temperature should be measured at diagonally opposed top and bottom corners and in the centre of a face. Insert the whole length of the probe between cartons, or between the flap and body of a carton, on the mid-line. Insert the probe between vertically stacked cartons rather than horizontally adjacent cartons as the weight of the cartons above ensures a good thermal contact with the probe. Record the minimum reading. Pushing the probe between cartons will result in some frictional heating, so 5 to 10 minutes may be required to reach equilibrium. When measuring temperatures of cartons, it is useful to have several probes, cover the stack to avoid heat loss, and allow 5 to 10 minutes before connecting the probes in turn to the thermometer.

Figure 38.12: Measuring temperature within a carton.

When cartons are loosely stowed, it is necessary to measure the temperature within cartons. If the contents are loose, such as individually quick frozen (IQF) fillets, the probe can be forced through the side of the carton into the product.

Thermal contact is poor in such cases and it may take 10 minutes, or more, to reach thermal equilibrium. If the cartons contain blocks, it should be possible to insert the probe between blocks or to drill a hole in a block and insert the probe through the side of the carton. The carton usually has to be split to locate gaps between blocks and the centres of faces of blocks.

Calibration of the thermometer and probes

Instruments are calibrated by their manufacturers, but it is possible to check thermometer/probe combinations at 0°C on the vessel.

Finely crush some ice made from fresh or distilled water and pack it tightly into a vacuum flask or jar. Add cold water to fill the flask and insert the probe to its full length in the ice/water mixture in the centre of the flask. Leave the flask and probe for a while in a cool place, perhaps a refrigerator or chill room, before taking a temperature reading. Since a mixture of ice and fresh water at thermal equilibrium has a temperature of 0°C, any deviation of the probe/thermometer combination from 0°C is the correction for that system.

Figure 38.13: Reefer cargo temperature probe calibration.

Chapter 39 –
Meat and Meat Products in Containers

39.1   Contamination by Odour

Meat is particularly vulnerable to foreign odours. Remedial treatment can be costly and substantial claims can result. If the intensity of the odour or its penetration of the meat surface is significant, the warehouse or cold store may reject it because of the risk of taint to other meat already in store. Modern cold stores usually have no facilities for carrying out remedial treatment for small quantities and it can be difficult and expensive to carry out the treatment at other premises.

39.2   Soft Condition

Damage may result from complete failure of the refrigeration plant, but is more usually brought about by incomplete closure of the vents at the connection point in controlled atmosphere containers, where the ship's refrigeration has been disconnected. Damage can comprise blood-stained and misshapen carcasses and the distortion and staining of meat in cartons in the area of the ambient airflow.

39.3   Chilled Beef

The shelf life of chilled beef is about 10 weeks from the time of slaughter and it may have been in store for some time before shipment. Occasionally, on arrival at destination, the amount of free blood in the vacuum pack is found to be in excess of normal. Provided there is no evidence of intramuscular icing at the time of discharge, any allegation that the transit temperatures were too low should be refuted. The cause could be that the meat has been kept below its freezing point of minus 2°C (−2°C) before shipment, in an effort to keep it as cool as possible and prolong its shelf life.

39.4   Vacuum-Packed Chilled Meat

The object of chilling is to provide meat that resembles, as closely as possible, fresh meat and to retain the maximum degree or flavour, texture, appearance and nutritive value. Chilled meat is often vacuum packed, a process used to reduce bacterial growth and surface dehydration activity and so prolong the storage life of chilled meat.

Meat is vacuum packed by first placing it in a gas impermeable plastic film bag at a temperature slightly above 0°C. The air is exhausted from the bag so that the film applies tightly to the meat surface. The temperature is then held at an appropriate level.

It should be noted that, because of the absence of air, chilled meat may show an abnormal discolouration and on removal of the vacuum packing can give off a distinctive odour. On exposure to air, the colour of the meat reverts to normal and the odour will disappear, so no immediate conclusions should be drawn as to the condition of the meat after removal of the packing.

In the past few years, a number of claims have been raised by receivers of chilled vacuum-packed meat, primarily in northern European ports citing that the meat had suffered a considerable depreciation as a result of the presence of ice crystals in the meat. The presence of ice crystals means that the meat can no longer be considered to be chilled (or fresh) meat but must be considered as 'frozen chilled meat'. The claims are for the difference in market value between chilled and frozen meat at the time of delivery at the discharge port, which may be as much as 20 to 25%.

> The usual carrying temperature will range from minus 1.4°C (−1.4°C) to +2°C, but on short voyages the shippers may require a carrying temperature as high as 0°C. The shippers should normally issue precise instructions on this point and, if they do not, Masters should press for instructions to be provided, preferably in writing.

As the meat is vacuum packed, spike temperatures cannot be taken upon loading, but spot checks on individual cartons, placing thermometers between the layers, is recommended. Should there be any significant variation above or below the recommended carrying temperatures, it is suggested that a competent surveyor be called in.

For significant ice crystal formation to occur within the meat requires exposure to temperatures lower than minus 2°C (−2°C) for prolonged periods because the meat contains various salts that lower its freezing point. Minor quantities of crystal near the surface within the meat should not be taken to demonstrate a deterioration in condition or value. Crystals may also form on the meat at temperatures of 0°C (the freezing point of water) and below. These crystals between the meat and the vacuum packing result from moisture migration and are not indicative of any deterioration in the quality of the meat or any fault in the carriage. Any claim presented on the basis of the presence of such crystals should be strongly resisted.

39.5   Transshipment

There have been isolated instances where, as a result of damage to the original container during transit, restowage of the cargo into a sound container has been necessary. If such a transfer is carried out without veterinary control, in a country designated as a 'disease pollution' area, the consignees in some countries may reject the consignment on the grounds that there has been a breach of their own health regulations.

39.6   Insulated and Integral Refrigeration Containers

The shipment of chilled meat in units has been accomplished with great success with carriage temperatures as low as minus 1.4°C (−1.4°C). However, when similar carriage temperatures are attempted in containers fitted with integral refrigeration equipment, problems with intra-muscular icing have been encountered. It is recommended that chilled meat shipments are not carried in integral refrigeration containers with temperature settings lower than minus 0.5°C (−0.5°C).

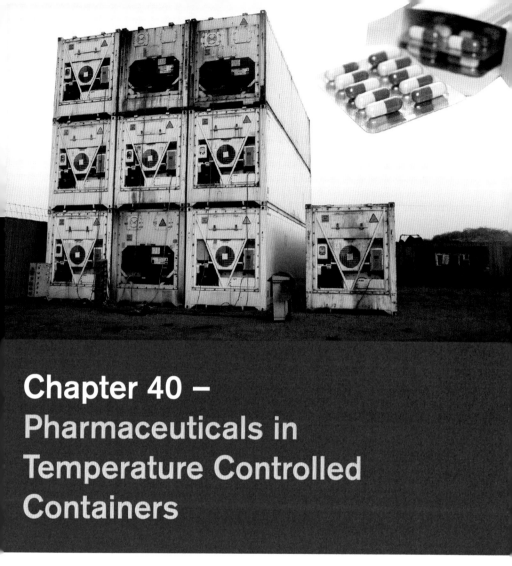

Chapter 40 –
Pharmaceuticals in
Temperature Controlled
Containers

Many different pharmaceuticals are supplied worldwide, some requiring temperature controlled storage and distribution to maintain their efficacy and other properties.

Until fairly recently, long distance distribution of products was undertaken by air, but there has been a trend to move some of them by sea in refrigerated containers. Due to their sensitivity to the atmosphere and limited storage life, they are referred to as Time- and Temperature-Sensitive Pharmaceutical Products (TTSPP).

The carriage of pharmaceuticals and intermediaries is already established on many trade routes with different transit times. Two examples are Ventolin (an aid to breathing) carried at chilled temperatures and blood products moved as frozen cargoes.

Some cargoes create significant cold chain challenges if they are temperature sensitive or have a very high value. When both the sensitivity and high values of a pharmaceutical shipment combine, a careful and systematic approach to its planning and carriage must be undertaken. The consequences of a failure to do so can be serious. The damage to cargo is one aspect that may lead to P&I claims, but timely delivery of pharmaceuticals may also be of critical importance for public health, eg during a pandemic.

40.1   Product Attributes and Challenges

Pharmaceutical product attributes have to be preserved through the cold chain to give the consignee the outturn expected after loading good quality product into the container. It is extremely helpful if shippers can explain the physical, chemical and biological attributes of sensitive products being carried. Products must have adequate storage lives for the transit phase and the next steps in the distribution chain to the patient or user.

Temperature control and times off refrigeration should be clearly specified and well controlled. Reefer containers are designed only to maintain the temperature and not to cool down any cargo. Shippers therefore need to ensure that appropriate procedures are followed prior to and during stuffing containers.

In the event of problems or claims concerning products whose characteristics are unknown, or not fully known, carriers/shipping lines should contact their P&I Club to identify experts to provide assistance.

40.2   Carriage Challenges

For the successful carriage of pharmaceuticals on long sea routes, carriers should ensure that:

- Cold chain requirements are met, using equipment that operates correctly
- procedures, information flows and operations are compatible and coordinated
- due diligence actions for quality control systems and security requirements are defined and followed
- careful work by trained personnel provides good quality control and assurance
- any ambiguity or lack of information is resolved prior to accepting a consignment.

Transport of pharmaceuticals in reefer container shipping is still relatively unusual and its requirements are less well understood. It may, therefore, be helpful to consider the features of an equivalent class of food product in transit.

However, many pharmaceuticals have a very much higher value than the equivalent volume of food products. They are also regulated by national or state medicines agencies that have several similar roles to foods standards agencies.

The World Health Organization (WHO) supports member States through the publication of international standards to ensure delivery of high quality finished products to the end user. Some examples are *Good Distribution Practices for Pharmaceutical Products* (Reference 62), *Guide to Good Storage Practices for Pharmaceuticals* (Reference 63) and *Supplement 13: Qualification of Shipping Containers* (Reference 64), a technical supplement to WHO Technical Report Series No. 961, *Annex 9: Model guidance for the storage and transport of time- and temperature-sensitive pharmaceutical products.*

40.3   Management Issues

Carriers should define the extent to which they are prepared to carry cargoes of certain materials on different routes, as they can differ significantly in sensitivity, monetary values and the levels of control that are possible. The onus, however, remains with the shipper to declare the goods accurately and to specify any special carriage requirements. If the carrier discharges their duty of care as per the prescribed procedures and precautions, any losses may have to be picked up by the shipper and/or the consignee.

Pre-transit risk assessments should be made, to include discussions with the shippers (and consignees if necessary). Accepted cargoes should initially transit as trial shipments, with review after outturn. One approach is to limit risks by only accepting 20 ft container loads of particular products until the transits have been established. Corrective actions can be taken, if necessary, for further shipments, and in extreme circumstances bookings may be refused.

40.4   Commercial Issues

Additional insurance premiums may be payable, depending on the risk limits and previous experience in carrying similar products. Special rates may be necessary to cover the additional work in carrying the cargoes successfully and the extra precautions taken against the risks. Careful wording on B/Ls is also required.

40.5   Operational Issues

Shippers define the set point temperatures required for the cargo. Other carriage requirements must also be agreed with the carriers when the containers are booked. There may be a need for additional instructions and checks in transit, depending on product sensitivities and the routes. Clearance by the appropriate authorities in importing countries may be specified, as well as compliance with consignees' due diligence standards.

Shippers may include their own independent data loggers in the cargo space to measure product or air temperatures. A few data logger types are able to calculate mean kinetic temperatures (a defined form of weighted average), while others record shocks and vibrations. Relative humidity is measurable, but the accuracy of the data must be considered carefully and large variations allowed.

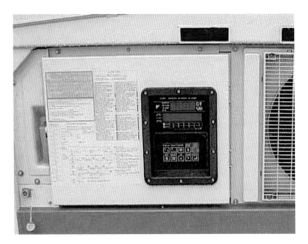

Figure 40.1: Temperature/data recorder.

40.6 Temperature

Pharmaceuticals should be carried in integral containers with good refrigeration capacity, high internal airflow rates and an ability to provide the required temperature control. Following the stuffing of the cargoes into containers, they require the capability to deal with the heat loads to which they may be subjected.

Warm cargo must never be shipped for cooling on board. All cargo must be pre-cooled to its temperature for carriage prior to stowing in a container, keeping in mind that reefer containers are only designed to maintain the temperature at which they are set.

Pharmaceuticals are often transported in reefer containers in nominated temperature zones. Many require an environment in the +2°C to +8°C range. These products must not freeze or become too warm in transit because this may impair their potency, or adversely affect colloidal suspension or other properties, potentially compromising product release. Pharmaceuticals vary in sensitivity, but the most sensitive could be considered somewhat similar to chilled meat for carriage. The container set point is normally in the +2°C to +8°C range, and +4°C or +5°C are often used.

Temperatures colder than minus 18°C (–18°C) are specified for some products. They are often sensitive to temperature fluctuations as well as needing a cold base temperature. A temperature set point of minus 25°C (–25°C) for containers is often requested. Serious thawing can often be observed by eye, but changes in protein structure or other changes caused by temperature fluctuations will require laboratory assessment. For example, frozen blood products could be compared to carrying a product with the combined properties of ice cream and individually quick frozen (IQF) prawns. Temperature fluctuations in ice cream can cause texture changes whilst prawns can incur protein denaturation and weld together. Ice crystals can form in both products. Similarly, blood products can suffer protein damage and separation if not stored correctly.

Temperatures cooler than +15°C or even +25°C are required for shelf stable products. Examples are powders, liquids and tablets. An equivalent food product is chocolate confectionery (usually carried with a set point of +10°C).

> The shipper may specify individual container set points outside the above general ranges to meet a product requirement. If the carrier is uncertain as to the shipper's requests, independent expert advice should be sought.

The shipper may request relatively dry air to be circulated in the containers. Many modern containers are fitted with a dehumidifier to reduce the relative humidity (RH). The RH is measured and controlled by a probe in the refrigeration unit. It does not represent the actual RH throughout the cargo space, which is difficult to measure accurately, and a tolerance of at least ±5% over the available range should be expected.

Fresh air ventilation is not expected for chilled pharmaceutical cargoes, but the need for any such requirements should be checked before bookings are accepted. Ventilation volumes should be kept as low as is essential.

Part 10 –

General Container Operations Including Waste Shipments

Chapter 41 –
Stuffing, Stacking and
Lashing Containers

There are three main categories of damage to cargo shipped by container:

1. The consignee receives the container with a broken seal. In such circumstances, the carrier may be held liable for damage and/or loss to the cargo.

The safety measure from the carrier's point of view should be to ensure they reject any containers found with a damaged/broken seal at the load port.

In theory, the seal must be checked at each stage in the logistic chain where a container exchanges hands. If found and unreported, the next entity in the chain who finds the broken seal may claim for damages from the previous one. It must be borne in mind at all times that a broken seal may mean more than damage or loss of cargo; it may also mean that criminals have introduced illicit items such as drugs or even humans into the container. The carrier is advised, therefore, to report any broken seal to the shipper as well as to their P&I Club. It may be appropriate to conduct a survey to establish any pilferage, loss or damage to the cargo, after which the container may be allowed for shipment.

2. The container and the cargo are damaged. In such a case, a joint survey by the shipper or consignee and the carrier (P&I Club) will be carried out to establish the extent of damage. This survey report will define the liability for both parties.

Courtesy of New Zealand Defence Force

Figure 41.1: The grounding of MV *'Rena'* off New Zealand in 2011 overstressed many container twistlocks, resulting in a partial collapse of container stacks.

3. The consignee opens the container and finds the cargo damaged. In this case, the carrier may repudiate the claim on the basis that the container was packed by the shipper, provided that the ship did not suffer extreme weather damage during the voyage.

Reference should also be made to the guidance and publications provided by the shipping lines, which contain practical advice on container securing components and securing systems. A widely used publication is the *Safe Transport of Containers by Sea: Industry Guidance for Shippers and Container Stuffers* which is published by the International Chamber of Shipping and the World Shipping Council (Reference 65).

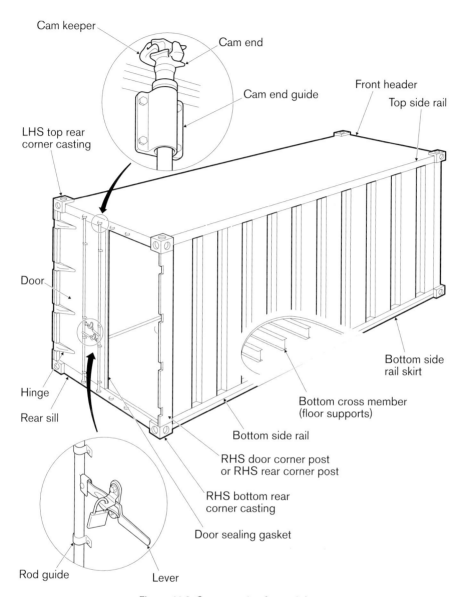

Figure 41.2: Components of a container.

41.1 Stuffing

Containers are often packed at places that are distant from the marine loading terminal, sometimes several days' journey. It is, therefore, important that everyone involved with the packing of containers, at whatever stage in transit, is fully aware of the stresses that can be generated in the structure of the container itself and in the cargo within it. It is essential that containers are in sound structural condition each time they are put into service and that they are suitable for the cargo to be carried.

It should always be borne in mind that the side panels, end panels and roof panels of an ISO container are not normally strength members.

Beneath the floor timbers, there are metal cross bearers and it is generally these bearers that provide the floor's strength. Additionally, the corner posts, front and rear headers, and front and rear sills provide the internal strength members. Whenever bracing is to be used in vertical, horizontal or diagonal form, it must act against those members and the floor bearers and no others. Bracing and/or end chocking against side, end and roof panels will result in disaster.

Unlike breakbulk cargo, the ship's Master and officers do not see, or have any control over, the contents of containers or the methods by which the contents have been packed and secured.

If the contents of just one container are improperly packed, lack adequate securing arrangements or are inappropriate for container carriage, they may break adrift when the ship encounters heavy weather, risking the safety of the other containers, their contents and the ship itself.

In one example, round steel bars, inadequately secured, broke adrift within a container third in stack on deck, pierced and went through the container's side panels and shattered a corner post of the adjacent container, creating a domino collapse of the other units. In another example, a single block of granite, lacking securing arrangements within the lower tier of a below-deck stack, broke through the container's side panel and fell corner down, piercing the double-bottom fuel oil tank below. The consequential fuel oil flooding of the hold and lower level damage to base containers was a costly business.

Figure 41.3: Poorly stuffed container – note the damaged packages, the pallet on top of cartons and the apparent lack of securing arrangements.

Courtesy of PO2 Prentice Danner, DVIDS

Figure 41.4: Inspection of goods in a container terminal.

Figure 41.5: Damage caused to a container by poorly secured coils.

Casualty investigation often reveals that horizontal spaces, ie fore-and-aft and longitudinally, are generally adequately chocked, but the vertical component is entirely neglected. When a ship is pitching and yawing in a seaway, vertical acceleration and deceleration forces acting on cargo components can attain values of 2 g, which means that, as the ship goes up and comes down, the load on the securing arrangements will be equal to twice the static weight of the cargo item. If there is no arrangement to secure the cargo to the floor of the container, the cargo will lift, and once it lifts it will start to shift, and once it starts to shift it will go on shifting!

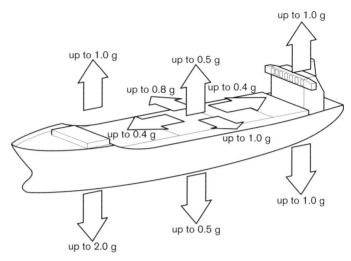

Figure 41.6: Potential accelerations at sea.

Where relatively lightweight cartons or good timber cases can be afforded tight block stowage, there will be little need for additional securing arrangements. However, where plastic jars, bottles, barrels or lightweight cartons with frail contents are to be stowed to the full internal height, it may be necessary to provide mid-height flooring so that the lowermost items do not suffer compression damage or collapse.

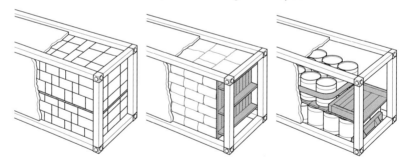

Figure 41.7: Flexible flooring arrangement.

Figure 41.8: Heavy machinery on a 'flat'.

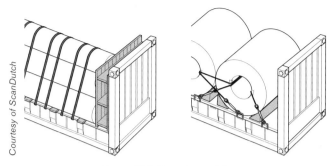

Courtesy of ScanDutch

Figure 41.9: Securing points.

Where bags, cartons or cases do not occupy the full internal space, chocking and bracing with timbers and/or air bags is necessary.

Where heavy items are involved, securing with downward leading wire lashings and/or strapping to 'D' rings attached to the upper parts of the floor bearers will be required.

It is important that the correct form of container is used, because not all have provision for mid-height flooring to be fitted, and not all are provided with 'D' rings.

Steel coils, steel pipes and bars, and heavy machinery items should be shipped on specially designed 'flat racks', 'flats' or 'sledges' (see Figure 41.8). These units are strengthened for such loads and adequate securing terminal points are provided (see Figure 41.9).

41.2   Container Stuffing Considerations

The packing and securing of goods inside a container plays a vital role in safe transportation of goods to their destination, but this is never in the control of the ship's officers. In some ports, some carriers require container stuffing to be sample checked to ensure that the contents, particularly if there are any dangerous goods, have been secured properly.

Further inspections of the goods may also be made by the harbour or customs authorities to establish correct application of customs duties and export taxes, etc and, where this is done, the carriers can utilise the opportunity to check the stuffing of cargoes.

The ship's officers must play their role in observing and reporting any abnormalities. Consideration should be given to the following.

1. Cargo may be containerised for a prolonged period, during which changes in temperature may lead to generation of mould, bacteria, fungus or other microorganisms, particularly where the cargoes are hygroscopic and there is a lack of proper ventilation. To avoid biological contamination, many countries require containers to be fumigated and then sealed prior to shipment.

2. When different commodities are stuffed together, the compatibility characteristics of each cargo should be noted. Some examples of non-compatible cargoes are:

   a) cargoes that emit odours stowed with odour sensitive cargoes

   b) hygroscopic cargoes stowed with cargoes that may absorb moisture. If unavoidable, hygroscopic cargoes should be loaded under other cargoes with a layer of dunnage and a protective cover such as a tarpaulin laid on top of the hygroscopic cargo.

3. Hygroscopic cargoes are likely to give off moisture during transportation leading to condensation, commonly referred to as 'container sweat' or 'container rain'. Condensation may damage the cargo and may lead to biological contamination. Desiccants may be provided, but these are not a failsafe means of preventing condensation.

4. Certain sensitive cargoes, such as wet hides or salted skins, require containers to be lined with plastic sheeting or packing paper.

5. Containers are fitted with lashing/securing points with the longitudinal beams on the floor or roof and also with the corner posts. Each lashing point has a predetermined SWL (safe working load), which is generally 1 T but may vary for older containers. Container walls are not designed to be load bearing, so nothing should be attached to them.

6. When palletised cargo is loaded into a container, the space utilisation will depend on the size of the pallet in relation to the size of the container. Generally, there will be some void spaces between pallets and these must be filled in with air/inflatable bags or dunnage. Where pallets are stowed more than one high, their longitudinal movement within the container must also be blocked by the use of appropriate lashing or chocking.

7. Distribution of weight within a container should avoid:

   a) loading heavier items at one end or side of the container

   b) stowing heaver items above light items. Impact on the centre of gravity of the container with respect to weight distribution should also be considered.

8. Cargo items with sharp edges, protrusions or awkward shape must not be stowed next to soft packages, to avoid damage during even the smallest movement within the cargo.

9. Any cargo that is liable to leak should not be stowed on top of other cargo.

41.3   Containers in Stack

Most ISO containers are designed to allow nine-high stacking when empty. They should be placed and must stand on the four lower and four upper corner castings alone, with the appropriate stacking/locking components between. The bottom and top side rails, the front and rear sills and headers, and the underside floor bearers should remain free of vertical stacking contact at all times if transient racking stresses are to be avoided.

There are many different securing systems and problems may arise if ships' officers/charterers' superintendents are unfamiliar with a specific system.

Container stack racking failures may occur in non-purpose-built ships if charterers insist on stacking containers in the holds and on the weather deck in a manner that would not be approved even in a purpose-built ship. Unfortunately, stack collapses within the holds, and within weather-deck stacks, occur just as frequently in purpose-built ships.

Container stack failures generally arise from three causes that involve unacceptable racking stresses in one form or another:

- Substandard components and seaworthiness
- weight management problems in stacks
- mixed unit sizes.

41.3.1   Substandard Components and Cargoworthiness

A ship's container stowage and securing arrangement can easily be undermined if substandard and/or incorrect components are utilised. Maintaining securing equipment in good order, both fixed and portable, requires considerable time and effort.

Whatever regulations, standards or codes of practice are issued, the integrity of a ship's container stowage and securing arrangement can only be ensured by regular inspection of the securing equipment. The securing arrangement can be undermined by one or more of the following:

- 'Rogue' securing equipment
- improperly maintained securing equipment
- complacency in inspection of the equipment and record keeping
- insufficient supply of correct securing equipment
- overloading of the securing equipment.

Portable securing equipment
If substandard equipment is used, it can fail at a lower load than its design rating, thereby resulting in failure of the overall securing system and possible collapse of the container stow.

The following aspects should be considered during periodic inspection of container securing equipment:

- Inspection of the twistlock complement to ensure that rogue twistlocks, ie ones with an opposite locking action to the ship's standard complement, have not been brought on board. When left-hand and right-hand locking twistlocks are fitted with similar shaped handles, which can be the case, it is not always possible to differentiate between them once used in the same stow. Even if the stevedores are aware of the difference, any subsequent checks by other people could result in disengagement if those people actuate all the handles in the same direction on the premise that some twistlocks had not been properly locked in the first instance.

  ISO Standard 3874, *Series 1 freight containers – Handling and securing*, includes the physical and functional requirements for various items of portable securing equipment as an appendix to the standard itself (Reference 66). ISO Standard 1161, *Series 1 freight containers – corner and intermediate fittings* establishes the basic dimensions and the functional and strength requirements of corner and intermediate fittings for series 1 freight containers (Reference 67).

For manual twistlocks, it is proposed that the unified direction of handling will be clockwise when viewed from above, ie lefthand locking

- checks to ensure that the spring holding the twistlock in the closed position is in a resilient condition. If a spring loses its resiliency, the cone(s) will not be held in position in a positive manner. The moving and flexing of a ship in a seaway has been found sufficient to allow twistlocks to unlock themselves if their spring action is failing or has failed

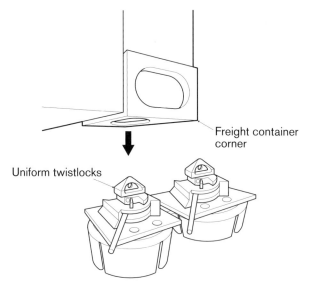

Figure 41.10: Uniform twistlocks.

- checks to ensure there are no structural defects that would compromise the proper use of the equipment, for example:
  - twistlocks with missing handles
  - twistlocks with fractured housings
  - double cones with fractured base plates
  - seized/buckled turnbuckles, bridge fittings.

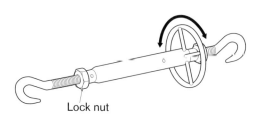

Figure 41.11: Fixed fittings.

Regular inspection of fixed fittings is also essential to establish whether progressive wear has undermined their integrity. Areas requiring particular attention include:

- Reduction in the thickness of securing points where, for example, a turnbuckle may have chafed
- wastage in the way of the key holes of deck foundations
- wastage and cracking of the plating to which fittings are welded
- distortion of dovetail deck foundations.

If a dovetail-type fitting and its associated part are compatible and in good working order, it should only be possible to slide a dovetail-type twistlock or locating cone in a horizontal direction into the deck fitting. However, if the deck fitting is damaged or its associated part is incompatible, it may be possible to lift a dovetail-type twistlock or locating cone out vertically. In such an event, there will be no vertical restraint to secure a column of containers to the deck.

Figure 41.12: Worn shoe fitting.

41.3.2 Weight Management Problems in Stacks

Courtesy of Danny Cornelissen/portpictures.nl

Figure 41.13: The stacking of containers.

The most potentially damaging stacking problem occurs when heavyweight containers are loaded into the upper tiers of container bays on deck.

The problem can occur with any container ship if the permissible stack/tier weights are ignored for a specific securing arrangement. For example, modern container ships feature deck stows comprising six or seven tiers of units, which appears to represent a huge carrying capacity. However, weight limits apply and, in the upper tiers (sixth and seventh layers), only empty containers may be carried.

The operating principle is that the weights of containers should not exceed the prescribed limits for the slots in which they are stowed. These limits should be set according to stack weight, tier position and the securing arrangement being used. In modern container handling systems, the loading model for a particular class of ship is usually sufficiently well detailed that it prevents an operator from planning the loading of a heavy container in a light slot. In a more sophisticated approach, the loading computer will calculate, on an individual stack basis, the resultant forces acting upon the containers and the lashing system. A maximum container weight will be determined for each position and it is possible that a heavy container could be received over a unit of lesser weight, provided that securing loads are acceptable. In both examples, if the weight is excessive for the specified position, the computer program will simply reject the container.

However, the container industry covers a broad spectrum and ships that incorporate the very latest technology run side by side with others from older generations. In all cases, it is the responsibility of the ship planning coordinator and/or the loading terminal ship planner to stow the containers into the proper and appropriate positions on the ship.

Another reason for exceeding the stack loads may be misdeclared weights by the shippers. As a consequence of continued accidents resulting from this practice, and pressure from the shipping industry, the IMO amended SOLAS Regulation VI/2 so that it requires shippers to weigh containers prior to shipping and provide verification to the carrier about the total mass of each container.

The verified gross mass of a container is the total gross mass of a packed container, which is obtained by either of the following methods:

- Weighing the container after packing and sealing it
- weighing all packages, dunnage, pallets and securing materials to be stuffed in a container and adding them to the tare mass of the container.

Upon receipt of verification of the gross mass of the container, the shipper must communicate it to the carrier (and Master) via a shipping document. The shipper must also inform the marine terminal operator. It should be noted that the obligation is for the shipper to provide the verified gross mass to the terminal operator, the carrier, the shipping company and the Master.

Under legislation laid down by the United States Department of Labor's Occupational Safety and Health Administration (29 CFR 1917.71 *Marine Terminals: Terminals handling intermodal container or roll-on roll-off operations)* (Reference 68), all cargo containers must be weighed before being hoisted for loading. Empty containers must be checked to ensure that they are indeed empty and marked or noted as such.

Figure 41.14: Collapsed container stacks as a result of bad stowage.

Bad stowage can occur as a result of a mistake, or it may be due to complacency. The following are the main reasons why heavy containers are sometimes placed in the wrong slots:

- Inexperience
  An inexperienced planner faced with a problem of container distribution might simply allocate stowage on the 'best possible' basis, ignoring good stowage principles and the ship's stowage and securing criteria.

- insufficient knowledge
  A planner who lacks specific knowledge of the tier limits for a particular ship, or class of ship, will not know whether a particular plan they have composed meets the criteria of the ship's lashing system. Lack of coordination between the planners and the lashing teams may not take into account the added complications resulting from the need for sufficient strength of lashing for heavy stows.

- late arrivals
  Errors often occur when containers are received late for shipment. The ship may be part loaded and stevedores may have abandoned a scheduled loading plan in place of a hybrid because some of the cargo was not available when the ship arrived. When containers arrive late, it may be the case that only relatively high positions remain available.

- third party stowage.
  In almost all cases, loading, stowage and securing of containers is carried out by third party stevedores with the ship's officers and crew only able to monitor their work. The quick operation of modern container gantries and the large number of containers being loaded/discharged in a short period of time mean that the ship's crew is physically unable to pay the same attention as they would otherwise on a smaller container ship with slower cargo operations. Historically, this situation has been complicated by lack of proper access to the top of container stacks, for example, to place the stacking cones or to properly lock the twistlocks. While some of these functions remain restricted due to the quick turnaround of container ships, combined with the large volume of cargo being loaded, some of the issues can be overcome by the crew's due diligence.

MSC.1/Circ.1353/Rev.2, first published in December 2014 and revised for the second time in December 2020 (Reference 24), requires that a Cargo Safe Access Plan (CSAP) is supplied within the Cargo Securing Manual to ensure that persons engaged in securing and stowage of containers are provided with safe access during their work. This plan details guidance for hand rails, platforms, walkways, ladders, storage facilities, fittings for specialised containers such as reefer plugs, first aid locations and any other information that may be relevant to provision of safe access. The requirement for a CSAP applies only to container ships built (ie keel laid or at a similar stage of construction) on or after 1st January 2015.

Addressing the issue on board ship

The ship's personnel should not allow loading operations to commence until they have received a copy of the proposed stowage plan. A relatively quick inspection of this plan should show whether heavy containers are proposed for stacking over light ones and whether the stack and tier weights are within the permissible limits.

Vigilance is key and the ship's personnel should be aware that mistakes are often accompanied by departures from the plan. Duty officers must not hesitate to report to the chief officer on any occasion when stevedores advise there is a change to the original plan and the chief officer should look carefully at what is proposed.

The ship's personnel should always check the pre-loading plan for heavy container stacks. These should be identified and, if possible, the container numbers in these stacks checked during loading. If a different container appears in the upper tier, it may be a heavy unit stowed by mistake and of sufficient weight to overload the stack and the lashing system.

Problems that may be created by incorrect stowage of this type include:

- The need for restowage of containers (and resulting delays and costs) if an overweight condition is ascertained
- collapsed container stacks
- containers lost overboard (both the overweights and containers that were not overweight)
- cargo liability claims
- chassis damage
- damage to the ship
- stability and stress risks for the ship
- risk of personal injury or death to seafarers and shore side workers
- last minute shut-outs of confirmed, booked and available loads when the actual weight on board exceeds what is declared and the total cargo weight exceeds the ship limit or port draught limit.

Container ship operators must instruct terminals to check weight against stowage slot before allowing a unit to be shipped late in a position other than that originally planned. In most cases, the plan will be sufficiently flexible to accommodate late loading, but in some instances it will not. Potential problems must be identified, and remedied, before sailing.

The most common method by which a stowage error of this type is discovered is when the chief officer updates their loading plan using the final plan, normally provided electronically. The update should tell them whether there are any changes from the pre-load plan. In more extreme cases, the discovery is made when the ship encounters moderate weather and starts to roll and pitch. The safety margins in lashing systems are very small and an excessively heavy stack will soon begin to challenge the integrity of the securing arrangements. Container structures will be overloaded, causing fittings to fail and movement to occur.

On a modern ship, the breakdown of the stowage usually commences in lower tiers, possibly at second tier level, where racking loads may cause failure of the door end structure. Alternatively, the compressive forces may cause buckling of a post. There may be excessive pull-out loads on twistlocks or base locks.

Once fittings have begun to fail, movement of the stack occurs and load is transferred to adjacent stacked containers and, in most cases, an entire bay of containers is at risk. Outcomes where heavy containers have been loaded in high positions have involved:

- The loss overboard and subsequent compulsory recovery of dangerous chemicals in 200 m water depths
- the capsize of ships alongside a berth
- the collapse of stacks and spillage of hazardous chemicals on deck.

Case studies
The loading of a container ship is a complex process. Weight must be evenly distributed at the same time as ensuring that hazardous cargoes are positioned appropriately and away from other cargoes with which they might react. There have been several instances where ships have capsized or heeled to severe angles during loading or unloading.

'Deneb'
In June 2011, the container ship 'Deneb' capsized at the Port of Algeciras during loading operations. There had been modifications to the stowage plan during loading because of safety concerns and, during the first part of loading, a heel of 10° was seen. As the final containers were being loaded, the ship listed to approximately 45°, resulting in the ship lying on the pier. Further listing was in progress when tugs managed to push the ship further onto the pier to avoid a total capsize. It is believed that this accident was due to the weights of containers being incorrectly declared.

'Repubblica di Genova'
In March 2007, the 'Repubblica di Genova' capsized as it was being loaded, while in berth at Antwerp. This ship was a RoRo vessel but was carrying a number of containers on deck. The cause was never determined, but a number of reports suggested that some of the containers on deck were heavier than had been declared and caused the ship to list to one side, eventually capsizing. The ship was partially under water for six months before salvage could be completed, at which point the ship underwent a total renovation and then returned to service.

41.3.3 Mixed Unit Sizes

Another cause of stack failure is where two 20 ft units are stowed on the weather deck in what would otherwise be a 40 ft unit position, making it very difficult, and sometimes impossible, to apply wires, chains or lashing bars to the adjacent end-butting corners. Their absence is not compensated for by using double or four-way interlayer stackers (spades) or longitudinally positioned screw-bridge fittings, tie-wires or similar (see Figure 41.15).

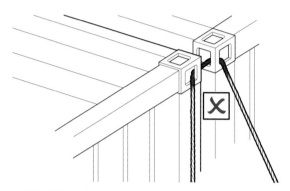

Figure 41.15: Adjacent corner castings should never be loop-lashed.

The container stack as a whole, and particularly units in the base tier, will be subject to excessive racking stresses should the ship start rolling in heavy seas or pronounced swell conditions. Some compensation can be applied by the use of anti-rack bands (two tensioned metal straps fitted diagonally across the corners of the 'free' ends of the base tier containers) but they suffer from the same inability to secure the 'butting' ends. Sometimes, anti-rack spacers are used (see Figure 41.16), but a full lashing system is preferred.

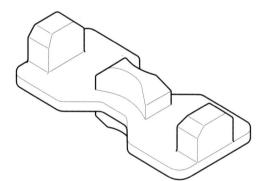

Figure 41.16: Anti-rack spacer.

41.4 Lashings

Figure 41.17: The safe lashing of containers.

In the early years of containerisation, existing general cargo ships were converted by the removal of tween decks and the addition of cell guides into the cargo holds. On deck, the hatch covers were strengthened and fittings added for lashings. However, the containers on deck were seldom stowed above one high and so were secured to the vessel by 'traditional' cargo ship methods.

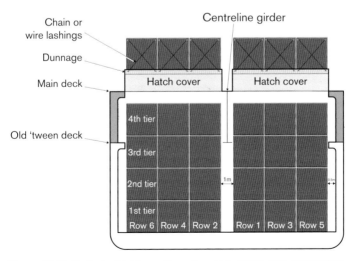

Figure 41.18: Typical midship section of an early cargo ship conversion.

The first generation of purpose-built container ships had holds and hatch covers that were as wide as possible, and container posts were fitted on deck to facilitate loading of deck-stowed containers out to the ship's side (see Figure 41.19).

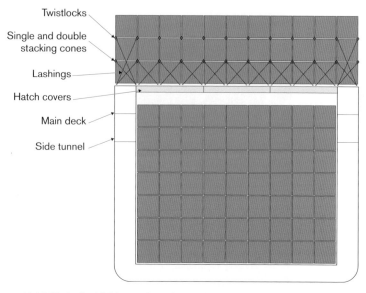

Figure 41.19: Typical midship section of an early generation cellular container ship.

Courtesy of Danny Cornelissen/portpictures.nl

Figure 41.20: 1990s 4,500 TEU cellular container ship.

For this generation of vessel, two systems of securing the cargo were common. One relied on the use of twistlocks in conjunction with lashing bars or chains, and the other made use of stacking cones and bridge pieces in conjunction with lashing bars or chains. Gradually, due to the increased use of containers of differing heights, the second method became redundant and it became common practice to use twistlocks throughout the stow. This usually allowed containers to be stacked three high and, in some cases, four high, if the fourth tier was light in weight or empty.

For first generation vessels, computer technology was not available on board to speedily calculate dynamic loads acting on container lashings and frames. The shipboard computer was only used to calculate stresses and stability for the ship itself. Therefore, shipboard personnel would ensure the ship was lashed according to a lashing plan taken from the lashing equipment manufacturer's manual, which tended to assume an ideal stow with respect to the distribution of weight in each stack.

With further development in the industry, the size of container ships continued to grow, with 9-high stowage in holds and 4-high stowage on deck becoming commonplace, and the industry began to realise that standards in lashing were required. Ships were at this stage still supplied with loading computers to calculate the ship's stability, shear forces, bending and, occasionally, torsion moments. Very few had the capability to calculate the dynamic loads on container frames and lashing systems caused by ship motions and wind forces, so the lashings were still applied throughout the stow in accordance with the manufacturer's manual.

Following incidents such as the loss of the MOL *'Comfort'*, it was queried whether the sheer size of these ships constituted a risk. If a fire started on one of these ships, potentially millions of pounds worth of cargo would be at risk, with only a relatively small number of crew available to try to get any such situation under control.

While the economies of scale demand larger container ships, the lashing systems in use on all types of container vessels are very similar and based on the twistlock and lashing bar/turnbuckle system. Large hatch openings mean that containers are partly resting on hatch covers and partly on stanchions located adjacent to the hatchway, but unequal deformities in the hull structure may lead to misalignment of container seating points. Even though the Classification Society rules provide for a certain allowance in any such misalignments, the extent of these will vary between ships and, in some cases, on the same ship between various stowage locations. This will have an impact on the stresses placed on lashings and, therefore, the resulting outcomes with respect to their ability to hold a container in position.

On post-Panamax vessels, where among other features the ship's large beam results in an unavoidable, relatively large metacentric height (GM), the practice is for the ship to be fitted with a lashing bridge, which is a substantial steel structure running athwartships between each 40 ft container bay. This allows the second and third tiers of containers to be secured to the bridge using lashing rods and turnbuckles, while the whole stow is secured throughout with twistlocks (see Figure 41.25). The lashing bridge allows the anchoring points for each stack to be moved higher up the stack, which allows the lashings to be more effective in reducing the tipping moments acting on a stack when a ship is rolling heavily. However, the practice of fitting the bridges between 40 ft bays means that the 20 ft containers can only take advantage of the lashing bridges at one end. So, in effect, the 20 ft stacks have to revert to the limits of a conventional lashing system. This is because the practice of estimating the forces acting on a stack divides the container weight equally between each end of the container.

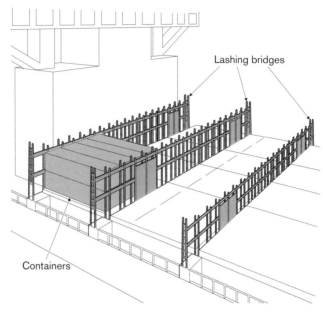

Figure 41.21: Lashing bridges.

Therefore, the weight in each 20 ft container is limited by the capacity of the lashing system at the container end, which does not have the advantage of being secured by a lashing bridge.

Courtesy of Cargotec

Figure 41.22: Top lashing bridge system for up to 9-high containers.

On smaller ships, the whole stow is also secured throughout with twistlocks, and the lowest three tiers are secured to the hatch cover or support post using the lashing bar/turnbuckle combination (see Figure 41.27).

Modern ships may have up to 9-high stowage on deck, and the use of onboard computers to check the dynamics of the stow in all weather conditions is vitally important for the safe carriage of the cargo. Development of ultra-large container ships (ULCS) has required ultra-secure lashing systems. The safety of containers on board not only depends on the speed at which modern container ships operate but also their direction of movement in relation to the height and direction of waves to control the ship's rolling and pitching motion, and so stresses on the container lashings. This type of development, combined with modification of lashing equipment such as lift-away hatch covers and fully automatic twistlocks (FATs), and the use of modern computerised systems to check loads on lashing points and equipment, together with full assessment of ship stability, can provide a complete solution.

MSC *'Napoli'* case study

In January 2006, the 276 m, 4,734 TEU container ship MSC *'Napoli'* was deliberately beached in the English Channel during a strong storm after parts of the ship became flooded. It was discovered that the hull had suffered severe fractures, although the ship remained in one piece.

The investigation determined that the hull fractures occurred because the ship had insufficient buckling strength. Whipping and hogging in the high waves caused heavier than usual loads.

Figure 41.23: MSC *'Napoli'*.

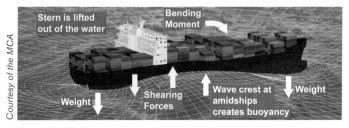

Figure 41.24: MSC *'Napoli'* – simulation of forces leading to hull fracture.

The use of a computer lashing program, together with the IMO requirement for every vessel to carry on board an approved Cargo Securing Manual, should theoretically mean a reduction in collapsed stows and losses overboard, provided the operators maintain the lashing equipment and comply with the requirements of the manual. The vigilance of the ship's personnel is, therefore, vital to ensure that lashings are applied correctly.

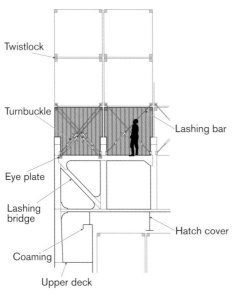

Figure 41.25: Typical post-Panamax lashing bridge arrangement (shown 4-high).

Figure 41.26: Lashing a container to the lashing bridge.

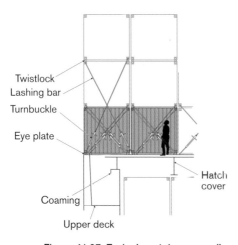

Figure 41.27: Typical container vessel's hatch cover lashing arrangement.

Figure 41.28: Tightening the turnbuckle.

41.4.1   Requirements of Lashing Systems

Figure 41.29: Typical 'on lid' loading.

The requirement to carry a Cargo Securing Manual is specified in:

- MSC.1/Circ.1352/Rev.1 – *Amendments to the Code of Safe Practice for Cargo Stowage and Securing* (CSS Code) (Reference 69), originally given in MSC/Circ.745(17) which has been superseded

- MSC.1/Circ.1353/Rev.2 – *Revised Guidelines for the Preparation of the Cargo Securing Manual*, (Reference 24) are based on, and supersede, provisions contained in the annex to MSC/Circ.745(17). The guidelines are expanded to cover safe access for lashing of containers, taking into account the CSS Code (Reference 22).

SOLAS Chapter VI: Regulation 5, Stowage and Securing states:

"Cargo, cargo units and cargo transport units carried on or under deck shall be so loaded, stowed and secured as to prevent as far as is practicable, throughout the voyage, damage or hazard to the ship and the persons on board, and loss of cargo overboard."

It goes on to say that:

"Freight containers shall not be loaded to more than the maximum gross weight indicated on the Safety Approval Plate under the International Convention for Safe Containers (CSC), as amended.

All cargoes, other than solid and liquid bulk cargoes, cargo units and cargo transport units, shall be loaded, stowed and secured throughout the voyage in accordance with the Cargo Securing Manual approved by the Administration. (...) The Cargo Securing Manual shall be drawn up to a standard at least equivalent to relevant guidelines developed by the Organization." (Reference 18)

Therefore, following MSC.1/Circ.1352/Rev.1 (Reference 69), any Classification Society that approves a Cargo Securing Manual will need to ensure the following:

- It is made clear that the guidance given in the Cargo Securing Manual cannot replace experience in stowage and securing and the principles of good seamanship

- the information in the manual is consistent with the requirements of the vessel's trim/stability and hull strength loading manual, the *International Convention on*

Load Lines, 1966 (Reference 25) requirements and the *International Maritime Dangerous Goods Code* (IMDG Code) (Reference 19), where applicable

- the manual specifies arrangements and cargo securing devices provided on board for the correct application to the containers, based on transverse, longitudinal and vertical forces that may arise during adverse weather and sea conditions

- such securing arrangements and devices shall be suitable for, and adapted to, the nature of the cargo to be carried and used properly with appropriate securing points or fittings

- there is a sufficient quantity of reserve cargo securing devices on board the ship

- the manual contains information on the strength and instructions for the use and maintenance of each specific type of cargo securing device

- the manual should be updated when new or alternative types of securing devices are introduced, and alternative cargo securing devices introduced should not have less strength than those being replaced

- the manual should consist of a comprehensive and understandable plan, providing an overview of the maximum stack weights and permissible vertical distribution of weight in stacks

- the manual should present the distribution of accelerations expected at various positions on board the ship based on a range of GM values. This information should be accompanied by a worked example showing the angles of roll and GM above which the forces acting on cargo exceed permissible limits for securing arrangements, along with examples of how to calculate the number and strength of securing devices required to counteract these forces. Calculations may be carried out according to Annex 13 of the CSS Code, as set out in MSC.1/Circ.1623 *Amendments to the Code of Safe Practice for Cargo Stowage and Securing* (Reference 70)

- the manual should provide information on the forces induced by wind and sea on deck cargo, and on the nominal increase of forces or accelerations with an increase in GM

- the manual should contain recommendations for reducing the risk of cargo losses from deck stows, by applying restrictions to stack weights or heights where high stability cannot be avoided

- the cargo safe access plan (CSAP) should provide detailed information for the safety of persons engaged in work connected with cargo stowage and securing. Safe access should be provided and maintained in accordance with this plan.

MSC.1/Circ.1352/Rev.1 also states that the cargo securing devices should be maintained in a satisfactory condition and that items worn or damaged to such an extent that their quality is impaired should be replaced. It is commonly accepted that obligatory survey of portable fittings is not generally pursued by the Classification Society, and so inspection and replacement should be the responsibility of the operators/Masters. Any inspections, maintenance, repair or rejection of cargo securing devices should be recorded and kept with the Cargo Securing Manual. When replacement securing devices are placed on board, they should be provided with appropriate certification.

Portable fittings should be certified by some form of type-approval system, usually coming from the manufacturer (when approved), a Classification Society or other accepted testing body.

Ship managers may request a Classification Society to approve their particular lashing system and the lashing program software, in addition to the requirement of approving the Cargo Securing Manual. However, until the Cargo Securing Manual and the computer lashing program are produced and approved together, in the same way as the ship stability loading computer and stability/loading manual are already used, there is bound to be confusion with respect to the safe capabilities of the on-deck container lashing system for each ship.

One note of caution: different Classification Societies have set their own standards for the minimum SWLs of lashing gear, the maximum allowable forces acting on a container, and the roll angle that any calculations should include.

Types of lashing failure
In general terms, whenever a vessel is working in a seaway, it will incur three main movements, described as rolling, pitching and heaving. These give rise to accelerations, and therefore forces, that act on the container frames and lashing system in use. Figure 41.30 illustrates the ship motions experienced by a container stack.

Of the forces acting on an individual container and its lashings as a result of these movements, the separation force is the tipping force that acts to pull out or separate the corner fittings or twistlocks. When the vessel is rolling heavily, if the separation force is excessive, it may pull the twistlocks out of the corner castings of the container, break the twistlocks at their weakest point or separate the corner castings from the main body of the container.

When the vessel is rolling heavily, and containers stowed on higher tiers are heavy, a racking force will be produced in the frame of the lowest containers. The larger the roll of the vessel, the larger the racking force will be.

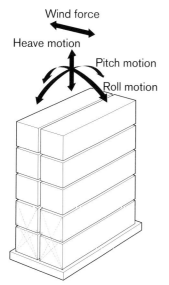

Figure 41.30: The accelerations acting on a container in a seaway.

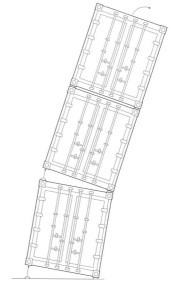

Figure 41.31: Excessive tipping moment or separation force on corner fittings.

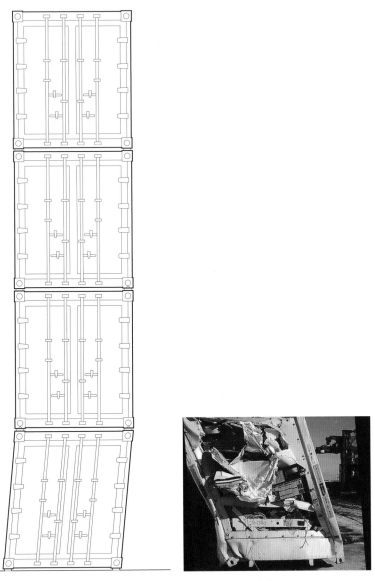

Figure 41.32: Excessive racking force on a container.

A large GM, particularly when coupled with a short roll period, increases the dynamic loadings caused by rolling, and all of the loads previously mentioned will increase the compression and tension forces acting at the corner posts of the containers and at the twistlocks between them. If excessive, they may result in structural failure of one or more of the corner posts (see Figure 41.33).

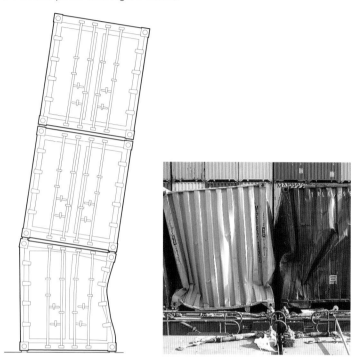

Figure 41.33: Excessive compression force on container corner post, leading to failure of the post.

Application of computer software

Analysis of incidents involving loss of containers overboard, despite correct stowage and securing, revealed that there was a lack of understanding of the combined static and dynamic loads that were present in adverse weather. In such cases, the bad weather caused severe ship motions, in particular a rolling motion. Of all the ship's motions, rolling is the most likely cause of overloading of the container frames and lashings.

It is interesting to note that the same difficulties with proper container securing and load distribution were being experienced in the mid-1980s. The solutions, in principle, are still similar but more recent difficulties are exacerbated due to the larger size of container ships, with higher stacks and increased loadings on lashings and securing points. Even though a number of computer programs are available to calculate a ship's stability and the forces experienced within a container stack, human error continues to play some part in their effective usage. Ship planners need to be provided with two vital pieces of information, ie the discharge port and the weight of the container. Any inaccuracies in this information will result in erroneous output, leading to the same old problems.

The situation is complicated when the chief officer, on behalf of the Master, continues to hold the responsibility for correct stowage and carriage of cargo but may not have enough time to study the information supplied by the planner in order to question any inaccuracies.

To aggravate the situation further, many ports supply the chief officer with an electronic bay-plan file of the pre-load plan, which should include all the relevant container data. Again, the onus is on the chief officer to check that the correct information about the container height and weight has been entered, as this affects the ship's stability and any calculation of the forces that may be experienced within the stack.

The benefits of using a computer loading program include the potential to achieve safer carriage of deck-stowed containers, saving on lashing requirements in terms of employment of lashing gangs, and the possibility of loading more cargo (depending on the voyage). Lashing equipment must be in good condition and certified as suitable because the calculations assume that all containers and lashing materials are in good condition and that all lashings are correctly applied, with equal tension on lashing bars, etc. These programs also calculate a theoretical angle of roll that a ship should not exceed.

Forces within a stack are affected by all ship motions, but the angle of roll is normally the most critical. Classification Society regulations assume certain values, which are generally the default values in loading programs. The natural period of roll can be determined using the rule of thumb formula:

$$Period\ (TR) = \frac{0.7\ Beam}{GM}$$

A detailed breakdown of the forces in each stack will be provided by loading programs, which include:

Racking force
This is the transverse force that tends to distort the container ends, primarily due to a rolling action. It should not exceed a maximum allowable force (MAF) of 15 T. If a lashing is applied, the force varies between the forward and aft ends of the container because of the different stiffness of the door and closed ends.

Corner shear
This is closely related to racking force, but is the force that tends to shear off the twistlocks. It should not exceed an SWL of 15 T for a standard twistlock.

Compressive force
This is the force acting on the container corner posts and fittings, which results from tilting of the stack and the vertical acceleration. It should not exceed 45 T for a standard 20 ft container corner post or 67.5 T for a 40 ft container corner post. Larger compression forces are allowed for corner castings at the base of a stack (83.8 T).

Separation force
This is the tipping force that is acting to pull out or separate the corner fittings. It should not exceed 15 T for the top fitting and 20 T for the bottom. This force does not refer to the tensile loadings on the twistlocks.

Lashing tension

This is the tension in the applied lashings. Lashing rods should only ever be applied hand tight, not overtightened with large spanners, as this induces unnecessary tension in the lashing rod, reducing the angle of roll at which the SWL would be exceeded. The Germanischer Lloyd (now DNV) limit for lashing rods is 23 T SWL; turnbuckles are rated at 18 T.

If a container or item of lashing equipment exceeds its SWL/maximum allowable force, this does not automatically mean that the item will fail. SWLs are mostly set at 50% of the breaking load. The use of an SWL is to give a safety margin, allowing for occasional overstressing. A container that has been highlighted as having exceeded the Class limits will not automatically be lost if the vessel rolls to 24.9°. However, while many container stacks remain on board after having suffered greater loadings than some of those lost, calculations cannot allow for the domino effect of an inboard stack collapsing, falling against its neighbour and inducing far greater forces upon it, which in turn causes collapse.

Correct application of lashing equipment is also important and one example of incorrect application of semi-automatic base twistlocks occurs when there is an element of fore and aft movement of the container immediately prior to landing it on board so the base locks tend to be placed in the deck fitting rather than the base of the container prior to loading.

Any fore and aft movement of the container as it is aligned over the base lock risks the actuating wire being caught under the container, rendering the twistlock inoperable unless the container is lifted and landed correctly. This highlights the necessity of continual vigilance by the ship's personnel during the loading process.

Figure 41.34: Twistlock failure. Figure 41.35: Unlocked twistlock.

41.5   Containers in the Holds of Conventional Ships and Bulk Carriers

The ongoing problem of collapse of unsecured container stacks in non-purpose-built holds provides ample evidence that such stacks will not stay in place on the basis of their total weight alone.

Firm securing of the stacks to the ship's structure as a block is essential. If slackness develops during adverse weather conditions, the containers will chafe and rack, leading to overall distortion and possible collapse, particularly if heavy units have been placed in upper tiers.

ISO containers are designed to be carried by stacking them one above the other in slots or cells below deck and on the weather decks in purpose-built ships, or ships converted for such carriage. The design of bulk carriers appears to provide large, unobstructed spaces for the safe stowage of containers. They are, however, prone to severe stresses arising in a heavy seaway and containers carried in block stowages below decks can create problems if adequate securing measures are not adopted. It is not infrequent that an entire stow of containers collapses, with serious damage to the boxes and to the cargo within them.

Generally, the cargo compartments of bulk carriers are not of the right dimensions to enable the container stow to be a perfect fit. In ships fitted with sloping hopper side tanks, for example, there will be a large area of unusable space between a block of containers and the ship's sides. Adequate measures must be adopted to ensure that the containers, as a result of rolling stresses, will not move or collapse into these spaces.

Whenever possible, the containers should be formed into one solid rigid block so that there will be no movement whatsoever. The bottom containers in the stacks should be secured to the ship's tank top plating by twistlocks or lockable locator cones and, in addition, twistlocks or lockable inter-layer stackers should be used between each container in the stack.

Not all the containers in a block will be loaded or discharged at a single port and, as a consequence, there may be parts of a voyage when the block will be irregular rather than cuboid in shape. The stow must be fully resecured as omissions of this nature have been the prime cause of a number of casualties. In the absence of such precautionary measures, the stacking of containers two high or more will produce racking stresses, which tend to distort containers laterally.

This problem will be aggravated during heavy weather, when the weight of the containers in the upper part of the stow may cause the corner posts of the lower containers to buckle, with the inevitable result that the stow collapses. This is more likely to happen in the forward holds, where the effects of pounding are more pronounced. Ideally, all ships converting to the carriage of containers in stacks two or more high should have the securing system and the strengthening requirements for the tank tops approved by the Classification Society.

In some systems, the spaces between the containers and the sides of the holds are taken up with portable or hinged steel girder chocks that insert precisely into the corner castings of the various heights of containers. Alternatively, and in addition to the provision of any form of inter-layer stackers or twistlocks, solid bar or wire lashings may be required, tautened on turnbuckles hooked into securing points at the tank top and at higher levels adjacent to the ship's shell plating.

41.6 Packing of Cargo Transport Units and the IMDG Code

Poor packing practices and improperly secured cargoes have increased the number of container related incidents, resulting in damage, loss and injury to personnel, both in port and at sea. In light of this, the *Code of Practice for Packing of Cargo Transport Units* (CTU Code) has recently been adopted as non-mandatory international guidance. The CTU Code is also referred to in the latest editions of the IMDG Code.

As of 1st June 2022, Amendment 40-20 (2020 Edition) is the current amendment applied to the IMDG Code. Note that although the 2022 edition of the IMDG Code (Amendment 41-22) has been published, it is not yet in force and compliance with its provisions is voluntary until 1st January 2024. Ensuring compliance with the latest mandatorily applicable version of the IMDG Code is essential as a minimum standard for all shipping of dangerous goods by sea.

The 2020 Edition includes significant changes and additions, including:

- New and revised provisions relating to the classification, packing, labelling, placarding, and marking of dangerous goods
- new and revised provisions relating to the handling, stowage, segregation, and transportation of dangerous goods
- amendments to various schedules and lists in Annexes A, B, and C.

Amendment 40-20 also refers to the use of the IMDG Code in a 'harmonised' manner with the International Maritime Organization's (IMO) new Regulations on the Carriage of Containers by Sea, which will come into effect on 1st January 2024.

Lithium battery carriage

There have been several shipping incidents recently where the evidence suggested that the carriage of lithium batteries was at fault for the initial fire breaking out on board.

In February 2022, the *'Felicity Ace'* sank while on route to the US from Germany. The car carrier had 3,965 vehicles on board, including 189 Bentleys, 85 Lamborghinis and nearly 2,000 Audis. It was suspected that a lithium battery within the cargo on board ignited and caught fire.

There was also a separate case in 2020 on board the *'Cosco Pacific'* where an undeclared container of lithium batteries caught fire. The ship was destined for India from China.

Changes to regulations involving lithium batteries include:

- Removal of the requirement to insert a telephone number in a lithium battery mark, but consignors can use their old marks with telephone numbers until 31st December 2026
- 'air mode' has introduced a requirement that packages of lithium ion batteries (UN 3480) and lithium metal (UN 3090) being shipped under specific thresholds (1B), must now be capable of withstanding a 24-hour stacking test.

Additional reading

The UK P&I Club and the TT Club have recently updated their joint best practice publication *'Book it right and pack it tight'* (Reference 57a), which takes account of IMDG Code Amendments, as of June 2022.

The guide provides key insights for all participants in the freight supply chain responsible for preparing unitised consignments for carriage by sea. The guide is intended to provide an overview of the key practical duties under the IMDG Code for each individual and entity, while not seeking to meet the mandatory training requirements.

Chapter 42 – Container Top Safety

Container top safety has been discussed in detail by various maritime organisations. The conclusions have brought about numerous changes in the applicable laws in a number of countries, most notably the USA and Japan. Both of these countries require all ships calling at their ports to comply with their legislation relating to the safety of dockworkers in the operation of loading and unloading containers. This includes the requirement that dockworkers are able to secure containers without going onto the top of containers that are stacked more than one high, whether on the quayside or on the ship. For ships to comply with the applicable law means that the equipment for fitting and securing containers on board the ship is operated from the deck level, or possibly a safe walkway level.

To ensure that containers are safely secured, automatic or semi-automatic twistlocks should be used and lashing rods need to be constructed such that they can be handled easily and safely, and secured properly, without the dockworkers having to be raised above the level of the deck or safe walkway.

The top tier of a stack of containers should be secured at the top of the container and the positioning of bridge pieces normally achieves this. Dockworkers do need to be positioned on the top of containers on the top tier to fit these bridge pieces. The port or terminal normally has specialised cages fitted with fall-arrester systems to facilitate this operation.

The ILO's *Code of Practice on Safety and Health in Dock Work*, Section 16 (Reference 71) specifies the guidance for 'access to the top of a container'. It requires purpose-built container ships to carry a safe means of access consisting of a stowable gantry frame fitted with suitable ladders and guarded walkways, and a means of locking the gantry against movement on deck. If such a frame is not carried by the ship, a similar arrangement should be available on the dock.

MSC.1/Circ.1263 (2008) *Revised recommendations on safety of personnel during container securing operations* (Reference 72) and amendments to the *Code of Safe Practice for Cargo Stowing and Securing* (CSS Code) through MSC.1/Circ.1352/ Rev.1 (Reference 69) further enhance the safety of workers when accessing containers. These amendments specifically require an approved Cargo Safe Access Plan (CSAP) for purpose-built container ships. However, all of these arrangements for loading and unloading ships are based on the ship being alongside a pier, quay or wharf and properly secured against unwarranted movement.

The fact that cargo operations usually take place in port terminals does not mean that the ship's crew can afford to be ignorant of the arrangements for safe handling of cargo and the special nature of the equipment involved, as they will need to be able to operate these items of equipment in an emergency while the ship is at sea. Training in the safe operation of these pieces of equipment is an essential part of the management and running of the ship as required by SOLAS. Initial training can be carried out at shore-based facilities, provided that a sufficient mock-up of the arrangement for stacked containers on board can be arranged, but training in the ship environment is likely to be more instructive.

All training should be practised frequently, in a safe environment, and should be reviewed after each session. This is essential as the requirement for automatic and semi-automatic equipment becomes more widespread in ports and terminals throughout the world.

The ship's crew should be wary of doing any part of the job that would normally be done by dockworkers. The correct fixing and lashing of containers, irrespective of whether they are on or under deck, is a specialised job and should always be left for the specialists. Ship's personnel, who ultimately have the responsibility for the safe carriage of the cargo, should oversee the fixing and lashing on board.

Ship operators must follow the rules and regulations applicable to each port and should be aware that these are likely to vary between ports.

Any ship that does not have the particular equipment in use for a specific country's requirements should never consider trying to undertake releasing or lashing work whilst at sea, in coastal waters, or manoeuvring within port limits, as this would be very dangerous both for the crew and the cargo.

The countries that operate 'safe dockworker' principles should still have facilities to handle all ships that call at their ports. There should be other methods of ensuring that their dockworkers operate in a safe way, even if this means going on the tops of containers to release twistlocks (assuming that a ship does not have automatic or semi-automatic units). How they do this work is not the direct concern of the ship, as long as the ship is loaded or unloaded effectively.

Dockworkers are provided with appropriate safety equipment, such as fall-arrester harnesses and ancillary equipment, and similar safety equipment should be provided for ships' crews, even though this may only need to be used in an emergency.

Chapter 43 –
Container Crime

UN statistics show that an estimated 500 million containers are transported annually around the world with only about 2% inspected at various stages of the shipment, which allows an opportunity for smuggling of weapons, drugs and other contraband. To mitigate such crime, the UN Office on Drugs and Crime (UNODC) and the World Customs Organization (WCO) initiated a Container Control Programme (CCP) in 2005. This programme provides a platform for all nations involved in trade to cooperate in fighting crime related to container traffic by involving entities such as customs, the police and port authorities. Crime prevention is managed through exchange of information, ensuring all personnel involved are trained to the same standards and follow a standardised approach.

The figures for cargo theft are estimated to be around US$30 billion per year and are forecast to continue to increase by 8% every year. The typical locations for this type of crime are at ports, terminals or during road or rail transport. There is less of a risk while the container is on board a ship, but ship operators often find that they are the focal point of a claim. This is due to the fact that:

- The operator may accept containers on board without actually checking the seal
- the contractual terms of the B/L provides coverage from door to door
- their assets are often more easily accessible than those of other parties.

Whatever type of container is used, its safety relies on its own security safeguards and those in place throughout its journey.

The introduction of containers was a technological advancement in the safe movement of cargo and it has had a major impact on the reduction of cargo pilferage. However, this type of transport has become a significant asset for organised crime, primarily due to the cargo involved, which offers substantial profits with minimal chance of detection.

Cargo in transit has always been the subject of crime. The distance involved in this type of movement, combined with the various handling procedures in place during the journey, presents a major obstacle to container security and it is extremely difficult to identify where a theft occurred and who carried it out. This is obviously very important when a B/L provides a door to door service.

If a container is correctly stuffed and its doors secured, there are only three ways in which unlawful entry can be gained:

- The removal of a section of the container's body
- interference with the seals on the outer container door
- interference with the container doors. The weakest links tend to be the pivot rivet connecting the door handle to the handle hub, the rivet to the swivel seal bracket and the rivets on the door hinges.

The presence of a seal on a container may provide evidence that its cargo has remained secure throughout its journey, but it is not an anti-theft device. Fortunately, there have been significant advancements in the design of seals to increase deterrence against the loss of cargo from containers while in transit.

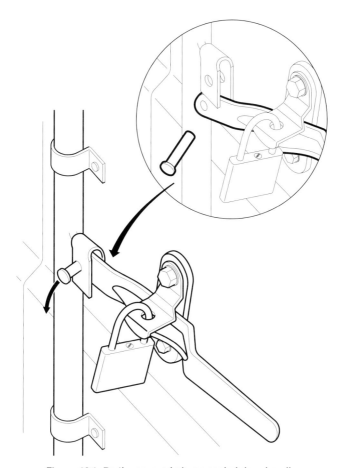

Figure 43.1: Partly removed pin on sealed door handle.

However, these improvements alone will not prevent an attack on a container because, if given the time, the opportunity and the tools, a criminal can remove virtually any seal or section of a container's door. The extent to which a seal offers protection is dependent on the system into which it is introduced.

For this reason, it is important that B/L issuers are satisfied that the procedures in place throughout a container's movement meet their requirements. Any discrepancies noted in the figures for container weight might be a good indication of loss of container contents, so the mandatory container weight verification requirement on shippers should be utilised. The IMO Guidelines categorically specify that the shipper named on the B/L is responsible for providing the container's verified gross mass. This requirement is likely to make stealing the entire contents of a container impossible provided the requirements are complied with diligently, particularly if the mechanism implemented requires the container to be weighed immediately prior to being loaded on the ship.

It is not only weight but also contents that need to be correctly identified to enable the crew to deal with any potentially hazardous goods in a safe manner. It has long been considered a problem in the container ship industry that shippers make false declaration of contents to avoid paying the extra charges associated with the carriage of dangerous goods.

In many instances, improved security procedures have reduced the opportunity of a loss occurring at a port or terminal, but they have not prevented the criminal from identifying a suitable cargo to steal once it has left that location.

There is, therefore, a need to constantly review procedures, for example, by working through the following checklist:

1. Have you received correct documentation that verifies a container's correct weight as required by SOLAS?
2. Are you satisfied that a container was correctly secured before departure from the shipper's premises?
3. Are you satisfied with the haulier contracted to move a laden container on your behalf?
4. Do they use sub-contractors? If so, are they suitable to undertake this work?
5. Are transport instructions issued to the haulier?
6. How efficient is the checking procedure of a container on its arrival at a port?
7. Is there a physical check prior to a container being loaded onto a vessel? (Weakness in the system, often due to operational or financial constraints, is constantly exploited by criminals, who remove cargo prior to loading.)
8. Is the seal physically checked when the container is offloaded at the destination port?
9. Is the seal checked when the container leaves the port?
10. Is there a procedure in place should there be an alleged irregularity on delivery? It is important whenever there is a potential loss that:
    - the seal sections are retained
    - special attention is given to the container's doors, in particular as to whether there are any different shaped rivet heads or signs of repainting.

Any irregularity should be noted, with consideration given to a surveyor's examination. It is imperative that a carrier's agent complies with the cargo release terms, which generally require presentation of the original B/L.

On occasion, agents show a lack of judgement in not complying with the release terms, but take an alternative approach without first obtaining the required authority. Such action usually relates to:

- A consignee's letter of credit
- a consignee's letter exonerating the agent from their action
- a bank guarantee confirming that sufficient funds exist in an account on a specific date
- agreement between agent and receiving party
- shipper's extended credit facility, minus the authority to release the cargo.

43.1 Drug Trafficking

During the last decade, the use of containers on board ships to illegally transport drugs has become the most common form of drug trafficking. It is estimated that 750 million containers are shipped every year, but approximately only 2% of these containers are inspected. South American countries, such as Brazil, Colombia, Peru and Bolivia, have extensive drug trafficking networks, and organised crime leaders often infiltrate ports, harbours, shipping companies and ship's crews in order to take advantage of this growing trend of mass cocaine shipments by sea. The drugs are primarily exported to Europe, but due to container ship trade can be delivered worldwide easily.

There are several different methods for drug trafficking. These include:

- **'Within the load'** – this method requires drug traffickers to own/run smaller companies that export products regularly. They hide the cocaine within their regularly traded products, in various forms. Anything from regular bricks of cocaine, to hollowed out fruit and hazardous chemical barrels have been discovered using this method. Suspicious trading patterns and irregular business methods have led to an increase in inspections of smaller companies attempting this method, which in turn drove drug traffickers to seek alternative means

- **'container contamination'** – this requires drug traffickers to have access to the loading port areas where the containers are located. This can be done in person, but is more likely achieved using mules or paid dock workers. The port workers find the required containers, break the customs seal, fill the container with the drugs to be shipped and replace the seal with a replica. This is a much more difficult method to detect as seals appear to remain in place throughout the voyage, however it can be detected via the weight difference of the container

- **'within the container structure'** – there has been an increase in the number of drugs found hidden within the walls, floors and ceilings of the container itself. This reduces the risk of drugs being discovered hidden within regular products and can be even harder to detect. However, they are still not hidden from x-ray machines, which is the main counter to this method of trafficking.

  This method requires the use of dock workers or personnel within shipping companies themselves, and often occurs after an initial customs inspection, just prior to the final loading onto a ship.

- **'drop off'** – smaller drug boats approach the vessel whilst underway, usually at night, and have the crew haul the products on board. The crew then store them in the containers on board. The following case study illustrates this method.

43.1.1 Case Study

In June 2019, the MSC *'Gayane'* container ship was boarded by federal agents in the port of Philadelphia, who spent several days using narcotics sniffer dogs, x-rays and fibre optic cameras to inspect thousands of containers on board. Seven containers were found to contain cocaine, totalling 20 T – one of the biggest seizures in US history. The investigation determined that drug traffickers had paid two of the crew members 50,000 euros to bring cocaine bricks on board from 14 smaller boats, then store them in the containers. The 14 boats approached the ship during the night off the Peruvian coast.

Chapter 44 –
Waste Shipments in Freight Containers

A container operator may face the following perils associated with the carriage of waste:

- Structural damage to the freight container due to improper stowage practices at the loadout point
- tainting of the inside of the container due to the waste having odorous properties
- imbalanced load resulting in the vehicle rolling over during road transportation
- rejection at the discharge port due to incorrect and/or incomplete documentation
- rejection at the load and/or discharge ports due to 'green waste' being contaminated with no possibility of its recovery in an environmentally sound manner
- risk of non-payment of storage charges at the load and/or discharge ports because the shipper/receiver fails to take timely and appropriate measures to mitigate the problems that arise following one or other of the above incidents
- the shipper/receiver abandoning their waste and the container operator being left to arrange disposal and/or return to the point of origin with the associated costs.

With the significant amount of waste now shipped in freight containers on some trades, the potential for problems can be high. For example, a ship loading in the UK for China may have up to 65% of its containers carrying various types of recyclable waste.

A major difficulty facing a container operator is that their client, the booking party, may not be the originator of the waste. The booking party will more often than not be a consolidator or NVOCC (non-vessel operating common carrier) and will themselves be dependent upon a third party for the quality and nature of the waste being supplied to them. Therefore, while a container operator may have a good relationship with their booking party, if that party then has a new supplier, problems may be experienced. Also, problems can be masked when, say, good bales of waste are stowed in the doorway of a container concealing poor quality/contaminated bales behind.

44.1 International Waste Disposal Legislation

In the late 1980s, a tightening of environmental regulations in industrialised countries resulted in a significant increase in the cost for disposal of hazardous waste, leading to unscrupulous practices such as shipping toxic waste to developing countries.

The Basel Convention, negotiated under the authority of the United Nations Environment Programme, was adopted in 1989 and entered into force in 1992. The Convention was originally designed to address the uncontrolled movement and dumping of hazardous wastes, including incidents of illegal dumping in developing nations by developed world industries.

Transboundary movements of waste have increased significantly over the last decades, primarily due to the international trade for recycling purposes.

The Convention has 176 member countries (parties) and regulates transboundary movement of hazardous and other wastes by applying the 'prior informed consent' procedure (shipments made without consent are illegal). Written consent must be obtained from the States of export, import and transit. The Convention also obliges parties to ensure that hazardous and other wastes are managed and disposed of in an environmentally sound manner. Parties are expected to minimise the quantities that are moved across borders, to treat and dispose of waste as close as possible to their place of generation and to minimise the generation of waste at source. Article 8 of the Convention requires:

> *"When a transboundary movement of hazardous wastes, or other wastes to which the consent of the States concerned has been given, subject to the provisions of this Convention, cannot be completed in accordance with the terms of the contract, the State of export shall ensure that the wastes in question are taken back into the State of export, by the exporter, if alternative arrangements cannot be made for their disposal in an environmentally sound manner ..."*

The Convention currently addresses 27 specific categories of waste and 18 waste streams. Annex I identifies the categories of waste to be controlled. Annex II identifies categories of waste requiring special consideration. Annex III provides a list of hazardous characteristics. Annex VIII, otherwise known as List A, identifies waste characterised as hazardous under Article 1, paragraph 1(a) of the Convention. Annex IX, otherwise known as List B, identifies wastes not covered by Article 1, paragraph 1(a) unless they contain Annex I material to an extent causing them to exhibit an Annex III characteristic.

Annex IX (List B) includes paper, paperboard and paper product wastes, provided they are not mixed with hazardous wastes, and covers:

- Unbleached paper or paperboard or corrugated paper or paperboard
- other paper or paperboard, made mainly of bleached chemical pulp, not coloured in the mass
- paper or paperboard made mainly of mechanical pulp (for example, newspaper, journals and similar printed matter)
- other, including but not limited to, laminated paperboard and unsorted scrap.

Among several other categories, Annex IX (List B) also details plastic or mixed plastic materials, provided they are not mixed with other wastes and are prepared to a specification, and electrical and electronic assemblies that are metals or alloys.

Further information on waste categories, waste containers and packaging, and the provisions of the Basel Convention, is available on the Cargo Incident Notification System (CINS) website at www.cinsnet.com, particularly in their *Awareness Paper for the Carriage of Waste in Containers* published in 2018 (Reference 85).

44.1.1 Illegal Traffic Under the Basel Convention

Statistics compiled by the Secretariat of the Basel Convention suggest that millions of tonnes of hazardous waste are shipped internationally each year.

For the purpose of the Convention, illegal traffic is deemed to be:

- *"Without notification pursuant to the provisions of this Convention to all States concerned; or*
- *without the consent pursuant to the provisions of this Convention of a State concerned; or*
- *with consent obtained from States concerned through falsification, misrepresentation or fraud; or*
- *that* [which] *does not conform in a material way with the documents; or*
- *that* [which] *results in deliberate disposal (eg dumping) of hazardous wastes or other wastes in contravention of this Convention and of general principles of international law".*

While many countries receive hazardous waste as a welcome source of business, others receive shipments for which there is no agreement and have difficulty in dealing with it properly.

Examples of 'illegal trafficking' incidents involving shipments in freight containers include:

- 60 freight containers containing 1,600 T of waste were seized by the Dutch port authorities. The waste was declared as recovered paper, on its way to China from the UK. However, it was found to contain bales of compacted household waste, food packaging and residues, plastic bags, waste wood and textiles. The waste was first transported to Dutch ports by lorry and ferry, where the bales were then transferred into the freight containers

- 95 containers of household rubbish were seized and the exporter involved was fined US$110,000

- a shipment of waste destined for India from the UK was declared to the customs authorities as containing paper. However, when opened by enforcement agents, it became clear, not only from the pervasive smell, that there was a mixture of wastes inside. As well as paper, there were also plastics, wood, metals and textiles, contaminated by food wastes. An attempt by the exporters to save fees payable under the correct procedure landed them with a fine of 10 times as much

Figure 44.1: Compacted and tainted soft plastics.

- 89 containers were exported from England to Brazil with the cargo declared as 'plastics for recycling'. However, upon investigation, the Brazilian authorities found the containers contained plastics, tin, paper, batteries, medical packaging and soiled nappies. The Brazilian government lodged an official complaint with the Basel Secretariat, leading to one of the UK Environment Agency's largest investigations, the return of all 89 containers to England and the prosecution of three companies and five individuals.

The import of electronic waste into mainline China is illegal, but it is alleged that legislation in Hong Kong provides loopholes allowing 'e-waste' to enter the country and make its way to scrap yards in China. The loopholes are said to include:

- No clear definition for 'reuse', 'reprocessing', 'recycling' and 'recovery operations'
- loose definition of the term 'contamination'

- lack of control of some types of electronic waste. While attention is given to old batteries and cathode ray tubes, printed circuit boards are given less attention.

Only about 50% of a computer can be recycled, comprising on average 32% ferrous metal, 23% plastic, 18% non-ferrous metal (lead, cadmium, antimony, beryllium and mercury), 15% glass and 12% electronic boards (including gold, palladium, silver and platinum). The toxicity of the waste is mostly due to the lead, mercury and cadmium. The non-recyclable components of a single computer may contain almost 2 kg of lead. Much of the plastic used contains flame-retardant materials, which makes it difficult to recycle.

44.2   Regional Information

44.2.1   Hong Kong

Regulatory control over the import and export of waste in Hong Kong comes under the Waste Disposal Ordinance (WDO), which is enforced by the Environmental Protection Department (EPD). The WDO provides for enhanced control on movements of wastes into and out of Hong Kong through a permit system, which corresponds with the Basel Convention.

Under the WDO, any import and export of prescribed hazardous, non-recyclable and contaminated waste for whatever purpose, and import and export of other waste for a purpose other than recycling, must be authorised by the EPD (Hong Kong Special Administrative Region) through a permit. A person who conducts controlled waste import/export activities without a valid permit, or disposes of any imported waste listed in the Sixth Schedule of the WDO, for which an authorisation is required, commits an offence that could be subject to a fine or prison term.

Waste movements between Hong Kong and mainland China are subject to the same control.

'Green waste' is commonly used to describe waste that can be readily recycled and is free from contamination. For the purposes of waste import and export, waste is considered to be contaminated if it is tainted by a substance to an extent that:

- Significantly increases the risk to human health, property or the environment associated with the waste
- prevents the reprocessing, recycling, recovery or reuse of the waste in an environmentally sound manner.

The following procedure is used to decide whether a permit is required to import/export waste into/from Hong Kong:

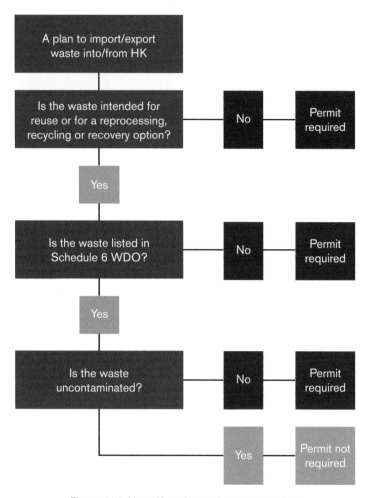

Figure 44.2: Hong Kong import/export procedures.

For green waste to be imported into mainland China from Hong Kong or elsewhere, the shipments concerned may need to be inspected by designated parties at the exporting countries or other places approved by the mainland authorities. Importers, exporters, traders or any parties concerned should confirm the latest requirement prior to effecting any shipments destined for the mainland.

44.2.2 China

China has a long history of importing recyclable waste, such as scrap iron and plastics, from other countries to compensate for the shortfalls of their own domestic resources. The demand for recyclable waste grew rapidly after China joined the World Trade Organization (WTO) in 2001.

Imported recyclable waste consumes less energy and uses up fewer natural resources, so was seen as the optimum choice as source material. However, the trade became so popular and profitable that China had to impose limits on the amount of recyclable waste it could import yearly.

Eventually, the China State Council declared that it would prohibit the importation of 24 types of recyclable waste, beginning at the end of 2017. In addition, China stopped importing wastes which could be supplied by its own domestic waste sector, as of the beginning of 2019.

The importation of household plastics waste was banned completely by the end of 2017, and the importation of various types of scrap metal and electrical appliance scraps was banned by the end of 2018. These policy changes have had a major impact on global trade in waste, particularly plastic waste.

The Ministry of Ecology and Environment (MEE) of the People's Republic of China, formerly known as the Ministry of Environmental Protection (MEP), is the designated authority for the environmental management of solid waste imports and is responsible for issuing import licences.

Imports should have:

- A Waste Import Licence issued by MEE – this is obtained by recyclers and/or utilisers of the imported waste in China prior to the waste import
- a License of Registration for Overseas Supplier Enterprise of Imported Scrap Materials issued by AQSIQ (AQSIQ Licence)
- a CCIC Pre-Shipment Inspection Certificate – pre-shipment inspection of scrap materials to China, to be used for the purpose of customs clearances. More information may be obtained from www.cciceu.com/en/ or www.cciclondon.com

CCIC is an inspection and certification company recognised by the General Administration for Quality Supervision, Inspection and Quarantine (AQSIQ) and accredited by the China National Accreditation Service for Conformity Assessment (CNAS). A number of CCIC offices have been set up around the world in countries that export waste materials to China. Container operators who accept waste product bookings to China should request the AQSIQ licence number at the time of booking, as it confirms that the shipper is approved by the Chinese Government authorities to ship waste products to China.

The Chinese Government continues to approve overseas scrap suppliers and at the same time monitors existing suppliers for the quality of waste supplies. During their inspections, if they find any anomalies, they may simply warn the suppliers and require them to rectify any issues. However, if these issues are not rectified or in the case of serious non-conformities, their licences may be cancelled. Container operators can check the AQSIQ website (www.aqsiq.net) for a list of approved companies with details of licences held. Container operators should not accept bookings from shippers who do not hold the relevant valid import licences as listed in this database.

It is good practice for the shipper to provide a copy of the documentation to the container operator as early as possible, but not later than the cut-off time for loading on the main line carrier. If a shipper has not submitted the export declaration, it is likely that they have not sold the cargo to a specific consignee. This increases the chances of cargo being abandoned at destination.

Following a revision of the solid wastes regulations in China in 2020, some types of MARPOL Annex II and III materials are prohibited from import from 1ˢᵗ January 2021. The list of prohibited solid wastes includes some 84 types, such as urban garbage, medical waste, waste organic solvent, waste clothes, waste tyres and tyre pieces, battery waste and scrap, used batteries, waste animal and plant products, waste rubber and leather, waste speciality paper, waste glass, as well as household appliances and waste electric motors including air-conditioners, televisions and computers (including their parts and accessories, dismantled parts, broken parts and scraps unless stipulated otherwise by the state). The container operator's booking department needs to be familiar with such prohibitions.

44.2.3   European Union (EU) Regulations

Commission Regulation (EC) 660/2014 amended Regulation 1013/2006 that had applied since 12ᵗʰ July 2007 covering the shipment of waste (Reference 73). Commission Regulation (EC) 1379/2007 amended Annexes 1A, 1B, VII and VIII of Regulation (EC) 1013/2006 (Reference 74). Annexes III, IIIA and IIIB of this regulation covered different types of non-hazardous waste, whilst Annexes IV and IVA covered different types of hazardous waste. These regulations were supplemented by Regulation (EC) 1418/2007 *"concerning the export for recovery of certain waste listed in Annex III or IIIA… to certain countries to which the OECD [Organisation for Economic Co-operation and Development] Decision on the control of transboundary movements of waste does not apply"*. Under these rules, stricter procedures must be followed (Reference 75).

Despite several EC regulations, gaps were identified relating to proper enforcement and inspections carried out by EU member States. Regulation 660/2014 is designed to cover these gaps by strengthening Regulation 1013/2006 and providing a mechanism for planning of waste shipment inspections and to prevent illegal shipments. It also requires member States to make publicly available the outcomes of inspections and any measures taken, including penalties imposed on any parties.

It also clarified that the inspection of shipments must include verification of documents, confirmation of identity and, where appropriate, physical checking of waste. Inspections could take place in particular at any of the following stages:

"a) at the point of origin, carried out with the producer, holder or notifier;

b) at the point of destination, including interim and non-interim recovery or disposal, carried out with the consignee or the facility;

c) at the frontiers of the Union; and/or

d) during the shipment within the Union".

Under the Regulation (EC) 1418/2007 (Reference 75), currently in force as amended, there are three options for controlling the export of wastes:

* Prohibition
* notification controls
* green list controls (lowest level of control).

Prohibition

Movements are not allowed under any circumstance, including almost all:

- Imports and exports for disposal
- exports of hazardous waste to developing countries, even if moving for recovery.

Notification controls

These apply to all allowed imports and exports of:

- Hazardous waste moving for recovery operations
- all types of waste moving for disposal
- some shipments of non-hazardous waste to non-OECD countries (includes Annex IIIB waste).

Green List controls

These controls contained in Article 18 of Regulation 1013/2006 (Reference 76) require that the exporters of waste must:

- Ensure that the Green List waste type can still be sent to that country under Green List controls
- know where the waste is going to be recovered in the destination country before shipping the waste
- ensure the waste is dealt with in an environmentally sound manner throughout its movement and recovery
- complete the Annex VII document specified in the rules with all the required information, including details of the producer or collector of the waste and the destination facility, before shipping the waste (a copy of this document must be retained for 3 years)
- ensure that a copy of the above document accompanies the waste
- enter into a written contract containing specified provisions for the recovery of the waste with the person receiving the waste before the waste is shipped
- ensure that the person receiving the waste in the destination country signs the document that accompanies the waste to confirm receipt.

Waste being exported under Green List controls must be accompanied by a completed Annex VII form. The person who arranges the shipment of the waste must complete and sign this form. It is good practice for the shipper to provide a copy of this documentation to the container operator as early as possible, but not later than the cut-off time for loading on the main line carrier.

44.2.4 United States of America

The Resource Conservation and Recovery Act (RCRA) is the public law in the United States that creates the framework for the proper management of hazardous and non-hazardous solid waste.

Since the United States is not a party to the Basel Convention, it can export waste to those countries with which the US Government has negotiated a separate waste trade agreement.

44.3 Shipments of Waste at the Load Port

The first indication for a container operator that there is anything untoward with a container load of waste is when it is received by the loading terminal and the container is damaged. This is most likely to be the sidewall panels bulging outwards beyond their accepted envelope. Figure 44.3 is a series of pictures that show different problems with waste shipments.

It is not always possible to identify the cause of damage to the structure of a container from a doorway inspection at the loading terminal. Identification of the cause may only be possible when the container is unpacked, which may take place some distance from the port.

The stow in the doorway when the container was opened. The container had been loaded with bales of waste plastics (eg bottles and packages). The bales were of rectangular shape with a long tack (right-hand bale) and a short tack (two left-hand bales).

This shows the right-hand side bales stowed tight to the underside of the roof panel. This was because two bales had been stowed with their long tack upright. This resulted in the roof panel bowing upwards. The bales were also of non-uniform size.

This picture is from an incident where the exporter had declared his shipment as being three container loads of electrical motors. However, these had been thrown into the containers with other rubbish that included plastic intermediate bulk containers (IBCs).

Picture 5 shows an incident where it was found that the top right-hand bale of waste paper in the row (marked by the red arrow) was 'canted' at an angle on the horizontal plane. This resulted in pressure being applied during the course of loading to the left and right-hand sidewall panels, resulting in them bulging outwards and being permanently deformed by up to 100 mm.

Picture 6 shows another incident where the cause of damage became apparent during unloading. The bale of waste paper in the top left-hand row was not stowed with its side parallel to the fore and aft line of the container, but was 'cocked' at an angle thereby increasing its width in the stow. This bale was stowed adjacent to the maximum bowing outwards of the left-hand sidewall panel.

Poor stowage of bales within the container was not the only problem. The waste paper was contaminated with tin cans, some of which had sharp jagged edges, plastic bottles, plastic bags, pieces of wood and twigs, and a complete inflatable rubber mattress.

Waste paper contaminated with other such waste cannot be recovered in an environmentally sound manner. This type of waste should not be moved under Green List controls.

The container in picture 8 was rejected by the ship's personnel at the time of loading because liquid was leaking out from the door seal. When inspected at the terminal's leaker bay, the front of the door sill was found to be heavily stained with a black oily substance.

When the container doors were opened, a distinct oily type odour was detected and emulsified oil was found on top of the door sill. Two solid plastic IBCs were stowed in the doorway, containing shredded plastic waste.

Behind these IBCs, shredded plastic waste had been stowed loose to approximately half the height of the container.

Other IBCs had been stowed on top of the loose shredded plastic waste. These IBCs were free to move, which would have made the container unstable during handling and transportation.

Figure 44.3: Different problems with waste shipments.

Part 11 –

Miscellaneous Cargoes

Chapter 45 –
Heavy-lift and Project Cargoes

Following a number of significant damage losses to ships and cargoes and a series of near-miss incidents in recent years, concerns have increased about the lack of expertise, skills and resources being deployed in this complex area of shipping.

The information in this publication is provided for guidance only and is not intended to replace, nor should it be used for, specific expert advice on the transportation of project/heavy-lift cargoes.

45.1   Project Cargo

Figure 45.1: Project cargo.

A wide range of cargoes fall within the definition of project cargo, from traditional breakbulk type cargoes to large single items such as cranes or oil and gas modules. It may be that large, heavy or out-of-gauge items require specialised stowage, lifting and handling, or there may be high value or critical items, or a quantity of goods connected to the same project, possibly loaded from different ports.

The cargo insurers will stipulate certain conditions (a warranty) for the purpose of insurance. If the cargo to be carried meets certain criteria (often referred to as 'critical items'), certain procedures will have to be followed under the warranty.

Critical items may fall under one (or both) of two broad headings:

1. Those that are critical because of the cost and difficulty of replacement.
2. Those that may require unusual provisions for safe loading, stowage, lashing and discharge.

The criteria for critical items take into account factors such as the replacement lead time, the value of the cargo (individually and/or in total), the size or footprint, weight, the centre of gravity and whether specialised transport, lifting and/or securing is required.

Cargo types that fall within the definition of a critical item may include:

- Oil and gas equipment for onshore and offshore infrastructure
- refinery and petrochemical plant equipment
- renewables equipment for onshore and offshore infrastructure
- modules and pre-assembled units
- port handling equipment

- port construction
- floating cargo
- rolling stock
- heavy machinery
- power plants and power generation equipment.

Critical items require special attention during transportation. Careful assessment and detailed planning is required for loading, stowage, securing and discharge.

Project cargo damages or loss can be very costly, often running into many millions of dollars. The risks involved can be largely mitigated with careful planning and attention, before the cargo is received for shipment.

The pressure to reduce costs is always high and, as the cost of shipment is essentially an overhead, there is a natural desire to reduce the shipping costs as far as possible. The use of unsuitable vessels to transport a cargo, poor quality or inadequate securing and dunnage, poorly trained crew and a lack of detailed planning can all lead to damage or loss.

Figure 45.2: Damage to project cargo during transportation.

Damage will likely lead to a claim against the cargo and/or liability insurance and, potentially, delays to the project (eg delay in start-up). With many other parties involved and the consequential costs high, these claims are often complicated and may result in lengthy and costly litigation.

45.2 Relevant Regulations, Codes and Guidelines

It is the Master's responsibility to ensure that all cargo is stowed, secured and handled (loaded/discharged) with care and in accordance with the requirements of the charterparty.

The charterparty may stipulate specific responsibilities of the vessel owner, charterer and shipper, such as the specific responsibility for stowage, lashing and securing of the cargo. There may be a requirement from the charterer and/or the cargo insurers for the appointment of an independent marine warranty surveyor (MWS) to review, approve and monitor all loading and sea fastening operations. These responsibilities should be carefully assessed as they can greatly affect the liabilities if the cargo is damaged or lost during the loading, voyage or discharge. It is important that all relevant persons are aware of these requirements and their responsibilities.

The following regulations are applicable and should be adhered to:

Flag State and Classification Society rules
These are always mandatory and, in particular, SOLAS Chapter VI: Carriage of Cargoes is relevant and must be complied with. Regulations for lifting gear and operations will be found within the flag State or Classification Society rules.

The rules of a vessel's Classification Society will also set out the requirements for maintenance of the vessel, including equipment required for the loading, stowage and securing of project cargoes. If these requirements are not followed, the vessel's owners may be liable in the event of an incident.

Cargo Securing Manual (CSM)
The vessel's Cargo Securing Manual (CSM) is a key document in the shipment of project cargoes. The CSM is a required document under SOLAS Chapters VI and VII and sets out the types of cargo that the vessel is properly suited to carry, as well as how it should be loaded, stowed and secured. It will also document the vessel's cargo securing equipment (inventory) and its maintenance and inspection procedures.

The CSS Code (IMO *Code of Safe Practice for Cargo Stowage and Securing, 2003, revised 2021*) (Reference 22)
This Code has been amended several times by MSC Circulars (eg by References 69 and 70). It sets out the general principles for the safe stowage and securing of a range of cargoes, including project cargoes and non-standard, heavy units that may require special attention. Annex 13 of the CSS Code, as revised by MSC.1/Circ.1623 in 2020 (Reference 70) sets out the method for calculating the required lashing forces for abnormal loads. The CSM will be based on the principles set out in the CSS Code.

One key aspect is that specialist knowledge and experience in the shipment of project cargoes is required to fully plan and engineer such cargo shipments safely. The CSS Code sets this out in Section 1.8, Special Cargo Transport Units:

"The shipowner and the ship operator should, where necessary, make use of relevant expertise when considering the shipment of a cargo with unusual characteristics which may require special attention to be given to its location on board vis-a-vis the structural strength of the ship, its stowage and securing, and the weather conditions which may be expected during the intended voyage."

In particular, the calculations involved often require specialist knowledge and appropriate expertise should be engaged.

Figure 45.3: The IMO CSS Code is the main standard to be applied for the stowage and securing of project cargoes.

The IS Code (IMO *International Code on Intact Stability*, 2008, as amended) (Reference 27)

The IS Code contains both mandatory regulations and recommended provisions, setting out the minimum stability standards for all applicable vessels. MSC.1/ Circ.1537/Rev.1 (Reference 27a) provides approved unified interpretations of the Code, agreed in 2019. Damaged stability standards should also be considered (SOLAS Chapter II-1).

The CTU Code (IMO/ILO/UNECE *Code of Practice for Packing of Cargo Transport Units*, 2014) (Reference 57)

This Code provides guidance and measures for ensuring the safe packing of cargo in containers and other cargo transport units (CTUs).

Guidance on best practice for the loading, stowage, securing and discharge of project cargoes may also be found in:

DNV *Rules for Planning and Execution of Marine Operations* (Reference 77)

The DNV Rules are mainly applicable to offshore operations, but there are sections on heavy lifts, lifting appliances, and loading and discharge operations that are relevant to project cargo shipments.

DNV-GL *Noble Denton Guidelines* (Reference 78)

The DNV-GL *Noble Denton Guidelines* provide the technical basis for marine operations, including the transportation of specialised cargoes. The guidelines include *Marine Transportation Guidelines, Marine Lifting Guidelines, Mooring Guidelines* and *Load-out Operations*.

All of these guidelines are specialist technical documents and appropriate expert advice on their content and implications should be sought before they are used.

45.3 Vessel Types and Suitability

Figure 45.4: Tweendecker.

A number of different vessel types are commonly used to carry project cargoes. These include:

- Tweendeckers: This old-style general or breakbulk cargo ship, with multiple hatches, fixed tween decks and cargo handling via derricks or cranes, has now largely disappeared
- general cargo ships: These carry a wide variety of cargoes, including industrial items, bagged cargoes, project cargoes, steel products, forest products, palletised cargoes, smaller breakbulk cargoes and containers. They are uncellular and have holds with movable/stackable tween deck pontoons
- multipurpose and heavy-lift vessels: These vessels usually have wall-sided (rectangular) holds and movable tween decks, providing efficient stowage for a range of cargoes using their own securing fittings. They are ideally suited to the carriage of project cargoes. Heavy-lift vessels are commonly defined as having cranes capable of a 100 T single lift. The cranes are usually sited to enable tandem working
- bulk carriers: These vessels have a number of holds designed to carry cargoes such as coal, grain, iron ore, etc. This type of vessel may vary in size from only a few hundred tonnes to around 200,000 T. The smaller sizes, up to around 50,000 T, may be fitted with cranes for self-discharge

Bulk carriers are sometimes chartered for project cargo transport, but are not well suited to this task as they do not have wall-sided holds, making safe and proper stowage difficult. The crews are often not familiar with the requirements for the stowage and securing of project cargoes.

Figure 45.5: General cargo ship.

Figure 45.6: Multipurpose vessel.

Figure 45.7: Bulk carrier holds are not designed for the carriage of project cargoes. The shape of the holds makes proper stowage and securing difficult and will require stacking and overstows. This can, and often does, result in cargo damage and sometimes damage to the ship.

- module carriers and semi-submersible heavy-lift vessels: These vessels have all accommodation forward and a broad, flat deck, designed for the carriage of large modules. Loading and discharging is via self-propelled trailers, skidding or, if semi-submersible, by float-on/off methods. The vessels are usually fitted with sophisticated and highly responsive ballast systems (sometimes with stability pontoons) to allow fine adjustment of draught, list and trim as heavy modules are loaded

Figure 45.8: A purpose-built heavy-lift ship.

Figure 45.9: The tween deck of a purpose-built multipurpose vessel.

- barges: A wide variety of barge types can be used for the transport of project cargoes, ranging from inland river barges to large ocean-going barges. Self-propelled, ballastable 'dumb' barges, requiring the use of pusher or tow tugs, are available in some regions. Some are equipped with holds and hatch covers. For larger project cargoes undergoing an ocean tow with a tug, a large 'classed' pontoon-type barge (with a flat watertight upper deck) would be utilised (spoon bow and raked stern with two box skegs). Careful consideration is required for the type of barge, tugs and towage arrangement. The condition of the barge should be carefully assessed, particularly the condition of the structure and essential systems (ballast system and manhole covers).

Figure 45.10: Loading heavy-lift cargo on to an inland barge.

45.4 Voyage Instructions

45.4.1 Summary of Master and Crew Responsibilities

The shipper's instructions may provide specific precautions that should be adhered to for the safe carriage of the cargo. These may be as simple as standard handling symbols indicating orientation or centre of gravity stencilled onto a packing case, or a large amount of information covering every aspect of carriage, from factory packing to onsite unpacking, and the conditions that must be met during transportation to ensure that a manufacturer's guarantee is honoured. Another aspect is the basis of design and design accelerations for heavy/project cargo (such as a transformer or module).

The cargo insurers may require the attendance and approval of a MWS during transportation and any recommendations made by the surveyor with respect to the transport must be adhered to. These do not remove or override the Master's ultimate responsibility for the safety of the crew, vessel and cargo.

Figure 45.11: A clear understanding of each party's responsibilities and good teamwork is key to the success of project cargo transportation.

45.4.2   Shippers' Instructions

The shippers may provide instructions for the safe and proper stowage and securing of the cargo. These instructions may refer to matters such as whether the cargo unit can be overstowed (ie whether other items may be stacked on top of it), the lashing and securing of the cargo (including the suitable lashing points on the cargo), the preferred stowage location (such as whether it can or cannot be stowed on deck) and the required packing to ensure the protection of any internal components and protection from the elements.

For more complicated shipments, particularly those for large, heavy items, a detailed transport manual or method statement should be provided. Owners should ensure that this is provided in a timely manner. It is normally provided by the shippers to all relevant parties and it should document all required procedures for the safe and proper shipment of the cargo, including:

- Management of the project, responsibilities and key contacts
- details of the cargo
- details of the vessel
- vessel strength and stability
- port details
- loading procedures, including any heavy lifts and, if necessary, any transportation to the loading berth
- stowage requirements
- lashing and securing requirements, including details of all lashing, securing and lifting gear
- voyage plan, including contingency procedures and ports of refuge
- discharge procedures.

The transport manual, or method statement, should be complied with as this defines the procedures for the entire shipment. It will have been reviewed by personnel with the specialist knowledge required for critical shipments, such as a MWS or cargo superintendent ('supercargo').

45.4.3   The Marine Warranty Surveyor (MWS)

The MWS is appointed on behalf of the cargo insurance underwriters, who insure the shipment of the cargo.

The MWS ensures that the terms of the warranty clause in the insurance policy are complied with and that the operations are carried out in accordance with the approved procedures, as defined in the transport manual or method statement.

Involvement of an MWS is common where shipment of the cargo forms a component of a larger project, including cargo comprising relatively small cases or cargo transport units (CTUs) through to complete modules for new infrastructure projects. In the latter case, the shipping operation will comprise a series of procedures, ie transport to point of shipment, lift plans and rigging calculations, sea fastening, and routeing of the ship or tow.

Subject to the approval of procedures and calculations, it is normal for the MWS to attend and observe loading, securing and possibly discharging operations, to ensure that approved procedures are adhered to and to be on hand to evaluate and approve any changes to procedures necessitated by the actual onsite conditions.

Where smaller quantities of cargo are being shipped on breakbulk or container 'liner' vessels, the MWS would typically consult with the chief officer and/or client's representative with respect to stowage position and method(s) of securing.

In cases where an MWS attends to approve loading and securing of cargo, it is usual for a certificate of approval (COA) or letter of approval (LOA) to be issued, on completion of operations, to confirm that the previously approved procedures have been adhered to or that the MWS is satisfied with onboard securing arrangements agreed with the ship's personnel or client's representative. The COA/LOA may have additional recommendations attached, such as specifying checks to be made on lashings, records to be noted in the vessel's log, etc.

45.4.4 The Client's Representative (Supercargo)

The supercargo, in many respects, plays a similar role to the MWS, but is usually appointed as the representative of one of the parties directly involved in the shipment such as the shipper, charterer or receivers.

45.5 The Cargo

Cargo group	Examples	Comments
Oil and gas equipment	Process modules, accommodation units, sub-sea equipment, topsides, decks, complete platforms/jack-ups	Can be very large units weighing thousands of tonnes
Refinery and petrochemical plant equipment	Cooling towers, flash towers, storage tanks, pipe-racks, reactors, towers and similar	May have large dimensions, often deck space intensive
Renewable energy equipment	Wind turbine blades (carried in racks), nacelles, foundations, mono-piles, tidal turbines, power cables (on non-specialist vessels)	Wind turbine blades (usually carried in racks) can be affected by longitudinal bending of the vessel due to their length. Careful stowage and securing are required to avoid this
Modules and pre-assembled units	Often for oil and gas installations or refinery/petrochemical plants, such cargoes may include living quarters, pre-assembled machinery, generator sets, large pipe racks	Often pre-assembled into large structural framework for which careful lashing, securing and bracing is required to avoid distortion

Cargo group	Examples	Comments
Port handling equipment	Typically, cranes and material handling equipment such as large container gantry cranes, ship-loaders, mobile harbour cranes, rubber tyre gantry (RTG) cranes, reach stackers	May consist of a framework, requiring careful lashing, securing and bracing to avoid distortion. Some units may have low lift stability
Port construction	May include pre-assembled items such as link-spans, jetty platforms, cat-walks, dolphins, single buoy moorings	
Floating cargo	A wide variety of vessels and craft, such as tugs, small ferries, yachts and super-yachts, small naval craft	Careful lifting sling positioning and restraint required
Rolling stock and heavy machinery	Locomotive engines and carriages, wheeled and tracked vehicles such as material handling lorries, excavators, trucked equipment such as mobile cranes, drilling rigs, etc. Mining equipment, factory equipment	Often included as breakbulk project cargo. Proper stowage and securing required
Power plants and power generation equipment	Large generators, conductors, transformers and similar	

Table 45.1: Different types of project cargo.

Project cargoes come in many different shapes and sizes.

Heavy lift
There is no standard definition of a heavy lift in weight terms, although the cargo insurance policy may set a weight figure as part of the critical item criteria (typically 50 T, but this may vary).

A 500 T lift on a specialised vessel, loaded/discharged at a safe berth, may present less risk than a 50 T lift at the limits of a vessel's safe handling capacity loaded/discharged at a berth not suited to handling such items.

Breakbulk cargo
Breakbulk cargo is a much broader group of cargo types and refers to cargoes that are loaded and stowed individually and not in containers or palletised. This includes certain project cargoes that are small enough to fit inside a vessel's holds, but which require individual loading, stowage and securing.

Problems often occur with breakbulk cargoes because there may not be a requirement for a surveyor to oversee and approve loading and securing. There has been a growing trend to use bulk carriers for such cargoes, which are ill-suited to the task and can result in extensive damage to the cargo.

Out-of-gauge

The term out-of-gauge refers to any cargo that has dimensions that exceed the normal dimensions of a standard shipping container.

Figure 45.12: Project cargoes require clear positioning and stowage. Care is required to ensure that all units in the stow can be properly secured.

45.5.1 Aspects to Consider for Project Cargoes

'Footprint' of the cargo

Where and how cargo will be stowed on the vessel must be considered to minimise the risk of damage and/or loss. The three-dimensional space and position must be considered in relation to the vessel structure and other cargo units; the stowage of project cargoes (particularly those in a breakbulk format) can often resemble a 3D jigsaw and must be planned as such.

The stowage plan should consider the following:

1. Is shoring required to hold the unit in position?

2. Can enough lashings with sufficient scope be run to resist the forces that will be experienced?

3. How should the cargo be orientated, with regard to any principal axes of strength in the cargo to the largest forces that will be applied to it?

4. Can the cargo have other cargo stowed on top of it (overstow)? What is the weight limit for overstow?

5. Does the cargo need to be carried on deck? Does the charterparty or fixture specify whose responsibility and risk this is (as often owners will not wish to carry the risk for deck cargoes)?

6. If carried on deck, is there a risk of green seas affecting the cargo? Is forward on the deck the right position for the unit? Does it overhang the vessel's sides (significantly increasing the risk of cargo damage)?

Figure 45.13: Lifting and securing lugs (pad-eyes) should not be subjected to forces out of plane of the eye as this will damage the eye and may lead to failure of the lashing.

Lifting and securing points

The cargo must be supplied with appropriate lifting and securing points, particularly for large and heavy items. If the cargo unit is not supplied with adequate lifting/securing points, attempts may be made to lift and secure the cargo in the best manner possible. However, if this is felt to present any risk of damage to the cargo (itself or surrounding), a note of protest should be issued at the time of loading. If the risk is felt to be significant (to the cargo unit, cargo as a whole or to the vessel), the cargo should be rejected.

The cargo lifting/securing points should be assessed to confirm that they are strong points and not merely attached to a protective cover, ie are they intrinsically part of the unit? They should also be checked to see that they are structurally sound and that they are in plane to the principal forces to which the cargo is going to be subjected, taking due account of the unit's position and orientation in the stow.

Figure 45.14: Cargo being lifted.

Cargo condition

The cargo unit, whatever its size, must be adequately packed and covered for its voyage to protect it from damage. If contained within an outer casing or protective packaging (eg a wooden box), the casing must be secure, well fixed to the cargo unit so it does not come loose, and cover all required parts of the unit. The unit should be well secured and packed within the casing.

Figure 45.15: Cargoes should be well packed and properly secured inside CTUs. Failure to do so can lead to extensive damage to the CTU, surrounding cargo and even the ship itself.

If shipped without an outer protective casing, careful packaging and covering of any vulnerable parts or components is necessary to prevent damage from impacts and corrosion.

Certain cargoes (such as coils, transformers, turbine components, etc) may be particularly liable to internal damage as they are sensitive to accelerations. These units must be properly packed, secured (including all internal components) and, if necessary, monitored during the voyage.

Advice from the manufacturer and/or relevant specialists should be sought.

Figure 45.16: Damage to the cargo observed on loading, even if only to packaging, should be noted and recorded.

Any project cargoes shipped inside containers or other cargo transport units (CTUs) should be adequately packed (stuffed), with appropriate shoring and internal securing, as with normal containerised transport (see Chapter 41).

The cargo should be inspected at loading and any damage recorded and noted, see Figure 45.16.

Cargo information

Heavy-lift and project cargoes tend to be more valuable than most and the consequence of their damage or loss proportionately more serious. Each cargo unit should be supplied with appropriate documentation that provides the necessary information to ensure safe transportation. The general standard for project cargo information should always be 'comprehensive and accurate'.

> The documentation must include the accurate weight of the cargo unit, the accurate location of its centre of gravity (particularly important for heavy lifts and possible off-centre units), its dimensions, and details of the safe slinging, lifting and securing points, as well as the nature of the cargo.

The weight and centre of gravity should be marked on each side of the cargo unit such that it is immediately visible.

45.6   The Vessel

45.6.1   The Cargo Securing Manual (CSM)

All ships carrying cargoes other than solid or liquid bulk cargoes are required to carry and maintain a ship-specific Cargo Securing Manual (CSM). This is a mandatory requirement of SOLAS (Reference 18) and the CSS Code (Reference 22). The CSM must be approved by the vessel's flag State.

The purpose of the CSM is to set out the procedures and standards for the securing of cargo, taking into account the type of cargo, the characteristics of the vessel and the conditions that may be encountered. It is intended to provide relevant information and guidance to assist the crew in properly securing the cargo.

Guidelines for the production of the CSM have been published by the IMO (Reference 24) and various Classification Societies. In general, the CSM should provide information on:

- The securing devices carried on board (number, strength, inspection regime and maintenance) and their arrangement
- the stowage and securing of non-standardised cargo, including evaluation of the forces and the appropriate calculation methods for determining the required cargo securing capacity
- the stowage and securing of standardised cargo units (such as containers), including securing devices, stowage requirements and evaluation of the forces acting upon the cargo units.

45.6.2   Vessel Stability

The vessel must comply with the *International Code on Intact Stability* (IS Code, Reference 27) at all times, including during loading and discharge operations. For large, heavy cargoes, the vessel's stability should be checked at all key stages of the proposed loading/discharge sequences. This will include any lifting operations (cargo unit at furthest extension and highest crane boom position), 'drive-on' (using self-propelled modular trailers for example) or floating operations (with semi-submersible vessels).

Figure 45.17: The IS Code, 2020.

Where relevant, the effect of a stability pontoon should be included in the calculations.

For high value/long replacement time cargoes and/or if the voyage route is deemed to be high risk, additional stability checks will be required for a damaged state (eg a one compartment flooded condition). Although a vessel may meet the IMO intact stability criteria, it may still be considered that the vessel has too little (tender) or too much (stiff) stability.

Vessels with heavy deck cargoes may have a high centre of gravity (CG) and a small metacentric height (GM). This will result in a slow roll period (tender) and the ship will linger at the maximum angle. The extended roll period increases the gravitational forces on the cargo and the securing devices.

Figure 45.18: Rough weather combined with a high GM can result in violent motions, which if not properly planned for, can result in damage to or loss of the cargo.

Vessels with heavy cargo stowed low in the holds may have a low CG and a large GM. This results in a fast roll period (stiff) and the ship may roll violently. This violent motion increases the dynamic forces acting on the cargo and the securing devices, due to the increased accelerations.

Project cargoes for the oil industry, loaded on conventional vessels, usually include a quantity of drill and casing pipe. This has to be bottom stowed in the holds and the result is always a high GM, with its associated short roll period, which in some cases is as low as seven to eight seconds, potentially resulting in violent rolling. High acceleration forces may be exerted on tween deck and deck cargo lashings and this should be taken into account during the planning and loading phase. Because project cargoes can be relatively light but have a high volume, there is usually insufficient deadweight in the whole consignment to bring the vessel down to a reasonable draught that will provide full propeller and rudder immersion. Therefore, some bottom ballast will still be needed, which further increases the GM. Pumping out this bottom ballast will make little difference to the roll period and will make the vessel difficult to handle in adverse weather.

With a lighter vessel, there is an added risk of main engine shutdown, as the governor will be working harder to avoid engine overspeed.

On conventional vessels, an ideal roll period would be in the region of 15 to 20 seconds. A longer roll period, resulting from a GM that is too low, will mean that the vessel will 'hang' at the maximum angle at the end of each roll and any shift of cargo could result in loss of GM and the vessel reaching angle of loll, with no prospect of recovery without resorting to ballasting bottom tanks.

The nature of the cargo will dictate the final GM, although consideration should be given during the planning phase to loading as many heavy units high up in the tween decks, or on deck if permitted, to counteract the effect of the drill and casing pipe consignments in the lower holds. This will not be possible in the case of bulk carriers being employed to load project cargoes, as the heaviest units will have to be stowed directly over the pipe stows, or on the remaining tank top areas in the holds, further increasing the GM.

Consideration should be given to the weather conditions that the vessel may experience on voyage. For exposed, open ocean voyages, where bad weather is a possibility, the effect of the loading condition (GM and draughts) on the vessel's motions should be considered and any negative effects mitigated as much as possible. It is important to minimise the motions of the vessel (including possible wind heeling) as far as practically possible.

Figure 45.19: When sea fastenings fail under excessive vessel motions, the violent motion of large, heavy project cargoes can cause extensive damage to the vessel structure. Side-shell plating (in way of cargo holds), deck structures and hatch covers are particularly vulnerable to damage. The repairs can cause extensive delays.

45.6.3 Vessel Strength Considerations

The vessel will have defined weight limits for the tank top, tween deck and hatch covers (expressed in tonnes per square metre). It is important that these limits are adhered to, particularly with heavy cargoes, and they must be considered in the stowage planning.

Heavier cargo units should be placed over the frames of the vessel and additional load spreading may be required. Methods of load spreading can range from dunnage or wooden mats, to steel grillages for heavier units. These spread the load into the surrounding structure of the vessel. The grillage should be designed to take both the static weight of the cargo unit and the dynamic loads to which it will be subjected on voyage. In many cases, sophisticated software is used to determine 'hot spots' in the structural members of the vessel while stowing heavy-lift cargo. This approach is usually used by naval architects or structural engineers, who are either employed internally or externally.

Figure 45.20: Load-spreading 'mats' to protect the structure of the vessel.

Where structural reinforcements, grillages or any other welded modifications are required, the proximity to the vessel's bunker tanks or any other flammable source must be considered and the appropriate hot work procedures followed. All appropriate work permits should be in place.

The longitudinal strength of the vessel in terms of shear forces and bending moments must be checked at all key stages of the loading and discharge operations and for the voyage conditions. Project cargoes are typically limited by volume (rather than weight) and so the shear forces and bending moments are usually within the vessel's permissible limits.

45.6.4 Securing Points

The securing points fitted to the vessel, and the surrounding structure to which they are fitted, must be strong enough to withstand the loads (static and dynamic) imposed by the cargo during the voyage. This is particularly important in the case of 'hard' sea fastenings such as welded stoppers.

Figure 45.21: Adding securing points to the deck of a heavy-lift vessel.

Figure 45.22: Lashing wires with sufficient scope and clear working space.

The securing points should be located such that there is adequate room for the securing device to operate effectively. For wire lashings, the lashing should have a clear line between the cargo unit and the securing points on the vessel and must not run around corners of the vessel structure or other cargo units.

Figure 45.23: Examples of D-rings properly welded to the deck (left) and poorly welded onto a bulkhead (right).

45.6.5 Cranes and Lifting Devices

The vessel's cranes and lifting devices are of critical importance in the loading and discharge of project cargoes.

Maintenance of cranes and the operational procedures applied are critical to their safe operation. There are numerous examples of heavy lifts being dropped due to failures of cranes and/or poor operational practices. The manufacturer's recommendations for maintenance should be followed and full records kept. Defective wires must be replaced as necessary. The Classification Society inspection history and maintenance records (eg 'rocking' test results) are often requested for review.

 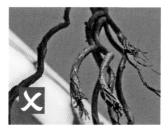

Figure 45.24: The vessel's cranes are of critical importance to the safety of operations and all components should be thoroughly maintained and regularly inspected. A crane failure during a heavy lift could be catastrophic.

The manufacturer's recommended operating procedures should be followed and the crane operating limits adhered to.

A significant factor in incidents relating to cranes is the competence of the operators. Heavy lifts, particularly tandem lifts (using more than one crane at the same time to lift a unit), require experience and appropriate training.

Figure 45.25: Cargo being unloaded using a tandem lift.

45.7 Loading and Discharge

The responsibilities of each party must be agreed and documented prior to commencement of operations and should set out the chain of responsibility, persons in charge and contact details for all relevant persons.

Instructions/information from shippers

The shipping note provides details of the contents of a cargo consignment to carriers, forwarders and receivers.

Industry guidelines and best practice

For any cargo movement, in particular for loading and discharge operations, a full and detailed plan must be produced and adhered to. The plan should take account of the requirements and recommendations of industry best practice guidelines and rules.

Heavy-lift equipment and relevant requirements

Lifting gear may include wires, shackles, spreader beams and lifting blocks/hooks and should be documented on board the vessel, or with the crane (if shore-side). All lifting equipment should be certified and its safe working load (SWL) or working load limit (WLL) and minimum breaking load (MBL) documented and marked visibly on the item itself.

Figure 45.26: Safe lifting equipment.

Lifting lugs/eyes on the cargo unit should be located so as to provide a stable lift, accounting for any offset of the unit's centre of gravity. They must also be strong enough for the lift, including any dynamic lifting loads. All lifting gear and lifting points on the cargo should be inspected before commencing the lift.

Figure 45.27: Unsafe lifting equipment.

Lifting and rigging plans

For any heavy lift, it is essential to properly develop and document a lifting plan, which should define the procedures for the lift and provide accurate information on the centre of gravity of the unit, the proposed lifting spread to be employed and the calculation of the rigging stability (the lifting triangle). It should document the loads expected to be experienced and the safety factors used in selecting the lifting gear. It should also assess the need for centre of gravity corrections (eg the use of water bags) and/or possible test lifts required to ensure stability (insurance policy coverage should be checked in this case).

The lifting of units with a high centre of gravity (CG) can be challenging. An incident occurred on board a ship where the rigging arrangement for a heavy-lift item was incorrect, and this coupled with a strong gust of wind, caused the crane to list. As the stability of the lift was marginal to begin with, once the crane had started to list, there was no means to restore it to its upright position. The load fell to the deck of the vessel and the quayside, causing significant damage.

All crane lifts should be carefully assessed to ensure adequate clearances between the cargo unit itself, the vessel, and the port infrastructure. Tandem crane lifts must be planned in detail to ensure the correct synchronous movement of the cranes.

Limiting conditions and external influences

The lift should have limiting conditions imposed on it to ensure that the design loads for which it is rated are not exceeded. These will include limiting wind conditions and vessel motions (which may differ for in-harbour and offshore operations) and, where positional accuracy is important, the lift may be limited to daytime hours only.

Significant crane slewing (rotation) and other horizontal motions should be assessed to ensure that the dynamic loads imposed are within the capacity of the lifting system. Similarly, lifting into and out of water imposes additional loads on the lift and must be assessed.

Reference should be made to the relevant industry guidelines for the determination of these loads.

Loading sequence and trim, ballasting
During loading and discharge operations, it is important to carefully manage the vessel's draughts and trim. This is particularly important for drive-on/off and float-on/off operations. Careful ballasting is needed to ensure that the required draughts and trim are maintained during the course of the operation and this should be properly calculated and documented in advance. The ballast tank and pump capacity of the vessel should be checked to ensure that they are adequate, particularly for barge transports. In addition to ballast water loads, the impact on stability of the free surface effect from slack tanks should also be taken into account.

Other loading methods
- Float on/off: This method of loading and discharging is employed by semi-submersible heavy-lift vessels and submersible pontoon barges. Cargoes may include offshore platforms, jack-ups, other vessels (eg barges, tugs, etc) and large project cargoes that are suitable for wet loading/discharging. These vessels can be expensive to charter, but provide a safe and relatively fast option for transportation

Figure 45.28: A float on/off vessel with an offshore platform as its cargo.

- skid-on/off: pontoon barges, module carriers and semi-submersible heavy-lift vessels are commonly loaded by cargo being skidded into position. Large oil and gas units (eg topside modules) are often loaded by this method. These are typically bespoke operations allocated to a specialist contractor

Figure 45.29: Barge transports and loading/discharge by non-lifting methods require specialist expertise and knowledge.

- roll-on/off: Wheeled cargoes can be driven onto and off the vessel. Many project cargoes are loaded/discharged using self-propelled modular transporters (SPMTs). SPMTs provide a flexible loading/discharge method and are capable of dealing with inclined and uneven routes.

45.7.1 Other Operational Issues

Ground-bearing pressure

Consideration should be given to the ability of the load path (ashore) to withstand the weight passing over it without undue deformation, which might result in damage to the load path and/or a loss of stability of the load-transporting equipment. This can also be a factor with lifted loads, particularly where a high capacity mobile crane is utilised. The loading capacity of port facilities should be determined and account taken of any damaged or degraded areas. Repair and/or consolidation may be required to provide a usable load-path over which a heavy unit can be skidded or driven, or a crane safely located. The transport of the unit to the load port and onwards from the discharge port must also be considered. A route survey may be required.

Transshipments

Transshipment of cargo should, under ideal circumstances, be avoided as generally the cargo is at its most vulnerable when being handled. However, there are circumstances when it cannot be avoided. Transshipment operations, particularly ship to ship (STS), require detailed and careful planning.

Barge transport

While there are heavy-transport vessels capable of carrying modules of 2,000 to 3,000 T, towed barge transport is often the only reasonable solution to move heavy-lift cargo, particularly where extremely large and heavy structures are concerned. These may include container cranes, large tanks, or jackets and decks for offshore installation. Barge transport is inevitably slower than the use of an equivalent vessel. It will also require the attachment of a suitable towing vessel and may need more sophisticated voyage planning where the tow route is lengthy or transits known hazardous or adverse weather areas. Barge transports should be carefully planned as they are generally a higher risk method.

Management of operations

For any loading and discharge operation, the planning of the operation must include provision for hold points during the operation and toolbox talks. These help to ensure the safe progression of the operation and that all persons involved understand the next steps, responsibilities, etc.

Appropriate risk assessments, including hazard identification meetings, should be carried out. These should involve all relevant parties and be approved by all. They should include management of changes (any deviations from agreed procedures) to be documented and agreed by all parties.

> Relevant authorities (such as the local Port Authority) should be informed of the operation and involved in the planning. There may be a need to restrict vessel movements nearby during an operation, for example, which will require the support and assistance of the port.

45.8   Stowage Requirements

All vessels have their specific advantages and disadvantages, but while specialist heavy-lift vessels will be more expensive to charter, they are generally better suited to the cargo types typically shipped, so the overall shipment is safer. Cheaper vessels, such as bulk carriers or general cargo vessels, are often employed for economic reasons. However, they are not designed to carry these types of cargoes and their use often ultimately leads to increased costs, either due to cargo damage claims or the extra design and work required to make the cargo shipment as safe as possible, which tends to nullify the perceived cost benefit.

Figure 45.30: Large cargo units will need to be carried on deck, requiring special planning of the stowage, required sea fastenings (to allow for the higher CG) and protection from the elements. Stowage on forward hatch covers is not advised unless absolutely necessary as vessel motions (in particular, pitch motions) are greater in this location and there is a higher risk of impact from seas shipped on deck.

Large cargo units require large amounts of deck space and this often dictates the choice of vessel. If the cargo can only be carried on deck and not in the holds, suitable protection from the elements is then required.

> Deck cargoes will often be specified as being carried at the shipper's risk and it is important to note this and take action accordingly.

45.9   Cargo Securing

Cargo securing equipment

Cargo securing gear may include lashing wires, web lashings, chains, D-rings, turnbuckles and shackles. In project cargo terms, these are often referred to as 'soft' lashings. As with lifting gear, all of the equipment for cargo securing should be certified and have its SWL and MBL documented and marked visibly on the item. If carried by the vessel, the CSM should provide a full inventory of these items.

Figure 45.31: Turnbuckles.

Also applicable are 'hard' sea fastenings such as stoppers, braces, etc, which are often constructed from steel plating and/or beam sections and welded to the vessel. These are typically used for larger, heavier cargo units and are usually used only once.

Figure 45.32: 'Hard' sea fastenings.

As with lifting gear, securing equipment should be well maintained and regularly inspected. Records of the inspections and maintenance should be retained. Prior to use, all securing gear should be inspected and, if damaged, should not be used and should be replaced.

45.9.1   Types of Securing

Wire lashings (direct or looped)

Wire lashing are the most common form of cargo securing. They are easy to stow (but must be wound/unwound properly), are easily adaptable to the shape of cargo compared to deck/hold lashing points, and tension can be maintained on voyage (using turnbuckles or similar). The wires are susceptible to damage and require regular maintenance. Care must be taken to ensure the wires do not damage the cargo and sheathing protection may be required. The wires must be rigged properly to get full load capacity and will need retensioning during the voyage. Large numbers of wires are required for larger, heavier items, and these can be difficult to handle. Separate wires should be used to counter sliding and tipping forces.

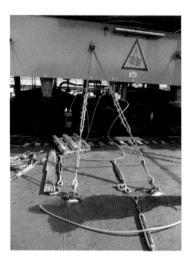

Figure 45.33: Wire lashings.

Web lashings

These are better suited to smaller/lighter cargo units and where the cargo unit does not have dedicated lashing points. They are re-usable, easy to stow and the soft material minimises damage to cargo. They tension with a ratchet and are easy to handle. They are prone to chafing damage and have limited strength so a large number are required, even for medium-sized units.

As a general rule, soft lashings have the greatest effect if attached close to the plane of the centre of gravity (CG) of the item (subject to the structure of the item being able to withstand the motion forces expected) with the angle of the lashings as close as possible to 45° to the deck.

Figure 45.34: Web lashings may sometimes be used for smaller, lighter project cargoes, typically because they are cheaper than wires. However, they do not provide the strength of wire lashings and are prone to chafing damage. Securing cargoes using web lashings as shown in the right-hand image will damage the webbing and reduce its effectiveness.

Chains

These can provide higher strength capacity and require less maintenance than wires but are harder to handle and stow, and difficult to keep taught. When using ratchet tensioners, the chain will loosen in steps (by link) rather than gradually, potentially resulting in loss of tension. They are suited to stronger securing points, with separate chains required for sliding and tipping resistance.

Figure 45.35: Lashing chains need to be properly tensioned and so need to be secured to appropriate securing points to enable the tension to be created. The chains shown provide good tipping restraint but minimal sliding restraint, due to their high angle.

Sea fastenings

These can include hard stoppers and braces, typically of steel construction and with welded connections to the decks. They can provide combined resistance to sliding and tipping and may be designed to resist very large forces. They are well suited to large, heavy units of non-uniform shape but require proper design and engineering. They will have a higher cost, require time to construct and will need qualified welding contractors and non-destructive testing (NDT). Care is required to ensure that the vessel's structure can withstand the imposed loads.

Figure 45.36: Sea fastenings.

Dunnage, shoring

Wooden dunnage must be placed on the decks underneath the cargo to provide greater friction between the cargo and the deck and to assist load spreading. Dunnage is not used where the cargo unit sits on a grillage or similar, which is designed to spread the load, but may be used as shoring or bracing to help position and maintain the cargo unit.

The dunnage should be of good quality solid wood and not of plywood or similar. Ideally, it should be of horizontal grain (and not curved) to minimise the risk of splitting.

Figure 45.37: Wooden dunnage.

45.9.2 Securing Methods

The options for securing the cargo unit should be assessed and the most appropriate selected. This is typically undertaken by the charterers but is subject to the provisions of the charterparty. It is, therefore, important that each party understands their specific responsibilities. The Master should ensure that they are satisfied with the cargo securing and should note any defect or concern about the proposed arrangements.

Certain cargo types, particularly large heavy items or units that cannot absorb any stresses, will dictate that certain types of sea fastenings are required and whether 'hard' or 'soft' sea fastenings should be used.

Hard sea fastenings include welded stoppers, braces, etc that are connected to the vessel's decks and provide restraint of the cargo and spread loads into the surrounding structure of the vessel. Equally, if there is a direct connection between the vessel and the cargo unit (eg welds, pad-eyes, etc), stresses on the vessel may be transferred to the cargo unit. In particular, this can occur with cargo units of sufficient length that longitudinal bending and deflections of the vessel are imparted into the cargo unit. Careful design of the sea fastenings is required to ensure that this is avoided or, if unavoidable, that the stresses imposed on the cargo are within the capacity of its own structure. Hard sea fastenings will typically provide a greater restraining capacity and so are better suited to larger, heavier units.

Figure 45.38: Where cargo units may incur deflections due to the longitudinal bending of the vessel, the sea fastenings must be carefully designed to minimise the loads imparted into the cargo unit. More complex sea fastening designs are required, based on specialist expertise. It is, therefore, important that sufficient time is allowed in the project for the proper design process to be carried out.

Soft sea fastenings include wires, straps, etc which provide some restraint, but also have some 'give'. This 'give' is useful in avoiding the transfer of vessel stresses into the cargo unit, but also means that the tightness of the securing needs regular checking to ensure it does not come loose. Soft sea fastenings are generally cheaper and more convenient to use.

The design of the sea fastenings must provide restraint against sliding and tipping in both transverse and longitudinal directions as well as against uplift. The design philosophy for sea fastenings is such that hard and soft types should not be mixed in each mode of restraint, eg use of sea fastenings for sliding or tipping restraint can each employ different methods such as hard for sliding and soft for tipping, but a mixture of both types of fastening for one mode of restraint should be avoided.

For soft restraints, the optimum angle for sliding restraint is about 25 degrees to the deck, while for tipping restraint, the optimum angle is about 45 to 60 degrees. Hard sea fastenings should be designed considering all relevant forces and stresses (and not just one mode of force).

Bracing may need to be installed on the cargo unit to prevent distortion of the cargo unit under the loads experienced in a seaway. This is particularly relevant for frameworks (eg modules for oil and gas installations) and large gantry cranes (eg container cranes, RTGs, etc).

Where welding is required to construct the sea fastenings, it must be ensured that this is not over or against any fuel tanks and that hot work procedures are followed. The welding must be of a high standard and specialist, fully qualified welders are normally required to complete the welding of sea fastenings. The welds must be tested to ensure that there are no defects and non-destructive testing (NDT) inspectors are employed for this. The amount of NDT required varies, depending on the complexity and criticality of the project/cargo, but testing of a minimum of 20% of all welds is normally required and, in some cases, 100% of all welds may require testing. In addition to any NDT, there should always be a 100% visual inspection of all sea fastening welds.

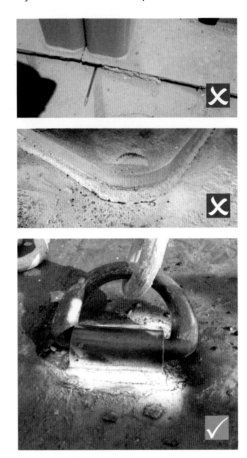

Figure 45.39: Examples of welds, showing very poor quality welding (top), a sea fastening weld to the deck that failed the NDT inspection due to the presence of weld cracks (middle) and a D-ring after NDT inspection that was passed (bottom).

45.10   The Voyage

45.10.1   The Voyage Plan

The voyage plan should be critically assessed for the route, proximity to areas of navigation danger, exposure to weather conditions (duration and how open the area is and its effect on cargo stowage and securing) and areas of known piracy activity. Different criteria will apply for open ocean voyages, compared to sheltered voyages of limited duration. Weather routing should be used where possible. Adequate fuel reserves should be maintained on board the vessel for the duration of the voyage. The usual recommended minimum reserve is 20% or five days' fuel reserves.

The voyage route should include contingency plans in case of emergency events or forecasted weather exceeding the limits defined in the stowage and sea fastening calculations. Ports and areas of refuge should be identified and should ideally be reachable within a reasonable accurate weather forecast timeframe (usually two to three days' sailing).

Where an MWS is involved, the vessel will be required to provide daily reports of voyage progress and a report on the condition of the cargo. This is usually a small addition to the normal reporting process for owners and charterers.

45.10.2 Voyage Reporting

An MWS may provide a certificate or letter of approval to confirm that the vessel can depart and that all procedures have been complied with. The certificate/letter may contain a number of recommendations that must also be complied with, as a requirement of the warranty for the insurance policy. The recommendations will typically include limiting weather conditions for the voyage, the requirement to regularly check the sea fastenings and reporting requirements.

A certificate or letter of approval may also be provided for critical operations such as heavy lifts or load-out/load-off.

It is important to keep records of the operations, both for log entries and future reference. It is recommended that the crew make notes of the operations as they progress and while on voyage. Handwritten notes (or crew's notebooks) should be retained and, for more complicated cargoes, the notes should be extensive and represent a proactive approach.

Duty officers should be encouraged/instructed to take as many photos as possible, particularly during loading. Video clips of critical heavy-lift operations can also be taken. Photos and video clips are particularly helpful to investigators and experts in case of cargo loss or collapse, and could help protect interests in case of litigation.

Chapter 46 –
Agricultural Produce – Insect
Infestation and Fumigation

Fumigant gases are poisonous to humans and should only be used by specialists, not by the ship's crew.

Insect and mite pests of plant products may be found within cargo spaces as:

- Introduced infestation (carried on board with the produce)
- cross infestation (moved across from one product parcel to another)
- residual infestation (remaining on board from a prior infested cargo to attack subsequent cargo).

The principal method of treating cargo spaces or their contents for the control of insects is by fumigation, which is the action of an insecticidal chemical in its gas phase. The chemical can be applied as a gas, liquid or in solid formulation, but after vaporisation from liquids or reaction from solids, will always act in the gaseous phase. Fumigants act either as respiratory poisons, or as suffocants in the case of controlled or modified atmospheres. On release, they mix with air at a molecular level and are capable of rapidly diffusing from one area to another and through commodities and buildings.

> Fumigants should not be confused with smokes (which are solid particles in air) or with mists, aerosols or fogs (which are liquid droplets, of various sizes, in air). Smokes, mists, aerosols or fogs are not fumigants as they are unable to diffuse (ie they do not mix with air at a molecular level) and do not reach deep-seated infestations in commodities or structures.

The most common fumigant is phosphine (PH_3), which is extremely toxic.

The effective and safe use of fumigants requires the space being treated to be rendered gastight for the period of exposure, which may vary from a few hours to several days, depending on the type of fumigant and concentration used, the pests, the commodities being treated and the ambient temperature.

The critical parameters that need to be considered for effective fumigation are:

- Nature of infestation (type of pest, eg rodent, insect or other invertebrate, and stage of its life cycle)
- type of fumigant applied
- concentration and distribution of gas
- ambient temperature
- length of time for which fumigant must be applied
- method by which fumigant is administered
- containment of fumigant
- nature of commodity
- nature of commodity packaging
- monitoring system
- ventilation system.

The other chemical used for fumigation on board ships is methyl bromide, also known as bromomethane.

Exposure to methyl bromide is highly irritating to the skin, eyes and airways. Irritation of the airways can cause coughing, chest tightness and a burning sensation in the nose and throat. It may also cause nausea, vomiting and abdominal pain if it is inhaled in large volumes. As of 2010, this chemical was banned within the EU due to its adverse effects on humans, health and the environment (it is also a greenhouse gas). However, as only the EU has banned its use, it may still be found in use as a fumigant in other parts of the world, or in cargoes loaded outside of the EU.

46.1 Aim of Fumigation

The aim of fumigation is to create an environment that will contain an effective concentration of fumigant gas at a given temperature for a sufficient period of time to kill any live infestations. Both the time measured (hours or days) of exposure and the concentration of gas are critical to fumigation efficiency. Dosages applied are usually expressed as grams per cubic metre. Concentrations measured during the fumigation are usually expressed in parts per million (ppm) or grams per cubic metre, and total concentrations actually achieved as concentration time products (CTPs). The fumigation process is not completed until ventilation has been effectively carried out and the removal of any residues is completed.

Evacuation of the space under gas treatment is essential and, in some cases, it will be necessary for the whole ship to be evacuated.

The Master will require the fumigator to provide written information on the type of fumigant to be used, to include the hazards involved, the threshold limit values (TLV) and the precautions to be taken.

The fumigation of cargoes with phosphine gas is by the use of tablets, pellets or solid preparations in other physical forms which are supplied by the manufacturers in hermetically-sealed containers. The active ingredient of these preparations is either aluminium phosphide or magnesium phosphide. These substances are highly reactive with water and, as the preparations are removed from their sealed containers, the active ingredient comes into contact with atmospheric water vapour and yields phosphine gas into the cargo space under fumigation. Phosphine is extremely toxic, so the crew evacuation procedures should apply. However, shippers or charterers frequently supply phosphine-releasing fumigants and request the Master to arrange for them to be applied to the cargo by the ship's crew during the course (often towards the end) of the voyage. Such requests flagrantly contravene IMO recommendations.

As well as this serious issue (applying apparently different procedural standards to the fumigation of goods according to which fumigant is employed), two further important points should be made in relation to requests to fumigate the goods while on passage:

- To fulfil such a request, it would be necessary to open the weather-deck hatch covers while at sea to apply the fumigant and then to release and re-secure them. This may involve considerable risk and is contrary to good practice
- fumigation is incompatible with the need to ventilate the cargo as may be required by the prevailing climatic conditions. This will exacerbate ship's sweat, if the prevailing conditions are conducive to its formation, and may lead to an adverse effect upon the cargo.

As well as being highly toxic, phosphine gas is also highly flammable with a low flammability level of 1.8% by volume in air.

Therefore, it is likely that potentially explosive mixtures of air and phosphine are encountered during the first 12 to 24 hours of phosphine fumigations when the phosphine concentration in the cargo hold reaches its peak. The high concentrations of phosphine then disperse by diffusion, with the gas diffusing into the less accessible portions of the cargo hold, removing the explosion risk.

Reference should be made to the following IMO guidance:

- The IMDG Code (Reference 19). The IMDG Supplement includes copies of the following three Circulars in 'Recommendations on the Safe Use of Pesticides in Ships'
- *Revised Recommendations on the Safe Use of Pesticides in Ships* (MSC.1/Circ.1358) (Reference 1)

- *Recommendations on the Safe Use of Pesticides in Ships Applicable to the Fumigation of Cargo Holds* (MSC.1/Circ.1264) (Reference 51)
- *Revised Recommendations on the Safe Use of Pesticides in Ships Applicable to the Fumigation of Cargo Transport Units* (MSC.1/Circ.1361/Rev.1) (Reference 52).

The relevant sections should be studied very carefully by Masters, always bearing in mind the following recommendations (Reference 51):

- *"Fumigation in transit should only be carried out at the discretion of the master*
- *in-ship in-transit fumigations with Methyl Bromide should not be carried out. Fumigation with Methyl Bromide should be permitted only when the ship is in the confines of a port (either at anchor or alongside) ... once crew members have disembarked".*

The IMO recommendations permit discretionary usage of phosphine in transit. It is possible that this has led to common misconception that phosphine gas is less toxic and that, consequently, non-specialists such as ships' crew may apply phosphine-releasing preparations prior to or during a sea voyage. It must be clear that this belief is incorrect and potentially dangerous. Masters should never agree to requests for the ship's crew to apply phosphine-releasing preparations in cargo spaces at any time, whether at sea or not.

46.2   Fumigation Continued in Transit

If fumigation that began in port is to be continued in transit, it is strongly recommended that the Master should have access to *Recommendations on the Safe Use of Pesticides in Ships* (Reference 1) and be familiar with all relevant sections. This will enable them to make suitably informed decisions as to whether or not to allow fumigation to be continued in transit and, if such fumigation is allowed, to be aware of and to implement the appropriate safety precautions that should be taken before the ship leaves port and during the course of the voyage.

When specialists apply phosphine in port with a view to the fumigation being continued in transit, they usually install flexible pipework in stows to circulate the phosphine gas better throughout the stow. This provides more effective fumigation of deep stows than would be achieved by applying the fumigant only to the surface of the stow and relying on diffusion alone to deliver the gas to the lower regions of the stow.

When the owners/charterers/Master agree to phosphine fumigation being carried out in transit, the Master should be clear both as to their own obligations and those of the fumigator:

Fumigator
The fumigator provides written documentation in respect of the following:

- Pre-fumigation inspection certificate
- standard safety recommendations for vessels with fumigated grain cargoes
- gastightness statement

- statement of vessel suitability for fumigation and fumigant application compliance
- manufacturer's information or safety data sheet
- first aid and medical treatment instructions
- fumigation certificate
- fumigation plan
- instructions for the use of the phosphine gas detecting equipment
- precautions and procedures during the voyage
- instructions for aeration and ventilation
- precautions and procedures during discharge.

Master

It is the Master's responsibility to:

- Appoint a competent crew member to accompany the fumigator during the inspections/testing of empty holds prior to loading, to determine whether they are gastight or can be made gastight and, if necessary, what work is to be carried out to ensure they are gastight
- ensure the crew is briefed on the fumigation process before fumigation takes place
- ensure that the crew search the vessel thoroughly to ensure there are no stowaways or other unauthorised personnel on board before fumigation takes place
- appoint at least two members of the crew to be trained by the fumigator to act as representatives of the Master during the voyage, to ensure that safe conditions in respect of the fumigation are maintained on board during the voyage
- provide, after the fumigant has been applied and appropriate tests have been completed, a representative to accompany the fumigator to check that all working spaces are free from harmful concentrations of gas
- accept responsibility for maintaining safe conditions in all occupied areas after the fumigator has discharged their responsibilities. The fumigator should formally hand over responsibility to the Master in writing
- fully understand that, even if no leakage of fumigant is detectable at the time of sailing, this does not mean that leakage will not occur at some point during the voyage, due to the movement of the ship or other factors. This is why it is essential that the Master ensures that regular checks are carried out during the voyage
- ensure that during the voyage regular checks for gas leakage are made throughout all occupied areas and the findings recorded in the ship's log. If any leakage is detected, appropriate precautions to avoid any crew being exposed to harmful concentrations must be taken. If requested to do so by the fumigator, the Master may, prior to arrival at the first discharge port, start ventilation of the cargo spaces
- inform the Port Authorities, prior to arrival at the first discharge port, that the cargo has been fumigated in transit
- only allow discharge of the cargo to commence after they are satisfied that the cargo has been correctly ventilated, any aluminium phosphide residues that can be removed have been removed, and any other requirements of the discharge port have been met.

46.3 Compatibility between Fumigant and Cargo

It should be borne in mind that compatibility between the fumigant and the particular cargo being carried needs to be determined. Decisions on this point should be left to specialists. However, it should be noted that, while fumigants are suitable for many different cargoes, they are not suitable for all.

46.4 Charterparties

Charterparties may provide the charterer with an option to fumigate cargoes (usually cereal grains and oil seeds or similar agricultural produce) on board after loading has been completed. While it is convenient for the charterer or the shipper to fumigate cargoes on board instead of ashore, problems may well be experienced as a result of this practice. Before considering the most significant problems that may be encountered, it is worth remembering that, although the goods may have been fumigated prior to loading, this will not necessarily mean they are free of all live insects. Insects in one or other of their metamorphic stages of development may still be present in the products because no treatment against insects is permanent.

A standard sale contract usually requires cargoes such as cereal grains to be free from 'live infestation' at the time of shipment. However, rarely, if ever, will such a cargo be absolutely free from insects.

Although the terms of the contract of sale may only affect the relationship between the buyer and the seller, it makes little sense to expect a Master to adopt a standard that is at odds with the standards anticipated in standard forms of contract.

> If the expectation of the standard contract of sale is that the goods should be 'free' of live infestation at the time of shipment but infestation is clearly apparent to the Master at that time, they are bound to conclude that the goods are not in apparent good order and condition.

If clearly infested goods are loaded on board, even though there is an intention to fumigate the goods upon completion of loading, it is advisable to clause the relevant mate's receipts and B/Ls in terms similar to the following:

"Some live insects detected at the time of shipment on board; cargo to be fumigated by shippers/charterers at their risk and expense upon completion of loading."

If the charterer intends to have the goods fumigated on board, it is also advisable to make a suitable provision in the charterparty in terms similar to the following:

"Charterers shall indemnify the owners in respect of any and all claims of whatsoever nature howsoever arising as a consequence of any infestation of the cargo at the time of shipment on board the vessel and/or the presence of dead insects in the cargo following the fumigation thereof."

Regulations applying in some countries will only allow the presence of limited numbers of dead insects in imported goods. In such circumstances, sale contracts will be drafted to reflect these limitations. However, the fumigation of goods on board anticipates a residue of dead insects remaining within the cargo following the fumigation and it is, therefore, doubtful whether the issuance of clean B/Ls in such circumstances can be justified.

The Master may be told by a representative of the shipper or charterer that the presence of live insects in agricultural produce is quite normal, and that any insects present will be killed during the fumigation process on board after the completion of loading. This is usually the basis of the request for clean B/Ls, notwithstanding the visible presence of insects at the time of shipment. It is, therefore, important to consider this point further.

46.5　Recommendations on the Safe Use of Pesticides in Ships

IMO Circular MSC.1/Circ.1358 covers the use of insecticide sprays, smokes and gaseous fumigants, and it is recommended that it is carried on board all dry cargo ships (Reference 1). Insecticide sprays and smokes can be used effectively on clean empty holds. However, the eradication of either insect infestation or rodents in loaded holds can only be effected with fumigant gas treatment.

Owners' and Masters' attention is drawn specifically to the following sections:

3.1.1.2
"The success of chemical treatments does not lie wholly in the pesticidal activity of the agents used. In addition, an appreciation of the requirements and limitations of the different available methods is required. Crew members can carry out small-scale or 'spot treatments' if they adhere to the manufacturer's instructions and take care to cover the whole area of infestation. However, extensive or hazardous treatments including fumigation and spraying near human and animal food should be placed in the hands of professional operators, who should inform the master of the identity of the active ingredients used, the hazards involved and the precautions to be taken."

When a cargo or empty vessel is to be treated with gaseous fumigation, the following requirement must be observed:

3.1.3.4
"A fumigator-in-charge should be designated by the Fumigation Company, Government Agency or appropriate authority. He should be able to provide documentation to the master proving his competence and authorization. The master should be provided with written instructions by the fumigator-in-charge on the type of fumigant used, the hazards involved, and the precautions to be taken, and in view of the highly toxic nature of all commonly used fumigants these should be followed carefully. Such instructions should be written in a language readily understood by the master or his representative."

Fumigation in port is covered in Section 3.1.4 of the Circular, and particularly important sections are:

3.1.4.1
"Fumigation and aeration (ventilation) of spaces on board a ship should always be carried out in port (alongside or at anchorage). Ships should not be permitted to leave port until gas-free certification has been received from the fumigator-in-charge."

3.1.4.2
"Prior to the application of fumigants to spaces, the crew should be landed and remain ashore until the ship is certified 'gas-free', in writing, by the fumigator-in-charge or other authorized person. During this period a watchman should be posted to prevent unauthorized boarding or entry, and warning signs should be prominently displayed at gangways and at entrances to accommodation."

3.1.4.3
"The fumigator-in-charge should be retained throughout the fumigation period and until such time as the ship is declared gas-free."

3.1.4.5
"The fumigator-in-charge should notify the master in writing of any spaces determined to be safe for re-occupancy by essential crew members prior to the aeration of the ship."

It is common practice to fumigate ships, both empty and loaded, with crew still on board and in some instances this requirement is incorporated in charterparties. However, in some ports, the authorities will not allow fumigation with crew on board. While evacuation of crew provides the safest option, if a Master is prepared or required to allow fumigation with crew on board, it is imperative that the Master is satisfied that the fumigator-in-charge is equipped with proper gas detection and measuring equipment for the fumigant gas being employed. When Draeger tubes are used, the Master should ensure that adequate tubes are available, bearing in mind that each measurement requires the use of a separate tube. The Master should also insist that the fumigator-in-charge remains on board throughout the whole operation, ie from initial closing to completion of ventilation and the issue of a gas-free certificate. The Master should also be satisfied that the fumigator-in-charge regularly checks for gas leakages in areas where crew may be working or resting.

MSC.1/Circ.1264 covers in-transit fumigation of cargo holds, which is now a fairly common practice, particularly for bulk cargoes of agricultural products. With this type of operation, the Master is responsible for the safety of all on board their ship.

3.3.2 *"Fumigation continued in transit"*

3.3.2.1
"Fumigation in transit should only be carried out at the discretion of the master. This should be clearly understood by owners, charterers, and all other parties involved when considering the transport of cargoes that may be infested. Due consideration should be taken of this when assessing the options of fumigation. The master should be aware of the regulations of the flag State Administration with regard to in-transit fumigation. The application of the process should be with the agreement of the port State Administration. The process may be considered under two headings:

.1   fumigation in which treatment is intentionally continued in a sealed space during a voyage and in which no aeration has taken place before sailing; and

.2   in-port cargo fumigation where some aeration is carried out before sailing, but where a clearance certificate for the cargo hold(s) cannot be issued because of residual gas and the cargo hold(s) has been re-sealed before sailing."

3.3.2.2

"Before a decision on sailing with a fumigated cargo hold(s) is made it should be taken into account that, due to operational conditions, the circumstances outlined in 3.3.2.1.2 may arise unintentionally, eg a ship may be required to sail at a time earlier than anticipated when the fumigation was started. In such circumstances the potential hazards may be as great as with a planned in-transit fumigation and all the precautions in the following paragraphs should be observed."

3.3.2.3

"Before a decision is made as to whether a fumigation treatment planned to be commenced in port and continued at sea should be carried out, special precautions are necessary. These include the following:

.1   at least two members of the crew (including one officer) who have received appropriate training (see 3.3.2.6) should be designated as the trained representatives of the master responsible for ensuring that safe conditions in accommodation, engine-room and other working spaces are maintained after the fumigator-in-charge has handed over that responsibility to the master (see 3.3.2.12); and

.2   the trained representatives of the master should brief the crew before a fumigation takes place and satisfy the fumigator-in-charge that this has been done."

3.3.2.4

"Empty cargo holds are to be inspected and/or tested for leakage with instruments so that proper sealing can be done before or after loading. The fumigator-in-charge, accompanied by a trained representative of the master or a competent person, should determine whether the cargo holds to be treated are or can be made sufficiently gastight to prevent leakage of the fumigant to the accommodation, engine-rooms and other working spaces in the ship. Special attention should be paid to potential problem areas such as bilge and cargo line systems. On completion of such inspection and/or test, the fumigator-in-charge should supply to the master for his retention a signed statement that the inspection and/or test has been performed, what provisions have been made and that the cargo holds are or can be made satisfactory for fumigation. Whenever a cargo hold is found not to be sufficiently gastight, the fumigator-in-charge should issue a signed statement to the master and the other parties involved."

3.3.2.5

"Accommodation, engine-rooms, areas designated for use in navigation of the ship, frequently visited working areas and stores, such as the forecastle head spaces, adjacent to cargo holds being subject to fumigation in transit should be treated in accordance with the provisions of 3.3.2.13. Special attention should be paid to gas concentration safety checks in problem areas referred to in 3.3.2.4."

3.3.2.6
"The trained representatives of the master designated in 3.3.2.3 should be provided and be familiar with:

.1   the information in the relevant Safety Data Sheet; and

.2   the instructions for use, eg on the fumigant label or package itself, such as the recommendations of the fumigant manufacturer concerning methods of detection of the fumigant in air, its behaviour and hazardous properties, symptoms of poisoning, relevant first aid and special medical treatment and emergency procedures."

3.3.2.7
"The ship should carry:

.1   gas-detection equipment and adequate fresh supplies of service items for the fumigant(s) concerned as required by 3.3.2.12, together with instructions for its use and the occupational exposure limit values set by the flag State regulations for safe working conditions;

.2   instructions on disposal of residual fumigant material;

.3   at least four sets of adequate respiratory protective equipment; and

.4   a copy of the latest version of the Medical First Aid Guide for Use in Accidents Involving Dangerous Goods (MFAG), including appropriate medicines and medical equipment."

3.3.2.12
"Upon discharging his agreed responsibilities, the fumigator-in-charge should formally hand over to the master in writing responsibility for maintaining safe conditions in all occupied spaces. The fumigator-in-charge should ensure that gas-detection and respiratory protection equipment carried on the ship is in good order, and that adequate fresh supplies of consumable items are available to allow sampling as required in 3.3.2.13."

3.3.2.13
"Gas concentration safety checks at all appropriate locations, which should at least include the spaces as indicated in 3.3.2.5, should be continued throughout the voyage at least at eight-hour intervals or more frequently if so advised by the fumigator-in-charge. These readings should be recorded in the ship's log-book."

It has been noted that some fumigations are unsatisfactory due to three basic causes:

•   Excessively heavy infestation or infestation with fumigant-resistant strains of various insect species

•   inadequate initial dosing

•   insufficient time allowed for total penetration of the fumigant gas.

It is impossible for Masters to have sufficient expertise to be able to decide whether a proposed fumigation operation should prove satisfactory. Although it is possible to obtain expert advice on this matter, it is difficult for anyone to advise other than in general terms when they have not seen either the ship or the cargo. It is the fumigators' duty to perform proper fumigation and, if they are employed by shippers or charterers, it is the latter's duty to ensure that the fumigators are competent. However, to safeguard the shipowner's position, the Master must insist on receiving a certificate of fumigation from the fumigators which states:

- The fumigant used
- the dose level in terms of weight of fumigant per volume of hold, eg g/m^3
- the dates and times when fumigation commenced and ceased (ie when either ventilation fans were turned on or hatches were opened, whichever was the earlier).

If insects and/or mites are observed in or on any cargo, it is helpful to take specimens, transfer them to a small bottle with a secure closure, such as an aspirin bottle, and place it in a refrigerator. The specimens can be supplied to experts at a later date if there are complaints at the time of discharge.

If heavy infestation is observed, surveyors should be instructed to draw substantial samples of affected cargo (1 kg lots), which should be sealed and refrigerated pending expert examination to determine the level and nature of the infestation.

Shipowners are particularly warned that receivers in certain countries, particularly in the Middle East, may reject cargo, with the backing of their government authorities, if minimal live infestation is detected, or even if the cargo is contaminated with a very small quantity of dead insect residues. It follows that, if a Master detects any insect infestation when cargoes are being loaded for Syria, Egypt and some other eastern Mediterranean countries, they should inform the shipowners immediately so they may seek advice from the Club.

46.6 Fumigation of Bulk and Bagged Cargo with Ventilation in Port

This procedure can be used either after loading and prior to sailing or on arrival at the discharge port prior to discharging.

After loading and prior to sailing
Phosphine fumigation and ventilation in port, prior to sailing, will normally take from 1 to 2 weeks to complete and therefore is only occasionally specified. All procedures as for in-transit fumigation should be followed to ensure safe and effective fumigation.

At discharge port prior to discharge
The crew should be landed and remain ashore until the ship is certified gas-free in writing by the fumigator-in-charge. The fumigator is responsible for the safety and efficiency of the fumigation, but crew members may remain in attendance to ensure the safety of the ship, provided they adhere to safety instructions issued by the fumigator-in-charge.

The ventilation of fumigant from cargoes can be a very slow process if sufficiently powerful ventilation is not available. The Master (or their representative) should confirm that the fumigator has ensured that residues of gas are below the TLV throughout all parts of the cargo and holds. All procedures as for in-transit fumigation should be followed to ensure safe and effective fumigation.

46.7 In-transit Fumigation of Freight Containers

Fumigation of containers is normally undertaken to ensure that, when the goods arrive at the discharge port, they are free from live pests/insects.

Containers are normally fumigated and then ventilated prior to being loaded on board the ship. Containers that have been fumigated and ventilated, and where a 'certificate of freedom from harmful concentration of gas' has been issued, can be loaded on board ships as if they had not been fumigated.

Frequently, containers are fumigated but not ventilated prior to loading and these containers are therefore fumigated in-transit, as the ventilation process will not take place until after they have been discharged from the ship. The carriage of containers in-transit under fumigation is covered by the IMDG Code (Reference 19) whereby these containers are classified in Section 3.2, Dangerous Goods List as *Fumigated Cargo Transport Unit Class 9 UN 3359*. Reference should also be made to MSC.1/ Circ.1361/Rev.1 (Reference 52) which may be found in the IMDG Code Supplement in the chapter entitled *Recommendations for the safe use of pesticides in ships*.

> **WARNING – Containers are sometimes shipped under fumigation with no warning notices attached and no accompanying documentation stating they have been fumigated. This process is in direct contravention of the IMDG Code. There may be dangerous levels of fumigant gas inside the container when it arrives at its destination, which is both illegal and dangerous.**

DANGER

THIS UNIT IS UNDER FUMIGATION

WITH: _____

APPLIED ON/DATE: _____

TIME: _____

VENTILATED ON/DATE: ____ _____

DO NOT ENTER

Obligations on the fumigator
- The fumigator must ensure that, as far as is practicable, the container is made gastight before the fumigant is applied
- the fumigator must ensure that the containers are clearly marked with appropriate warning signs stating the type of fumigant used and the date applied and all other details as required by the IMDG Code and MSC.1/Circ.1361/Rev.1 (Reference 52)
- the fumigator must ensure that the agreed formulation of fumigant is used at the correct dosage to comply with the contractual requirements.

Obligations on the exporter
- The exporter must ensure that the containers are clearly marked by the fumigator with appropriate warning signs stating the type of fumigant used and the date applied and all other details as required by the IMDG Code and MSC.1/Cric.1361/Rev.1 (Reference 52)
- the exporter must ensure that the Master is informed of the fumigation prior to the loading of the containers
- the exporter must ensure that shipping documents show the date of fumigation, the type of fumigant and the amount used all as required in the IMDG Code and MSC.1/Cric.1361/Rev.1, specifically Section 5.5.2.4.

Obligations on the Master
- The Master must ensure that they know where containers under fumigation are stowed
- the Master must ensure availability of suitable gas detection equipment on board for the types of fumigant present, and that instructions for the use of the equipment have been received
- prior to arrival of the vessel at the discharge port, the Master should inform the authorities at the discharge point that the vessel is carrying containers under fumigation
- if the Master (or their representative) suspects that unmarked containers may have been fumigated and loaded on board, they should take suitable precautions and report their suspicions to the authorities prior to arrival at the discharge port.

Obligations on the receivers
- The receiver (or their agent) must ensure that any fumigant residues are removed and the container checked and certificated as being free from harmful concentrations of fumigant by a suitably qualified person before the cargo in the container is removed.

46.8 Phosphine Methodologies

The various methods of phosphine application that can be considered for in-transit fumigation of bulk or bagged cargoes in ships' holds include the following. The actual method to be used will be specified by an expert.

1. Application of tablets or pellets to the cargo surface (or into the top half metre).

   High concentrations of gas build up in the headspace, potentially resulting in a lot of leakage through the hatch covers unless these are very well sealed. There is very little penetration down into the cargo and powdery residues cannot be removed. This method produces a good kill of insects in the top part of the cargo but has negligible effect on eggs or juveniles or even adults in the lower part of the cargo.

2. Application of tablets or pellets by probing into the cargo a few metres.

   There is less loss of gas through hatch covers than in method 1 and better penetration of gas than when applied on the surface only. However, it is unlikely to be fully effective unless holds are relatively shallow and voyage time relatively long. Powdery residues cannot be removed.

3. Application of tablets or pellets by deep probing into the full depth of the cargo.

   This is difficult to achieve and currently practically impossible if the cargo is more than 10 m deep. However, it ensures effective fumigation provided voyage time is long enough to allow gas to distribute. Powdery residues cannot be removed.

4. Application of aluminium phosphide in blankets, sachets or sleeves placed on the surface of the cargo (or into the top half metre).

   All points are the same as for method 1, except that, with this method, powdery residues can be removed prior to discharge.

5. Application of tablets or pellets by probing into the cargo a few metres in retrievable sleeves.

   All points are the same as for method 2, except that, with this method, powdery residues can be removed prior to discharge.

6. Fitting of an enclosed, powered recirculation system to the hold and application of aluminium phosphide tablets or pellets to the surface.

   This method will ensure the gas is distributed throughout the cargo evenly and rapidly making maximum use of the fumigant in the shortest possible time. Powdery residues cannot be removed.

7. Fitting of an enclosed, powered recirculation system to the hold and application of aluminium phosphide in blankets, sachets or sleeves on the surface or probed into the top 1 or 2 m.

   All points are the same as for method 6, except that, with this method, powdery residues can be removed. Also, gaseous residues can be removed more easily than with other methods as, once the powdery residues have been removed, the recirculation system can be used to assist this to happen rapidly.

8. Deep probing into the full depth of the cargo (however deep) with tablets or pellets (in retrievable sleeves when required).

   This method is being developed in Canada but is not yet available. Deep probing could also utilise pre-inserted pipes. It will enable good distribution of gas to be achieved without the requirement for a powered recirculation system, provided the voyage is long enough.

9. Use of powered recirculation system with phosphine from cylinders.

This method is not yet available but could be in the future and will enable phosphine fumigation to be carried out without using aluminium phosphide. This will mean no powdery residues to deal with and therefore residue and safety problems at the discharge port will be minimised. A powered recirculation system will be needed to enable this system to work with maximum efficacy.

Chapter 47 –
Fishmeal Cargoes

If an insufficient quantity of antioxidant is added to fishmeal products at the time of production, oxidation will start at some stage. This can result in carbonisation and/or fire.

Fishmeal is a product made from fish, as well as bones and offal from processed fish. It is a brown powder or cake obtained after cooking, pressing (particularly important for oily fish, to extract as much oil as possible), drying and then grinding the fish trimmings. It is nutrient rich and high in protein, and primarily used in the diets of domestic animals. Four or five tonnes of fish are needed to manufacture one tonne of dry fishmeal.

In some areas of the world where industrial processing plants are not available, fish are simply dried out in the sun before grinding them into fishmeal. However, the end product is poor in comparison to modern methods. Fishmeal can be made from almost any type of seafood but is generally manufactured from wild-caught, small marine fish that contain a high percentage of bones and oil, and are therefore usually deemed not suitable for direct human consumption. The fish caught solely for fishmeal purposes are termed 'industrial'. Virtually any fish or shellfish in the sea can be used to make fishmeal, although rare/poisonous species are avoided.

The standard products are classified as hazardous cargoes and are included in the IMDG Code (Reference 19) in Class 4.2 (Substances liable to spontaneous combustion) or Class 9 (Miscellaneous dangerous substances and articles), UN numbers 1374 and 2216.

Figure 47.1: Small fish, deemed unsuitable for human consumption, ready to be processed at a fishmeal processing plant.

The original fishmeal trade involved products now falling into the Class 4.2 category. The basic requirements for the carriage of cargo of this type were that it was bagged and aged, for a period of not less than 28 days, between production and loading on the carrying ship. Stowage was by the double strip stow method, where the bags were stowed longitudinally in the cargo spaces with transverse channels every two bags. Cargo stowed in this way was to be ventilated throughout a voyage, weather permitting. There were also requirements in terms of maximum oil content, maximum and minimum moisture contents and temperature at the time of loading. Strict adherence to these conditions permitted generally uneventful carriage of fishmeal over protracted voyages. However, the stowage requirements resulted in a high stowage factor and were expensive in both labour and materials (dunnage).

47.1   Self-heating

It has been known for many years that heating of fishmeal to the point of fire is due to aerial oxidation of reactive chemical sites on fish oil molecules. All oxidation reactions are associated with the production of heat, so in the double ship stow method the most reactive material was oxidised during the aging process prior to loading and the residual oxidisable material reacted with atmospheric oxygen at a rate at which the heat produced could be removed by ventilating air.

Certain shipowners approached the problem of reducing the rate of oxidation by using inert gas. Special ships were built, which were equipped with onboard inert gas producing equipment similar to that used on tankers and with hatch cover systems that were substantially airtight. This system works satisfactorily provided the number of load and discharge ports served on a single voyage is limited. However, each time a hatch cover is opened, part of the inert atmosphere is replaced by air and the inerting operation must be repeated when the hatches are closed.

The fishmeal industry sought to resolve the problem by modifying the product to render it inert or less susceptible to oxidation. This was achieved by the addition of antioxidant during the production of the meal. Fishmeal treated with antioxidant is categorised under Class 9 in the IMDG Code (Reference 19). Antioxidant-treated oily fishmeal, conforming to the requirements of the Code, can be carried either as a bulk cargo or in bags in block stow. This has permitted relaxation of both stowage and ventilation requirements during ocean carriage. Introduction of antioxidant-treated fishmeal on a large scale roughly coincided with drastic fall in the annual production of fishmeal on the west coast of South America. However, sufficient cargo was shipped for it to be apparent that the process could provide a stable product for carriage in bulk or block stow.

Fishmeal is produced by cooking the fish and extracting oil and aqueous fluids mechanically. The cake that is produced is then dried and milled. The milled meal is cooled and treated with antioxidant, usually by spraying the meal as it passes through a trough. Antioxidants used are ethoxyquin, BHT (butylated hydroxytoluene) or tocopherols.

Heating of fishmeal is due to atmospheric oxidation, but the chemical process is complex and involves a series of reactions. The amount of heat produced by these reactions varies and those producing most energy are those towards the end of the series. The addition of an antioxidant stops the reaction chain before these later reactions can occur.

As treated fishmeal ages, the antioxidant additive is used up. If an insufficient quantity is added at the time of production, it will be depleted before the condition of the fishmeal has been stabilised. As a result, and at some stage after production, oxidation will start, producing substantial quantities of heat and the risk of a serious rise in temperature in the affected meal. However, this will not be evident until some time after loading. This was the case in shipments from both Chile and Peru during the 1980s.

When serious heating occurs, it can result in carbonisation and/or fire. Many small isolated pockets of bags may be involved. Incident investigations have identified these pockets in regions of maximum ventilation and also in the interiors of large block stows, and it follows that the primary cause is the intrinsic reactivity of the contents of a few bags rather than unsuitable stowage or ventilation.

47.2 Bagged Fishmeal

Bagged fishmeal presents the majority of problems.

47.2.1 Documentation

The Master should have on board a copy of the latest edition of the IMDG Code (Reference 19), which includes entries for unstabilised fishmeal and for stabilised (ie antioxidant treated) fishmeal. The Master should also have a copy of the International Maritime Solid Bulk Cargoes Code (IMSBC Code) (Reference 17), where there is an entry for stabilised fishmeal.

> The Master must obtain and retain certificates for antioxidant-treated fishmeal, as required by the IMDG Code, covering all the cargo loaded. These certificates should include all the information required to ascertain that the product conforms with the requirements for temperature, weathering and packing, as set out in the special provisions in Volume 2 of the Code.

Since deregulation of the fishmeal trade in Peru, certificates may be issued by a person or company recognised by the Government of Peru, the competent authority. Certificates for Chilean fishmeal, which very rarely gives problems, are issued by the Instituto de Fomento Pesquero (IFOP), the Chilean Institute of Fisheries Development, a government agency that supports the sustainable development of the country's fishing and aquaculture resources.

47.2.2 Action to be Taken by the Ship or Surveyors Acting for the Ship During Loading

The temperature of the contents of as many bags as possible should be measured. Where these do not comply with the requirements under the IMDG Code, the relevant bags must be rejected. If high temperatures are observed, it may be necessary to stop loading the relevant parcel to allow more extensive temperature checking. The Code states that fishmeal *"shall not be transported if the temperature at time of loading exceeds 35°C or 5°C above the ambient temperature, whichever is higher."* Any wet, water-stained or caked bags should be rejected. It may be difficult to detect staining when fishmeal cargoes are packed in black woven polypropylene bags, so it may be necessary when such staining is observed to slow or suspend loading to allow a proper examination. Torn bags should also be rejected.

47.2.3 Stowage

Standard stowage practice for bagged cargoes should be adopted, ie use of double dunnage on decks and tank tops and provision of a spar ceiling or adequate dunnage to prevent the cargo coming into contact with the ship's sides, pipes and bulkheads, particularly those that are liable to become heated.

Details of stowage precautions for fishmeal can be found in the IMDG Code (Reference 19). For UN 1374 fishmeal, where loose bags are carried, double strip stowage is recommended provided there is good surface and through ventilation. For UN 2216 fishmeal, where loose bags are carried, no special ventilation is required for block stowages of bagged cargo. Flammable materials, such as paint, should be removed from store rooms immediately above or adjacent to cargo spaces loaded with bagged fishmeal.

47.3 Bagged Fishmeal Carried in Containers

Bagged stabilised fishmeal (ie UN 2216, Class 9) may be carried in freight containers as indicated in Volume 1 of the IMDG Code (Reference 19). Containers will usually be delivered alongside already sealed. However, if the Master is in a position to see the containers being stuffed, he or she should ensure that they are clean and that the maximum quantity of bags are placed in each container to restrict the free air space to a minimum. In any event, the Master should ensure that the container doors and other openings are properly tape-sealed to minimise possible air ingress.

On the voyage, the temperature of the outsides of containers, if stowed in accessible positions, should be checked regularly by feeling them, in any event as indicated in Volume 1 of the IMDG Code: *"Temperature readings in the hold should be taken once a day early in the morning during the voyage and recorded"*. If any container becomes hot, it should be cooled using water; *"... and the consequent risk to the stability of the ship should be considered."* If smoke is seen issuing from a container, a hole should be punched in the side at the top of the container, a hose nozzle fitted and the container flooded.

Masters must ensure there is reasonable access to any containers stowed under deck.

47.4   Installation and Operation of Temperature Sensors

The IMSBC Code (Reference 17) requires that the temperature of cargo in each hold is monitored throughout the voyage. This can only be satisfactorily performed by the installation of remote reading sensors that are normally connected to a switch box that also has a connection for a readout meter. The installation is usually carried out by a specialist survey organisation employed by the shippers or charterers. It is generally recommended that installation is not performed by the ship's crew as they should be solely engaged in observing loading operations. It is common to install sensors at two or three levels in a lower hold and one or two levels on a tween deck, depending on the depths of the relevant spaces. Between four and eight sensors are distributed at each level, depending on the cross-sectional area of the cargo spaces.

The Master should obtain a drawing from the installation operator indicating the locations of sensors in each cargo space. At completion of loading, once all sensors have been installed, the Master or chief officer should check the temperature as indicated by each sensor, in the presence of the installation operator. This will ensure that the ship's command is conversant with the equipment. It will also show whether each sensor is functioning correctly.

Abnormally high or low figures will indicate malfunction from the outset of the voyage. At this stage, it is impractical to replace sensors and such an operation should not be attempted. The installation operator should be asked to sign the entry covering the first set of recordings, which should be entered, as read, in a book. Subsequently, the figures for each sensor should be read and recorded in the book each watch for the first few days of the voyage. If they are more or less stable, they may subsequently be read at eight-hourly intervals, as required under the *Carriage* requirements for UN 2216 (stabilised fishmeal) in the IMSBC Code (Reference 17). If some temperatures in a space start to rise, temperature reading should revert to four-hourly intervals for all sensors in the space.

From experience, it is known that there can be some increase in temperature at the outset of a voyage (possibly up to a value of 34°C) as recorded from some sensors, after which the temperature stabilises. This situation need not give rise to concern. If, however, the temperature of one or more sensors exceeds 40°C and continues to rise, the Master should take steps to seal the relevant hatch covers using sealing tape and, if necessary, plastic or foam sealant or cement. Consideration should be given at this stage to sealing ventilation openings. Owners and charterers should be informed of the temperature figures and their advice/instructions sought. Expert advice should be requested to advise owners or charterers when this situation arises and advice is normally given on the basis of temperature trends over a time period. Therefore, when a Master is forwarding information, they should ensure it is clear and the temperature figures for each cargo space are always reported in the same sequence.

In any event, the instructions under *Ventilation* for UN 2216 in the IMSBC Code (Reference 17) should be followed, ie if any temperature sensors indicate a cargo temperature in excess of 55°C, the cargo space and any interconnecting cargo space should be sealed effectively and ventilation stopped. If self-heating continues, CO_2 or inert gas should be injected as stipulated in the fire-fighting manual provided by the installers of the system. The injection should take place slowly over a 24-hour period. It is undesirable to inject less gas than is recommended in the manual, even though this means that only a few cargo spaces can be so treated.

It should be appreciated that any cargo heating results from an oxidation process. This means that the oxygen concentration in a hold is depleted and the concentration of nitrogen (an inert gas) increases. Therefore, in a sealed hold, cargo heating tends to be self-quenching.

It is of paramount importance that the Master has all necessary materials on board to allow very efficient sealing of cargo spaces to minimise atmospheric interchange. Efficient sealing may be a time-consuming operation, but should never be skimped.

Technically, provided that hold sealing is adequate, it would be possible for a ship with cargo heating in all her holds, to sail safely with her CO_2 supply exhausted (assuming a sufficient reserve for the engine room). However, such an action would only be recommended if effective sealing could be guaranteed. Under normal circumstances, where there is obvious progressive heating, a ship would be best advised to go to a port of refuge to obtain adequate CO_2 supplies. This often involves fitting a bulk tank containing several tonnes of CO_2. If considered necessary, further sealing should be performed while the ship remains in port.

Unless special circumstances prevail, sealed hatch covers should not be opened until the first discharge port for that hold is reached.

An accurate assessment of the situation in any cargo space can be obtained by measuring the oxygen concentration via a pipe connected to an oxygen meter. This is introduced ideally via dedicated points of access, or alternatively by slightly opening an access manhole. The manhole should be closed and secured immediately after measurements have been taken. Although some ships have oxygen meters on board and have crew conversant with their use, it is generally recommended that, where possible, measurements of oxygen levels are made by surveyors. If they are made by the ship, the instrument should be checked immediately before use by measuring the oxygen concentration of the external atmosphere (20.8%). When oxygen levels are below 10%, heating is greatly restricted. Even without the use of CO_2, oxygen concentration may drop to this level in a few days where hatches are effectively sealed and there is a substantial quantity of cargo heating in a hold.

47.5   Discharge

Heating cargoes (if any) should be discharged first. However, where this is not practicable, the rate of spread of heating in a cargo space can be drastically reduced by maintaining a low oxygen concentration. This is preferably by the use of CO_2 or, when supplies are not available, by keeping the holds sealed. It must be appreciated, however, that once the holds are opened for discharge and the oxygen concentration is allowed to rise to at least 20.8%, which is necessary for safe working in the hold, heating will resume at an accelerating rate. Therefore, attempts should be made to discharge pockets of heating cargo as soon as possible. This can sometimes be achieved without difficulty. However, on occasion, smoke generation becomes excessive and prevents manual operations. There are several options for dealing with this problem and the choice depends on the circumstances prevailing.

The first option is to reseal the hold and inject CO_2, the minimum quantity injected being that recommended by the installers of the ship's CO_2 system. Again, this operation should take place over a 24-hour period. The hold should then be left sealed for at least four days. The oxygen concentration must again be allowed to rise to 20.8% before personnel are allowed into the space to resume discharge. This option, when successful, results in the minimum amount of cargo damage but extends the discharging period. It may be considered impractical if it has to be repeated several times.

The second option is to control smoke evolution by the use of water applied through a fine spray directly onto the smoking cargo, while discharge proceeds. This procedure, if undertaken properly, results in limited water damage to part of the cargo. However, excessive water is often applied, particularly when the local fire service intervenes, and the amount of cargo wetted can then be substantial.

The third and last option, which should only be used when other methods have failed, is to use a water spray to control smoke evolution or fire, and discharge heating pockets by grab. The procedure obviously results in more cargo damage.

If the cargo ignites, the flames should be extinguished with a water spray. Fires in fishmeal may ignite flammable cargo in adjacent spaces with disastrous results. It is reiterated that flammable materials should not be stored in storerooms adjacent to or above holds loaded with fishmeal.

Damaged and apparently sound cargo should always be separated at the time of discharge. However, even badly heated cargo has feed value and can be incorporated in cattle feed.

Chapter 48 – Palletised Cargoes

Wooden pallets are used extensively for the transportation of cargo, both in containers and in conventional breakbulk seagoing ships. Palletising of cargo helps to speed up cargo handling operations by consolidating merchandise into units that can be easily and rapidly handled. Both the efficiency and the reliability of the system depend upon the quality of the construction of the pallet and on the measures taken to protect the goods and to secure them in place.

Care should be taken not to stow pallets of inadequate construction as this is likely to lead to widespread collapse of the stow and damage to the cargo.

When pallets were first introduced into the trade, they were generally of robust construction. As experience was gained, it was found necessary to secure the goods adequately to the pallet by means of metal strapping bands and to protect them by providing a covering.

Nearly all palletised cargoes are received directly from the producers/manufacturers of the goods, and shippers and shipowners should appreciate that, while pallets may appear to be adequate when stacked ashore in a warehouse, they must be strong enough to be transported to the docks, unloaded, picked up by forklift trucks, carried over uneven surfaces and finally loaded on board ship.

There are formal recommendations covering the design, construction and strength of pallets. These are set out in ISO 6780:2003 (Reference 79). Some freight conferences specify the standards they require to ensure that a pallet will be capable of handling its proper load adequately and supporting four tiers of similar pallets.

Flimsy pallets, constructed from soft wood and designed for storage of lightweight cargo in warehouses, are sometimes presented for loading onto ships. They may be dangerously overloaded and unable to withstand the rigours of an ocean voyage or stevedoring operations. In some cases, the design of the pallets may be adequate, but the materials used and the standards of workmanship are poor.

Experience shows that little consideration is given to whether the strength of the pallet matches the weight of the goods it is to carry. Often the dimensions do not match, resulting in bags or cartons projecting beyond the edges of the platform. Frequently, the merchandise is badly stacked or badly secured and is in danger of shifting.

Other inadequacies relate to the methods of securing goods to the pallets. One form is the shrink wrap plastic cover, which is applied by placing a large piece of plastic over the stack of cartons or bags on the pallet and then applying heat at the folds to shrink the plastic onto the load.

It is a common misconception that this method alone ensures adequate packing, and that the entire load is therefore secured to the pallet. If the load is secured to the pallet by any other means, this is often in the form of weak plastic strapping that may stretch easily.

During the various stages of transportation, as a result of the forces acting upon the ship and its cargo, pallets can break or fall apart. Loads can also become lopsided and unstable, potentially ending up as damaged breakbulk cargo.

The method of handling pallets within dock areas may also cause damage to the pallets and/or goods. Where forklift trucks are used, the forks may be misdirected, penetrating the goods rather than passing beneath the pallet. This is particularly important if the cargo on the pallet consists of a liquid or some form of granular material (in bags) that shifts or runs easily. The stability of the load can be compromised by leaking cargo. When bagged cargo bulges through the gaps of the planks forming the pallet base, or where the planks in the pallet base break in weak pallets, damage can occur when the pallet is picked up.

Figure 48.1: Example of best practice when transporting palletised items by sea. The contents of the heavy duty bag do not overhang the pallet, they are wrapped in plastic to avoid weather damage or items spilling, and the item is secured to the pallet with plastic strapping. The ship's crane can then lift the heavy duty bag/pallet by its lifting strops.

48.1   Handling of Pallets

* Where slings are utilised, particularly wire slings, they should be of adequate strength. At the very least, wide nylon belts and spreaders should be utilised

* where forklift trucks are utilised in handling pallets, care should be taken to ensure that the forks are not pointing parallel to the base boards of the pallets, otherwise there is a danger of tearing the longitudinal timbers from the base

* where it is necessary to load pallets in twos, this should be achieved by utilising special lifting equipment

* where pallets are handled singly, perhaps because of the low safe working load (SWL) of the crane, they should be handled on solid pallets with suitable pallet-lifting gear attached

* the use of C-hooks, originally developed for the handling of fruit cargoes, is now widespread on palletised goods and has proved very successful

* where holds are completely filled with pallets, the incorporation of 'key pallets' in the stowage will assist at the time of discharge. This may be achieved by pre-slinging the pallets with strops or other similar suitable appliances to gain access to the remainder of the stow.

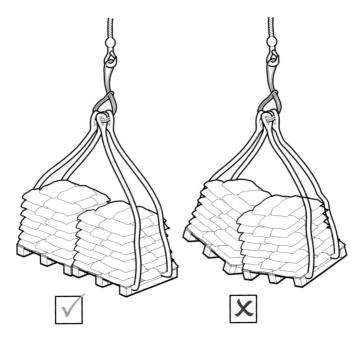

Figure 48.2: Example of best practice for handling palletised cargoes.

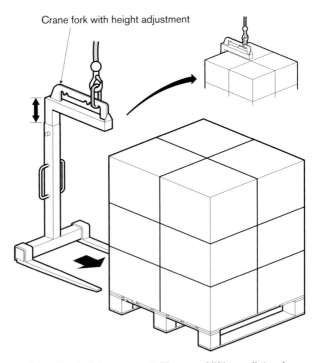

Crane fork with height adjustment

Figure 48.3: A 'C-hook', which is a more stable way of lifting pallets when compared to strops and slings.

48.2   Stacking of Pallets

When stacking goods on pallets, a number of steps can be taken to prevent or reduce some of the more obvious problems:

* The platform of the pallet should be covered with a sheet of cardboard to prevent bulging bags or damage by contact with the sharp edges of the timber platform

* to prevent stacks of polypropylene or paper bags sliding, a square of strong kraft paper can be inserted between each horizontal tier to bind the layers of bags together

* where multiple paper bags are concerned, the bags can be attached to each other by a patch of glue on the centre surface of each bag

* to prevent the secure strapping from damaging the bags when tightened, a thin square plywood sheet or a sheet of strong cardboard should be placed on the outer perimeter edge of the pallet platform and inserted between the securing bands and the bags. This will also provide protection against the fork ends of the lifting trucks.

Figure 48.4: Engine spares and equipment are regularly stored and transported on pallets. These can be hard to rig and lift due to the centre of gravity (CG) of the item being unknown.

Chapter 49 –
Radioactive Cargoes

If a radioactive cargo is not 'excepted matter', the consignment is not covered by P&I Club Rules and the consignor must arrange nuclear liability insurance and produce a certificate of financial security.

Transport of radioactive materials is a well-regulated international activity and it may be surprising to many people to know that approximately 15,000,000 radioactive packages are transported around the world each year, with up to 1,500,000 of these by sea. Records show that the transport of radioactive material is a highly safe activity in terms of people and the environment because of the regulatory standards to which the carriage is subject internationally, and the careful application of them by industry and transporters. As with the transport of all hazardous materials, the carrier places great reliance on the consignor to declare the materials correctly. In the case of liability insurance, there is an additional question of whether or not the consignment is 'excepted matter'. If it is not 'excepted matter', the consignment is not covered by P&I Club Rules and the consignor must arrange nuclear liability insurance and produce a certificate of financial security from their government before the consignment can be moved.

The following case involving an international shipment highlights the fact that, while Members may think they know that a certain shipment is probably 'excepted matter', they should always consult the Club for their nuclear consultant's confirmation.

Two consignments of uranium – one of uranium trioxide and one of uranium metal ingots – were shown on the dangerous goods note as being *Radioactive Material, Low Specific Activity (LSA-II),* and as being *'fissile excepted'.* However, the dangerous goods note also showed that, from the weights of uranium and of the U_{235} fissile isotope, the uranium trioxide was 5.55% fissile and the uranium ingots were 1.23% fissile. In each case, the limit for the quantity involved to be fissile excepted was 1.0%. When the Member refused these consignments, the consignor reverted with revised weights for the U_{235} fissile isotope that brought both consignments within the 1.0% limit. The Club's nuclear consultant was able to confirm that the revised figures were correct by obtaining the relevant data independently from the consignee, asking them what they were expecting to receive.

In this case, the outcome was satisfactory, but if the U_{235} fissile isotope weights in the first dangerous goods note had been correct and the packages had been stowed on a vessel in the proximity of other fissile material, there would have been a real risk of a 'criticality excursion' (chain reaction).

The Association's Rule 5, Exclusion of Nuclear Risks, applies.

49.1 The Regulatory Framework (IAEA – UN Model Regulations – IMDG Code)

Transport of radioactive materials is subject to comprehensive and strict regulation. The International Atomic Energy Agency (IAEA) has developed and continuously revises these regulations, which are used as the basis for relevant sections of the IMDG Code (Reference 19). The IAEA approach is that the safety of radioactive material transport is defined by the design, construction and operation of the packages used and that the level of package safety is proportional to the hazard of the material it contains. UF_6 packages, as an example, must be able to withstand normal and/or accident conditions during transport. They are designed in accordance with ISO Standard 7195 (Reference 80), which is specific to UF_6 packages.

The packages must be approved by the Competent Authority, and this includes quality assurance during construction and operation, and periodic testing during use.

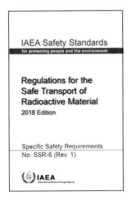

49.2   UOC and UF₆ – Production, Processing and Use

The raw material to make fuel for nuclear power stations is uranium ore. The ore is first ground and purified at the mining site using chemical and physical processes to produce a dry powder of natural uranium oxide, known as uranium ore concentrate (UOC).

This material contains 0.72% of the uranium 235 isotope (U_{235}), which is fissionable. The rest consists of non-fissionable uranium 238 and small traces of other naturally occurring isotopes such as thorium.

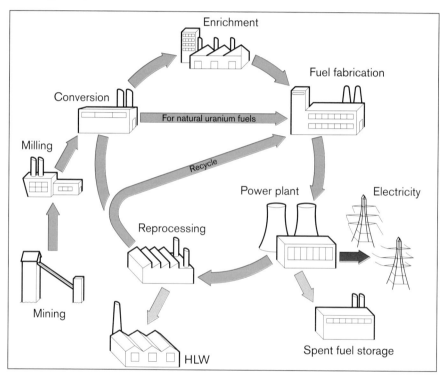

Figure 49.1: Nuclear fuel production processes.

To be manufactured into nuclear fuel for pressurised water or light water reactors, the fuel needs to contain 1 to 5% U_{235}. This is achieved by 'enriching' the proportion of U_{235} in a centrifuge enrichment plant. The feedstock needed for this process is in the form of natural uranium hexafluoride (UF_6).

Uranium ore concentrate is transported worldwide to conversion plants in Europe and North America, where it is converted into uranium hexafluoride by reacting it with fluorine gas. Commercial enrichment plants are in operation in North America and Western and Eastern Europe, which gives rise to the international transport of UF_6 between conversion plants and enrichment plants.

Following enrichment, UF_6 is transported worldwide to nuclear fuel manufacturing plants, where it is processed back into the form of uranium dioxide powder. The powder is processed into nuclear fuel pellets by pressing and sintering. Depleted UF_6, the residual product from the enrichment process, has the same physical and chemical properties as natural UF_6 and is transported in the same way.

For transport, following the conversion process, large cylindrical steel cylinders 48 inches in diameter each holding up to 12.5 T are filled with natural UF_6. The UF_6 solidifies inside the cylinder on cooling to room temperature. On reaching the enrichment plant, the cylinders are heated, which turns the solid into the gaseous form needed for the enrichment process. After enrichment, the enriched UF_6 is transported in 30 inch steel cylinders inside a protective structural package to provide protection against transport accidents. Enriched UF_6 packages are designed in accordance with ISO Standard 7195 (Reference 80), which is specific to UF_6 packages. They are required to withstand hydraulic tests to 2.76 MPa, including a drop test from 9 m onto the most vulnerable part of the package and a thermal test consisting of immersion in a fire at 800°C for 30 minutes.

49.3   The Hazards of UF_6

UF_6 presents a radioactive, toxic and chemical hazard but, for the purposes of transport regulation under the IMDG Code (Reference 19), the radioactive nature of the material takes precedence and it is therefore categorised as radioactive Class 7.

Radioactive effects
UF_6 poses potential health risks due to the radioactive nature of the uranium and the other radioactive elements it decays into. For natural UF_6, the radiological hazard is low and the main hazard is due to the chemical effects of a release. Enriched UF_6 poses an increased but still low radiological hazard and a low risk of a criticality excursion.

Chemical effects
If UF_6 is released to the atmosphere, the uranium compounds that are formed by reaction with moisture in the air are chemically hazardous. Uranium is a heavy metal that, in addition to being radioactive, can have chemical effects, principally on the kidneys, if it enters the bloodstream by ingestion or inhalation. When UF_6 comes into contact with water vapour in the air, it reacts to form hydrogen fluoride and uranyl fluoride, which are intensely corrosive to the skin and toxic if inhaled.

Figure 49.2: UF_6 cylinder being loaded onto a flat-rack container.

Figure 49.3: 48 inch cylinder for natural UF_6.

49.4 Current Levels of Uranium Ore and UF_6 Transport

There are no official figures, but the current annual level of uranium ore transport worldwide is believed to be about 40,000 to 50,000 T from the source to the plants that convert it to UF_6. As these conversion plants are in Europe and North America, this means that most of this material is transported by sea. When converted to UF_6, about 8,000 to 13,000 T are believed to be transported by sea to enrichment plants. This represents up to 2,000 packages annually. After enrichment, about 3,000 T of enriched UF_6 are transported from enrichment plants to the fuel fabricators, located everywhere in the world. Cylinders returning from these transports often contain residues of UF_6, known as 'heels', and some cylinders are classified under the IMDG Code as UN 2908 empty packages after washing. Uranium enrichment costs are largely based on the cost of electricity which is influenced, among other things, by variations in monetary exchange rates that are difficult to predict. Fluctuations in these costs can cause significant variation in transport levels.

49.5 Accidents Involving UF_6

Two significant accidents have occurred during sea transport of UF_6.

On 25th August 1987, a French cargo ship, the *'Mont Louis'*, sank in the English Channel after a collision with a car ferry. The *'Mont Louis'* was carrying 30 cylinders of UF_6 containing 12 T of material each. Although there was damage to some of the cylinders, no significant release of UF_6 occurred. The recovery campaign was complex and lengthy because of the sea conditions and the need to carry out extensive checks to the cylinders before their onward transport. In addition, there was a very large programme of environmental testing carried out by the French and UK authorities.

Figure 49.4: Nuclear fuel assembly being loaded into nuclear power plant.

On 23rd May 1989, a container vessel carrying nine cylinders of UF_6 residues was involved in an incident while on passage from Rotterdam to Montreal. During a mid-Atlantic storm, three cylinders, which were inadequately secured inside a closed 40 ft freight container, broke loose, damaging the freight container and two adjacent containers. The valves of two of the cylinders were broken off and UF_6 residue escaped, contaminating the deck of the ship, other equipment and cargo in the adjacent containers. A section of the dock area was also contaminated when the freight containers were unloaded in Montreal.

The accident was caused by improper stowage of the UF_6 cylinders inside the freight containers. Each of the cylinders had been tied to straps on the wall of the freight container using half inch thick polypropylene rope, which snapped during the storm. Although there was no significant radiological risk to the crew, workers or the public, there was a very large insurance claim for the subsequent monitoring and clean-up operation.

49.6   Club Cover and the 'Excepted Matter' Regulations

UF_6 transport presents particular difficulties in assessing whether it is 'excepted matter' under the Nuclear Installations (Excepted Matter) Regulations 1978. If it is 'excepted matter', it is covered by the Club, but if it is not then the consignor, or in some cases the consignee, is required to arrange nuclear liability insurance in place of Club cover and provide the carrier with a certificate of financial security to demonstrate this. The certificate must be countersigned by the government of the country concerned.

UF_6 is transported in a variety of quantities, enrichments and activities and, unlike chemical products, which have a single UN number for each material, UF_6 may be categorised as UN 2978, 2977, 2919, 3331, 2910 or 2908. Natural, non-fissile UF_6, in quantities greater than 0.1 kg, is transported as UN 2978 and, although this should always be, 'excepted matter', it is necessary to check that consignments are not misdeclared.

Enriched UF_6 is transported in full, partially full, or emptied cylinders. It is, therefore, always necessary to check the total quantity of U_{235} in a consignment to determine whether it is more or less than the limit of 600 g, and therefore whether it is covered for 'excepted matter' by the Club. This is achieved by converting the net quantity of UF_6 to the weight of uranium and then, knowing the % enrichment, calculating the weight of U_{235}, eg 5 kg of UF_6 enriched to 4% contains $5 \times 0.6761 = 3.3805$ kg of uranium. The quantity of U_{235} is 3.3805 kg $\times 0.04 = 0.13522$ kg or 135.22 g of U_{235}.

Members should contact the Club for advice if there is any doubt as to whether or not the cargo is 'excepted matter'.

49.6.1 Other Radioactive Cargo

Plutonium, fission products, uranium and other transuranic elements combine to form used nuclear fuel. To decrease heat and radiation levels, used fuel is stored on site for up to five months. It can then be transported by land or sea to a reprocessing plant. Sea transportation requires purpose built ships containing Type B casks, composed of either steel or steel and lead. Approximately 300 used fuel transportations have been made by sea to date.

Over one-third of the energy produced in nuclear power plants come from plutonium, which has two different isotopic categories:

- 'Reactor-grade' plutonium, a by product of used fuel from nuclear reactors after it has been irradiated for around 3 years

- 'weapons-grade' plutonium, which is recovered from uranium that has been irradiated for a short period (2–3 months) and is made for military purposes.

Once irradiated (burned), reactor plutonium is transported as an oxide powder, ie in its most stable form. Cargo packages must be of a specific design and weight to be transported by sea. A typical container holds several packages, in weights ranging from 80 to 200 kg of plutonium oxide.

49.6.2 Naturally Occurring Radioactive Material (NORM)

Although NORM potentially includes all radioactive elements found in the environment, it usually refers to all naturally occurring radioactive materials where human activities have increased the potential for exposure. Therefore, NORM can be detected in industry, such as the production of oil and gas, mining and mineral sands extraction. NORM includes long-lived radioactive elements, primarily uranium, potassium and thorium, and their decay products such as radon and radium. Exposure to these naturally occurring elements contributes to a person's annual radiation dose, on average making up the majority of that dose.

Hydraulic fracturing (fracking) for gas production increases the release of NORM in water and drill cuttings. NORM causes operational safety issues for oil and gas industry workers during maintenance, decommissioning and waste transport. This is particularly problematic when pipe internals are exposed to Pb-210 deposits. However, external exposure tends to be low enough to keep workers below annual limits and prevent serious health risks.

Chapter 50 –
Seed Cake Cargoes

50.1   Carriage of Seed Cake Cargoes

Commodities such as soya bean meal, sunflower seed pellets, palm kernel expellers, and others have been shipped for many years in large volumes. These are the solid residues left behind when oil is removed from oil-bearing seeds. The amount of residual oil in these materials varies substantially depending on the technology used to extract the oil. Like all agricultural commodities, these materials have inherent moisture. They are used as ingredients in animal feed materials.

Although the oil level in these commodities is invariably much lower than the oil level in the original unprocessed seed or plant, the fact that these feed materials have been processed and the underlying plant cellular structure disrupted means that the residual oil is more prone to undergoing oxidation reactions with the air than is the case in unprocessed seeds. Because of the possibility of chemical oxidative reactions in the oil, these commodities have the capability of self-heating to much higher temperatures than do the seeds themselves.

For years, the universal name used to describe these commodities was simply 'seed cake'. Although it is a strange term to use for a group of commodities which are very widely traded and are well known under their individual names, until recently seed cake was the only recognised bulk cargo shipping name in use. The term seed cake can be found throughout the harmonised UN system for carriage of cargos in bulk and packaged forms with UN numbers 2217 and 1386 applying where these materials are Class 4.2 (spontaneously combustible) because the oil is sufficiently reactive to give rise to the risk of eventual spontaneous fire.

Figure 50.1: 'Seed cake' when not used to describe cargo.

50.2   New Schedules

Previous editions of the IMSBC Code have contained four schedules relevant to the carriage of seed cake cargoes in bulk. Three of these were Group B cargoes, being Class 4.2 spontaneously combustible, and one was a Group C cargo – seed cake (non-hazardous). With the introduction of the 2020 Edition of the IMSBC Code, which came into force in January 2021, there are several changes. The schedules which have UN numbers retain the name 'seed cake' – to give SEED CAKE UN 1386 (a), SEED CAKE UN 1386 (b), and SEED CAKE UN 2217. These categories are retained in the 2022 Edition of the Code.

As has been the case for many years, the schedules each contain an identical list of commodities to which they apply. These lists include the more common feedstuffs (soya bean meal, sunflower seed pellets, etc) but they also list materials such as citrus pulp pellets and bran pellets. The description in the Code says the seed cake schedules are for the *"residue remaining after oil has been extracted… from oil-bearing seeds"*. Commodities such as citrus pulp pellets and bran pellets are not actually produced in this fashion, but as plant-based materials with residual oil and moisture content they behave in a very similar way.

The potential for confusion arises because the 2020 Edition of the Code introduced two new schedules headed SEED CAKES AND OTHER RESIDUES OF PROCESSED OILY VEGETABLES. Although this title explicitly references other types of residues, the description only mentions residues produced after extraction of oil. No list of the commodities included appears in the two new schedules.

The naming of schedules in this way is thought to arise from the need to retain the description 'seed cake' for materials with a UN number. All five schedules in the IMSBC Code (three SEED CAKE schedules and two SEED CAKES AND OTHER RESIDUES OF PROCESSED OILY VEGETABLES) should be taken as encompassing any processed plant material with residual oil and moisture. The applicable schedule should be selected based on the properties of the material, not whether it happens to be produced by extraction of oil from seeds.

50.3   Hazard Categories and Testing

The two new schedules relate respectively to hazardous Group B cargoes, designated MHB (material hazardous only when in bulk) because they have self-heating properties (although not to the extent that would require them to be categorised as Class 4.2), and to Group C cargoes that are deemed not to have a chemical hazard because there is insufficient self-heating tendency. The relevant test is a UN standard test known as the N4 test in which a cube of the commodity in question is held at high temperature in an oven and its tendency to increase in temperature above the oven temperature is measured.

Figure 50.2: 100 mm sample cube used for N4 test.

If a sample of a seed cake type undergoes dangerous self-heating, it would be categorised as Class 4.2 and covered by one of the three SEED CAKE schedules (UN 1386 (a), UN 1386 (b) or UN 2217). If it does not exhibit dangerous self-heating but does increase in temperature by more than 10°C then it is a MHB (material hazardous in bulk), category SH (self-heating), and would be covered by the SEED CAKES AND OTHER RESIDUES OF PROCESSED OILY VEGETABLES, Group B MHB schedule. If it showed a rise in temperature of less than 10°C then it would not be either MHB or Class 4.2 and would come under the provisions of the SEED CAKES AND OTHER RESIDUES OF PROCESSED OILY VEGETABLES Group C schedule. This latter schedule is effectively the replacement for the previous SEED CAKE (non-hazardous) schedule that formed part of the more recent editions of the IMSBC Code prior to 2020.

50.4 Documentation and Certification

The criteria for determining which of the schedules is appropriate have, in the past, been based on the oil content, the moisture content, the process which was used to produce the cargo, and the type of plant involved. These criteria still apply to distinguish between the three SEED CAKE schedules and are set out in those schedules, the form being unchanged from previous editions.

However, the rules regarding whether one of the three SEED CAKE schedules applies, or one of the two new schedules (MHB or Group C SEED CAKES AND OTHER RESIDUES OF PROCESSED OILY VEGETABLES) are more complex and will place additional requirements on a shipper. There is therefore potential for confusion regarding what testing and documentation is required, and shipowners and Masters may be presented with conflicting information.

The Group B MHB schedule will apply to a cargo of this type (ie plant material with residual oil and moisture) which gives a temperature rise of more than 10°C when subjected to the UN N4 test described above, but for materials which are not considered Class 4.2 (ie would not be considered hazardous under the provisions of the IMDG Code).

There is no requirement in the Group B MHB schedule for any proof or other certification to be provided to the ship along with the cargo declaration. Therefore, a Master will have no means of verifying whether the cargo being presented is not one which should be considered a SEED CAKE under Class 4.2.

The provisions for exempting a cargo from the Class 4.2 SEED CAKE schedules focus on the material not exhibiting sufficient self-heating properties in the N4 test to merit that hazard class. The following cargoes qualify for exemption – solvent-extracted rape seed meal, sunflower seed extraction, soya bean meal, cotton seed meal, expelled citrus pulp pellets, corn gluten meal, corn gluten feed and beet pulp pellets under the criteria for oil and moisture listed in the SEED CAKE UN 1386 (b) and SEED CAKE UN 2217 schedules.

There is also potential for confusion regarding the extension of the provisions for exemption from Class 4.2 SEED CAKE to other types of commodities – such as palm kernel expellers. They have never been listed as a material which can be exempted from Class 4.2, and the text of SEED CAKE UN 1386 (b) states that it applies to all extracted and expelled seed cakes with oil and moisture below certain limits. Shippers may assume that a seed cake cargo of any plant or vegetable origin can be carried under one of the two new schedules provided it does not show Class 4.2 behaviour in the N4 heating test.

The Group C schedule for SEED CAKES AND OTHER RESIDUES OF PROCESSED OILY VEGETABLES, unlike the corresponding MHB Group B schedule, does place a requirement on shippers to provide a certificate indicating that the requirements for exclusion from SEED CAKE UN 1386 (b) or UN 2217 are met, and that the material does not meet the criteria to be classed as MHB. In practice this means that certification will be required to indicate that when the material is subjected to the UN standard N4 test, no temperature rise of more than 10°C is experienced.

The certification needs to be issued by a *"person recognised by the competent authority of the country of shipment"*. This phrase has formed part of the seed cake schedules for many years but can be problematic. Most countries do not have lists of approved persons or laboratories issued by the competent authority. In such countries, and in places where there may be no functioning competent authority, there appears to be no guidance to a ship's Master regarding which organisations are permitted to issue such documentation.

Figure 50.3: Heated and discoloured seed cake cargo (corn gluten feed).

50.5 Potential Confusion and Conflict

For a shipment of a parcel of solvent-extracted rape seed meal, sunflower seed extraction, soya bean meal, cotton seed meal, expelled citrus pulp pellets, corn gluten meal, corn gluten feed or beet pulp pellets, it would appear that these remain Group C cargoes but with the added requirement of provision of certification demonstrating that when subject to the self-heating N4 test, the material does not exhibit a rise in temperature of over 10°C and is therefore not to be considered MHB.

There is also scope for problems in relation to cargoes of commodities which have not previously been able to be considered Group C. These include materials such as palm kernel expellers. They are not listed in the SEED CAKE UN 1386 (b) schedule as being potentially exempt from the provisions of Class 4.2. It is possible that tests will be carried out on some such materials using the UN standard procedure which shows that they are insufficiently capable of self-heating and should therefore be considered Group C or MHB under the new SEED CAKES AND OTHER RESIDUES OF PROCESSED OILY VEGETABLES schedules.

Although the Group C schedule specifies the documentation required for presentation so that the schedule can be applied, the MHB schedule does not. The latter simply says it applies to cargoes which do not meet the criteria required to be Class 4.2 under the IMDG Code.

A Master presented with a cargo declaration for, eg palm kernel expeller, under the SEED CAKES AND OTHER RESIDUES OF PROCESSED OILY VEGETABLES MHB (Group B) schedule should request proof that the cargo has indeed been tested according to the UN N4 test and it does not have sufficient self-heating properties to be Class 4.2. While such a request would be justified, there is no requirement in the IMSBC Code for such proof to be supplied, and this may give rise to disputes. It is not yet clear how many cargoes are likely to come under the provisions of the new MHB schedule.

Figure 50.4: Fire in corn gluten feed.

50.6   New Loading and Handling Provisions

The provisions covering loading and carriage for the three SEED CAKE Class 4.2 schedules are unchanged from previous editions of the Code.

The new SEED CAKES AND OTHER RESIDUES OF PROCESSED OILY VEGETABLES MHB schedule contains a requirement that the cargo should only be accepted for loading when it is at a temperature which is either (at most) 10°C above ambient, or 55°C, whichever is lower. This provision has been a part of the SEED CAKE UN 1386 (a) schedule but as that relates to a cargo which requires special permission, is rarely referenced. However, a cargo reaching a temperature of 55°C during a voyage and continuing to increase in temperature has always been the criteria set out generally in the SEED CAKE schedules for taking emergency action, and that is also in the new schedules. Experts recommend that seed cake cargoes are not loaded at elevated temperatures, and so the new provision of *"at most 10 degrees above ambient or 55°C, whichever is lower"* reflects good practice.

The MHB schedule also contains the requirement to take temperature measurements at depths in the cargo on a regular basis. Unfortunately, in practice this is very difficult to achieve – the simplest method is to lower thermometers down sounding pipes; however, this does not take measurements of the actual bulk cargo itself.

Both new schedules (MHB and Group C SEED CAKES AND OTHER RESIDUES OF PROCESSED OILY VEGETABLES) contain requirements that cargo needs to be substantially free from flammable solvent residues and that the cargoes need to be aged. No guidance is given as to what length of ageing is likely to be required and there is no necessity to provide documentation in respect of the amount of time the cargo has been allowed to age.

50.7   General Comments

It is recommended that Masters carrying any of these cargoes exercise caution during carriage, even if the cargo is being shipped under one of the two new schedules. Although these include cargoes in the Group C category, experience shows that they can still self-heat on board ships and damage cargo as a result. It is also worth remembering that if fuel oil tanks immediately adjacent to such cargoes are overheated, any of these commodities can be ignited. Fires tend to be slow-burning and do not spread readily, but they can be challenging to extinguish.

Carriage of all seed cake cargoes can also cause oxygen depletion in enclosed spaces. No entry into enclosed spaces containing any seed cake cargo should take place without thorough atmosphere testing and the appropriate permits to work put in place.

Part 12 –

Cargo Planning and Securing (Including Hatch Covers)

Chapter 51 –
Preparing Cargo Plans –
Structural Limitations

51.1   Strength of Tank Tops, Tween Decks, Hatch Covers and Weather Decks

When preparing cargo loading plans, it is important that the ship is loaded as close as possible to its maximum deadweight or capacity, but it is equally important to consider the implications of loading any high density cargo. In the early stages of planning, it is essential to establish not only the physical dimensions of the cargo but also the maximum permissible weight that can be loaded into any compartment. In general terms, there is a common failure to fully understand the strength limits of tank tops, tween decks, hatch covers and even weather decks. The knowledge of many Masters in this matter is often superficial.

The strength limits that are to be applied to tank tops are calculated and approved by the Classification Societies. The maximum limits are expressed in tonnes per square metre and are included in the ship's technical manuals and capacity plans. To calculate the number of tonnes that can be loaded on the tank top without exceeding the limit, the area of the tank top in square metres is multiplied by the permissible number of tonnes per square metre. To ensure that the limits are not exceeded, the cargo must be spread evenly over the area of the tank top. The volume of the space above the lower hopper tanks should also then be calculated and the figure obtained included in the total quantity to be loaded. A typical calculation might be as follows:

Maximum tonnage to be loaded:

(L)ength × (B)readth × PL (permissible load) = 27 m × 21 m × 12 T/m^2 = 6,804 T

(where L and B represent the dimensions of the tank top excluding the hopper tanks)

Maximum volume to load:

6,804 T at 3 T/m^3 = 2,268 m^3

Height of stow:

2,268 m^3/567 m^2 = 4.0 m
(567 m^2 = 27 m × 21 m)

When discrete items are to be loaded, such as billets, steel coils, slabs, etc, it is recommended that the load should not exceed the equivalent tonnage shown above.

When other homogeneous cargoes are loaded, which may safely be stowed over the hopper tanks, additional weight may be carried, but always with the proviso that the overall height of stow should never exceed the original figure as arrived at in the example.

In such cases, the amount of weight that can be safely added can be calculated by using the formula:

0.5 (L × B × PL) T, where L = the length of hopper tank and B = the horizontal width of tank and PL = permissible load.

Thus, if L = 27 m and B = 4 m then 0.5 (27 m × 4 m × 12 T/m^2) = 648 T at each side. At 3 T/m^3, 648 T would occupy 648 T ÷ 3 T/m^2 = 216 m^3. Over a base area of 108 m^2 (27 m × 4 m), this would take the height to 2 m (216/108) or, allowing for the wedge of a 45° hopper tank, to 4 m height. Thus, the final result of the calculation would be that the total weight of cargo to load would be 8,100 T at an overall height of 4 m.

In any case, when making these calculations, Masters should consult the IMSBC Code (Reference 17) Section 2.1, Cargo Distribution.

Figure 51.1: Bulk cargo loaded in a heap in the centre of the hold.

When bulk cargo is poured into a ship's hold, it tends to form a heap, thereby increasing the load on the tank top towards the centre of the hold. The result is a tendency for the double bottom to sag and for the ship's sides to be drawn in, as indicated in Figure 51.2.

Total cargo: 8,100 T

Cargo of iron ore stowing at	3 T/m²
Width of tank top	21 m
Length of hold	27 m
Peak of hopper tanks above tank top level	4 m
Base width of hopper tanks above tank top level	4 m
Classification Society permissible load	12 T/m²

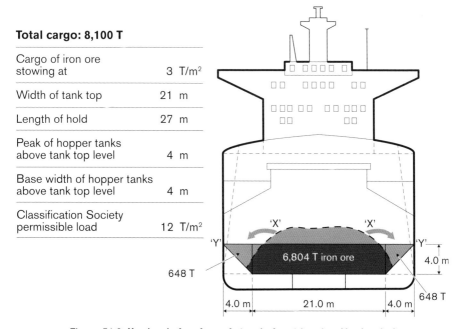

Figure 51.2: X = level of surface of stow before trimming, Y = level of surface of stow after trimming.

Such stresses can seriously weaken the ship's structure. It is possible that the effects of such stowage procedures over a number of years may have contributed to the losses of loaded bulk carriers. During loading, the aim should be to maintain an even distribution of weight both transversely and longitudinally so that the specified tank top limits are not exceeded.

The procedures outlined above are simple, but more complicated situations may arise if breakbulk cargoes are to be loaded where large, heavy pieces of cargo may be offered for shipment.

A 200 T transformer with base dimensions of 5 × 3 m (15 m²) is to be loaded into the hold illustrated in Figure 51.2. The spot load on the tank top would be 200 T ÷ 15 m² = 13.3 T/m². This load would be excessive if the limit were 12 T per square metre. To spread the load and reduce the pressure to within the specified limits, it is customary to build a grid-like timber frame on the tank top. The timber selected should have its grain running the length of the timber and be of uniform quality. The area over which to apply the timber can be calculated by dividing the weight of the transformer by the tank top limitation, ie 200 T ÷ 12 T/m² = 16.7 m². This would be the minimum area to be covered by the frame. 2 × 2 inches and 3 × 3 inches timber is commonly used with the loading of many cargoes, particularly steel. Square timber of greater cross-section is extensively used for supporting heavy lifts.

Ideally, a complete floor should be constructed, with baulks of timber placed next to the steel surface of the tank top and with no spaces between the timbers. In practice, this would be costly and uneconomical. Any procedure is likely to involve compromise, but it is in any case recommended that, with heavy lifts, the baulks used should be of substantial sized timber with cross-sectional areas of not less than 9 square inches (58 cm²). The timber may compress under the applied weight and, as an alternative, a steel frame may be used. Before deciding the exact stowage position for a heavy lift, it is advisable to check the nature of the hull construction. A heavy lift should be placed with reference to the longitudinal reinforced structure (longitudinal girders). The placement of timber baulks should be considered with reference to the internal double-bottom structure, always bearing in mind that an important function of dunnage is to spread the load to the primary structure of the hull.

Other complications are likely to arise when loading steel cargoes. When loading steel coils, it is usual to load not more than three tiers high with individual coils weighing up to 10 T. If the unit weight is more than 10 T, only two tiers are loaded and, if more than 15 T, only one tier is loaded. Usually, two lines of double dunnage measuring 6 × 1 inches are laid athwartships between the coil and the tank top. Applying the formula above, the pressure exerted over the small bearing surface of the lowest coil is about 30 T. Without due care, the customary dunnage may not be sufficient to effectively spread this weight and there is a risk that the tank top will be overloaded beneath each unit.

Figure 51.3: Steel coils (loaded three high) in a cargo hold.

Every possible precaution should be taken to ensure that the spot load does not exceed the limit, bearing in mind that the load spread is improved if the pitch of dunnage is reduced and that the dunnage must be laid across primary structures and must not terminate in between members (ie between double-bottom longitudinal girders).

The stowage of steel slabs poses similar problems. A typical slab may measure 6 × 1.25 × 0.25 m and weigh 14.75 T. The area of such a slab is 7.5 m² and, when stacked 7 high, there would be 103 T bearing down on the tank top. Assuming the slabs were stowed flat, this would indicate a load of 13.74 T/m², ie 14.5% in excess of a 12 T permissible limit. However, the lowest slab is likely to be supported by three or four baulks of timber in order to facilitate handling by forklift truck. This means that the entire stack is supported on a maximum of four points, resulting in a tremendous concentration of weight on a small area. Unless larger dunnage is utilised, thereby spreading the load to within satisfactory limits, the tank top will be overloaded when such cargo is loaded in the manner described. Bearing in mind the manner in which steel billets and slabs are usually dunnaged and stowed, it should be clear that little or no weight of that stowage will be distributed to the sloping tank sides unless special dunnaging arrangements are constructed to do so. It is more likely that the flat tank top area alone will be supporting the entire cargo weight, even though billet/slab ends/ sides may be touching the plating of the sloping tanks.

Masters are again encouraged to consult the IMSBC Code (Reference 17), referring particularly to Section 2.1.2 which states:

"A general cargo ship is normally constructed to carry cargoes in the range of 1.39 to 1.67 cubic metres per tonne when loaded to full bale and deadweight capacities.

When loading a high-density solid bulk cargo, particular attention shall be given to the distribution of weights to avoid excessive stresses, taking into account that the loading conditions may be different from those found normally and that improper distribution of such cargo may be capable of stressing either the structure under the load or the entire hull. To set out exact rules for the distribution of loading is not practicable for all ships because the structural arrangements of each vessel may vary greatly. The information on proper distribution of cargo may be provided in the ship's stability information booklet or may be obtained by the use of loading calculators, if available."

The data provided for iron ore in the individual cargo schedules of the IMSBC Code indicates that the very densest iron ore has a stowage factor of 0.29 m^3/T, which is considerably lower than that shown in the schedule at the upper limit of the range, ie 0.80 m^3/T. When compared with reported dimensions for billets, their stowage factor may be not greater than 0.25 m^3/T (allowing for dunnage, margin plate areas, interstitial spacing, etc), on the basis that a mild steel billet will have an inherent density of 7.86 T/m^3. If it were possible to stow billets without any interstitial spaces, the stowage factor would be 0.127 m^3/T, demonstrating that billets constitute a very heavy cargo which stows denser than the densest iron ore.

In purpose-built container ships, the tank tops and double-bottom structures are specially strengthened where container corner castings are to be positioned. Here, the guiding principle is the stack weight, where four, six or even nine units per stack are involved. When containers are carried in the holds of non-purpose-built vessels, such as general cargo ships and bulk carriers, great care must be taken to use adequate dunnage to spread the point loading, generated by the stack load, at the corner castings. For instance, a single stack of two units, 20 T each will exert a down loading of 40 T. Beneath each corner casting, the point loading will be about 345 T/m^2. Failure to appreciate the magnitude of such stresses has sometimes resulted in tank tops becoming pierced, followed by flooding of the hold by fuel oil or ballast water.

Figure 51.4: A collapsed tween deck.

When loading high density cargoes, there is a risk of overloading tank tops and proper precautions must be taken. Provided that the tank top is not overloaded, the pressure on the hopper tanks should be within acceptable limits, but in any case, if the density of the cargo is sufficiently high, the surface level of the stow will be below the upper limits of the sloping sides and no problems should arise. When high density bulk cargoes are loaded, the cargo should be levelled to ensure an even pressure over the tank top. Heavy lifts require plenty of strong, good quality dunnage, laying as much dunnage as feasible on the tank top in order to spread the load evenly. The tank top limitations are laid down when the ship is built and, provided that the structure remains within class specifications, remain unchanged throughout the life of the ship. If, through damage or wastage, the structure is reduced, reduced limitations may well have been imposed as a condition of class.

Masters should be aware that tween decks can collapse even when overloading is marginal. There are no safety margins and all cargo must be carefully trimmed. Where ships are fitted with twin hatchways (port and starboard), the cargo should be loaded in equal quantities on each side, unless there are specific instructions in shipyard plans that dictate otherwise.

51.2   Weather Decks and Hatch Covers

Similar caution should be exercised when loading heavy cargo and containers on weather decks and hatch covers.

Unless the weather deck has been specially strengthened, it is unlikely to have a loading limit in excess of 3 T/m^2. Similarly, unless hatch covers have been specially strengthened, it is unlikely that they would have a limit greater than 1.8 T/m^2, and maybe half that value in vessels less than 100 m in length. Hence, it is of great importance to consult and confirm the relevant data from the ship's documentation. When exceptionally heavy cargoes are to be carried, it may be necessary to shore up the weather deck from below, but in such cases care should be taken to ensure that the load on the tween deck plating is properly spread.

Ships should avoid loading to the maximum permissible limit on the weather deck. Heavy weather, and seas across the deck, can add additional weight, which may then exceed the weather deck limits.

It is good practice to add 5% to the weight to be loaded before calculating the dunnage area, to act as a safety margin.

Generally, containers should be stowed on deck two or more high only on those ships that have securing arrangements specially provided. At no time should the deck-loaded containers overstress the hatch cover or the hatchway structure. In cases of doubt, details of stress limitations should be obtained from the Classification Society. As mentioned above, where bulk carriers or dry cargo ships are used for the carriage of containers on the weather deck and/or the hatch covers, it should be borne in mind that it is the stack weight and the resultant point loading beneath the corner castings that must be taken into consideration. This aspect is relevant not only in terms of the structural capability of the ship, but also the ability of the lower tiers of containers to support the superincumbent weight.

Where containers are to be stacked two or more tiers high on the hatch covers or weather deck, the base tier should be provided with permanent footlocks for the lower corner castings. The containers should be secured one above the other by means of twistlocks and/or lockable inter-layer stackers and the upper corner castings of a block of units should be locked into each other transversely by means of screw-bridge fittings and/or tension clamps. Containers so carried must be treated as deck cargo and secured in accordance with the deck cargo rules and recommendations.

> The total holding power of the lashing arrangements, properly disposed and attached to appropriate terminal points, should be not less than three times the static gross weight of the containers and contents.

If circumstances demand a twin tier stack in the absence of footlocks or welded restraints, properly rigged foot lashings should be used. The units must be twist locked together and lashed as discussed above. In such instances, the correct use of dunnage, both as to size and application, beneath the base corner castings is of paramount importance, as illustrated in Figure 51.5 (see also Section 53.2).

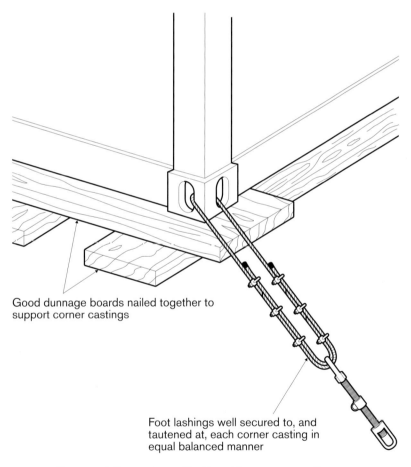

Good dunnage boards nailed together to support corner castings

Foot lashings well secured to, and tautened at, each corner casting in equal balanced manner

Figure 51.5: Dunnaging and lashing at base corner casting.

Chapter 52 –
Cargo Pre-loading Surveys

Instructing a surveyor to 'carry out a pre-loading survey' is inadequate and leaves the surveyor in doubt as to how far their duties extend.

In most contracts of carriage, the shipowner's responsibilities begin at the time of loading and it is, therefore, important to inspect the cargo at this stage. Pre-shipment inspection of cargo is undertaken to determine and document the condition of the cargo at this time. This inspection is commonly referred to as the pre-loading survey. This survey can be carried out by the ship's Master and officers, or the owner's representatives or surveyors instructed by the owner, depending on the trade and nature of the cargo. If the cargo is not as described in the shipping documentation, a decision will have to be made whether to reject the cargo or accept the cargo and adequately describe any differences on the mate's receipts and bills of lading (B/Ls). Early notification of any deficiencies to the shippers is desirable, together with the owner's intentions to either reject the cargo, or clause the mate's receipts and B/Ls. This notification can be given direct to the shippers but is more commonly given to the agents, stevedores or charterers, depending on the owner's contractual relations.

Masters and deck officers employed by owners who trade their ships in liner services are usually trained to undertake pre-shipment inspections. Liner companies usually employ cargo superintendents, who can be called upon to assist if there is a problem.

They may also have their own network of contracted surveyors who can be called upon quickly if an unusual cargo is to be loaded. Ships employed in the main bulk trades, (oil, grain, ore, etc) or specialised ships such as gas carriers and RoRo vessels, usually have competently trained Masters and officers on board to take care of any pre-shipment inspections that are necessary. However, problems may arise if a tramp operator is chartered to carry, for example, steel products, paper products or breakbulk cargoes, but the Master and the ship's officers have little or no experience of these products. In many instances, loading operations commence immediately upon the ship's arrival and there is little time for the ship's personnel to inspect the cargo.

The ship's personnel may be unfamiliar with the port and the system of loading, they may not know the agents, who almost always will be the charterer's agents, and they will be put under pressure by the charterers and possibly a cargo superintendent employed by the charterer to load their ship as quickly as possible. In these circumstances, employment of a competent local surveyor should be considered.

If owners decide they require a surveyor to attend their ship to carry out a pre-loading survey, the instructions given should be comprehensive, precise and given as early as possible to allow sufficient time for the surveyor to conduct an efficient survey. This will avoid confusion and disagreement at a later date when the surveyor presents their report and invoice. A general instruction that the surveyor should 'carry out a pre-loading survey' is inadequate and means the surveyor has to decide the extent of their duties. In these circumstances, the surveyor would simply inspect the cargo on the quay, possibly prior to the ship's arrival if all the cargo had been delivered, and report to the Master on its condition, presenting a written report. Most surveyors would take their duties a little further and advise the Master on the clausing of the mate's receipts and they might offer guidance on loading and stowage if it was requested by the Master. More precise advance instructions would, however, avoid any potential confusion and ambiguity. Instructing and informing the surveyor should therefore include the following:

Relevant details in the contracts of carriage (charterparties)
These include:

- Clauses relating to damaged cargo, eg sometimes clauses state that damaged cargo should not be loaded or that specific clausing only is permitted on the B/Ls
- clauses relating to the responsibility for loading and stowage
- clauses relating to the issue of the mate's receipts and B/Ls.

Precise instructions on the survey
- The surveyor should be instructed whether the cargo is to be inspected on the quay just before loading or in the transit shed or elsewhere prior to the ship's arrival, etc. The nature of the cargo and time factor will probably determine this. In many cases, the owners, charterer or ship's agent will not know where the cargo is stored in the port or when it is to be delivered, so the surveyor should be instructed to survey all cargo to be loaded as near to the time of shipment as possible
- instruction is also required on the information to be given to the Master before the signing of the mate's receipts and whether the surveyor should formulate suitable clauses relating to any damage. Usually, the surveyor should be instructed to be present when the Master signs the shipping documents. At this time, the surveyor

can assist with any language problems and any disputes with shippers, agents or charterers in the clausing of mate's receipts and/or B/L.

Other additional services connected with loading

* Inspection of ship's hatch covers and ventilation system. (The findings of this inspection should be provided in a separate report or confidential side letter. This is to avoid any adverse information being disclosed if the pre-loading report is used in a cargo dispute)

* advising the Master on loading, stowage and securing

* monitoring the loading, stowage and securing

* advising and reporting on handling damage caused by stevedores

* advising on the tallying of the cargo and the issue of cargo documentation

* advising whether the cargo can be loaded in rain.

If early instructions are given, the surveyor will have time to contact the agents and stevedores to find out the exact nature of the cargo, when it is arriving at the loading berth and the proposed stowage on the ship.

Most shipowners will be aware that the employment of a competent surveyor for a 'precautionary' pre-loading survey in certain circumstances can eliminate or reduce problems and claims. The UK P&I Club and correspondents can assist and advise owners in arranging these surveys and in some exceptional circumstances will pay for the survey. This is particularly the case with finished or semi-finished steel products when the Club will always pay for a pre-loading survey if notified by the owners but not any associated services.

Chapter 53 –
Stowage of Breakbulk Cargo
(General Cargo)

In recent years, there has been a general decline of standards in the stowage of breakbulk cargo, resulting in cargo damage and claims.

There are various reasons for the decline of standards, namely:

- Use of bulk carriers for the carriage of breakbulk cargo
- improper dunnaging
- inadequate packing
- inadequate stowage skills of ships' officers.

53.1 Bulk Carriers

Figure 53.1: Medium-sized bulk carriers often replace tweendeckers on trades that have not been containerised or where, because of the type of cargo, it is impossible to use containers.

A ship fitted with tween decks is ideal for the carriage of breakbulk cargo. The many compartments facilitate the carriage of different commodities and make port rotation easier, usually avoiding overstows. Provided care is taken over the stowage, cargo damage, particularly crushing damage, should be avoided. Unfortunately, tweendeckers are in short supply and cannot compete economically with the medium-sized bulk carrier. Medium-sized bulk carriers have, therefore, replaced, or are replacing, tweendeckers on trades that have not been containerised or where, because of the type of cargo, it is impossible to use containers.

The bulk carrier's two main disadvantages, as compared with the tweendecker, are the height of the holds (about 12 m as compared with 6 m for the lower hold of a tweendecker) and the sloping lower wing ballast tanks. Most breakbulk cargo is stowed using forklift trucks, but the sloping lower wing ballast tanks prevent the forklift trucks manoeuvring close to the side of the holds, making stowage difficult. The height of the holds also prevents stowage from the tank top to the deckhead using forklift trucks. These problems are usually overcome by loading the cargo in horizontal tiers on top of which are placed steel plates on which forklift trucks can manoeuvre to load the next tier. It is clear that crushing damage may occur, not just because of the height of the stow, but due to the use of the steel plates and forklifts.

53.2   Dunnaging

Proper and adequate dunnaging materials must be used during the stowage of breakbulk cargo. This applies to all cargo ships, and is particularly important for bulk carriers.

Timber and timber products, such as plywood, are the main types of dunnage materials in use, even though timber products have risen in price over the past few years. Other cheaper materials are sometimes used as a substitute, but are generally found to be inadequate. Because of the price of timber, charterers, or whoever is paying for the dunnage, are often reluctant to provide dunnage that is adequate both in quality and quantity.

Dunnage is used for the following reasons:

*   To spread the load over the surface area of the tank top, tween deck or deck, and also between horizontal tiers of cargo
*   to increase friction between steel surfaces (tank top and cargo, etc)
*   to tie the cargo together to prevent any movement in the stow
*   to keep the cargo away from the tank top or deck and away from the steel structure at the ship's sides, thereby preventing contact with moisture formed on, or running down or across, steel surfaces and permitting the water to flow to the bilges
*   to block void spaces, brace and support cargo, and block cargo to prevent movement
*   to create a divide, an auxiliary deck or level surface.

Figure 53.2: An example of timber dunnaging for steel plates.

Dunnage is an absolute necessity for proper stowage of breakbulk cargo and, when cargo damage occurs, the failure to use adequate or good quality dunnage may make it difficult to refute allegations of bad stowage by cargo interests and liability for cargo claims. Due to the difficulties in the stowage of breakbulk cargo in bulk carriers, proper and adequate use of dunnage is vital and, although cost is a consideration, this is usually minor in proportion to potential claims.

When timber dunnage is supplied, the Master and the ship's officers should check that the timber is properly seasoned. Green or wet timber contains up to 35% water. Shrinkage of green timber results in the loosening of nails and could mean that any blocking or bracing structure collapses. Timber should also be without dry rot, without infestation, without splits (split timbers cannot be fastened properly and lack strength) and of adequate scantling.

> Poor quality timber should be rejected and, as the ship's officers will probably have to sign for the timber supplied, they should check that the amount supplied corresponds to the receipt they sign.

53.3   Packing

One of the main causes of damage to breakbulk cargo is inadequate packing. Pallets, boxes, crates and other forms of packing are usually designed for a single transit. During the course of this transit, the unit must survive initial storage, loading onto a road or rail vehicle, transit to a port, handling at the port into temporary storage, loading onto the ship, stowage, static and dynamic forces related to the ocean passage, breaking out of stow and unloading, handling into temporary storage, handling onto a road or rail vehicle, transit to the receiver's premises and handling at the receiver's premises. There are regularly at least 10 handling operations involved with every transit, but by far the most arduous is the sea voyage. It is therefore very important that packaging is taken into account when planning the stowage of breakbulk cargo, particularly when a stow could be as high as 12 m on a bulk carrier. Packaging should be inspected prior to loading and, if inadequate, the cargo should either be rejected or the B/Ls properly claused with regard to the inadequacy of the packing. It is difficult to generalise on what should be considered as inadequate packing, but some examples are:

- Flimsy pallets that bend and break when lifted
- the cargo on the pallets is laterally greater than the surface area of the pallet platform, which results in the cargo projecting over the sides and becoming torn or split on the pallet edges, causing the load to become unstable
- the load on the pallet is only secured with shrink-wrapped plastic sheeting, which is not acceptable as a securing material and leads to instability of the cargo on the pallets
- some of the bottom bags of the pallets lose their contents due to being pierced by the forks of forklift trucks, which impairs the stability of the stow on the pallet
- packages on pallets are not interlocked making the whole unit unstable, particularly if the goods are slippery
- bundles of pipes secured with wire are wrongly arranged in the bundles, causing slackness in the bundles resulting in bending and end damage

- heavy drums loaded on pallets that are only secured with flat metal strapping bands which eventually become slack and the load becomes loose

Figure 53.3: Heavy drums that have broken loose from inadequate strapping.

- wooden cases that have a strong base but with weak covers that lack rigidity because they are not fitted with a frame. This can result in the cases collapsing in a stow and the stow collapsing. It is difficult to see this weakness at the time of shipment
- plywood bundles that are packed in such a manner that the packing is too light for the weight of the bundle and the bearers.

Figure 53.4: Plywood bundles that have broken out of packing that is insufficient for the weight of the bundles and bearers.

If the packing is inadequate and incapable of withstanding the rigours of an ocean voyage, good stowage may not prevent the cargo from sustaining damage. Furthermore, inadequate or weak packing can undermine the stability of a stow and in extreme cases lead to its eventual collapse. Without proper supervision during loading, inadequate or weak packing is often only discovered at the discharge port when the cargo is unloaded in a damaged condition. It is difficult to determine at the discharge port whether the cargo was damaged due to bad stowage or as a result of inadequate packing. Cargo claims will eventually be directed to the shipowner and may prove costly and impossible to defend, which is why identifying poor packaging at the point of loading is crucial.

It is far more difficult to cater for stowage of cargo with weak or inadequate packing on a bulk carrier than on ships with tween decks. On a tweendecker, top stowage either in the lower hold or tween deck can be arranged for suspect or weak packing. However, top stowage on a bulk carrier is far more limited, particularly when there are many loading or discharge ports.

Figure 53.5: Wooden cases that lack structural rigidity.

Even if packing is adequate, it is only designed to withstand certain pressures, and usually these pressures are determined for static conditions. Packing crates and cases of medium size should be able to withstand the superincumbent load of five similar items stowed above. Properly designed palletised units of 1,500 kg should be capable of supporting a 6,000 kg load under static conditions, which would result in a five-tier pallet stow of about 6 m in height. Steel drums are designed to survive under a static load of a 3 m height of units of the same weight. Proper stowage of these types of commodities can be arranged on a tweendecker, but the problem is far more difficult on a bulk carrier, even if vast quantities of dunnage are used to spread the loads evenly.

Various international and national organisations issue guidance stipulating the strength and construction of packing. These include the IMDG Code, British Standard, USA Packing Standard and the German Industry Standard (DIN) (References 19, 81, 82 and 83). For example, under DIN, cases have to withstand a static vertical pressure of 1.0 T/m^2 during sea transit. Ships' officers cannot be expected to test packaging to see whether it complies with these standards, but they should be aware that standards do exist and that shippers are under an obligation to comply with the rules and regulations of national and international organisations. Also, packaging has to be properly marked, particularly if there are special requirements for lifting or stowage. It is important to comply with wording or markings on packages such as:

- Stow away from heat
- top stowage only
- position of weight point
- marks for lifting points
- marks for forklift handling
- this way up arrows.

If it is impossible to comply with the instructions on the package, particularly with regard to stowage, that particular package or parcel of cargo should not be loaded.

53.4   Stowage Skills

The huge increase in containerisation has brought about a gradual decline in the traditional seafaring skills of loading and proper stowage. The result is that a Master or chief officer on a medium-sized bulk carrier may have never seen a general cargo loaded or stowed, and they may also have never received any tuition or training in a shore-based establishment. If a bulk carrier is chartered to load general cargo, the Master and chief officer will probably rely on the charterer's supercargo, if any, to advise on stowage, or on the stevedores' expertise. The result may be a series of expensive cargo claims.

53.5   Recommendations

It is recommended that when owners know that their Masters or deck officers do not have the necessary expertise to properly load and stow general cargo, particularly on bulk carriers, expert advice should be obtained. Club correspondents have the local knowledge to advise Members on experts and surveyors in their area. Even if the Master and deck officers have some skill in the loading of breakbulk cargoes, expert advice should be sought if it is suspected that the packaging of any commodity is inadequate.

Chapter 54 –
Lashing and Securing Deck Cargoes

For the purposes of this chapter, reference should be made to the IMO *Code of Safe Practice for Cargo Stowage and Securing* (CSS Code, Reference 22) and the requirements under SOLAS for a Cargo Securing Manual (CSM) (Reference 18).

54.1   Cargo Securing Manual (CSM)

Regulations VI/5 and VII/5 of the 1974 SOLAS Convention require cargo units and cargo transport units to be loaded, stowed and secured throughout the voyage in accordance with the CSM approved by the administration and drawn up to a standard at least equivalent to the guidelines developed by the IMO (Reference 18).

The guidelines have been expanded to take into account the provisions of the CSS Code (Reference 22), the amendments to that Code, the *Code of Safe Practice for Ships Carrying Timber Deck Cargoes* (TDC Code, Reference 23) and the codes and guidelines for RoRo vessels, grain cargoes, containers and container vessels, and ships carrying nuclear waste and similar radioactive products. Such individual publications are subject to amendments that need to be carried into the appropriate section of the CSM as they occur.

As from 1st January 1998, it is a mandatory regulation for all vessels, other than exempted vessels such as dedicated bulk solid, bulk liquid and liquefied gas-carrying vessels, to have on board an approved and up-to-date CSM. Some administrations may exempt certain cargo-carrying ships of less than 500 gross tons and certain very specialised ships, but such exemption should not be assumed in the absence of a formal exemption certificate.

It is a mandatory requirement for Masters and ships' officers to be conversant with the CSS Code and the CSM guidelines to understand their applications for the vessel in which they are serving and to be capable of deploying correctly the hardware that goes with them. The CSM and its associated hardware are subject to Port State Control (PSC) inspection. Violation of the CSM guidelines may give rise to vessel detention and/or prosecution of the Master and owners.

The CSS Code and the CSM guidelines and their amendments contain much sound and well-tried advice and should not be treated lightly. There are, however, a number of anomalies and in some instances the applied text is difficult to reconcile with safe practice and sound seamanship.

54.2   Deck Cargo

The term 'deck cargo' refers to items and/or commodities carried on the weather deck and/or hatch covers of a ship and thereon exposed to sun, wind, rain, snow, ice and sea, so that either the packaging or the commodities themselves must be fully resistant to, and not denatured by, such exposure. Even in RoRo vessels, many areas above the actual hold space can reasonably be considered as 'on deck' even though they are not fully exposed to the wind and sea. The combined effects of wind, sea and swell can be disastrous. Where damage and loss occur to cargo shipped on deck at anyone's risk and expense, the shipowners, the Master and ship's officers, and the charterers, must be in a position to demonstrate that there was no negligence or lack of due diligence on their part.

Deck cargoes, because of their very location and the means by which they are secured, will be subjected to velocity and acceleration stresses greater, in most instances, than cargo stowed below deck. When two or more wave forms combine, a high wave preceded by a deep trough may occur. This may be referred to as an 'episodic wave', ie a random large wave, noticeably of greater height than its precursors or successors. This occurs when one or more wave trains fall into phase with another so that wave(s) of large amplitudes are produced, giving rise to sudden, steep and violent rolling and/or pitching motions of the ship. The risk is widespread and prevalent, as such waves have the potential to occur in any sea area. The stowage, lashing and securing of cargoes therefore require special attention as to method and detail if unnecessary risks are to be avoided.

Courtesy of Danny Cornelissen/portpictures.nl

Figure 54.1: Many areas above the actual hold space on RoRo vessels can reasonably be considered as 'on deck' even though they are not fully exposed to the onslaught of wind and sea.

54.3   Causes of Losses

Unfortunately, despite all the loss prevention guidance available, there is a continuing incidence of the collapse and/or loss overboard of deck cargo items. Losses include large vehicles, rail cars, cased machinery, steel pipes, structural steelwork, packaged timber, freight containers, hazardous chemicals, boats, launches, etc. When investigated fully, the causes of such losses generally fall into the following categories, which are neither exhaustive nor mutually exclusive in occurrence:

- Severe adverse weather conditions
- lack of appreciation of the various forces involved
- incorrect application of the relevant rules and guiding recommendations
- cost limitations for appropriate securing methods
- insufficient time and/or personnel to complete the necessary work before the vessel leaves port
- dunnage not utilised in an effective manner
- inadequate strength, balance and/or number of lashings
- wire attachment eyes and loops rigged incorrectly, including incorrect methods of using bulldog grips
- lack of strength continuity between the various securing components
- positioning lashing materials around unprotected sharp edges
- incorrect/unbalanced stowage and inadequate weight distribution
- securing arrangements, both supplied and approved, not fully utilised on the voyage under consideration.

This last point is particularly true of ISO freight containers and timber cargoes carried on the weather deck, and of large commercial vehicles carried in RoRo vessels.

All interests involved in the lashing and securing of deck cargoes should bear in mind that high expense in the purchase of lashing materials is no substitute for a simple design and a few basic calculations before lashing operations commence.

Figure 54.2: An example of best practice when securing cargo within a container.

Other than in RoRo and purpose-built container operations where standardisation of gear and rapid loading and turnaround times pose different problems, Masters should be encouraged, on completion of lashing operations, to make notes of the materials used, to produce a representative sketch of the lashing system, to insist upon being provided with the test/proof certificates of all lashing components involved and to take illustrative photographs of the entire operation. These will be of great assistance to the ship's interests in the event of related future litigation.

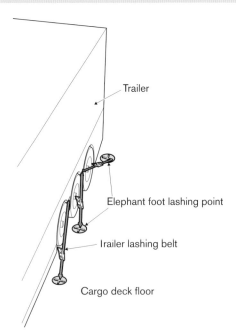

Trailer

Elephant foot lashing point

Trailer lashing belt

Cargo deck floor

Figure 54.3: Lashing of cargo RoRo.

54.4   General Guidelines

The *Merchant Shipping (Load Lines) (Deck Cargo) Regulations, 1968* (United Kingdom Statutory Instrument No 1089 of 1968) (Reference 84) set out guidelines to be followed when securing deck cargoes. Although the 1968 Regulations have been formally revoked by the *Merchant Shipping (Load Line) Regulations 1998* and their provisions are no longer requirements, the list of elements they set out for consideration in relation to deck cargo (although not exhaustive) is useful to provide further understanding, as reproduced below:

"2. Deck cargo shall be so distributed and stowed:

1) as to avoid excessive loading having regard to the strength of the deck and integral supporting structure of the ship;

2) as to ensure that the ship will retain adequate stability at all stages of the voyage having regard in particular to:

   a) the vertical distribution of the deck cargo;

   b) wind moments which may normally be expected on the voyage;

   c) losses of weight in the ship, including in particular those due to the consumption of fuel and stores; and

   d) possible increases of weight of the ship or deck cargo, including in particular those due to the absorption of water and to icing;

3) as not to impair the weathertight or watertight integrity of any part of the ship or its fittings or appliances, and as to ensure the proper protection of ventilators and air pipes;

4) that its height above the deck or any other part of the ship on which it stands will not interfere with the navigation or working of the ship;

5) that it will not interfere with or obstruct access to the ship's steering arrangements, including emergency steering arrangements;

6) that it will not interfere with or obstruct safe and efficient access by the crew to or between their quarters and any machinery space or other part of the ship used in the working of the ship, and will not in particular obstruct any opening giving access to those positions or impede its being readily secured weathertight."

54.5   Dunnage

If all deck cargo items could be structurally welded to the weather deck using components of acceptable strength, this would remove the necessity to consider coefficients of friction between the base of the cargo and the deck or dunnage it is resting on. As the large range of deck cargoes have various securing arrangements, the possibility of a cargo sliding across the deck is high, which means friction should be considered in securing calculations.

The values given for the coefficient of friction between dry timber and dry steel vary from 0.3 (17°) to 0.7 (35°). Sliding between steel and steel can occur at angles of inclination as small as 6°.

Due to the lack of available data on the relative sliding properties of materials (in relation to deck cargoes at sea), an experiment was carried out using 9 inch × 3 inch × 8 feet sawn pine planks, some of which had earlier been allowed to float in water. Others had been stored in covered conditions to conform as closely as possible to normal atmospheric moisture conditions.

The experiments were carried out on hinge-opening hydraulic-powered steel MacGregor hatch covers in clean, painted condition, free of any unusual roughness and/or obstruction. The tests used dry timber on dry covers, wet timber on dry covers, dry timber on wet covers and, lastly, wet timber on wet covers. The lowest value, 0.51 (27°), occurred with wet timbers on wet covers; the highest value, 0.645 (33°), occurred with wet timber on dry covers.

On the basis of such results, the lowest value of 0.51 (27°) should be accepted as relating to the most common condition likely to be found on the weather deck of a seagoing ship, ie wet timber on wet decks. Hence, with inclination, and without any effects likely to be introduced by velocity and/or acceleration stresses due to rolling and pitching, timber dunnage alone will start to slide of its own accord at angles of inclination of 27°. Thereafter, sliding will continue at progressively smaller angles. It follows that, when the vessel is rolling and pitching and timber dunnage is unsecured, it will begin to slide at angles of inclination considerably less than 27°.

Normal practice of utilising timber dunnage and of keeping downward-leading lashings as short and as tight as possible should be encouraged. A near vertical lashing is of great benefit in resisting the cargo item's tendency to tip; a near horizontal lashing will greatly resist sliding forces.

It is important not to overload lashing terminals and/or shackles, and consideration should be given to the 'effective strength' of a lashing – its 'holding power'. The 'slip load' of an eye in a wire should be balanced with the strengths of a shackle, a bottle-screw and a chain. A lashing is no stronger than its weakest part.

54.6   Spread the Load

Point loading and uneven distribution of cargo weight can cause unnecessary damage to decks and hatch covers. Unless the weather deck has been specially strengthened, it is unlikely to have a maximum permissible weight-loading of more than 3 T/m^2. Similarly, unless hatch covers have been specially strengthened, it is unlikely they will have a maximum permissible weight-loading of more than 1.8 T/m^2. The ship's capacity plan and/or general arrangement plan should always be consulted. If the specific values are not available on board, allow no more than 2.5 T/m^2 for weather-deck areas; and no more than 0.75 T/m^2 for hatch covers in small vessels; and 1.30 T/m^2 in vessels over 100 m in length.

The adverse effects of point loading are not always fully appreciated. For example, a 6 T machine with a flat-bed area of 3 m^2 will exert a down load of 2 T/m^2 (see Figure 54.4).

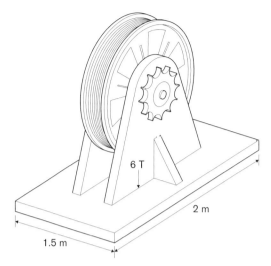

6 T

2 m

1.5 m

Figure 54.4: The 6 T weight is exerting a down loading of 2 T/m².

When exceptionally heavy weights are to be carried, it may be necessary to support the weather deck from below, but care must be taken to spread the load on the tween deck in order not to overload the plating. Cargo units in the range of 20 to 40 T are common and stacking of unit weights is widespread.

For example, if a piece of machinery weighing 30 T, with a base area of 6 m², is placed directly onto the weather deck, the point loading will be 30/6 = 5 T/m². If, however, the deck plating has a maximum permissible loading of 2.5 T/m², the minimum area over which that 30 T load must be spread is 30/2.5 = 12 m².

Good dunnage must be used to spread the load, and it is always good practice to add 5% to the weight to be loaded before working out the dunnage area. For the 30 T weight, for instance, 31.5 T would be used for the calculation and the dunnage area required would increase from 12 to 12.6 m².

Dunnage timber is often no more than 6 × 1 inch (150 × 25 mm) rough planking but, where weighty cargo items are involved, dunnage should be not less than 2 inch (50 mm) thickness × 6 inch (150 mm) width, and preferably 3 inch (75 mm) × 9 inch (225 mm). Thicker pieces of dunnage are frequently referred to as 'bearers'. A dunnage width greater than 150 mm is always acceptable, eg 9 inch (225 mm) to 12 inch (305 mm), but where the thickness is 3 inch (75 mm), care must be taken to choose straight-grained timbers of as great a width as possible and to ensure that they are laid with the grain horizontal and parallel with the deck. A singular piece of poorly constructed dunnage can set off a chain reaction in which the timber breaks, followed by a slackening of the lashing arrangements. This can cause increased cargo acceleration moments, culminating in the breaking of the lashings.

Because of the random nature of grain configurations in the thicker dunnage timbers, it is acceptable to achieve thicknesses by nailing planks together. A 2 inch thick dunnage timber can be made up using 1 inch thick planks, and a 3 inch thick dunnage timber can be made up using 2 inch and 1 inch thick timber planks, all securely nailed together. To a large degree, this will correct the tendency for separation in timber with a badly-aligned grain.

If load-spreading dunnage is to remain fully effective, it will be as important to install good lower-level foot lashings as it will be to install downward-leading lashings. See Figure 51.5 in Chapter 51 for an example of a good foot lashing arrangement.

54.7   Rolling Periods

The roll period of a ship is the time taken to make one complete transverse oscillation, ie from the upright position to starboard inclination, from starboard inclination back to upright and through to port inclination, then back to upright. Hence, if the roll period is 15 seconds and if the roll to starboard is 10° and the roll to port is 11°, the total 'sweep' within the 15 second roll period will be 10° + 10° + 11° + 11° = 42°.

When a ship rolls, the axis about which the rolling takes place may not be accurately determined, but it is accepted as being near to the longitudinal axis passing through the ship's centre of gravity. The time period of the roll is generally independent of the roll angle, provided that the roll angle is not large. Therefore, a ship with a 15 second roll period will take 15 seconds to make one full transverse oscillation when the roll angle (to port and to starboard) is anything from, for example, 2° to 30°. From a cargo lashing viewpoint, a roll angle of 2° and a roll period of 15 seconds involves a sweep of no more than 8°, whereas a roll angle of 20° and a roll period of 15 seconds involves a sweep of 80° (10 times the arc) within the same time period. This will involve large transverse acceleration stresses, particularly when returning to the upright position.

Equally important is consideration of vertical acceleration as the ship pitches and ascends. Calculation of this force is difficult, but measured values give results varying from 0.5 g (gravitational acceleration) amidships to 2 g at the bow.

A 'stiff' ship is one with a large metacentric height (GM) that is difficult to incline and returns rapidly to the upright (and beyond). This imposes excessive acceleration stresses on cargo lashings. A 'tender' ship is one with a small GM that is easy to incline and returns slowly to the upright. Although acceleration stresses are small, the inclined angles may attain 30° and the simple gravitational effects of such angles and slow returns may impose equally excessive stresses on cargo lashings. Extremes of either condition should be avoided. It is worth working on the assumption that, if deck cargo is to remain safely in place during severe adverse weather conditions, the lashing arrangements should be sufficient to sustain 30° roll angles associated with 13 second roll periods, and 5° pitch angles associated with not less than 1 g vertical acceleration.

54.8   Rule of Thumb for Lashing Strength

A general rule for securing cargoes that may move during moderate weather on a voyage is that the sum of the minimum breaking loads (MBLs) of all the lashings should be not less than twice the static weight of the cargo to be secured. For example, a single item of 10 T weight requires the lashings to have a total breaking load of not less than 20 T, on the assumption that the lashings are all positioned in a balanced, efficient and non-abrasive manner. This rule may be excessive below decks.

Where winds of Force 6 and upwards together with associated wave heights are likely to be encountered during a voyage, the increased stresses arising are those considered here, allowing for 30° roll angles with not less than 13 second roll periods (also see Tables 54.3 and 54.4, taken from the CSS Code and the CSM guidelines).

In these circumstances, it is usually recommended that the SWL of all of the lashings should equal 3 times the weight of the cargo to be secured, ie a cargo of 10 T would require 30 T worth of lashings. This is again subject to the lashings being deployed in a balanced, efficient and non-abrasive manner.

This approach is derived from the *International Convention on Load Lines, 1966,* within which framework the then UK Department for Transport, in earlier instructions to surveyors, gave the following guidance:

"When severe weather conditions (ie sea state conditions equal to or worse than those associated with Beaufort Scale 6) are likely to be experienced in service the following principles should be observed in the design of the deck cargo securing arrangements:

(iv) Lashings used to secure cargo or vehicles should have a breaking load of at least 3 times the design load, the design load being the total weight of the cargo or cargo plus vehicle subjected to acceleration of:

0.7 'g' athwartships,
1.0 'g' vertically and
0.3 'g' longitudinally,
relative to the principal axis of the ship.

When sea state conditions worse than those associated with Beaufort Scale 6 are unlikely to be experienced in service, a lesser standard of securing such items of cargo might be acceptable to approval by the Chief Ship Surveyor.

The equipment and fittings used to secure the deck cargoes should be regularly maintained and inspected."

Using the term 'holding power' to indicate breaking load/slip load/holding power, this means:

- The total holding power, in tonnes, of all lashings holding the cargo item vertically downward to the deck should be equivalent to three times the ordinary static weight of the cargo item in tonnes, ie a 10 T cargo item requires total lashings having a holding-down potential of 30 T

- the holding power, in tonnes, of all lashings preventing the cargo item moving to port and to starboard should be equivalent to seven-tenths of the holding-down potential of item 1 above, ie a 10 T item requires lashings with holding power preventing transverse movement of 21 T

- the holding power, in tonnes, of all lashings preventing the cargo moving forward or aft should be equivalent to three-tenths of the holding-down potential of item 1 above, ie a 10 T item requires lashings with holding power preventing longitudinal movement of 9 T.

The IMO 1994/1995 amendments to the CSS Code (Reference 22) (which were carried forward into the requirements for the preparation of the CSM) changed the emphasis as follows.

The CSM rule of thumb varies with the maximum securing load (MSL) of the different lashing components, as listed in Table 54.1. Vertical acceleration is replaced by a 1 g transverse acceleration, and vertical and longitudinal accelerations are not quantified except in the instance of containers of radioactive wastes.

The rule of thumb method given in Section 5 of Annex 13 of the current CSS Code (2021) indicates that the MSL values of the securing devices on each side of a cargo unit (port and starboard) should equal the weight of the unit, and Table 1 of Annex 13 of the Code now provides MSLs as follows:

Material	MSL
Shackles, rings, deckeyes, turnbuckles of mild steel	50% of breaking strength
Fibre rope	33% of breaking strength
Wire rope (single use)	80% of breaking strength
Web lashing	50% of breaking strength (was 70%)
Wire rope (re-usable)	30% of breaking strength
Steel band (single use)	70% of breaking strength
Chains	50% of breaking strength
Annex 13 of the CSS Code also notes that: *"Particular securing devices (e.g. fibre straps with tensioners or special equipment for securing containers) may be marked with a permissible working load, as prescribed by an appropriate authority. This may be taken as the MSL. When the components of a lashing device are connected in series (e.g., a wire to a shackle to a deckeye), the minimum MSL in the series shall apply to that device."*	

Table 54.1: Determination of MSL from breaking strength.

Consider a cargo unit of 18 T mass which is to be secured using only shackles, web lashings, chains and turnbuckles – all MSLs of 50% breaking strength (BS). The unit will require 18 tonne-force MSL on each side, or 36 tonne-force total MSL (72 tonne-force BS for these items), representing a total lashing breaking strength to cargo mass ratio of 72/18 = 4.

If the same cargo unit is secured with steel band only, the total MSL required will still be 36 tonne-force (72 tonne-force BS), but the MSL of steel band is nominated as 70% of its breaking strength. So this gives a total lashing breaking strength of (36 × 100)/70 = 51.42 tonne-force, representing a total lashing breaking strength to cargo mass ratio of 51.42/18 = 2.86.

If using re-usable wire rope to secure the same cargo, the answer is (36 × 100)/30 = 120 tonne-force: ratio 120/18 = 6.67. For wire rope, single use, the answer is

(36 × 100)/80 = 45 tonne-force: ratio 45/18 = 2.5, and for fibre rope the ratio is 6. These ratios (or multipliers) remain constant for equal cargo mass.

The CSS Code changes the commonly held understanding of the term 'rule of thumb' – a single multiplier easy to use and general in application – by inserting the MSL percentages to produce a range of rule of thumb multipliers.

Making use of Table 54.2, and in respect of any cargo mass, it is possible to use the multipliers without going through all the calculations previously described. More importantly, it can easily be seen the extent to which the MSL multipliers degrade or upgrade the generally accepted three-times rule.

In the instance of the 18 T cargo unit given above, the lashings' total breaking strength would be 54 tonne-force when the three-times rule is applied. Expressed simply 18 × 3 = 54 tonne-force total BS, that is:

Cargo mass × rule number = lashings' total breaking strength

Material	MSL	ROT multiplier
Shackles, rings, deckeyes, turnbuckles of mild steel	50% of breaking strength	4.00
Fibre rope	33% of breaking strength	6.06
Wire rope (single use)	80% of breaking strength	2.50
Web lashing	50% of breaking strength (was 70%)	4.00
Wire rope (re-usable)	30% of breaking strength	6.67
Steel band (single use)	70% of breaking strength	2.86
Chains	50% of breaking strength	4.00
(Compare with overall general component)	(60.67% of breaking strength)	(3.00)

Table 54.2: Determination of MSL from breaking strength, including rule of thumb multipliers.

54.9 Correction Factors

While the three-times rule may be considered adequate for the general conditions considered above, Section 7 of Annex 13 of the CSS Code (2021) provides Tables 3 and 4 where GMs are large and roll periods are less than 13 seconds. These tables, reproduced in this section, provide a measured way of applying that extra strength.

Length (m)	50	60	70	80	90	100	120	140	160	180	200
Speed (kn)											
9	1.20	1.09	1.00	0.92	0.85	0.79	0.70	0.63	0.57	0.53	0.49
12	1.34	1.22	1.12	1.03	0.96	0.90	0.79	0.72	0.65	0.60	0.56
15	1.49	1.36	1.24	1.15	1.07	1.00	0.89	0.80	0.73	0.68	0.63
18	1.64	1.49	1.37	1.27	1.18	1.10	0.98	0.89	0.82	0.76	0.71
21	1.78	1.62	1.49	1.38	1.29	1.21	1.08	0.98	0.90	0.83	0.78
24	1.93	1.76	1.62	1.50	1.40	1.31	1.17	1.07	0.98	0.91	0.85

Table 54.3: Correction factors for length and speed.

B/GM	7	8	9	10	11	12	13 or above
On deck, high	1.56	1.40	1.27	1.19	1.11	1.05	1.00
On deck, low	1.42	1.30	1.21	1.14	1.09	1.04	1.00
Tween deck	1.26	1.19	1.14	1.09	1.06	1.03	1.00
Lower hold	1.15	1.12	1.09	1.06	1.04	1.02	1.00

Note: The datum point in Table 54.3 is length of ship 100 m, speed of ship 15 knots and, in Table 54.4, B/GM <13.

Table 54.4: Correction factors for B/GM <13.

For all factors less than 1, it is safer to use 1 as the multiplier. For values greater than 1, Table 54.3 can be applied.

Section 6 of Annex 13 of the current CSS Code (2021) states:

"6 Safety Factor

6.1 When using balance calculation methods for assessing the strength of securing devices, a safety factor is used to take account of the possibility of uneven distribution of forces among the devices or reduced capability due to the improper assembly of the devices or other reasons. This safety factor is used in the formula to derive the calculated strength (CS) from the MSL and shown in the relevant method used.

$$CS = \frac{MSL}{safety\ factor}$$

6.2 Notwithstanding the introduction of such a safety factor, care should be taken to use securing elements of similar material and length in order to provide a uniform elastic behaviour within the arrangement."

54.10 Breaking Strengths

The term 'breaking strength' is not defined in the CSS Code and the CSM guidelines, but within the context of those two documents, it could reasonably be taken to mean *the point at which the component, material or element can no longer support or sustain the load,* pending some possible amendments by the IMO.

The CSS Code (Reference 22) defines the values of MSLs of mild steel components for securing purposes as 50% of breaking strength (see Table 54.1). Chapter 2 of the CSM requires such components to have identification marking, strength test result or ultimate tensile strength result, and MSL[1] all to be supplied by the manufacturer/supplier with information as to individual uses. The CSS Code requires that manufacturers should supply strengths/MSL values in kilonewtons (kN). (To convert kN to tonne-force, multiply by 0.1019761 or, for a rough value, divide by 10.)

This mix of terms is likely to raise questions about the validity of the CSMs issued and/or approved to date. If the components are not identifiable by at least their MSLs, they are not compliant with the CSM guidelines. To overcome this problem, it has been suggested that all aspects could be safely met by attaching, with suitable wire, small coloured metal tags stamped with the MSL of the component, such as used for securing components for timber deck cargoes. Responses received from the industry support this proposal.

It is recommended that ships' officers and others trying to apply the requirements of the CSM/CSS Code should, if the chains, shackles, rings, etc available are not clearly identified as to their MSLs, use the stamped SWL of a lifting shackle as required by the CSM/CSS Code. This means using a component that may have a breaking strength two times greater than is needed but ensures compliance with the regulations. Alternatively, multiply the stamped SWL value by 4 to obtain the breaking strength and apply the percentages given in Table 54.1 to obtain the MSL; then remove that component from any possibility of use for lifting purposes by tagging it. This fulfils the spirit of the regulations without resorting to the use of massively oversized lashing components.

54.11 Wire Rope

For efficient lashing purposes, wire ropes should be round-stranded, flexible and easy to handle/manoeuvre. The most commonly used general purpose wire is 16 mm diameter (2 inch circumference) of 6 × 12 construction galvanised round strand with 7 fibre cores having a certificated MBL of 7.74 tonne-force. This wire will turn easily around thimbles and lashing points, can be spliced or bulldog gripped without difficulty and is easily handled.

Other wires of different construction and of varying sizes or strength may be needed for particular lashing purposes and the certificated MBL should always be verified before bringing such wires into use.

---

[1] Chapter 1.1 of the CSM gives the following definition:
"Maximum securing load (MSL) is a term used to define the allowable load capacity for a device used to secure cargo to a ship. Safe working load (SWL) may be substituted for MSL for securing purposes, provided this is equal to or exceeds the strength defined by MSL."

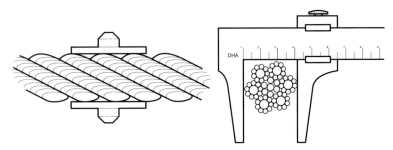

Correct method by which to measure the diameter of wire rope

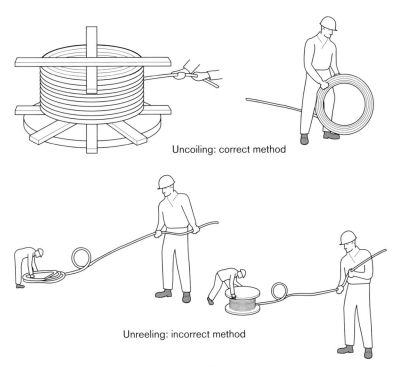

Uncoiling: correct method

Unreeling: incorrect method

Figure 54.5: Wire rope.

Wires intended for use as lashings may be supplied pre-cut to a precise length and with eyes or attachment devices already formed in one or both ends. Such purpose-made items are usually sold with certificates stating the test load and minimum break load applicable. If test certificates are not supplied, they should be requested. More commonly, the wire is supplied in coils and must be cut to length on board ship with eyes and attachment devices formed and fitted as required. Where this is the case, eyes formed by bulldog grips must be made up in accordance with the manufacturer's instructions. If they are incorrectly fitted, they may slip under smaller forces than stated in the MBL.

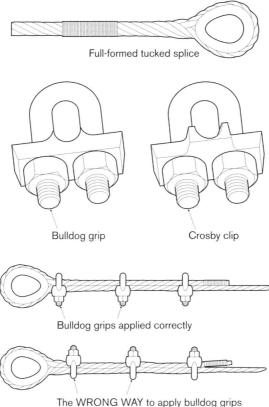

Full-formed tucked splice

Bulldog grip   Crosby clip

Bulldog grips applied correctly

The WRONG WAY to apply bulldog grips

Figure 54.6: Grips and clips.

54.12 Bulldog Grips

The most common cause of lashing failure is incorrect application of bulldog grips. Where an eye is formed around a thimble in the correct manner, the lashing arrangement will hold secure with loads up to or even in excess of 90% of the nominal break-load (NBL) of the wire before slipping or fracturing, although it is usual and recommended to allow not more than 80%. Without a thimble, the eye, when made up correctly, can be expected to slip at loads of about 70% of the NBL. Where the correct procedures are not followed, slippage is likely to occur at much reduced loads.

Under strictly controlled conditions, more than 100 tests were applied on a licensed test bed on 16 and 18 mm wire rope lashing configurations (see Figure 54.7a, b and c). As a result of such tests, the recommendations in this section are made.

It should be stressed that these recommendations relate to cargo lashings only. Lifting gear and other statutory applications require a minimum of 4, 5 and 6 grips for 16 mm diameter wire and upwards, respectively. It is also most important to ensure that the bulldog grips are of the correct size in order to correspond with the diameter of the lashing wire.

Diameter of wire rope (mm)	Wire rope grips
Up to and including 19	3
Over 19, up to and including 32	4
Over 32, up to and including 38	5
Over 38, up to and including 44	6
Over 44, up to and including 56	7

Table 54.5: Recommended minimum number of bulldog grips for each eye – lashing purposes only.

An allowance of 150 mm should be made between the last bulldog grip and the end of the 'dead' wire. It is important to ensure that the lashing wires are not cut short immediately next to the bulldog grips. The end of the dead wire should be tightly taped.

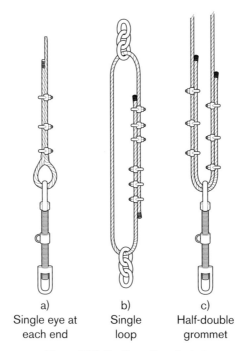

a)
Single eye at
each end

b)
Single
loop

c)
Half-double
grommet

Figure 54.7: Configurations tested.

- Bulldog grips have a grooved surface in the bridge piece which is suitable for a standard wire of right-hand lay having six strands. The grips should not be used with ropes of left-hand lay or of different construction. Crosby grips have a smooth surface in the bridge piece. The first grip should be applied close to the thimble or at the neck of the eye if a thimble is not used. Other grips should be placed at intervals of approximately six rope diameters apart (ie 96 mm with a 16 mm diameter wire, 108 mm with an 18 mm diameter wire)

- the grips must all face in the same direction and must be fitted with the saddle or bridge applied to the working or hauling part of the rope. The U-bolt must be applied to the tail or dead-end of the rope. If the grips are not applied as indicated, the effectiveness of the eye can be seriously affected

- ideally, all the nuts on the grips should be tightened using a torque wrench so that they may be set in accordance with the manufacturer's instructions. In practice, it may be sufficient to use a ring spanner, although thereafter all the nuts should be checked periodically and adjusted as necessary

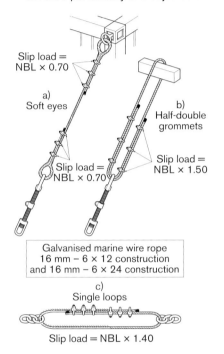

Figure 54.8: Correct application of Bulldog grips.

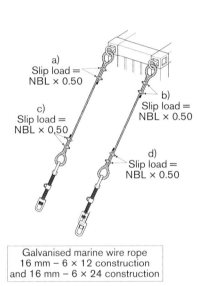

Figure 54.9: Soft eyes – some other representative slip loads.

- should a connection slip under load, it is likely that initially the rate of slip will be accelerated. The rate may then decrease but, until the load is removed, the slip will not be completely arrested

- the use of half-double grommets is common. Tests have shown that the slip load of this arrangement is only 1.5 × NBL (see Figure 54.8b). The holding power also decreases as the number of grips is reduced (see Figure 54.12)

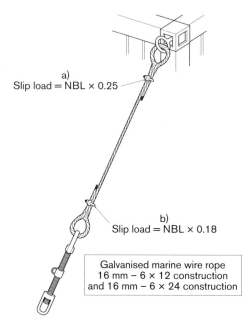

a)
Slip load = NBL × 0.25

b)
Slip load = NBL × 0.18

Galvanised marine wire rope
16 mm − 6 × 12 construction
and 16 mm − 6 × 24 construction

Figure 54.10: Soft eyes − UNSAFE application of Bulldog clips.

- the use of bulldog grips to join two ends of wire rope should be avoided. It is wrongly assumed that this will provide a holding power of 2 × NBL. In a single loop with six grips being used (see Figure 54.8), the slip load will be approximately 1.4 × NBL. The holding power decreases as the number of grips is reduced (see Figures 54.10 and 54.11)

- in a soft eye, with two grips and one or both used in the reverse manner (see Figure 54.9), the eye can be expected to slip at loads of about 50% of the NBL. These configurations are the least efficient

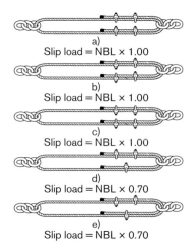

a)
Slip load = NBL × 1.00

b)
Slip load = NBL × 1.00

c)
Slip load = NBL × 1.00

d)
Slip load = NBL × 0.70

e)
Slip load = NBL × 0.70

Figure 54.11: Half-double grommets − some other representative slip loads.

- with a soft eye, using only one grip, the slip load was found to be 0.25 NBL with the grip positioned correctly (see Figure 54.10a) and 0.18 NBL with the grip reversed (see Figure 54.10b)

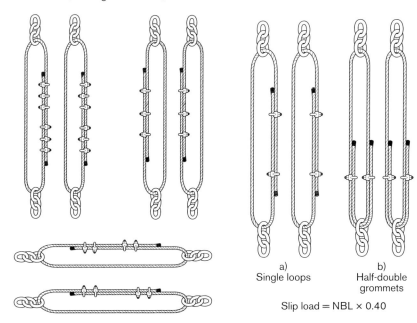

a)
Single loops

b)
Half-double grommets

Slip load = NBL × 0.40

Figure 54.12: Single loops – some other representative slip loads.

Figure 54.13: NOT recommended.

- a turnbuckle with a thread diameter of 24 mm or more can be adjusted to set up a pre-tension of about 2 T. If such a turnbuckle were attached to an eye made up in 16 mm wire, full tension in the wire would not be attained and the eye would slip at the grip under the pull of the turnbuckle alone.

Before deciding to use half-double grommets (NBL × 1.5) and single loops (NBL × 1.4) as opposed to single eyes (NBL × 0.7), it must be remembered that, at one terminal end in the instance of a half-double grommet, and at each terminal end in the instance of a single loop, there is no more material than at the terminal end of a soft eye.

If a properly made up single loop or half-double grommet breaks, this equals a loss of twice the holding power allowable for a soft eye. Therefore, it is most important to ensure that the terminal ends are connected by shackles or some other form of smooth component with no sharp edge.

Eyes and similar terminal ends in wire lashings should never be formed by the use of round turns and half hitches. Turns and hitches may slip and create sharp nips, leading to failure of the wire at loads well below those expected for eyes properly formed using bulldog grips.

When attaching wires to lashing terminals on the ship's structure or the cargo itself, every means should be taken to avoid hard edges, rough chafing points and sharp nips at the eye. Even where thimbles are not used, the attachment of the eyes of the wire to lashing terminals may best be accomplished by using shackles of the appropriate size and break load.

It must be ensured that the lashing points on the ship are sufficient in number and adequate in strength for the lashings they will hold.

54.13 Plastic-coated Wires

Plastic (PVC) coated galvanised standard marine wire of 18 mm diameter and 6 × 24 construction is commonly used for various purposes where there is a need to avoid the risk of cutting or chafing. Such wire should be used with caution because, if plastic-covered wire is used in conjunction with grips, slippage is likely to occur at lower loads than would be the case for unprotected wire of the same size and characteristics. The plastic coating should be stripped from the wire where the bulldog grips are to be applied and from the surface of any wires coming into contact with each other.

54.14 Fire and Explosion Hazards

Great care should be exercised if lashing terminals are to be welded during or after loading cargo. Before undertaking any hot work, it is important to obtain a hot work certificate from the local Port Authority. The authority should also be in possession of all relevant information relating to the ship and cargo. The welders themselves should be properly qualified and competent and, if welding is taking place either on deck or under deck, a proper fire watch should be mounted, both at and below the welding site. Adequate fireproof sheeting should be spread below welding points. On deck, fire hoses should be rigged with full pressure on the fire line.

A watchman should be posted for at least four hours after the completion of welding and a ship's officer should examine all spaces before they are finally battened down. These precautions should never be neglected and, if there is any doubt about safety, the welding must not go ahead.

54.15 Positive Action

It is important to be vigilant at all stages of the operation. If an officer or crew member sees a job being carried out incorrectly, the work should be stopped and reassessed.

54.16 Chain

Chain is widely used in the securing of freight containers, timber cargoes and vehicle trailers.

The use of chain alone for the securing of general deck cargoes is not widespread. Where chain lashings are used, they are usually supplied in precise lengths already fitted with terminal points and tightening devices.

The advantage of using chain is that, under the normal load for which the chain is designed, it will not stretch. Therefore, if all chain lashings are set tight before the voyage and the cargo neither settles nor moves, nothing should cause the chain to lose its tautness.

In general, chain for non-specific uses is awkward to handle, tiresome to rig, difficult to cut to length and does not render easily. For general purposes, it is most effectively used in relatively short lengths in conjunction with, or as a part of, lashings otherwise composed of wire or webbing.

54.17 Webbing

The use of webbing slings and webbing lashings for cargo securing purposes has steadily increased over the past years, but operational results differ widely. There are instances where webbing is ideal for securing deck cargoes and there are other instances where it should be used with caution.

Special large bore pipes made of reinforced plastic, or provided with contact sensitive outer coatings, make webbing an ideal securing medium. The broad, flat surfaces and reduced cutting nature allow the webbing to be turned around and tightened against the pipes, producing a highly secure form of stowage.

Large, heavy, crated items or high standing heavy machinery, where relatively long spans may be involved, require wire or chain lashings. Sufficient unsupported tension is difficult to apply with webbing alone.

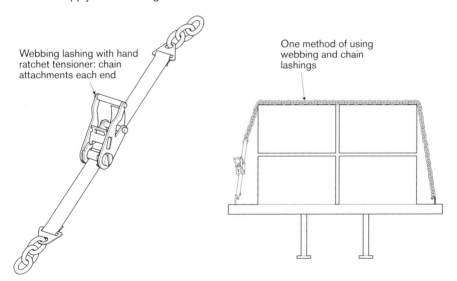

Webbing lashing with hand ratchet tensioner: chain attachments each end

One method of using webbing and chain lashings

Figure 54.14: Webbing.

Webbing is usually manufactured from woven polyester fibre, therefore will stretch more than wire rope. It is supplied in reels and may be easily cut and fashioned to any required length.

Webbing should not be used without first confirming from the manufacturer's manual its nature, breaking load and application. Tension on a hand ratchet can be obtained easily up to 0.54 T and then with increasing difficulty up to a maximum of 0.60 T. A spanner or bar must never be used to tighten a hand tension ratchet since recoil could cause serious injury.

Webbing should be kept away from acid and alkalis and care taken to ensure that it is never used to secure drums or packages of corrosive materials or chemicals because any leakage may damage and weaken the webbing. All webbing should be inspected frequently and, if re-used, care taken to ensure that all lengths are free from defects.

Protective sleeves should be used between webbing and abrasion points or areas. ISO freight containers should only be secured using webbing systems designed for such a purpose.

54.18 Fibre Rope

Ropes of up to 24 mm in diameter are handy to use but are more likely to be found on cargoes that are stowed below deck. The use of fibre ropes for weather-deck cargoes should be restricted to light loads of limited volume, in areas that are partly sheltered by the ship's structure. Where such ropes are used on deck, difficulty is likely to be encountered in maintaining the tautness of the lashings when they are subjected to load stresses and the effects of wetting and drying out in exposed situations. The use of turnbuckles should be avoided as they may easily overload the rope lashing. The tautening of rope lashings is best achieved by the use of bowsing ropes and frappings. At 24 mm diameter, a sisal rope has a breaking strain of 7.5 T and a polyester rope of 9 T.

Composite rope, frequently referred to as 'lashing rope', is made up of interwoven wire fibres and sisal or polypropylene fibres. The breaking strain of composite ropes should be considered as about 0.8 T for sisal-based and 1.8 T for polypropylene-based ropes.

Nylon fibre absorbs water and when under load this can reduce its effective strength by about 15%. Premature failure of nylon rope occurs under limited cyclic loading of up to 70% of its effective strength. Therefore, nylon rope is not recommended for deck cargo securing purposes.

The figures for breaking strain refer to new material and not to rope that has been in use for any length of time.

54.19 Shackles

Shackles are supplied in several shapes, sizes and strengths. The two shapes most commonly used in general cargo lashing are the D shackle and the bow shackle, each with an eyed screw pin. When using shackles, it is correct to define their strength in terms of the safe working load although, as indicated in Table 54.1, the CSS Code (Reference 22) and the CSM guidelines define their MSL as 50% of the breaking strength. Therefore, when preparing combined cargo lashings, it must always be ensured that the MSL of the shackles selected is not less than the effective strength of the eyes or other configurations formed in the wire rope and similar materials.

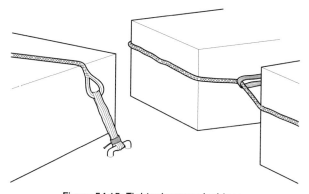

Figure 54.15: Tightening rope lashings.

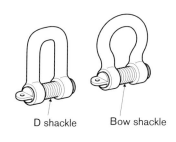

D shackle   Bow shackle

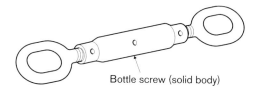

Bottle screw (solid body)

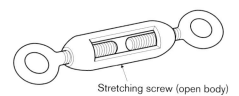

Stretching screw (open body)

Figure 54.16: Shackles and screws.

54.20 Turnbuckles

The precautions for shackles also apply to the use of turnbuckles. The word 'turnbuckle' is used collectively to include solid-cased bottle screws and open-sided rigging screws or straining or stretching screws. These are most commonly used for general cargo lashing and are supplied in a range of sizes and strengths with a closed eye at each end. Open-sided rigging screws and straining screws tend to have noticeably lower strengths than solid bottle screws of the same size. The suppliers or manufacturers should be asked to provide the relevant test data so that the correct MSL or SWL can be ascertained before commencing lashing.

Solid bottle screws are typically sold by size of screw pin diameter. Those of 24 mm diameter have a proof-load of 4 T and those of 38 mm have a proof-load of 10 T. Special-purpose turnbuckles are available with much greater strengths than those given above. These may have particular fittings and modifications, such as those used in the container trade. Again, it is important to consult the manufacturer's manual before equipment is used.

Turnbuckles should always be used with the pulling forces acting in one straight line. They should never be allowed to become the fulcrum of angled forces.

Care should always be taken to ensure that the screws are at adequate extension when the cargo is finally secured. In this way, scope is provided for further tightening if this is required during the voyage as the cargo and lashing arrangements settle. Where high torque upon a main lashing is involved, the eyes of the turnbuckle should be seized or stopped against its own body in order to prevent the screws working back under load during the voyage.

Chapter 55 –
Steel Hatch Covers

The steady increase in the size of ships, and particularly bulk carriers, has been accompanied by a steady increase in the cost of manning and running them.

Figure 55.1: Steel hatch covers.

As a partial counter to this escalation in costs, equipment such as steel hatch covers was developed and introduced on board ship, shortening the turnaround time in port and enabling larger ships to be manned by smaller crews.

This chapter is based on a UK P&I Club report that considered steel hatch covers in general and the MacGregor-Navire hatch covers in particular. It examined claims for seawater damage to cargo carried in ships fitted with steel hatch covers, to analyse the causes of leakage and to suggest solutions.

The fitting of steel hatch covers on the weather deck of seagoing ships is now the rule rather than the exception, and so it is essential to eliminate the underlying causes of cargo damage from ingress of seawater through these hatch covers. The additional weight of seawater in the tanks may also overload the ship and threaten stability.

55.1   Advantages of Steel Hatches

The advantages of steel hatch covers include:

- Greater strength than traditional hatch covers, which contributes to the safety of the vessel
- easier and quicker to open and close
- fewer crew are required to operate them compared to traditional hatch covers.

Against these advantages must be placed the high costs of initial purchase and routine maintenance.

55.2   Development of Automatic Steel Hatch Covers

The hatch openings of ships were traditionally covered with beams, wooden boards and tarpaulins. Metal was used for slab-type pontoons, but the MacGregor-Navire Organisation had the idea of using an eccentric wheel to lower and raise these pontoons and, in the raised position, to move them to one end of the coamings, lifting them at that point into a vertical position. In the lowered position, they would rest on a rubber gasket and, by the use of cleats, become weathertight. This revolutionary but simple modification was still in operation in the mid-1940s.

Subsequently, these simple individually moved panels were linked together and counterbalanced in such a way that one wire could be used to move them to one end of the hatch, where they would automatically assume a vertical position and stow in a small area. This principle became internationally known as the 'single pull hatch cover' and, on the weather deck, it is still the most widely used means of cargo protection. Refinements and modifications have been incorporated to include automation and folding hatch covers motivated by hydraulic or electrical means, piggy back covers, stacking covers, coiling covers and sequential or non-sequential multi-panel covers. However, for illustrative purposes, this chapter covers just the single pull type of operation.

55.2.1   Coamings

The sealing round the edge of the hatch, to prevent the ingress of water, consists of a hard rubber gasket strip retained on three sides in a channel bar within the hatch cover framework and resting on the compression bar, which is a square section steel bar welded onto the coaming bars (see Figures 55.2 to 55.4). A double drainage trough is designed inboard of this compression bar to safeguard against minor localised sealing problems.

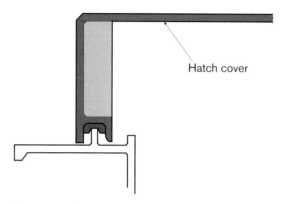

Figure 55.2: Section through side or end of hatch cover.

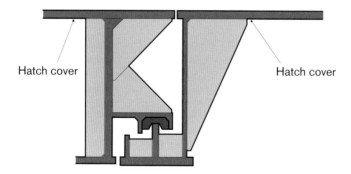

Figure 55.3: Section through cross joint.

Figure 55.4: Details of cross joint rubber inserts.

Should anything be trapped on the coaming during the closing operation or a local deformation in the compression bar be caused by, for example, a derrick runner wire, then in this local area there is a small opening for the possible entry of water which, while not being dangerous, could damage a fairly large amount of cargo.

55.2.2 Moving Parts

Maintenance for the continuance of original weathertightness is essential and correct maintenance of moving parts, such as wheels, chains, gypsies, etc, will alleviate the possibility of the assembly being subjected unnecessarily to rough treatment because of undue wear on these parts.

55.3 Weakness in Hatch Covers

55.3.1 Strength

Each automated steel hatch cover panel, consisting of steel plate, sections, beams, etc, is designed and assembled to the strict requirements of a Classification Society and is expected to be immensely strong. However, this can be a disadvantage under certain circumstances, particularly when the vessel is labouring in a seaway. Although ships give the impression of great strength, when the weather is adverse any ship that does not yield to the force of the waves would quickly founder. In fact, the ship must ride those blows that cannot be avoided to absorb the greater part of the energy directed at it. In so doing, the ship 'works' along its length and across its width.

In these conditions, the strength and rigidity of the steel hatch covers can cause the weathertight joints between the vessel's structure (hatch) and the covers to move as the ship works in a seaway.

With the average freeboard of ships considered as being approximately 2.75 m, and with a combination of wave heights, a deadweight cargo and strong winds on passage, most ships will have the decks and hatches awash at frequent intervals.

In an analysis of claims for cargo damage when hatch covers had failed, bad weather had been experienced on every voyage, but in no case was it of such severity as to offer certain defence of 'perils of the sea' under the Hague-Visby Rules, neither was it severe enough to justify penetrations of the rubber seals of the hatch joints, provided that the seals were in good condition. However, in many cases, survey reports from the discharge port criticised the condition of the hatch covers and coamings, indicating a poor standard of maintenance.

The results on analysis of claims showed:

- Usually, the only vessels involved were those carrying bulk and deadweight cargoes
- their freeboard was not very large
- all voyages included a period of heavy weather
- hatch survey reports indicated that some hatches and coamings were in poor condition.

55.4 Suggested Remedies

55.4.1 Proper Securing

When hatches were secured with boards and tarpaulins, the need for care in their securing was very obvious. The ships were also much smaller and there were more seafarers to perform the tasks connected with leaving port, such as the lowering and securing of derricks and the battening down of hatches. The crew had to work as a team because the various jobs could not be done by one or two seafarers alone and, with teamwork, there is less risk that the job will be improperly done. Lastly, a poorly secured hatch was immediately apparent to the ship's officers and steps could be taken to remedy the situation.

However, on modern bulk carriers, there are fewer crew members. For the one or two seafarers concerned, the prospect of securing a long line of hatch covers stretching away along the weather deck is not an inviting one, and when there are added discomforts of wind and rain it is not surprising if the securing is not always carried out as conscientiously as it ought to be. Steel cleats and wedges are not as interesting as canvas tarpaulins and wooden wedges, even if they are stronger and more efficient and, therefore, safer. There are also a great many of them; hatches of say 40 × 30 ft will probably have six panels secured around the edges by about 40 cleats and further secured by about 50 cross-seam wedges.

When securing hatch covers, the joints cannot be effective if insufficient pressure is applied and the pressure must be evenly distributed along the whole length of the joint.

Type of cargo stresses

The type and distribution of cargo carried can affect the stresses experienced by a ship in a seaway and the degree of bending and twisting suffered. In this respect, homogeneous cargoes of low density, such as bulk grain, are better than high density cargoes, such as ore concentrates or steel products. Bulk carriers are designed as single-deck vessels, which means that high density cargoes will be stowed at the bottom of the holds, causing severe racking strains of hogging and sagging.

These racking strains may well cause the hatch covers to leak if the cleats and wedges are not secured properly. In these conditions, it is important to ensure that the cleats remain tight.

Case Study – 'Sabine Howaldt'

In severe weather, leakages can and will occur through steel hatch covers even if they are properly secured. This was illustrated by the decision of the US Court of Appeal in the case of the 'Sabine Howaldt', 1971 AMC539.

The 'Sabine Howaldt' was a vessel of 2,300 gross tons, 306 ft in length, a beam of 40 ft, her bridge amidships and her engines aft. The four cargo holds were served by two hatches only, one forward and one abaft the bridge. The fore deck hatch was about 60 × 18 ft and had the protection of solid bulwarks at the ship's side, while the after deck with open rails at the ship's side was 3 ft higher than the fore deck and had a hatch of about 68 × 18 ft. The holds were separated by bulkheads with the forward hatch serving Nos 1 and 2 and the after hatch serving Nos 3 and 4.

At the time, the 'Sabine Howaldt' was 7 years old and her classification, which was the highest in Germanischer Lloyd, had been maintained at her annual survey in April 1965. The charter voyage during the following December was from Europe to the USA with a full cargo of steel products, which were loaded in good condition but were rusted and pitted from contact with seawater when discharged from No 4 hold and also, but to a lesser extent, from No 1 hold.

Before completion of loading, the surveyor for the charterer inspected the hatch covers and found them in good condition with no dents, bending or other damage and no staining on the inside of the coamings to indicate previous leakage. His report found the ship seaworthy. After the hatches had been closed and tightened down, they were inspected by the chief officer together with another officer and a log entry was made by the chief officer that the MacGregor-Navire hatch covers were 'closed and wedged'.

The *'Sabine Howaldt'* sailed from Antwerp on 15th December at a draught less than permitted as she was not down to her winter marks. By midnight on the third day, the wind had risen to force 9 on the Beaufort Scale. It increased to force 10 by 09:00 hrs on the 18th, blew with that force until about 17:00 hrs and then began to ease. During the whole of this period, the ship pitched and rolled heavily in the high seas and waves were continually breaking across the decks.

On the 20th, the wind reached force 9/10, but it abated the following day and did not exceed force 7/8. On the 23rd, the ship was hove-to for 12 hours trying to reduce the battering from hurricane force winds, heavy confused swells and huge seas breaking over her forecastle deck hatches and upper works; bending, twisting and vibrating her continuously.

The violence of the weather was severe enough to cause structural damage. After the worst of the storm was over, it was discovered that the pedestal holding the master switch control for the capstan had been torn loose leaving a hole in the deck, a galley port hole was smashed and the catwalk gangway from amidships to poop was torn loose and destroyed, denting a ventilator at the same time. Several parts of the ship's superstructure and fixtures were dented and the covers from two winches had been ripped off and lost.

When the weather first deteriorated at the beginning of the voyage, the chief officer, in the company of another officer, made a second inspection of the hatches from inside the cargo holds. He found no leakage through the hatchway although waves were washing across the covers. He also examined the covers on arrival in the USA on 3rd January and found hatches, covers and gaskets all in good condition, as did the surveyors for both the owners and the charterers. Nevertheless, seawater had entered the hold and it was decided that the severe stresses to which the ship had been subjected had momentarily deformed the rectangular opening of the hatch, thereby disturbing the seal between the gasket and the compression bar on the coaming, allowing seawater, which was pouring over the decks and hatches, to enter the hold.

After considering all the circumstances, including the fact that on both the previous and following voyages the hatch covers had not leaked in spite of heavy weather, the Court of Appeal decided that the violence of the wind and the confused cross swells that had wrenched and twisted the ship during the voyage were a 'peril of the sea' and that the owners were not liable for the damage to cargo resulting from the leaking of the hatch covers.

Had the *'Sabine Howaldt'* been equipped with wooden hatch boards and tarpaulins, the situation would have been far more dangerous. The collapsing of the amidships catwalk would undoubtedly have torn the tarpaulins covering the hatch over Nos 3 and 4 holds, allowing a much larger volume of seawater to enter those holds to the certain detriment of the cargo and possibly to the ultimate danger of the ship itself.

55.4.2 Proper Maintenance

It is absolutely crucial for hatch covers to be maintained at the highest standard if cargo damage is to be avoided.

It is not easy to achieve this standard because the modern bulk carrier has a smaller crew for its size than the older type general cargo ship and spends little time in port. Adequate maintenance is difficult to carry out in port because of cargo being worked, or at sea because the hatches are then secured for the passage.

Figure 55.5: Folding hatch cover.

Systematic and well-documented inspection is an essential part of onboard maintenance and will aid identification of defects at an early stage. The ship's planned maintenance system should include ship/hatch-specific checklists that have been drawn up in accordance with the equipment manuals.

Working parts

The marine environment is extremely corrosive and every opportunity must be taken to minimise its effect, particularly in respect of the cleats that secure the pontoons. It is the shipowner's/operator's responsibility to undertake the required maintenance.

Figure 55.6: Hatch coaming and cleat arrangement on a container ship fitted with pontoons.

Hatch panels

Regular inspection and maintenance of hatch panels is essential because any defects, cracks, holes or corrosion will invariably lead to water leaking into the hold. Properly painted hatch top plating contributes only to cosmetic appearance and should not be taken as proof that the panels are in good condition.

Cracks and holes may be repaired with doublers, but these should be considered as a temporary repair and never a substitute for a proper insert repair. Doublers will cover the damage and prevent water ingress, but will not restore the original strength or stop corrosion. Welding on hatch covers should be carried out by trained and qualified personnel as excessive heat may cause distortion of the panel structure, which is very difficult to correct.

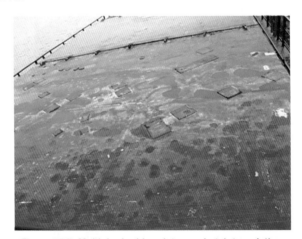

Figure 55.7: Multiple doubler plates on hatch top plating.

Care must be taken if sealing tape has been applied to the hatch cover. This adheres strongly to the surface and may lift off the paint when removed. This leaves the surface unprotected and exposed to the elements, with corrosive action setting in if not dealt with quickly and in the proper manner.

Hatch covers are type-approved equipment and repairs involving modifications or changes to the design can only be made with the approval of the Classification Society or the flag State.

Hatch cover repairs should be properly and promptly reported to the Classification Society or flag State. As well as being a Class requirement, this enables the ship to obtain correct repair information that is in line with Class rules.

Figure 55.8: Damaged hatch cover which cannot be repaired at sea.

Rubber seals

The most important factors determining the ability of the hatches to remain weathertight are the rubber seals on the underside of the panels and the compression bars with which the seals make contact when the hatches are in a closed and secured position.

The effectiveness of the rubber seals can be reduced in several ways:

- Accidents occurring while the hatches are being worked and during the opening and closing of them can physically deform the seals
- careless painting of channels can cause hard spots on the seals, locally reducing their resilience
- rust scale can form underneath the seals in an uneven thickness, causing high spots and resulting in non-uniform compression of the rubber
- particles of cargoes, such as grain or ore, can become compressed between the seals and the compression bars
- overcompression of the rubber will result in permanent damage in the form of a groove where the rubber meets the compression bar
- age will cause seals to perish or harden, with a tendency for them to crack and break.

Any of these can result in the covers leaking when under stress.

Figure 55.9: Permanent groove in packing rubber caused by overcompression.

Good management, careful inspection and routine maintenance at every opportunity will help to prevent all but the ageing of the rubber. This cannot be prevented but it can and ought to be recognised and remedied before it has progressed too far. The only remedy is the replacement of the old seals with new, and the opportunity should be taken at the time of renewal to remove all traces of rust scale from the channels before preparing them and reseating the new seals.

Any seals more than two years old should be inspected regularly for signs of deterioration due to ageing.

Whenever packing is to be renewed, whether because of damage or old age, it is essential that the whole strip is replaced, or there will be different compression strengths between the new and existing rubber. In hatch cover tightness, compression is the governing factor, not contact.

Last minute repairs should be avoided, particularly if they focus on passing a tightness test rather than the quality of repair. Improper repairs are unlikely to withstand ocean passage and overlook the important issue of due diligence.

> Under the due diligence principle, owners are required to carry out a reasonable inspection to ensure that hatch covers are in good condition. If a defect is found during this inspection, repairs should be carried out in line with good industry practice to restore the condition of the hatch covers and their sealing and securing arrangements.
>
> If a claim for wetting damage is filed against the ship, a well-prepared maintenance file will be of great value in defending the owner's interest and proving that due diligence was exercised.

Improperly maintained or adjusted hatch covers will generally cause accelerated wear and deep permanent imprint to the rubber seal. Replacing the rubber seal alone will not solve the problem and identifying the root cause of the problem is necessary to ensure that repairs will be efficient.

Compression bars

The compression bars along the top of the hatch coamings are solid steel and there is a tendency to assume that no harm can come to them and that they need no maintenance.

The most common cause of damage to these bars is impact from cargo moving into or out of the hold. This is particularly the case if the ship carries cargoes of constructional steel, when each lift will be awkward to handle and probably heavy as well. A load of this type striking the compression bar can easily dent, score or bend the bar.

The bars may also become damaged over a period of time by cargo wires continually passing across the same area, with the result that the original right-angled edge of the bar becomes rounded. If care is not taken to combat corrosion, the top surface of the bar will, in time, develop high and low spots that will prevent the proper seating of the rubbers.

This corrosion is particularly likely to affect the compression bars of the cross joints. Close attention should be paid to the cross joints between the panels as, in many instances, leakage has occurred at these joints or at some other position as a result of them being defective in some way. The cross joints must be pressed firmly and evenly together, and the cross wedges, whether manually or automatically operated, are of paramount importance as the tightness of the joint mainly depends on them. If the cross wedges do not provide an effective seal, either the seals have become too heavily compressed and require renewal, the compression bar on the adjacent panel has become bent or worn down, or there is a combination of both these defects. The situation is often rectified by welding a small plate onto the adjacent panel edge at a position where the manual wedge end rides up and over the panels to put pressure on the cross joint. If the wedges become strained or bent, new wedges should be fitted.

Bearing pads

Figure 55.10: Bearing pad.

Bearing pads have two parts, one attached to the side of the hatch cover and the other attached to the coaming. Their purpose is to:

- Assist with alignment/adjustment of the hatch cover
- transfer loads into the deck structure

- prevent the hatch cover sitting too low on the coaming
- prevent loads being transferred to other structural parts such as wheels and axles.

Bearing pads come in different sizes and materials and their wear will depend on their position and loads. This means that not all bearing pads will wear down to the same extent simultaneously and they require regular inspection to determine whether allowable wear limits have been exceeded.

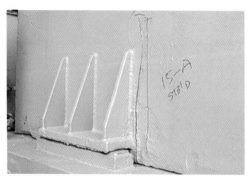

Figure 55.11: A crack developing in the side plating due to advanced bearing pad wear.

Care must be taken when replacing bearing pads and it is not just a case of restoring them to their original height. Original spares of the correct size should be used and the two parts must be of compatible materials. Low-friction material is recommended to allow smooth movement between the panel and the coaming. Manufacturers or specialists should be called in for bearing pad adjustment.

Figure 54.12: Improper repair to a bearing pad.

Hatch covers fitted with bearing pads usually have an operational clearance of 10 to 15 mm between the panel side lower edge and the coaming. The exact distance should be checked in the manual and noted on inspection sheets as it is one of the first indicators of bearing pad wear.

Locators

Locators guide the panel into its correct closing position and ensure the panels are kept properly positioned during the voyage.

Locator wear should be regularly monitored because slight wear in one place may result in significant loss of compression or improper positioning in another place.

Figure 55.13: Properly maintained and adjusted locator.

Some locators have replaceable mating surfaces and allow for the use of shim plates to facilitate installation and adjustment in case of wear down.

Figure 55.14: Excessive wear on the locator.

Stoppers

Hatch panels may be subjected to heavy loads and accelerations when the ship is rolling and pitching in a seaway. Stoppers (restraints) are fitted to keep the panel in its correct position. Stopper wear must be closely monitored and the manual should be consulted for advice on allowable wear limits.

Figure 55.15: Stopper.

Draining system

The coamings and covers of steel hatches are designed to clear away moisture, but general cleanliness of drain holes, waterways and coamings is important because any accumulation of cargo residues or dirt may trap condensation and rainwater. This could result in sweat damage to the cargo and steady deterioration of the covers by corrosion.

Maintenance of the draining system should include regular cleaning of the drainage channels, drain holes, drain pipes and drain valves, particularly following cargo operations.

A wooden bung may be placed in the drainage system to prevent blockage during cargo operations. This is fine as long as removal of the bung is not overlooked on completion of operations.

Figure 55.16: Blocked drainage systems.

Securing mechanism

The primary function of the securing mechanism (cleats) is to hold the panels down when the ship is at sea. Whatever cleating system is used (eg manual, hydraulically operated), it is vital that it is structurally sound. This includes not only the cleat itself, but also the component parts to which the cleats are engaged (eg coaming table, crutches, snugs/panel side plating). The system should be checked regularly for wear and corrosion.

Figure 55.17: Corrosion of quick acting cleat crutch (left), thinned down snugs (right).

The cleats should never be overtightened to obtain a tighter seal. This would make the system too rigid and eventually result in damage to the cleats. In addition, steel to steel contact between the panels and the coaming would make it impossible to compress the rubber seal to achieve an adequate seal.

After completion of securing operations, a final check should be made to ensure that the cleats are all in place and correctly positioned. Crooked or poorly fitting cleats may be an indication of improper closing or alignment of the panel. This should be investigated and corrected before commencement of the voyage since faulty securing will affect the holding power of the system.

Figure 55.18: Improper vertical alignment of quick acting cleat.

Tape or foam

Sometimes, additional safeguards against leakage are applied. The usual method is the covering of cross joints with heavy adhesive tape. A more recent procedure is to use expanding foam, which when sprayed onto the joints produces a hardened barrier to water. The use of additional safeguards does not negate the need for hatch cover testing and inspection.

Some charterers, particularly in the steel trades, require the Master to apply tape to the hatch cover joints and may even supply the tape. However, the use of temporary sealants allows claimants to assume that the Master/shipowner was aware of a tightness problem, but disregarded due diligence by opting for the cheapest and quickest repair.

Maintenance manuals

Vessels fitted with steel hatch covers should carry manufacturer's manuals that provide detailed information relating to the construction, operation and maintenance of the covers, together with lists of spare parts that should be carried on board for remedial repairs. In addition, leading manufacturers may have representatives in major sea ports available both to advise and also to carry out repairs and maintenance as required.

It is strongly recommended that major overhauls and inspections are carried out by manufacturers' representatives, at the very least each time the vessel dry-docks, in order that the high original standard of the covers is maintained throughout the life of the ship. As the trend is for ships to spend less time in port and to carry a relatively small crew, it is reasonable to say that shore maintenance must be the standard, with crew maintenance being used as remedial, as and when necessary. In this way, claims on the shipowner for damage to cargo should be reduced to a minimum.

55.5   Testing Weathertight Integrity of Dry Cargo Vessels' Hatch Covers

Regulation 3.12 of the *International Convention on Load Lines, 1966* states:

"Weathertight. Weathertight means that in any sea conditions water will not penetrate into the ship".

Regulation 16 of the Convention concerns hatchways closed by weathertight covers. The *"means for securing weathertightness"* is defined in Regulation 16.4 of the Convention, which states:

"The means for securing and maintaining weathertightness shall be to the satisfaction of the Administration. The arrangements shall ensure that the tightness can be maintained in any sea conditions, and for this purpose tests for tightness shall be required at the initial survey, and may be required at periodical surveys and at annual inspections or at more frequent intervals."

55.5.1 Traditional Methods

The light test

This is the simplest means of establishing whether a defect exists and its location. The hatches are battened down fully and properly for seagoing, then the surveyor/observer enters the hold and views the underside of the covers from below. In strong sunlight, defects should be readily visible, with daylight shining through any gaps in the packing. If the test is undertaken during poor light conditions, strong torchlight properly directed from above will serve the same purpose.

The chalk test

Chalk is applied to the compression bars of the coamings and the individual panel cross seams. The hatches are then battened down fully and in the proper manner, after which they are immediately re-opened and the rubber packing (joints) carefully examined. Where a clean regular chalk mark is observed on the packaging, it is assumed that sufficient pressure exists between the joint and the adjacent compression bar. If the chalk mark is found to be intermittent or less pronounced at some points than at others, it is assumed that weathertight integrity does not exist over those areas. This method can only be considered as indicative of a possible problem, with likely inconclusive results even after rectification of possible defects that may have been exposed by the test. The International Association of Classification Societies (IACS) advises in their Recommendation No. 14: Hatch cover securing and tightness (Reference 86) that:

"Upon completion of installation of hatch covers, a chalk test is to be carried out. This is to be followed by a hose test with a pressure of water not less than 200 kN/m². "

The hose test

In this test, a strong jet of pressurised water is directed at the seams and joints of the hatch covers. Hatch covers are battened down fully in the proper manner and with the surveyor stationed in the hold. A survey assistant must be stationed on deck/on top of the hatch covers to ensure that the water, usually supplied from the vessel's fire main, is directed at a constant and sufficient pressure in the proper direction. Ideally, the hose should be held at a distance of no more than 1 m from the joint under test with a pressure of not less than 200 Kn/m². The disadvantages of this method include:

* It is time consuming
* it is difficult to ensure adequate water pressure
* excessive water may drain from the decks when the vessel may be alongside a wharf, pier or jetty
* the test cannot be safely carried out when the vessel is laden for fear of wet damage to the cargo
* two surveyors are required to conduct the test
* the test cannot be carried out if weather conditions/air temperatures are at or below 0°C.

A high-pressure jet of water may break apart on top of the panel rather than entering the interpanel void space, thus producing an unreliable test result. A second method would be to close the panel's side guttering and fill up the cross joint interpanel void space with water from a low-pressure hose. This allows hydrostatic pressure to build up on top of the packing rubber/compression bar interface. Any water that passes through the seal will be expelled on deck through the drain valve (note that perimeter joints will still require water jet testing). As a lot of water is generated during the test, it is recommended that a plastic bag is placed at the discharge end of the drain valve to collect water expelled during the test.

Ultrasonic test

There has been debate concerning the efficiency and acceptability of ultrasonic testing equipment but the technique is widely used throughout the industry to test and prove the weathertightness of hatch covers.

The advantages of this method include:

* The test identifies the exact location and extent of leakage
* it indicates the compression status of the rubber seal; if compression is good, the rubber will be able to compensate for movements at sea and maintain a tight seal
* the equipment is quick and easy to operate. One person operation is possible

- the test may be carried out in loaded or empty holds

Figure 55.19: Ultrasonic testing of hatch cover.

- there are no weather/temperature limitations and the test may be carried out during the day or night
- there is no pollution risk.

The procedure comprises placing a transmitter in the cargo hold, switching it on, and properly closing and securing the hatch covers (or other access equipment) to seaworthy requirements. The ultrasonic waves emitted by the transmitter within the enclosed space will leak through the smallest of apertures. Any leakage of sound may be detected by a receiver or detector between frequencies of 36.7 and 40.7 kHz and converted into aural frequencies or into digitally reproduced information. The location of leaks can be precisely detected from outside the hold by moving a hand-held detector along the periphery and cross seams of the covers. Evaluation of the extent of leakage can be established from reading a digital scale.

Class type approval and operator training is undertaken by some manufacturers of ultrasonic equipment used in the testing of hatch covers. The training courses include:

- Principles of the technique
- the ultrasonic equipment
- hatch cover types
- typical defects identified
- testing and reporting procedures.

It is impossible to say that hatch covers are weathertight merely by testing the seal. Although the condition of the seal plays a major part, it is also necessary to visually inspect all parts of the cover.

Records

A record should be kept of the location and extent of any leakages detected during testing. The hatches should then be opened, the causes of leakages, if any, identified, the defects rectified, covers resecured and further weathertight testing undertaken.

Hatch cover safety

Hatch covers are heavy, moving pieces of machinery and crew must be trained in their safe operation and maintenance.

Chapter 16 of the *Code of Safe Working Practices for Merchant Seafarers* (2015 Edition, amended 2022) identifies areas of operation that need particular attention to protect the health and safety of operators.

As there are many different types of hatch cover, shipowners should draft ship-specific operating guidelines based on the manufacturer's manuals. This should include the operational limits due to trim, heel, and transversal and longitudinal coaming deflection. The OOW/cargo officer should monitor these operational limitations closely because failure to do so may cause the hatch covers to derail.

Evidence to produce in the event of a claim

If a claim for wetting damage is filed against the ship, the following documentation should be produced as evidence of due diligence:

- Work schedules
- maintenance logs and test reports
- work specifications
- accounts
- standing instructions
- reports and correspondence
- logbook entries
- hatch patentee manual
- relevant certificates
- evidence of voyage planning and weather reports
- proof that the ship was operated in a seamanlike manner during the voyage.

A note of protest should also be prepared. A local P&I surveyor will be able to assist with further survey and test requirements.

References

References

1. IMO. *Recommendations on the Safe Use of Pesticides in Ships* (MSC.1/Circ.1264 and MSC.1/Circ.1361/Rev.1),

2. Isbester, Captain J. *Bulk Carrier Practice: A Practical Guide.*

3. IMO. *International Code for the Safe Carriage of Grain in Bulk* (International Grain Code).

4. Oxley, T A. *The Scientific Principles of Grain Storage.*

5. European Commission. *EU Register of authorised GMOs.*

6. European Commission Joint Research Centre. *European Union Reference Laboratory for Genetically Modified Food and Feed* (EURL GMFF).

7. Biosafety Clearing-House, Convention on Biological Diversity. *BCH Central Portal.* https://bch.cbd.int

8. *2004/787/EC: Commission Recommendation of 4 October 2004 on technical guidance for sampling and detection of genetically modified organisms and material produced from genetically modified organisms as or in products in the context of Regulation (EC) No 1830/2003.*

9. International Organization for Standardization (ISO). *ISO DIS 21568: FOODSTUFFS – METHODS OF ANALYSIS FOR THE DETECTION OF GENETICALLY MODIFIED ORGANISMS AND DERIVED PRODUCTS – SAMPLING.*

10. *Regulation (EC) No 1829/2003 of the European Parliament and of the Council of 22 September 2003 on genetically modified food and feed.*

11. *Directive 2001/18/EC of the European Parliament and of the Council of 12 March 2001 on the deliberate release into the environment of genetically modified organisms and repealing Council Directive 90/220/EEC – Commission Declaration.*

12. *Directive (EU) 2015/412 of the European Parliament and of the Council of 11 March 2015 amending Directive 2001/18/EC as regards the possibility for the Member States to restrict or prohibit the cultivation of genetically modified organisms (GMOs) in their territory.*

13. *Regulation (EC) No 1830/2003 of the European Parliament and of the Council of 22 September 2003 concerning the traceability and labelling of genetically modified organisms and the traceability of food and feed products produced from genetically modified organisms and amending Directive 2001/18/EC.*

14.   *Commission Recommendation of 23 July 2003 on guidelines for the development of national strategies and best practices to ensure the coexistence of genetically modified crops with conventional and organic farming (notified under document number C(2003) 2624).*

15.   Biosafety Clearing-House, Convention on Biological Diversity. *The Cartagena Protocol on Biosafety.* https://bch.cbd.int

16.   INTERCARGO/Lloyd's Register/UK P&I Club. *Carrying Solid Bulk Cargoes Safely.*

17.   IMO. *International Maritime Solid Bulk Cargoes Code* (IMSBC Code), 2022.

18.   IMO. *International Convention for the Safety of Life at Sea* (SOLAS), 2020.

19.   IMO. *International Maritime Dangerous Goods Code* (IMDG Code), 2022.

20.   N I Dowling and J B Hyne. 'Controlling Corrosion of Steel by Wet Elemental Sulphur.' *NACE Canadian Region Western Conference,* 1987.

21.   International Group of P&I Clubs. *Circular: Direct Reduced Iron.* 1982.

22.   IMO. *Code of Safe Practice for Cargo Stowage and Securing* (CSS Code), 2021.

23.   IMO. *Code of Safe Practice for Ships Carrying Timber Deck Cargoes,* (TDC Code), 2011.

24.   IMO. *Revised Guidelines for the Preparation of the Cargo Securing Manual* (MSC.1/Circ.1353/Rev.2).

25.   IMO. *International Convention on Load Lines 1966,* 2021 Edition.

26.   UK P&I Club. *Carefully to Carry: Packaged timber deck cargo – dangerous densities.*

27.   IMO. *International Code on Intact Stability* (IS Code), 2020.

27a.   IMO. *Unified Interpretations of the 2008 IS Code* (MSC.1/Circ.1537/Rev.1).

28.   ASTM-IP-API. *Petroleum Measurement Tables.*

29.   *International Convention for the Unification of Certain Rules of Law relating to Bills of Lading* (1924)/*First Protocol* (1968)/*Second Protocol* (1979) (the Hague-Visby Rules).

30.   IMO. *International Convention for the Prevention of Pollution from Ships* (MARPOL), Consolidated Edition 2022.

31.   United Nations. *International Convention on the Carriage of Goods by Sea* (the Hamburg Rules), 1978.

32.   British Standards Institution. *BS EN 627:1996 Specification for data logging and monitoring of lifts, escalators and passenger conveyors.*

33.   Department for Transport. *Renewable Transport Fuels Obligation.*

34.   ASTM. *ASTM D6751 – Standard Specification for Biodiesel Fuel Blend Stock (B100) for Middle Distillate Fuels.*

35. European Committee for Standardization. *EN 14214 Biodiesel fuel standard.*

36. The Federation of Oils, Seeds and Fats Associations Ltd. *Carriage of Oils and Fats.*

37. Ministry of Defence. *Defence Standard 91-91.*

38. European Committee for Standardization. *EN 590 Automotive fuels – Diesel – Requirements and test methods.*

39. The Energy Institute. *HM 50. Guidelines for the cleaning of tanks and lines for marine tank vessels carrying petroleum and refined products.*

40. International Organization for Standardization (ISO). *ISO 8217:2017: Petroleum products – Fuels (class F) – Specifications of marine fuels.*

41. European Committee for Standardization. *EN 228 Automotive fuels – Unleaded petrol - Requirements and test methods.*

42. IMO. *International Code for the Construction and Equipment of Ships Carrying Dangerous Chemicals in Bulk* (IBC Code), 2020.

43. IMO. *Guidelines for the Carriage of Blends of Petroleum Oil and Biofuels, as Amended, 2011* (MEPC.1/Circ.761/Rev.1).

44. IMO. *International Code of Safety for Ships Using Gases or Other Low-flashpoint Fuels* (IGF Code), 2016.

45. IMO. *International Code for the Construction and Equipment of Ships Carrying Liquefied Gases in Bulk* (IGC Code), 2016.

46. IMO. *Code for the Construction and Equipment of Ships Carrying Liquefied Gases in Bulk* (GC Code), 1983.

47. IMO. *Code for Existing Ships Carrying Liquefied Gases in Bulk* (EGC Code), 1976.

48. IMO. *International Convention on Standards of Training, Certification and Watchkeeping* (STCW Convention), 2017.

49. OCIMF. *Mooring Equipment Guidelines, 4th Edition* (MEG4), 2018.

50. SIGTTO. *Liquefied Gas Handling Principles on Ships and in Terminals, 4th Edition* (LGHP4), 2016.

51. IMO. *Recommendations on the Safe Use of Pesticides in Ships Applicable to the Fumigation of Cargo Holds* (MSC.1/Circ.1264, as amended by MSC.1/Circ.1396).

52. IMO. *Revised Recommendations on the Safe Use of Pesticides in Ships Applicable to the Fumigation of Cargo Transport Units* (MSC.1/Circ.1361/ Rev.1).

53. The International Group of P&I Clubs and CINS (the Cargo Incident Notification System). *Guidelines for the Carriage of Calcium Hypochlorite in Containers,* 2018.

54. Gray, B F and Halliburton, B W. *The thermal decomposition of hydrated calcium hypochlorite (UN 2880).* Fire Saf. J. 2000, 35.3, 223–39.

55.   The Expandable Polystyrene (EPS) Transport Group of Plastics Europe. *Guidelines for Transport and Storage of Expandable Polystyrene Raw Beads,* 2007.

56.   The Office of the Federal Register. *Title 49: Transportation.* The Code of Federal Regulations.

57.   IMO/ILO/UNECE. *Code of Practice for Packing of Cargo Transport Units* (CTU Code), 2014.

57a.   UK P&I Club/TT Club. *Book it right and pack it tight,* 2022.

58.   Container Owners Association (COA). *Code of Practice for Flexitanks.*

59.   British Standards Institution (BSI). *PAS 1008 – Specification for the performance and testing of a single-use flexitank.*

60.   International Organization for Standardization (ISO). *ISO 1496-1 Series 1 freight containers – specification and testing.*

61.   International Council on Clean Transportation (ICCT). *Recommendations Regarding Carriage Instructions for Refrigerated Cargoes.*

62.   World Health Organization (WHO). *Good Distribution Practices for Pharmaceutical Products.* (Annex 5 to WHO Technical Report Series, No. 957, 2010).

63.   World Health Organization (WHO). *Guide to Good Storage Practices for Pharmaceuticals.* (Annex 9 to WHO Technical Report Series, No. 908, 2003).

64.   World Health Organization (WHO). *Supplement 13: Qualification of Shipping Containers.* (Technical Supplement to WHO Technical Report Series, No. 961, 2011, Annex 9: Model guidance for the storage and transport of time- and temperature-sensitive pharmaceutical products).

65.   International Chamber of Shipping (ICS) and The World Shipping Council (WSC). *Safe Transport of Containers by Sea: Industry Guidance for Shippers and Container Stuffers.*

66.   International Organization for Standardization (ISO). *ISO/DIS 3874 – Series 1 freight containers – Handling and securing.*

67.   International Organization for Standardization (ISO). *ISO 1161:2016 – Series 1 freight containers – Corner and intermediate fittings – Specifications.*

68.   The Office of the Federal Register. *Title 29: Labor.* The Code of Federal Regulations.

69.   IMO. *Amendments to the Code of Safe Practice for Cargo Stowage and Securing* (CSS Code). MSC.1/Circ.1352/Rev.1.

70.   IMO. *Amendments to the Code of Safe Practice for Cargo Stowage and Securing* (CSS Code). MSC.1/Circ.1623 (2020).

71.   International Labour Organization (ILO). *Code of Safe Practice on Safety and Health in Dock Work.*

72.   IMO. *Revised recommendations on safety of personnel during container securing operations,* 2008 (MSC.1/Cric.1263).

73. *Regulation (EU) No 660/2014 of the European Parliament and of the Council of 15 May 2014 amending Regulation (EC) No 1013/2006 on shipments of waste.*

74. *Commission Regulation (EC) No 1379/2007 of 26 November 2007 amending Annexes IA, IB, VII and VIII of Regulation (EC) No 1013/2006 of the European Parliament and of the Council on shipments of waste, for the purposes of taking account of technical progress and changes agreed under the Basel Convention.*

75. *Commission Regulation (EC) No 1418/2007 of 29 November 2007 concerning the export for recovery of certain waste listed in Annex III or IIIA to Regulation (EC) No 1013/2006 of the European Parliament and of the Council to certain countries to which the OECD Decision on the control of transboundary movements of wastes does not apply,* as amended.

76. *Regulation (EC) No 1013/2006 of the European Parliament and of the Council of 14 June 2006 on shipments of waste,* as amended.

77. DNV. *Rules for Planning and Execution of Marine Operations.* www.dnv.com

78. DNV-GL. *Noble Denton Guidelines.* www.dnv.com

79. International Organization for Standardization (ISO). *ISO 6780:2003 – Flat pallets for intercontinental materials handling – Principal dimensions and tolerances.*

80. International Organization for Standardization (ISO). *ISO 7195:2020 – Nuclear energy – Packagings for the transport of uranium hexafluoride (UF$_6$).*

81. BSI. British Standards Institution. www.bsigroup.com

82. ANSI. American National Standards Institute. www.ansi.org

83. DIN. German Institute for Standardization. www.din.de/en

84. *The Merchant Shipping (Load Lines) (Deck Cargo) Regulations 1968* (SI 1968/1089).

85. Cargo Incident Notification System (CINS). *Awareness Paper for the Carriage of Waste in Containers,* May 2018. www.cinsnet.com

86. International Association of Classification Societies (IACS). *Recommendation No 14 Hatch cover securing and tightness.* Rev.2 Corr.1 October 2005.